The Edinburgh Companion to Contemporary Scottish Literature

to Mr Smith

The Edinburgh Companion to Contemporary Scottish Literature

Edited by Berthold Schoene

Edinburgh University Press

Edinburgh University Press Ltd
22 George Square, Edinburgh

Typeset in 10/12 Goudy
by Servis Filmsetting Ltd, Manchester, and
printed and bound in Great Britain by
Antony Rowe Ltd, Chippenham, Wilts

A CIP record for this book is available from the British Library

ISBN 978 0 7486 2395 2 (hardback)
ISBN 978 0 7486 2396 9 (paperback)

The right of the contributors
to be identified as authors of this work
has been asserted in accordance with
the Copyright, Designs and Patents Act 1988.

The publisher acknowledges subsidy from the Scottish Arts Council
towards the publication of this volume.

Scottish
Arts Council

Scotland's New
Literary Heritage

From Earliest Times
to the 21st Century

Contents

PART IV: Topics

Introduction

Post-devolution Scottish Writing

In *The Scottish Novel since the Seventies*, published in 1993, Gavin Wallace described contemporary Scottish literature as 'a grey and morose beast prone to lengthy fits of self-pity' (Stevenson and Wallace 1993: 220). As the chief reason for the pathos and disaffection pervading late twentieth-century Scottish culture Wallace cited the general listlessness of Scottish affairs in the aftermath of the unsuccessful referendum on national self-rule in March 1979. Ten years after the successful second referendum in September 1997 and following the opening of the Scottish Parliament on 1 July 1999, the present collection of forty-two essays on the 'state' of post-devolution Scottish writing revisits Wallace's rather defeatist characterisation of Scottish literary culture from a post-devolution perspective, and it strikes me as particularly propitious in this context that Wallace himself has agreed to be one of the contributors. The project takes its cue also from Christopher Whyte's proposition, made in 1998, that 'in the absence of an elected political authority [in Scotland], the task of representing the nation has been repeatedly devolved to its writers'. The *Companion* aims at a critical stocktaking of the ways in which the cultural and political role of Scottish writing could be said to have changed after devolution. Has it come true that, as Whyte predicted, 'the setting up of a Scottish parliament [would] at last allow Scottish literature to be literature first and foremost, rather than the expression of a nationalist movement' (Whyte 1998a: 284)? And if so, what exactly might it mean for a 'minor' literature to become primarily 'literary' instead of self-consciously fulfilling the ancillary role of a subnational counterdiscourse? In what ways would such a literary 'turn' be desirable? According to Tom Devine, 'when the first Scottish Parliament since 1707 met in Edinburgh in July of 1999, the Scottish nation undeniably embarked on another exciting stage in its long history' (Devine 1999: 617), and it is this excitement and 'newness' which ought also to be palpable in the recently devolved nation's literature. What the *Companion* seeks to provide against the background of Scotland's transition from subnational status to devolved home-rule independence is a literary history of the present identifying and defining a new period in Scottish literary history. As Robert Crawford asserts in *Devolving English Literature*, 'Scotland and Scottish culture, like all nations and cultures, require continual acts of re-imagining which alter and develop their natures' (Crawford 2000: 14–15), and the present project aspires to be not only such an act of critical re-imagining, but also a sourcebook of ideas on how, as a collaborative project of the nation's people, 'Scotland' might be devised and pursued in the future.

When I first arrived in Scotland from Germany as a visiting student in the late 1980s, what struck me was that in Scotland nationalism did not appear to be a problem. 'Of course' it was 'good' to be Scottish and entirely 'natural' to say so with pride, whereas similarly unselfconscious expressions of German-, English- or American-ness, for instance, would undoubtedly have been met with outrage and contempt. The accident of being born into a certain nationality either bestowed upon someone the loathsome burden of totalitarianism's, colonialism's or neo-imperialism's ineradicable shame, or the awesome gift of nationalist exhilaration propelled by a strong sense of minoritarian resistance to political injustice and oppression. Whereas I had been brought up to wince at the slightest stirring of even the most minute and innocuous nationalist sentiment, in Scotland nationalism was not a problem.

This has changed fundamentally. Following devolution, both Scottish critics and creative writers have begun to issue reminders that Scotland's assumed moral superiority as a victim of historical circumstance must not be permitted to persist uninterrogated. Most powerfully perhaps James Robertson's award-winning novel *Joseph Knight* (2003) discloses Scotland's complicity in the slave trade while also revealing Scotland's profound immersion in the wider British imperial enterprise. Neil Davidson goes a critical step further by suggesting that the very idea of pre-British Scottish nationhood, which successful devolution is allegedly intended to re-install, constitutes a grave ideological fallacy. According to Davidson, Scottishness 'is at least partly the product of imperialism and ethnic cleansing' and it is therefore 'futile to imagine that merely setting up a Scottish nation state will *by itself* remove the attendant poisons of racism and hostility towards cultures which are perceived to be "different"' (Davidson 2000: 202). Furthermore, in *Modern Scottish Culture* Michael Gardiner reminds us that devolution must be understood not as a primarily Scottish-, Welsh- and Northern-Irish-owned prerogative but as 'the *last* British political process' also involving 'England [which], as part of the UK, is also a *minor* [stateless] nation crippled by the idea of its own *majority*, but it is having a much harder time [than the other three] identifying a specific national culture' (Gardiner 2005: ix, 4). As Gardiner convincingly argues elsewhere, for the sake of justice and credibility devolution must be prevented from becoming a wondrously rejuvenating devolving away from Britishness, which might exculpate all four formerly British nations from their historical accountability and effectively 'leave no agent of colonial violence' (Gardiner 2004a: 96). All the more pertinent it appears therefore to discover that the very date of the 1997 devolution referendum (11 September) was chosen because it marked the seven hundredth anniversary of William Wallace's defeat of the English at the Battle of Stirling Bridge (Edensor 2002: 153).

It is imperative that post-devolution Scotland cease once and for all to identify itself in opposition to all things English; not only were the histories of the two nations intimately entwined for almost 300 years, they continue to be so, and it would be nonsensical to deny that these days the two countries do 'in fact . . . have a good relationship' (Gardiner 2005: 3). Accordingly, while discussions of Scottish nationalism and nationhood feature prominently in the present volume, they are conducted invariably with reference to other debates on contemporary 'identity', such as class, sexuality and gender, globalisation and the new Europe, cosmopolitanism and postcoloniality, as well as questions of ethnicity, race and postnational multiculturalism. The problematisation of 'Scottishness' is enhanced further by adding an international perspective, incorporating 'foreign' viewpoints and analysing the reception of Scottish literature, as well as dominant images of Scottishness, both in Europe and overseas. This volume also makes a point of addressing Scotland's internal heterogeneity by commenting on literary activity in the different regions of Scotland, both urban and rural, and examining recent trends in all the traditional generic domains of fiction, drama and poetry. Literary production and critical practice are placed within the broadest possible cultural context, including history, economics, national and international politics, as well as the literary marketplace and literature's relationship with the media and issues of topical significance, such as ecology or town-planning. The project has also been driven by the desire to broaden the focus of Scottish literary studies by introducing work on popular genres, such as children's literature and crime fiction, and establishing links with closely affiliated areas of scholarly interest, such as film, television and the ongoing tradition of Scottish storytelling. Last but not least, the *Companion* revisits the role of language within Scottish self-representation by including enquiries into contemporary writers' use of vernacular Scots, the canonical position of literature in Gaelic, and the 'double realm' of Scottish literary translation.

Throughout the present volume the work of established authors is re-evaluated alongside that of relative newcomers who have entered the scene since the mid-1990s, and that of emergent writers, with their first or second books, who are currently getting noticed as an avant-garde or 'renaissance' movement in twenty-first-century Scottish writing. After devolution, what has become of postmodern Scottish literature's predilection for literary innovation and linguistic experimentation as markers of political subversion and resistance? And how does a new generation of writers define its relationship to Scotland's literary tradition? Similarly, do younger cultural and literary critics tend to situate their voices within, or in conflictual opposition to, the academic establishment of Scottish literary studies? The task is not only to demonstrate how political devolution is being represented and theorised, but also to determine what exactly might have been its impact on Scottish conceptualisations of the value and function of literary practice *per se*, both creative and critical, as well as the relationship between the individual intellectual or artist and the state and, by extension, the nation and global politics. To ensure a sense of *telos* within the collection, all contributors were asked to reflect on at least some of these issues and contextualise their specific readings within an analysis of contemporary Scottish literature's affinity with various pro-, anti- and post-nationalist discourses before and after 1997.

The forty-two essays collected here under four main headings – 'Contexts', 'Genres', 'Authors' and 'Topics' – encompass the whole spectrum of scholarly enquiry in post-devolution Scottish literary studies. As explained above, the *Companion's* chief motivation is to open up a new chapter in Scottish literary history by capturing and commenting on manifestations of 'the contemporary' in early twenty-first-century literature, re-addressing the relationship between literature, culture and national politics, and promoting a vibrant dialogue between prominent and emergent critical and creative voices. The collection provides a comprehensive stocktaking of what is at present being researched and debated in academic Scottish studies, as well as a detailed account of what is 'troubling' popular cultural politics in post-devolution Scotland. The contributors include critics, creative writers, journalists and art administrators from Britain, Canada, Germany, Ireland, Italy, New Zealand and the United States, ranging from eminent scholars to younger voices at the beginning of their academic careers. The volume also includes chapters by two creative writers, Zoë Strachan and Suhayl Saadi, who have chosen to become involved in the project beyond their traditional role as mere subjects of study, as well as chapters by novelist-critics Alan Bissett, Andrew Crumey and Christopher Whyte. It seemed fruitful not only to allow but actively to encourage significant overlap between individual chapters. Thus various prominent themes, authors and individual literary works make recurrent appearances throughout the collection, identifying contemporary Scottish studies not as docile choir practice but as a busy parliament in which critics take each other to task, passionately contradict each other and, more often than not, come to markedly different conclusions. The formation of Scottish studies, now released for good from its traditional subsumption within the subject of English, must in itself be regarded as a devolutionary act, but it was never predicated on homogeneity or consensus and, as demonstrated by the *Companion*, the vociferous devolutionary dynamic that brought it into being in the first place continues.

To illustrate in greater detail exactly what kind of impact devolution exerts on the sensibility of the nation, and to what extent it can indeed be expected to inaugurate a new era in Scottish literature, it seems useful to make reference to Raymond Williams's influential term 'structure of feeling', which he coined in order to capture 'the distinct sense of a particular and native style' of any given culture, nation or historical period. Profoundly pervasive, yet notoriously elusive and difficult to pinpoint, what Williams means by 'structure of feeling' is 'the particular living result of all the elements in the general organization [of a community]', which 'any formal description would be too crude to express' (Williams 1961: 65). Most pertinently in the present context, to conceive of nationhood as a structure of feeling inscribes it with possibilities for dynamic generational change, as capable of incorporating cultural transmutability instead of cherishing culture simply as a homeostatic tradition of national self-constancy. As Williams explains,

> one generation may train its successor, with reasonable success, in the social character or the general cultural pattern, but the new generation will have its own structure of feeling . . . The new generation responds in its own ways to the unique world it is inheriting, taking up many continuities . . . and reproducing many aspects of the organization . . . yet feeling its whole life in certain ways differently, and shaping its creative response into a new structure of feeling. (Williams 1961: 65)

Undeniably, then, devolution has changed and will continue to change Scotland's structure(s) of feeling, and the nation's present preoccupations and priorities are bound to differ markedly from late twentieth-century political concerns. Hitherto unforeseeable perspectives have opened up on the world and Scotland's position within it. Literary and other cultural representations of the personal and the political, the self and the nation, are assuming new guises and rehearsing previously unheard-of crises and emergencies. It is these current developments, the manifold political circumstances and aesthetic agendas that propel them, as well as literature's indefatigable envisioning of possible solutions that the present volume seeks to record and critically contour.

I am indebted to Jackie Jones at Edinburgh University Press for her faith in this project and to my colleagues in the English Research Institute at Manchester Metropolitan University for generously supporting its completion. Special thanks are due to Sue Zlosnik and Peter Gilroy. It would quite obviously have been impossible to put the *Companion* together without the enthusiastic commitment, effort and team spirit of all its contributors – many thanks to all of you! My gratitude goes also to Keith Harvey, Kate McGowan, Shafqat Nasir, Chris Perriam and Helen Rogers for their friendship and support, and to Stephen Smith for his love and patience.

Part I
Contexts

Chapter 1

Going Cosmopolitan: Reconstituting 'Scottishness' in Post-devolution Criticism

Berthold Schoene

Rather than stunting cultural activity in Scotland, the failure of the first referendum on national self-rule resulted in an 'unprecedented explosion of creativity . . . often seen as a direct response to the disastrous "double whammy" that had been inflicted upon the Scottish people in 1979' (Petrie 2004: 2). What Duncan Petrie refers to here is the frustrating defeat of Scottish nationalist ambition, followed only a couple of months later by the new British prime minister Margaret Thatcher's enduringly ominous rise to power, which seemed then to be cementing Scotland's subnational status for good. Not only did post-1979 Scottish literature – and, by extension, Scottish cultural life as a whole – prove that 'fruitful literature is made from reaction to unpropitious cultural circumstance' (Carruthers 1999: 61); their disenfranchisement and representational elision by an anachronistic politics of Anglo-British homogeneity only induced the Scottish people to pull more closely together and develop a more clearly defined and morally superior sense of national identity. As Richard Weight explains in *Patriots*:

> The more the English revelled in the benefits of Conservative rule, the more the Scots and Welsh saw them as a nation of callous, selfish individuals. In contrast, they saw themselves as peoples with a unique sense of community and compassion; a belief which the nationalist parties encouraged . . . Thatcherism and Conservatism in general came to be synonymous with English nationalism in north and west Britain. (Weight 2002: 589)

Albeit thematically often bleak and pessimistic, in terms of quality and sheer volume post-1979 literature rapidly developed into a vibrant and characteristically unruly vehicle for Scottish self-representation. As Liam McIlvanney has observed, 'by the time the Parliament arrived [in 1999], a revival in Scottish fiction had been long underway . . . Without waiting for the politicians, Scottish novelists had written themselves out of despair' (McIlvanney 2002: 183). Devolutionary Scottish writing – that is, writing produced and published between the referenda of 1979 and 1997 – was always, of necessity, politically informed, or at least it was received and critiqued that way, and only considered a success if it made – or could be construed as making – some kind of case for Scotland. In this light Christopher Whyte's query whether after devolution it might be possible to relieve Scottish writing of its burden of nationalist meaning-making and 'at last allow [it] to be literature first and foremost' (Whyte 1998a: 284) seems timely. Notably, Whyte's promotion of an aesthetic turn in Scottish literature and criticism goes far beyond Robert Crawford's caveat that 'the word "Scottish" must not come to seem a restriction [but merely] a factual description.' As Crawford continues, 'just as it is absolutely valid to engage closely with the grain of one's own culture, so it is equally fine to fly free of local contours' (Crawford 2000: 329). Whyte is not simply after securing an author's or text's entitlement to momentary self-extrication from the national culture; rather, he regards it as imperative to strip Scottish literature radically of its context and apply purely aesthetic parameters of critical enquiry. In *Modern Scottish Poetry* Whyte voices his intention 'to reclaim a degree of autonomy for the creative (in this case, specifically literary) faculty' and deny 'both history and politics . . . any privileged status as tools for the interpretation of Scottish literature' (Whyte 2004a: 7–8). Representation, both creative and critical, is no longer to be impaired by the interference of any extra-literary interests.

In my view Whyte's renegade gesture must primarily be understood as the post-devolution manifesto of a Scottish poet, novelist and critic intent on extricating *himself*, let alone Scottish literature, from the tenaciously traditionalist grasp of his fellow writers and critics (as well as erstwhile departmental colleagues) Douglas Gifford and Alan Riach. In *Scotlands: Poets and the Nation*, published in the same year as Whyte's *Modern Scottish Poetry*, Gifford and Riach not only persist in championing Scottish literature's preoccupation with Scotland as its most eminent trait but also rather unhelpfully reinscribe the oppositioning of Scottish and English writing before invoking, quite feebly I find, the alleged heterogeneity of 'Scottishness':

> Scotland is a major theme in the poetry of Scotland. This might appear self-evident, yet it is the most obvious that is most easily overlooked, and this theme is a distinctive and differentiating feature of Scottish literature . . . and nothing in English literature compares in consistency and continuity with the theme of the matter of national identity in the poetry of Scotland . . . Scottish nationality nourishes many differences within itself – and after all, recognition, understanding and celebration of difference is the principal work of culture and the arts. (Gifford and Riach 2004: xvii)

Clearly, one task for critics of contemporary Scottish literature is to determine whether after devolution 'Scottishness' still remains a useful quality marker, viable identity descriptor, or suitable criterion for gauging the canonical eligibility of an author or text. What does a critical invocation of Scottishness achieve, or intend to achieve? Equally worth investigating is the question whether post-devolution Scottish literature is about to lose its distinctive 'Scottishness', or if it is now more 'typically Scottish' than ever. Ought Scottish literature to continue to be burdened with an alleged national specificity, or should it be allowed to go cosmopolitan rather than native? What if it is indeed the case that, as suggested by Alan Bissett, for a whole new generation of Scottish writers 'Scotland barely exists now. It's just a name we give to the place where we live. Scotland or something' (Devine and Logue 2002: 22)? While seemingly progressive and without doubt well-intentioned, Gifford and Riach's reflection that 'national identity can now be accommodated in literary discourse as a concept encompassing diversity and pluralism' (Gifford and Riach 2004: xxviii) fails to explain exactly what purpose the invocation of nationhood in post-devolution literary appraisals is meant to serve in the first place.

Throughout the twentieth century Scottish literary criticism has been deeply troubled by questions of national authenticity, such as (a) whether, despite Scotland's loss of statehood in the eighteenth century, it might still be possible to argue for the persistence of a coherent Scottish literary tradition, or (b) how truly and unmistakably 'Scottish' Scottish literature really is, and (c) if Scotland's literature is indeed marked by an essential differ- ence, then what exactly might be the most salient attributes of this essence. All attempts at definitively identifying Scottish literature's Scottishness by detecting continuity in dis- continuity, construing homogeneity from evident heterogeneity, or finding signs of a gen- uinely autonomous development in relations of cross-cultural indebtedness inevitably resulted in finding Scottish culture lacking, 'odd' or even 'mad', its particular sensibility characterised in turn by antisyzygy, dissociation and paradox (see Carruthers 1999). Pertinently, however, in devolutionary times – coinciding with the ever-increasing cultural currency of postmodern, postcolonial and other politically eccentric artistic movements and debates – this apparent centuries-old shortcoming of Scottish culture would reveal itself as thoroughly advantageous. Under the aegis of a new zeitgeist not only suspicious of neat unities and entitative truths, but deeply responsive to processes of apparent cultural disintegration as conducive to democratic diversification, Scottish culture and politics came significantly to benefit and prosper. As Cairns Craig acknowledged very early on:

> The 'real' Scot, the 'true identity' was entirely unstable: its was an instability which, in com- parison with the surety of other cultures' certainties – and particularly England's – gave rise to the conception of the Scot as, in some sense, schizophrenic, self-divided . . . The fragment- ation and division which made Scotland seem abnormal to an earlier part of the twentieth century came to be the norm for much of the world's population . . . Scotland ceased to have to measure itself against the false 'norm', psychological as well as cultural, of the unified national tradition. (Craig 1988: 7)

Similarly dismissive of nationalist fetishisations of holistic unity, Gerard Carruthers has praised 'the fluidity and dynamics of the Scottish nation and Scottish culture since their beginnings' (Carruthers 1999: 63), and in *Understanding Scotland* David McCrone argues that since 'throughout its history Scotland's survival and identity have been the product of compromise and negotiation . . . its "identity" is not under threat of extinction' (McCrone 1992: 220). Discontinuity and adaptability have become Scotland's cultural trademarks. 'Statelessness' and a postcolonial disposition no longer signify lack and inferiority, but harbour a resourceful flexibility.

From this powerful critical paradigm shift, which champions the cultural authenticity of the fragmented, marginalised, shadowy and wounded over that of the allegedly intact, wholesome and self-contained, Scottish culture has emerged as from a distorting mirror. No longer regarded, or led to regard itself, as exclusively Scottish and thus found or finding itself lacking, it becomes free to reconceive of itself in broader terms, with reference to other cultures (not just English culture), indeed as situated within a vibrant network of interdependent cultural contexts. As Carruthers explains in *Beyond Scotland*, the very notion of a nation's cultural independence must be regarded as a fallacy:

> Interdependence is not the opposite of independence, but in fact reveals the folly of recourse to the latter term in the cultural domain. Independence is little more than an illusion or an aspiration that has been projected onto the cultural sphere through its persistent lack in the political sphere. The philosophy of 'ourselves alone', rather than entrenching a coherent sense of national identity, is more likely to deform the very idea of Scottishness itself – to mistake a complex, forward-looking, heterogeneous identity for one that is narrow and reductive in its nativism. (Carruthers et al. 2004: 15)

Of course, the opening up of such a decisively international angle on Scottish literature is only truly 'new' when viewed from within a British context. In *The Scottish Tradition in Literature*, first published in 1958, the German philologist Kurt Wittig already displays a very good grasp of Scottish literature's heterogeneity and multicultural interdependence. Categorising Scottish literature as at once 'part of our European heritage' and 'a product of that particular community in which it originated', Wittig is at pains not 'to separate things that are better joined, or to erect an invisible barrier that would isolate Scottish literature itself from the larger world to which it inseparably belongs' (Wittig 1958: 3).

Post-devolution Scotland finds itself embedded within a multicultural, international context, signalled also by the Scottish National Party's programmatic aim to achieve independence *within* Europe (see MacAskill 2004). Meanwhile Scottish nationalism has effectively ceased to be a minoritarian counterdiscourse, raising manifold questions regarding Scotland's internal interdependencies and alliances. How has Scotland's newly devolved status influenced Scottish nationalism's often idealised, quasi-coalitional relationship with other emancipatory movements and initiatives, such as feminism, gay liberation, or ethnic-minority and working-class resistance? What is the position of politically subordinate voices, and their desire for further socio-cultural diversification, within Scotland's new political environment and literary canon?

In his study *Postethnic America* David Hollinger envisages a form of nationhood that favours 'voluntary over involuntary affiliations, balances an appreciation for communities of descent with a determination to make room for new communities, and promotes solidarities of wide scope that incorporate people with different ethnic and racial backgrounds' (Hollinger 1995: 3). Post-devolution Scotland evidently holds postethnic potential, mainly due to its relatively flexible views on what constitutes a Scottish person, as detailed by its civic citizenship legislation, which values an individual's choice of residency as highly as their familial descent. As Michael Keating explains, ethnic citizenship 'presents membership of the national community as given, or ascriptive', whereas civic citizenship 'sees individuals voluntarily constituting themselves as a collectivity' (Keating 1996: 3). Pertinently, Hollinger's conceptualisation of postethnicity is derived from a contrastive juxtaposition of pluralism with cosmopolitanism:

> Pluralism respects inherited boundaries and locates individuals within one or another of a series of ethno-racial groups to be protected and preserved. Cosmopolitanism is more wary of traditional enclosures and favors voluntary affiliations. Cosmopolitanism promotes multiple identities, emphasizes the dynamic and changing character of many groups, and is responsive to the potential for creating new cultural combinations. Pluralism sees in cosmopolitanism a threat to identity, while cosmopolitanism sees in pluralism a provincial unwillingness to engage the complex dilemmas and opportunities actually presented by contemporary life. (Hollinger 1995: 3–4)

The chief difference between a pluralist and a cosmopolitan society is that the latter is never closed or whole, never fearful or tired of evolving, never conclusively devolved or assembled, remaining continually keen 'to absorb as much varied experience as it can'. In order to live up to Hollinger's ideal of 'a civic nation . . . built and sustained by people who honor a common future more than a common past', post-devolution Scotland must not be allowed to rest at having achieved 'home rule', but must continually aim to make it the best possible – that is, the most inclusively convivial and hospitable – rule ever (Hollinger 1995: 84, 134).

While future debates on Scottish culture and politics will no doubt benefit greatly from imported theorising – not only Hollinger's postethnicity model, but also Jacques Derrida's essays on cosmopolitanism and hospitality (Derrida 2001a, 2001b), Paul Gilroy's recent work on conviviality and postcolonial melancholia (Gilroy 2004), and Homi Bhabha's current project on 'global dwelling' – Scotland does in fact possess its own indigenous theoretical resource in the unjustifiably neglected work of John Macmurray (1891–1976), described by his biographer John Costello as 'the best kept secret of British philosophy in the twentieth century' (Costello 2002: 16). The most radically innovative axiomatic of Macmurray's thinking resides in a dismissal of the Cartesian *cogito* as the assumed core of human subjectivity. Keen to release not only our selves, but our basic understanding of reason and rationality *per se*, from the deformative grasp of traditional thought, Macmurray reproaches the Enlightenment for forging a standardised view of the human that is fundamentally warped, since it 'isolates the self from others, splits mind from body, the spiritual from the material, and separates thinking from sense experience, feeling and action' (Kirkwood 2005: 21). As indicated by the titles of his two most famous works, *The Self as Agent* and *Persons in Relation*, originally delivered as the Gifford Lectures at Glasgow University in 1953 and 1954, Macmurray insists we view the self not as 'an isolated individual [but as] a *person*, and that personal existence is *constituted* by the relations of persons' (Macmurray 1969a: 12). Macmurray's elementary reconfiguration of the human, which is at once religiously motivated and appealingly secular, demands no less than 'a radical modification of our philosophical tradition' and is striking in its anticipation of deconstructionist discourse as well as much influential postcolonial theory. Resolute in its rejection of 'the traditional distinction between the subjective and the objective' (Macmurray 1969a: 38), Macmurray's work is particularly interested in eradicating deeply ingrained epistemic mechanisms of recognising the other person only as object and hence not recognising – let alone relating to – him or her at all.

Macmurray does not propose to replace reflection and reason with the allegedly greater spontaneity of agency and feeling; neither is it his aim to ensoul thought and action in a mystifying 'New Age' plea for perfect remedial embodiment. In his view modernity's idealisation of pure thought has led to a fundamental impairment of the human, rendering it disembodied, unemotional and solipsistic. The mind needs reminding that it has hands and a heart and, in fact, that its thoughts will remain entirely abstract and inconsequential unless they translate into conscientious, ethically informed action. Put differently, thought needs re-embedding within an all-round post-Cartesian reconciliation of the human with itself, tolerating no hegemonic discrimination between mind, heart and body and in fact comprehending 'reason' as an amalgamation of all three. If in his work Macmurray recurrently accentuates the primacy of action over thought, then this is because he perceives the former to be encompassing the latter, regarding action as 'a full concrete activity of the self in which all our capacities are employed; while thought is constituted by the exclusion of some of our powers and a withdrawal into an activity which is less concrete and less complete' (Macmurray 1969a: 86). Macmurray does not intend to reinvent the human, but to repossess humanity of all its faculties, making it whole again by remedying its disabling Cartesian specification. The ultimate aim is to 'set man firmly in the world which he knows, and so restore him to his proper existence as a community of persons in relation' (Macmurray 1969b: 12).

Agency and relational personhood take priority in Macmurray's understanding of the human and, as Craig has indicated, an integration of his ideas into our conceptualisation of post-devolution Scottish nationhood might have certain quite remarkable repercussions:

> Conceptions of the nation which start from the notion of an 'imagined community' mistake the nature of their object, for the nation, as much as the person, is an agent. To begin from the agency of the nation, rather than its imagination or self-perception, would be to bring us back to a world in which nations are the media of our practical and ethical endeavours; a world in which nations, as constituted by the relations of agents, would be neither totalitarian 'imagined communities' nor our open-ended pluralistic habitats; they would be, like all intentions, a constant redefinition of the 'beyond' from which they emerge and to which they are directed. Scotland, like any other nation, exists not as an expression of our essence, nor as the by-product of our hybrid graftings, but as the object of our intentions. Scotland is already 'beyond', was always 'beyond', because as long as we wish it to be so, it is the medium for translating into action our communal intentions. Scotland is our intended nation. (Craig 2004a: 251)

Macmurray encourages us not to conceive of – and hence ineluctably idealise – the nation as an act of the imagination; rather, we are to experience it as our immediate, entirely tangible, concrete and practical here and now, forever unpredictably evolving into the future rather than monotonously replicating itself from past blueprints. In this way, then, the nation is always more than its present state; neither a historical or institutional given, nor a people's unavertible fate, it is at the same time what we intend it to be and what we ultimately succeed in making of it. By boldly incorporating Macmurray's philosophy into post-devolution Scottish studies, Craig puts a definitive end to a critical tradition of tautologically measuring all things Scottish by their degree of 'Scottishness'. Instead, Scottish identity has become performative, at once solid and 'in process', clearly intelligible and impossible to pinpoint, historically embodied and promisingly suspended in the grasp of the people's intentions. Importantly, Craig's appraisal of Macmurray's philosophy results in a theoretically astute vision of (the new) Scotland; it must not be confused with impulsive neo-nationalist invocations of nationhood, such as Joy Hendry's, in which (the old/the eternal) Scottishness rematerialises like some recently legalised intoxicant hitting the people's bloodstream and leaving the people incapable of speech or thought: 'There is less and less the need to talk about [Scottish identity], because we can *be* it, and . . . *do* it. Whatever it is. If *Scottishness* is at last set free in the blood, it can express itself, without striving for disingenuous and rationalising articulation' (Devine and Logue 2002: 99).

I shall now look at two very different literary renditions of Scottishness in the works of two very different post-devolution writers – Kevin MacNeil's debut novel *The Stornoway Way* and Ewan Morrison's first collection of short stories, *The Last Book You Read*, both published in 2005. The aim is to compare their envisionings of Scotland's intra- and international relations, the local and the global, as well as tradition and its impact on contemporary national identity.

Complete with author's note, an upside-down map of Scotland, ample footnotes, two sets of acknowledgements, plus a 'Letter for Kevin, with Permission to Publish', MacNeil's novel poses as the author's edition of a manuscript by *Leòdhasach* R. S., also known as Roman Stornoway. From the first page *The Stornoway Way* connects with two traditional strands of modern Scottish writing, that of the drug-fuelled nationalist invective and that of the tale of the doppelgänger, converging in a well-rehearsed portrayal of true (albeit 'backwater') Scotland's indigenous culture pitted more or less hopelessly against an encroaching imperialist world that threatens to assimilate its uniqueness. Portraying his native island of Lewis as 'indeed conforming, both subtly and overtly, to the spread of globalization', which appears to be synonymous with both Anglicisation and Americanisation,

MacNeil continues to describe it as 'a quietly vicious irony that R. S. – whose proud individuality and determination not to be culturally colonized are clear from the start – has written a book that is influenced at times by American culture and language' (MacNeil 2005: x). Indeed, after a very short prologue R. S.'s narrative opens with:

> Fuck everyone from Holden Caulfield to Bridget Jones, fuck all the American and English phoney fictions that claim to speak for us; they don't know the likes of us exist and they never did. We are who we are because we grew up the Stornoway way. We do not live in the back of beyond, we live in the very *heart* of beyond. (MacNeil 2005: 15)

What is remarkable about this passage is not so much MacNeil's protagonist's vituperative stance, or the author's apparent failure to recognise that to identify oneself, however self-assertively, against some other culture's hegemony is not to extricate oneself from it but in fact to confirm the inescapability of its ubiquitous influence. Neither does it seem surprising that the much-cherished 'Stornoway way' never actually assumes particularly appealing shape, making R. S.'s declaration of parochial pride look somewhat vacuous and his invocation of Celtic sensitivity frustratingly clichéd. (Evidently, MacNeil's 'beyond' denotes a traditionally fixed locale and mental disposition rather than the evolutionary national dynamic invoked by Craig in response to his reading of Macmurray.) What is most remarkable about R. S.'s opening protestations is that in terms of style, target readership and authorial intention his novel actually displays precious little resemblance to the works of J. D. Salinger or Helen Fielding. If 'colonised' by anyone or anything, then it is surely the markedly urban, 'in-your-face' voice of Irvine Welsh, perpetuated by Highlands and Islands novelists such as Alan Warner and Luke Sutherland, which has contributed most enduringly to 'de-authenticating' Hebridean writing. As indicated by the novel's final sentence, this irony – that these days globalisation might actually come in the guise of the kind of bestselling Scottish writing most fêted for its local authenticity – appears to elude MacNeil. 'I sincerely hope', he concludes, 'that R. S. is the first of many diverse new Hebridean voices, Gaelic and English, old and young, classical and wild, to square up to the world' (MacNeil 2005: 252). But exactly what diversity the explicit parochial singularity of the 'Stornoway way' might be prepared to accommodate, let alone be able to promote, is left to the reader's conjecture; so, too, is the question of what would ultimately be gained if all Hebridean writing paid heed to MacNeil's recommendation and cultivated a belligerent attitude to 'the world'.

Its ostensibly dialogic style of self-conscious fragmentation clearly signalling the author's postmodern aspirations, MacNeil's novel ultimately appears dishearteningly out of time, a self-defeatist swansong unattuned to the majority of new Scottish literature's experimentation with less isolationist and more cosmopolitan and 'planetary' modes of narration. No fruitful countervision emerges from *The Stornoway Way*; nothing new enters the Scottish world. Instead, the novel heaps scorn on MacNeil's 'globalised' fellow islanders for wearing a 'new York Yankees baseball cap, spray-on jeans and a hooded sweatshirt declaiming the might of a triggerhappy black Los Angeles gang. A true product of the times. Insular Lewis smotherhugged by global America. Black pudding meets black power' (MacNeil 2005: 127), quite as if effective resistance to neo-imperialism were a matter of sartorial preferences. One is left to wonder if, in R. S.'s view, traditional Highland dress would make a more appropriate outfit for a twenty-first-century *Leòdhasach*. In terms of a creative response to British devolution MacNeil seems equally unforthcoming. Post-devolution Britain is referred to as 'D. Q. (= Disunited Queendom)' (MacNeil 2005: 18), testifying to little more than the protagonist's juvenile wit even though, admittedly, as far as the implied slight of effeminacy is concerned, it remains unclear if it is aimed at discrediting English culture, or whether it constitutes a rare authorial comment on R. S.'s own latent hysteria and emasculation. Most frustrating, however, is the centrality assigned to R. S.'s friend Johnny Banana's recitation of his much-applauded ceilidh-piece, 'Neighbours We Could Have Had', which involves the chanting of the names of all independent nations from Afghanistan to Zimbabwe (MacNeil 2005: 81–5). While possibly intended to demonstrate the survival of an oral tradition of indigenous merry-making, it effectively puts a lid on the novel's self-obsessed interiority and irremediable postcolonial pathos, signalled by its oblivious blindness to the fact that in the twenty-first century these countries *are* of course Scotland's neighbours, or at least they could be if the Scots so chose.

By cultivating a hopelessly anachronistic self-image, markedly lagging behind that of the rest of contemporary Scotland, MacNeil's portrayal does not do Hebridean culture any favours. Notably, the novel's greatest achievement is delegated to its footnotes, in which MacNeil successfully advertises the peculiar expressiveness of the Gaelic language as unrivalled. What sticks in the reader's mind after having read the novel, however, is R. S.'s pertinent musing on the purpose of his (and MacNeil's) literary endeavour: 'Am I elegizing, prematurely-but-only-just, my own demise and the death-rattles of my culture, my language? Do I, after all, *care?*' (MacNeil 2005: 94)? What *The Stornoway Way* most desperately needs is an unequivocal, self-assured answer to these questions.

Although prominently adorned with a blurb from the *Sunday Times* designating it as 'the most compelling Scottish literary debut since Irvine Welsh's *Trainspotting*', Ewan Morrison's *The Last Book You Read* could not be any more different from Welsh's debut, both stylistically and thematically. What the texts do have in common is that both oscillate generically between constituting a novel and a collection of short stories, *Trainspotting* representing the former forever on the brink of irreparable self-dispersal, whereas Morrison's narrative appears only minutely removed from aggregating into a larger whole. Similar to ambitious American film projects such as Robert Altman's *Short Cuts* (1993), Paul Thomas Anderson's *Magnolia* (1999) or Paul Haggis's *Crash* (2005), *The Last Book You Read* brings together a kaleidoscopic ensemble of different characters, relationships and places – most notably New York and Glasgow – within a sequence of fourteen stories intimately interlinked by theme, tone and experience. While many of the stories are excruciatingly perceptive in their portrayal of the characters' broad spectrum of emotional dispositions and quandaries, the collection remains indefatigably optimistic in its refusal to let any one of its characters persist in isolation – that is, its cosmopolitanist effort to relate individuals, and induce them to relate to each other, across the restrictive parameters of sex, gender, class, race or nationality. Unlike in MacNeil's novel, there are no old axes to grind; Morrison's stories attend to more important, contemporary and *personal* matters. Embracing globalisation as the new human condition, Morrison contrives to wrest from it a strong sense of planetary commonality among people, no matter whether they are male or female, gay or straight, white or black, Scottish, British, European or American – and it certainly does not matter what anyone happens to be wearing.

Most poignant are three stories at the heart of the collection – 'The Piers', 'Fuck Buddy' and 'Her Body' (Morrison 2005: 110–13, 114–26, 150–66) – all of which reveal the pitfalls of failing to relate by commodifying both oneself and one's other(s). Intuitively implementing Macmurray's ethical imperative to think, feel and act in wholesome combination, Morrison is concerned with the indispensable necessity of personal relationships, the heroic effort it takes to initiate, trust and maintain them, as well as the common everyday trials inherent in being generally human in our globalised twenty-first-century world. In 'The Piers', overwhelmed by late-capitalist mass culture, which eradicates individuality at the same time as it appears to be promoting it, and confronting his inability as a writer to 'make this city [New York] stop – stop and see itself', we find Morrison's narrator ruminating on retrieving the personal: 'Perhaps, if each person treated every other as a different species, as totally different and other, then we would could [*sic*] begin to care for each other' (Morrison 2005: 113, 111). In the unstoppably increasing absence of genuine individual uniqueness, it is imperative not to lose sight of our common humanity. The joggers watched by Morrison's narrator appear all the same and yet it is possible to relate to the personal life experience of every single one of them:

> So many people racing in the same direction. So many people. Needing exercise, rest, alcohol, distraction, danger or a moment alone to stare at the water, before they continue running again. Headphones on. All of them. Everyone with different music but they all look the same. When they jog, they measure their pace against that of strangers. Thousands of people, following each other, without even realizing it. Thousands of people looking for a reason to do what they're doing. If I jogged, I would follow them too. (Morrison 2005: 112–13)

Morrison's collection is about the difficulty of establishing and maintaining intimate relationships, of becoming a person by relating to another, in a world that has long confused individuality with self-commodification. As highlighted in 'Fuck Buddy', ours is a world in which affection ('now that he's made me feel somethin'') is equivalent to pain ('now that he's hurt me'), and in which orgasm as the most intimate physical expression of love has become part of a transaction that might drain rather than fulfil the self: 'I no longer let him make me come. I try to give away as little as possible about myself' (Morrison 2005: 126, 156). To use Macmurray's terminology, Morrison's characters struggle to love and be loved as persons in a world that has reduced people to selves and driven an irremovable wedge between them. Thus 'Her Body' concludes with what is simultaneously a declaration and a denial of intimacy, a realisation of love that must not speak or recognise itself in order to remain at all bearable: 'Tell him that, in spite of everything, in spite of even myself and all I know about love, I can see it there in his eyes and it makes me love him in return. But I know that if I say this he will run' (Morrison 2005: 166).

In Morrison's *The Last Book You Read* Scotland no longer features as an issue, but this is not to say that the novel is devoid of Scottishness. Morrison's sense of national belonging is not entirely left behind in the jet-lagged commotion of self-representational transit. While cosmopolitanism, in order to manifest experientially, inevitably requires the specificity of a locale and personal encounter, many of us feel most conscious of our national difference when elsewhere: I am most Scottish to myself whilst outside Scotland, in unfamiliar surroundings, which is when perceptions of me as a 'foreigner' are likely to interfere with my indigenous sense of self. In her reopening of the feminist debate on 'what is a woman' Toril Moi has tested the usefulness of such terms as 'situation' and 'background' to adumbrate the existential vicissitudes of modern 'identity', and I wonder whether her terminology may be fruitfully applied to the Scottish question also. Might it be useful to conceive of Scottishness as every Scottish person's 'situation', which fundamentally defines them, even if fervently disavowed? *At the same time* Scottishness never constitutes more than a mere 'background' to anybody's life, which no one ought to be obliged to foreground unless they choose to do so; in fact, having one's Scottishness foregrounded without one's consent, or out of context, might be experienced as constrictive and even personally injurious. Scottishness as lived experience must always precede and prevail over Scottishness as a fixed, definitive given, even though existence and essence will remain forever inextricably entwined. In Moi's more general terms, 'each concrete human being is involved in an open-ended process in which she constantly makes something of what the world makes of her' (Moi 1999: 188). This is very much what is at stake in Morrison's stories, in which identity is at once experientially palpable – that is, either pleasurable or painful or, more often, a mixture of the two – and, in Craig's terms, 'already "beyond" . . . always "beyond" ' (Craig 2004a: 251).

Undeniably Morrison's collection of short stories makes a contribution to contemporary world literature at the same time as it remains transfused by Morrison's particular situation, perspective and sensitivity as 'a Scot', even if, for most of the time, his Scottishness passes unmentioned. His stories' central focus is on human experience, at once common and personal, within an open-meshed cosmopolitan network of interpersonal relations; instead of receiving them on purely aesthetical, cultural-historical, socio-political or nationalist terms, I suggest we read them first and foremost ambassadorially.

Chapter 2

Voyages of Intent: Literature and Cultural Politics in Post-devolution Scotland

Gavin Wallace

An impartial observer of post-devolution Scotland might be forgiven for concluding that the position of the nation's literature within the new political establishment is both a prominent and secure one, and that its relationship with the new 'body politic' is close. The fundamental contribution Scottish literature has made to national identity was conspicuously celebrated in the Opening Ceremony of the Scottish Parliament on 1 July 1999. The poetry of Robert Burns (1759–96), together with that of Amy Linekar, a young schoolgirl, and Iain Crichton Smith's 'The Beginning of a New Song' ('Let our three-voiced country / Sing in a new world' [Gifford and Riach 2004: 245]) featured prominently in the ceremony. The new MSPs peppered their pronouncements with quotations from Sir Walter Scott (1771–1832), Sir David Lindsay (c.1490–c.1555) and Hugh MacDiarmid (1892–1978). Five years later, the long-awaited new Parliament building boasted an exterior inscribed with Scottish aphorisms, past and present, and its propinquity to Malcolm Fraser's visionary new Scottish Poetry Library building in the Canongate made the country's legislators – acknowledged and unacknowledged – symbolic neighbours. The centrepiece of a second ceremony in October 2004 to mark the Parliament's official opening was 'Open the Doors', a new poem by Scotland's greatest living poet, Edwin Morgan, recited by Liz Lochhead. Morgan himself had been appointed the first 'Scots Makar' or 'Poet for Scotland' – Scotland's equivalent of the Poet Laureate – by the Scottish Executive in February 2004. In November 2005, the inaugural artist-in-residence at the new Parliament building was James Robertson, one of Scotland's most successful contemporary writers, and it is from his *Voyage of Intent* (2005), a series of sonnets and essays he composed out of his experience, that the title of this chapter is taken.

To deduce, however, that a sequence of symbolic gestures is firm evidence of a rapprochement between the country's literary and political communities would be seriously mistaken. Scotland's distinguished literary tradition of vociferous dissent and opposition, radicalism, and scourging of the political establishment is as vibrant and sharp as it was in Burns's time. This was made manifest in the irreverent notes of warning that underlined Morgan's 'celebratory' Parliament-opening poem:

WHAT DO THE PEOPLE WANT of the place?
They want it to be filled with thinking people
as open and adventurous as its architecture.

A nest of fearties is what they do not want.
A symposium of procrastinators is what they do not want.
A phalanx of forelock-tuggers is what they do not want.
And perhaps most of all the droopy mantra of 'it wizny me' is what
they do not want.

(Morgan 2004b)

The ironic subtext of this particular sequence of reiterated negatives is of course that 'what they do not want, they may very likely get'. Morgan's cheeky manifesto is an apt reminder that since 1999 Scottish politicians' slow struggle as to how best to support literature has amounted to a symposium of procrastination. This was symbolised by two major post-devolution faux pas, the first being the Scottish Executive's publication of 'Creating Our Future, Minding Our Past', Scotland's first national cultural strategy, from which, to the literary community's considerable dismay, literature, even in the broadest sense, was omitted or, to be more precise, occluded (see Scottish Executive 2000). The second one was a result of the weary debacle of delay and spiralling expenditure surrounding the Parliament building. Deeply sympathetic to the centrality of literature to the life of the country, its Spanish architect Enric Miralles (1955–2000) had intended that newly commissioned and ambitious interior artwork for the building would be inspired by this theme. However, following Miralles's untimely death and the ensuing costs controversy, his scarcely insignificant vision was unceremoniously dispatched. In the meantime, as if in polite defiance, Scotland's literature sector was undergoing an unprecedented period of rapid, sustained and dramatic expansion; in a process paralleled by the growing profile of Scottish writers internationally, in Scotland itself public interest in and enthusiasm for literature continued to swell unabated. When in January 2006 the Scottish Executive at last unveiled 'Scotland's Culture', its new cultural policy responding to the Cultural Commission of 2005, the prominent place afforded to literature in both the document and within the remit of Creative Scotland, the proposed new body of support for the arts in Scotland, was welcomed, even if it did seem as if politicians and civil servants had been playing a game of catch-up (see Scottish Executive 2006). The prediction of many cultural-policy gurus that literature was poised to secure for itself a centre-stage position had been proved correct, at least in Scotland.

The Literature Department of the Scottish Arts Council (SAC) has been providing direct support for Scotland's literary culture for almost four decades. Its extensive portfolio of support programmes has played a major role in nurturing Scotland's writers, either by awarding them writing bursaries or by helping their work into publication through grants to literary magazines and publishers. The SAC also awards its own literary prizes, now the largest of their kind in Scotland. Many leading writers acknowledge early support from the SAC, including Janice Galloway, Andrew Greig, Bernard MacLaverty and Alan Warner. SAC grants also helped publish the early work of James Kelman and Ian Rankin. In addition, many established and emergent writers have benefited from the reciprocity of the SAC Writing Fellowships scheme, a network of which operates throughout the country in partnership with a range of organisations, predominantly local authorities, and since the late 1990s a parallel network of literature development workers has begun to emerge. The wider literature and storytelling sector is similarly sustained through SAC's core funding of the infrastructure of the ten national literature and language organisations, including the Association for Scottish Literary Studies, the Edinburgh International Book Festival, the Gaelic Books Council, Scottish Book Trust, the Scottish Poetry Library and the Scottish Storytelling Forum (see Table 1). All of these organisations are core providers of

Table 1 Scottish Arts Council literature budget, 2006–8

	2006/7 (£)		2006/7 total (£)	2007/8 (£)		2007/8 total (£)
	Voted	Lottery		Voted	Lottery	
Organisations:						
Association for Scottish Literary Studies	40,745	0	40,745	70,475	0	70,475
Edinburgh International Book Festival	139,587	0	139,587	170,000	0	170,000
Gaelic Books Council	160,172	0	160,172	190,000	0	190,000
Moniack Mhor	56,701	0	56,701	56,701	0	56,701
Scots Language Resource Centre	28,855	0	28,855	43,855	0	43,855
Scottish Book Trust	154,254	0	154,254	284,254	0	284,254
Scottish Language Dictionaries	95,909	0	95,909	115,909	0	115,909
Scottish Poetry Library	163,198	0	163,198	203,198	0	203,198
Scottish Publishers Association	172,779	0	172,779	204,779	0	204,779
Scottish Storytelling Forum	67,255	0	67,255	150,000	0	150,000
Organisations total	*1,079,455*	*0*	*1,079,455*	*1,489,171*	*0*	*1,489,171*
Projects:						
Creative development – writers bursaries	105,500	92,500	198,000	205,500	82,500	288,000
Edinburgh UNESCO City of Literature (New)	0	0	0	70,000	0	70,000
Itchy Coo (New)	0	0	0	0	30,000	30,000
Literature festivals and events	0	75,500	75,500	175,500	0	175,500
Programme publishing	65,000	0	65,000	165,000	0	165,000
Writing fellowships	50,000	97,500	147,500	150,000	97,500	247,500
Book awards	0	30,000	30,000	0	30,000	30,000
International (translation)	30,000	0	30,000	30,000	0	30,000
Live Literature Scotland	0	154,500	154,500	0	154,500	154,500
New work – literature	0	50,000	50,000	0	0	0
Professional development – literature	0	20,000	20,000	0	40,000	40,000
Publications	209,500	0	209,500	202,500	0	202,500
Research and development	28,000	0	28,000	0	0	0
Storytelling live/storytelling bursaries	46,000	0	46,000	46,000	0	46,000
Projects total	*534,000*	*520,000*	*1,054,000*	*1,044,500*	*434,500*	*1,479,000*
Total	**1,613,455**	**520,000**	**2,133,455**	**2,533,671**	**434,500**	**2,968,171**

support, nationally and internationally, to individual writers and storytellers, in education, as well as with regard to readership and audience development. In many ways these three areas represent overlapping virtuous circles: activity and support in one of them invariably impacts on and benefits the others.

This, however, is a brief outline of the core business only; to enumerate all developmental work and new initiatives undertaken in the past two decades – such as the establishment of the Canongate Classics series or the Readiscovery National Book campaign in the 1980s – would take another chapter. Moreover, in the closing years of the twentieth century it became increasingly clear that it would be impossible to contain the major burgeoning of Scottish literature within the tight parameters of the SAC literature budget, the mediation of overwhelming demands upon which constituted an increasingly hairraising, high-wire challenge for successive literature directors. Finally, while the total budget for literature has risen consistently since 2000, and is set to increase substantially in 2007, the sums have remained at approximately the same level of only 4 per cent of the SAC's total expenditure on the six 'artforms' it supports: crafts, dance, drama, literature, music, visual arts.

By 1999 there was strong consensus among the literature community that 4 per cent was unacceptably low; concomitantly, there was a growing recognition that due to its substantial social and cultural benefits, as well as the size and reach of its 'audience', public investment in – as opposed to 'subsidy of' – literature was remarkable value for money. To cite just one compelling example, in 1997 a modest production grant was awarded to Scottish Braille Press for the first Braille edition of a recent children's novel. The publisher organised a small launch event in an obscure Edinburgh hotel. There could not have been more than twenty people present, and both press and media were conspicuous by their absence. The author was a shy, awkward and little-known J. K. Rowling, and the book was *Harry Potter and the Philosopher's Stone*. What promised to be a rather routine tepid-sausage-roll occasion was made unforgettable when a blind boy read from the opening pages of the book in a voice of such preternatural beauty that the author was not alone in being moved to tears. In retrospect, it was a powerfully symbolic moment of literature's unique ability to overcome the most insuperable of barriers, and how the most meagre of resources could effect an appropriately magical transformation. Bringing the book to life for both audience and author, and expressing so palpably the imaginative transport it represented to him, the boy had 'seen' for us the alchemy of the mass-media miracle that was just around the corner. Another part of this parable has become modern folklore: only a few months before the book-launch event, an impoverished Rowling had successfully applied for a writer's bursary of £8,000 to complete the second Potter volume, a lifeline without which, as the author herself graciously acknowledged, *Harry Potter and the Chamber of Secrets* (1998) together with the rest of the series would most probably have sunk without trace. Less than £10,000 of public money laid the foundations to the greatest ever global phenomenon in the history of publishing.

Between 1999 and 2005 the SAC Literature Department conducted a programme of research into almost every aspect of literature in the country, starting with an audit of the SAC-supported national literature organisations, which not only confirmed the deleterious effects of decades of structural underfunding, but also helped identify hitherto unrealised potential for these organisations to collaborate in a more strategically 'national' and long-term fashion. The most significant result of the audit was the establishment of the Literature Forum for Scotland in 2001, an independent body comprising the ten corefunded national literature and language organisations, as well as other national agencies representing the interests of writers and libraries, ranging from the National Library of

Scotland and Scottish Book Trust to Scottish PEN and Scotland's Playwrights' Studio. The Forum would play a seminal role in the first years of the twenty-first century in formulating, in partnership with the SAC, a national policy for the development of literature in Scotland, and in determining, not without some controversy, what might be the most appropriate support structures for sustaining Scottish literature's success in the future. The continuing rise of that *succès d'estime* – embodied by such figureheads as Rowling, Rankin, Warner, Welsh and latterly also Michel Faber, Alexander McCall Smith and Louise Welsh – took Scotland's literary profile onto a new plane. Such pinnacles, however, could be attained only through the luckiest of breaks, or the longest and most arduous of ascents. For a majority of writers life down in the foothills remained a precarious slog. A comprehensive consultation with Scottish writers in 2000 confirmed the rigours of that pilgrim's progress: over 50 per cent of the 500 writers surveyed earned less than £5,000 a year from their work, while a much smaller number earned over £100,000. Over 50 per cent of writers did not have a literary agent. Yet strikingly, the majority of respondents felt confident about their future careers, and more than a third rated the profile of writing in Scotland as 'high' or 'very high'. Over 50 per cent were also happy – underfunding apart – with the SAC's models of support. The majority of respondents exhorted the government to introduce tax breaks for writers, and an 'honours' system, following the example of the Republic of Ireland. The consultation revealed a profession bruised by adversity, but unbowed in its commitment to the craft – pilgrims all right, but with a tough love.

At last the road was beginning to level out somewhat. In 2002 a £500,000 cash injection into the Writers' Factory – a large raft of initiatives to support training for screenwriting – significantly widened the SAC's remit and passed on extensive benefits to a whole range of writers, publishers and organisations. This was followed by a clever SAC-corporate conjuring act, which saw the Council's governmental grant-in-aid and its National Lottery funding reconfigured in such a way that serious amounts of additional money became available for all artforms. Coinciding with the SAC's publication of 'Literature, Nation' – its five-year strategy plan for literature, produced in collaboration with the Literature Forum and robustly underpinned by the research programmes referred to above (see Scottish Arts Council 2002) – the majority of literature agencies began to expand ambitiously. In 2003, the Scottish Book Trust, for example, moved to the remarkable Sandeman House, nestling in an urban glade in the heart of Edinburgh's Old Town behind the Netherbow. The Trust trebled its capacity and remit, establishing BRAW ('Books Reading and Writing'), a new network for the children's book, as well as words@work, a groundbreaking new training and mentoring programme for writers. Serendipitously, the adjacent Netherbow and its occupant, the hugely dynamic Scottish Storytelling Forum, secured major lottery funding in the same year to metamorphose stunningly into the world's first purpose-built National Centre for Storytelling in 2006. Meanwhile, the Edinburgh International Book Festival (EIBF) also underwent spectacular growth and maturation between 2001 and 2005, surpassing its own ticket- and book-sale records each successive year, trebling its visitor numbers, and emerging with great panache and professionalism not only as the biggest festival of its kind in the world, but also as a major national and international cultural institution: an arena for serious critical and intellectual debate and 'a place where thought happens', to use its own motto.

The public's keen appetite for contact with authors and complex ideas revealed the general paucity of intellectual and imaginative stimuli in mass-media popular culture. The book-festival phenomenon – closely linked to the mushrooming of readers' and writers' groups – did not remain confined to the capital; new literary festivals, most of them

SAC-funded, sprang up across the nation in Glasgow, the Borders, Perth and Kinross, Pitlochry, Inverness, Ullapool, Orkney, Shetland and Lewis. At the same time, longer-established events such as WORD at the University of Aberdeen, the StAnza Poetry Festival in St Andrews, and the Wigtown Book Festival grew into national fixtures. By 2005 barely a calendar month would pass without a book festival of some kind somewhere in the country. Scotland had become a book nation.

Scottish literature's growing national momentum was reflected by a sharper international profile. Applications to the SAC for supporting the translation of contemporary Scottish writing increased four-fold, with writers like John Burnside, Ron Butlin, Faber, Gray and Kelman attracting major media coverage overseas and winning distinguished translation prizes in Europe. In the case of Burnside, media coverage in France of the first French translation of one of his novels dwarfed the total UK coverage of the title's original publication. But quite how firmly Scotland had imprinted itself on the world map through its literature, past and present, was acknowledged by UNESCO's historic designation of Edinburgh as the world's first City of Literature in October 2004. The fact that the designation was announced six months earlier than anticipated, and only hours after the city's presentation to UNESCO of an elaborate dossier setting out its case, testifies to the timeous and powerful originality of this ambitious project, pioneered by EIBF and the Scottish Publishers Association (SPA). Designed to maximise Edinburgh's literary pre-eminence on behalf of the whole literature community in Scotland by creating partnerships with other aspirant literary cities across the globe, Edinburgh as UNESCO City of Literature is not just a vision for literature, but also a paradigm of how art and culture can be used imaginatively to promote a nation and engage its citizens. It is unique in that the designation is a permanent one, rather than a transient accolade such as the European City of Culture honour, thus allowing for a slow-burn momentum of great potency.

With a further injection of additional funding to the national literature infrastructure in the form of a 40 per cent increase to the SAC's literature budget following rigorous planning and campaigning, the total expenditure for Literature now stands at just under £3m, double its level in 2000. Thus 2007 marks the beginning of a new era of support, development and expansion, introducing a major structural reconfiguration of the sector in collaboration with the Literature Forum. As laid out in 'The Word on the Streets', an as yet unpublished statement of the Literature Forum, the chief aims are to create 'clear, integrated and transparent structures which are understood by the general public, the education sector, and writers themselves' and to maximise 'public awareness and social and commercial engagement'. The precise form of Creative Scotland, SAC's successor, has yet to be determined, but the prominence afforded to literature and the creative industries in its remit, as specified by the Scottish Executive, has the potential to position literature a great deal more centrally within the nation's cultural landscape. Indeed Scotland's literature community, strengthened by its remarkably fruitful unanimity since devolution, is highly unlikely to acquiesce to anything less. Its contention that literature's particular dynamic, its centrality to literacy and education, its underpinning of democracy, as well as the special symbiosis between readership and citizenship combine to make it fundamentally distinct from the other arts is powerfully persuasive (see Carey 2005). One might even want to go further and argue that literature's uniqueness is obscured by being subsumed within the generic catch-all category of 'the arts'. As Donald Smith, convenor of the Literature Forum, has asserted, 'the period when Scotland's literature could be adequately served as a junior partner in SAC's funding line-up is over . . . it is time for literature in Scotland to help make time for literature globally' (Smith 2003: 8).

There can be little doubt that one of the chief catalysts in making the twenty-first century a 'time for literature' in Scotland was the landmark win by Canongate Books of the Man Booker Prize for Yann Martel's *Life of Pi* in 2002. It was a triumphant vindication of the need for independent vision, innovation, and sheer chutzpah in a sector increasingly driven by transnational multimedia centralisation. The fact that the author was Canadian, and not a Scot, added sweetness to the taste of success; here was the ultimate accolade to a publisher that, while committed to Scottish content, had insisted on situating it within a cosmopolitan context.

In an odd way, the book and the win were the conjoined fruits of the best available support structures for publishing in both countries, Scotland as well as Canada, even although the two models in question could not have been more unalike. Canada's exemplary support programmes are so expansive and shamelessly interventionist that when Gordon Platt, head of publishing with Canadian Heritage, presented the details to a small gathering of Scotland's publishing professionals at a Royal Society of Edinburgh symposium in 2004, there were (literally) gasps of astonishment – and embarrassment. As Platt revealed, Canada was pouring an extraordinary $47 million per year into publishing, helping sales of books of indigenous origin in Canada to rise to almost 30 per cent in 2000, not to mention its largesse in the direct support of authors. In Canada the state rewarded commercially successful publishers, and an exquisite equilibrium appeared to have been achieved also in the government's support for the industrial and cultural imperatives of the industry. Meanwhile, Scotland greeted its publishing entrepreneurs with a Calvinist wince and threats of claw-backs. Even allowing for the two countries' disparities in economy, population and geography, as well as their common heritage of minority languages and coexistence with powerful anglophone neighbours, Scotland's equivalent overall support for literature of only £2 million per annum (approximately 25 per cent of this devoted to publishing) resembled a dugout canoe next to a luxury cruise liner. The disparity also highlighted the severe limitations in state support beyond the SAC for the creative industries in general. Scottish Enterprise, the country's leading economic development agency, has steadfastly resisted pressure to widen its parameters of support to include aid to SMEs (owner-managed, small-to-medium-scale enterprises, of which Scottish publishing is largely comprised) and thus embrace the cultural as well as economic spheres of the creative-industries sector.

Subsequent to Canongate's Booker Prize win – as well as other stratospheric successes such as Alexander McCall Smith bankrolling Polygon (acquired by Birlinn, now Scotland's second largest independent house, in 2002) and the decision by two metropolitan colossi, Penguin and Hodder Headline, to open branches in Scotland – the SAC published its 'Review of Scottish Publishing' (Scottish Arts Council 2004). Its consultants, PricewaterhouseCoopers and Napier University, found the sector to be diverse and operating in highly competitive markets, yet significantly hampered by a lack of capital, investment and general business skills. Particular attention was given to the relevance of the Canadian model to Scotland, and a new investment vehicle for publishing in Scotland was recommended, together with legislative measures such as a minimum purchase scheme for indigenously published titles for Scottish libraries. Other recommendations – such as an e-commerce portal for Scottish books, a think-tank on kick-starting educational publishing, and a new magazine to promote Scottish books – were swiftly implemented by the SPA and the *Sunday Herald*, which launched the *Scottish Review of Books* in 2004. All these developments resulted in an optimistic, buoyant and productive time for an industry well known for its defeatist view of Scotland's position in a globalised anglophone marketplace as a disadvantage rather than an opportunity, and prone to its periods of depression (in both senses of the word). The SPA reflected the positive mood in its decision to undergo a major restructuring in 2006 to provide more direct services to writers, expand training and develop overseas rights sales.

But was there a spectre at this modest banquet? The Publishing Review's emphasis on the global industry's growing centralisation became a prophecy fulfilled in the latter half of 2005 by the takeover of Ottakars by HMV Waterstones, which hung over Scotland's publishing and literary community like a funereal shroud. The affectionate nicknaming of the venture as 'Wottakars' did little to dispel the gloom felt at how sharply this threw into relief the true vulnerability of a central part of Scottish culture, and indeed how fragile many of its recent achievements had been. The Competition Commission was asked to ascertain if the bid was fair, and it agreed to a request from the new Cross-Parliamentary Group on Scottish Writing and Publishing, established in 2005, to hear evidence from the sector. The case for considering Scotland separately was argued persuasively by the SPA, who in their (unpublished) submission to the Competition Commission of 2005 identified the crucial issue as 'whether the production of material relevant to Scotland could continue to be published if the merger of these two businesses were to happen, given the concentration of buying power for Deep Range bookshops which would result'. Despite firm consensus that the Commission ought to respect the need for the book market in Scotland to reflect adequately national expectations and preferences in cultural, educational and general-interest content, the case was dismissed in March 2006, as was a subsequent SPA appeal.

In the light of this baleful example of the power of corporate capitalism to elide rather than respect national boundaries and culture, it is clear that writing and publishing in Scotland are now facing their biggest threat since the early twentieth-century collapse of its once-mighty publishing domain and the concentration of conglomerate-publishing ownership from the late 1980s onwards. In fact, the present predicament is infinitely more acute, as the country's literature has never had more to lose. What is at stake is not merely the issue of writing, publishing and selling books, but the degree to which a nation should exert control over the expression and mediation of its identity. What is needed is that clever Canadian equilibrium: while carefully minding its own borders, Canada has also cautiously welcomed conglomerate giants like Pearson and Bertelsmann, which provide an international market for Canada's literary stars. Ironically, although a threat similar to 'Wottakars' visited Canada in recent years with the arrival of Chapters/Indigo, the country's culturally interventionist legislation, the like of which would be illegal under European law, mitigated the potential damage significantly. 'Wottakars' has exposed the inadequacy of the Scottish Executive, who failed singularly to act on a matter of profound import to Scotland's identity and national culture, disclosing disturbingly the real extent of the limitations and inherent contradictions of Scottish devolution.

There has been since 1997 a critical orthodoxy, subscribed to also by writers, that Scotland's literature played a central role in articulating the pressures towards political change that led to devolution. As Roderick Watson observes, 'the main "state" left to a "stateless nation" may well be its state of mind, and in that territory it is literature which maps the land' (Watson 1995: xxxi). Territory and maps presuppose journeys; literature has provided both the vessel and the 'voyage of intent' towards the Parliament, and beyond. Such metaphors are gracefully conjoined and enacted in one of Robertson's parliamentary sonnets:

For in the end a Parliament is not
a building, but a voyage of intent,
a journey to whatever we might be.
This is our new departure, this is what
we opted for, solid and permanent,
yet tenuous with possibility.

(Robertson 2005: 24)

Robertson's politicised aesthetic equally validates Christopher Whyte's contention that 'in the absence of an elected political authority, the task of representing the nation has been repeatedly devolved to its writers', suggesting that 'the setting up of a Scottish parliament [would] at last allow Scottish literature to be literature first and foremost, rather than the expression of a nationalist movement' (Whyte 1998a: 285). But what kind of 'parliament', one wonders? Indisputably, devolution and the Scottish Parliament have done nothing to change one fundamental fact: Scotland remains a stateless nation within the anomalous polity of the UK as, indeed, does England itself (see Gardiner 2005).

It is therefore legitimate to ask to what extent contemporary Scottish literary culture's profile, reach and growth have actually benefited from devolution, and emancipated it from an alleged obligation to re-channel thwarted political aspirations and bear the yoke of the identity question. According to Eleanor Bell, there has been a significant shift. 'If the predicament of the Scottish writer in the 1980s involved the need to incorporate Scotland into her or his own work, to reflect upon the political predicament', Bell writes, 'then in the 1990s and afterwards it seems the writer has been allowed some respite from this' (Bell 2004: 41). However, if it is true, as Douglas Gifford and Alan Riach argue, that 'national identity can now be accommodated in literary discourse as a concept encompassing diversity and pluralism' (Gifford and Riach 2004: xxviii), then one is prompted to query who determines the parameters of what constitutes the 'diverse', who polices the 'plural', and on whose behalf. Might the new postmodern configuration of Scottish identity possibly be guilty of perpetrating the very essentialism it purports to deconstruct?

As Bell continues to assert, 'for many writers [devolution] is no predicament at all. Rather it provides a long-awaited and much-needed potential for Scottish literature to look beyond the often overly fixed boundaries of 'home'' (Bell 2004: 41). Indeed, it is striking how unanimously many eminent Scottish writers have recently warmed to this theme. For example, Robertson concludes in 'Scotland's an Attitude of Mind' that 'the most exciting thing about recent Scottish literature is its sheer diversity of voice, accent, language, ethnicity, genre, style, sexuality' (Robertson 2005: 55). With characteristic directness Janice Galloway asks 'who wants to write about *nation* all the bloody time', adding that 'cross-fertilized soil is always richer, and it might help us get off some of the rather tedious single-track roads this country's writers are often expected to go down' (Galloway 1999: 70–1). Galloway's view is mirrored in Kathleen Jamie's somewhat gentler meditation on the constraints of representational orthodoxy:

For some years issues around 'identity' have been . . . energetic, but really, I feel it's over now, for me at any rate – I mean, those issues are resolved. There is no more poetic energy in them. Mined out. So to carry on would be . . . they'd risk becoming an orthodoxy. There was a short term task to do, it had to be done, a political task, but now it's time to move on. (Fraser 2001: 15)

'Time to move on': time to cross and transcend, not heed or reinscribe borders. Ironically, Jamie's cultural perspective resembles, however benignly, the increasingly global capitalist forces driving the selling, as opposed to the writing, of books. The extent to which the paradigm of 'Scottish literature' as a necessary political, devolutionary act has shifted and turned into the supra-national, supra-territorial concept of 'literature *in* Scotland', or Bell's literature '*from* Scotland' (Bell 2004: 41), must be regarded as possibly the most conspicuous and far-reaching characteristic of contemporary literary identity in the country.

A brief synopsis of three prize-winning literary works of the past five years produced 'from' Scotland, yet not explicitly 'about' it, may serve to confirm this dramatic enlargement of compass. At first glance Galloway's *Clara* (2002), a fictional biography of the German composer Clara Schumann (1819–96), could not appear any more detached from Scotland, until one recognises its preoccupation with creativity, insanity, love and gender as perfectly congruent with that of Galloway's Scotland-specific debut *The Trick is to Keep Breathing* (1989). Also, could one possibly find a novel more cosmopolitan than Meaghan Delahunt's *In the Blue House* (2001), the debut of an Australian resident in Scotland, set in New Mexico but concerned with the Russian Revolution or, to be more precise, the last days of Leon Trotsky (1879–1940) and his relationship with the Mexican painter Frieda Kahlo (1907–54)? And then there is Rory Stewart's extraordinary travelogue *The Places in Between* (2004), about the author's walk across Afghanistan in the aftermath of the collapse of the Taliban, which is an exquisitely understated indictment of contemporary imperialism, a book whose global significance is finally and movingly 'grounded' in the author's epiphanic return to his native Perthshire.

The dominant trend in post-devolution Scottish literature has become the displacement and not a definitive fixing of identity, and in this respect contemporary Scottish writing provides an exemplary illustration of Geoffrey Harpham's conceptualisation of literary 'movement':

> The essential thing about a text is that it is portable. Not only can it be carried, but it seems at a deeper level to be *made to carry*, to bear the word out from the culture of origin into the wide world, to speak to others. Just as literature integrates and filters group identity, it also constitutes a lesion in the bounded cultural self-imagination, a principle of communication that presupposes otherness, and others. The text itself 'imagines' readers far away, who must in turn imagine the original world of the text as well as the possible community of other readers. (Harpham 1999: 5)

As a generation of younger critics has begun to recognise, even Scottish writers whose work is renowned for invoking 'the local' are integrated within these cosmopolitan imagined communities of writers and far-away readers, and engage with equally profound aesthetic and philosophical dichotomies, not entirely unrelated to Harpham's paradox of movement. As A. J. P. Thomson argues in his reading of Kelman's fiction:

> His use of the vernacular is not however an assertion of a pride in his nationality, or of a given Scottish identity, but a recognition of a more involved paradox. A parable of the local can only have significance elsewhere in the extent that it asserts itself as *general*, and thereby reinvents the appropriative logic of the system against which Kelman's characters find themselves thrown, which effaces the individual's identity in the name of the general. (Thomson 1999: 151)

The local-within-the-general will be forever offset by the general-within-the-local; correspondingly, the universally parochial is the parochially universal, as in Hugh MacDiarmid's classic long poem *A Drunk Man Looks at the Thistle* (1926): the further the poem travels into the narrator's consciousness, the further out into the cosmos it ventures. Every voyage inward is a voyage out: with a vitality and vigour unprecedented since the twentieth-century literary renaissance, post-devolution Scottish writing is being inwardly nourished by the deep, outward-reaching international taproots of Scottish culture. However 'tenuous with possibility', if Scotland as a small nation is to find a meaningful place within the world, it is literature that will take it further on that voyage of intent into the community of nations, and it is likely to get there before the politicians do.

As Duncan McLean shrewdly observes, 'writers aren't bound to follow' (McLean 1999: 74).

Chapter 3

In Tom Paine's Kitchen: Days of Rage and Fire

Suhayl Saadi

I am currently writing a stage-play about violence and secrets, including those surrounding the partition of India in 1947, the independence war of Bangladesh in 1971, and the ongoing territorial dispute about Kashmir. If less than ten years after the first two of these massive political upheavals one were to have attempted to gauge their literary repercussions, one would naturally have missed Salman Rushdie's *Midnight's Children*, published in 1981. Similarly, perhaps 'The Great Post-Devolution Novel of Scottish Autonomy', should such a thing at all be conceivable, has already been published or else may emerge sometime in the not-so-distant future. However, if one views the entire post-World War II period in Scotland as devolutionary, then one could argue that virtually everything written during that time has contributed in some way to the post-devolution literary-historical dynamic of national self-determination. But concepts such as 'autonomy', 'rights', 'representation' and so forth are fluid and tend to flow in complex tides between the individual, the world of ideas, and societal and political structures.

Together with the restructuring of governmental sponsorship of the arts, which may lead to greater investment in the sector, literary organisations such as the Scottish Arts Council, Scottish Book Trust, the Scottish Poetry Library, the Edinburgh International Book Festival and the Scottish Publishers Association have in recent years become collectively engaged in developing, promoting and selling Scottish literature globally. If one must enmesh oneself in the transnational capitalist mainframe and become a chip in the great 'cultural industries' complex, as opposed to being a shaman, a plumber of words, a petty bourgeois quasi-revolutionary, a heuristic wastrel, an anti-Benthamite sponger, then one might as well do it effectively. Writing is a broad church and the corporate requirements placed on a writer may not accord with the literary needs of a society. The effects of transnational corporatisation are complex and multivalent: a successful Scottish arts sector may be engendered by implementing a coherent cultural policy aimed at making Scotland an attractive environment in which creative people and companies would wish to invest. However, such a shift in consciousness would require that the whole process be seen not in the *passé* sense as 'subsidising the arts', but as investing in a 'rising tiger' business which has become crucial to the development of twenty-first-century civil society and a healthily diverse economy. The great positive about the arts is that the people involved in them are not normally alienated from their work; they have all the best features of both the 'innovation adopter' (Rodgers 1995) and the classic capitalist entrepreneur. All they need, in essence, is the means to pursue their craft, whether in the form of micro-grants or the parleying of larger, institutional dynamics.

One major problem of adequately appraising and appreciating Scottish literature resides in the British post-Thatcherite denial of contemporary class-conscious narrative. Those who shape literary discourse in the UK overwhelmingly are from, or have bought into, the social and political attitudes of an *über*-class, which feels threatened by such narratives, much more so than by similar narratives from 'exotic' countries, in whose case an imperial liberalism may be invoked. In the multicultural utopia of London, the 'movers and shakers' – who know neither how to move nor how to shake – have been openly scathing of class-conscious Scottish writers, referring in public to one colleague of mine as 'a performing monkey' and to another, in a now-famous national newspaper article, as 'an illiterate savage' (Jenkins 1994). It is not deemed unacceptable to make such comments about working-class writers because the whole issue of class, and hence of economic disparity and its link with contemporary corporate-military colonialism, has become taboo, thus allowing for the masking of a veritable legion of sins, including structural and archetypal racism and the perpetuation of foreign wars. The impermissibility of resistant class discourse at once maintains imperial dominance and contracts public space (see Mitchell 2006; Saadi 2006). Of course, it is one of the key harmonics of late capitalism that people come to believe that there is no such thing as social class. 'Celebrity culture' is premised on this presumption. In the West, many people really do believe that they are free, when in fact, as John Lennon reminded us a long time ago in 'Working Class Hero', they are only hallucinating (Lennon 1970).

My first published novel was *The Snake* (1997), a literary erotic fiction in the vein of Georges Bataille, penned under the pseudonym 'Melanie Desmoulins'. To my knowledge, this was the first novel by a black Scottish person, or Muslim Scot, ever published. It was followed by an eclectic short story collection, *The Burning Mirror* (2001), and *Psychoraag* (2004), another novel, in all of which I aimed to promote syncretism, liminality and heteroglossia in order to dynamise ideas of social class, ethnicity, history, musicality, geography and consciousness. The title of *Psychoraag* could poetically be translated as 'symphony of the mind' or 'symphony of madness'. I wanted to avoid the inertia of, as Stuart Kelly has expressed it in conversation, 'safe multiculturalism' by employing a multiplicity of referents – language, identity, history, song, reality – in the text, writing as a writer and not simply posing as a storyteller. To me, language must be mobilised, otherwise it is as though a classical composer were thinking only of the melody. I love the multilayered, rhetorical poeticism of many Arabic, Persian, Hebrew and Urdu texts, where a single word, phrase or idea, balancing on an incipient paradox, can come to mean many different things and thus link up with other ideas elsewhere in the text. To use a poetic terminology in a semiotic way, my stories strive not so much for rhyme as for assonance, or for even looser linkages, perhaps similar to Charles Baudelaire's *correspondances* between superstructure and substructures. Much of my fiction is not so much allegorical as employing symbols which operate simultaneously on literal and suggestive levels. In Sanskrit poetics, this process arouses in the reader that essence, *rasa*, which is central to attaining a state of knowledge. The reader becomes a *rasik*, a lover. In societal terms, as Rusmir Mahmutcehajić explores in a very different context, such processes can induce the reader to explore notions of tolerance and concepts of 'The Other', not in the liberal-materialist sense but on a syntagmatic, metaphysical plane (Mahmutćehajić 2003).

Far from being a regressive linguistic-political statement, the glossary in *Psychoraag* represents both a hypertextual, etymological exposition and a creative deviance from the psychological intensity of the narrative itself. For example, *hijaab*, the Arabic word for a woman's headscarf (but metaphysically speaking also the term for a protective spiritual 'covering'), sits next to *hijerah*, the Urdu word for 'transvestite'. Similarly, *khotay ka lun* (Punjabi for 'you're a donkey's prick') nestles up alongside *Khuda hafez*, which is Persian/Urdu for 'God go with you', and *khuserah*, the Urdu term for 'effeminate homosexual'. I did not intend to be outrageous; these juxtapositions are alphabetical and I have picked them at random. None the less, the effect is subversive and egalitarian: *Psychoraag* becomes an *hommage* to the work of Diderot's encyclopedists. Throughout the novel I would have preferred not to have italicised the non-Standard English words. I aimed to debunk the dominant London-Oxbridge text, the shrine by which even the most supposedly progressive narratives are framed, and to shatter the mirror of decorum, linguistically, culturally and in terms of a regressive class dynamic that defines most corporately published literary novels in the UK. I believe the positioning of my work within the post-Kelman context of contemporary Scottish literature has made such a critique both possible and necessary. I wanted to tear away the comfortable tropes of 'The Multicultural Novel' and to say it like it is. My influences evolve, but bar some exceptions they tend not to be from the nineteenth- or twentieth-century literatures of England. *Psychoraag* is not an exotic theme park of 'The Asian-Scots experience'; rather, it traverses the rivers of history and memory and the courses these rivers take through our lives.

Predictably, my stance, my place and my history have excluded my work from the sources of capital in the corporate publishing industry and, outside Scotland, from the media-literary complex which services this industry (see Alibhai-Brown 2003; Chakrabarti 2003/4; Dolan 2004), and this has made it increasingly difficult financially for me to continue to write. We are not in the hip, multicultural utopia which many metropolitan commentators seem to mistake for a postcolonial situation. Scotland has recently witnessed the emergence of a vibrant, relatively egalitarian and emotionally unrestrained literary scene, a 'stand-up' scene, possibly encouraged by the nature of literary discourse in Scotland going back to the Enlightenment as well as from strong radical-political movements of the past. Listening to Alasdair Gray expound, one could be right back there, in Tom Paine's kitchen. Although they may not be fully aware of it, many gatekeepers of English mainstream literary discourse are still living in either the 'long' nineteenth century or the 1950s, which partly explains the relentless obsession with the works of Jane Austen and the persona of Elvis. Symptomatically, both periods are quintessential epochs of white cultural hegemony and modernity. It is crucial to recognise that just as (they say) even in the apparently tidiest metropolitan centre one is never more than six inches removed from the skin of a rat, so contemporary western culture is never more than a snake's kiss away from colonialism, slavery, scientific and artistic supremacism, which should make us wonder 'where have all the mongooses gone' (Seeger 1956).

In school during the 1970s I had some very enlightened English and history teachers and I have worked with and lived among all social classes in Scotland. All this helped my mind expand, take root and develop a sense of an infinite canon. When I began to write, in the early 1990s, I did not wish to parrot the machismo urban style which by then was already becoming hackneyed, gratuitous and denuded of power. Instead, I explored mystical, transcontinental vistas, hoping that they would take me out of both my head and my life. I read, for example, Gustav Meyrink, Hermann Hesse, Vladimir Nabokov, James Joyce, Patricia Duncker, Doris Lessing, Mihail Bulgakov, Edward Synnott, Sheikh Nefzawi, Anaïs Nin, Juan Rulfo, Yukio Mishima, Jorge Luis Borges, Primo Levi, Jesus Ignacio Sanchez, Ben Okri, Naguib Mahfouz, Italo Calvino, Julio Cortazar, Juan Goytisolo and Thomas Mann as well as mystical and wisdom literature by Jalaluddin Rumi, Sheikh Saadi and Hafez Shirazi, old texts from Arab Andalusia, and experimental and political writing from the

USA and elsewhere. This literary fare played well with my love of psychedelic music, which goes back to 1979, the Winter of Hate; no one yet seems to have perceived the links between *Psychoraag* and Donald Cammell and Nicolas Roeg's film *Performance* (1970). I then returned, as it were, to urban Scotland and used some of this experience when I wrote *The Burning Mirror* and *Psychoraag*. In an appropriate circularity, having been invited by my old school recently to deliver a Burns Immortal Memory speech, I drew comparisons between hallucinatory religious themes in my short story 'The Dancers' (Saadi 2001: 121–30), set in a contemporary kirk-cum-nightclub in Glasgow, and Robert Burns's 'Tam o'Shanter'. In some senses, I see myself as the inheritor of Tam's mare's tail.

Every tongue talks into being a universe; so, allowing tongues to dance up close with one another results in a raag of lunacy, a cosmic song. Most mainstream anglophone writers and publishers cannot grasp this essential instability of language. Take Rushdie, for example. Of Kashmiri origin, he was brought up in India, but I have never heard him speak either Urdu or Kashmiri. Whereas my Urdu is instinctual and fragmentary, Rushdie – even though technically more multilingual than I – is likely to sound like a late 1940s' goon (Saadi 2005). There probably exists a class analysis of Rushdie's work somewhere in a high tower of academe, but I have never seen one in the press. Language is political always and everywhere, but in Britain we have the added ontological nuance of language as the mediator of social class. The English *über*-class of white upper- and upper-middle-class southerners remains the driver of empire. In the subconscious vistas of fiction, one plays around with this elite at one's peril. However, the increasing diversification and tendency to immanence of English around the globe, apart from raising economic, educational, political, cultural and ethical issues, also catalyse exciting and challenging developments in the evolution of anglophone consciousness. Broadening the range of the sextant enlarges its possible horizons. In this ocean of words, Kelman is Khair ad Din Barbarossa and I am a bathyscaphe.

Unfortunately, in the UK many gatekeepers are neither equipped nor willing to engage with the new global phenomena. One anonymous publisher's reader recently stated that in my work 'the use of unusual words and foreign words is a difficulty' and 'they seem to be drawn from such a broad range of languages and traditions that their impact and meaning became lost'. This reader also found the footnotes 'truly bizarre' and 'disturbing'. Signalling acute (partly sexual) anxiety at the dissolution of old boundaries, this kind of response is no less than fundamentalist monocultural rearguard action disguised as a sensible plea for decorum and aptitude. By contrast, in respect to the same work, the Scottish Arts Council assessors 'were unanimously impressed by . . . the quality of [the] writing, [which was] considered outstanding'. In a recent British Council research report David Graddol predicts 'the Doom of [English] Monolingualism', suggesting that 'Asia, especially China and India, probably now holds the key to the long-term future of English as a global language' (Graddol 2006: 16–17); in other words, the boot will be well and truly on the 'Other' foot. Graddol also posits that in the linguistic sense, the dynamic begun during the period of British imperial ascendancy ended in 1989 with the close of the Cold War, and in Kabbalistic synchronicity it was in the fall of that very year that I began to write. Just as Graddol argues that 'we need a "paradigm shift" in our perception of language and of the place of English in the rubric of world languages', so – in my view – we require a revolution with regard to the corporate comprehension of the potential of English-language fiction. Fiction-writing should be in the van of this 'innovation diffusion' (Rodgers 1995). As Graddol continues, 'in many countries, English still forms a key mechanism for reproducing the old order of social elites – especially those originally constructed by imperialism' (Graddol 2006: 22), and in my view, in the UK as well, the very template, so to speak, of this process – that is, the system itself – will not reform itself. There is a fundamental disconnect between the relatively open, noisy panoply of democratically accountable 'soft power'-liberal state institutions, which hold some degree of devolved autonomy (such as the British Council, the BBC, local authorities, the Arts Councils), and the nepotistic, iron-wrought, class-defined apparatus of corporate power. A new structure, with entirely different dynamics, must be kicked into being.

Colonial hierarchies of power – linguistic, racialist, class-oriented, geographical – dissemble, but remain definitive. Literary censorship in the UK today is not monolithic; there is no man-with-a-blue-pencil (I am referring here only to fiction and not to non-fiction, in particular non-fiction written by whistleblowers, without which blue-pencil manufacturers would go out of business). Yet, just as in the internal world of fiction one is constantly shadow-boxing, so its external environment consists of a series of filters that are reflective of the nodes and flows of knowledge and power in our society, and these are based on both deliberation and ignorance, not only with respect to language but manifold other contexts as well – in fact, with regard to everything informing even the most basic understanding of the role of art in the world. To change, or even prove, this is extremely difficult. Well done, the Lancaster Litfest (2005) for being the only England-based literary festival ever to invite me to read. In the current climate, being a male from what is one of the most despised, undereducated and excluded minorities in the UK – that is, the Pakistani community – living in what is from the Thamesian elites' viewpoint a peripheral region, writing narratives which challenge both liberal-imperial and multicultural-metropolitan received wisdoms, and being neither foreign enough to be deemed 'exotic' nor tamed enough to be seen as 'one of us', comes pretty close to being delegated to the bottom of the neo-colonial slushpile. As Ali Smith has commented on *Psychoraag*, 'the critical silence that met it down south is an interesting reaction in itself to a book about race and invisibility, voice and silence, whose central theme is the question of whether anyone out there is actually listening' (Smith 2004).

One might expect large, corporate publishers to entertain cosy relationships with large, corporate media outlets. But the filters are more complex. Assuming one has developed the talent and craft of writing, the five essentialist-totemic rate-limiting steps seem to be class, politics, ethnicity-faith, language and location. If you and your work have three or more of these on board, then you are in with a chance. If you have none of these, then regardless of the quality and significance of your writing and potential saleability of your book, you will find yourself (to be euphemistic for once) in a very difficult position. Fiction is politics, but politics is not fiction. On a personal level, this systemic pathology is exemplified by the experience of Yasmin Alibhai-Brown, a British journalist of Ugandan-Asian origin who has lived in the UK since the early 1970s and is the author of a regular column for the *Independent*. Recently, so Alibhai-Brown informs me, she was approached by an editor from a liberal paper, who said to her: 'You have done well, haven't you? Great touch that, having the Brown at the end of your name, certainly helps.'

Agents, publishers, librarians, festival programmers, arts officers, booksellers and so forth permitting, even a challenging book like *Psychoraag* might be able to do things with readers, even turn some sort of tiny wheel, and this again proves that unlike many publicly owned or publicly financed institutions, which seem to have a much broader conception of possible literatures, too often corporate entities have their heads screwed on the wrong way, their mouths wide open and their minds tightly shut, waiting for the latest Bollywood-dream vindaloo sensation to come along and spice up their taste-buds. But even in the anti-entrepreneurial, private business world, incremental progress does occur: Asian writers are being published in Britain. However, too often, in the hallucinatory multicultural utopia of London, the work of the latest groovy writer of Asian origin comes to be worshipped by the (white) gatekeepers of the literary salons as little more than an innocuous bogus cipher for colonial redemption. Yet beggars and whores – which even after Mahatma Gandhi, Malcolm X, Martin Luther King, Nawal el Saadawi, Che Guevara, Angela Davis and Jim Kelman is still what most of us are at the end of the day – can't be choosers, and to disable further any critique of this whole, festering psychodrama, it is no longer seen as good form to get angry about anything other than semantics. This emotional and linguistic manipulation is a direct consequence of the corporatisation of our societal mentality. It is as though the carpet-baggers had buried both Jesus and the Word in snake oil under their temple and then obliterated the slab of his grave so they might endlessly take his name in vain. So we must keep on pushing! One day, we may no longer be 'emergent' writers from 'developing' countries, purveyors of tourist maps to unknown territories or bow-tied waiters supplying bellyfuls of chillies and brain-pans of endorphins. One day, our unmodulated voices will be listened to on a par with those of middle-class white writers. One day, we may even own the chain(s) of production. And as wishful prophecies go, quite possibly it will take the fulfilment of the latter to deliver the former.

In these days of rage it seems I lack the equanimity to compose an academic-style essay, and so I have bashed out a diatribe. No doubt I run the risk of landing in Dante's Ninth Literary Hell. I would prefer the Eighth, as then at least I would be in good company, since in the psychotic cosmogony of *L'Inferno*, the Ninth Bolgia of the Eighth Circle is the bloody ditch to which for eternity the Prophet Mohammad and other 'Sowers of Discord' were banished. Cultural war is all-consuming. I cannot just go off to a monastery or sleep on friends' floors for seven years, or cut cane with the natives in some exotic locale, or live in a garret while I pen the masterpiece, or do any of the romantic nonsense about 'writers' put out by publicity departments. Dante's vision has been transfigured from the diabolic to the ridiculous: his celebrated inferno is now a termite mound. No wonder, historically, so many black artists have self-destructed. In the smouldering fires of their kitchens, Tom Paine, Camille Desmoulins, Frantz Fanon, Robert Burns, Malcolm Shabazz, MLK, W. E. B. Du Bois and the rest knew that the rationale, establishment and perpetuation of freedom necessitate constant struggle. But before struggle, there is the requirement first to rise from Dark Age cerebration and to recognise that one is in a state of unfreedom, and at best this recognition can be a tangential achievement of literature. In my view, whether one is talking about freedom for the peoples of Scotland, South Asia and the Middle East, or for humanity as a whole, in this Aeon of Kali the essence of building – or indeed, of permitting the survival of – both a progressive politics and a meaningful literature must be about enabling the possibility of dissent against the sources of power.

Chapter 4

The Public Image:
Scottish Literature in the Media

Andrew Crumey

In 1846 Edgar Allan Poe published 'The Literati of New York City', a series of articles in which he discussed thirty-eight writers well known and admired at the time. Poe wrote:

> The most 'popular', the most 'successful' writers among us, (for a brief period, at least) are, ninety-nine times out of a hundred, persons of mere address, perseverance, effrontery – in a word, busy-bodies, toadies, quacks. These people easily succeed in *boring* editors . . . into the admission of favourable notices written or caused to be written by interested parties . . . In this way ephemeral 'reputations' are manufactured which, for the most part, serve all the purposes designed – that is to say, the putting money into the purse of the quack and the quack's publisher. (Poe 1984: 1118)

Public taste, in Poe's view, was generated by a cosy collusion between the press, publishing houses and enterprising authors, all acting more in the interests of self-promotion, or out of sheer laziness, than the advancement of art. Similar claims are made today; but while there undoubtedly will always be authors whose success owes as much to entrepreneurship as literary talent, the more interesting question concerns the nature and operation of a commercial-critical nexus which nowadays includes not only publishers, booksellers and a greatly expanded media, but also festivals, funding bodies, prize givers, universities and other sectors, all serving to produce public taste while at the same time responding to it. I shall examine this question in the Scottish context focusing, after some preliminary remarks, on the reception of Irvine Welsh's *Trainspotting* (1993), and although much of what will be said here about public taste in literature is by no means unique to Scotland, two special features will be worthy of note. The first is Scotland's peculiar status of semi-autonomy within the United Kingdom, leading to an ambiguity between 'local' and 'national' identity which has important ramifications. The second is Scotland's small population, roughly a tenth that of the United Kingdom as a whole, meaning that Scottish writers – and book buyers – form a sample whose small size makes statistical variance a significant issue. As we shall see, these features become intimately bound up with attempts, in the period since *Trainspotting*, to define Scottish books as a distinct literary and marketing entity.

Poe held the traditional view that aesthetic value, judged ultimately by the test of time, need not match economic value, measured by sales, media attention and so on, and the fact that all his thirty-eight authors are nowadays forgotten (while Poe alone is remembered) would appear to bear him out. Marxism, however, introduced the idea that aesthetic value is itself a product of socio-economic conditions, and this is a matter of continuing debate. Many people have an intuitive sense, grounded in historical experience, that often the most innovative artists struggle initially to gain recognition. But there is also a commonly held feeling that literary canons reflect the interests of an elite, and that works which achieve mass popularity should be accorded the same critical attention as those aimed at a more specialised audience. Whatever one's view, it is evidently important to be able to distinguish between the aesthetic, economic, political or other significance of artistic works. The present chapter will restrict itself entirely to the economic and political. There will be no discussion of aesthetics, not because I consider this the least important or interesting element in literature (quite the reverse), but rather because – as Poe recognised – it plays the least important role in public taste. Poe's analysis of literary reputation was, however, overly reductive, and a useful innovation of Marxist theory was its recognition that social and economic systems are self-interacting and not reducible to simple causal chains. Public taste, like all social phenomena, arises from a complex network of feedback loops, the crucial factor being the extent to which any person's judgements or actions are influenced by those of other people. Viewed in this way, public taste is a measure of the non-independence of personal opinion, and with this in mind, we can consider how literature differs from the other arts in the way that reputations are constructed. Anyone can form an opinion of a film in ninety minutes or of a television show in half an hour. Books take longer, and this is the principal reason why literary opinions are more likely to be of the received kind. When our newspapers and other media inform us about 'leading' writers whose books are 'acclaimed' or 'award-winning', there is every possibility that the adjectives are being deployed by people who have not personally read the works in question, and it is equally likely that these terms of praise will be accepted at face value by readers happy to be freed from having to form an independent view.

In purely economic terms, the value of a newspaper to its owner or shareholders resides in the profits which can be raised from selling advertising space, and from sales of copies to readers. Thus a newspaper can be thought of as an advertising medium whose news, features and opinions provide added value which will attract readers and hence advertisers (the same being true for any commercial content provider on television, radio, the internet or elsewhere). The various forms of content used to do this result in the familiar, if blurred distinction between 'quality' and 'tabloid' newspapers, as well as between 'local' and 'national' ones, and the high journalistic standards attainable in all these fields explain why most people are happy with a free press based on private ownership. Scotland's main quality papers are the *Scotsman*, based in Edinburgh (together with its Sunday version, *Scotland on Sunday*, of which I am former literary editor), and the *Herald* (and *Sunday Herald*), based in Glasgow. All four papers carry book review pages which are the main literary forum in the Scottish media. There are also Scottish versions of UK papers, for example the *Sunday Times*, which carry specifically Scottish material in addition to UK content. The spectrum of 'local', 'regional' and 'national' newspapers is as blurred as that of quality and tabloid: all newspapers are in a sense local, so that a disaster in a foreign country, for example, will be reported in relation to how many Britons/Scots/Glaswegians were victims. Historically, the Scottish press was regarded, in Scotland, as being regional, and there remains some uncertainty in people's minds about its status. What, for instance, should be the balance between Scottish, UK and international coverage, both in news and in the arts? Every newspaper must strike a balance between parochialism and cosmopolitanism that will appeal to its readers' expectations. With regard to book coverage, there is a general understanding that Scottish books are likely to have particular appeal, and these are therefore well covered in Scotland's quality press. Certainly, books get reviewed which, if they were not Scottish, would receive no such attention.

The necessity of carrying specifically Scottish content as an appeal to reader expectation means that in news coverage a Scottish angle is forever being sought. If a writer was born in Scotland or sets a book there, this might provide the required angle, but whether it counts as news, to be covered outside the books pages, depends on the writer's perceived status; and for living authors, lacking the benefit of a 'classic' aura, the primary measure is economic or political rather than aesthetic. For newspapers generally, there is really only one reason, other than *fatwah*, why a contemporary novel will become a news item, and that is money. A million-pound advance is a story (usually an inaccurate one emanating from an agent or publicist), particularly if the recipient is the kind of 'ordinary person' readers can relate to, such as a bus driver or former waitress. Most literary authors, though, make very little money from books, so prizes are one of the few ways they can break into wider public recognition: the Man Booker Prize gets global press coverage, always with an emphasis on the expected income from increased sales. Inevitably, public figures are usually recognised as local heroes only once their fame and wealth are established: we have seen this, for instance, in the case of J. K. Rowling – and not only in Scotland. The Portuguese press have run stories on the café in Lisbon where Rowling's writing career allegedly began while she was resident there, reflecting the political desire within small nations for famous role models who enhance the national image.

From an economic perspective, the purpose of publishing book reviews in newspapers is to offer content which will attract readers from the required target audience. For authors and publishers, reviews serve in most cases as the sole form of advertising that a book will receive, and among the reading public, reviews are typically seen as a guide to which books might be worth reading. Poe alleged that review space goes mainly to those writers who make most noise, but the biggest noise-makers nowadays are publicists. The book industry, like the rest of the entertainment industry, is dominated by a small number of conglomerates whose various publishing imprints bear the names of once-independent houses that have been taken over. These imprints retain varying degrees of editorial independence, and in many cases maintain the highest standards of quality and integrity. They also have at their disposal the full array of modern marketing and promotional tools, and in the effort to maintain profit margins, the usual emphasis is on putting maximum resources into a small number of products which have the greatest likelihood of giving a healthy return on investment. The result is a strategy which is highly focused and risk-averse: a writer's first book increasingly becomes his or her one real shot at success, buoyed by expectation and unhindered by past performance. Many journalists and pundits like to be seen as spotting 'the next big thing', and hence are highly responsive to this strategy. If the book fails it can be quietly forgotten along with its author – there are always plenty of other first-time writers.

Over the last decade, independent booksellers have been supplanted by a small number of chains, with the HMV Group (owners of Waterstones, Dillons and Ottakars) having a major share of the high-street quality-fiction market. The issue of 'local' versus 'national' is of particular relevance with regard to bookselling. In any bookshop in the United Kingdom one usually finds a section devoted to 'local interest', stocking guidebooks, histories, memoirs and humour (such as books on local dialect). In the Scottish branches of high-street stores, the 'local interest' sections are typically replaced by 'Scottish' ones, often positioned prominently near the front of the store. The UK-wide technique of promoting a small number of selected titles through strategies such as 'Book of the Month' campaigns finds its counterpart in 'Scottish Book of the Month' initiatives. The front-of-store tables of new titles, which generate the majority of sales, are joined by tables devoted exclusively to Scottish books. This is a distinctly Scottish phenomenon: no English bookshop, for example, has an 'English' section; nor is it usual for 'local interest' sections to be dominated by fiction, as has happened with Scottish books. Yet the identification of Scottish books as a distinct marketing entity has evident commercial implications. Just as some books get reviewed which otherwise might not, we find books put on sale in the most prominent part of a bookstore which might otherwise be relegated to the unprofitable shelves. The case in favour of this is economic and political: the practice stimulates sales of Scottish books within Scotland. One could say that anything that makes books sell is a good thing; the question, though, is which books. There is no clear definition of what constitutes a 'Scottish' book, and within bookselling the concept is best thought of as a form of branding.

To see how this has grown historically, let us go back to the early 1990s. James Kelman was shortlisted for the Booker Prize in 1990 and won it in 1994. Alasdair Gray's *Poor Things* won the 1992 Guardian Fiction Prize and the Whitbread Award, and the Whitbread First Book Award went to Jeff Torrington for *Swing Hammer Swing*. Granta's list of 'best young British novelists' in 1993 included A. L. Kennedy and Iain Banks. It was a time when the British book world became aware of Scottish writing as a distinctive entity; like the Indian subcontinent, Scotland was a part of the Booker-eligible Commonwealth which offered something colourfully different from most English fiction. London publishers Jonathan Cape and Secker & Warburg (now both part of the Random House Group) were particularly keen to acquire Scottish writers. Duncan McLean signed up with Secker, and on his recommendation they also acquired Alan Warner and Irvine Welsh. The latter's first novel, *Trainspotting*, received considerable pre-publication publicity, as can be seen in the following extract from the first Scottish newspaper interview with Welsh, which ran eight days prior to the novel's official release:

> It has to be said that *Trainspotting* is a bum title for a would-be bestseller – just try asking for it in Waterstone's and watch the funny looks from other customers. Undaunted, PR people from Welsh's London publisher, Secker & Warburg, are waging a campaign of hype unprecedented for a debut Scottish author, enthusing breathlessly that the book will be huge and that Irvine is 'just a lovely man'. A Secker executive makes known his belief that Welsh will 'do for Edinburgh what Jim Kelman did for Glasgow'. Jeff Torrington, winner of the Whitbread prize, calls the debut novel 'wickedly witty . . . a bad day in Bedlam'. This month's *Literary Review* hails a 'wonderfully sordid depiction of how the other half dies and why it matters'. All this flannel usually has self-respecting journalists reaching for the vitriol. But not this time – *Trainspotting* turns out to be a genuine wonder . . . Imagine Jim Kelman with a sense of humour and six cans of superlager, and you will be close. It is revolting, funny, scary and deeply affecting. Best of all, it destroys the myth that the only Scottish urban working-class culture worth a damn can only be found a pub crawl's distance from Parkhead and Ibrox: the east coast keelie has arrived. (Farquharson 1993: 55)

As well as quoting a wide range of favourable opinions, the piece places *Trainspotting* within an established context of 'Scottish urban working-class culture'. Thus, the largely middle-class readership of *Scotland on Sunday* were made aware of the literary importance of the novel before it went on sale. Poe might have seen this as another of those 'favourable notices' by which 'reputations are manufactured', but the inadequacy of Poe's view is seen in the way the *Scotland on Sunday* writer both reports and distances himself from 'hype' and 'flannel', considering them in this case justified. We also see that from the outset, an important part of the book's appeal was political in that it offered an east-coast alternative to the Glasgow writers who dominated Scottish public literary taste at the time – something that was of particular interest to Edinburgh-based newspapers. The following weekend, *Scotsman* literary editor Catherine Lockerbie previewed Welsh's forthcoming appearance at the Edinburgh Book Festival as follows:

> [*Trainspotting*] abounds with a fierce wit and a full-frontal use of the demotic (there are passages here which make James Kelman sound like Anita Brookner). This is a young writer of wild talent. His session in Charlotte Square, light-years removed from the milieu of his work, should be of intense interest, and just what the Book Festival should be doing: providing a platform for the cutting edge of the new amid the comfort of the established. He reads on Monday, 30 August, at 12.30pm with another vigorous young author, Duncan McLean, also percipiently picked up and published by Secker & Warburg and whose last volume, *Bucket of Tongues*, was the winner of a Somerset Maugham award. It will be interesting [to see] how the various award-givers, after their inital gulps, honour *Trainspotting*. (Lockerbie 1993: 13)

The scheduling of two authors from the same publisher at a reading together is not unusual at book festivals, since publishers have control over authors' promotional appearances and see festivals and bookshop events as important marketing tools. Lockerbie herself went on to become a highly successful and well-regarded director of the Edinburgh Book Festival, achieving record ticket sales in an increasingly crowded market: over the last decade, new book festivals have sprung up in Glasgow, Aberdeen, Wigtown and elsewhere, all competing for the same top names who attract the largest audiences. The delicate nature of such mutual economic dependency can be illustrated by the recent example of a major Scottish festival organiser, who was offered an author who, for some reason, was not wanted. A phone call from the publisher, gently threatening that other authors might not be made available in future, was sufficient to make the organiser give way. The press is equally vulnerable to such symbioses: freelance journalists known for writing flattering and uncritical profiles are the most likely to be offered first interviews which they can readily sell. The situation is familiar in the film and music industries, and inevitably recurs as literature succumbs to the same celebrity system.

The *Scotsman* article also mentions the annual round of prize-giving, whose UK season runs from the early-autumn Booker shortlist to the Whitbread award in January. Since 2001 the Booker (now Man Booker) longlist has also been made public, offering a boost to the languid late-summer book market. As the single most important factor in generating mass sales for literary authors, prizes are a crucial, if unpredictable part of any publisher's marketing strategy, and the talking-up of books as likely contenders is an integral part of pre-publicity promotion for lead titles, even though, as always, a delicate balance must be drawn between advantageous 'hype' and counterproductive 'flannel'. At the weekend of the publication of *Trainspotting*, the pseudonymous 'Harvey Porlock' column in the *Sunday Times* led with Welsh's debut, offering a round-up of the extensive coverage the book had already received, and when the Booker Prize shortlist was drawn up some weeks later, *Trainspotting* – so it emerged later – made the final ten.

Prizes in Scotland serve much the same function as elsewhere, though what is particular to Scotland is the notion that a Scottish prize has to be for a Scottish book. As with the 'Scottish' sections of bookstores, this reflects the continuing ambivalence of regional versus national identity. *Trainspotting* failed to win either a Scottish Saltire award (announced annually in November) or the then privately sponsored Scottish Book of the Year award. But Welsh did win a Scottish Arts Council award in May 1994, by which time he had already published his second book, *The Acid House*. In a pre-publication interview in the *Scotsman*, the Edinburgh-versus-Glasgow theme was again prominent:

> 'We're the cultural equivalent of the casuals,' says Irvine Welsh, with a big happy smile. He's talking about a new grouping on the Scottish literary scene: young east-coast writers whose violent energies make the macho west-coast hard men seem suddenly old and tame. These boys, and girls, are out to administer a kicking to tradition, and – better watch your step, pal – Irvine Welsh is leader of the pack. (Lockerbie 1994: 13)

The article failed to name any other members of the 'new grouping', but during the following months, when *Trainspotting* was staged at Glasgow's Citizens Theatre and Edinburgh's Traverse Theatre, the Glasgow-based *Herald* was able to offer a more conciliatory comment on east–west relations: '*Trainspotting* proves that theatre can be the new rock'n'roll . . . Edinburgh and Glasgow can produce work that is world-beating when they join forces' (Bruce 1994: 15).

By now Welsh's work was already a familiar cultural commodity and a source of national pride, though it was not until the summer 1994 release of the Vintage paperback edition of *Trainspotting* that the book began selling in truly large numbers, being picked up by readers beyond the usual literary fiction audience, who had been made aware of it by the stage version and attendant media interest. Welsh rose to the top two places in the Scottish bestseller list, compiled at that time by the Scottish Book Marketing Group, which appeared in the *Herald* on 27 August 1994:

1. *Trainspotting*, Irvine Welsh, Vintage 1994
2. *The Acid House*, Irvine Welsh, Cape 1994
3. *Teach Yourself Doric*, Douglas Kynoch, Scottish Cultural Press 1994
4. *Para Handy Tales*, Neil Munro, Birlinn 1992
5. *The Wee Scottish Book Of Facts*, A. Scott, Straightline 1994
6. *Scottish Island Hopping*, Vivien Devlin, Polygon 1994
7. *The Wasp Factory*, Iain Banks, Abacus 1992
8. *The Sporting Urban Voltaire*, Jack McLean, Neil Wilson 1994
9. *Glenkiln*, John McEwen, Canongate 1993
10. *Scottish Clans And Family Encyclopedia*, edited by George Way and Romilly Squire, Collins 1994

Apart from Iain Banks's *The Wasp Factory*, first published ten years previously, all the other books are of the humorous, historical or topographical kind traditionally classed under 'local interest' and issued by Scottish-based publishers. Now fiction was being seen as part of Scottish books. Alongside this list, however, there was also a 'general' one, based on sales in Scotland of all types of book, and one of its highest places went to William Boyd's *The Blue Afternoon* (1994). Boyd was educated in Scotland; so should his novel have been in the 'Scottish' list? A book about tartan or Doric evidently fitted in, as did Welsh and Banks. Novelists whose work was not recognisably 'Scottish', even if they were born or lived in Scotland, did not. Given the promotional advantage of bestseller listing and prominent bookshop positioning, it began to make commercial sense for a novelist to be branded as Scottish, at least within Scotland; though elsewhere, such branding might have little effect, or even an adverse one, if the writer came to be seen as local or regional. Thus Scottishness became an issue, with many novelists, including myself, being routinely asked to what extent their work was 'Scottish'.

The idea that *Trainspotting* emerged from an Edinburgh-based literary movement was a response to what was already by then something of a foundation legend for modern Scottish writing, namely the creative-writing group run at Glasgow University during the early 1970s, whose participants included Kelman and Gray. A memorial to an even earlier epoch is Sandy Moffat's painting *Poet's Pub*, showing Hugh MacDiarmid and others in a meeting that never happened, set in a non-existent venue. As Stuart Kelly has commented, *Poet's Pub* is 'fundamentally a fiction, a response to some yearning for a "group" or "movement" that Scotland could hold up against Bloomsbury Square, the Cabaret Voltaire or the Algonquin Hotel' (Kelly 2005: 188). The international media proved eager to share this yearning: in February 1996, some months prior to the release of the film version of *Trainspotting*, the *New Yorker* sent photographer Richard Avedon to Glasgow to make a group portrait of Scotland's leading writers, assembled in the Clutha Vaults pub. The following month, the *New York Times* ran a feature by Lesley Downer titled 'The Beats of Edinburgh', describing her meeting with

> writers who have smashed their way out of rave culture onto the British literary scene. In a cyber era in which literary circles are usually metaphors, they hang out together in Edinburgh's pubs, clubs and rave bars . . . They live the life of Edinburgh beats – get up at noon, drink, talk and write the day away, and party through the night. All are young and fiercely working class. They write about people on the margins of society: the young, the poor, the dispossessed, junkies, Ecstasy users, football hooligans and people who live on the dole in housing projects. (Downer 1996: 42)

Downer reported that 'in Scotland, writing is a form of protest by the alienated, a subversive act'. She found her Edinburgh beats in a Leith pub, though of the 'dozen or so' making up the group she named only Alan Warner, Duncan McLean, Gordon Legge and Paul Reekie, as well as Kevin Williamson, her host for the evening, who anthologised all four writers in *Children of Albion Rovers* (1996). Not present was fellow contributor Irvine Welsh, 'the undisputed star', whom she interviewed in London. Literary movements – real or imaginary – make great newspaper copy, but the narrow definition of Scottish writing presented in Downer's piece, as well as countless others, did not match the diversity of work being produced. Over the next decade, important Scottish novels were written with historical themes, middle-class settings, fantasy elements or other factors echoing the concerns of literary writers everywhere. Within Scotland – particularly since devolution – there has been a conscious reaction against restrictiveness and an urge to conceive 'Scottishness' in the widest possible terms, replacing alienation with multicultural modernity. This, however, has created new anomalies.

When *The Life of Pi*, by Canadian author Yann Martel, won the Man Booker Prize in 2003, publisher Canongate quickly made it known that this was a victory for Scotland, since Canongate are based in Edinburgh. Such distinctions are muddied by the fact that the United Kingdom remains a single publishing territory, and whereas a book may have separate American and British editions, it cannot have distinct English and Scottish ones. For a publisher to count as Scottish in the eyes of the Scottish Publishers Association (SPA), it is sufficient for it to run an office north of the border. The SPA is a major shareholder of the e-commerce site BooksFromScotland.com, launched in 2005 with Scottish

Arts Council funding to sell and promote books which are 'of Scottish interest' or 'by a Scottish author', or which have been 'published in Scotland'. At the time of the launch it was found that *Case Histories* (2005) by Kate Atkinson, long resident in Scotland though published in England, was not listed on the site, despite the fact that the novel had been awarded the Saltire Award for best Scottish book not long previously. The omission was quickly rectified, but it highlighted the subjective and imprecise nature of the inclusion criteria. If residence in Scotland makes a writer Scottish, we could count Pierre Ronsard, Poe and Orwell alongside Atkinson and Rowling. If publication in Scotland makes a book Scottish, then the Bible is presumably German, thanks to Johannes Gutenberg. Outside Scotland, ancestry is seen as the main qualification for Scottishness, but this view is less prevalent within Scotland, where Ian McEwan, for example, is never considered a Scottish writer, whereas the Canadian Alistair MacLeod often is.

When it comes to the notion of Scottish bestsellers, other complexities arise. For a British hardback literary novel to enter the UK bestseller list, sales of only a few hundred can suffice. Scaling that to Scotland we arrive at a figure of tens: a book that sells one or two copies in the right branch can end up with 'bestseller' status. This was illustrated when journalists compared the official lists produced by the SPA with electronic sales figures from Nielsen BookData. The journalists found that in one week, five top ten titles had recorded fewer than a hundred sales throughout the UK, while in another instance, a top ten title had registered no sales at all, prompting the claim that 'the official Scottish bestseller list has been exposed as a sham' (Goodwin and Legg 2005: 8). The article also quoted an unnamed SPA spokesperson as saying the list was compiled from information supplied by a number of Scottish bookshops, and 'as a publicly funded body we can't justify spending thousands of pounds a year on buying information from Nielsen . . . We make no claim that it is completely accurate, but we do take it as an average indication.'

The rise of the internet and text messaging has created new forums of public taste. In 2005 the results of the poll of 'Scotland's 100 Best Books' were announced, a campaign sponsored by Orange and headed by Professor Willy Maley of Glasgow University. At the launch in Edinburgh Maley said that the intention was to provide a 'road map' of Scottish literature that would benefit schools in Scotland and universities around the world. Others involved in the project insisted it was not an attempt to create a new canon but only a means of stimulating interest in books. As ever, the question arose which particular books would attract interest. One controversial feature of the poll, whose initial list of 200 books was drawn up by a team headed by Maley, was the preponderance of living authors, some of whom had only published a single book: the test of time evidently conflicted with the more pressing desire to be contemporary and forward-looking. Equally contentious were the inclusions of Joseph Conrad's *Heart of Darkness* (1902) and Virginia Woolf's *To the Lighthouse* (1927), as well as the Authorised Edition of the Bible. Of the final top ten, most were by living authors, four had been published since 1993, and the oldest were James Hogg's *Private Memoirs and Confessions of a Justified Sinner* (1824), George Orwell's *1984* (1948), and Lewis Grassic Gibbon's *Sunset Song* (1932), which was also the overall winner with around 400 votes. The booklet accompanying the campaign was distributed to schools throughout Scotland (Maley 2005). Scaling arguments suggest that a similarly representative list of great 'English' writers would need to contain at least 1,000 names, with Robert Louis Stevenson presumably being among them.

In the period since *Trainspotting* Scottish public literary taste has been torn between the overly restrictive and the overly inclusive, reflecting the old dilemma of parochialism versus cosmopolitanism. Restrictiveness gave rise to a recognisable international brand, while the ensuing combination of inclusiveness and triumphalism has resulted in manifestations of national aggrandisement whose appeal can only be domestic, and it is fortunate that such global ambitions are not matched by any ability to do genuine international harm. To the practising writer for whom aesthetics are paramount, such political and economic questions need be of no concern; however, to anyone interested in the mechanics of public taste – a subject pondered so provocatively by that famous 'Scottish' writer Edgar Allan Poe – the issues are intriguing, puzzling and not infrequently amusing.

Chapter 5

Literature, Theory, Politics: Devolution as Iteration

Michael Gardiner

Scottish literature since the 1960s has inherited – but also been critical of – earlier native traditions of thought, which find their most salient expression in the Enlightenment and the Empire. Once we accept Scotland's centrality to the intellectual architecture of the British Empire, we must also accept that Scottish thought has been proactive in leaving imperial ideals behind. Looking back into critical history, one finds that a detached reliance on universal aesthetic standards was strongest in imperial times, but imploded after empire. In this chapter I will introduce and discuss some of the properties via which we can identify Scottish models of thought as 'postcolonial' and hence trace a general way of understanding the motives recurrent within recent, post-devolution Scottish writing.

The extent to which Scottish Enlightenment aesthetics relied on the conception of a stable and separate, judging viewer for its universally valid constructions of civility, cultivation and beauty depends on how much we believe David Hume (1711–76) modified the form of the subject-self he had inherited from René Descartes (1596–1650). Opinions on this vary; for some Hume's theorising points towards a critical self which is less detached and more active (see Kemp Smith 1941). Generally speaking, however, in Hume's work the self's relation to art is described along objective lines, and the critic and artist are not normally understood to be active at the same time, even if one might want to argue that a critic completes a work of art by registering its beauty. This leads to an aesthetics which is primarily visual and spatial in orientation, which in turn relates to the definition of certain imperialist properties, such as the idea of race, deemed to be derived from 'objective' judgement through vision at its least sympathetic – and race, of course, has more wide-reaching Scottish implications than most of us would like to admit. Moreover, in the nineteenth century we see how these cognitive modes, which were originally designed for classification and judgement, crucially contribute to emergent discourses on anatomy, eugenics and imperial management. The *philosophes* of the Enlightenment were also primarily unionist, culturally at least, and a British standard was often embraced as the natural final stage of national development; we see this in the creation of English literature as an academic discipline, conceived of as a set of standards for the correct use of language to be found in a small canonical group of English writers.

It is this effort of consolidating Britishness, rather than a general lack of enquiry by individual intellectuals, which accounts for the blankness in literary culture from the 1830s to the 1890s. Although there are certainly theorists who are sceptical of British, universalist approaches to Hume, even in the twentieth century the Scottish tradition of critical thought is most commonly associated with a practical imperialism subsumed under the pan-British discipline of English literature. The post-Enlightenment period of consolidation of objective aesthetic goodness ran from the time when Scotland first began to benefit from imperial investments in America – that is, the 1740s – to the mid-nineteenth century when Scottish social climbers would appear with disproportionate regularity on a wider imperial stage. In the first half of the twentieth century the British movement of logical positivism attempted to reappropriate Hume in terms of his scepticism over any experience threatening to intervene in the relationship between viewer and object, but this time Scottish thinkers reacted. For John Macmurray (1891–1976) in particular the rejection of experience in favour of logical truth was '*prima facie* a pure receptivity' (Macmurray 1969a: 43). Macmurray also makes the link between this receptivity and visual, spatial understanding, as well as drawing a parallel connection between knowledge based on touch and social action, since touch provokes an active, real-time resistance in the other (Macmurray 1969a: 106). In visual-spatial understanding, cultural forms which are outside the normative standard are identified as past; thus popular guidebook assertions that some cultures are stuck in another century, or the pronounced fascination of native intellectuals like Hume with English history, which seemed to indicate a more advanced or progressive stage of civilisation. Within such a standardised framework, art in Scots, for example, will always be perceived as 'backward' and deficient, and is expected to do its best to 'catch up' with the norm. This division corresponds with what postcolonial criticism has called a colonial time-lag which, once identified, led to an EngLit critique of the primacy of vision to understanding. What has until recently remained less explored are similarly postcolonial threads in modern Scottish literary thought, even though Scots are at the centre of the whole objective schema, and postcolonial strategies are widespread in recent Scottish literature and theory, Macmurray being one prominent example.

Macmurray's criticism of the primacy of visual knowledge, particularly in his criticism of logical positivism's use of Humean thought, has a deeper affinity with EngLit theory than one might expect. For example, on being presented with the following passage on an unmarked page one might easily be persuaded that it was authored by Jacques Derrida: 'From the time of the Greeks, and especially through the influence of Plato, "vision" has tended to be the model on which all *knowledge* is construed. Thought is taken to be an inner vision' (Macmurray 1969a: 105). This markedly un-British thinking also pulls away from the notion of organic society which we find in New Criticism of the mid-twentieth century, and which was absolutely reliant on objective standards and the belief in teleological evolution towards perfect civility. For Macmurray, society is not organic, but intentional and moral; it does not unfold naturally but needs persons to enact it experientially (Macmurray 1969b: 128). His agent is an acting self who generates experience intentionally, and history is always experienced rather than merely watched (Macmurray 1969a: 140). Macmurray's recovery of the present tense of action strikingly resembles Homi Bhabha's distinction, influenced by Frantz Fanon (1925–61), between anterior nations – that is, those which have always somehow been in existence, like the UK – and performative nations, which are understood in terms of action, like the four nations which are currently beginning to (re-)emerge from post-British devolution (see Bhabha 1994: 139–70).

Once the interaction between the person and the institution had become a central theme in the postcolonial era, knowledge of the other's experience was less likely to be described in terms of spatial distance. Scottish aesthetics also abandoned ideas of seeing and judging from a viewpoint backed up by objective truths. Neither the literary work nor the reader is now typically thought to exist in a purely subjective bubble; rather, they determine one another, and any aesthetic standards that are applied can always be related back to the social context of the critic. Criticism is an active process, a process which is always political as well as conducive, in its own turn, to the articulation of new forms of representation. The destination of Hume's universalism in this sense is not logical truth, as the British logical positivists believed, but rather recognition (John Macmurray), engagement (Alexander Trocchi) and empathy (R. D. Laing). Since the 1950s, always mindful of the legacy of the Scottish Enlightenment, Scottish critical thought has worked towards an ethical self-extrication from British imperialism. But this was, as one might perhaps expect, missed by the unionist governments responsible for devolution, which, as a result, was erroneously defined as a new form of managing *British* identity. Meanwhile, the breakdown of transexperiential standards has led to a recovery of experience which we might call the Scottish form of the postcolonial. This does not mean that Scotland can be identified as coloniser or colonised – to believe it was definitively identifiable as either would be to misunderstand it fundamentally as a nation. Rather, given the way in which objective standards have traditionally been used, a reworking of Enlightenment ideas is always liable to be postcolonial, and notably Scotland was more heavily invested in the Enlightenment than any other nation. Once we abandon the idea that postcolonialism must be limited to identifying definite victims, we are free to acknowledge that Scottish literary thought since the 1960s has been thoroughly underscored with postcolonial motifs.

Macmurray's personalist philosophy in particular shows a surprising affinity with post-colonial models. His celebrated Gifford Lectures, delivered at Glasgow University in 1953 and 1954, have much in common with Fanon's *Black Skin, White Masks* (1952), which has been massively influential in postcolonial cultural studies. Whereas since the Enlightenment the nation had been conceived of as static background, giving way to a form of state based on defence, Fanon described the nation itself as the collectivised action of personal change. Correspondingly, for Macmurray, the nation (rather than the state) is key in rescuing and pooling the political resourcefulness of active selves capable of recognition, or mutual understanding; in the work of both Fanon and Macmurray, the self becomes a 'person' by reaching beyond his or her own subjectivity towards a recognition and acceptance of the other. By contrast, the British gifting of devolutionary powers from one region to another involves little recognition, since it is not reciprocal. In Macmurray's view mutual recognition is a basic condition without which a society as a whole lacks the experience of otherness and, as a result, becomes fearful, negative and defensive (Macmurray 1969a: 123). Interestingly, Macmurray's theorising also finds an echo in the first chapter of Cairns Craig's *Modern Scottish Novel*, which bears the title 'Fearful Selves: Character, Community and the Scottish Imagination' (Craig 1999: 37–74). According to Macmurray, in personal intercourse the self is both subject and object, yet always being subject only 'negatively' or defensively; hence, personal and impersonal relationships are productive of two different types of knowledge, and of these two impersonal knowledge has traditionally claimed the upper hand while obfuscating its reliance on any specific experience or emotion. Logical positivism has been obsessed with objectivity, denying personal experience any significance or impact, and taken to the extreme would surely render literature either impossible or redundant, since literary representation has an acute interest in the speculative and the personal. Logical positivism certainly was a fiercely unliterary movement, positing a world untouchable by action, one in which 'nothing is ever done; in which everything simply happens' (Macmurray 1969a: 219). Its standardised aesthetic proposition petrifies into a certainty predicated upon a sustained denial of experience, which is entirely irreconcilable with literary expression.

In healthy societies literature and politics (as 'activism') ought to be in dialogue with one another. Extrapolating from Macmurray's distinction, devolution-as-action and devolution-as-activity are opposite tendencies in representing 'the relationship between the person and society' (as in Tony Blair's perplexing paraphrase of Macmurray [see Wheatcroft 2004]). Correspondingly, throughout postcolonial literature native populations are redefining themselves in terms of their own action and speech, released and removed from the political structures which have governed them. Gradually, since the 1950s, Scottish literary thought has learned to deal with the way British conceptions of devolution as management tend to contrast with indigenous ideas of devolution as community. As far as the British government is concerned, devolution constitutes little more than a reshuffling of local power with no active change in the relation of self to society, whereas, understood from a personalist perspective, devolution is far more political, saving the representation of relationships from becoming a mere managerial activity (see Nairn 2000). Put another way, for the ultra-centrist governments of devolutionary times, prone to conceiving of devolution as previous governments conceived of empire, devolution simply results in more empowerment for individual Britons rather than instigating or necessitating a complete social rethink. Within the UK government's grasp, the 'self' of 'self-rule' remains an enlightened subject, perfectly separated from the world, rather than an agent continually being redefined by action.

The two conceptions of devolution – as individual empowerment or as recovery of community – exist side by side in both London and Edinburgh. However, when we think in terms of the relation of the self to the social, we find that Scottish descriptions, in literature and in parliamentary politics, are more 'active' and 'political'. Yet what precisely does it mean to say that a certain form of representation is 'more political'? I would like to cite one fundamental example. In postcolonial terms Winnie Ewing's speech, which opened the Scottish Parliament in 1999, may have been problematic, since it claimed to 'reconvene' the institution, begging the question of whether the nation had remained entirely unchanged in the interim. At the same time, however, it conveyed a clear sense of some kind of political action taking place (see Ewing 1999). Not so with the newly 'devolved' Regional Assembly of London in 2000 when, in his inaugural speech, Trevor Phillips warned Ken Livingstone that the Assembly was not to be used for 'ideological purposes' (Phillips 2000). In Phillips's view, there was a danger the Assembly might be used solely for streamlining governance without much time for an ethical recasting of the relationship of the government to the people. Effectively appropriating the rhetoric of US foreign policy, Phillips makes his views very plain to Livingstone, concluding with the warning that 'if you decide to . . . choose to use the platform for other political ends, we will, I promise, kick your ass' (Phillips 2000). Nairn's description of British devolution as an institutional sleight of hand becomes even more ominous if one contemplates it not simply as a change of location but, as Phillips suggests, a move from political to non-political representation. From this angle it looks as if the citizenry were being trained to lose sight of the personal in society and allow 'political ends' to be expunged for abstract efficiency. However, giving up the political means also giving up any possibility of personal recognition and must result inevitably in a 'fearful' collapse into a society obsessed with its need for security. It appears the British press noticed nothing unusual about the first London Assembly proceedings, but Phillips's speech is momentous in so far as it dares invoke devolution as the creation of political assemblies in which no political action is likely ever to take place.

Scottish postcolonialism attempts to recover the potential for action which is buried within devolution; hence, postcolonial Scottish literary criticism must be committed to socio-political contextualisation rather than subscribing to timeless aesthetic standards. Close-reading criticism, as it was established by New Criticism from the 1920s, is now hard to practise with a straight face; seeing a text in isolation from any socio-political processes which have gone towards its writing or reading becomes pointless at best, and a liability at worst, obscuring any class, ethnic or gender assumptions which may have had an effect on production and publication. Scottish literature seems less bound by precedent than English literature, especially since it has begun to assume a critical stance to the universalism of Scottish Enlightenment aesthetics. Unlike the EngLit canon, heaving under the weight of its great writers, Scottish literature remains open to frequent democratic reshuffles, since it is not beholden to a catalogue of absolute values. In my view, it is most productive to understand the pulling away from precedent, which has recently opened up Scottish literature, as a post-Enlightenment and postcolonial effect enabled by a specific national and socio-political context in which representation continues to be active and political.

The British understanding of devolution might be described in terms of 'transport' or 'metaphor', that is, as ultimately purely vehicular, always referencing something more than itself which is posited to exist in an objective beyond. This understanding leaves devolution devoid of political content, reducing it to a mere metaphor for actual politics. Significantly, in *Anti-Oedipus* (1972) Gilles Deleuze and Felix Guattari define the metaphorical as that aspect of literature which is the least literary, always referring to something ideally absent rather than experience, and so having nothing to say about society (see Deleuze and Guattari 1983). As it takes power 'up' and 'down' between individuals and governments, at first glance devolution as 'metaphor' or 'transport' does seem democratic; however, since there is no personal relationship which might act as resistance, the metaphor has no resting place and its alleged political power is left without a personal destination and hence devoid of social meaning. As long as it remains simply in motion, and metaphorical, it does not signify politically how mobile power becomes. In *Art and Fear* (2000) Paul Virilio describes this ambush on democracy as an 'aesthetics of disappearance' or, put differently, the eclipse of the human for and by a logic of efficiency (Virilio 2000). As Macmurray realised, objective societies are maintained by a kind of perverted, albeit seemingly flawless democracy as people's needs are answered at an individual level without reference to the person's place in society, redolent of the multi-voicedness of 'spin' or of call centres. This kind of democracy is not political at all since it does not actually represent anyone. It is not based on personal experience, but derives from a position so centrist it owns no political position at all, even though of course it opens up the ideal space for the 'third way'. The centre is the path of least resistance.

So this has been the British conceptual framework through which devolution has been presented to the public, and it has proved such an irritant to Scottish literary studies that stocks in English literature, its cultural analogue, have plummeted. In turn, 'British culture' has become notably uncomfortable with national – that is, Scottish and Welsh and, less obviously, English and Northern Irish – ideas of devolution, which are far more active and less individualist. This is ultimately to do not with any specific governmental fib but with the general British tendency to separate politics from personal experience. Literature has the urgent political duty of putting the personal back, and it will do so without referring to a canonical set of properties. Consequently, if we lose sight of the particular context of the late twentieth-century boom in Scottish literature, we will never get to ask some very basic questions: in what sense is devolution a political happening? When is it action, when merely activity? What form of representation of the self would lead to the person being valued in society? Is there some ground degree of experience at which efficiency gives way to ethical content? How do we find and secure the right kind of mutual resistance, which will enable us to share experience and give history its human texture? When and how is the personal smoothed out of history altogether? All these issues are worried away at by the protagonists of Scottish fiction since the 1960s, though obviously not always encapsulated in devolutionary terms. They are central to the work of writers as diverse as Muriel Spark (in an overtly postcolonial context in *Robinson* [1958]), Kenneth White (in an overtly Deleuzian context in his privately published and distributed 'Jargon Paper #1' [1964]) and Alexander Trocchi (in an overtly personalist context in *The Sigma Portfolio* [1968]). Character development in fiction and rhetorical development in the literary essay often crucially hinge on whether other people are seen functionally, leading to alienation, or personally, allowing for mutual experience. (And this must not be misunderstood as a truism on literature in general: British literature has been much more market-led than many of its international counterparts while displaying a markedly less urgent interest in changing selves.) Characters are either bound by some abstract idea of progress, or struggle to represent themselves in active terms. Experience is often either pointedly visual, isolating individuals within separate spaces and times, or primarily based on touch, allowing individuals to share a single time of experience with others. As we read concretely back into Scottish literature, we find that it has increasingly moved towards the mutual, the active and the tactile.

Allow me now to introduce one more key term. The emergent Scottish literary tradition strongly corresponds to what Deleuze and Guattari have described in terms of a 'minor literature'. A minor literature exists within and despite of a major literature, and is quite similar to what we understand as postcolonial literature, in which personal relationships are often worked out through a non-universal, non-standard use of language. For Deleuze and Guattari – as also, later, for Bhabha – as a literature of effect and becoming rather than one of static assumptions, the minor is invariably more literary than the major. Scottishness could easily be described as a minor nationality, having few formal boundaries – being Scottish is an elective identity – and always becoming anew, its literature continually diversifying into new 'canons'. The minor is also the active: significantly, in Deleuze's view expressed in 'Literature and Life', the form of representation afforded by literature is nothing less than the creation of a people (Deleuze 1997). In *Kafka* (1975) Deleuze and Guattari summarise the three characteristic traits of a minor literature: (a) 'the impossibility of not writing because national consciousness, uncertain or oppressed, necessarily exists by means of literature', (b) 'that everything in [it] is political', and (c) 'that in it everything takes on a collective value' (Deleuze and Guattari 1986: 16–17). These properties – the linguistic, the politicised and the communitarian – are also typical of postcolonial writing, and Deleuze and Guatarri's ideas were of course strongly influenced by the context of the revolutionary events in Paris in May 1968, which should be understood as postcolonial, driven as they were by an Algerian diaspora. 'French theory', as it came to be known in EngLit circles, largely arose from France's relation to its ex-colonies. The three minoritarian literary properties defined by Deleuze and Guattari can also be seen at work in Scottish literature's use of Scots or Scottish English, as well as its emphasis on action and the personal. Once again, this correspondence does not require the Scottish nation to be identified as either coloniser or colonised; rather, it demonstrates that post-imperial, devolutionary literature is predicated upon a radical rethinking of Scottish Enlightenment ideas. Whereas the Enlightenment ideally separated the qualities of the iterative, the engaged and the communitarian, recent Scottish writing makes iteration a form of political action which is always directed at mutual understanding. This must be regarded as a general tendency in post-devolution Scottish literature, as illustrated by the following three examples.

James Kelman's Booker-Prize winner *How Late It Was, How Late* (1994) opened up a debate on representational aesthetics as no other work of fiction of recent years has done. Kelman's storyline is Deleuzian in that it rejects 'lack', that is, the idea that experience is never quite enough. Sammy, the novel's blinded protagonist, is perpetually in action, battering on, forced to 'feel' the streets in order to understand them, and ultimately basing a whole new cultural topology on touch. In *Anti-Oedipus* Deleuze and Guattari argue that lack is not, as Freud described it, necessary to desire, but in fact a blockage of desire, produced by capitalism and concretised in the law. Correspondingly, from the outset of Kelman's novel the law enacts various kinds of violence on Sammy, physical as well as personal; suggesting there is something originally wrong with him, the law tries to transport Sammy onto a quest for something that is ultimately missing, a universal, pre-experiential metaphor which is also supposedly experience's true destination. Sammy is literally beaten and blinded into this quest. The novel, however, resists Sammy's impersonal determination by re-alerting him to actual, physical, present concerns; even his blindness is not questioned beyond the novel's representation of it as an integral part of Sammy's present experience: 'He was definitely blind but. Fucking weird. Wild. It didnay feel like a nightmare either, that's the funny thing. Even psychologically. In fact it felt okay, an initial wee flurry of excitement but no what you would call panic-stations. Like it was just a new predicament' (Kelman 1994: 10). The law sets up a series of questions designed to force Sammy to catch up. The police demand that he 'clarify' himself (Kelman 1994: 15; see also Deleuze and Guattari 1983: 12–14). If he gave up his personal ability to act, Sammy would be obeying the law, just like the kafkaesque characters described elsewhere in Kelman's work (see Kelman 2002: 264–334). But Sammy walks away from any metaphor promising an explanation beyond his own immediate experiential grasp, enacting the Deleuzian proposition that the literary is what is not metaphorical but effective. Rather than accepting his present lack according to rules of precedent, Sammy takes each of his problems as a singular starting-point and begins to act out a series of new becomings. He is an agent rather than a subject, and his struggle is a miniature version of the movement from objective visual values to an un-metaphorical, direct representation of devolution.

As I have suggested, minor and postcolonial literatures tend to be strongly focused on the tactile, as demonstrated by Sammy's feeling his way out of the city. The 2003 Vintage cover of A. L. Kennedy's *Indelible Acts* (2002) is even more emphatic in this respect, showing a hand pressed against glass in darkness, and many of the collection's twelve stories clearly elevate the tactile over the visual. The title of one of the stories is 'Touch Positive' (Kennedy 2002: 91–106), while 'Awaiting an Adverse Reaction' (Kennedy 2002: 27–30), in which a doctor helps a patient reject both foreign diseases and her partner, exemplifies Macmurray's push-and-pull dynamic of mutually resistant personal relationships. The doctor is shown to administer a vaccination which allows the patient to go abroad, a 'prick' which is in itself poisonous and painful (the doctor's push) followed by her taking a tablet, which decides her on leaving (her own push). The brief bond gives the patient the ability to resist while also reminding her of the primacy of personal relationships. This kind of correlation of body, speech, and action is reworked in terms of iteration in 'An Immaculate Man' (Kennedy 2002: 33–52), in which the narrator struggles with his feelings towards his immediate office senior. Obviously ill at ease with his clients and unable to tell much about them from sight only, the narrator struggles to find a voice to speak to either his clients or his boss, reminding us of Sammy's stuttering towards self-representation in Kelman's novel – until, that is, his admission of wanting to touch his boss leads to a moment of personal understanding. In the end he feels an affirmative sensation course through his body, which is described as 'hot'. Also, throughout the story, the act of seeing is frequently depicted in tactile terms, as in turns of phrase such as 'reflections snagged his attention' or 'the effect was not untidy but it drew the eye' (Kennedy 2002: 38, 39). The space between persons is broken down, and it is in mutual recognition that experience occurs: '*I'll touch him. How can I not . . . Touch him as if he were me*' (Kennedy 2002: 41, 45). Through iteration a possibility is enacted; the struggle has been to say and recognise it, to allow the language to inhabit the body. In Kelman's work we find that narrators are stuck in quasi-autonomous space and often unaware of whether or not they are speaking. By contrast, in Kennedy's work the need to speak beyond subjective boundaries becomes a narrative principle.

The work of Alan Warner equally shows a physical working out of the becoming-political of representation. In *The Man Who Walks* (2002) the Nephew's mission of walking and climbing is most notable in its immediate physicality, as the landscape becomes ever more inseparable from his being within it (see Schoene 2006a). Similarly, the Uncle, out in the lead, lays his foot on the mountain towards unknown territory, both literally and figuratively. The pronounced physicality of the Uncle is extraordinary:

> Using two fingers, he reached up to his left eye and removed it. It was a glass eye. After he'd taken out the glass eye he poked into the dark recess of the socket and from beneath the little flap of skin he removed a small tin-foil package of cannabis resin. He unwrapped it, used his thumbnail to split away more than half, then swallowed the lump of resin. (Warner 2002: 89)

Beyond the undoubtedly entertaining aspects of the Uncle's drug-taking habits, what should interest us here is the high degree of corporeal physicality, the thumbnail on resin. The Uncle does away with his eye at will, and posts his abstention, like Sammy in Kelman's novel, from the world of surveillant, objective knowledge. The action of walking surpasses the activity of watching, setting in motion a self which is consistently being remade, a self not fixed visually or topographically dependent. Grounded in bodily resistance, these protagonists of recent Scottish literature are 'in touch' with the political rather than gauging the political by detached, absolute standards.

Chapter 6

Is that a Scot or am Ah Wrang?

Zoë Strachan

Scotland desperately wants to be a big city, albeit one with tourist-enticing mountains and glens, but in many respects it is still a small town. Just look at this phenomenon as described by Jeremiah Brown in James Kelman's *You Have to Be Careful in the Land of the Free* (2004):

> One usually associates it with small towns but it happens in major cities as well: stray into a new district and ye discover it is a homogenous hotbed of poisonous fuckers all staring at ye because ye are the wrong 'thing': religion, race, class, nationality, politics; they know ye as soon as look at ye, boy, you is alien.
>
> Even in places where it isnay obvious and ye think it is okay, suddenly the atmosphere shifts. It can even be your fault, you say something out of turn and the fucking roof caves in. (Kelman 2004: 27)

In a fresh millennium and new political era the endeavour is to redefine how we feel about Scotland, to decide what is means to us to be Scottish. Almost a decade ago Peter Kravitz wrote that 'the impossibility of staying and the difficulty of leaving is a constant refrain in Kelman's fiction' (Kravitz 1997: xxv). Some writers leave home, others enjoy the sensation of being a big fish in a small pond, and still others nurture a curious love–hate relationship with their muse, a muse they may sometimes want to kick in the balls, if I may gender Scotland as masculine for a moment.

You do not have to be a 'Celtic male with pink skin, fair hair (receding) and blue eyes (watery)' (Kelman 2004: 20), or to have inadvertently strayed into a spit-and-sawdust pub after a nil–nil Old Firm game, in order to empathise with the protagonist of *You Have to Be Careful*. The sensation of being 'alien' is familiar to any emergent Scottish writer, and the 'new district' referred to in the above-quoted passage can easily stand for the Scottish literary community as a whole. Not, I hasten to add, that I consider my colleagues, critics or readers to be 'poisonous fuckers', and certainly not because our culture is 'homogenous', but rather because there seems to be a pressing need to slap labels on writers and see what sticks. I would say that there are two 'wrang things' deliberately missing from Jeremiah's list. In all but the most specialised contexts, he is unlikely ever to find himself accused of being the wrong gender or sexual orientation. Although Jeremiah does note that of the gays in a bar 'a couple did gie me looks, but nothing new in that' (Kelman 2004: 41), the dominant context remains heterosexual. I am particularly interested in gender and sexuality in relation to literary constructions of Scottishness, so that is what I will focus on here, before commenting on various other elements of the wider cultural context.

In *Rewriting Scotland* Cristie March comments that

Kelman and Gray present what Keith Dixon suggests are 'post-feminist' men who engage in 'almost Calvinist self-flagellation in their relations with women', such as Jock's solitary and lonely sexual fantasies intended to mask his lost relationships in Gray's *1982 Janine*. Similarly, Galloway offers 'post-feminist' women who over-analyse and second-guess themselves in their attempts to build stable relationships with men, assuming the burdens of both feminist and traditional agendas but successfully carrying neither. (March 2002: 7; see also Dixon 1993: 103)

Dixon was writing in 1993; March was writing in 2002. Now, in 2006, we cannot claim either a social or theoretical climate which can usefully be described as 'post-feminist'. Third-wave feminism may have ebbed, but it did not disappear. Now it is surging again – in grassroots collectives, internet communities, books and newspaper articles – and there are plenty of foosty little corners in Scottish society and the Scottish psyche ready to be washed out. Would we say, for example, that Galloway's *Clara* (2002) is about Clara Schumann (1819–96) as a 'post-feminist' woman over-analysing and second-guessing herself in order to build a stable relationship with a man, her husband Robert? No, because the novel is set in the nineteenth century, a time when the beginnings of first-wave feminism were just about to ripple out from America. *Clara* is a novel praised for its humanism, but the historical context allows for a feminist reading to emerge far more clearly than if Galloway had chosen to write a similar story about a contemporary creative couple, never mind a Scottish one. It is worth noting that Galloway herself would not necessarily welcome any of her work being labelled 'feminist'. When asked if feminism was central to the writing of *Clara* she replied:

> No. I don't use the word 'feminism' if I can help it because it so often means automatic dismissal from talk of aesthetics or meaning or craft. You could say I've been bullied out of it, but for sure the word has become a corner for any writer . . . Besides, Clara herself was a great believer in men first – men as more valuable and valued. (Morton 2004)

Of course, rejecting the label 'feminist' in this context can amount to a feminist stance in itself – in terms of a rejection of the dominant perception of the creative act as originally masculine – though I suspect this is precisely the kind of statement Galloway would find frustrating.

Post-feminism is a dangerous term because it allows us to gloss over what is really going on. There exist many androcentric places in literature where women still appear as simulacra for Scotland and bear the brunt of masculine frustration at its own intransigent Scottishness. Some male writers are very knowing, such as Duncan McLean in *Bunker Man* (1997), but in the post-devolution context others produce work which is open to ambivalent interpretations. In *Porno* (2002) Irvine Welsh may be writing more in the tradition of the great satirists than the great social-realists, but I remain unconvinced by his female narrator Nikki Fuller-Smith (as well as by the participation of Spud, my favourite Trainspotter, in a meticulously described rape scene). Although Welsh takes care to introduce conflicting forms of feminism through the characters of Nikki, Lauren and Dianne, post-feminists may be disappointed that in the end Nikki is forced to realise the limits of her sexual liberation. As Welsh himself comments, 'if you're Nikki, you can be as radical a porn star as you like, but if you've got Sick Boy holding the purse strings and the camera, you end up another capitalist product in the marketplace' (Martin 2002). Not the least of Simon's exploitations of Nikki is that he edits his porn film to make it appear as if she had anal sex when this was the very act she refused to perform. Foregrounding male-on-female anal intercourse above all other forms of sexual activity, as Welsh consistently does, highlights the attitude of his male characters towards women: the fact that the orifice penetrated is not specifically gendered comes to signify a profound rejection of the female. Female characters are disenfranchised at the most basic level in a world where men call their male friends 'cunts', refer to women as 'it', and prefer anal penetration, with or without consent. *Porno* illustrates just how fine is the line between misogyny and the representation of misogyny, and how perilous it is to tightrope-walk. An interesting comparison can be made with Alan Warner's *The Man Who Walks* (2002), which not only portrays Scottish literary masculinity as lacking the priapism of yore, but hacks another dent in it by making its hero Macushla the Nephew impotent. Scotland may have been fucked, as Jock McLeish claims in Gray's *1982 Janine* (1984), but there is a key sense in which the Nephew is not 'one of the fuckers who fucked her' (Gray 1984: 136; see also Schoene 2006a).

In his preface to *And Thus Will I Freely Sing*, the first anthology of Scottish gay and lesbian writing, Toni Davidson noted that Scottish writers sending their work to publishers in London had to worry not only about seeming 'too gay' but also 'too Scottish' (Davidson 1989: 9). The lesson seemed to be that you could be gay until it was coming out of your ears as long as you were English, male and posh. Alan Hollinghurst's *The Swimming-Pool Library* (1988) had burst into print the year before, and it may very well have sold out in formerly independent bookshops like John Smith's on St Vincent Street, Glasgow, and James Thin's on South Bridge, Edinburgh, but Scottish equivalents were much thinner on the ground. The tendency towards repressed queer characters and subtexts in pre-devolution Scottish literature was linked to class as well as homophobia, and in societal terms it seems sometimes as if we have not progressed all that much. For example, what answer will we give Joanie in John Maley's *Delilah's* when he asks 'when was the last time you saw two guys walkin' arm-in-arm down Sauchiehall Street? When was the last time you saw two women winching in Argyle Street' (Maley 2002: 204)? Simple gestures of affection may occur in Glasgow's tiny Pink Triangle and other small liberal enclaves across the country, but anywhere else they still require a certain amount of bravery. The poignancy at the end of *Delilah's* derives not from the fact that the characters are brought together by a lesbian wedding but rather from our realisation that the ceremony exudes a false sense of liberation: it takes place within a closet, the closet of a dingy gay bar, the only safe option available to Glasgow's 'invisible lovers' (Maley 2002: 204). It is not through choice that Bobbie and Rae experience 'the happiest day of their lives' in a place where the staff work 'shitty hours [for] shitty pay', and the customers come 'in a fog of booze and smoke . . . looking for love but unable to love themselves, hiding from their families and exposing themselves to strangers, crying like rivers and screaming like banshees. Drinking to kill the fear and free the fairy in themselves' (Maley 2002: 4, 208). Maley was writing three years before civil partnerships were approved, and even when in 2005 they were, we learned that Scottish registrars are not obliged to officiate if they find the idea distasteful. Nor need registry offices conduct civil partnerships with the amount of ceremony usually expended on heterosexual weddings, and yet the February 2006 edition of Glasgow City Council's *Glasgow Magazine*, bearing the title 'The Wedding Planners', can hardly contain its excitement at welcoming same-sex couples to the city's expensive council-owned venues. As ever, the dominant discourse is that of the marketplace, and social acceptance follows in the wake of the pink-pound potential for economic gain.

The popular notion of a gay club is of a place packed with camp, handsome young men in pristine clothing, talking wittily to their (straight) female friends about shoes and *Will & Grace*. This notion fails to take into account that every single one of these boys will grow up to be a gay man who may wish to set up a gay household, or even become a gay parent.

Worse still, he may wish to stop talking about shoes and sitcoms, if indeed he did in the first place. That is when society comes to face a challenge, when people leave their carefully labelled boxes and move into the wider sphere of public activity. It also signals the moment when sexuality ceases to be the most defining characteristic of a literary character, which points up a pertinent trend in contemporary Scottish writing, and it is female (and not necessarily lesbian) writers who are most engaged with it: recent works by Jackie Kay, A. L. Kennedy, Ali Smith and Louise Welsh all feature lesbian and gay characters who are not ghettoised. An interesting example of the power of labelling is the story 'Physics and Chemistry' in Kay's *Why Don't You Stop Talking* (2002). The Physics and Chemistry teachers at Bishopbriggs High School sometimes have dinner with Rosemary and Nancy, 'PE and Music, who also, like them, lived together and bought each other comfortable slippers for Christmas', but they never, 'ever, ever, mentioned the nature of their relationship to each other' (Kay 2002b: 217), not even when it is expressed sexually:

> Physics had never said the dreaded word out loud for fear of it. The word itself spread terror within in her. Chemistry was like her flesh and blood, heart of her heart, a part of her . . . Everything was relative. What they did in the dark at night in their own small house in Gleneagles Gardens was immaterial. (Kay 2002b: 219)

However, the label 'lesbian' is inescapable, forced upon them from outside 'their own small house'. A parent complains and the school gossips, 'saying that they had a lesbian relationship, shared a house, a car, a bed' (Kay 2002b: 221), and eventually both teachers are sacked. And yet, being identified as lesbian proves ultimately liberating as the couple begin to kiss 'in the kitchen over a sizzling wok', are seen 'arm in arm at the traffic lights' at Bishopbriggs Cross, and finally open a wool shop in Milngavie called 'Close Knit'. As the story concludes, being outed 'was a strange relief really' (Kay 2002b: 222).

Kay also writes a good deal about immigrant and adoptive Scots, alerting us to the fact that our country is made up of many different Scotlands, and increasingly we hear more varied voices from Scots who are not fair-haired, blue-eyed Celtic males. One day soon a marketing department will discover 'the Scottish Monica Ali', a writer who will tell us what it is like to grow up female and Pakistani (or Chinese, or Somali, or Serbian) in Glasgow (or Aberdeen, or Dundee, or Cumnock). The comparison might be a tad irksome for the writer in question – as doubtless the comparisons with Zadie Smith were for Monica Ali – but hopefully it will result in the empowerment of many others. Writers are seeking asylum in Scotland right now (with limited success), and there are plenty of stories to which the white middle classes are never exposed. In our new nation, we need to hear these voices loud and clear.

Although we cannot afford to get complacent, about either our literary or our political situation, I find all this very encouraging. In fact I would say that Scottish fiction is looking decidedly chirpy. A flurry of new novels and short story collections by world-class Scottish writers – Laura Hird, Jackie Kay, Denise Mina, Andrew O'Hagan, Alan Warner, Irvine Welsh, Louise Welsh and others – is due out this summer, which makes it rather odd that literary agent Jenny Brown, who has been a staunch advocate of Scottish writing for many years, complained at last year's *Aye Write!* Conference in Glasgow that

> we write typically dark fiction in an age where people want feelgood novels . . . Scots are really good at feeling bad . . . The humour is black comedy, the sex is dark too. Maybe that's why it doesn't translate to the big screen or feature in Richard and Judy's book club. (Boztas 2005)

Black comedy and dark sex? That's us on a good day! However, perhaps most damning of all, Brown insisted that 'writing is also commerce, and in terms of income from sales, we have a long way to go'. Writing may be commerce, but in my view it is art first and foremost. If our work is a political act as well, then that is all to the good. If it sells lots of copies, no one will complain, least of all the author. But we are not bound by duty to be flag-wavers for the new Scotland, or to produce saleable products for its economy.

If indeed we do have a culture of failure – as Stuart Cosgrove claims, singling out the work of Kelman as a prime example of Scotland's 'obsession with' and 'indulgence of' poverty (Martin 2005) – then that is partly due to the notion that real success is achieved elsewhere, whether on the *New York Times* bestseller list or in the corridors of Westminster. It will take a hell of a lot of positive reinforcement campaigns from the Scottish Executive to get rid of self-doubt as deeply entrenched as ours. Unfortunately we cannot turn Scotland into a *tabula rasa*, eliding the parts of our culture we dislike, such as Buckfast, deep-fried Mars bars and parochial old gits, and then champion the parts of which we approve: James Hogg, potato scones, the Jesus and Mary Chain – who decides? In the end, the things we value may be as much a product of our shortcomings as our strengths.

Brown also bemoaned the lack of 'gorgeous, sexy novels from Scotland', the absence of 'a Scottish Jilly Cooper' (Boztas 2005), leaving me intrigued as to what aspirations a Scottish Jilly Cooper would reflect, though given that *No. 1* magazine – Scotland's 'top celebrity read' – has just been launched, a market may be about to open up for the Haggis'n'Harvey Nics bonkbuster. Although it might all be harmless fun, the values promoted by such publications are not necessarily healthy. We are not meant to be interested in what the women who appear in these magazines think, only in what they are wearing, what they weigh, who they are sleeping with, and most of all, what it all costs. Sick Boy's next business venture, perhaps? While we may not agree with Brown or Cosgrove, there is a great deal to be said for setting the grouse-beaters among the grouse once in a while. Which is why I am looking forward to Alan Taylor's *The Scots*, forthcoming from Penguin. I am hoping for a stooshie like that raised by Hugh McDiarmid and Alexander Trocchi at the Edinburgh International Writers' Conference in 1962. Perhaps my local bookie will take a bet on whether the shouts of 'cosmopolitan scum!' will drown out those of 'parochial old git!' when the feathers start to fly.

I began this piece with a quotation from Kelman's most recent novel because reading his work changed my perception of what could be done in fiction and what could be done in Scotland. Although he wrote about women with that Calvinist self-flagellation identified by Dixon, I did not see any point of reference between myself and his women characters, aside from the most obvious common denominators of Scottishness and femaleness. It was the male characters who compelled me. I admired and identified with their yearning, their angst. It was a while before I realised that all the novels I loved were by men. When I did, at first I thought that, as a feminist, I should write about women, and particularly to claw back some of the experiential potential which seemed to have been packaged up and labelled 'male'. That was a driving force behind the writing of *Negative Space* (2002), my first novel, and thankfully many wonderful books by Scottish women writers had by then elbowed their way to the front of my reading list to encourage me. Now I have given myself permission to tackle those sacred thistles of Scot Lit – masculinity and class – head on. It is a prickly business, but I shall keep at it. In the future, I hope the labels I mentioned above will disappear. How nice it would be to be known not as a 'woman writer' or a 'lesbian writer' or even as a 'Scottish writer', but simply as a writer! You cannot deny the factors that influence your work, or that sometimes labels can indeed give you a leg up. As Scottish writers we are coming from a place – an intellectual and emotional place – that is not English, and of course we want review coverage in the Scottish press (while it still exists as a significant presence at a national level). We need it because we start out at a disadvantage; we are far from London and not born with silver pens in our hands. That for such a small nation we have one of the most exciting and varied literary scenes in the world is something of which to be proud. Who knows, soon we might almost be ready not only to figure out who we think we are, but to get above ourselves.

Part II
Genres

Chapter 7

The 'New Weegies': The Glasgow Novel in the Twenty-first Century

Alan Bissett

The period from 2004 to 2005 might be described as something of a high tide in the history of Glasgow literature, witnessing the publication of seventeen novels by writers who hail from, or have written in or about, the city, as well as *The Knuckle End* (2004), an anthology of work by recent Glasgow University creative-writing graduates. The novels include Des Dillon's *The Glasgow Dragon* (2004), Alan Kelly's *The Tar Factory* (2004), Laura Marney's *No Wonder I Take a Drink* (2004) and *Nobody Loves a Ginger Baby* (2005), Colette Paul's *Whoever You Choose to Love* (2004), Nick Brooks's *My Name is Denise Forrester* (2005), Rodge Glass's *No Fireworks* (2005), Alison Miller's *Demo* (2005), Ewan Morrison's *The Last Book You Read* (2005), Will Napier's *Summer of the Cicada* (2005) and my own *The Incredible Adam Spark* (2005), as well as new publications by Kelman and A. L. Kennedy, and recent work by Suhayl Saadi, Zoë Strachan and Louise Welsh. It is hard to imagine any British constituency beyond London with an output to rival contemporary Glasgow's. Of course, it would be folly to coagulate these many writers under any one banner; the diversity of their material is testament to a place which Moira Burgess has called 'Kaleidoscope City' (Burgess 1998: 181). Given the nature of Glasgow's strategic importance to the British Empire, its sectarian divide, former industrial might and subsequent affiliation with socialist politics, the city has an identity quite distinct from other urban centres in Britain, or Scotland, and a literary tradition very much of its own. Whereas this heritage is relatively well documented, its present literary profusion has so far remained undiscussed. In this chapter I will examine the contemporary Glasgow novel's marked discontinuity with the themes and styles of the 'Glasgow tradition', as well as its necessarily contiguous links with it. I will contextualise the works of four new authors – Louise Welsh, Anne Donovan, Suhayl Saadi and Alison Miller – and will do so with reference to a city very much altered from the one experienced by previous generations of writers.

In an attempt to recast Glasgow as a shopping, business and tourism magnet the city has been subject to a slick rebranding exercise loudly proclaiming 'the transformation of Glasgow from its inward-looking, post-industrial slump to a confident, outward-looking, economically regenerated destination city' (Glasgow City Council 2005). According to Deborah Stevenson, such rebranding inevitably involves a shift towards commodity-based capitalism. 'What distinguishes urban tourism from traditional tourism', she writes, 'is the way in which what is on offer has been packaged and marketed', and instead of 'being centres of production [localities] take on the task of reinventing themselves as centres of consumption' (Stevenson 2003: 99–100). Indeed, consumption is what has risen in the wake of the city's manufacturing decline engendered by Thatcherite policies in the 1980s. Like other old industrial conurbations, Glasgow has been forced to 'raise its profile in the marketplace of visitors and substantially improve its attractiveness' (Law 1992: 599). The first stirrings of this imperative showed in Glasgow's City of Culture strategy in 1990, railed against by the city's writers (Kravitz 2001: 26). 'The Friendly City,' scoffs also one of Suhayl Saadi's characters in *Psychoraag* with reference to Glasgow's rebranding. 'Aye. Friendly so long as you were a tourist' (Saadi 2004: 196). But changes in the character and self-image of Glasgow have also been wrought by various other processes and events such as devolution, the founding of New Labour, the 'war on terror' and American imperialism, corporate globalisation, and a widespread political consensus 'exemplified in neo-liberalism' whereby, according to Don Slater, 'consumer choice [is] the obligatory pattern for all social relations' and 'collective and social provision [gives] way to radical individualism' (Slater 2000: 178). In this climate even Kelman's invective against the British state and English linguistic hegemony now seems curiously historical, which might explain the author's switch of attention to the dominion of the United States in his latest novel, *You Have to Be Careful in the Land of the Free* (2004).

What is also new about the wave of noughties' writers is that it is spearheaded by women; never before have so many female Glaswegian novelists simultaneously achieved such prominence. Louise Welsh has been the most successful in this respect. Her novel *The Cutting Room* (2002) quickly became an international bestseller, translated into numerous languages and garlanded with awards. Its marked contemporariness provides us with an unequivocal indication of Glasgow's changing profile:

> The industrial age had given way to a white-collar revolution and the sons and daughters of shipyard toilers now tapped keyboards and answered telephones in wipe-clean sweatshops. They shuffled invisible paper and sped communications through electronic magic. Dark suits trampled along Bath Street, past the storm-blasted spire of Renfield St Stephens . . . Cars crept at a sluggish pace towards curving slip roads and the motorway miles below, where three lanes of paralysed traffic shimmered in a heat haze. Buses forced their way to obedient queues of defeated commuters . . . Elevator buildings that inspired the Chicago skyline disgorged men and women crumpled by the day . . . And all around me mobile phones. People talk, talk, talking to a distant party while the world marched by. (Welsh 2002: 65)

Welsh's Glasgow is a city transformed by de-industrialisation and its economy's shift towards the tertiary sector. Welsh not only invokes industrial images from Glasgow's past, but also acknowledges both religion ('Renfield St Stephens') and labour emigration ('the Chicago skyline'). Glasgow's traditional heritage has been supplanted and erased by Thatcher's 'white-collar revolution', which augured much but has delivered only, according to Welsh, a life of gridlock, alienation, commuting, computing, stress and long hours in 'wipe-clean sweatshops'. It is an economy of consumption which barely slows by night:

> We slipped through a fluorescent white tunnel, then climbed high over the city on the curving expressway; the River Clyde oil-black and still beneath us, a backdrop to the reflected lights of the city; the white squares of late-night office work; traffic signals drifting red, amber, green, necklaces of car headlamps halting then moving in their sway . . . scarlet neon sign of the Daily Record offices suspended in the dark sky to our right . . . On the radio a Marilyn Monroe sound-alike whispered an invitation to an Indian restaurant, where, her voice intimated, she would fuck and then feed you. (Welsh 2002: 98–9)

Welsh's Glasgow comprises a restless, postmodern panorama of neon light, 'late-night office work' in tower blocks, and twenty-four-hour media and advertising, resembling a perpetual simulacrum which, as Welsh intimates through her reference to Monroe, promises and commodifies sexuality as a consumer good as much as it recycles literally 'dead' images. But this is, of course, the novel's central motif: Rilke, an antique dealer, discovers pornographic photographs of a murdered girl, or so it seems, and then traces her identity through the clandestine labyrinth of a city restlessly displaying new facets of itself to the reader. There is an extensive interplay of identities and cultures on parade in the novel, referencing a multitude of historical periods and styles which comprise both postmodern Glasgow and postmodern aesthetics *per se*. Not only does Rilke deal in antiques – that is, the exchange of objects divorced from their historical context – but he leads us on a tour through a Glasgow continually recycling its past for commercial purposes:

> The Chelsea Lounge looks like a club for dubious gentlemen, designed by a Georgian poof with a Homeric bent . . . Chaises longues and high-backed sofas, upholstered in wine velvet, group round tables. Corinthian columns flower into the fondant cornicing of the high ceiling. The effect is expensive, somewhat austere, and spoilt by the sheer twenty-first-centuryness of its clientele.
>
> Some people hold that ancient Greece was a golden age for inverts. Old men and boys walked hand in hand through Elysian fields, and Sapphic love flourished in an island paradise. Personally, I see many reasons why youth should be attracted to old age; all of them can be folded and put in your wallet. (Welsh 2002: 99)

The 'twenty-first-centuryness' of the Chelsea Lounge can only command an expensive 'effect', a clearly inauthentic, commercialised reproduction of the historical. Whenever Welsh is not rigorously examining the correlation between Glasgow's homogenised 'rebranding', on the one hand, and its many submerged and marginalised identities, on the other, she is exposing capitalism as divesting all communities, and other repositories of the past, of their authenticity and value. Notably, for J. K. Galbraith in *The Affluent Society* (1963) the desire for consumer goods was merely an illusion stimulated by an economy of production (Galbraith 1963: 121–30). Jean Baudrillard goes a step further, suggesting that 'everything is finally *digested* and reduced to the same homogeneous fecal matter [which is] everywhere diffused in the indistinguishability of things and of social relations' (Baudrillard 1988a: 34–5). Consumption is a flattening and, finally, an evacuation of identity and value, and so Rilke's search through an intricacy of economic exchanges is a search *through* Glasgow for the delayed meaning *of* Glasgow, taking place in a postmodern, eternal present layered by shifting histories and styles: industrial Glasgow, post-industrial Glasgow, Gothic Glasgow, pornographic Glasgow, Romantic Glasgow, decadent Glasgow, bourgeois Glasgow, commercial Glasgow, criminal Glasgow. It is the semiotics of the city itself which is the novel's concern, like the photographic image of the anonymous girl who perpetually eludes identification.

In *The Condition of Postmodernity* David Harvey argues that postmodernism produces simulacra of history in city environments, fabricated traditions presented as authentic (Harvey 1990: 87). Given its plunge into de-industrialisation, attended by a cultural collapse of meaning, Glasgow as a signifier is now detached from any lasting and definite signified beyond consumerism itself, that is, beyond the eternal ingestion of images, the purchasing of objects divested of their history, the exploitation of anonymous, unidentifiable bodies. According to Stephen Knight, in crime fiction 'anxiety about city living, itself a product of a commodity-based culture, is felt in and through objects' (Knight 1980: 179), and in Welsh's novel it is the anonymous girl's body and its photographic reproduction that induce this anxiety.

The Cutting Room, then, is thematically more Marxist even than many novels by Kelman, as every relationship in the novel is mediated through the exchange of money. Photographs, information, antiques, art objects and even flesh pass between men in a seemingly endless cash nexus which stretches throughout the city. Sexuality is expressed as exploitation. Voyeurism denotes possession and control. Love itself, Welsh tells us, 'can be folded and put in your wallet'. A model, who looks like 'a pretty primary schoolteacher, an air hostess, a weather girl', dresses by request as 'a nineteen-fifties pin-up, naughty, but wholesome', any fixed identity of her own lost among those projected onto her by the equally anonymous voyeurs bred by late capitalism to be consumers of pornography. Anonymity is further emphasised by Welsh's framing of the scene: 'The door to the room was made of dimpled glass. It held a thousand distorted reflections repeated in honeycomb, an impression of people and white light, pink faces and dark suits, a crush of bodies' (Welsh 2002: 99). Unsurprisingly, on photographing the model, Rilke tells us '[he] felt like an assassin' (Welsh 2002: 87): women in the novel are literally and figuratively 'killed' in the camera gaze, emptied of meaning, self and signified for the gratification of those empowered to control the image. The legitimate market economy, which Welsh alludes to through Rilke's antiques business and the repeated spectre of the 'white-collar revolution', mirrors the network of underground transactions which exists beneath the city's façade, all of it aggressively capitalist in nature. 'Rebranded' Glasgow, it seems, is itself up for auction.

However, not all of the new Glasgow writers share Welsh's pessimism concerning consumerism and its threat to social integrity. Anne Donovan's work, for example, while retaining a sense of continuity with the Glasgow tradition in its deployment of the vernacular, indicates how Glasgow might, through developing an awareness of consumerism, begin to search for new definitions. The immediate question the novel asks is how to bridge gaps between religious faiths blighting both the city and a wider post-9/11 world. The sectarian divide has provided much material for Glasgow novels – as in Hugh Munro's *The Clydesiders* (1961), Gordon Williams's *From Scenes Like These* (1968) and Alan Spence's *The Magic Flute* (1990) – but Donovan recasts these religious tensions by focusing not on the conflict between Catholics and Protestants or, as one might expect, between Christians and Muslims, but between Catholicism and Buddhism. In *Buddha Da* (2003) the life of the McKenna family is thrown into crisis when painter-and-decorator Jimmy discovers Buddhism, alienating him from his Catholic wife and daughter. Donovan depicts the family unit as inhabiting four separate ideological spheres: if Buddhism and Catholicism stand in opposition, so too do inherited Glaswegianness – manifest in the characters' use of the vernacular – and new, globalised youth culture, as documented by daughter Anne-Marie's obsession with pop music. Donovan occasionally attempts to funnel this territorial conflict of spheres linguistically: 'Hey, listen tae you,' Jimmy tells his daughter, 'it's cool man. Where d'you think ye are – New York?' (Donovan 2003: 6).

Vying ideological oppositions such as these, Donovan suggests, are not compounded but erased by the levelling effects of an omnipresent popular culture. As Anne-Marie cheerfully points out, 'some folk like meditatin, some prefer Eastenders' (Donovan 2003: 23), a relativism giving each equal weight. Dreaming of becoming a star like her idol Madonna, Anne-Marie is also being interpellated by a new American individualism. Yet Madonna's value as a cultural artefact represents not only a triumph of American commodity capitalism (Donovan reminds us that Madonna is, of course, 'The Material Girl'); it also bears

Catholic connotations. Donovan's approach to religion, like Madonna's, is highly post-modern: Anne-Marie and her best friend Nisha, who is of Indian descent, produce a song which mixes Latin and Tibetan chants, thus bringing together radically different faiths through the simple, democratising promise of pop music. Indeed, Donovan highlights the success of contemporary popular culture where religion and tradition have failed: for example, Nisha's brother's DJ-ing involves a synthesis of European House music with Hindi lyrics, a cross-cultural transposition layered further by a recognisably Scots idiom:

> [Dad] wanted us tae speak the mother tongue – but Kamaljit and me just speak English maist of the time. Even my ma doesnae really speak it tae us a lot. But Gurpreet [Nisha's brother] likes tae mix it in, especially when he's DJin. Thinks it makes him a bit different fae the others. (Donovan 2003: 102)

For Donovan, it is through music and the sudden relativising effects of cultural consumption that a postcolonial consciousness can assert itself both alongside and within the host culture, effacing religious differences and annulling the legacy of colonial relationships by allowing Scottishness, Britishness and Indianness to commingle in a complex ideological melange. Donovan's answer to the identity crisis blighting postcolonial nations like Scotland is literally to 'sample' from and 'remix' the output of other agencies, specifically dominant ones, thereby eradicating political, racial and national disparities.

The hip-hop conceit of 'sampling' referenced by Donovan is an important one in the light of the present discussion. Despite hip-hop being part of a transatlantic culture spread by globalisation via corporate media such as MTV, it retains its original subversive potential. According to the African-American rapper Chuck D, hip-hop promotes identification across race–class lines while signalling disaffection with the structures of capitalism (Potter 1993). Borrowing and cutting from other sources, hip-hop is also by nature a heteroglossiac medium, and this is a trait it shares with the Scottish novel, which, woven of both indigenous and superimposed voices, has equally been described as a heteroglossiac form (see Craig 2002). Given Glasgow's complicity in the history of American slavery, as merchant city and imperial workshop, it would be disingenuous to insist on any facile comparisons between the experience of Glaswegians and African-Americans. None the less, many Glaswegians have latterly become victims of capitalist expansionism, placing them at least economically in the vicinity of other disenfranchised cultures.

As it chronicles the urban experience in a politicised and vernacular mode, much Glasgow literature since the emergence of Tom Leonard's poetry in the 1970s, and including the novels of Kelman, Des Dillon and Alan Kelly, as well as Saadi, Donovan and Miller, could be read as the Scottish equivalent of hip-hop. Some new Glasgow writers – most notably Ewan Morrison and Suhayl Saadi – are not content simply to emulate Kelman's vernacular achievements but have taken on the practice of 'sampling', thus helping the Scottish novel adjust to a century saturated with pop culture, iPods, the internet, shopping and brand names. 'Mixing' contemporary youth culture's commodity language with a Glaswegian syntax and lexicon, they produce a new aesthetics, at once local and global, which successfully subverts late-capitalist consumerism's signifiers by appropriation and recontextualisation. As Russell Potter explains:

> By taking . . . musical sounds, packaged for consumption, and remaking them into new sounds through scratching, cutting and sampling, what had been consumption was transformed into *production*. Such a cut-and-paste valuation of the hitherto unvalued put hip-hop in a unique

relation with commodity capitalism, and concomitantly with cultural production in general. If consumption could be productive, it could never again be regarded as merely passive. (Potter 1995: 36)

In the novels of Welsh and Donovan we find at work what Eleanor Bell describes as 'a certain permeability of borders . . . [an] urge to get beyond the reductive, to challenge the "nature" of Scottishness and to explore its "lesions"' (Bell 2004: 122), a taste for multifaceted inclusivity which appears congruent with the pick-'n'-mix agendas of postmodernism and also – in Donovan's case – hip-hop. No contemporary Scottish writer explores these 'lesions' more fiercely than Suhayl Saadi. While Donovan makes mere reference to the culture of sampling, Saadi integrates it into the very politics of his art. As the first novel to chronicle the life of Glasgow's Asian community, Saadi's *Psychoraag* makes an important contribution to contemporary Scottish literature. Throughout, Saadi employs a voice blending English, Glaswegian and Urdu, interspersed with quotations from the lyrics of the songs aired by Zaf, Saadi's protagonist, who works as a DJ for an Asian radio station. The songs comprise a mixture of eastern music and western artists influenced by eastern sounds, such as the Beatles, Led Zeppelin and Kula Shaker, a cultural conjunction which Saadi goes on to explore in a thematic way.

If we give credit to Tom Nairn's proposition that Britain's relationship to the United States 'has fossilised into a form of self-colonization . . . of "indirect rule"' (Nairn 2004a: 27) and that thus, as a subnational component of Britain, Scotland has become doubly colonised, then the Scots-Asian experience is one of three-fold colonisation: by white Scotland, by England, and by Britain's current self-colonisation under the aegis of American imperialism. Saadi explores the complexities of cultural integration as experienced by immigrant populations in a host country still grappling with its own 'postcolonial' crisis, using pop music (relentlessly cross-fertilising between cultures) and radio transmission (extending the grasp of interpellating agencies from media 'centres') as his main metaphors. Little wonder then – given Saadi's ceaseless unpacking of the Russian-doll sets of (post)colonial power relations, voices and multiple Glasgows in the novel – that 'it wasn't just Zaf who was on multiple wavelengths, the whole bloody population of Glasgow wis tunin in on totally different levels' (Saadi 2004: 19). For Saadi the trope of 'sampling' serves at once as a technical device and a major theme in his writing, demonstrating the matrix of deconstructed identities which emerge from a mixed backdrop of postcolonial, globalised and consumerist relations. As such, sampling constitutes a form of politicised (re)production in which 'true' identities become inextricable from commercial or assimilated ones. '[Zaf] liked samples,' writes Saadi, 'felt comfortable with them. He was a sample of Pakistan, thrown at random into Scotland, into its myths. And, in Lahore, he had felt like a sample of Glasgow in the ancient City of the Conquerors' (Saadi 2004: 227).

Psychoraag is as much a representation of Glasgow as a whole as of the specific Scots-Asian experience of Glasgow. Visiting the slums of the East End and the Gorbals, the Orange heritage of Govan and Kinning Park, as well as the legacy of generations of Irish, Jewish and East European immigrants – all 'sampling' from each other as they began to integrate – Saadi records the changing rhythms of popular music and commodity-based fashion: the Teddy Boys of the 1950s, the biker gangs of the 1960s, the rock music of the 1970s, Acid House in the 1980s, drum 'n' bass and Britpop in the 1990s. Saadi highlights the ways in which 'identity' becomes consumable, the extent to which even race and nationality are commodified into mere fashionable 'items'. 'Until recently,' he writes, 'Latino had been hip and Paki hadn't' (Saadi 2004: 73). Saadi interweaves the highly visible white history of Glasgow – one so well documented by Glaswegian writers reacting against superimposed grand narratives that it has become a grand narrative in its own right – with the suppressed Scots-Asian history of the 'sons and grandsons ae the *kisaan* who had powered the buses, the underground trains, the machines of the sweatshop under-wear-manufacturers' (Saadi 2004: 242). *Psychoraag* demonstrates how either group inter-acts with, informs and ultimately transforms the other. Glasgow literally consumes Asian culture, while Asians become assimilated into Glasgow, with language acting as the viscous, mutable adhesive in-between:

> They had clothed the lily-white bodies of whole generations of Scots and then, later, they had filled their stomachs too. You are what you eat. If that was the case, then Glasgae wis Faisalabad a hundred times over. But their sons and daughters had gone in the opposite direc-tion and become Scots. Right down to their gangs and their dancin and their chip-bhatti *sahib* footba tops, they had sipped the water of the Clyde and had become cold killers. And they were swearin at him and Ruby in a mixture of Glaswegian and Faisalabadi. (Saadi 2004: 242)

Like *Buddha Da* and *Psychoraag* Alison Miller's *Demo* represents a Glasgow riven with racial and class divisions; however, it seems markedly less sure of finding resolutions between the warring faiths and cultures. The novel's main achievement is its capture of the mood of anti-capitalist discontent in the noughties, a decade which has witnessed Scotland's largest ever public protests: 80,000 anti-Iraq War protestors marched in Glasgow in February 2003, and 225,000 people joined in the 'Make Poverty History' demonstration in Edinburgh in July 2005. Miller seems sympathetic to Nairn's contention that 'supine' Scotland is implicated in the crimes of its colonial masters. As a banner in one of the novel's 'demo' scenes reads, 'GUANTANAMO. BELMARSH. DUNGAVEL. END SCOTLAND'S SHAME' (Miller 2005: 178). Like Saadi, Miller crams in a civic history of Glasgow, re-evaluating 'received' history and promoting the hitherto unrecorded narra-tives, yet she is concerned more with the city's radical rather than ethnic traditions. *Demo* takes us from Red Clydeside to the corporate gentrification of the Clyde, encompassing anti-nuclear protests at Faslane Naval Base, the Iraq War demos and public dismay at the re-election of George W. Bush, as well as more recent events, such as the appointment of Mordechai Vanunu, whistleblower on Israel's nuclear-power programme, to the rectorship of Glasgow University and the G8 convention at Gleneagles. Concomitantly, Miller also addresses existing tensions between the 'Old' Left of trade unions, on the one hand, and the 'New' Left, marked by a post-Thatcher, post-Berlin Wall focus on globalisation, racial issues and American militarism, on the other. Thus, in an argument over the emergent sweatshop labour of call centres, leftist Danny asks his father: 'So where's your politics now? The big socialist, eh? The Big Red Clydesider. That kinda work's crap and you know it . . . Some a they boys in there have never even *heard* of a union' (Miller 2005: 4).

Unlike his father's, Danny's twenty-first-century Glasgow constitutes a co-opted culture, in which even socialists wear Calvin Klein, trade unions have become hobbled, and para-noia over terrorism renders the city's own citizens suspect. Instead of solidarity between Glasgow's citizens, in *Demo* Muslim Farkhanda, a Glaswegian herself, comments dispirit-edly to Clare, a white girl, that 'we threaten civilisation as you know it' (Miller 2005: 229), while another disillusioned Scots-Asian states: 'If you're no a Suspected Terrorist, you're a Bogus Asylum Seeker, the new Bogeyman. Best you can hope for is economic migrant status and gettin snapped up by some capitalist bastard to do the jobs nay other cunt wants. Sweepin streets and shovellin shit' (Miller 2005: 177). These exchanges sound like echoes from *Psychoraag*, where Zaf recounts his immigrant parents' experience of wading through 'the shit of Empire' on first arriving in Scotland (Saadi 2004: 157). In *Demo* Miller's focus shifts between wealthy urbanites Julian and Letitia, the politicised proletarians Danny and Clare, and those anonymised by the machinery of globalisation. 'Did you audition for this role?' asks Julian of a beggar, 'Archetypal Glasgow Drunk?' – 'No, son,' comes the reply, 'I was born tay it' (Miller 2005: 145).

Unlike Donovan's Glasgow, Miller's is one in which economic and racial disparities are exacerbated by transnational forces and made epidemic. According to Stevenson, this is ultimately a phenomenon of capital movement itself:

> Cities and urban cultures continue to be constructed, deconstructed and reconstructed by powerful commercial interests (predominantly those of white, middle-class men) which, increasingly, are global in scope. Thus the major forms of social inequality, such as class and gender, continue to be reproduced and inscribed locally in the landscape. (Stevenson 2003: 50–1)

It is the inscription of these inequalities in post-devolution Glasgow (or, rather, their *re-inscription*, since Miller makes it clear that they pre-existed globalisation) that constitutes Miller's major concern in *Demo*. Just as in *The Cutting Room* Welsh draws connections between sexual and economic exploitation, so Miller demonstrates how power disparities determined by class, ethnic and gender differences operate in and through each other: for instance, the wealthy Englishman Julian rapes working-class Scot Clare while – most importantly in a world in which popular consent is massaged by political imperium – convincing her that no such thing is actually taking place.

That Glaswegian writers continue to write about working-class characters may be less to do with left-wing politics than the fact that, as Manfred Malzahn writes, 'the assertion of a working-class identity in a Scottish context is likely to appear also as the assertion of a Scottish identity, in spite of the cosmopolitan aspect of industrial culture, which favours a kind of basic global uniformity' (Malzahn 1988: 230). By writing from a working-class perspective, then, Glaswegians resist this 'basic global uniformity'. Moreover, by providing vernacular renditions of Glasgow, Donovan, Miller and Saadi interlink both the historical city and the tradition of its novel with the global idiom of a projected future discourse in which, one imagines, Glasgow's integration into a postmodern matrix of commodity values will make the city decreasingly 'Glaswegian'. Along with novels like *The Cutting Room*, the work of these writers interrogates the change from what was to what is and what may well be, gradually re-imagining Glasgow, however reluctantly, within a new globalised context. If, as Baudrillard argues, brand names and products increasingly form a global language of signs (Baudrillard 1988b: 14), then the future of vernacular literature is very likely to depend on an innovative appropriation of postmodern techniques – such as hip-hop's dissection and eclectic reassemblage of a global code – for the creation of a new local dialect, culture or tradition capable of transforming passive consumption into politicised (re)-production and subversive resistance. Hopefully, so Stevenson speculates, rather than globalisation eroding locality, 'the artefacts and practices of the globalizing culture will in some way be transformed or subverted in the very act of coming into contact with a particular local culture', with the effect that 'although this local culture may well be changed . . . it will not be destroyed' (Stevenson 2003: 48).

In my view, contemporary Glaswegian novelists – still aligned to the ethos of industrial socialism while finding themselves immersed within a distinctly cosmopolitan milieu – are very well equipped not only to partake in but to instigate this kind of cultural transformation. The 'New Weegies' are keen to preserve and develop the tradition of formal innovation and political engagement initiated by the twentieth-century Glasgow novel while also, of necessity, having to reach beyond it. As such, their work is an act of regionalism at once hostile to and consistent with globalisation.

Chapter 8

Devolution and Drama: Imagining the Possible

Adrienne Scullion

Just weeks after the opening of the first Scottish Parliament to sit for 292 years leading Scottish playwright David Greig's new work *The Speculator* premiered at the Edinburgh International Festival. In the play Greig's fictional impersonation of the eighteenth-century French playwright Pierre de Marivaux (1688–1763) challenges his contemporary dramatists to acts of bold speculation and civic action:

DUFRESNY   We are not – playwrights – really we're gamblers.
MARIVAUX   Not gamblers.
   Speculators.
DUFRESNY   What's the difference?
MARIVAUX   Gamblers stake blind.
   Speculators imagine a possibility
   And have the courage to force it into existence.

(Greig 1999: 85 – II.vi)

Close to two complete parliaments later – and with the new National Theatre of Scotland (NTS) successfully launched – it appears timely to review the repertoire of post-devolution Scottish theatre to see how Scotland's playwrights have responded to the challenge of imagining and bringing into being a new world. Whereas 1999 represents a watershed in the political history of Scotland, its impact on the theatrical meanings of Scotland seems more evolutionary. The year itself saw a number of unexpected revivals, ranging from James Bridie's *The Anatomist* (1930) to Iain Heggie's *An Experienced Woman Gives Advice* (1995), both at the Lyceum, as well as adaptations and translations, such as Robert David MacDonald's *Death in Venice* and Harry Gibson's *Filth* (both for the Citizens' Theatre), and Peter Arnott's new translation of Bertolt Brecht's *Mr Puntila and His Man Mati* (Dundee Rep). There was also a raft of new plays, including Greig's *Mainstream* (Suspect Culture), *The Cosmonaut's Last Message to the Woman He Once Loved in the Former Soviet Union* (Paines Plough) and *Danny 306 + Me Against the World (4 Ever)* (Traverse), as well as David Harrower's *Begin Again* (KtC), Linda McLean's *Riddance* and Aileen Ritchie's *The Juju Girl* (both Traverse). Amongst this work, however, it is Greig's *The Speculator* that stands out as a particularly important, if perhaps unusual new point of departure in post-devolution Scottish drama.

One reason why *The Speculator* makes such an unusual beginning for a new era of Scottish drama is that it is a history play; one might argue that in the past the hegemony of the history play constrained and deformed both the development and appeal of modern Scottish drama. Greig's play, however, is a confident re-imagining of the genre. Just as its chief characters Law and Islay leave Scotland to test themselves in new places and undergo new experiences, so Greig re-energises a failing genre by rebuilding it furth of Scotland. The play is set in Paris in 1720, capturing a historical moment poised precariously between a failing world order of traditional rules, structures and hierarchies and a shocking new world marked by pioneering economic innovation, re-imagined social relations and new cultural practices. In the play the banker John Law is controlling a huge project of economic speculation that will modernise Europe's monetary infrastructure, creating new markets and facilitating the building of new worlds. The tension between the old and the new, between looking back and looking forward, underpins Greig's diegesis and opens up a dramatic parallel with the political speculations of 1999. In his speech at the opening of the Parliament on 1 May 1999, Donald Dewar (1937–2000), Scotland's first First Minister, similarly sought to activate history by identifying the 'new voice . . . of a democratic Parliament' that would 'shape Scotland as surely as the echoes from our past' (Dewar 1999). In this speculation (that is, Dewar's wish for the new Parliament) as well as those articulated in *The Speculator* (that is, Marivaux's new theatre, Law's modern monetary system, and Islay's new love) what is at stake is a vision for the future that is forward-looking, aspirational and exploratory. In short, contextualised within the summer of 1999, Greig's play challenges a new Scotland to grasp a new kind of future.

As its title suggests, Greig's play is an elaborate fantasy, huge and sprawling, telling many stories and filled with dozens of characters. As well as a number of subplots, the play interweaves three key narratives: (a) Marivaux's writing of a new play for the *Comédie Italienne*, (b) the romantic adventures of Lord Islay of Islay, a young Scottish nobleman on his grand tour, and (c) the cautionary tale of John Law, the Scot whose scheme to move away from a gold standard of currency made him, for a time at least, the richest and most powerful man in Europe. These stories are intricately linked through narrative and metaphor. For example, Islay's love for Adelaide is paralleled by the frustrated relationships of Marivaux, his wife and his mistress, which reappear in reworked form in the plays Marivaux writes for the *Comédie*, and by a third narrative strand concerning Law, who is loved by both his bodyguard Philippe and his housekeeper-cum-consort Catherine. In addition to these love stories the play is shaped through monetary imageries as well as actual debates on money, wealth and credit, and – particularly important for my present analysis – ideas of the future, the forces and meaning of modernisation, and national identity. Greig boldly re-imagines a socio-historical anxiety of conflicting cultural identities at the heart of eighteenth-century Europe:

ISLAY   Why do you want to go back [to Scotland], Mr Law?
    You're in Paris, man.
    Paris is the centre of the fucking world –
    You'd need to be fucked up to want to go back to Edinburgh.
LAW   I don't need Paris, Islay.
    I'm a rich man.
    It's not physically possible to be richer than me. I control the assets of a quarter of the
    world. I can satisfy any desire it's possible to imagine.
ISLAY   I suppose that could fuck you up.
LAW   There's no end to me, Islay.
    No night, no day, no possible, no impossible.

> I'm limitless . . .
> French princes begging at the door.
> And we're here.
> Scots – the pair of us.
> ISLAY   And proud of it.
> LAW   – weightless.
> ISLAY   But fucked up about it as well.
>
>   (Greig 1999: 29–30 – I.viii)

The tension between local identities and international forces, as articulated here in Law and Islay's exchange, is comparable to the particular challenges of contemporary global politics and the context of a simultaneously expanding and fragmenting twenty-first-century Europe.

Greig's heroes are all speculators of some kind. Law is most obviously engaged in a complex financial speculation that will modernise the global economy, but he clearly needs the practical, and complementary, loves of Philippe and Catherine to protect him from mundane reality. Marivaux defines his professional identity as that of the speculator, while his personal life – his marriage to the heiress Colombe and his affair with the actress Silvia – is full of wishes, promises and masquerades. In her professional life Silvia acts the ingénue, fantasising that her affair with Marivaux will achieve the happy match of the archetype she plays. In contrast, Colombe has no illusions as to her marriage – she knows Marivaux has married her for her money and position alone – but still she insists on the terms of the marital contract: 'If you want to fuck around, / Fuck around with whores. / But you're contracted to me' (Greig 1999: 40 – I.xi). Marivaux refuses to confront the reality of his marriage and affair, being content with the fantasy of his imagined staged worlds. The main tension is between being limited to the fantasy only, ultimately as constraining as Colombe's appeal to the letter of the law, and being able to act on it and seek its implementation. Islay's speculation is an 'all-or-nothing' romantic commitment to Adelaide, an affair which also has an element of financial speculation as he spends all his resources on gifts for his lover. Recently escaped from the patriarchal authority of a convent, Adelaide, too, speculates about the future and what it may hold in store for her. Arguably, it is the lovers Islay and Adelaide who are, at least in Marivaux's terms, the most successful speculators, acting together to force into being a new order, made manifest in Greig's most incongruous symbol of modernisation and metaphor of a new world (*the* New World), a Harley Davidson motorcycle. Malleable to the force of Islay and Adelaide's speculation, the theatre itself dematerialises in favour of the open roads of a new set of cultural references: 'ADELAIDE *puts the keys in the ignition.* / *The engine starts.* / *The entire theatre opens up.* / ADELAIDE *and* ISLAY *drive into the night*' (Greig 1999: 119 – II. xiii). For Greig, then, fantasy and image and wish are one thing; acting on them is quite another, requiring a deliberate will that can indeed change the world.

Greig's cultural exploration deliberately looks beyond Scotland, transporting the Scots Law and Islay to the new and unfamiliar surroundings of Paris. In *The Speculator* all the cities of Europe – Paris, London and Edinburgh – are ageing and failing; none of them can successfully connote the modern or the new. Both London and Edinburgh are portrayed as small, insular and limiting, and despite the promise it initially holds to the Scottish itinerants, Paris is experienced as equally constraining – its spaces are limited and enclosed, and its perceived freedoms prove illusory. Greig's Paris may indeed be 'the centre of the fucking world', as Islay claims (Greig 1999: 29 – I.viii), but as Law and Adelaide realise, it is the centre of an old world, impossibly hierarchical and controlled by an old elite, and as a result they each look to create – to 'force . . . into existence' (Greig 1999: 85 – II.vi) – new worlds. The efforts of Greig's characters to call into being these new places stretch from Law's financial manipulation to Islay's romantic wooings, from the wholly pragmatic to the exclusively opportunistic, but what each aspires to is agency and action. Accordingly, Greig's post-devolution thesis appears to be that what matters most is the possibilities afforded by an aspirational future bold enough to confront and progress away from the assumptions and prejudices of the past. In this way *The Speculator* might be read as a metaphor for a new Scotland – 'an awful small place' perhaps (Greig 1999: 13 – I.iii), but one pushing at the edges and distinguished by an outward-looking, internationalist dynamic.

Ironically, while such an internationalist reading now seems so appropriate and comprehensible, utterly containable within both contemporary Scottish theatre criticism and practice, it was, in previous decades, at the very least problematic. For example, Arnott's *White Rose* and John Clifford's *Losing Venice* (both Traverse 1985) emerged into a culture with distinctive national and cultural identities, but also into a society and industry struggling with their role as peripheral, marginal and other. The remarkable originality of these earlier plays, so closely tied to their bold political and dramaturgical internationalism, rendered them isolated within contemporaneous criticism. Other plays of the late 1980s and early 1990s, which had a more obvious link to ideas and issues of Scottishness, such as Liz Lochhead's *Mary Queen of Scots Got Her Head Chopped Off* (Communicado 1987), Tony Roper's *The Steamie* (Wildcat 1987) or Sue Glover's *Bondagers* (Traverse 1991), could be more easily incorporated into a critical orthodoxy and the producing repertoire (see Crawford and Varty 1993; Koren-Deutsch 1992; McDonald 1997; Maguire 1995; Varty 1997; Scullion 1995, 2000a). Naturally, this historical note raises the question as to what exactly might be so different now.

During the 1985 'Points of Departure' season at the Traverse Theatre a new generation of writers – Arnott, Clifford, Simon Donald, Chris Hannan and Stuart Paterson – burst onto the scene with plays of unexpected eclecticism, robust politics and dramaturgical internationalism; however, both academic criticism and theatre production failed to understand or engage sufficiently with them. As a result, few of the plays were published, even fewer were studied, and fewer still revived. Twenty years later the Scottish theatre industry, as well as theatre criticism, may be about to catch up with the dramaturgical internationalism of some of its playwrights and become similarly outward-looking. The 1990s saw a significant increase in international touring, collaboration and exchange; more international work was seen in venues such as the Glasgow Tramway, while established companies like the Traverse and the Tron developed strong international links and started a regular trade of theatre imports and exports, with several new plays – centrally those by Harrower and Greig – entering an international repertoire. At the same time, new companies like Suspect Culture and Theatre Cryptic were established with a demonstrable international commitment. All this helped shift the aspiration of indigenous theatre-makers and their audiences. Arguably, however, while these changes in the industry do matter hugely, the conceptual tipping point came with devolution, the Scottish legislative revolution that holds the potential to change everything hitherto taken for granted about representation and identity in Scotland's cultural and critical outputs.

Scottish theatre in the 1990s was also marked by a tendency to oust the 'old' in favour of the new, wilfully neglecting established and mature talent in favour of the prodigious and the youthful. In the 1990s playwrights who had emerged strongly in the previous decade, such as Arnott, Clifford and Hannan, were cast aside, with little or no new work by them reaching the major stages of the country. While this did have the positive outcome of opening the field to a new generation of writers – to Stephen Greenhorn, Greig, Harrower, Nicola McCartney and Anthony Neilson – it was also the mark of a flawed industry, in which it seemed impossible to grow, develop and sustain a career. In marked contrast to the nearby theatres of England and Ireland, where senior figures saw their earlier work revived and new work produced alongside the outputs of younger talents, it stretched the memory of even the most committed of Scotland's theatre-watchers to name but a single Scottish-based playwright in their sixties or fifties (or even, it sometimes seemed, in their forties) whose new work was being produced, while it was even less common to see revivals of earlier work revisited by new directors and companies. One feature of recent Scottish theatre is that this narrow vision and wasteful profligacy have disappeared and that, arguably for the first time, there is a range of voices, experiences and ages all writing for and within the industry. The Traverse continues to bring new writers to production – and tour them nationally and internationally – and the Playwrights' Studio Scotland, launched in 2004, supports talent at whatever stage of development. Devolution has also led to direct shifts within Scotland's cultural infrastructure, which has been the subject of much governmental scrutiny and attention, including a 'National Cultural Strategy' and the aforementioned launch of the NTS in early 2006.

The role and future impact of the NTS must remain largely imponderable at this stage, but its early balance of new commissions, revivals and workshop activities clearly seeks to enhance support for key writers across various degrees of experience and accomplishment, including tempting John Byrne back to writing for the stage, with an adaptation of his BBC television series *Tutti Frutti* (1987) scheduled for a major production in autumn 2006. Remarkably, the post-devolution period has also seen the production of work by temporarily 'forgotten' voices. Since 2000 Arnott, Clifford and Hannan have all returned to the stage with work encompassing a broad range of dramaturgies and modes of production, including bold statements in the context of the Edinburgh International Festival (for example, Clifford's translation of *Celestina* in 2004), a new play from one of Scotland's smallest theatres (Arnott's *Cyprus* for Mull Theatre in 2005), plays for community and outreach work (Arnott's *Full of Noises* [2002], *Court of Miracles* [2003], *House of Murders* [2004] at the Citizens') and finally, successful revivals – and, indeed, rewrites – of earlier plays, principally Hannan's *Shinning Souls* (Tron 2003) and, more controversially, his *Elizabeth Gordon Quinn* for the inaugural season of the NTS in 2006. Even elder statesman Tom McGrath premiered new work, with his eccentric *My Old Man* dividing critical opinion in a production by Magnetic North in 2005. In addition, writers who emerged in the 1990s – such as Greig, Harrower and Neilson – have not only been able to sustain their careers, but won international esteem and are now spearheading a new generation of talent. Henry Adam, Gregory Burke, Zinnie Harris, Douglas Maxwell, Iain F. MacLeod and Linda McLean have all proved much more than one-hit wonders, with strong production records at the Traverse and beyond, and of course such a vibrant context bodes well for the currently emergent talents of writers such as Davey Anderson and Selma Dimitrijevic.

Against this backdrop of infrastructural investment and change a number of key dramaturgical questions arise, particularly surrounding politics, representation and identity. Arnott's *A Little Rain* (2000) was premiered by 7:84 in the immediate post-devolution context. It was the third in a loosely connected trilogy of political plays, commissioned by the company's then artistic director Iain Reekie, which began with Greig's *Caledonia Dreaming* (1997) and Greenhorn's *Dissent* (1998). Arnott's final piece eschewed the potential bombast of a state-of-the-nation address to follow a subtler path, shifting between base lyricism and acerbic banter. In a series of encounters in a Glasgow pub, Arnott charts the territory of post-devolution Scotland played out against a daringly mythologised cityscape, which is drowning after forty days and forty nights of rain. Failed student Phil returns to a Scotland caught between mythology and harsh reality. Reflecting on the cultural responsibilities of home rule, beery newspaperman Michael confides in him that 'this is a new Scotland, no longer protected from its own ugliness by the alibi of Westminster. We are ourselves again. And this is who we are. Cunts . . . There are no excuses anymore. Officially, from now on, it's all our fault' (Arnott 2000: 43).

The frustration of politicised writers and theatre-makers, like Arnott, with the early reality of post-devolution Scotland was matched by a realisation, articulated in *A Little Rain*, that a new democracy demanded not just 'the same old' solutions but a revised world view. What was required was a view of Scotland that was speculative in Greig's terms, but also kept track of a similarly aspirational theory of a new Scotland as 'the template from which other nations can learn how to develop a non-threatening conception of nationalism, one that is tolerant both of internal plurality and of a flexible submersion of its sovereignty in larger forms of social organisation that have positive benefits for its citizens' (Craig 2002: 27–8). Theatre's rather more pragmatic appeal to collective and social responsibility, and the push to understand the consequences of political decision-making for both society as a whole and individuals, became recurrent themes in new Scottish drama, explored in plays of personal experience and testimony (Greig's *When the Bulbul Stopped Singing* [Traverse 2004]), heightened realism (Anderson's *Snuff* [Arches 2005] and vicious satire (Heggie's scabrous *King of Scotland* [Theatre Babel 2000], an indecorously post-devolution deployment of *Diary of a Madman* [1834] by Nicolai Gogol [1809–52]). However, for all the innovation of a new, contemporary Scottish drama of politics, one major aspect of the post-devolution repertoire remained virtually unchanged from previous decades. Despite strong work from Glover with *Shetland Saga* (Traverse 2000), Harris with *Further than the Furthest Thing* (RNT/Tron 2000), *Midwinter* (RSC 2004) and *Solstice* (RSC 2005), McCartney with *Home* (LookOut 2001) and *Cave Dwellers* (7:84 2002), McLean with *Word for Word* (Magnetic North 2003) and *Shimmer* (Traverse 2004), and Rona Munro with *Iron* (Traverse 2002), Scottish theatre has largely remained dominated by male voices and representations of male experience (see Scullion 2001).

Through a bold borrowing of J. M. Barrie's *Peter Pan* (1904), Adam's *Among Unbroken Hearts* (Traverse 2000) portrays a hard-edged reality of rural Scotland by exploring the alienating potential of place, youthful disillusion and a rural drug culture. *The People Next Door* (Traverse 2003) continues Adam's deconstruction of contemporary masculinities by way of an impish re-imagining of generic convention and wicked Brookmyre-style violence. Similar concerns with modern male communities underpin Maxwell's most successful plays, *Our Bad Magnet* (Tron 2000), *Decky Does a Bronco* (Grid Iron 2000) and *Helmet* (Paines Plough/Traverse 2002), each of which describes exclusively male communities. Maxwell's subsequent plays, *If Destroyed True* (Paines Plough 2005) and *Melody* (Traverse 2006), have been set within a wider community and more successfully integrate his characteristic tragicomedic tone. Burke pursued an edgier attack on the shibboleths of Scottish masculinity in *Gagarin Way* (2001) – a tour de force of razor-sharp, demotic dialogue – and he delivered a subtle revision of the history play with *The Straits* (2003). Set on Gibraltar during the Falklands War of 1982, the latter was a complex exploration of masculinity and nationhood choosing the rather unexpected subject of Englishness. The media prominence afforded Martin J. Taylor's *East Coast Chicken Supper* (Traverse

2005) – an energetic, if rather derivative and overwrought tale of boy-bonding and drug-taking in small-town Fife – re-emphasised the significance of the gender-specific community as a key locus in modern Scottish drama, the particular twist here being that the male community has retreated into the domestic sphere (see Scullion 1995). Macleod's *I Was a Beautiful Day* (Traverse 2006) was also built around a concern with masculinities under pressure; the central relationship is between Dan, a former soldier who saw violent action in the first Gulf War, and Lube, a fellow inmate of a psychiatric hospital. Conspicuously, the play borrows from the Irish playwright Brian Friel's *Translations* (1980) the motif of map-making as a mechanism to chart society and the individual's place and position within it: Dan spends his days composing meticulous descriptions, and drawing huge and detailed maps, of his island home, a place to which he cannot bring himself to return.

In recent years, mainly due to the emergence of new political and ethnic nationalisms in Europe, critical thought on the idea of identity, and in particular national identity, has shifted, leading historians, social scientists, artists and critics to interrogate the orthodoxies of cultural imperialism, colonialism, marginalisation, and their neat binary oppositionings. The idea of nations as 'imagined communities' and of identity in modern society as hybrid, fragmentary and 'fuzzy' have significant ubiquity when considering the evolution of identity politics and its impact on our critical vocabulary. Against this backdrop Nadine Holdsworth has analysed the conceptualisation of borders and border-crossings in Greig's *Europe* (Traverse 1994) and Greenhorn's *Passing Places* (Traverse 1997), assigning to their authors the perspective that 'there is something residually important about the nation, something that is worth trying to hold on to, worth trying to articulate amidst the increasing encroachment of globalization into all areas of economic, political and cultural life' (Holdsworth 2003: 39). Holdsworth's observation affords the delineation of a distinctive, if porous and inclusive, Scottish theatre culture as well as dramaturgy. In a useful parallel development exploring the borderlands of theatre history, practice and theory, Michal Kobialka finds that contemporary border theory has 'subverted the notion of the border as the limit that defines and contains' and transformed it into a site of connectivity (Kobialka 1999: iii). Such articulations of cultural hybridity and fruitful instability are demonstrably useful ways of conceptualising post-devolution Scotland, and Scottish theatre indeed ubiquitously deploys a catalogue of relevant metaphors of mutable edges and liminal terrains, the space between, as well as the 'here' and the 'there'.

A significant group of contemporary Scottish plays – such as Riccardo Galgani's *The Found Man* (Traverse 2005), Glover's *Shetland Saga*, Greig's *Outlying Islands* (Traverse 2002), Harris's *Further than the Furthest Thing* and McLean's *Shimmer* – are set on islands or coastlines, at the edge of the world and on the brink of things, describing encounters in the fissures, peaks and hollows of geological and psychological pressure, movement and erosion; their characters survey landscapes, map places, describe topographies, chart events. Other plays are concerned with interior landscapes: mind-maps appear as structuring devices, while narratives enact psychological journeys back to what is barely memorable, out to the edge and beyond, into the unconscious and back. McCartney's *Home*, Macleod's *I Was a Beautiful Day*, Neilson's *The Wonderful World of Dissocia* (EIF 2004), Greig's *Pyrenees* (Paines Plough/Tron 2005) – in which the physical edge of the world is a mountain-top rather than an island – and Harrower's *Blackbird* (EIF 2005) all explore the boundaries and limits of identity through metaphors of psychoanalysis and memory. These plays are hugely different – and I do not want to force comparisons where there are none – but, returning to this chapter's point of departure, they are united by a concern with possible realities, and the internal and external factors that curtail or delimit the extent of speculation. In *Blackbird* and *The Wonderful World of Dissocia*, for example, the exploration of identity is painful, violent and clinical, yet understood to be necessary and inescapable, while in Greig's *Pyrenees* the objective is similar, but the mechanism for exploration turns out to be rather different.

In *Pyrenees* The Man, Greig's nameless hero, seeks to escape his quotidian self initially through rather prosaic affairs with younger women, then through a staged suicide and self-imposed exile on a remote island, and finally, through an extended odyssey across Europe, which ends as he is discovered unconscious in a snowdrift in the Pyrenean mountains, seemingly embarked on the traditional itinerary of penitents and pilgrims walking to Santiago de Compostela. He claims to have lost his memory – the play is equivocal as to the authenticity of his amnesia – and with it his identity. Another character, Anna, has been sent from the British Consulate to determine if he is British and hence her responsibility. Her own identity painfully confused, she is attracted to the *tabula rasa* of The Man. The Proprietor, the play's third character, adopts a more flexible approach to identity, claiming multiple nationalities and roles, each of which can be deployed or discarded at a moment's notice. The final character is Vivienne, who claims that The Man is her husband, Keith Sutherland, whom she has been tracking across the continent, but The Man resists her claim on him: 'This Keith, he sounds like – / It sounds like he should have got out more' (Greig 2005: 85 – II). The Man's identity remains elusive; various signs are proposed as the carriers of his identity, but for Greig words clearly possess much more authority than images or pictures. Vivienne's evidence of photographs is dismissed as unreliable, while spoken language is valorised as the true conveyor of meaning. According to The Man, 'the words are a clue', and he allows Anna to record his voice for analysis (Greig 2005: 19 – I). However, at the end of the play the aural and visual evidence remains equivocal: it may be that Vivienne's interpretation of the signs is correct and the characters will return to the identities signified by them; alternatively, the signs might be reinterpreted to negotiate new identities, and 'Keith' might be shed in favour of something new.

Greig's plays tend to problematise the proscriptive aspects of identity rather than celebrating its emancipatory or empowering capacities (see Nesteruk 2000; Reinelt 2001). In *Pyrenees* identity may be inescapable, but it is also negotiable and even playful. When it was first produced in March 2005, the play was seen as something of a nascent NTS dress rehearsal: its author, Greig, is the NTS's dramaturge, and its director, Vicky Featherstone, is the artistic director of the NTS. Indeed, without question, the key theatre event of the post-devolution period is the establishment of the NTS as Scotland's new national flagship company. After a long period of anticipation and extensive politicking, combining governmental commitment with a collaborative agreement of the Scottish theatre sector, the NTS was launched on 25 February 2006. Up to the time of writing the NTS has been focused mainly on two interconnected concerns: (a) the actual work on stage, and the aesthetic and political agendas the new company might adopt and come to disseminate through its theatre-making activities; and (b) Scotland's cultural infrastructure and the changing relationship between politics and culture. As a national flagship company, which has chosen deliberately not to be bound to, or identified with, any one particular 'home' building or locale, the NTS is expected to deliver influential new thinking in respect to both.

To date the NTS's on-stage story comprises ten *Home* events over the launch weekend, a musical adaptation of Neil Gaiman's children's book *The Wolves in the Wall* (2003), directed by Featherstone and Julian Crouch at the Tramway and on tour (indeed the first NTS production to play outwith Scotland), and a long-awaited revival and controversial rewrite of Hannan's *Elizabeth Gordon Quinn* by John Tiffany, as well as *Falling* by Poorboy in the underground spaces beneath Glasgow's Queen Street Station, *Roam* by Grid Iron at Edinburgh Airport, and Arthur Miller's *The Crucible* (1953) by TAG, involving community groups across Scotland. This astonishingly broad repertoire has been complemented by the recruitment of a 'Young Company' currently working towards its first outputs, and numerous other education and outreach events, workshop initiatives and new talent labs. The choices made by the NTS in this very early phase of its operation have been well received as thoughtful, bold, strategic and tactical in more or less equal measure. This is best exemplified by *Home*, the event that launched the NTS simultaneously across the whole of Scotland over one long weekend at the end of February. Ten directors had been commissioned to respond to the concept of 'home' in ten very different locations: Alison Peebles worked in Aberdeen, Matthew Lenton in Caithness, Graham Eatough in Dumfries, Kenny Miller in Dundee, Gill Robertson in East Lothian, Anthony Neilson in Edinburgh, John Tiffany in Glasgow, Scott Graham in Inverness, Stewart Laing in Stornoway, and Wils Wilson in Lerwick.

Distinctively, the logistics of *Home* meant that no one person – no one critic – could see all the productions. It meant also that no one production constituted in itself the launch of the NTS, and no one production 'stood for' the NTS or carried the entire weight of popular and critical expectation. The project was designed to reflect the geographical, social and cultural diversity of Scotland while also marking the rather new take on national self-representation and representativeness envisaged by the NTS; accordingly, the 'whole-ness' of the project was not accomplished by seeing or contributing to it in its totality, but by fully engaging in the production of a part or parts of it. As both the NTS's original point of departure and its declaration of intent, *Home* concerned the necessity of exploding pre-conceived expectations, of getting 'out there' among the people, and of taking risks, sig-nalling that the NTS is interested in testing and exploring the boundaries of 'national' theatre. The *Home* project also showed that the NTS intends to raise the level of debate about theatre in Scotland, which is to be achieved by producing more theatre for a greater number of people in more places, by strategic dramaturgical and theatrical choices involv-ing both new plays and newly devised revivals, and by political lobbying and active par-ticipation in policy-making.

The NTS is the first national theatre of the new millennium and, as such, its functions, responsibilities and choices are expected to differ significantly from the national theatres conceived by the nineteenth-century nationalist movements or mid-twentieth-century modernist discourse. It is a national theatre created by consensus within an existing theatre community as well as by the political will of a new parliament. In 1997, in response to the successful referendum on devolution, Harrower and Greig wrote in the *Scotsman* that 'Scotland has voted to redefine itself as a nation. To redefine ourselves we need to under-stand ourselves, exchange ideas and aspirations, confront enduring myths, expose injustices and explore our past. The quality, accessibility and immediacy of Scottish theatre make it one of the best arenas in which these dialogues can take place' (Harrower and Greig 1997: 15). In 2001 the report of the National Theatre working group took the two playwrights' aspiration a step further, envisaging 'a Scottish National Theatre which can reflect an inclu-sive and outward looking sense of identity' (Scottish Arts Council 2001: 5). By 2004 the particular challenges of creating a national theatre for a new Scotland had become even clearer and were tested by Greig, among others: 'What purpose . . . does a national theatre serve in a borderless Europe? What identity does it articulate in a globalised, multi-cultural, media-saturated Scotland?' (Greig 2004: 1). The NTS has aimed to create an innovative and practical national theatre fit for purpose within twenty-first-century Scotland's globalised small-nation context, not a gerrymandered replica of something designed for nineteenth-century nation-building or end-of-empire retrenchment. Accordingly, emerging from the original conceptual structures of the NTS, the *Home* project must be seen as the clearest manifestation so far of what this vision might be able to deliver theatrically.

Two new NTS-commissioned plays – Neilson's *Realism* and Burke's *Blackwatch* – are scheduled to premiere at the 2006 Edinburgh International Festival and Edinburgh Fringe Festival respectively. Playing in multiple contexts and to multiple audiences has already become a hallmark of NTS activity; its ambition to promote a range of different types of theatre has the potential to create a new Scottish repertoire. With this in mind, the conceptual potential and bold speculations of 1999, supported by recent investments, interventions and initiatives in and by the NTS, may very well take more concrete and fruitful shape.

Chapter 9

Twenty-one Collections for the Twenty-first Century

Christopher Whyte

The critical impulse is rooted in generosity, in a capacity for profligate attention. If it is essential to set limits and impose a framework, this can also feel like self-sacrifice. How could one possibly exhaust what requires to be said about even a single poet, never mind one generation, or several? More than a chorus of praise, uncritical in its very essence, poets demand to be read and look for honest articulation of one's experience in reading their work. Occasionally wrongheaded and inevitably biased, such responses can none the less constitute the basis for an ongoing debate. In *Modern Scottish Poetry* (2004) I was eager to avoid pontificating about Scottishness and the Scottish tradition, or offering support to any canon constructed on the basis of essentialist concepts. As a result I refrained from even naming anyone not included among the twenty poets I had selected for aleatoric and agnostic treatment. The present essay was at one stage conceived of as the final chapter of that longer study, where I would throw caution to the wind and offer thumbnail assessments of a wide range of collections published within the space of only half a decade. Poets dealt with there are ignored here. The following texts have not yet had time to sediment in readers' consciousnesses. If the views expressed are at times stringent, even harsh, that ought to be taken as evidence of the passion and commitment with which the poems have been read.

It is not enough to write, discovering in turn how each new work demands to be written. Writers must also regularly reinvent for themselves the very possibility of writing, against the background of their daily lives and a network of relationships and obligations. Particularly for poets living in highly developed consumer societies, the problem of appropriate subject matter just will not go away. The pervasive awkwardness of tone marring Stewart Conn's latest volume, *Ghosts at Cockrow* (2005), thus appears to issue from a problem with entitlement. It is as if a member of the Calvinist elect – talented, tolerant and self-questioning – were pondering how an existence such as his, notoriously blessed by God and undeservedly privileged, could relate to poetry and the need to make poetry. Does such good fortune bring with it an implicit injunction to silence? Trivial incidents like leaving one's varilux glasses on the plane, or losing the cusp from an upper molar while on holiday in France, are symptomatic. Conn avoids finite verbs, preferring participles and apposition, thus de-energising his verse. Chunks of prose crop up undigested in a manner verging on the provocative. In a section devoted to a holiday in Burgundy, foreign travel offers one means of escape, while Raoull of Corstorphine, the poet's alter ego, concedes the possibility of both an admirable, deflected modesty – 'more likely lack of merit than Fate denied me // a drooling posterity' – and direct, untrammelled utterance: 'Is not our progress through life / a search for harmony, amidst darkness?' (Conn 2005: 70, 63). Most convincing, however, are Conn's poems to his wife, in which a sense of connectedness, won through determination and day-to-day commitment, of facing dangers rather than unaccountably being spared them, briefly dissipates the poet's concerns about entitlement.

Noteworthy Poems (2002) by Tessa Ransford covers the entire range of her career. Consistently illuminating postscripts highlight the rich interconnections between poetry, reading and experience. What Ransford says of 'Sacred City' is applicable to her work as a whole: 'The language is of declaration or statement. Others may disagree with the stance taken, but it is not presented as a debating point. It is taken without apology and is authoritative' (Ransford 2002: 37). A poem in terzinas, a sestina, and an Alcaic ode carefully transmuted from the Greek with unobtrusive precision show Ransford's lively interest in form, while 'A Poem About a Concrete Poem' embodies the vision which gave birth, after nearly two decades, to the outstanding building by Malcolm Fraser which now houses the Scottish Poetry Library. 'Not in a Garden' sets three agonies alongside one another, without sensationalism or any attempt at ranking: of the self-frustrating poet, of Christ, and of a Kurdish woman refugee. Unashamedly intellectual in its approach, Ransford's work acknowledges no limitations of gender and is about as far as one could get from conventional expectations of 'women's poetry'. That it should so far have found a limited circle of readers is a matter for speculation.

Though his was a round trip and hers was not, it is tempting to see the English engraver, the protagonist of the title sequence from *Bewick Walks to Scotland* (2004) by Sally Evans, as the poet's alter ego, allowing her to represent her encounter with a different culture – 'I feel the country change, law change' – in a landscape where 'the stag / (who does not know he is Scottish) / speaks rarely and perfectly' (Evans 2004: 13, 39). Evans has a talent for teasing the remarkable from the unremarkable, notably in 'Fireside', where 'flames / are more worth watching than / the road or television', but also in 'Blind Man by the River', which 'whispers its metric philosophy' as he 'tastes the articulate water on his fingertips' (Evans 2004: 47). The surface amble of her prosody is deceptive. Unobtrusive rhyming hints at a steely, hidden discipline, and her unassuming poems have a surprisingly experimental quality. Because 'I cannot recount my life / in a regular series of I-sentences' (Evans 2004: 10), experience is conveyed indirectly through the object of the gaze rather than the gazer. The juxtaposition of landscapes, 'this outlook on Lomond / and that view of the Tyne', of discovery and familiarity, is endlessly fertile: 'Otter! What next? / Me, with a quicksilver text' (Evans 2004: 22, 46).

Simplicity and frank openness of utterance characterise many of the poems in *Saoghal Ùr* (2003) by Maoilios Caimbeul. Medieval allegory is not far away in his 'Deasbad eadar a' Ghrian 's a' Ghealach', a dialogue in couplets between opponents with irreconcilable claims: 'Chan eil do shòlas ach air iasad', mocks the sun, 'mur b' e mise, càite d' ìomhaigh', while 'màthair chiùin na h-oidhche' rejoins that 'nuair bhios m' fhaileas ciùin san uisge, / nì esan 's ise gàir làn tuigse' (Caimbeul 2003: 4). Despite its title 'Ceòlraidh Ùr' resonates with old song – 'is thus' a mhaighdean iongantach / cur sèideadh na mo shiùil' (Caimbeul 2003: 6) – while Caimbeul makes local people's acquisition of a wood in Sutherland the basis for new lyrics to a well-known tune, recalling the tragic events which took place there at the time of the Clearances. Lightness and playful wit are evident in seven bird poems, imitating the thrush's song and with a powerful conclusion for the heron: 'Ach nuair a charaicheas mi / mo sgiathan mòra cudthromach / bidh na marannan fhèin a' gluasad' (Caimbeul 2003: 34). 'Rud a Thachair' intriguingly brings together a range of stimuli – a small press pamphlet picked up from the table by chance, a chat show on the radio accompanying morning coffee – as a verbal echo becomes pregnant with surprising meaning: 'a' coinneachadh mar siud anns an fhalamhachd / agus ag èirigh gu chèile às an t-sruth do-sheachanta' (Caimbeul 2003: 11). But a weightier note of spiritual wrestling and determined faith, familiar from Caimbeul's previous volumes, also occurs, as in 'Ùrnaigh – ann an àm a' bhuairidh' and 'Briseadh na Cloiche', bringing ballast to a varied and technically accomplished volume.

In a country that had not been denied an internal political forum during much of her lifetime, Valerie Gillies's fascination in *The Lightning Tree* (2002) with the land (specifically, the Scottish Borders), folk tradition, and what many would dismiss as superstition might carry disturbingly reactionary implications extending far beyond the field of poetry. Wild hares compete with aircraft in 'Runway Lights', and in 'I am Speaking to my Saint' St Fillan is implored to cure a daughter with his healing stones, as Gillies subjects a faith best labelled pagan to the grim tests of modernity. Similarly, having bidden farewell to one of her breasts in a silent ritual involving sun and hill in 'Golden Breast', the poet images radiation therapy as 'The Charmstone', making an amulet of a pebble: 'Hang it on your bedpost, keep / Away the nightmare from your sleep. / Mare stone washed up by the sea' (Gillies 2002: 35). By contrast, when going wholeheartedly for the contemporary, her diction is self-conscious: 'kinky kinetic / slinky prophetic // alien abduction / astral seduction' (Gillies 2002: 49–50). Gillies must urgently pursue the fundamental question whether her favoured preoccupations can ever be more than a stubborn retreat from contemporary reality, if her voice is not to become trapped in a permanent oscillation between the desperate and the ever so faintly twee.

To observe that what Tom Pow's poems in *Landscapes and Legacies* (2004) have to say is infinitely less important than how it gets said sounds like dispraise; yet it is intended as the highest kind of praise. The tonality achieved here is that of an almost indefinitely sustainable music, pointing to an acute technical grasp which, within a form whose medium must also be its message, proffers its own human and ontological certainties. To convey a feeling for Pow's verse requires extensive quotation: for example, 'as one heron, then another, / heave themselves from the shadows and, / trailing the grainy daylight, take // all the time two blue herons need / to sew darkness onto darkness / across the bay', or 'one of a pair of swans, / circling its young, raises itself from the river // and lifts up its wings. A slab of white light / hits Caravaggio with a shock of pleasure // like a lover's open thigh' (Pow 2004: 37, 41). The transition to silence requires deft management, which may be why Pow's closes occasionally dissatisfy. 'Simon in the Vegetable Patch', however, culminates in an immensely enjoyable resumé of its own frustrated content. Poetry of celebration is a treacherous undertaking; if Pow so amply succeeds, this must be because he understands that the very act of writing a poem is in itself a celebration.

Any account of Frank Kuppner's *A God's Breakfast* (2004) which fails to raise the issue of length would be less than serious: 'Thirty-five lines. Good God! And one more makes it thirty-six' (Kuppner 2004: 174). It is not just a matter of why use two words when you can use twenty: 'not one but two – no: not two but three. / Not three, but four. (No, wait a moment: not four)' (Kuppner 2004: 164). If concision is a virtue, should expansiveness be treated differently? After all, Hugh MacDiarmid's *In Memoriam James Joyce* (1955) made clamorous demands for an aesthetic of the long. Like Sydney Goodsir Smith (1915–75), Kuppner experiences an irresistible pull towards the 1920s, Ezra Pound, and the aftermath of European Decadentism. 'The Uninvited Guest' works as the pastiche of a classical anthology composed mainly of distichs, at times uproariously funny and showing off a persistent strand of schoolboy smuttiness. Presumably no Greek or Roman author could get quite so worked up about pederasty ('The universe is a pederast pretending to be a clock' [Kuppner 2004: 89]), while Kuppner's misogyny bespeaks a later age, when women have attained a degree of social power: 'While Sulpicia bounces her noble old boobs in my face, / I sigh at the thought of the chances I have lost in life' (Kuppner 2004: 50). If the recurrence of windows means he presents himself as both flâneur and voyeur, his engaging, pervasive facetiousness is transcended, however briefly, in a love poem: 'we may get used to anything, even staggering joy. / And talk as little as possible about what matters most' (Kuppner 2004: 167).

Pentameter rhythms are so automatic for John Burnside that he attempts to conceal them by splitting lines or dividing them across the page. One wonders what would happen if he were to challenge his facility rather than dissimulating it. Technical restrictions willingly confronted can lift a poet's voice beyond the personal into a different realm. In *The Light Trap* (2002) Burnside longs to transmute the banal and everyday, uncovering another level, even if this should mean no more than spying on a schoolteacher who takes a private swim at night and briefly embodies 'a life beneath the life / I understood' (Burnside 2002: 26). Harrowing existential doubt – 'Sometimes I am dizzy with the fear / of losing everything' (Burnside 2002: 41) – is also an urge to move beyond the boundaries of the individual, 'that foreign self, who never leaves / the middle-ground // yet never fully / hoves into view' (Burnside 2002: 75), if necessary through transmigration. Women become deer, 'slip between two lives / in skipping rhymes', and 'the borderland through which they pass' might have been his 'if I could have chosen anything / but this inevitable self' (Burnside 2002: 10). Burnside is fascinated by animals and plants, forms of life from which a mere difference of category separates him, and stresses the importance of not trying too hard: 'Though what we know is mostly the agreed / and measured, what we are is something else // and never comes / without some inattention' (Burnside 2002: 52).

If speculation can turn to naked certainty of threat as 'what we most love reveals itself as danger' (Burnside 2002: 34), that may be why Burnside's more soothing conclusions have an air of prevarication. When he claims 'this is the problem: how to be alive / in all this gazed-upon and cherished world / and do no harm' (Burnside 2002: 42), one wonders if human aspiration should be limited to such carefully schooled inhibition and hankers after direct utterance in a poetry made from the half-seen and the half-intuited. Will the vision, finally evoked, add up to more than the sum of its glimmers? 'Love' and 'soul' are crucial terms in Burnside's work, and a meticulous study of their occurrences might help clarify what struggles towards definition there. How many uses of the word 'love' are adequately earned? In *The Good Neighbour* (2005) the reader is constantly tantalised, left tussling with statements such as 'what we mean when we talk about love / is probably not what we think', or 'the real unmakes itself in every hand // that reaches out to touch and grasps thin air' (Burnside 2005: 70, 80). If Burnside is drawn to evening and nightscapes, the mist arising from his words, though it feels like enchantment, could also be befuddlement. Perhaps '*self* is metaphor', and 'a world around the world we understand' is indeed 'waiting to be recovered and given names' (Burnside 2005: 53, 43). Yet the moment when the vehicle, for which these scenes are the tenor, can manifest is postponed indefinitely.

One might expect the things familiar to a poet to tell us most about him. But *A Place in the World* (2005) by Iain Bamforth is a search for precisely that, an exile's book, fascinated by what can sustain life ('Pig Melon Incarnation'), elitist yet idealistic. The wealth of cultural references scattered throughout hints at a potential community of readers; not places only, but possible alternative selves are reviewed: Rainer Maria Rilke in Paris, Diogenes the cynic, Paul Gauguin and Robert Louis Stevenson. While exploring territories 'where Calvin never dared legislate' (Bamforth 2005: 63), Bamforth's Calvinist inheritance is never far away: 'hitching the problem of who you are to where you're going', he sets off to find a heavenly city for the twentieth century, determined 'not to minister to his needs, not to sell his birthright', yet ending up in 'the echoey labyrinth of his own mind' because 'the traveller sees as horizon what is, in fact, his own aggregate' (Bamforth 2005: 53, 87, 55). Even if Strasbourg cannot be that city, Bamforth's poems inhabit with at times frustrating doggedness a fault line between French and German civilisation hard to identify with Europe. Exhibiting not just learning but language – 'the wafer words of inner drought: / infecund, sere, drained, leached, sucked dry, barren, issueless, jejune' (Bamforth 2005: 53) – his work has a studied detachment rarely displaced by more sensual tones, as in 'Ten Years: a Psalm'. After all, charity is 'negating what you value most: / your self' (Bamforth 2005: 34). Evocations of Charles Baudelaire, Arthur Rimbaud and Hugh MacDiarmid serve to locate him as an unrepentant child of classic modernism.

The reek of testosterone that lifts off the opening sonnets in *Madame Fifi's Farewell* (2003) makes Gerry Cambridge's polemical setting of his face against the contemporary – 'put out the light of modernity' (Cambridge 2003: 91) – less convincing than might otherwise have been the case. This is a man with a problem: 'if you want me again look for me among the suspenders' (Cambridge 2003: 34). At its best, sex achieves reciprocity, a temporary dissolving of the boundaries between individuals and genders, as 'when I die in your earth and self-hood breaks / and we flow together' (Cambridge 2003: 30). More perceptible, however, is a polarisation that makes sonnet writing itself resemble an assault: 'We / spark such opposites, you and me; my blood-heat / blazes here in my red-bearded face; neat, / you sit like the form for a sonnet, whitely' (Cambridge 2003: 39). Yet the volume also has a wondrously tender, painfully erotic poem about a Spanish pomegranate, a 'chapel / packed with its ruby congregation' (Cambridge 2003: 19). In an enjoyable rejoinder to a free-verse sestina (now there's a contradiction!) by David Kinloch, Cambridge insists that 'I have more in common with Whitman than any free-verser, in a time of sonnets he wrote rhythmical free verse based on the prose in the Bible' (Cambridge 2003: 34). Were one to look abroad, to Europe and beyond, such dogged espousal of closed forms would not seem anachronistic. But it is no accident that Cambridge's longer poems, in pentameter or tetrameter rhymed couplets, depict a man wilfully isolated from broader society, pitting himself against the elements and only occasionally sallying forth to seek community: 'that street's air, / its ruddy faces, gutter leaves, shop windows, / the absolute earthly end of all rainbows' (Cambridge 2003: 50).

David Kinloch is in all likelihood verbally the most exciting poet of his generation. Thus, *Un Tour d'Écosse* (2002) inhabits an interlanguage between Scots, English and French, at times even moving beyond – 'do not slam the door on South Germany's *trooskel*, Denmark's *taerskel* or Iceland's *throskulldur*' (Kinloch 2002: 48) – though Gaelic is resolutely confined to a ghetto of place-names. Besides such playful brilliance comes a plentiful dose of humour, as in a cockroach's verse epistle 'To a Bardie'. Elsewhere, Scots sits awkwardly, its precise ventriloquism of a different social class insufficiently framed or distanced, as in 'Jacob and the Angel'. Gay themes loom large, and Kinloch does not shirk the scandalous sides of gay existence: cruising in 'Brompton Cemetery', blow jobs in public places. 'An Epistle to Robert Burns' smacks of one-upmanship, and what better position for penning such a missive than 'supine on the *far niente* of a Capezzano / Lounger', holidaying 'in Tuscany on pasta and Chianti' while your lover dives into the pool? Though being caught in the wrong place at the wrong time looms as the ultimate catastrophe, Kinloch does ordinariness best ('Bed'), along with a plangent note indicating the darker side to such hedonistic consumerism ('Customs', 'Walls'). However, his approach to AIDS is spectacular – '"Watayaseekid? Watayasee?"' (Kinloch 2002: 94) – and peculiarly emotionless. The conceits underpinning his longer sequences, in prose and verse, as when Walt Whitman and Federico García Lorca make a cycle tour of Scotland, are too flimsy to sustain them or let these hybridisations cohere into some larger meaning. Would it be wrong to suggest that, for Kinloch, Scots functions as a subset of English, an additional register? He never makes us forget – as any language should, however briefly – that other languages exist. Good as it is to have Paul Celan in Scots, one wonders where this leads, what purpose it can have within the larger framework of Kinloch's poetry. A fine prose piece, 'Painting by Numbers', offers some enlightenment while implying that Scots will always be, for this poet, a matter of exhumation.

The family elegies of *In My Father's House* (2005) use a sparer, more sober idiom than Kinloch's earlier book. He reaches a new high point with 'Baines His Dissection'. The historical setting deepens and chastens the expression of a thoroughly masculine tenderness, focusing and honing rather than rendering it remote: 'we'll move as we have always done in one harmonious / cavalcade, two bodies, one soul, the craft of love' (Kinloch 2005: 84). Though when 'passion left us . . . we discovered, together and separately . . . Persians . . . Armenians . . . silver-chested Greeks', the poem ends with a *Liebestod* in cascades of glittering, poignant and disorienting verbal brilliance: 'he sees and seizes me / in sound' (Kinloch 2005: 88).

Exile is the burning issue in Bill Herbert's *The Big Bumper Book of Troy* (2002), both in terms of place – 'I can't yet find that comfort of a curve, / the harbour shelf at Broughty Ferry' – and (with a neat zeugma) language: 'What is the Scots word I once knew for "throw" / that's neither "lob" nor "hoy" nor in my mouth?' (Herbert 2002: 18, 35). Poetic origins in Scotland's industrial central belt ('doon the waater past Greenock, past Davidson / and B. V. Thomson and Sydney Graham, all sharing / a silver flask among the rope coils of the docks') link Herbert to empire no less inexorably than Robert Crawford (see Whyte 2004a: 211), provoking a nervousness about intellectual engagement 'between a pint of Belhaven and / Jo's copy of Bachelard' as well as a moving tribute to Edwin Morgan: 'I was thinking about Morgan, how I love him / and I never said, the him I only know through words: / his work is my work's master' (Herbert 2002: 52, 20, 50). Tautology somewhat mars the sections dealing with Moscow and Spain. Herbert gets invited to these places because he produces poetry. The upshot of the invitation is more poetry. The whole process has an inevitability that can appear machine-like. The tautology points to a further difficulty: is the day-to-day life of a poet, with all its accidents and banalities, the most appropriate subject matter for his poetry? The overall effect is of a pervasive and effortless egotism, the sleight of hand so imperceptible one risks losing sight of the oddity of such an approach.

Herbert behaves as if he had rediscovered James Watson's *Choice Collection* (1706), and Allan Ramsay lives again not just in the resurrection of older forms but in the awkward relation to classical precedent Homer concluding a poem in Christ's Kirk metre as 'thon blind auld pogue, / that DJ'd ancient raves / and mixed / thigither tales o Troy' (Herbert 2002: 134). Robert Fergusson is 'a Northern Keats' and, finely, 'oor Jimmy Dean o thi canty beats / oor ain Kit Smart', his removal to Bedlam likened to MacDiarmid's legendary fall from the top deck of a London omnibus: 'he landed oan his lyric snoot / and banged, fowk sey, his rhythms oot – / they dwyned tae prose' (Herbert 2002: 143). Herbert's prognostication is no less damning than Kinloch's – 'Eh nearly ken noo hoo tae be thi last / tae write in Scots' (Herbert 2002: 119) – and the finest poems in this stimulating, exasperating, uneven collection are elegies, with the singer Billy MacKenzie splendidly 'Duveted in overdose'. Herbert's choice of English (language again a substitute for physicality) to lament his grandmother is startling: 'the act of breathing was reduced / to gasps and ratchets, clutchings and / embraces for our best attempts // at language who had never touched / to show our love' (p. 154). 'The Fall of the House of Broon' is a sustained parody of Book II of the *Aeneid*, elevating Dundee as much as it diminishes Troy, its epic treatment of comic-strip characters unfailingly entertaining. But if 'Oor Wullie' does stand in for Herbert, how are we to interpret Dido's closing exhortation? Where can this poet's Italy be located?

Jackie Kay's poems have tended to be interesting not merely in themselves but for the issues they raise. In *Life Masks* (2005) the painful ending of a love relationship broadens, as it were, the range of those she speaks for and to, while also inducing a degree of nervousness in the reader. Someone who writes so consistently and ruthlessly from her own experience gives the impression of a car driver going perilously close to the kerb. How long can she keep it up? And what role is reserved for the imagination? Familiar, less attractive characteristics of Kay's work come regularly to the fore: niceness, a wheedling tone, and formal inconsistencies. A poem in tercets, 'Notice', seems to want to be terzinas, while in 'Childhood, Still' couplets rhyme erratically. The danger of sentimentality looms: 'Old Tongue' is pure Kailyard, Scottish pawkiness at its worst. And yet, individual lines and phrases soar with irresistible authority towards a lapidary eloquence: 'But all of us are less than ourselves / in the days when we need to be more', or 'I say, you are never the same woman twice', and 'nobody – no other love – will likely / ever have the same slow charm, / that smile that was just about to happen' (Kay 2005: 28, 30, 22).

Don Paterson's staggering formal abilities shine forth in 'St Brides: Sea Mails' from *Landing Light* (2003), seven stanzas which open and close visually in tune with their rhyme scheme (*abcacba*), mimicking the wing movements of the birds that are their subject – a subject presented hermetically, full of ellipses, constraining readers to a labour of filling out and recreating a context for such tight-lipped utterance. Paterson's prosodic craft, his mastery of rhyme and half-rhyme, never aims at sensual delight. One thinks repeatedly of Byron while missing that poet's relish for excess, his irrepressible revolutionary idealism. Like 'The Landing', some of Paterson's poems tend towards clipped quatrains which, if strictly speaking in ballad metre, are more redolent of the Calvinist metrical psalms, didactic in tone, rigidly eschewing any verbal flourish, and rendering this particular poem's closing word – 'auditorium' – all the more of a shock. Set alongside these poems are what might be called anti-poems, such as 'A Talking Book', which is generically unresolved, infinitely extendable, yet the very opposite of generous, as if the poet regretted in the act of making it the concession of articulate utterance: 'It gives me no joy / to tell you this', or 'What work is so defeated / by itself, as all our scribbling on the air?' (Paterson 2003: 22, 37). Paterson, like so many others, writes 'after Cavafy', 'after Rilke', presumed reworkings of existing English versions by one with no knowledge of the original, where no boundaries are crossed, no different languages brought into contact. Could one call these anti-translations? Paterson's love poems concentrate on break-up recording 'the vast / infinitesimal letdown of each other', making one all the more thankful for two splendid tributes to the poet's sons: 'See how the true gift never leaves the giver . . . I kissed your mouth and pledged myself forever' (Paterson 2003: 39, 5).

Angela McSeveney comes over as something of a young Turk. The poems in *Imprint* (2002) lack traceable intertextualities, steering clear of references to existing forms or indeed to other poems. However, anyone who imagines such unadorned, stark utterance to be craftless, a mere matter of putting pen to paper, should have a go and see how they match up against McSeveney. Poems about her mother's death carefully frame the volume and, though clumsiness and naiveties recur, what look like chunks of prose have in fact been tirelessly refined and trimmed: consider 'jade' and 'jaded', the recurrence of 'sensible', or the acute observation of an infant's 'knuckles four stars / across the back of each hand' (McSeveney 2002: 33, 37, 30). In 'Flumes' and 'Bile' McSeveney writes the body with a vengeance: 'Launched like a stool / down yards of convoluted gut . . . Spat out at the other end, / it's birth speeded up' (McSeveney 2002: 13). Suicidal thoughts and sexual fantasy receive equally unflinching contemplation in 'Paracetamol' and 'Imprint', while uncurtained windows provoke dreams of different and happier families in a wistful passer-by 'choosing my foster home / by the arrangement of their photo frames, / their yards of bookshelving' (McSeveney 2002: 15).

What more skilled gambit for the market than a collection focusing in edulcorated form on pregnancy and childbirth? This is what every mother feels, or so *Newborn* (2004) by Kate Clanchy would have us believe. And naturally it is not and we do not. The claim to be ordinary – 'commonplace', borderless', 'glorious' (Clanchy 2004: 29) – is a claim to representation, indeed for delegation. What possible connection can there be between opening up the Ceremonial Road in China and breast-feeding, except that both are – in this poet's view – 'right'? This is one of the rare points in a blatantly political collection where the steely ideological fist shows through the attractive glove Clanchy has clothed it in. What about mothers lacking fathers? Mothers who do not like their babies? Postnatal depression? There are some fine descriptive moments – for example, the down on a baby's head compared to 'the innermost, vellum layer / of some rare snowcreature's / aureole of fur' – as well as some awkwardnesses: 'The willows toss their heads / like pettish girls' (Clanchy 2004: 12–13). Who, according to Clanchy, could be more pitiable than the woman who has lost her man and, with him, the possibility of being fertilised: 'her teeth were old, / had that yellow sheen like Bakelite // or piano keys, and I thought / of her last eggs, / the womb staying empty, folded // like an evening purse' (Clanchy 2004: 41)? One comes up for air from time to time at the glimpse of a potential space for questioning, as at the close of 'When You Cried', but this is not a book that encourages, or leaves room for, any manner of dissent.

Richard Price's method in *Lucky Day* (2005) is both minimalist and hermetic, as he avoids filling out a stanza or committing himself to any definite pattern, preferring half-phrases and hints instead. His poetry of love and sex – 'our bodies / a greedy mouthful / on the hungry bed' – bespeaks an easy confidence about pleasing women: 'As you're anxious but asking / to open up your shivering legs / I'll own up – / I'm out of myself / with nervous excitement' (Price 2005: 55, 58). He relies on similar indulgence from his readers, filtering individual experiences to an allusive idiosyncratic code, though Price is skilled enough for it never to become impenetrable. 'Lick and stick', an extended poem whose theme of non-committal mimics his own approach to form, shows an aptitude for visual play that is also, tentatively, aural, with fragments displaced across the page. Truncations and silences, half-statements and interjections work powerfully in the section on his daughters, in which he warns the one with Angelman syndrome that 'people will not love you / when we are dead', confessing 'Truth is, I was ashamed. / I'd rather not say // on what count' (Price 2005: 83, 82). His view of pregnancy – '"just" nine cricked months / (say sickness, say sciatica, / and that's for short)' (Price 2005: 95) – offers a useful corrective to Clanchy's more rhapsodic approach.

Page upon patient page, Tracey Herd raises through *Dead Redhead* (2001) her pallid iconostasis of victimhood, and one's sense of the intended audience as female makes the project all the more disquieting. America and Hollywood assume the mythogenic potential of the House of Atreus and the Trojan War. Marilyn Monroe 'lie[s] in a cold bath for hours' so her new jeans can shrink to fit while Jackie Kennedy 'stand[s] there in the bullet's acrid light' (Herd 2001: 15, 41). Herd's heroines foretaste a violent death ('The Empress Dreams in Miniature'), relive suicide ('Ophelia's Confession', which appropriates Diana's death in Paris), or realise a dreamed one in the waters of the Forth. Her celluloid Gothic makes for grim reading, the morgue-like atmosphere intensified by a sequence concerning a mass murderer whose victims' bodies have 'rocks removed from their vaginas', 'their necks raw from the makeshift ligatures' (Herd 2001: 26). Sadly Herd cannot always muster a tautness of line and diction to match the acuteness of the attitudes being struck. Her passion for the ambivalent icons of a land she must keep firmly at an oneiric distance can make one feel stranded in a ghoulish fan club whose coded references shoot far above one's head. Her writing about prize horses – 'Bombshell' and 'Lyric Fantasy' can instructively be set alongside one another – evokes catwalks of a different kind, whose triumphs and tragedies remain irretrievably beyond the human.

There can be no mistaking the sheer linguistic verve and passionate commitment to his language in *Kate o Shanter's Tale* (2003) by Matthew Fitt, avoiding capital letters and apostrophes while making a valiant attempt at a logical spelling for Scots ('geist'), which does justice to his Dundee vowels. At its best, Fitt's poetry bursts dramatically off the page, so acutely and authentically observed one can identify the voices that declaim it, as in the title poem, but also 'ken', a philosophical treatise which is at the same time a crippling denunciation: 'breenie cannae see the wudd fur the trees / – eh, eh ken / the word for cundie in bulgarian is okap / – eh, eh ken' (Fitt 2003: 31). What then provokes that troubling sense of someone running on the spot? The problem may be that Fitt is still writing at a time when using Scots cannot be taken for granted and, consequently, his choice of the language and the (tired?) agenda it draws after it have to be the subject matter of his poems. Even a Czech sequence, focusing on the assassination of the Nazi functionary Reinhard Heydrich by partisans in 1942 and the horrendous reprisals that ensued, remains faithful to the pattern of heroic, small nation pitted against a ruthless neighbour endowed with overwhelmingly superior forces. While Fitt's command of lexis is breathtaking – 'be guid tae yirsel / sic a drochle / a peeliewally / there's nae meat on ye at aa / mair bouk on a deid spuggie' – and he also effortlessly straddles the contemporary, as in 'eftir the pairty' (Fitt 2003: 29), the impression lingers of someone (more likely his language rather than Fitt himself) beating on the resounding walls of a metallic cell and begging to be let out. Where can they have put the key?

Twenty-one collections of poetry may sound like a generous ration, but there are regrettable omissions here. No space could be found for the fruits of Donny O'Rourke's German exploits *On a Roll: A Jena Notebook* (2001) and *Aus dem Wartesaal der Poesie: Nürnberger Notizen/From Poetry's Waiting Room: Nürnberg Notebook* (2005), or for *Stirling Sonnets* and *Fae the Flouers o Evil: Baudelaire in Scots* by James Robertson (both 2001), or for Elizabeth Burns's pamphlet *The Alteration* (2003). *Toithín ag Tlaithínteacht* (2003), the latest publication by prolific, multilingual Rody Gorman, is in Irish, and therefore beyond the scope of this chapter. Edwin Morgan once remarked in conversation that, having started out as a 'young' poet, he subsequently became a 'younger' poet. With Matthew Fitt and Tracey Herd already approaching forty, one's thoughts inevitably turn to the next generation: to texts which may be little more than an untidy sheaf of mismatched printouts on an obscure desk, which dropped this week into the rejections tray of a literary magazine, or else subsist as the merest, subliminal tingle at the edge of a mind or sensibility, like the imagined drop of water Osip Mandelstam kept trying to shake from his ear during the final stages of resistance before sitting down to write a poem. If one can only gesture in their direction, then that is none the less a fitting way to end this chapter.

Chapter 10

Shifting Boundaries: Scottish Gaelic Literature after Devolution

Máire Ní Annracháin

Devolution to an English-speaking Scotland has done little to redress the marginalisation of Gaelic. Scottish Gaelic, unlike Irish in Ireland, was not called upon to express cultural nationalism at any point in the twentieth century, nor was its literature charged with seeking or saving the soul of Scotland. There was no pressure to remain undiluted by contact with other languages and cultures. By the end of the twentieth century no great expectations of benefits for the language from devolution or independence had been built up, so that there have been no particular hopes either to dash or to fulfil.

The socio-linguistic situation of Scottish Gaelic remains grave. There have been some positive developments, including the Gaelic Language (Scotland) Act 2005, followed by the establishment of the statutory language board Bòrd na Gàidhlig. Although welcome as a sign of state support, these lack muscle and would need to be strengthened if the language shift towards English were to be effectively slowed or reversed. Census data and socio-linguistic research show a continuing decline in speaker numbers, as well as in the levels of competence and frequency of use within the speech community (see McLeod 2006). At a more general level, the surest grounds for hope may ironically flow from the globalising trends of late modernity. Smaller cultures, whether indigenous or migrant, show signs of organisation across the world. They are increasingly invested with moral and cultural authority, and in some cases receive badly needed resources. With regard to Gaelic, some benefits have accrued from membership of the European Union, and others are expected from the European Charter on Regional or Minority Languages. All this can be seen as part of a move to counterbalance the globalising impetus of multinational companies and organisations, as well as the seemingly inexorable spread of English (see Cronin 2005).

The death of Somhairle MacGill-Eain (Sorley MacLean) (1911–96) shortly before devolution might arguably represent a potent turning point for Gaelic literature. The demise of a writer of magisterial stature can be unpredictable in its effects, but it has certainly not resulted in any discernible fresh flowering of poetry, whether traditional or modern. During the last decade of the twentieth century a good deal of the energy available to Scottish Gaelic literature was channelled fruitfully into fiction, various state-funded arts projects and, to a lesser extent, television. While some developments have drawn down the opprobrium of traditionalists, the recent policy of support for writers of prose fiction has led to the development of genres of fiction, most significantly the novel, of which there had hitherto been quite a dearth. This chapter will focus mainly on these developments in fiction, with some mention of poetry towards the end.

A welcome stream of Gaelic fiction has emerged since 2003 out of Ùr-Sgeul, a project coordinated by the Gaelic Books Council to promote writing for adults. (*Ùr-Sgeul* literally means 'new story', but it has in the recent past also been taken to mean 'myth' or 'novel'.) Ùr-Sgeul both commissions and invites the submission of novels and short stories, which are then published by Clàr in Inverness. Authors are offered editorial advice and support, a modest but encouraging fee, royalties, and some efficient post-publication publicity. So far ten volumes have appeared, including a previously unpublished novella by Iain Mac a' Ghobhainn (Iain Crichton Smith).[1] Collectively these represent an increase of real significance in the volume of modern Scottish Gaelic fiction. Less than a score of novels were published over the course of the twentieth century, although there had been a number of collections of short stories. Neither did Scottish Gaelic produce more than a tiny fraction of the scores of regional autobiographies that formed one of the unfortunate staples of Irish prose for much of the twentieth century. Taken in conjunction with the relatively small harvest of poetry over the last decade, the Ùr-Sgeul project has brought about a significant change of emphasis in the current phase of literary production. No English translation of any of the more recent texts is available (with the exception of Mac a' Ghobhainn's novella), although extracts of two (*Ath-Aithne* and *Tocasaid 'Ain Tuirc*) have been translated into Irish (MacLochlainn 2006). Therefore, not only are they likely to be unfamiliar to many readers, they have also appeared so recently that it must seem premature to attempt a full critical appraisal. However, since they constitute the main area of growth in Scottish Gaelic writing at present, and a notable change from the traditional predominance of poetry, I shall offer some preliminary thoughts on their composition and prospective import. Stylistically, the range is not overly ambitious but, equally, these works are not pot-boilers designed simply as reading material for adult learners of Gaelic. Hence, they deserve consideration as works of fiction which form an integral part of the overall fabric of contemporary Scottish literature.

Lesser-used languages are frequently stereotyped as ethnocentric, provincial, and closed to any cultural alterity other than their own in relation to the dominant culture out of whose shadow they wish to escape. Scottish Gaelic, however, cannot be characterised in that way, partly because it was never asked to carry the agenda of cultural nationalism, but also because Scottish Gaelic writers have had ample experience of a world beyond the boundaries of Gaelic Scotland. In the last half-century or more, prominent revival writers,

---

[1] The texts are Aonghas Pàdraig Caimbeul (Angus Peter Campbell), *An Oidhche Mus Do Sheòl Sinn* (2003) and *Là a' Dèanamh Sgèil Do Là* (2004); Iain Fionnlaigh MacLeòid (Iain Finlay MacLeod), *Na Klondykers* (2005); Tormod MacGill-Eathain (Norman MacLean), *Dacha Mo Ghaoil* (2005); Màrtainn Mac an t-Saoir (Martin MacIntyre), *Ath-Aithne* (2003) and *Gymnippers Diciadain* (2005); Donnchadh MacGillIosa (Duncan Gillies), *Tocasaid 'Ain Tuirc* (2005); Iain Mac a' Ghobhainn (Iain Crichton Smith), *Am Miseanaraidh* (2006); Norma NicLeòid, *Dìleas Donn* (2006); and Tormod Caimbeul, *Shrapnel* (2006). Not all the titles are readily translatable: *An Oidhche Mus Do Sheòl Sinn* is taken from a boating song ('Oran a' Chiaora') and translates as 'The night before we sailed'. *Là a' Dèanamh Sgèil Do Là* is derived from Psalm 19: 'Day unto day uttereth speech'. *Na Klondykers* is 'The Klondykers', a name for Russian fishing-fleet boats. *Dacha Mo Ghaoil* is a pun on 'Dachaigh mo Ghaoil', which means 'my beloved home' and is taken from a Gaelic song of exile, but here 'home' is replaced by the Russian word for a holiday house in the country. *Ath-Aithne* denotes 'recollection'. *Gymnippers Diciadain* translates as 'Gymnippers Wednesdays', referring to a children's playgroup; *Tocasaid 'Ain Tuirc* is the nickname of the main character, metonymically constructed from his adventure with a barrel (*tocsaid*) as a child, followed by a version of his grandfather's and great-grandfather's names. *Am Miseanaraidh* translates as 'The Missionary'. *Dìleas Donn* means 'my brown-haired love' and is taken from the title of a well-known love song about separation ('Mo chailin dìleas donn'). *Shrapnel* is the novel's much-loathed eponymous villain's nickname.

such as Dòmhnall MacAmhlaigh (Donald MacAulay) and Somhairle MacGill-Eain, gained this experience through a metropolitan university education and, like earlier generations before them, service in the British army. Most of the current wave of fiction shows all the centrifugal openness to the world outside Gaelic which was such a characteristic feature of mid-twentieth-century poetry; ironically, however, a small number – and in particular those works which might be considered the best of the crop – seems to have a centripetal trajectory as well, which has also been discerned in current poetic activity (and in the bulk of television programmes). Of course, what precisely should be considered external to the Gaelic world is in itself problematical. It is absurd, though not uncommon, to question the authenticity of all those aspects of a minority culture which it shares with the wider world. While at best disrespectful, because it requires minority cultures to define themselves as exotic, at worst this view is a form of racist ghettoisation. It is also ahistorical, because Gaelic culture has been in contact with, and a part of, the wider European culture for millennia. For the purposes of this chapter, I shall confine myself to an analysis of the phenomena that are flagged up by the texts themselves as belonging to the external world, even if this sometimes turns out to be simply a particular character's perception. Thus, working on an oil rig may pass without comment, whereas aromatherapy comes to represent an entirely different world.

Whereas most Ùr-Sgeul fiction is brand new, Mac a' Ghobhainn's novella *Am Miseanaraidh* dates from an earlier period; an English version of the novella was published under his English name in *The Hermit and Other Stories* (1977). It is not known when it was written, or which version was written first. What it shows is that an interface between Gaelic culture and other worlds is not exclusive to the most recent fiction. The novella tells of Dòmhnall, a Scottish missionary who takes up a position in Africa. He blunders through his first few days with remarkable cultural insensitivity, causing a string of disasters, including the murder of a local woman and her children as well as the destruction of one of his host tribe's major food sources. However critical of the missionary's cultural and religious naivety and arrogance, the narration remains focused entirely on Dòmhnall's thoughts and feelings; with regard to all the other characters' views and perceptions we rely on what the missionary sees or hears. It is not until the very end that the narrative escapes from what appears to be a simplistic, superficially drawn tale of a well-meaning westerner doing more harm than good in a third-world country. Eventually, the missionary relinquishes both his authority and belief in the law to adopt the Africans' faith in what is *nàdarra* ('natural'). Ironically, his new position allows him to find and bestow Christian forgiveness, which is now seen to derive from nature rather than the law of God. However, his new identification with the Africans is only partial and does not prevent him resuming a role of authority at the end; neither does his identification result in a change in narrative style. The omniscient narrator continues to privilege Dòmhnall's perspective, although he stays clear of any experimentation with 'free indirect style', which would allow the reader to experience Dòmhnall's thoughts and feelings as they occur. The irony of a member of an oppressed culture inflicting a similar form of oppression on another people is not explicitly highlighted in the text, so that a complacent reader, unaware of the political implications of Mac a' Ghobhainn's representation, might well finish this novella unchallenged. Only through its subject matter does the narrative acknowledge the impact of Scottish Gaelic missionary zeal.

Moving on to more recent writing, Màrtainn Mac an t-Saoir's *Gymnippers Diciadain* breaks new ground in its representation of the encounter between DJ, a Gaelic-speaking taxi driver from South Uist, and Caroline, a middle-class music teacher and 'new Gael', originally from the edge of the Highlands, who has learnt Gaelic. Most of the novel comprises casual meetings between DJ and Caroline in the coffee shop of a weekly children's playgroup. Neither of their marriages is entirely healthy, and for a while a half-hearted romance blossoms. DJ finds himself in a largely feminine, child-centred suburban world in Edinburgh, in which the working-class canteen staff speak Scots and the middle-class parents speak English. Caroline temporarily steps out of this environment when she visits Skye and DJ's family home on Uist, but the romance never develops into a sexual relationship and eventually fizzles out. Caroline's second trip is a holiday to France with her husband, and it is to this relationship that she ultimately commits herself. Her future will be in Edinburgh, marked by the rediscovery of her French mother's cultural heritage. Caroline's toying with Gaelic culture is unfulfilling, abortive, and threatening to her previous identity. DJ's experience, on the other hand, is more positive. Through his relationship with Caroline, he achieves a rapprochement of sorts with his community of origin, from which he had been alienated for many years.

Russian culture features disproportionately in the Ùr-Sgeul texts: two novels explore the ramifications of the arrival of Russian workers employed as trawler fishermen and ostrich-farm workers respectively. The first novel is Iain F. MacLeòid's *Na Klondykers*, set in 1989, which focuses on the relations between a Gaelic fishing community and a large Russian fish-factory out in the bay. Soon love and violence break out. Beyond the obvious linguistic barriers, the emphasis is on stereotyped cultural similarities including laddish humour, drunkenness, brawling, black-marketeering and academic underachievement. Possibly to confound these stereotypes, and in marked contrast to the mundane conversations forming most of the dialogue, one of the Scotsmen's young Russian girlfriend has a well-informed political discussion about the events surrounding the break-up of the Soviet Union with her boyfriend's mother. Gaelic readers know well the fragility, as well as the macho qualities, of life at sea, and so the violence and the drowning tragedy at the centre of the plot are more than familiar, in literature as in life. The drowning in *Na Klondykers* connects it poignantly to a recurrent anxiety in Gaelic life, and to a long literary tradition of songs of lament. As so often with contemporary renditions of older themes and motifs, however, modernity demands a twist; in this case the drowning is followed by the birth of a Scottish-Russian child, who unexpectedly arrives at his Scottish grandmother's door sixteen years later, looking exactly like his dead father. Thus hope is eventually salvaged from the calamitous first encounter of two cultures, if admittedly at a high price. The Russian theme is taken up again in *Dacha Mo Ghaoil*, Tormod MacGill-Eathain's third novel, but this time the tone is one of burlesque irony. Once again a romantic liaison takes place between local men and Russian women, but the marriages are a sham, contrived to secure work permits for the women. While the humorous writing may act as a counterweight to the occasionally earnest tone of some of the other texts, it also leaves this novel lacking in substance, especially when compared to MacGill-Eathain's second, more darkly violent novel *Keino* (1998).

Two further Ùr-Sgeul texts engage with the non-Gaelic world, but in addition they give full attention to core elements of the Gaelic tradition, some of which are less obvious than the invocation of the boating tragedy in *Na Klondykers*. The first of these texts is *Ath-Aithne*, a collection of short stories by Màrtainn Mac an t-Saoir, whose language alternates between Gaelic and English from story to story, while its subject matter moves from the specifically local to the experience of Gaels in other settings. Most importantly, the stories span a range of approaches to cultural difference. Some of the stories are purely interlingual so that, were they ever to be translated into English, they would be most unlikely to show any discernible evidence of their Gaelic origin; others are searching encounters between traditional Gaelic culture and efforts at innovation clearly perceived as non-indigenous by the characters. The second text is Aonghas Pàdraig Caimbeul's *An Oidhche Mus Do Sheòl Sinn*, the most complex novel to have appeared under the auspices of Ùr-Sgeul to date. At one level, it is a realist tale about a large family across two generations, centred on a single character, but following the fortunes of several members of his family to England, the Spanish civil war and Canada, while shuttling back and forth between their native South Uist and these new and different cultural milieux. The novel is generous in its treatment of those who leave: Eòin in the Catholic seminary, one of his sisters settling in Spain during the civil war, and his brother who joins the British army and ends up in an unhappy marriage in the south of England. They are not presented simply as emigrants, whose sole interest is their ongoing connection to the native island; however, not quite every aspect of the plot holds to verisimilitude.

An Oidhche Mus Do Sheòl Sinn reaches out to the Gaelic linguistic and literary traditions almost as though, within its frame of reference, they too constituted a different 'other' to be encountered. At the simplest level, there is a clearly self-conscious appropriation of the author's local South Uist dialect with its cornucopia of vocabulary, some of which is presented in the form of list-like litanies. On a broader scale, the text is interwoven with echoes from traditional and modern poetry that must elude all but the most alert and erudite of readers. The presence of Somhairle MacGill-Eain, in particular, can be felt from the opening scene and goes on to punctuate the whole text. At one point, describing the passage of dogs across a frozen wasteland, the text simply breaks into lines from MacGill-Eain's poem 'Coin is Madaidhean-Allaidh' ('Dogs and Wolves') (MacGill-Eain / MacLean 1989). A third intertextual aspect of the novel is its evocation of certain conventions of the folktale tradition, which it unravels. An example of the type of tale that is dismantled is the story of the spoiled priest. A priest's sexual alliance with a woman, for whom he abandons his religious vocation, is one of the stock stories of eternal perdition in Catholic folklore. There are many folk stories about the ghosts of priests haunting their communities and vainly seeking to extirpate their guilt. By contrast, in this novel, Eòin's reincorporation into the community is achieved without repentance.

It is not immediately clear why the three Ùr-Sgeul texts that are most clearly centripetal in their subject matter – Norma NicLeòid's *Dìleas Donn*, Donnchadh MacGillIosa's *Tocasaid 'Ain Tuirc*, and Tormod Caimbeul's *Shrapnel* – should be written in the most effortless, fluent Gaelic and also possess the greatest artistic control. To the extent that the world outside Gaelic impinges on their stories, the authors contrive to integrate it seamlessly within their own worlds, without shifting attention outside or allowing external events and characters to disrupt the lives of their characters seriously. *Dìleas Donn* presents a love triangle, in which a middle-aged man re-encounters his first wife, who left him when they were in their early twenties, finding his religious conversion suffocating. He subsequently married Muriel, who sacrificed a life of music in order to join her husband's church in a somewhat half-hearted way and with whom he has remained childless. Their marriage comes under pressure when the husband's first wife falls pregnant with his child, he suffers a kind of breakdown, and all three characters must set out on an emotional journey in search of healing. There is sufficient cultural resilience and creativity in this novel to prevent the outside world from engulfing the life of the characters, which is most obvious in the case of Muriel, who takes up aromatherapy, unheard of in her community, but does so in a way that is neither threatening nor disruptive. Equally, certain elements in the life of the other female character are either passed over (we hear little about the years she spent in Canada) or, as in the case of her psychotherapy sessions, presented simply as developmental phases integral to her eventual return home to Lewis. NicLeòid is critical of the main high-status sources of healing, deeming the church morally and emotionally bankrupt and the conventional medical system at least partially compromised. Accordingly, her characters must find alternative routes to healing and happiness – music, parenthood, alternative therapies, unconventional sexual and emotional liaisons, and leaving the church – none of which ever causes any serious ripples in the community. Without doubt this places a certain strain on the uncomplicatedly realist style of her narration, because the unconventional living arrangements proposed at the end of her novel are as improbable as the community's re-acceptance of the scandalous priest in *An Oidhche Mus Do Sheòl Sinn*.

Donnchadh MacGilllosa's *Tocasaid 'Ain Tuirc* will be seen by many, and with good reason, as a jewel of recent Gaelic fiction, oscillating somewhere between a novel and a series of interlinked stories. Though centred largely on a single character, many of the episodes could stand on their own. One of the great strengths of the text lies in its opening up of an interface with another world, not that of other cultures or countries, but of the supernatural otherworld. Metaphorical treatment of the supernatural otherworld is a common device in literatures which have not been entirely alienated from their pre-modern roots by a long spell of high realism; in *Tocasaid 'Ain Tuirc*, however, the debt is mainly to the narrative techniques of the folktale. These are skilfully woven into the text, partly through the story-within-a-story device, and interact with realist elements of plot and character, generating an exquisitely controlled touch of irony and a recognisably Gaelic atmosphere. While it is impressive enough to entertain the traditional otherworld so effortlessly within a fully modern context, to do so in an entirely untroubled way is certainly a major achievement, primarily due to the subtlety of MacGilllosa's narrative voice. *Tocasaid 'Ain Tuirc* also employs stylistic echoes of sermon rhetoric, which infuse the text at a much subtler level than that of plot or theme. Gaelic prose is inevitably influenced by ecclesiastical rhetoric, and tensions between Gaelic secular culture and church culture pervade many of the texts assembled here. *Tocasaid 'Ain Tuirc* is a clear example, although it remains much more obviously influenced by Gaelic folklore.

It would be difficult to overestimate the importance of Tormod Caimbeul's only very recently published *Shrapnel*, whose depth and resonance make it one of the most significant Scottish novels of the modern period, and possibly ever. Mostly an encounter with the heart of darkness, as experienced by a Gaelic speaker in the hard-drinking, chaotic world of Lowland pub-and-drug culture, it is also part wonder-tale and part flood-tide of biblical and other traditional literary references. Featuring defining moments of heart-breaking lyricism, in which the call of home becomes audible from beyond the horrors of the abyss, Caimbeul's novel represents an eloquent moment in the abundant Scottish literature of homesickness and exile. Narratologically, too, it is the most sophisticated of all the texts discussed so far. Decentred almost from the start, the novel's first half is written in the first person, but the identity of the narrator, confused by alcohol-induced stupor and hospitalised after a pub-brawl beating, is largely withheld and virtually no personal details on him are given. The story spirals ever further downwards from pub brawl via infirmary to squat, interspersed with what may be blurred memories, hallucinations, even visions. There is violence and depravity – a sixteen-year-old girl is assaulted, people are knifed and shot – representing the full gamut of urban underbelly violence. Halfway through the novel the first-person narrator vanishes, and his voice is replaced by a nuanced series of scenes and third-person descriptions, as well as some rewrites of episodes and events from earlier in the text. It is not always clear what is happening: someone – perhaps some version of the original narrator – may be dreaming, or it might all be part of a vision, or a garbled childhood memory is opening up, or a fantasy may be assembling itself from biblical and other intertexts. There may even be a suggestion of near-death or posthumous experience. Despite the irony and confusion, Caimbeul's narrator is also very human; fastidious about cleanliness, both physical and verbal, he has other touching characteristics such as a love of birds. It is as if beyond a certain level the sordid outside world cannot reach him. Similarly, the many influences from the world outside Gaelic do not really impinge on him either; they are acknowledged, Buddhist-like, as existing 'out there' as part of the larger picture, but they are not something with which one needs to engage. What saves him is his love of home and flickering memory of a woman he once loved. Words in Arabic script, lines from an opera, Irish idiosyncrasies, references to exotic eastern train destinations, as well as Lowland racist abuse of the Gaelic community – all these somehow pass him by, or he accepts them unquestioningly as part of his personal landscape.

The significance of the sheer volume of new fiction in Scottish Gaelic can be grasped only from an awareness of the dominance of poetry over the past sixty years. Poetry has undoubtedly been the glory of Scottish Gaelic literature while also representing one of its chief weaknesses. The common practice of publishing Gaelic poetry in tandem with its English translation is regarded by certain critics, including this author, as a spancel, albeit one nowadays hardly noticed by Gaelic poets. Translation may of course expand the poet's readership and hence increase their visibility, but at the cost of directing their creative and emotional attention to a readership largely unfamiliar with their language or cultural tradition. From this perspective, it is heartening that Diehard publishers have launched a new venture in Gaelic-only publication, the timing of which would appear to confirm that a climate of greater globalisation can, if confronted carefully and sensitively, enhance the position of minority cultures.

Since the Scottish Gaelic literary revival exploded into being with MacGill-Eain's poetry at the end of the 1930s, two anthologies of poetry have commonly been held to mark the flowering of two consecutive generations of poets. The title of the first of these – *Nua-Bhàrdachd Gàidhlig / Modern Gaelic Poetry* (1976) – was not as bland as it may initially appear. Rather, by echoing the title of *Bàrdachd Gàidhlig / Gaelic Poetry, 1550–1900*, a canonical collection of vernacular poetry encompassing three and a half centuries, edited by W. J. Watson in 1918, it incorporated a status claim by a modern poetry movement in which some traditionalists could see nothing worthy of the name Gaelic. The publication of *An Aghaidh na Sìorraidheachd: Ochdnar Bhàrd Gàidhlig / In the Face of Eternity: Eight Gaelic Poets* (1991) signalled the arrival of a second generation as an identifiable group. Christopher Whyte, the editor of the latter collection, situated it in a clear line of descent from the two earlier anthologies, thus giving further impetus to the movement away from what had hitherto been considered the definitive traditional hallmarks of Scottish Gaelic poetry. Since *An Aghaidh na Sìorraidheachd* no further generation of poets has been constituted as a discrete group, and the bulk of new poetry since the early 1990s has consisted of individual volumes by the featured poets, plus one or two others. Foreseeably, their work matured with time; less predictable, however, was the slowing down of their output, given the dominance of poetry since the middle of the twentieth century as well as the traditional notion of poetry as the quintessential expression of Gaelic verbal creativity throughout the entire history of the language. The poets of the previous generation, with the exception of Dòmhnall MacAmhlaigh, had been relatively prolific. There was a flurry in 1996, when Polygon produced new books by Aonghas MacNeacail, Meg Bateman and Rody Gorman. In addition, many other poets, such as Whyte, Maoilios Caimbeul and Fearghas MacFhionnlaigh, published volumes after devolution, and Kevin MacNeil's *Love and Zen in the Outer Hebrides* (1998) sporadically forays into Gaelic, but this is still not a great harvest for a full decade, even if new works are said to be currently nearing publication.

According to Ronald Black, the three main developments in Gaelic poetry in the final quarter of the twentieth century were the arrival of women poets, the appearance of poets who were learners of Gaelic rather than native speakers, and the re-emergence of myth (Black 1999: lvii). However, Gaelic Scotland had a relatively high proportion of vernacular women poets and anonymous female voices in the seventeenth and eighteenth centuries; so the recent emergence of women is by no means without precedent. Moreover, the rewriting of myth is now a common feature of contemporary western literature, and the question must be asked whether the last quarter of a century has really witnessed a retreat from 'modernism' into 'myth', as though these were mutually exclusive categories. Black may be overstating the extent to which mythic sources were ever truly abandoned. Various modernist tendencies on the part of MacGill-Eain's generation are well known, including a devotion to international politics; however, the mere presence of such an international dimension ought not to be taken as indicative of a rejection of tradition. As even a very cursory reading of the work of MacGill-Eain and his generation reveals, it was deeply and solidly anchored in the indigenous traditions, and therefore the alleged redirection of attention to myth over the past twenty-five years cannot be described as a totally new departure. By contrast, what does become evident in the work of many contemporary poets is the loss of the particular type of public responsibility incorporated within MacGill-Eain's magisterial, pastoral voice, even though MacNeacail has gone some way to inherit his predecessor's mantle. Add to this the freedom – which many of the current generation, both men and women, have insisted on – to probe issues of domesticity in their work, and it is perhaps not surprising one should win the impression of a general retreat from the wider world.

An important development since devolution has been the arrival of often sizeable editions of poetry from the seventeenth to the twentieth centuries, which is indicative of a further inward-looking tapping of indigenous roots. This editorial work of almost visionary proportions has developed under the aegis of Edinburgh-based Birlinn publishers; most of the material had been published before, but was not widely available and in some cases had been long out of print. The project must be regarded as an act of canon-formation, granting ready access to large tracts of the poetic heritage that were in danger of receding from view, and thus re-establishing a tradition within which current and future poets can position themselves. *An Tuil* ('The Flood'), Black's twentieth-century collection, will undoubtedly provide such an immediate backdrop for future poets. With its impeccable, if occasionally perhaps overwhelming apparatus of referencing and annotation, it is a definitive portal into the world of recent Gaelic poetry, the range of which might surprise the previously uninitiated. Demonstrating the slow process of innovation in the early years of the century, *An Tuil's* additional merit is that it refuses, correctly in my view, to polarise contemporary poetry into 'modern' and 'traditional', thus correcting the common view that MacGill-Eain's poetry represented a complete break with tradition. A further strengthening of the tradition in recent years has been the publication of a series of collections by local poets from diverse Gaelic-speaking areas (see MacLeòid 1998; Mhàrtainn 2001; Lobban 2003). It is remarkable how few stylistic concessions can be made to modernity without inhibiting the choice of topic. One of the most lyrical of these local poets, for instance, Dòmhnall Aonghais Bhàin (Donald MacDonald), makes flawless use of traditional forms, and yet one of his best known poems is in praise of the then Camilla Parker-Bowles (Dòmhnall Aonghais Bhàin 2000: 24–5).

This chapter has aimed to show that in so far as fresh ground has been broken in Gaelic literature since devolution, it has been unconnected in any obvious way to constitutional change. Rather, it has primarily been the result of two publishing projects pioneered by Ùr-Sgeul and Birlinn publishers. What this indicates is the important role played by a sensitive publishing infrastructure in releasing creative energy; it also signals the urgent need for further development of this infrastructure, which at present remains seriously under-resourced. The body of work that has emerged from these ventures, which embraces the wider world while staying loyal to its own roots, displays an artistic strength that must give pause to the prophets of linguistic and cultural doom, and bodes well for the continuing vital contribution of Gaelic to literature in the new Scotland.

Chapter 11

Pedlars of their Nation's Past: Douglas Galbraith, James Robertson and the New Historical Novel

Mariadele Boccardi

There is an inherent tension in the very concept of the Scottish historical novel, which can be traced back to the earliest practitioner of the genre, Sir Walter Scott. On the one hand, his example led British and European novelists to become more self-conscious in their exploration of historical issues; on the other, his legacy to the Scottish novel has consisted largely of a disengagement from the actualities of history and the modern world in favour of anachronistic romanticisation. In a study of Scott's impact on later novelists, Francis Hart emphasises his role as a 'Scottish mythmaker' (Hart 1971: 62), which would make him the opposite of a Scottish historian. Similarly, commenting on the process by which the Stuart myth was created, Murray Pittock highlights Scott's central role in the depoliticisation of the Jacobite sensibility, suggesting that Scott's romantic engagement with the past ultimately resulted in the imaginative impossibility of a Scottish national-historical continuity independent of England (Pittock 1991: 84). Scott's influence on the tradition of the Scottish novel and his leading role in delegating the Scottish past to a realm outside of history also underpin Cairns Craig's *The Modern Scottish Novel* (1999), which is focused on a re-examination of the interaction between political and imaginative representations of the nation. According to Craig, following the post-1746 reconfirmation of the country's union with England, Scotland's past as an autonomous nation-state could only be related in romance form, that is, within the confines of a genre which, unlike the novel, desires to transcend rather than accurately represent history (Craig 1999: 117).

Indebted to Craig, the present chapter will apply his work specifically to an examination of Scotland's contemporary historical novel by reflecting on the conditions of Scottish history and its narrative representation, as well as the construction of a coherent Scottish national identity. National identity is understood here as the result of the various inter-actions between the cultural, political, economic, legal and religious institutions of a country, on the one hand, and the people's sense of the nation's common purpose and tra-jectory, on the other. As I will argue, this collective sense of purpose is crucially fostered by the nation's production of credible imaginative accounts of its historical trajectory. Against this background Scotland must ultimately be deemed 'unrelatable, un-narratable' (Craig 1999: 21) because its histories appear as a discontinuous, fragmented, episodic chronicle of traumatic events, with the loss of independence in 1707 being exacerbated by the loss of even the hope of independent statehood at Culloden in 1746. From another per-spective, of course, these cataclysmic disruptions in the Scottish national narrative constitute moments of increasing union and cohesion, as they mark the gradual articulation and consolidation of the supranational narrative of Britishness. Significantly, today's Scotland is no longer 'a country which lacks even the façade of conflict in terms of a politics fought out through a parliament' (Craig 1999: 120). Labour's electoral victory of 1997, which carried with it the commitment to a national referendum on political devolution, led to the opening of the new Scottish Parliament – the first since 1707 – in July 1999.

Yet, as Liam McIlvanney suggests, the actual reassertion of Scottish national identity did not originally occur in the realm of parliamentary politics:

> The point about the Parliament, from a cultural perspective, was how little it now seemed to matter. Its coming was welcome, certainly, but hardly seemed critical to the nation's cultural health. Above all, it was belated: by the time the Parliament arrived, a revival in Scottish fiction had been long underway . . . with the novel itself becoming a centre of sorts, taking up the political slack, filling the space where Scottish politics ought to have been. (McIlvanney 2002: 185)

According to McIlvanney, in the absence of an autonomous national politics, the Scottish novel developed into a political force that shaped the Scottish people's self-image and national identity. Historical fiction in particular must be regarded as closely related to the country's reacquisition of an institutional political dimension. Exploring the conditions for a national narrative and hence the imaginative recreation of the nation's history, historical fiction draws new, meaningful links between the past and the present rather than romantically engaging with discrete historical events in anachronistic isolation.

Douglas Galbraith's *The Rising Sun* (2000) and James Robertson's *Joseph Knight* (2003) must be read within the context of this new Scottish tradition of fictional historiography. Taking up the challenge of writing historical novels in and about this 'place without a history' (Craig 1999: 118), both texts open up a narrative space in which self-conscious reflections on storytelling in general coincide with a refreshingly sober reconstruction of the nation's history. Arguably the most productive aspect of both authors' engagement with the particular challenges of the Scottish historical novel is their revision of the complex correlation between national identity, empire and exile – the three elements identified by Timothy Brennan as absolutely indispensable for a proper understanding of 'the national longing for form' (Brennan 1990: 59–60). Interestingly, in *The Invention of Scotland*, his study on the treatment of the Jacobite rebellion in British writing, Pittock equally emphasises the prevalence of national identity, empire and exile as important identity-bearing descriptors peculiar to Scotland's literary imagining of its past (Pittock 1991: 72).

Douglas Galbraith's *The Rising Sun* tells the story of Scotland's attempt to create its own empire by establishing a trading colony in Darien on the isthmus of Panama in the late 1690s in order to rival the economic and political might of England. Not only did this remote spot of Central America prove totally inadequate to the task, mainly due to its location and climate, but the architects of the project had also underestimated the repercussions of a recent English embargo on independent trading. The subsequent failure of an enterprise in which, after years of famine, the nation had invested all its meagre savings resulted in Scotland's bankruptcy and its inevitable acceptance of the union with England after the latter's offer to bail, or buy, out its neighbour (see Devine 2003: 40–8). In the hands of Galbraith, and through the voice of his narrator Roderick Mackenzie, these historical events are transformed into a parable on the history of Scotland. Hope, trust and naivety come into conflict with the need for financial housekeeping and the harsh realities of economic exploitation, but the novel also highlights the political opportunities that become available to Scotland by yielding to England and joining its highly successful imperial enterprise. The title of the novel is ironic in its undertones and refers to the name of one of the vessels that are part of the colonial expedition. Mackenzie calls the ship 'a Britishman' (Galbraith 2000: 6), thereby ambiguously conflating the type of ship introduced at the start of the novel with what by its end will have become the new national identity of the story's narrator. The two meanings create between themselves what is at once a gap and an overlap, as Mackenzie's narration circuitously defers the novel's inevitable self-fulfilment, intimated from the beginning by the semantic richness of the term 'Britishman'.

The narrative of *The Rising Sun* appears structured around a double temporal dimension: in so far as the action is geared towards the Act of Union as a kind of climactic event that shapes the nation by negating it, it is prospective. However, in so far as the novel is told from a future, post-Union point of view, it is retrospective. This double dimension derives from the fact that the novel's narrator is a naive young man prone to readjusting his perspective whenever he gains insights into the actual state of affairs, as opposed to his initial understanding of it, while his narrative is implicitly informed by a retrospective knowledge of the eventual outcome of the historical events it relates. Mackenzie's position as a narrator thus mirrors the novel's position with regard to the historical events that constitute its subject matter: it is a story that unfolds only to reach an already known and experienced end. In a corroboration of this analogy, Mackenzie's comments on his role as 'the original Scots pedlar, the chapman of my own and my people's past' (Galbraith 2000: 5) become metanarrative statements on the composition of Scotland's historical narrative. Galbraith's particular choice of words points to an intersection of telling and selling, that is, the hope entrusted in effective narrative delivery, on the one hand, and the far more material power of money, on the other. Interestingly, Galbraith presents the very founding of the trading company as a storytelling exercise, emerging 'from its chrysalis of paper and dreams' and heralded by ballad-sellers who 'stood at every second street-corner selling heroic execrations of the King, the East India Company, the Continental war, the Navigation Acts, the English grain merchants, the English weather' (Galbraith 2000: 118–19). The condemnatory poignancy of this description gives us a good idea of the novel's view on the Scottish past and its customary rendition in the romance format. It would be misleading to read Galbraith's novel as a case study of 'the mythopoetic faculty of the Scottish imagination . . . creating pasts to mourn the loss of' (Pittock 1991: 5). Rather, Galbraith protests that the futures projected by the Scottish imagination are congenitally undermined by the romantic paradigm in which their existence is imagined.

Mackenzie's role in the novel participates in the ambiguity of telling as selling, of romance as economics. He is originally recruited to the enterprise as a clerk keeping a record of the goods taken on board at the start of the voyage, bought with the people's subscriptions and representing the nation's actual investment in the company, as well as the goods for which the colonists intend to trade them in, which never materialise. The irreconcilable clash of unreasonable hopes of financial gain with the reality of hard figures is encapsulated in the trajectory of Mackenzie's career. His interest in the prosaic accountancy elements of his job progressively decreases to be replaced by a penchant for the romance of storytelling. What remains of the enterprise when it fails is a narrative which, not dissimilar to Scott's fictional histories, seals it off in a sphere of Scottish romance utterly discrete from the British reality that follows. Indeed, from the outset the contradictory impulses that guide the Darien experiment – that is, economic reality and romantic adventure – are barely kept separate in the description of Mackenzie's first encounter with the world of colonial business: 'Kings, wars, Acts of Parliament, tobacco, grain, Mexico! It was a poem, an enchantment. "Affairs," I repeated to myself "Affairs, affairs!"' (Galbraith 2000: 55). The inextricability of romance and economics finds yet another expression in the phrases Mackenzie employs to define his role as chronicler, referring to himself, in the same dash of the pen, as 'the historian of these numbers' and 'the Herodotus of our comic tragedy' (Galbraith 2000: 3). These epithets hint at both the factuality of his account and its inherent contradictoriness, a mixture which the parameters of pure history cannot capture and which needs the greater flexibility of literature to find an appropriate means of expression.

Mackenzie's search for a suitable literary medium opens up an interesting perspective on the relationship between individual and national consciousness or, put differently, between the storyteller's act of narration and the impact of his narrative on his audience or readership, who perceive themselves as his 'imagined community'. Early on, Roderick Mackenzie's journal is introduced as an epic poem, 'the Scotiad (perhaps even the Roriad?)' (Galbraith 2000: 12). According to Brennan, epics are verse-narratives that establish the origins of the nation for its descendants; in other words, they are narratives directed at future readers (Brennan 1990: 50). By contrast, the novel addresses members of the nation in the here and now, providing them with 'a medium by which a common past and a common stock of cultural memories can be defined, and by which a possible route towards the future can be charted without loss of continuity with a founding past' (Craig 1999: 11). Mackenzie positions his journal firmly in the tradition of the epic; his record is kept because 'not a grain of what we do now must be lost' (Galbraith 2000: 12). Even though he takes pride in recording the story of his nation's attempt to project itself into the future by joining the modern colonial enterprise, Mackenzie displays a peculiarly Scottish tendency to regard his historical account as all the more valuable because it constitutes a memorial to what has irrevocably been lost. The same irresolvable ambiguity is evident in Mackenzie's double formulation of the subject of his epic: the nation (Scotiad) or himself (Roriad)? There appears to be no formal ground in the epic that could possibly encompass, let alone reconcile, both the nation and the individual. The sense of a common trajectory shared by individual and community, which is absent here, is precisely what characterises the imaginative range of the novel and its construction of a national narrative. The narrative of the novel co-opts individual lives into the fate of the nation by producing 'those symbolic systems which would provide readers with a sense of the fundamental unity and purpose of their social world' (Craig 1999: 9).

Clearly, in Galbraith's view, the fateful Darien expedition represents a significant watershed in Scotland's past, as it can be construed to lead directly to 1707 and the loss of independent statehood. National aspirations and imperial expansion are inescapably intertwined because, as Brennan explains, 'the markets made possible by European imperial penetration motivated the construction of the nation-state at home' (Brennan 1990: 59). Scotland's attempt at empire-building in competition with its English neighbour appears perfectly consistent with this description. Mackenzie's narrative, however, progressively becomes the story of a nation losing its statehood as a result not simply of the colonial project's material failure, but also of an imaginative failure to articulate adequately the nation's encounter with its colonial other, who – in the form of the native inhabitants of Darien – remains largely invisible.

When the convoy of ships leaves Edinburgh, it represents symbolically the nation itself, internally homogeneous (since the conditions on board erase the distinctions between

Highlanders and Lowlanders, country-or city-dwellers) and externally distinct from England. Moreover, with the ships described as 'neighbouring villages' and the flotilla as 'an archipelago of our own creation' (Galbraith 2000: 18), the novel employs the evocative image of the nation as an island, which Gillian Beer has described as 'the perfect form of [national] cultural imagining . . . Defensive, secure, compacted, even paradisal – a safe place; a safe place too from which to set out on predations and from which to launch the building of an empire' (Beer 1990: 269). The departure of the convoy literalises the national desire for a Scotland 'apparently unattached to anything – to, for example, England – . . . floating on its own sea' (Stirling 2001: 137). This symbolic image of Scotland moving towards an encounter with the alien colonial space also reflects Homi Bhabha's 'ambivalent figure of the nation' consisting of 'the *heimlich* pleasures of the hearth [and] the *unheimlich* terror of the space or race of the Other', which results in the nation's creation of an identity by virtue of its indelible sameness (Bhabha 1990: 2).

In *The Rising Sun*, however, the colony is not envisaged as a space of otherness, nor is the voyage perceived as a journey towards difference. The Reverend Mackay, one of the leaders of the expedition, delivers a complex argument identifying Gaelic as the language closest to the 'Original Tongue' of pre-Babelian times and linking this to unconfirmed reports that Darien is inhabited by 'white Indians'. Mackay concludes that these Indians are in fact original Scots who settled in America centuries before Columbus, so that 'it may be that we are not going abroad at all. No, indeed. It may be, sir, that we are going home' (Galbraith 2000: 148–50). Hence, rather than a narrative of progress, the colonial adventure is imagined as a return to one's origins, a mythical homecoming.

According to *The Rising Sun*, if Scotland is to achieve a narrative thrust forward, it can do so only as part of the larger narrative of Britain; in other words, only by joining the very enterprise against which Darien was conceived, planned and imagined. By recounting the events that led to the Union, Galbraith seems to conclude, like Scott, that 'the evolution which may help [Scotland] to develop is to come through Britishness' (Crawford 2000: 131). As James Minto, a friend of Mackenzie's, puts it in the novel, 'he had no past and from this day he would have nothing but a future' (Galbraith 2000: 515), words aptly uttered on the way to London, where he and his companion intend to make a future for themselves in a different, commercial form of empire-building. On his return to Scotland after the final debacle in America, Mackenzie accepts the offer of a job in 'the business . . . in the Gold Coast' (Galbraith 2000: 503) by a former member of the company, whose shift from an ideological investment in colonial trade to purely economic pursuits exemplifies a similar move on the part of Scotland. With the Act of Union, Scotland gained access to, and made the most of, existing English – now British – overseas possessions. The changed framework for the imperial operation becomes evident in the following exchange between Mackenzie and the businessman offering him employment:

> 'What sort of business?'
> 'Trade.'
> 'No complications?'
> 'Such as?'
> 'National companies, empires, flags, patriots?'
> He shook his head firmly. 'They don't know the meaning of the word. Just merchants.'
> (Galbraith 2000: 503)

As its location in the African Gold Coast signals, the new 'business' is the transatlantic slave trade, an uncomfortable topic to insert in the conventional emplotment of Scottish history as a tragedy whose protagonist is in every respect a victim.

Notably, Mackenzie's final acceptance of his new reality is literal but not imaginative; he chooses to engage with his prospective employment on purely practical terms, relinquishing any impulse to romanticise either the business or his role in it. Indeed, at the end of his narrative, as he is thrust into the modern world at the careering speed of the London coach, his Scottish self rests with the journal, 'a shelter, a home of sorts' (Galbraith 2000: 493). And before he can take a full part in the future course of events that awaits him beyond the 'home' of his journal, he must close the latter. At the end of the novel the initial correlation of selling and telling, finance and narrative, commerce and the nation returns, but their roles seem now significantly reversed:

> The lure of completion and, with that, never having to write another word. The consummation is horrible, no doubt, and I would shrink from it were it not for the thought of making a perfect end, of laying down the burden, paid to the last penny. Now is the time to cover the last few pages . . . I shall end with an oath never to take up the pen again if not for the honest simplicities of the ledger and the bill. (Galbraith 2000: 493)

James Robertson's *Joseph Knight* resembles Galbraith's novel in that it follows a similar trajectory from national to individual consciousness, but one which ultimately concludes that, whereas one may reach a compromise regarding one's nationalist ideals, compromising on individual standards of morality and conscience is destructive. Both novels are illustrative of 'the project of Scottish culture in the eighteenth century . . . to exploit the benefits of the British Empire through the creation of a culture of "Britishness"' (Craig 1999: 28): as Galbraith chooses to recover the history of Darien to explain and justify modern Scotland's embrace of the Act of Union, Robertson takes as his point of departure the quelled rebellion of 1745. *Joseph Knight* spans the period from 1746 to 1803, almost exactly the 'sixty years' to which Scott alludes in the subtitle of *Waverley*, a novel whose vision addresses the Jacobite enterprise only to accentuate the disruption it caused in the continuous progressive flow of Scottish history. In an essay on the very events *Waverley* eschews to explore, Claire Lamont suggests that 'the silence is eloquent' because 'it is out of the silence, and the gap in time, that the subject-matter comes, the loss of a culture' (Lamont 1991: 25). *Joseph Knight*, by contrast, proceeds to articulate the gap left open by its famous predecessor, unveiling the aftermath of the events of 1745 as well as the less salubrious aspects of Scotland's participation in British imperial expansion, and concludes where Scott's narrative opens. The novel's epigraph cites Ben Okri to remind readers of the need for nations to 'tell themselves stories that face their own truths [in order to] free their histories for future flowerings'. *Joseph Knight* thus introduces itself as a programmatic reaction against the elegiac treatment of Scotland's past by asserting itself as a representation of both the horrors of defeat and the moral ambiguities of imperialism.

The novel's relationship to *Waverley* is compounded by Robertson's choice of both subject and form: *Joseph Knight* depicts the defeat of the Jacobite army, which the earlier author expunged from his novel in favour of a celebration of Bonnie Prince Charlie's victory at Prestonpans. Robertson's principal character, seventy-three-year-old Sir John Wedderburn – who as a seventeen-year-old lad fought at Culloden with his father – is introduced to us as a frail, old man sitting in his drawing-room and reading Scott's ballads as an expression of 'the rusted, misty half-dream that was Scotland's past' (Robertson 2003: 5).

Joseph Knight illustrates the political and imaginative gulf that separates the events of 1746 from Wedderburn's comfortable and secure position in 1803: he has been knighted and become a fully respectable member of the (now British) aristocracy. The gulf also manifests itself in his daughter Susan's perception of history: 'All that Jacobite passion belonged in another age, it had nothing to do with her. The Forty-five might have been tragic and stirring but it was also hopeless and useless and ancient' (Robertson 2003: 20). Finally, the fact that in the novel Sir John's appearance as an old man precedes that of his younger self, and that only after he has commented on the romantic nature of Scotland's recent history do we witness the gore of battle he actually experienced in person, sheds an ironic light on the oblivious stance of romancers.

Like *The Rising Sun*, the central knot Robertson's novel seeks to untangle is the relationship between the individual's nationalist convictions and the exigencies of economic advancement. After Culloden, the Wedderburn sons leave for Jamaica, a place where the political strife and sectarianism at home are eclipsed by the colonists' avid pursuit of wealth. As one of Wedderburns' Jamaican acquaintances puts it, 'we're an island of tolerance – we're only here to get rich, after all' (Robertson 2003: 57). In Jamaica John and his brothers acquire a plantation worked for them by Gold Coast slaves, gradually accumulating the wealth that will enable them to reclaim their Scottish legacy, lost in the aftermath of Culloden. However, their eventual social rehabilitation is not purely due to their economic success; while the former rebels are away overseas, 'in Scotland their politics were becoming not only forgiven but positively romantic' (Robertson 2003: 68).

By tracing the Wedderburns' progress, *Joseph Knight* explores the problematic issues of Scotland's participation in the British imperial project; thus, the novel describes the Wedderburns as extremely keen to recreate an ideal Scottish home within what to them is a doubly alien environment: alien ideologically because it is British and alien geographically because it is colonial. Significantly, the land the Wedderburns acquire for their plantation is described as 'wilder, and yet somehow comfortingly familiar . . . If you discounted the abundance of the vegetation, you could almost believe yourself to be in a Scottish glen . . . The refuge-like feel of it had led [John] to name it Glen Isla' (Robertson 2003: 66). Perhaps unsurprisingly, the men's attempt to create a Jamaican replica of Scotland in order to preserve the sense of nationhood is centred on similarities of space because, as Craig explains, landscape is a parameter of the nation that persists even after its more transient counterpart – that is, national narrative – has lapsed into oblivion or anachronicity:

> The associations of place . . . are the location in which it is possible to glimpse those associations of time that go beyond history, and that can bring back into history values denied by the very processes of history. The region is the location of the 'golden age' in the sense of a place where it is still possible to glimpse a world as yet unmoved by the destructive forces of history. (Craig 1999: 159)

Of course, the Wedderburns can only begin to recreate their ideal home once they have become complicit in the modern historical process that is the British Empire. By moulding his colonial possessions after the image of the Mother Country and then proceeding to exploit them systematically, John appears to be at once accepting and disavowing his exile. Ultimately, he and his brothers live out the Jacobite ideal of 'Scotland's agricultural purity', which is no longer an option in the country where it originated, and in so doing they contribute to 'the luxuries of imperialist Britain', against which the local rural ideal was originally designed as a pure, uncorrupted form of Scottishness (Pittock 1999: 36).

While the Wedderburns' compromise in terms of their nationalist commitment manifests itself in their whole-hearted and ruthless exploitation of the Empire's economic possibilities, the moral ambiguities of Scotland's involvement in British expansion express themselves at a more individual level, most centrally in the relationship between John Wedderburn and his slave Joseph Knight. Signally, Knight claims his liberty with reference to Wedderburn's ideals – that is, the inalienable right to fight for one's freedom and that of one's people – yet is denied by his master in the name of economic principles. Although he is the novel's eponymous hero, Knight appears only fleetingly at the very end of the text and even then largely as a mere subject of representation. Similarly, he is the missing figure erased from an amateur painting by one of John's brothers, and he also features as a 'character' in the journal of Sandy Wedderburn, which graphically records the shocking aspects of life on the plantation and its brutalising impact on the colonists. John's eventual burning of the journal, leaf by leaf, is clearly an effort to expunge from his memory the entire Jamaican period and replace it with the romance of an adventure in foreign lands or a lament of exile, in exactly the same vein in which the events of 1745 were recast by Sir Walter Scott. Finally, Knight appears in a double representation: described in a letter by another black Scotsman, who likens him to a character in one of Robert Burns's poems, Knight is drawn into the literary construction of Scottish identity-bearing ideals, so that Burns's well-known line 'a man's a man for a' that' from 'Is There for Honest Poverty' (1795) could be paraphrased as 'a man is a man for all that he is black'. As Wedderburn's behaviour towards Knight reveals, however, this fine Scottish humanist sentiment has never had any more than purely rhetorical validity.

When Joseph is finally introduced to us at the end of the novel, we find him reflecting on the loss of his history and his life as an exile in Scotland. In other words, his experience parallels that of Wedderburn, as a Scottish nationalist in post-Jacobite Scotland, at the beginning of the novel. For Knight, however, it is the personal aspects of his narrative that have been erased by his forceful removal from Africa: he cannot retrace his life to its origins; indeed, his earliest memories are of the slave ship. As a result, the collective memories of his people sold and deported into slavery have come to define him as an individual. Neither Knight nor Wedderburn then, albeit for different reasons, is able to reconcile his individual life story with a narrative of the nation. Even after sixty years, Sir John's life and career are yet to become safely embedded within a larger national trajectory of progress and reconstitution, and the friction between the personal and the historical remains unresolved:

> There were anniversaries scattered through the calendar that Sir John always observed with a sombre heart: so far this year there had been the martyrdom of Charles I, at the end of January, and the death of his first, dear wife Margaret in March; and late in November he would mourn, yet again, his father. But tomorrow it was Culloden. (Robertson 2003: 26)

The preservation of the Scottish past has become the prerogative of personal memory rather than communal narrative. Even in the wake of worldly success and within the context of a prosperous British state, the memories are of loss, at both a personal and national level. In their exploration of two of the most critical and disruptive moments in Scottish history, and in their articulation of the nexus between the private and the public, as well as political ideals and economic expediency, both *The Rising Sun* and *Joseph Knight* seek to dispel the romantic mists that have traditionally enveloped Scotland's past. Theirs is not simply an attempt to explain the reasons for Scotland's double failure to preserve or reassert its political independence, but rather a manifestation of the 'desire, deeply inscribed in the tradition of the modern Scottish novel, for the reintroduction of historical dynamic into the suspended world of . . . Scotland' (Craig 1999: 125). This imaginative reintroduction of history as rehearsed by the two novels is accompanied, and arguably motivated, by the actual resumption of Scotland's historical autonomy since the successful referendum on national self-rule in 1997.

Chapter 12

Scottish Television Drama and Parochial Representation

Gordon Gibson and Sarah Neely

Since the publication of Colin McArthur's edited collection *Scotch Reels* in 1982, the conceptual framework it offered has become powerfully influential among academics and critics commenting on Scottish cultural production. The volume's categorisation of such production (especially in cinema and television) into a number of distinct strands – Kailyard, Tartanry and Clydesidism – has been widely adopted, providing commentators with a critically informed means to express their exasperation at what passes for an authentic representation of Scotland in film and television today. Despite attempts by some programme-makers to move forward, enduring stereotypes and myths of Scottish life continue to proliferate. Disguised behind a contemporary façade of mobile phones and four-by-four vehicles, or set within familiar Scottish locations and utilising a dialogue conducted in thin and hence internationally comprehensible Scots, much television drama still fails to investigate the particularities of Scottish experience in favour of a more marketable, implied universality. As John Caughie reflects, while cinema tends to refer to the classical narratives of Hollywood as a benchmark, television has traditionally stuck to a fixed repertoire of the local (Caughie 2000: 16–18). In his view, this privileging of the local over the universal and globally appealing has both positive and negative repercussions. On the one hand, television operating on a local level offers 'resistance to universalization', while on the other, a locally specific mode of representation inevitably encounters difficulty in generating interest outside its immediate catchment area. This duality of 'universalism' and 'parochialism', visibly at work in much recent Scottish television drama, constitutes a dilemma not only for producers of television, but for the entire cultural industry, which increasingly operates under the aegis of transnational economies and mass consumerism.

Citing the particularly prolific year of 1980 in combination with the creative output of BBC Scotland and the launch of Scottish Television's popular soap opera *Take the High Road*, in 1990 Gus MacDonald reflected nostalgically how the previous decade had allocated far more room to local television drama than was available at present. Television, MacDonald explained, was facing a new challenge, namely 'to expand beyond . . . borders, while simultaneously finding ways of telling stories . . . that don't need the approval of UK network patrons' (MacDonald 1990: 202). While this challenge remains, other challenges arise from the success of new communication technologies – such as the internet, satellite and digital television – as well as concerns over the ability of locally specific programmes to speak to non-Scottish audiences, which are mainly to do with the increasing necessity of productions to sell overseas in order to stay economically viable. Since new technologies often tend to give rise to anxieties regarding the survival of local programmes and audiences, the popular success of programmes such as *Still Game* (BBC Comedy Unit/F'n'G Productions), a comedy following the day-to-day life of two pensioners, ought to be seen as reassuring. Local television drama continues to have its appeal, a trend that is by no means specific to Scotland. As Glen Creeber writes, 'despite the doom-laden prophets of globalization, there is much evidence to suggest that home-produced programming in Europe is still strongly favoured against foreign imports' (Creeber 2004: 34). However, such success is not always welcomed uncritically. In a recent seminar organised by the BBC, Stuart Cosgrove criticised the general misconceptions about 'successful' Scottish programming that circulate within the BBC. Referring specifically to *Still Game*, he criticised the way the programme's success has often been interpreted as partial and typical of 'parochial' programming, well-funded and popular with local audiences, who watch these productions mainly because they are of local interest rather than for reasons of 'quality' (BBC 2004: 5). Cosgrove regards such interpretations as indicative of the resentment towards regional programming's absorption of production funds away from traditional pathways associated with a more centralised vision of the BBC.

Scottish devolution has prompted various responses from broadcasters, but it is the new technologies and their regulation which have had the greatest impact on television production in twenty-first-century Britain. Thus, the establishment of Ofcom (Office of Communications) in December 2003, and its review of public-service broadcasting, have given rise to considerable concern and provoked a number of debates. Ofcom's remit stretches across the whole of the UK communications industries and incorporates what were previously the responsibilities of the ITC (Independent Television Commission), the Radio Authority, the Radiocommunications Agency, Oftel (Office of Telecommunications) and the BSC (Broadcasting Standards Commision). ITV (Independent Television Network), for which the Scottish Media Group operates both the Scottish and Grampian Television franchises, has undergone various changes in response to Ofcom's review. In accordance with Ofcom's agenda, STV (Scottish Television) has not only continued to put local news coverage at the forefront of its agenda, but also renewed its commitment to 'regional drama' (STV 2004–5: 24). In the recent past, STV programming has also been increasingly dedicated to consumer-led drama. Thus, while the 'Chairman's Statement' from 2003 emphasised the broadcaster's response to the Communications Act and the various groups consulted – such as PACT (Producers Alliance for Cinema and Television), the Scottish Arts Council, politicians and the ITC – the greatest importance was placed on increasing viewer consultation (STV 2003–4: 2), providing clear evidence of the continuing shift from public-service to consumer-driven models of production.

In 2003 Scottish Television saw the end of *High Road*, a programme that had been on air for over twenty-one years, but was deemed to lack relevance in contemporary Scotland. Its last series ended with a telling metaphor, depicting Glendarroch, its fictional setting on the banks of Loch Lomond, like many other rural communities, as withering away in the absence of local facilities and the general pull towards (sub)urban centres. At the same time, STV was increasing its commitment to promoting new talent by commissioning five new scripts of regional drama to be broadcast over the coming year. Although STV's increased focus on new drama was evident, it also continued building on the success of existing favourites, such as the crime drama *Taggart*, which, after twenty-three years on screen, has attained a status akin to that of a national institution. Persisting with the format of a traditional police investigation, the Glasgow-based series has enthralled audiences within and beyond Scotland by creating a strong sense of place, as well as using well-written scripts and featuring a cast of actors that brings together experienced television professionals with up-and-coming talent. In the most recent series, DCI Burke – played by Alex Norton, a relative newcomer – leads the police team with a gruff aggressiveness reminiscent of Mark McManus's Jim Taggart in the programme's early days. At the other extreme, Blythe Duff's character DC Jackie Reid remains, having appeared in more than forty episodes. Against expectation, the changes in personnel over the years appear to have strengthened the programme, but although the interplay of characters within the team constitutes an integral part of the programme's enduring success, the solution of crime with its attendant twists of plot is still the main attraction for viewers. Remarkably, the series has never dwelt on stereotypes of Glasgow as a violent working-class city. In fact, the opposite is the case. As Duncan Petrie comments, 'the series contributed significantly to establishing the motifs of "the new Glasgow" . . . that have re-inscribed the city in the popular imagination as successful, confident and welcoming' (Petrie 2004: 147).

The same cannot be said for the STV comedy-drama series *High Times*, which was originally regarded as a risk production, mainly due to its move away from prime-time, popular programming towards niche marketing. However, *High Times* received a Bafta Scotland award for television drama in 2004 and was also shortlisted for the Montreux Festival's Rose d'Or in 2005. Set in a Glasgow tower block, the six-part series follows the interacting lives of ten tenants. The representation is of a 'new' Glasgow only inasmuch as twenty-first-century contexts create an occasion for the exploration of idleness, venality and dishonesty – all longstanding attributes of stereotypical Scottish urbanites. The critical success of the series rests upon its genuinely funny and authentic-sounding dialogue, and the consistently strong performances delivered by the cast. As declared by the programme's website, the aim of the series is the production of original drama effecting a departure from previous forms of Scottish television drama, including 'no murders, no car chases, no forensics, no soft soap . . . just life'. Yet comments like Steven McGinty's, first published in the *Scotsman* and repeated in the series's DVD cover blurb, question the programme's originality by clearly identifying some of its precursors. According to McGinty, 'the elevated set reminds viewers of *Still Game*, its strong language of *Tinsel Town* (Raindog Television) and its fat, corpulent wasters of *Rab C. Nesbitt*. There is also a smack of [Channel 4's] *Shameless*.' McGinty might also have added the novels of Irvine Welsh to his list. While all television drama is to some extent built upon what has gone before, *High Times* – despite the freshness of its scriptwriting – perhaps lacks the essential spark of originality required to outweigh its conspicuously derivative roots. *High Times* was written by John Rooney, whose career began as a contributor to STV's extremely successful New Found Land development scheme. Over the years, Scottish television has played a crucial role in developing new talent, and the remit of New Found Land, originally established to produce new half-hour dramas, now also includes feature-length films. In 2003, two award-winning feature films were made – Alison Peebles's *Afterlife* and Eleanor Yule's *Blinded* – followed in 2005 by Robbie Fraser's *Gamerz* and Adrian Mead's *Night People*, which won the Bafta Cineworld Audience Award.

Many critics have noted the impact of television on feature-film production in Scotland. In 1990 Gus MacDonald identified nine feature films backed by Scottish Television (MacDonald 1990: 194). Channel 4's commitment in particular has had an immense impact on the development of new film talent. In his exploration of the channel's influence, Caughie claims the success of British cinema to be 'almost entirely dependent on the convergence of film and television' (Caughie 1997: 35). Following the demise of Film Four's production sector, the channel continues to nurture new talent through its Ideas Factory initiative. However, while Channel 4's influence on film-making in Scotland is beyond doubt, its role in promoting Scottish television drama appears negligible. In fact, in 2005 Singh Kohli, the creator of Channel 4's *Meet the Magoons*, accused the channel of 'anti-Scottish' bias after it dropped his Bafta-nominated sitcom that had attracted over a million viewers (Ritchie 2005: 13).

In recent years, however, Channel 4 has commissioned at least one significant drama series set in Scotland: *The Book Group*, penned and directed by American Annie Griffin. *The Book Group* – about a lonely American woman in Glasgow who organises a book group in the hope of meeting people – proved a successful programme with UK and overseas audiences alike. Carrying many of the tropes of recent British television drama, such as the footballer's wife and resident 'ned', it also offered a degree of originality, mainly by including a hotchpotch of characters, (sub)cultures and class stereotypes not normally associated with a book group, which usually belongs to a particular vision of middle-class life. Also, literally set up from a foreign tourist's point of view, it offers a quirky view of contemporary Glasgow, tempering its representation of outlandish stereotypes with an ironic undertone provided by the tension between the American main character's preconceptions of Scotland and its actual reality. The joke is on the American: for example, when her mother phones to ask how she is, she claims to be going to a party at a friend's castle, then off climbing in the hills with her friends, when in fact she is staying in her flat, on her own. Her idealised vision of Scotland is consistently undermined and unmasked as a fiction. Just like the book group members, who are ultimately more interested in potential romantic liaisons than their reading, the exported face of Scotland, as everyone – even the lonely American – knows, has little bearing on reality.

Like Channel 4, the BBC has also been influential in Scottish film production. Over the years, the corporation has been involved in films such as Lynne Ramsay's *Ratcatcher* (1999) and *Morvern Callar* (2002) as well as Ken Loach's *Sweet Sixteen* (2002). Recently, the BBC has also demonstrated an increasing commitment to its Nations, Regions and Communities initiative. On 10 December 1998, less than one month after the Scotland Act 1998 received Royal Assent, paving the way for the setting up of a Scottish Parliament, the BBC's board of governors announced the broadcaster's intention to respond to the devolution of Scotland, Wales and Northern Ireland by investing over £20m, with £10m going to Scotland, £6m to Wales and £5 to Northern Ireland. The expiration of the BBC's Royal Charter also increased the urgency for a wider remit. In 2005, promises were made to boost spending across the nations and regions from £600m to £1bn by 2012, an initiative intent on rectifying the previous imbalance in the distribution of resources and the predominance of London-based activity. A review of the BBC's Royal Charter published in March 2005 reconfirms the BBC's original mission statement 'to inform, educate, and entertain' while also introducing five additional key purposes, the last two of which, most pertinently, concern 'representing the UK, its nations, regions and communities' and 'bringing the UK to the world and the world to the UK' (Department of Media, Culture and Sport 2005: 4). These additions are designed to differentiate the BBC from other channels, which have arguably come to fulfil the same duties as those outlined in the BBC's original mission statement. However, despite the BBC's increasing commitment to its Nations and Regions sector, the shift away from the dominance of a London-based infrastructure is far from complete. Financial investment and policy are one thing, reality is another. As Cosgrove puts it, 'unfortunately within the BBC the concept of regions is where you're sent to die', adding that 'until the BBC manufactures fundamental change in that area, and that's cultural change within the organisation, then we'll still have this debate and we'll still be talking about the edges of it' (BBC 2004: 14).

Recent statements issued by BBC Scotland, expressing its intent to produce material that would reflect 'Scottish experience', raise even more complicated issues, perhaps best exemplified by *Monarch of the Glen*. In September and October 2005, BBC 1 broadcast the sixth and final series of this drama series in its peak Sunday evening slot, attracting large audiences. Made by Ecosse Films, the series displays quality with regard to strong casting, beautiful locations and high production values, and its success certainly played a major part in securing the 2005 Silver Thistle award from VisitScotland for its executive producer Douglas Rae. (Notably, this award recognises excellence primarily in the tourism industry.) The programme's depiction of a supposedly impoverished aristocratic family, struggling to maintain its title to a Highland estate, offers an image of Scotland that is unashamedly nostalgic and romantic, clearly catering as much to overseas tourist markets as mainstream viewers in Britain. As far as overseas markets are concerned, the imagery of a beguiling Scotland as a potential place to visit is without doubt the main audience attraction, while narrative politics becomes incidental. Symptomatically, on BBC America's noticeboard, a moderator had to intervene to remind posters that discussion ought to focus on the series itself, not on travel to Scotland. Despite the superficial trappings of modernity, each episode of *Monarch of the Glen* portrays a land where the benevolent Laird presides over a family of lovable eccentrics, supported by faithful retainers. Glenbogle Estate is like a time capsule where the class structure of the nineteenth century is still in operation. Remarkably, in the opening episode of the 2005 series a shepherdess is introduced, displaying an attitude critical of the Laird and his management, taking the chair of the crofters' committee and agitating for necessary home repairs. However, not only is this shepherdess quickly assimilated into the Laird's household, but the series concludes with their marriage.

Threats to the stability of the closed society of the glen come from the remote outside world, and invariably each emergency is resolved within a single episode, deploying old-fashioned plot devices which are predictable and often glib. Most extreme in its dependence on tea-towel mythology is an episode centred on the discovery of a monster in the local loch. This episode sees a fraudulent scientific investigator returned to honesty and tourist cash rejected in favour of maintaining the idyllic tranquillity of the glen. However, a profit is still generated by the manufacture of chocolate novelties in monster shape. Although the programme displays what Petrie calls 'the tenacity of various tropes central to Kailyard/tartanry' (Petrie 2004: 209), it also conforms to a style of television drama that Lez Cooke identifies as 'consumer led', typified by 'marketable projects which would win and retain audiences' (Cooke 2003: 163–5). In this respect, *Monarch of the Glen* can be seen to share attributes with a string of other successful, yet undemanding series such as *Heartbeat* (Yorkshire Television), *Where the Heart Is* (Meridian Broadcasting) and even *All Creatures Great and Small* (BBC). Its popularity, sustained for seven years, is undoubted: the website features devoted message contributions from around the globe, and press publicity makes sure it records that, despite the continuing criticisms of academics, Scots viewers are no less enthusiastic than those from overseas (McQuillan 2003). This kind of marketing of Scotland as a tourist destination, reinforced by programmes like *Monarch of the Glen*, may well comply with the Scottish Executive's wishes by contributing to the economic well-being of the nation; however, due to its perpetuation of longstanding myths, *Monarch of the Glen* does very little to promote Scotland as a twenty-first-century nation.

At present, *River City*, BBC Scotland's flagship soap set in the fictional neighbourhood of Shieldinch in Glasgow and following a rather conventional format structured around the lives of a community, surrounding a local pub and shops, represents the BBC's biggest drama production outside London. Despite the soap opera's rocky start and critics' predictions of the programme's early demise, ratings and viewing figures have dramatically turned around. Indeed, early on the BBC identified the soap as 'too parochial' for broadcast outwith Scotland (Crawford 2003). By 2005 the BBC had changed its mind, acknowledging the programme's potential appeal to expatriate Scots worldwide. While concern continues to be expressed over *River City*'s large budget, draining money from new development schemes, even reviewers doubtful of its cultural value are inclined to praise it, if only for its awfulness. 'River Shitty' is now deemed 'a term of affection' (Mills 2005).

Similarly, the praise for other programmes on the BBC menu, such as *Sea of Souls* or *Two Thousand Acres of Sky*, is often mingled with contempt. The latter two programmes draw on the triumphant success of recent 'cult' television drama. Thus, *Sea of Souls*, centred on a parapsychology unit in the fictitious Clyde University, is a Scottish variant of Twentieth-Century-Fox's *The X-Files* and CBS's *CSI*. As in the popular US series *Twin Peaks*, its beautiful landscapes and backdrop serve as an ironic counterpoint to the darkness of its narratives. The series picked up a Scottish Bafta for Best Drama in 2005, yet its acclaim is not always agreed upon among reviewers: 'Hilarious . . . it is a comedy, isn't it?' (Stephen 2005). *Two Thousand Acres*, focused on an Englishwoman's relocation to a remote Scottish island, builds on the success of other thirty-something narratives like *Cold Feet* (Granada Television) while also sharing similarities with American programmes such as *Party of Five*, with its unlikely friend/family groupings, or *Northern Exposure*, with its quirky depiction of a remote community and its people. The narrative's preoccupation with the introduction of an outsider into a small community also proves fruitful terrain for explorations of belonging and cultural identity. Yet the reception of the series in the press labelled it a guilty pleasure. Thus, one Scottish reviewer, confessing to 'actually lov[ing] it', begs for his readers' sympathy ('Please don't be disappointed in me'), justifying his positive response by arguing the programme is edgier than 'Celtic charmfests like *Monarch of the Glen* or *Ballykissangel*' (Stewart 2002). Indeed, the island community depicted has definitely arrived in the twenty-first century, and the programme gives prominence to present-day economic and social issues alongside the exploration of modern relationships.

Generally speaking, it seems rare for Scottish programming to be met without a degree of critical cynicism. Press reviews often seek out the well-worn Kailyard and Tartanry tropes and, as a result, remain blind to the actual merits of the individual drama. At the same time, any programme's effort to revisit and capture Scotland's repressed histories finds itself at risk of being derided for digging up old ground. As early as 1982 Caughie referred to the Hogmanay specials of the period as 'fascinating in their awfulness' while trying to explain their regressive tendency to consolidate traditional – as well as anachronistic or downright fictitious – notions of 'Scottishness' (Caughie 1982: 120). Part of the problem, Caughie suggested, was the apparent taboo on trying to venture beyond the given Tartanry/Kailyard tradition. Any such attempt, he wrote,

> would involve an active engagement with other traditions and other versions of history; the traditions, for example, of the literature and theatre based in working-class experience which, since the twenties, have seemed to offer the only real and consistent basis for a Scottish national culture; and the histories of resistance and struggle exemplified by Red Clydeside, the Crofters' Wars, or the Lanarkshire weavers. (Caughie 1982: 121)

Accordingly, BBC2's tripartite serial *The Key* (2003) by Donna Franceschild takes a number of considerable risks in turning against recent trends in television drama by recasting

Scotland's narratives of political change and continuity against a background of shifting mores, gender roles and industrial decline. In this realist drama, which follows the lives of one family's successive generations of women from the Glasgow rent strikes of World War I to the first general election victory of New Labour, Franceschild interweaves the personal and the political in a way that draws on various traditions of popular television drama from the 'Wednesday Play' to the soap opera. Franceschild combines these different genres with direct political didacticism, attacking the on-the-street actuality of the New Labour project in a way that seems now like a premonition of the public distrust demonstrated in the general election of May 2005. Although *The Key* received a certain degree of praise from the press, the *Herald* tagged it a 'socialist realist soap' (Bell 2003) often resorting to cliché (see Sutcliffe 2003). *The Key* belongs to the discourse described by Petrie in *Screening Scotland* as 'Clydesidism', which is usually associated with brutal masculinity, poverty, urban squalor and leftist political aspirations, eventually to be dissipated by education and a move to middle-class compromise, or crushed into disillusionment by the cynicism and chicanery of professional politicians. In Clydesidist drama, the role of women has tended to focus on the degeneration of romance into victimhood, or the sentimentalisation of motherhood. Rather than avoiding these stereotypes, Franceschild reconfigures them, placing women of resilience at the heart of her representation. She also revisits the socialist project in a way that depicts it as a thoroughly realistic option for twenty-first-century life in a devolved Scotland rather than the graveyard of dinosaurs which it has consistently been represented as by politicians and in the media.

The richness of contextualisation in the drama is impressive. From the industrial unrest during World War I to Thatcherism and the Miners' Strike, the personal lives of the characters are enmeshed in politics and history. The exploration of political ideas is similarly broad, albeit at times perhaps burdening the realism of the dialogue with more than can be artistically sustained. Franceschild portrays a contemporary urban Scotland where employment depends on call centres and care homes – dual symbols of worker exploitation – and where New Labour politicians work hand in glove with private entrepreneurs to undermine the resistant potential of trade unions and women's solidarity. Effective parallels are drawn with earlier times, and earlier forms of exploitation, such as the ruthless factory owner or the abusive husband. In addition to adopting and adapting the critically suspect discourse of 'Clydesidism', Franceschild implements a direct appeal to the emotions of the viewer, risking the other charge so often levelled at Scottish screen drama – that of sentimentalism. To draw the viewer into the world of the drama, she does not hesitate to blend soap-operatic emotionality with overtly political didacticism. Love and death, passion and poetry heighten lives above the mundane and, in the end, direct political action is taken by soon-to-be lovers in defiance of cynical employers and politicians alike. *The Key* unashamedly displays its affinity with a style of British television drama, recurrent from the 1960s to the end of the twentieth century and stretching back via *Our Friends in the North* (BBC) to *Days of Hope* (BBC) and even *Up the Junction* (BHE Films/Crasto), but now deemed unfashionable. This is realist work, overtly polemical and challenging the political orthodoxy of its time by historicising it and thus seeking to criticise it for its perpetuation of old injustices in new guises.

In the 1989 preface to *Determinations*, a Polygon project which also included Craig Beveridge and Ronald Turnbull's provocative volume *The Eclipse of Scottish Culture* (1989), the series editor Cairns Craig insists that although the 1979 devolution referendum was unsuccessful, the disappointment meant that 'the 1980s proved to be one of the most productive and creative decades in Scotland this century – as though the energy that had failed to be harnessed by the politicians flowed into other channels'. But if political discontent is likely to foster a creative and cultural revolution, how exactly might this equation apply to the production of television drama in post-devolution Scotland? Martin McLoone has expressed a general optimism regarding British cinema's increasing attempts to explore the complexities of identity, arguing 'that peripherality has moved towards the cutting edge of contemporary cultural debate' (McLoone 2001: 190). However, in television, a trend towards 'peripherality' cannot necessarily be gauged in the same way. Traditionally rooted in the local, the medium is continually pushed in new directions by developing technologies. The demise of Thistle Television, the last local station in Scotland, happened in 2005 and although we are unlikely to see its return, Ofcom is currently reviewing the value of local stations. It should also be noted that only a year before its closure, Thistle Television was praised in the Scottish Parliament for its potential to serve as an immediate link to the community (Fabiani 2004); however, concerns over adequate investment in 'quality' programming to guarantee wider appeal and increase export potential must eventually have weighed more heavily. Clearly, the double-bind quandary caused by 'universalist' and 'parochialist' interests and requirements, as detailed by Caughie, continues to constitute a key tension in Scottish television.

The projected switchover to digital provision between 2008 and 2012 is anticipated as ensuring both greater choice and increased quality of television drama. At present, STV is due to broadcast another series of *High Times*, in addition to two new adaptations of *Rebus*, while *Taggart* continues. *River City* remains the primary focus of the BBC, but new drama series are currently in development, and *Sea of Souls* made a reappearance in 2006. Investment in regional production is undeniably increasing but financial and institutional constraints represent only one half of the battle. Twenty-five years on, what Caughie identified in *Scotch Reels* as 'one of the most massive inadequacies of Scottish television' remains and, as the present chapter illustrates, the majority of recent Scottish drama continues to lack any real 'engagement with a developed notion of national culture or national identity which goes beyond the reflection of an always already constructed "Scottishness"' (Caughie 1982: 115). While a programme like *The Key* is criticised for its alleged parochialism, it goes some distance towards broadening existing representations. In our view, universalism and the export of Scottish culture need not be a stumbling block; the challenge of addressing Scottish culture with the topical complexity it deserves often is. If less time were spent fretting over global translations of the particularities of Scottish culture, and replaced instead by a real and honest engagement with it, the rest would no doubt fall into place.

Chapter 13

Scotland's New House: Domesticity and Domicile in Contemporary Scottish Women's Poetry

Alice Entwistle

The idea of a House of Parliament, a locus in which the strands of a nation's political, economic and socio-cultural interests intersect, enshrines a powerfully dual trope: in its promise of a more autonomous future, Scotland's new government building offers a visible focus for the nation's conflicting expectations, which are cultural coherence and stability, on the one hand, and socio-economic and political transformation, on the other. In Joanne Winning's words, the building registers 'a Scotland poised now at the edge of a new stronger sense of identity; looking for its coordinates both backwards into the past, and forwards into the future' (Winning 2000: 226). At the same time, the Parliament marks out the equivocal space in which a freshly self-conscious nation turns simultaneously inward (to its domestic agenda) and outward (with a newly clarified and confident sense of statehood). Thus, with conspicuous cultural implications, the metaphorical and functional processes of devolution manifest and formalise the interpenetration of a nation's internal and external affairs.

Such implications resonate in Kathleen Jamie's two-line poem 'On the Design Chosen for the New Scottish Parliament Building by Architect Enric Miralles': 'An upturned boat / – a watershed' (Jamie 1999: 48). The image of the inverted boat gestures broadly at a resiliently self-sufficient Scotland, a survivor witnessing, or poised on the brink of, momentous change, not least in pointing towards cultural practices, as Susanne Hagemann observes, at once archaic and current, since 'the crofting and fishing economy exemplifies both continuity and transformation' (Hagemann 1997: 322). The poem deftly configures the convergence of security and risk, the collapsing of interior into exterior, over which – Miralles's design appears to suggest – the new Parliament presides. Jamie's gender, meanwhile, discreetly sharpens this gnomic little poem in two further ways. Implicitly contesting the status quo, the 'watershed' threatens to unsettle the 'masculinist bias in Scottish culture and nationalism' (Winning 2000: 227). 'Like gender, nations are constructs' (Hagemann 1997: 317), and Jamie invests Miralles's design with the potential to reconstruct gender roles as well as redefine the nation. Moreover, in all its ambiguous brevity, the poem can be read as self-referential, its 'watershed' signalling a turning point marking the aesthetic resituating of the Scottish woman writer and, specifically, the woman poet.

As one of Scotland's leading contemporary poets, Jamie accepts that her own claim on her native poetic tradition must be carefully negotiated. Writing about 'Mother-May-I' (Jamie 2002c: 114), a poem whose title derives from a childhood game, she draws a parallel between the game and her own progress towards poetic self-determination:

> In our game, by the accretion of permissions and consequent moves, we made our way toward the authority-figure, Mother, until eventually we tapped her on the shoulder. Symbolically, we became adults ourselves. As poets, something similar pertains. We accrue permissions, and consequently make poems, which in turn grant us permission to extend into new, scary areas. Through that we develop poetic authority. (Herbert and Hollis 2000: 278)

The authority of the Scottish woman poet having been long contested, Jamie and her generation make shrewd examiners of a political paradigm shift they have reason to understand differently from their male counterparts. Centralising and circling the figure of Jamie, this chapter examines the response of Scotland's women poets to their changing national context. It draws a parallel between the trope of the house *qua* 'home' – that is, the conflicted space of the traditionally female 'domestic sphere' – and the 'House' *qua* public or communal institution, focal signifier for a 'homeland' with a newly reinvigorated sense of cultural identity.

Women's poetry testifies to the way in which domesticity constrains but also – paradoxically, by offering emotional security – both anchors and stimulates women's creative lives (see Dowson and Entwistle 2005; Entwistle 2003). Likewise, Scotland's new political 'House' invites a revitalised cultural identification which promises to benefit its female citizens, yet retains the power to entrench the nation's historical failure to recognise women's contribution to, and claim on, their homeland's political and aesthetic life. If '[a] national culture is a *discourse*', then that discourse demands to be acknowledged, as Kathryn Kirkpatrick argues in her discussion of Irish women writers, as 'a dialogue in which women have always spoken, though their voices have not often been heard' (Kirkpatrick 2000: 6). Otherwise there is little hope of achieving the political transformations upon which any lasting reconfiguration of women's cultural status depends. While it has been claimed that 'Scottish poetry radiates, to a degree unmatched by any other substantial national literature, a passionate love of country, a sense of joy in its belonging' (Crawford and Imlah 2001: xxviii), this is only partly true of poetry by Scottish women, their work often complicated by a sense of estrangement from the aesthetic traditions embedding their nation's communal imagination and memory. In her poem 'Scotland's New House' (McMillan and Byrne 2003: 205–8), Mary Montgomery predicts that 'there'll be noise from the tent / As the house gets built / Before everybody can enter'. Scottish women poets' contribution to this 'noise' demonstrates at once their profound alienation and their hopeful faith in the aesthetic potentialities of a semi-autonomous situation as richly indeterminate as their own. In this respect, as Donny O'Rourke puts it, 'poetry can help focus and foment feeling that has no parliamentary outlet' (O'Rourke 2002: 282).

'Home' remains a problematic idea for creative women in the twenty-first century, forced to juggle the routine exigencies of domesticity and the demands of their professional lives. Their predicament leaves them weighing the manifold pleasures of home and family, a frequent source of inspiration, against the constraints and frustrations accompanying these pleasures. Thus, in 'On Not Writing Poetry' Ellie McDonald's 'Muse' grouchily complains about how domestic work invades and interferes with the woman poet's pursuit of her craft:

> This is yer Muse talkin.
> Ye're on yer final warnin.
> Nae mair sclatchin i the kitchen,
> nae mair hingin out the washin,

nae mair stour soukin.
This is yer Muse talkin
fae the wyste paper basket.
I kent it wis a bad idea
makin weemin poets.

(McMillan and Byrne 2003: 128–9)

McDonald's use of the vernacular makes the issue of domesticity here a specifically Scottish one, gesturing linguistically at a tradition in the habit of defining – and sidelining – female experience as primarily domestic.

Whether contesting, investigating or simply recording it, McDonald's peers can often be found probing their essentially separate history. The speaker of Margaret Gillies Brown's 'Scottish Woman', for example, impassively describes the country's 'women renouncing, when they conceive, / A separate existence, / Teaching the children, nursing the sick, / Cleaning, cooking, sewing / Making life smoother and rounder' (McMillan and Byrne 2003: 120). An extreme version of this traditional paradigm is dramatised by Dilys Rose in the pitiful, drudging figure of 'No Name Woman', her child 'grubbing in the dirt for bugs' at her feet, as

>   Steaming pots
> And hot fat spit their hiss at her.
> She wears the same rag constantly
> A hand-me-down print wrap, the pattern
> Washed away, the hem a tatter –
> Eats her dinner standing up
> Then clears and lays more tables
> Cradling plates to hush their clatter.

(Macmillan and Byrne 2003: 191)

The paradigm is nourished and guaranteed by women's self-censorship, reproached by Margaret Elphinstone in 'Potato Cuts': 'be sure you do it properly – / Tidy potatoes, without smudges / . . . Not using too much paint . . . And don't spill / Anything' (McMillan and Byrne 2003: 170–1). This is the world Alison Fell rejects so emphatically in 'Women in the Cold War', where a speaker 'still pockmarked with envy and a thousand wants' confronts a peer group 'dreaming of marriage':

> 'I'll be an artist' I said
> and bristled for the skirmish; quite slowly
> their eyes scaled and their good sense
> bunched against me.
> 'That's no' for the likes o' us.'
> Elizabeth, Elaine, Rhoda of the long legs,
> all matrons, mothering, hurrying
> their men to work at 7am.

(McMillan and Byrne 2003: 139–40)

But there are other ways of representing women's domestic experience. The idea of the house has remained a productive leitmotif throughout Jamie's shaping poetic idiom, connecting the early female-centred poems about her travels in Pakistan, Tibet and China with the more overtly Scottish work of *The Queen of Sheba* (1994) and *Jizzen* (1999) as well as, perhaps more unexpectedly, the nature poems of *The Tree House* (2004). Troubling the relationship between women's public lives and their personal experiences, Jamie's interest in house and home habitually results in depictions of the confined and confining domestic interior as an enabling and even transgressive space. Poems like 'Abir', 'For Paola' and 'Rooms' (Jamie 2002c: 18, 104, 155) reveal women questioning, challenging and subverting the beliefs and practices which determine the very structures of their disenfranchisement. Similarly, in 'My Grandmother's Houses' (Kay 1991: 40–1) Jackie Kay pays tribute to the fierce independence of a woman who appears to take her social disadvantages for granted. A lifetime spent in the shadows, literally, of successive mass-housing solutions (first the tenement-block, later the high-rise) has helped to define this ageing stalwart, her domestic skills transferring smoothly between home ('she makes endless pots of vegetable soup') and working life ('even at 70 she cleans other people's houses'). The details of her private existence ('the sideboard shiny as a coffin') both comfort and unsettle, throwing her domestic job into stark relief. A brief glimpse of the house which her grandmother cleans, and the awkward encounter which follows with its 'posh' owner, reinforce upon the poem's speaker the ways in which domestic work simultaneously divides and binds women. For all the hardship she has known, against the enervated middle-class employer who sends her so coolly 'back to your work', the speaker's grandmother comes to epitomise a freer and more autonomous model of womanhood.

Like Fell, McDonald and Jamie, for Kay the Scots language proves a flexibly suggestive political resource. The dialect connecting Kay's child and grandmother ('hoch', for example) is deployed by Fell at once to highlight and extricate herself from the menace of a parochialism all too useful to patriarchy. On the other hand, 'language loyalist' Catriona NicGumaraid uses Gaelic both to earth her sense of cultural identity and protectively to circumscribe the community with which it is shared. As NicGumaraid explains, 'I think in my imagination I'm living in a Gaelic world all the time. I know that most of my thoughts are concerned with Gaelic and certainly as I go about the house, I always sing Gaelic songs' (Somerville-Arjat and Wilson 1990: 39). In 'Playing at Houses' NicGumaraid's persona is similarly consoled by her native tongue, asserting her cultural identity against the threat posed to the Gaelic community by English-speaking incomers. Any warmth in the poem is reserved for an unexpected Gaelic-speaking visitor: 'That's it, tidy the hearth, / put a peat on the fire – / in this house at least / we'll talk as we used to' (McMillan and Byrne 2003: 164). According to Helen Kidd, 'Lallans, Doric Scots, Gaelic, standard English with regional syntax and idioms . . . There is no single essential Scottish voice. Women poets recognise this, and there is an unabashed espousal of, and fidelity to, regional differences' (Kidd 1997: 99). This idiomatic hospitality accompanies a common determination to interrogate the homogenising effect of a predominantly patriarchal culture and history. Scotland's linguistic pluralism is manipulated to distinguish a particular (that is, female) cultural identity with its own set of political and aesthetic expectations from the nuances, codes and conventions of other, more hegemonic versions of 'Scottishness'. Thus, language offers a subtle way of linking the private 'home', an ambivalent site of frustrated purpose and creative energy, with the equally conflicted terrain of the national and topographical 'homeland' in which it is secured. Like the home, which both anchors and imprisons, the homeland offers an uneasy domicile, promising a sense of cultural connectedness it can never properly fulfil. The relationship between the two spheres is important not least because, as Robert

Crawford is everywhere applauded for noting, 'where do you come from? is one of the most important questions in contemporary poetry – where's home?' (Crawford 1993a: 144).

Scottish women poets appear to respond as strongly as their male counterparts to the 'strange potency' of a landscape evoked by Kathrine Sorley Walker, in 'Scottish Legacy', in powerfully human-relational terms:

> Does it derive
> from the long line of generations
> whose human dust, mixed with the burial earth,
> scattered in ashes on the hills and glens,
> speaks to me, in this land, of love of place,
> kinship and ancestry?

(McMillan and Byrne 2003: 104)

For Sorley Walker, nationhood emerges from a deep-rooted sense of familial and implicitly domesticated history or, in her own words, 'the long skein of genealogy . . . / that ends in me'. And yet, as the Scots-speaking Muse of Ellie McDonald's 'On Not Writing Poetry' reminds us, so romanticised a construction of female cultural place overlooks how readily women, invariably immured in the complexities of 'home', have been absented from their nation's civic and cultural life. Such apparently different views as Sorley Walker's and McDonald's combine in a literature which firmly reproaches, even as it subverts, the persistent view that 'the Scottish nation and its heritage are essentially the concern of men' (Gifford and McMillan 1997: 320).

The extent to which women are encouraged or permitted to feel 'at home' in Scotland is examined in a clutch of recent poems condemning their effacement and exclusion from some of the nation's most definitively public places and institutions. The collection of statues housed in Glasgow's Botanic Gardens prompts Anne MacLeod, for example, into a suggestively gendered study of motion and constraint. In 'In the Kibble Palace: Sunday Morning' (MacLeod 1999: 34–5) a group of statue-like old men silently watch the restless children, who 'escape into the inner swell / of palm and fern and moss, a green confusion'. This juxtaposition of stasis and movement frames the struggles of a 'tired mother / stuck with the push-chair' as the speaker (who might or might not be the mother herself) witnesses, in relentlessly enjambed lines, the potential drama of her toddler striking out after the other children. Unpunctuated lineation makes for phrasing as stifling as the heat enveloping the 'stranded' parent. Poised for different reasons between motion and stasis, mother and child alike seem obstructed, if not endangered, in this claustrophobic environment: 'No due momentum / without clear support'.

Similarly, if situated in a very different public space, Jamie's 'Arraheids' mischievously critiques the certainties of a male-dominated cultural heritage:

> See thon raws o flint arraheids
> in oor gret museums o antiquities
> awful grand in Embro –
> Dae'ye near'n daur wunner at wur histrie?
> Weel then, Bewaur!
> The museums of Scotland are wrang.
> They urnae arraheids

but a show o grannies' tongues,
the hard tongues o grannies
aa deid an gaun . . .

(Jamie 2002c: 137)

The poem gleefully permits a subversive female chorus to assault an unsatisfactorily androcentric perspective on history from within; the 'muttering' of the arrowhead-like 'sherp /
chert tongues' waspishly undermines the inaccurate one-sidedness of 'wur histrie' recycled
in 'oor gret musems' down the centuries. Smartly reinserting the voices of the nation's
female ancestry into the historical record, Jamie evokes and exploits the muted, largely
private and habitually secretive nature of female experience. Meanwhile, the use of the
vernacular scornfully rebukes the decorous, formalised language of the nation's elite, rendering the more democratically oral and informal traditions of female self-expression peculiarly effective.

The poem makes it enjoyably clear that for women there is no better weapon than
(their own) language, and no more vulnerable target than Scotland's self-deluding masculinist (mis)representation of its cultural and intellectual identity. 'Arraheids' insists that
more often than not Scotland's museums proffer a decidedly partial interpretation of the
nation's cultural experience. The role of the curator (like the poet) is to mediate and transform the relationship between past and present, intervening in history by making the
strange familiar and the familiar strange. Exhibits are positioned and contextualised in
ways which inevitably recontextualise and reconfigure them, the coalescence of known
and unknown, public and private, exposing history-making as a deeply provisional and
unreliable process.

Unlike Jamie, Gerrie Fellows reflects without much humour on the obliteration of
female experience from Scotland's public life and the nation's historical record. Written in
2000, her poem 'A Woman Absent from the Museum Muses on her Life in South Dunedin'
reproves the formalised gaps and silences of a profoundly gendered and impoverished
chronicle with carefully positioned lacunae: 'Those of us whom no one thought to photograph / Are here as ghosts to give the lie / To bread without scarceness freedom by / Honest
toil' (McMillan and Byrne 2003: 194).

Noting the critical tendency 'to belittle women's cultural productions as lesser, subjective, dealing in daily trivia rather than universals and "eternal verities"', Kidd insists that
'it is precisely those relational, interactive and heterogeneous processes that form societal
and cultural texture, and provide the material for transformation into art' (Kidd 1997:
101). Accordingly, when Fellows and Jamie problematise the gender-sensitive space of the
museum, it is to rehabilitate a female aesthetic which has no cultural standing. Obliterated
from history, women's sense of estrangement from their homeland is deepened; moreover,
without influence on the nation's cultural and political psyche they can do little to repair
or reconstruct their position, let alone their homeland's. Following critics like Winning,
then, who take literature as a central 'index of national identity' (Winning 2000: 228), it
seems telling that the denouement of 'The Queen of Sheba', one of Jamie's best-known
poems, should hinge on the moment that the Queen demands 'the keys / to the National
Library':

Sure enough: from the back of the crowd
someone growls:
whae do you think y'ur?

and a thousand laughing girls and she
draw our hot breath
        and shout:

THE QUEEN OF SHEBA!

(Jamie 2002c: 113)

Like 'Arraheids', 'The Queen of Sheba' rehearses Jamie's abiding conviction in the political power of the poetic text. As she has declared, 'if poetry is a method of approaching
truths, and each of us with a human soul and "a tongue in oor heids" can make an approach
toward a truth, poetry is inherently democratic' (Herbert and Hollis 2000: 281). This poem
in particular represents something of a manifesto. As Jamie explains, 'we were having one
of our occasional convulsions of proud despair and I was able to wonder what kind of
Scotland we could/would have, were we brave enough' (Brown and Paterson 2003: 125).

'Republic of Fife', also from *Mr and Mrs Scotland Are Dead*, offers an alternative view on
the same question. Interestingly, in this poem, it is 'my house' which provides a vantage
point from which to interrogate the position of the fledgling republic:

on whose roof we can balance,
carefully stand and see
clear to the far off mountains,
cities, rigs and gardens,

Europe, Africa, the Forth and Tay bridges,
even dare to let go, lift our hands
and wave to the waving citizens
of all those other countries.

(Jamie 2002c: 147–8)

At its conclusion 'Republic of Fife' contrives to summon Julia Kristeva's envisioning of the
twenty-first century as 'a transitional period between the nation [state] and international
or polynational confederations' (Kirkpatrick 2000: 5). At the same time, however, in balancing the drama of political secession on the ridge of a house-roof, the poem surrept-
itiously collapses the political back into the personal again.

Commissioned by the National Museum of Scotland, inaugurated in the year of the 1997
referendum, 'Lucky Bag' from *Jizzen* cheerfully weighs in on the reinstitutionalising of the
nation's imaginative and cultural life. In playfully poststructural mood, the poem assembles a proliferating array of official and unofficial signifiers exposing how Scotland's public
and private, secular and spiritual, historical and contemporary experiences intrude on one
another: 'Tattie scones, St Andra's banes, / a rod-and-crescent Pictish stane, / a field o
whaups, organic neeps / . . . a Free State, a midden, / a chambered cairn – yer Scottish
lucky-bag, one for each wean; / please form an orderly rabble' (Jamie 1999: 42). Its double-
jointed couplets reminiscent of Anglo-Saxon poetics, the poem begins to resemble some
kind of religious incantation. It might even be a blessing intoned over the 'weans' at its
centre which, with an eye to posterity, formally assigns them the cultural birthright it
deconstructs. As Helen Boden percipiently remarks, 'a new present does not . . . need to
reject older definitions entirely: to do so would mean a loss of defining continuity with the
past that has shaped the present' (Christiansen and Lumsden 2000: 31). Exposing a nearly

autonomous Scotland as a productively indeterminate space ripe for political and aesthetic reappropriation, *Jizzen* delicately and deliberately sutures a heterogeneous female self – and the 'herstories' she reifies – into the core of the nation's cultural memory, while the arrival of the nation's devolution is paralleled with, and thus lightly feminised by, the experiences of pregnancy, parturition and maternity. *Jizzen* connects with work by poets as diverse as Gillian Ferguson – especially 'Scan' ('*it* becoming *you*') and 'Everything is More' ('you are my second chance at the world') – and Kay, who remains relentlessly conscious of the special complexities of her own cultural origins and affiliations, and who, like Jamie, ascribes to domesticity intensely productive potentialities, however closed-in or closed-off it might seem (McMillan and Byrne 2003: 244–5, 245–6).

Politically 'clear-headed', 'historically sophisticated', 'sensitively internationalist' and laced with a cautiously 'conditional affection for one's native place', recent poetry by Scottish women evinces the principal elements of O'Rourke's 'new patriotism' (O'Rourke 2002: 287), but not uncritically so. As the mysterious, archaic persona of Liz Niven's 'Devorgilla in the Borderlands' remarks with suggestive equivocation: 'Not living at the heart of the matter, / skirting peripheries brings / its own perils; / Like finding your own centre' (McMillan and Byrne 2003: 184). Throughout *Jizzen*, Jamie's recuperative incursions into her nation's historical record gesture at a female poetics as self-consciously interested in its survival as its origins. Yet, by concentrating on 'experiences which are wholly female – in an art form which still, at times, likes to imagine that real, proper poetry cannot have women's experience at its centre' (Brown and Paterson 2003: 127), the collection also dramatises how literary tradition threatens to compound the Scottish woman poet's sense of cultural alienation. This alienation persists despite the increasingly well-documented involvement of women, over the centuries, in Scottish poetics, primarily through the oral, often domesticated, traditions of ballad and song. Catriona NicGumaraid even argues that 'in Gaelic society the better poets were the women. They wrote the wonderful work songs when they waulked the tweed, when there would be only women present' (Somerville-Arjat and Wilson 1990: 40). Situating women at the intersection of ancient Scotland's economic and aesthetic life, such songs were – significantly – culturally and aesthetically defiant or, in Kidd's words, 'political, bawdy and challenging' (Kidd 1997: 101).

In certain respects, then, women's poetic utterances have continued to shape and be shaped by a tradition of their own. As Kerrigan notes, 'in its power to tell a story, in providing a place for unrecorded experience, the ballad became for many women poets the home of their history' (Kerrigan 1991: 5). This reference to an indigenous female-authored poetic tradition in Scotland helps to explain Meg Bateman's 'To Alexander Carmichael', her poetic tribute to the Scottish folklorist and original editor of the *Carmina Gadelica* (1900): 'You gave us the prayer of ordinary things / which I hear now in the thrum of the wipers, / waiting at the lights' (McMillan and Byrne 2003: 217). It also illumines the jaunty determination of Montgomery's 'Scotland's New House', which lends this chapter its title:

> There'll be noise from the tent
> As the house gets built
> Disputes
> Statutes
> Firm foundations
> Income
> Outcome
> Institution

And constitution
As the house gets built
To an independent design

. . .

And when the house is ready
We'll have a party
And we'll have a *ceilidh* too.

(McMillan and Byrne 2003: 207–8)

The availability of Bateman's and Montgomery's poems, originally composed in Gaelic and published alongside English translations in Dorothy McMillan and Michael Byrne's *Modern Scottish Women Poets*, confirms McMillan's much-quoted assertion, made almost a decade ago, that 'Scottish women's poetry is probably having a better time of it now than it has ever had' (Gifford and McMillan 1997: 549). Arguably, however, any improvement in the status and critical appraisal of Scottish women poets over the last ten years has been piecemeal. Only eleven of the thirty-six poets in O'Rourke's re-issued *Dream State* are women. Framed by an introduction proclaiming that 'Scotland's artists did more than its politicians to dream up a new Scotland' (O'Rourke 2002: 2), *Dream State* leaves the impression that Scottish women poets have less to offer to the literature of a devolved twenty-first-century nation-state than their male peers. While McMillan has counselled against presuming that an entire generation of poets is absorbed by 'battles that they are not always fighting and certainly not only fighting' (McMillan and Byrne 2003: 549), women's impoverished poetic ancestry continues to haunt their attempts to converse with literary tradition: there are few instances of Scottish women poets writing self-consciously to and about themselves and their predecessors as *literary* figures.

Arguably, Liz Niven has produced the most daring female poet's engagement with tradition in her riposte to Hugh MacDiarmid's *A Drunk Man Looks at the Thistle* (1926), 'Extracted fae a Drunk Wumman Sittin Oan a Thistle', first published in 1997 in *New Writing Scotland*. Niven's 148-line poem (its epigraph, naughtily, proclaiming 'misquoted is a' body's property') converses only semi-humorously with a text it relocates into post-devolution times: 'The tension ower the votes aw coontit, / Wir Parliament formed, the right wing routit.' As her poem's title warns, Niven's highly gendered response to MacDiarmid's original explicitly contends with it, not only on political grounds ('Tae be a wumman—an tae hae aw men's equal richts / Nae harder job tae wumman is in sight'), but also in literary terms. Niven's antagonistic predecessor is mockingly exposed as oblivious to the advantages he enjoys, in stark contrast to generations of women whose poetic skills have been undervalued, or overlooked, on account of their sex:

But thon kinna wumman's jist a slut
An should only write clean lyricals.

Could ye jist hae seen the history books if Rabbie wis a lass?
She'd o fun hersel wi child, cut off at the first pass
    An wrote nae poems
An nivver hid the chance tae write like Rantin Rovin Rabbie,
Who didnae try tae pen a poem while stuck at hame wi babbie.

(Niven 1997: 118)

What Niven's poem demonstrates is that the poet feels comfortable enough in, and confident enough of, her own contemporary poetic context to displace MacDiarmid's insensitively gendered literary trail. At the same time, perhaps more revealingly, the very existence of the parody suggests that Niven, one of the most innovative and experimental of a group of younger female voices, does not yet feel sufficiently 'at home' in her literary surroundings to be able to resist the opportunity to confront MacDiarmid on his own terms.

The epigraph of Jamie's 'Meadowsweet', which concludes *Jizzen*, cites the tradition 'that certain of the Gaelic women poets were buried face down', retraced by Bateman to 'a custom introduced by the Norse for the burial of witches' (Kerrigan 1991: 16). The poem opens as the burial party turn away, unaware that 'the liquid / trickling from her lips / would' result in the germination of the 'summer seeds'

> showing her,
> when the time came,
> how to dig herself out –
>
> to surface and greet them,
> mouth young, and full again
> of dirt, and spit, and poetry.

(Jamie 1999: 49)

Not so much hostile as defiant, the closing line boldly re-inscribes the self-exhuming woman poet into the literary history which she contests. However, the poem's narrative also dramatises the part played by nature in guaranteeing the survival of a female aesthetic. Art, in the form of poetry, emerges from – or rather, is revived by – the land itself, instructed and charged by nature. This is a view which might also helpfully illuminate the direction taken by Jamie in her most recent work, *The Tree House*. The title poem of the collection resonates intriguingly with 'Uncertainty', a poem by Gaelic-language poet Anne Frater and, in my view, an appositely unresolved female self-positioning with which to conclude the present chapter: 'Walking across the beach, / My eyes on my destination; / Not knowing if the tide / Is turning / Setting me walking / On quicksand' (Frater 2001: 49).

Chapter 14

Redevelopment Fiction: Architecture, Town-planning and 'Unhomeliness'

Peter Clandfield and Christian Lloyd

On 12 September 1993 the slab-block flats of Queen Elizabeth Square in Glasgow's Gorbals were destroyed in a controlled explosion (see Glendinning 1997: xii; Glendinning and Muthesius 1994: 327). The two twenty-storey buildings were less than thirty years old, completed in 1966 as Hutchesontown Area C, a prominent part of the modernist redevelopment programme that transformed Glasgow, along with other parts of Scotland, after World War II. The 'Queenies' were designed by Sir Basil Spence, a leading figure in postwar Scottish (and British) architecture, as highly visible symbols of urban and national rejuvenation (see Robertson 1997). In the views of many of their latter-day residents, though, flawed planning and escalating neglect had made the tower-blocks even more unhomely than the cramped and unsanitary nineteenth-century tenements they originally replaced. The demolition was a traumatic and controversial event – made worse because one onlooker was killed by flying debris – and a particularly dramatic manifestation of ongoing uncertainties about the development of Glasgow and Scotland as a whole.

Redevelopment features as a major concern in contemporary Scottish fiction, and 'redevelopment fiction' may be treated as a particularly, though not uniquely Scottish sub-genre. The variety within this category deserves emphasis in itself, and the parallels and resonances among works of diverse approaches and styles highlight the centrality of urban-renewal efforts to recent Scottish history and culture. Accordingly, this chapter examines literary works that read social and political developments by exploring more concrete kinds of (re)development in architecture and urban planning. Two types of redevelopment fiction converge in the works to be discussed. One type, dealing mainly with concrete conditions and relying mostly on metonymic and synecdochal detail, treats the failures of grand modernist urban schemes of the 1950s, 1960s and 1970s as foci and loci for disaffection and cautionary lessons to counter post-devolution idealism; another, emphasising the psychological effects of built spaces and often operating through allusion and metaphor, looks further back in architectural and social history to warn that pre-modernist iniquities and inequities may have uncanny descendants that haunt emerging postmodernist developments.

In his introduction to *Rebuilding Scotland* Miles Glendinning suggests that the ideas which drove Scotland's post-1945 reconstruction had roots in the nation's prewar efforts to move beyond its role as a partner in the British imperial enterprise and redefine itself according to ideals of social welfare (Glendinning 1997: 1). Scottish redevelopment projects became part of what Anthony Vidler in *The Architectural Uncanny* describes as a 'therapeutic program', inspired particularly by the Swiss architect-theorist Le Corbusier (1887–1965) and 'dedicated to the erasure of nineteenth-century squalor in all its forms' through, among other things, 'a polemical equation between art and health' (Vidler 1992: 63). Modernist architectural 'art', emphasising clean-lined forms and 'encouraging the ceaseless flow of light and air', became a prescription for physical and mental health: 'If houses were no longer haunted by the weight of tradition ... if no cranny was left for the storage of the bric-à-brac once deposited in damp cellars and musty attics, then memory would be released from its unhealthy preoccupations to live in the present.' Inevitably however, so Vidler continues, 'this house-cleaning operation produced its own ghosts, the nostalgic shadows of all the "houses" now condemned to history or the demolition site' (Vidler 1992: 63–4). Moreover, in Scotland, as elsewhere, the shortcomings of modernist theorising were compounded by more material failings. Some problems with the design and execution of Scottish redevelopment projects can be attributed to the urgency with which new housing was needed. As Michael Pacione reports, following World War II 'one-seventh of Scotland's population was crowded into three square miles of central Glasgow, and houses often lacked basic sanitary amenities' (Pacione 1995: 161–2). Accordingly, large sections of the city were designated as Comprehensive Development Areas and completely rebuilt, with their inhabitants relocated either to the tower-blocks that replaced older housing or to new developments in outlying areas.

Functionalism – the modernist doctrine that 'all elements of architecture could [and should] be explained in relation to construction and "function"' (Glendinning and Muthesius 1994: 9) – was not accepted wholesale by planners or political leaders, but its connotations of efficiency suited their priorities. According to Beatrix Campbell, 'the Tory governments of the Fifties and Sixties [were] bewitched by the promise of Corbusier's utilitarian urbanism' (Campbell 1993: 24). However, planners may also have been inspired by Scandinavian social housing and 'the 1950s dream of being able to design everything in society and everyday life – from the whole to the smallest detail' (Rudberg 2002: 163). What such planners overestimated was the extent to which it might be possible to transfer design principles appropriate to one place to the different lived experience of another.

As Glendinning notes, the very success of modernist architects became problematic, as their designs were imitated, sometimes hastily, by planners and building contractors interested less in details of design than in economies of scale, which leads him to conclude that the problem with Scotland's modernist projects resided primarily in their execution (Glendinning 1997: 22–4). Similarly, echoing Pacione's claim that the economic problems of the 1970s and 1980s compromised both the design and the maintenance of housing developments in Scotland (Pacione 1995: 170–1), Charles Robertson, architect for Spence's Queen Elizabeth Square project, acknowledges that its designers did not take account of its very high maintenance cost (Robertson 1997: 101). Robertson's remark also evokes what Peter Hall has identified as a fundamental flaw of Corbusian modernism, and that is the conception of buildings as autonomous works of art, or art theory, rather than products destined for material lives in space and time (Hall 1988: 214).

Significantly, Glendinning's *Rebuilding Scotland* includes documents from 'Visions Revisited', a 1992 conference concerned with what chairperson Kirsty Wark called 'our own uneasy present-day relationship with the relics of Modernism – monuments of a lost era of utopian dreams'. Spence's Queen Elizabeth Square blocks, whose future was then still up for debate, were discussed from 'a variety of views'. Wark even suggests that 'I don't think we have anyone who has ever lived in Hutchesontown "C", but ... it would be interesting to have their views as well' (Glendinning 1997: 144). However, the idea that residents might be able to offer 'interesting' views on Spence's blocks appears to have been little more than an afterthought, replicating the biases and blindspots of those responsible for projects like Hutchesontown C. While Glendinning suggests that present-day orthodoxy in housing design prioritises the needs of 'users' over the ideals of 'providers' (Glendinning 1997: xii–xiii), the very terms insinuate that residents of publicly supported housing are parasitically dependent on the generosity of enlightened architects and planners. As Campbell says of the 'Queenies', 'the exterior of livid grey slabs forbade any adornment or alteration. They spoke only of their author, not of their inhabitants' (Campbell 1993: 24). Part of the value of redevelopment fiction, then, is the space it creates not only for exploring alternative definitions of homeliness, but also for speaking of the everyday experiences of inhabitants of projects like Queen Elizabeth Square, as these places have come to be haunted not only by ghosts from the structures they replaced, but also by the 'nostalgic shadows' of their own unfulfilled promise.

Few fictional treatments of Scotland's redevelopments see them as success stories, and the material and ideological shortcomings of high-rise, high-density flats or isolated suburban estates are often registered briefly but effectively in works whose main narrative attention is on other matters. Helpful here is Mikhail Bakhtin's concept of chronotope, by which he means 'the intrinsic connectedness of temporal and spatial relationships [which] provides the ground essential for the . . . representability of events' in narrative (Bakhtin 1981: 84, 250). Modernist architecture's failed utopia can be seen as a distinctive chronotope of both crime and satirical fiction. Bleak housing projects provide natural settings for crime narratives; however, leading Scottish writers in the genre, such as Denise Mina in her *Garnethill* trilogy and Ian Rankin in his Inspector Rebus series, have used Scottish housing schemes not only for generic purposes but also to point metonymically to social and political dysfunctions. By comparison, satirical fiction – from the extravagantly provocative novels of Irvine Welsh to the understated and underappreciated works of Dilys Rose – has drawn more direct and sustained attention to connections between ill-designed housing and social problems.

In *Marabou Stork Nightmares* Welsh's protagonist, Roy Strang, describes the toxic housing estate of his youth as 'a systems built, 1960s maisonette block of flats, five storeys high, with long landings which were jokingly referred to as "streets in the sky" but which had no shops or pubs or churches or post offices on them' (Welsh 1995: 19), thus likening it to a degraded realisation of the Corbusian vision. In Roy's view, 'the scheme was a concentration camp for the poor' (Welsh 1995: 22). It is the very ahistoricity of this hyperbolic metaphor that appears to speak to the social dysfunctionality of rehousing schemes, which removed communities from their histories and thus effectively denied them the chance to grow organically. Comparably excessive in their rhetoric are Roy's reflections on his family's return to Scotland after a temporary emigration to South Africa. According to Roy, the only difference between the Scottish capital and Johannesburg is that here 'the Kaffirs were white and called schemies or draftpaks. Back in Edinburgh, we would be Kaffirs; condemned to live out our lives in townships like Muirhouse or So-Wester-Hailes-To or Niddrie, self-contained camps with fuck all in them, miles fae the toon' (Welsh 1995: 80). Roy's acceptance of the personal metonym 'schemie', as well as the concomitant notion that he is formed entirely by scheme life, suggests he is unlikely ever to take full responsibility for his actions. Sexually abused by an uncle in South Africa, as an adult in Scotland he himself commits a particularly vicious rape. The novel recognises implicitly that unhomely housing may contribute to launching violent careers like Roy's without insisting it is their sole cause, or suggesting that social deprivation is as fundamental a form of iniquity as apartheid. Thus, the extravagance of Roy's descriptions of the 'scheme' allows Welsh to dramatise the detrimental shortcomings of such places and disclose the modernist vision as unconscionably naive

Dilys Rose offers an alternative and more low-key account of the pathologies of Scottish housing estates. In 'Snakes and Ladders', from *Our Lady of the Pickpockets*, Lily Marsh of '125 Hill View, 14/B, Easter Drumbeath' (Rose 1989: 132), an address which reads like a composite of several well-known Scottish scheme-sites, submits a relocation request to her housing officer in order to escape her damp, decaying residence. However, even the revelation that her son has been hospitalised after discovering the hanged body of a despondent fellow tenant fails to sway the bureaucrat: '"I do sympathise with you, Mrs. Marsh. I'll try to do what I . . ." – The clerk's condolences were cut short by another irrepressible sneeze' (Rose 1989: 135–6). The sneezing humanises the official while also hinting at something unhealthy about the whole housing system. As Lily returns to Easter Drumbeath, she begins to contemplate 'how easy [it] would be' to take matters into her own hands. As the story ends, she is attempting to buy paraffin from 'one of the few shops which wasn't an off-licence or a betting shop' (Rose 1989:137), implying that such places as 'Easter Drumbeath' contain the ingredients of their own destruction.

Alternating between the interior monologues of a tower-block resident who hears voices and the woman psychologist monitoring his condition, 'Friendly Voices' from Rose's *Red Tides* employs a similar blend of pointedly satirising officiousness and sympathetically evoking the human fallibilities that inform it. The resident appears menacing, contemplating with apparent glee the visitor's exposure to the building's stinking lifts and looking on with inward approval as his dog accosts her: 'Ah let him sniff about a bit until she starts to get panicky' (Rose 1993: 11). By contrast, the psychologist's thoughts assume the form of detached, sometimes formulaic reflections about her work and its limitations: 'We take certain routes through the city, avoid others . . . We're not heartless but practical, having learned from experience that we can only function efficiently by maintaining a certain distance' (Rose 1993: 12). Never directly addressing her client's material or psychological conditions, she cultivates a disconnected attitude which, in the absence of any dialogue, dramatises the mutual detachment of her theory and practice. The resident ultimately proves to understand the psychologist better than she understands him; as his aggressive mood passes, he recognises her good intentions: 'Ah mean, she could've gone for one a they plum jobs in the private sector.' However, when he concludes that 'she could really dae wi a big hug' (Rose 1993: 15, 17), his clumsy effort to bridge the distance between them only precipitates her departure, leaving him to confront even greater isolation.

Apart from establishing dysfunctional housing schemes as apt metonyms for contemporary urban life, fictional renditions of the human cost of grand utopian schemes of postwar communal reconstruction, such as Welsh's and Rose's, implicitly recommend a cautious view of any new scheme – be it social, political or material – for Scotland's future. A particularly noteworthy example of redevelopment fiction in this context is Andrew O'Hagan's *Our Fathers* (1999), which not only gives an account of postwar redevelopment, but also looks towards an imminent era of re-redevelopment, that is, a post-devolution future in which Scottish space, physical as well as ideological, will be reconfigured. *Our Fathers* invites comparison with *Swing Hammer Swing* (1992), Jeff Torrington's novel about Scotland's changing urban landscape, which depicts the Gorbals in 1968 during the slum clearances that made way for projects like Queen Elizabeth Square. Torrington's narrator, Gorbals resident and aspiring writer Tam Clay, denounces the new buildings. 'Much imbued by the so-called merits of functionalism the planners and architects had taken wardrobes and tombstones to be their thematic design models', Tam observes, adding that 'surely it was with such a sense of transience that Basil Spence had sat down to fashion yon concrete spike he'd driven into the Gorbals' vitals' (Torrington 1992: 317). Torrington's analogy evokes both the unhomely qualities of the tower-blocks and the faulty, warped imagination of their designers. However, the novel critiques architectural modernism not only through such robust localised attacks, but also through narrative techniques that draw on the innovations of Joyce and Woolf by similarly accentuating the digressive propensities of individual consciousness. Tam explicitly rejects conventional narrative structure: 'Plots are for graveyards' (Torrington 1992: 162). *Swing Hammer Swing* makes formal untidiness the basis for its critique of over-schematic redevelopment 'plots', leaving readers to find their way through the disorderly text just as much as Tam is left to negotiate everyday life in his rapidly changing city (see also Clandfield and Lloyd 2002). Torrington's emphasis on Tam's tactical, ground-level use of the city also confirms Michel de Certeau's view of the town-planner as a culpable and even slightly ridiculous 'voyeur-God', whose model of a city – seen from above as a fully knowable space – must inevitably be severely flawed (Certeau 1984: 93)

Like Torrington, in *Our Fathers* O'Hagan uses the techniques of literary modernism, including disorienting shifts in time and point-of-view, to critique the assumptions of architectural modernism. However, O'Hagan's main method is quite distinctively different from Torrington's: most of *Our Fathers* is composed of sentences that are structurally simple and often fragmented, yet cumulatively imposing in their resonance. The resulting poetic qualities help the novel register not only the shortcomings of Scotland's recent redevelopment schemes, but also the genuine aspirations and ideals that helped inspire them in the first place. Thus, *Our Fathers* ultimately not so much demolishes as eulogises modernist ideals of housing. The novel focuses on the careers of Hugh Bawn, a city councillor in postwar Glasgow, and Jamie Bawn, O'Hagan's narrator, who is Hugh's prodigal grandson. Hugh has believed fervently in architectural design as a means of social re-engineering, yet missionary zeal mixed with a loss of perspective caused by his initial success has led him to compromise on his building standards and ethics in a bid to produce as many new homes as possible. The present tense of the novel finds Jamie returning to Scotland as the discredited Hugh is dying slowly in the high-rise flat where, in stubborn adherence to his own principles, he lives with his wife. In reaction partly to Hugh's excesses, Jamie has abandoned Glasgow (for Liverpool) and dismissed Hugh's ideals: he has become a demolition engineer and indeed is advising on the 'blowing-down' of one of Hugh's pet projects, 'a block in the Gorbals, at Florence Square' (O'Hagan 1999: 189), which looks like the novel's version of Queen Elizabeth Square. Gradually, Jamie grows determined to make his peace with Hugh as well as Scotland's recent architectural past. First, though, he offers a detailed diagnosis of the flaws of Hugh's Corbusian modernism:

> [Hugh] would draw on the great cities of the world as examples. This disaster zone in Helsinki. That excellent housing estate in Madrid. The example of Brooklyn, the model of Denver. 'As illustrated by the northern suburbs of Tokyo.' In his high-housing days, he would mention these places as if they were theories, to be deemed useful, or else rejected. (O'Hagan 1999: 148)

According to *Our Fathers*, too theoretically high and ambitious a perspective results in a hyperopic inability to see places and people in their small, quotidian individuality.

Rather than attacking town-planning theory in general, O'Hagan's evocation of Hugh's presumptuous views appears to contain a critique of architectural theorising which, like that of Le Corbusier and his followers, aspires too hastily to bring about a perfect translation of idealised virtual space into the built world of three-dimensional human reality. In what follows we will read O'Hagan's account of the legacies of Glasgow's tower-blocks alongside Gaston Bachelard's influential *The Poetics of Space* (1958), which provides an in-depth theory of houses, homes, and the role of poetic language in making such 'intimate places' legible.

In an effort 'to determine the human value of the sorts of space . . . that may be defended against adverse forces' Bachelard coins the term *topophilia* (Bachelard 1994: xxxv). Due to its stark lack of such defensible space capable of accommodating human individuality, Corbusian housing could be described as blatantly 'topophobic'. Yet O'Hagan moves beyond such a critique to show that even modernist flats can have homely qualities. According to Bachelard, not only is it impossible for 'space that has been seized on by the imagination [to] remain indifferent space subject to the measures and estimates of the surveyor', but 'an entire past comes to dwell in a new house' (Bachelard 1994: xxxvi, 5). This formulation corresponds with the apparent change in Jamie's view of his family and their past, culminating in his realisation that he has believed wrongly 'that only old houses could be haunted' (O'Hagan 1999: 255). Contemplating Hugh's Gorbals block in the moment of its demolition, Jamie reflects upon the event's more subtly private implications:

> All those sitting rooms and painted walls, gone in an instant, as if the hours that passed inside meant nothing much, as if they never happened. The shape of those rooms will always remain in the minds of those who lived there. People will grow up with a memory of their high view over Glasgow . . . The thought of the rooms will bring back conversations, the theme-tunes of television shows; they'll remind them of parties and arguments and pain. And above all that they will bring back innocence: a memory of the day-to-day; a time when the rooms felt modern and good, when no one imagined their obliteration. (O'Hagan 1999: 200)

Despite the given evidence of Bachelard's alleged 'rejection of urban contemporaneity' and the 'geometric cube' of modern architecture (Vidler 1992: 65), Jamie's thoughts clearly resonate with the theorist's evocation of the psychic repercussions of more traditional kinds of home-space. 'Even when we no longer have a garret, when the attic room is lost and gone', Bachelard writes, 'there remains the fact that we once loved a garret, once lived in an attic' (Bachelard 1994: 10). In showing that topophilia occurs, and can find a home, even in modernist spaces, O'Hagan renders his critique of the shortcomings of modernist redevelopment more poignantly true to life. *Our Fathers* gently insists that even 'once-modern houses' (O'Hagan 1999: 56), as well as the recent past they metonymise, must still be reckoned with as Scotland moves through the reconstructions of the present. 'I wanted my own day, but not at the expense of every day that preceded my own', Jamie decides at Hugh's bedside (O'Hagan 1999: 227). Significantly, after Hugh's death, Jamie also initiates a reconciliation with his father, who is struggling to recover from the violent alcoholism that has estranged him from his family (O'Hagan 1999: 281). In suggesting that what needs to be overcome and cleared away in Scotland may be not only the errors of the recent past, but also any excessive reaction against that past, *Our Fathers* exemplifies the kind of forward-looking and provisionally optimistic work that has been called paradigmatic of contemporary Scottish fiction. Thus, Douglas Gifford, Sarah Dunnigan and Alan MacGillivray count *Our Fathers* among a group of recent novels that illustrate 'the predominant theme of current Scottish writing, that of the emergence from a traumatised personal – and modern Scottish – past' (Gifford et al. 2002: 960).

Yet there are other, more daunting fictions problematising the prospect of Scotland's renovation. Both Rose and Rankin have not only addressed the practical and material problems of Scotland's built legacy; in recent works, whose generic and stylistic divergence makes their similarities all the more noteworthy, they have conjured perspectives in the light of which unhomeliness appears to be not just a matter of bad design and the nation continues to exude the air of a haunted house. *Pest Maiden*, Rose's first novel, unfolds from a multifaceted crisis in the life of an Edinburgh man, Russell Fairley. Its title alludes both to his estranged girlfriend, Arlene, who is trying to force Fairley out of their flat so that she can renovate and sell it, and to an ancient plague-bringing figure, which may be haunting the redeveloped cellar where Arlene runs a trendy restaurant. Suggesting that redevelopment is likely to resuscitate past trauma, this figure haunts Russell's dreams: '*Here I have always been, waiting in the dark. My time has come again*' (Rose 1999: 66). Several of Rankin's Inspector Rebus novels draw up comparable analogies. For example, centred on the renovation of Edinburgh's Queensberry House for the new Scottish Parliament, *Set in Darkness* (2000) concerns the discovery of a skeleton, which leads to the exposure of a network of criminal activities taking advantage of the disorder associated with political and architectural change. At the same time as it occurs to Rebus that 'the city was changing for the worse, and no amount of imaginative construction in glass and concrete could hide the fact' (Rankin 2000: 331), Rebus's nemesis, the canny gangster 'Big Ger' Cafferty, is optimistic about prospering in post-devolution times. In *Fleshmarket Close* (2004), another Rebus novel, the skeletons discovered in the cellar of a bar prove to have been planted there, and the action – inspired, so the author's acknowledgements suggest, by real events – is focused more crucially on the plight of criminally exploited refugees living illegally on an Edinburgh housing estate. This is 'Knoxland', whose towers are memorably described as 'reaching skywards with all the subtlety of single-digit salutes' (Rankin 2004: 4). As the novel suggests, Scotland's problems with its Knoxlands must now be seen and tackled within a global context, and Scotland's renovation therefore cannot take place in isolation from political and ideological redevelopment elsewhere.

In *The Architectural Uncanny* Vidler suggests that it is not buildings *per se* that are inherently unhomely, but the qualities with which they are imbued by particular political climates and social functions. 'Estrangement and unhomeliness have emerged as the intellectual watchwords of our century, given periodic material and political force by the resurgence of homelessness itself', Vidler writes, 'a homelessness generated sometimes by war, sometimes by the unequal distribution of wealth.' Vidler leavens his theorising with comments on the ongoing material scandal of actual homelessness in wealthy societies, which he sees as indicative of the uncanny persistence of 'questions that have stubbornly refused solutions in politics as in design and that still seem pertinent to our late twentieth-century [or early twenty-first-century] condition' (Vidler 1992: 9, 13). The contemporary importance of the unhomely in a broader intellectual context is also signalled by Jacques Derrida's 'spectre', the figure that emerges from the past to make a claim on the present. In Derridean terms, the insurrection against the Parisian authorities by the socially excluded groups of the *banlieue* in November 2005 was a spectral action, manifesting the likelihood that this issue would powerfully recur throughout, and come to haunt, the twenty-first century. Vidler's and Derrida's theorisings resonate strongly with Rose's and Rankin's examinations of unhomeliness, demonstrating that what the latter conjure in their fictions is not just a Scottish problem but in fact identifies their work, in however unsettling a way, as truly international in both outlook and topicality.

International contexts are also invoked in Rose's 'Out of Touch' (2000), which casts the cold eye of its anonymous first-person narrator on various Scottish developments currently 'in progress', including the efforts of the heritage industry to reinvent 'more or less any old pile of stones' as a tourist destination (Rose 2000: 188). The story's implication is that, no matter how boldly they may attempt to push into the future, both physical and ideological attempts to reconstruct Scotland are inevitably haunted by residues of the past:

> When it comes to nations, there is no such thing as new, only the old with a face-lift and slathers of make-up to mask the ravages of history, geography, economics, religion and so on. Like a bygone star whose public appearances are limited by how long the pan-stick will stay in place and cover the surgeon's scars, this revived, renovated nation poses for the world's press holding a tense, slightly startled smile. (Rose 2000: 188)

Our final example of redevelopment fiction is taken from the work of Ali Smith, a Scottish writer whose English residence and characteristic avoidance of explicitly Scottish settings may already signal her international outlook and disposition. Unusually, for Smith, set in either Edinburgh or Glasgow, her short story 'Gothic' (2001) uses the first-person narrative of an obtusely self-absorbed bookstore employee to voice a hauntingly suggestive account of the literal as well as figurative place of literature in the contemporary world. From her managerial position in a new chain bookstore, the narrator looks back to the mid-1990s and her previous post as a clerk in a Gothic building that had been a bookshop for hundreds of years, where she encountered an array of troublesome customers. However, even the most sinister of these – a man touting revisionist, Nazi-sympathising accounts of World War II – seems to have made no more impression upon her than other much less malignant figures. Indeed, her new position appears to have awakened in her authoritarian instincts of her own, as she expresses pride in her power to police the new store, with its armchairs left 'as company policy suggests . . . in open positions so people won't be comfortable in them for too long' (Smith 2001: 21). The story implicitly challenges any easy equation of renovation or redevelopment with social or political progress, suggesting that iniquitous forces can find accommodation in new styles of architecture as readily as in more traditional haunts. Smith points to a daunting kind of cultural devolution, in which literature is at risk of becoming so purely itself – so discretely housed – that it becomes complicit in an apolitical amnesia which sees all cultural products simply as commodities. Smith's story finds an echo in *Fleshmarket Close*, in which Rebus reflects uneasily on changes in the area around Edinburgh's George IV Bridge, whose 'weird bookshops' have been replaced by 'Subway and Starbucks' (Rankin 2004: 377).

Whereas devolutionary Scottish fiction was at least in part the displaced expression of a frustrated nationalist movement, recent fiction reverberates with cautious scepticism regarding the dangers of yielding to a facile post-devolution utopianism. Rather than cultivating pathos or disaffection, the works discussed in this chapter acknowledge the inevitability of redevelopment and insist that literature can help map and guide the process of renovation, as well as challenge any grandiose, ideologically motivated attempts to channel and dictate its course.

Chapter 15

Concepts of Corruption:
Crime Fiction and the Scottish 'State'

Gill Plain

Crime writing has been a vibrant dimension of Scottish literary culture since the 1980s, when a range of writers adopted the genre as a means of exploring systemic rather than individual criminality. The alienated figure of the detective was a trope well suited to the articulation of opposition to Thatcherism, and from these polemical roots crime fiction developed into an ideal formula for investigating the state of Scotland. Writers such as Christopher Brookmyre, William McIlvanney and Ian Rankin constructed fictions that exposed the harsh realities of urban Scotland, examining the disenfranchisement of both individual and nation. In the 1990s new voices emerged to critical and popular acclaim: Manda Scott's *Hen's Teeth* was shortlisted for the 1997 Orange prize, while two disturbing dystopias, Paul Johnston's *Body Politic* and Denise Mina's *Garnethill*, won the Best First Crime Novel of the Year Award in 1997 and 1998 respectively. But as these bleak visions were striking chords with the crime-fiction market, a new spirit of optimism was taking hold of Scottish politics. This chapter will consider the impact of devolution on Scottish crime writing and ask whether governmental change has brought about a shift in national self-perception and a movement away from the oppositional politics of anti-Conservatism. How does the fiction of a devolved Scotland occupy its new centrality? Has Holyrood replaced Westminster as the *éminence grise* behind the crimes of social injustice? Or have writers turned away from the political towards a more introspective examination of crime? Crime fiction as a genre feeds upon concepts of corruption: to what extent, then, might a thriving national crime fiction find itself at odds with twenty-first-century visions of a brave new Scotland?

As I have argued elsewhere, Scottish crime fiction emerges from a hybrid tradition that owes more to American than English popular culture (see Plain 2003). From the existential isolation of McIlvanney's Laidlaw to Rankin's introspective, anti-establishment Rebus, Scottish crime fiction has adopted and adapted the hard-boiled private investigator of modernist American legend while also, of course, drawing upon an indigenous tradition of Scottish urban working-class fiction. When Raymond Chandler praised the 'revolutionary debunking of both the language and material of fiction' that he found in the writing of Dashiell Hammett (Chandler 1950: 194), he was seeking to distinguish the vibrant vernacular voice of America from the staid and conservative voice of the coloniser – a voice embodied by the traditions of 'classical' detective fiction. Set against cosy 'English' narratives, indelibly tarnished by association with women writers such as Agatha Christie and Dorothy Sayers, hard-boiled detective fiction represents an assertion of both masculinity and national identity: it constitutes a manifestation of the frontier spirit in the modern age, and its detectives are hard-edged but honourable, tough-talking, blue-collar figures uncorrupted by power and intractably opposed to the decadent forces of wealth. This is the fiction of identities forged in opposition, and its legacy offered an ideal template for the fiction of pre-devolution Scotland.

Scottish crime fiction, then, has had a clearly defined oppositional identity, but it is also shaped by a wider Scottish literary tradition. From James Hogg's *Private Memoirs and Confessions of a Justified Sinner* (1824) to R. L. Stevenson's *The Strange Case of Dr Jekyll and Mr Hyde* (1886) to Muriel Spark's *The Prime of Miss Jean Brodie* (1961), Scotland has produced a rich literature of duality, deceit, repression and hypocrisy. The recurrence of these themes is significant. As Michael Gardiner suggests, literature enables the writing of a national consciousness silenced by the absence of constitutional specification, and his first example in support of this thesis is *Dr Jekyll and Mr Hyde*: 'the story most often associated with Scots' split personality, their "strandedness" between nation and state' (Gardiner 2004a: 131–2). Through fiction, the inarticulable resentments of a stateless nation find form and expression, and this symbiotic relationship between text and context is equally manifest in crime fiction. Furthermore, Scottish crime writing draws extensively upon its literary forebears: nearly every self-respecting crime novel carries an obligatory reference to Stevenson or his seminal novel. These references are often satiric, challenging the increasing commodification of the past and the branding of Scotland. In Johnston's imagined future, for example, the Usher Hall has been renamed Stevenson Hall, and tourists watch the daily public hanging of Deacon Brodie before being encouraged to 'pick up a souvenir edition' of *Dr Jekyll and Mr Hyde* (Johnston 1997: 7). Louise Welsh also uses Stevenson as a shorthand for duality in her successful debut novel *The Cutting Room* (2002), offering a pair of brothers called John and Steenie Stevenson, one of whom is a pornographer and the other an evangelical Christian. She also adopts 'Gilmartin' – Hogg's seductive, chimerical demon – as her name for the simulacrum of Scottishness that is a renovated working-man's pub packed with hideously mismatched antiques (Welsh 2002: 133–5).

The haunting of Scottish crime fiction by the ghost of *Dr Jekyll and Mr Hyde* thus continues into the twenty-first century, suggesting its ongoing relevance as a trope of national identity. However, beyond the pervasiveness of dualism, what can crime fiction tell us about Scotland on the verge of devolution? A snapshot of 1997 reveals a range of anti-establishment fictions focusing on the margins, on misfits and outsiders drawn into situations beyond their control. Johnston's and Mina's dystopian novels are typical of this pattern. Johnston's *Body Politic* is the first of a series of novels set in the world of 'Enlightenment' Edinburgh, an autonomous city-state founded after the UK's collapse into anarchy. His novels explicitly set the utopian impulse of a 'new' society against the sordid reality of political survival. As one of the city's original 'Guardians' observes, 'once we were in power, people's priorities changed' (Johnston 1997: 89), and after eighteen years of Tory rule, it is hard not to see the novel as a warning to New Labour. Power corrupts, and it is no surprise to investigator Quintillian Dalrymple that his attempts to investigate a series of brutal murders are compromised by spin, 'commercial considerations' and the vital imperative of attracting tourists to the city.

Mina's *Garnethill* trilogy, by contrast, offers a more mundane contemporary dystopia in its depiction of poverty and social deprivation. Hers is a world in which those systems central to a healthy body politic – the law, medicine, social services – have broken down or been withdrawn, leaving the individual to negotiate a corrupt society as best they can. Mina's detective, Maureen O'Donnell, is as much concerned with preserving her own sanity as with investigating crime; indeed, so far is she from traditional conceptions of the truth-bearing detective figure that she ends *Garnethill* accused of 'false memory' by her abusive family. This unreliable agent variously occupies the textual space of investigator, victim and criminal, blurring the traditional boundaries of crime fiction, and this ethical instability is typical of the devolutionary moment. By 1997, even the police, as incarnated by Rankin's Rebus, seem to have become 'outsiders', non-conformists struggling against a higher authority repeatedly revealed as both corrupt and corrupting. Rankin's *Black and Blue* (1997) is, arguably, the exemplary crime text of this time. Literally and metaphorically massive, the novel takes its dubious police hero on a tour of the nation, from the housing estates of Glasgow and Edinburgh to the oil-rich heart of Aberdeen and the bleak frontier of the Shetlands. Over the course of his grand tour, Rebus investigates not just the present but also the past, looking into the histories of corruption, betrayal and violence upon which contemporary Scotland is built. The past contaminates the present, leading the detective to be read as a suspect by those who do not recognise that his obsession with the victims of crime is not a sign of guilt but rather a sentimental masochism articulating the impotence of the individual in the face of evil and indifference (see Plain 2002).

In 1997, then, the 'state' of the nation left much to be desired and Scotland voted for change, investing in a devolutionary ideal that enfranchised at least some of the voices silenced by the unwieldy state of Britishness. Devolution is, in theory at least, a utopian concept, speaking to an ideal of self-determination and healthy governance that responds to the needs of the nation rather than the demands of a distant colonial power. By contrast, hard-boiled crime fiction is, characteristically, not utopian. Indeed, it is generally actively dystopian in its depiction of an alienated modernity permeated with greed and violence, overseen by corrupt and contaminating institutions. This disjuncture between fictional form and political ideal gives rise not so much to the question of what is post-devolution crime fiction as to whether such a concept is at all possible. Writing in the wake of two reports identifying Scotland as the 'most violent place in the developed world', Irvine Welsh asks:

> What is going on here? It's almost as if the Glasgow City of Culture reinvention and Edinburgh's continued status as international festival city are a mirage and nothing substantial has happened since the 70s when Scotland and Finland regularly went head-to-head on the major indicators of social instability: murder, suicide and alcoholism. (Welsh 2005: 10)

Welsh comes to a grim conclusion which echoes the imagined future of Johnston's Edinburgh dystopias, asserting that 'social problems have been removed from the city centre to the peripheries, out of sight and out of mind of tourists and professionals' (Welsh 2005: 10). In Johnston's world, too, the centre of Edinburgh is closed to its citizens and reserved for the international tourist who keeps the city's economy afloat. However, the problems shaping Welsh's Scotland are not confined to economics; rather they are rooted in a structural malaise pervading both concepts of nation and fictions of crime.

As Welsh's portrait of urban Scotland suggests, the crisis affecting the community is a masculine one. Opening with a funeral – a family mourning 'another youth who went to town and didn't come back' (Welsh 2005: 8) – in Welsh's article, 'young people' and 'Scots' are synonymous with men. The world he describes, offering a career trajectory of drink, drugs, violence, prison and hardened criminality, is a male world, reminding us that Scotland, like most nations, is constructed and understood through reference to masculinity. As Berthold Schoene observes, nationalism is 'a profoundly gendered discourse that interpellates men as "insiders" while at the same time excluding and quite literally alienating women' (Schoene 2002: 83–4). It is the Scottish male who stands as the defining feature in the landscape of Scottish identity – an association which crime fiction has done little to undermine. The hard-boiled American tradition, so valuable for the articulation of opposition to a corrupt and decadent centre, carries its own dark legacy of misogyny, racism and homophobia. The literary-political coalition between the tough-guy detective and the Scottish hard man is ultimately a limiting and destructive one, constructing Scottish masculinities as inevitably alienated, inarticulate and violent. In examining crime fiction's response to the changing 'state' of Scotland, then, we must also ask whether crime fiction can rewrite its own tropes and imagine alternatives to masculine modes of investigation.

Three distinct trends can be discerned in the output of Scottish crime writers since 1997. The first is the delineation of continuity rather than change. For Rankin in particular, devolution has meant business as usual: *Set in Darkness* (2000), his first clearly post-devolution novel, features a murdered MSP and a long-buried skeleton in Queensbury House, part of the New Parliament building site. As if this were not enough, the novel ends with the triumphant return of 'Big Ger' Cafferty, once again 'in charge of *his* Edinburgh' (Rankin 2000: 414), and a horrific vision of the new democracy's foundations: 'The Old Town: the building works around Holyrood – Queensbury House, Dynamic Earth, *Scotsman* offices . . . hotels and apartments. So many building sites. Lots of good, deep holes, filling with concrete' (Rankin 2000: 413). The second option for Scottish crime writers is a social or geographical shift away from urban Scotland and its characteristic problems. *Sanctum* (2002), Mina's first stand-alone novel after the *Garnethill* trilogy, is set in Scotland, but the location of the action has little bearing on what is essentially a masterly exercise in unreliable narration. Mina's taut psychological examination of self-deception and duplicity may have resonances with Scotland's familiar literary concerns, but in its claustrophobic domestic focus, it displaces the political for an examination of middle-class masculinity. A similar transformation has overtaken Johnston's work: after five novels featuring Quintillian Dalrymple (including an investigation in the much-feared democratic city-state of Glasgow), he produced *A Deeper Shade of Blue* (2002), in which the Edinburgh of the future is replaced by contemporary Athens and the corrupt microcosm of a small Greek island. The hero is Alex Mavros, a private investigator whose Greek-Scottish heritage works to throw the construction of both national identities into relief. Inevitably, the novel reveals paradise to be rotten to the core, but by transporting his fiction to Greece and focusing on Mavros's unresolved mourning for his missing older brother, Johnston – like Mina – has moved away from the writing of a national consciousness characteristic of the 1990s.

The third option adopted by twenty-first-century Scottish crime writing is a generic shift to a more optimistic model of crime writing, which has been the strategy of Alexander McCall Smith, whose books now dominate the high-street book chains as Rankin's did in the late 1990s. McCall Smith writes in the classical mode, utilising aspects of the clue-puzzle formula so vehemently rejected by Chandler. This model of crime fiction, previously little seen in Scottish writing, can arguably be defined as one that preserves the integrity of society and respects its structures of authority. The suspects inhabit a relatively small or enclosed community disrupted by a criminal act. The detective outsider, a detached, specialist figure, reads the community, identifies the criminal and restores society to health and happiness. This is the mode of writing perfected by Agatha Christie, whose all-seeing spinster sleuth Miss Marple is clearly the template for McCall Smith's Precious Ramotswe and Isabel Dalhousie. Miss Marple was set apart from her fellows by her remarkable capacity to read human nature, a talent that enabled her to suggest that essential types reappeared the world over and that these types were inherently predisposed to certain behaviours. In adopting Miss Marple as his model, McCall Smith displaces the hard man from his customary centrality and constructs a significantly different ideological framework for detection. But what conclusions can be drawn from these trends? In the following I will consider both the ongoing success of Rankin's Rebus novels and the unexpected triumph of McCall Smith's Precious Ramotswe. Does the remarkable success of *The No. 1 Ladies' Detective Agency* (1998) and its many sequels suggest that neither contemporary writers nor readers want to look too closely at the state of the nation? Or are these fictions deceptive in their geographical displacement of the state, constructing their politics through parables of community rather than the exposure of corruption?

Above I asked whether, in response to the changing 'state' of Scotland, crime fiction might be able to rewrite its own tropes by imagining alternatives to masculine modes of investigation. The recent developments in Rankin's fiction suggest an awareness of this need, made evident through two related strategies: the breakdown of the male detective (already well under way by 1997) and the development of a new female detective figure, Siobhan Clarke. The Rebus of *Set in Darkness* is a far less conflicted, guilt-ridden and self-destructive figure than he was in the novels of the late 1990s. Although he remains an introspective outsider, slowly drinking and eating himself to an early death, the extreme crisis of masculinity that characterised his struggles in *Black and Blue*, if not entirely over, has at least abated. Rankin has taken a step back from the personal traumas he chose to inflict upon his character and relented in his exposure of the emotional inadequacy of Scottish masculinity. There have also been changes in the patterns of detection: in *Black and Blue* everything was focalised through Rebus or the serial killer Bible John whereas, since *Set in Darkness*, Rankin has increasingly made use of a range of perspectives. Rankin now also introduces his readership to a world of new technologies and global networking, a world wholly alien to the corporeal authority of both traditional masculinity and the traditional detective. This redundancy is most fully examined in *Resurrection Men* (2001), in which the hard-man detective is entirely superfluous to requirements. Seemingly disgraced, Rebus is one of a group of men sent back to the schoolroom to learn the rules of 'modern' policing. Consigned to the police college, the men perform their tough-guy roles in a safely contained environment that verges on the parodic in its testosterone-fuelled posturing. Rebus is ultimately elevated above his dinosaur colleagues, but not sufficiently to align him with the modern police service. By *Fleshmarket Close* (2004) his 'stateless' condition has been made explicit: without a desk or any clearly defined remit, Rebus has become a marginalised figure haunting the investigations of his colleagues. Yet, conversely, his outsider status is also liberating, leaving him free to see beyond the limited horizons of the other detectives. Rebus, then, has become a mobile, disruptive and creative force, improbably feminine in his distance from the officially sanctioned masculinities of the twenty-first century.

The most significant transition in Rankin's fiction, however, has been the creation of Siobhan Clarke, who is posited as the inheritor of whatever legacy it is that Rebus can offer, a legacy read in wholly positive terms by Duncan Petrie, who argues that the companionate relationship between Rebus and Clarke 'erases the gulf between the professional and domestic spheres that Rebus, like many other fictional policemen, has conspicuously failed to reconcile' (Petrie 2004: 158). In addition, Clarke also epitomises a political reconciliation: given the inclusive aims of the Scottish Parliament, it seems singularly appropriate that an English policewoman should gradually replace the homegrown hard man at the heart of a series of novels about contemporary Scotland. However, what are the conditions of Clarke's rise to prominence? Does this transition create a viable detective double act, combining old and new modes of detection with old and new embodiments of the Scottish nation?

Certainly, Rankin is ambivalent about Rebus as a post-devolution crime fighter, and in recent novels he has often been dispatched to examine historic cases, crimes that are in some way or another outside the temporal or physical space of contemporary Scotland. Clarke, by contrast, has evolved into a curious version of the double agent, carrying the legacy of Rebus's hard-boiled integrity into a 'new' world which she can, and does, read effectively. Similarly, her status as an adoptive Scot disrupts the limited and potentially dangerous concept of an 'authentic' national identity by problematising the traditional linkage of man and nation and by imagining the possibility of fluid and diverse national identities. But this potential enfranchisement remains undermined by the persistent handicap of gender, which remorselessly renders her 'other' within the obstinately patriarchal structure of the police force. In order to survive, Clarke must become a shapeshifter: 'She'd been a bit of a mimic even at school and college, knowing she did it so she'd fit in with whoever she was talking to, whichever peer group. Used to be she could hear herself switching, but not now' (Rankin 2000: 118–19). To speak of fluid identities is to open up a space that challenges the notionally fixed bourgeois subject; however, it remains doubtful whether mutability is a viable long-term option for the female detective. The empowering image of the double agent can equally be regarded as a no-win situation, a crisis most starkly exposed in *Resurrection Men*, where Clarke's indeterminacy suggests that, rather than opening up a new detective space, she is being offered a choice between two modes of masculine identification. Beginning the novel by aspiring to the institutional authority embodied by DCI Gill Templer, she ends it in the counsellor's office, contemplating her status as an outsider. Her mentors – Templer or Rebus – represent a choice between the New Labour vision of a modern service economy and the historic, but still potent, legacy of urban working-class Scotland. For women working in a patriarchal institution, it seems that any truly 'new' mode of subjectivity remains impossible.

Rankin, then, seems pessimistic about imagining alternative modes of investigation, suggesting that women's entry into patriarchal structures can only end in corruption or marginalisation. Is he any more optimistic about the 'state' of twenty-first-century Scotland? In *Fleshmarket Close*, focusing on the twin horrors of the aptly named 'Whitemire' detention centre and the 'Knoxland' housing scheme, Rankin depicts an 'aging country dispatching its talents to the four corners of the globe . . . unwelcoming to visitor and migrant alike' (Rankin 2004: 170). Although the novel remains concerned with the power of a faceless political establishment, there is a greater focus here on the complicity of the nation *per se*. What Rebus sees is an ignorant, white, racist society in which old hatreds are exploited to new ends. Knoxland is at the heart of this civic failure, but events at the dying West Lothian village of Banehall perhaps provide even greater insight into Rankin's fears for the 'state' of the nation. The villagers' belief in the value of Whitemire prison and their resentment of the immigration debate disguise a deeper 'national' dislocation. Concentrating their anger on the incomers, the residents of Banehall unwittingly service and support the less tangible invasion of global capital: Whitemire is run by an American company portrayed as making profit out of poverty and pain. Forced by the collapse of traditional Scottish economies to welcome the prison in their midst, the inhabitants of Banehall risk becoming victims of colonisation. Ethically compromised by economic need, they are incapable of empathy or hospitality. Theirs is not a convivial or open society, but one built on envy, deprivation, need and despair.

As suggested above, in order for the utopian ideal of devolution to find a suitable reflection in crime fiction, a shift to a different generic model is required, and the fiction of Alexander McCall Smith provides exactly such a shift. Closer to Christie than Chandler, McCall Smith's work has revitalised the conservative structures of classical detective fiction, making an unlikely bestselling icon out of a middle-aged Botswanan woman. The phenomenal success of *The No 1. Ladies' Detective Agency* and its sequels hints at a broad readership keen to escape from parochial Scottish concerns, but does this fictional displacement also suggest that all in the national garden is rosy, or might it represent yet another mode of articulating disaffection with the Scottish 'state'?

Fictions implementing the classical detective formula usually end with a restoration of communal order; however, prior to this the narrative demands that every character become a plausible suspect. Typically, the detective's investigation will reveal anti-social desires and violent impulses to be the norm, exposing the society that is eventually preserved as both corrupt and hypocritical. While aspects of McCall Smith's work are clearly shaped by this generic 'Golden Age' template, there are also significant differences providing insight into the relationship between text and national context. What McCall Smith shares with writers such as Christie is a specific methodology of detection: both Precious Ramotswe and Miss Marple detect through close observation and an understanding of human nature. Beyond this, however, McCall Smith does not concern himself with the elaborate plotting typical of Christie's oeuvre; indeed, he is not writing ratiocinative detective fiction at all. The Mma Ramotswe novels are closer to interwoven short stories, parables and vignettes that serve a moral or character-development purpose within the series. Furthermore, McCall Smith seems determined not to reveal the community as corrupt. Although assistant detective Mma Makutsi rails against the idle apprentices and Mme Ramotswe bemoans the decline of the 'old Botswana morality', the novels repeatedly reveal unexpected goodness and the ongoing strength of communal values, offering the reader a degree of emotional investment notably absent from the classical model. The central characters are not clinically detached from their investigations and frequently have problems of their own. Where the two models reunite is in the resolution of these problems: just as Christie's fiction would habitually end with a symbolic marriage, so McCall Smith's conclude with what Muriel Spark might have termed 'the transfiguration of the commonplace' (Spark 1961: 35). As Mma Ramotswe concludes in *The Kalahari Typing School for Men*, 'it was astonishing how life had a way of working out, even when everything looked so complicated and unpromising' (McCall Smith 2002: 201).

At the level of narrative structure, then, McCall Smith's novels seem designed for reassurance, and yet the sheer extent of their commentary on government and community inevitably invites an allegorical reading. One is left in no doubt as to the virtues of an independent Botswana functioning as part of the British Commonwealth. Each book contains a paean to Sir Seretse Khama, the country's first president, while *The Full Cupboard of Life* includes Mma Ramotswe's tribute to Queen Elizabeth II, who has 'been on duty for fifty years' (McCall Smith 2003: 199). The general approval of Botswanan government is accompanied by a celebration of the cultural specificity of this small nation, reiterated in comments on morality, education and the value of the Setswana language, and rooted in a valorisation of the local and a fundamental resistance to economic globalisation. Advances in technology are seldom seen to benefit the ordinary citizen: for example, Botswana's finest mechanic, Mr J. L. B. Matekoni, imagines writing to Japan to complain about the overcomplexity of modern car manufacture, protesting that 'they are trying to make cars into space ships . . . we do not need space ships here in Botswana. We need good cars with engines that do not mind the dust' (McCall Smith 2004b: 244). Similarly, Mma Ramotswe, on visiting her home village, concludes that in 'that world, nobody needed to be a stranger; everybody could be linked in some way with others, even a visitor; for visitors came for a reason, did they not? . . . There was a place for everybody' (McCall Smith 2003: 27). McCall Smith's Africa is an exercise in nostalgia for a world in which 'people like their places' (McCall Smith 2003: 133), and in which sensible citizens take comfort and stability from a sense of living in a 'knowable' world. By contrast, those who move away from family and community are revealed to be shallow, misguided, or led astray by the lure of modernity.

There is a tension here between the celebration of nationhood and a resistance to the modernity that the nation-state itself represents. The antipathy towards large-scale government evident in the valorisation of village life is a constant of the series, suggesting discomfort with a contemporary world infected by the disturbing attributes of postmodernity: fluidity, flux and the absence of boundaries. To set against this, McCall Smith offers a return to 'common sense' and a communal fantasy that challenges the obliteration of local cultures and the increasing anonymity of global networks. That he might imagine this knowable, tangible world also to be a Scottish one is evident from his more recent Isabel Dalhousie novels. Isabel, who first appears in *The Sunday Philosophy Club* (2004), is the editor of the *Review of Applied Ethics*. She has a horror of relativism and a respect for good manners that would earn her the respect of Precious Ramotswe. Her belief that 'international law . . . was simply a system of manners writ large' (McCall Smith 2004a: 158) returns us to the world of Miss Marple, where everything under the sun can be understood through reference to the microcosm of village life.

What conclusions can be drawn from this brief account of McCall Smith's writing? In terms of the politics of genre, he has certainly disrupted the established relationship between masculinity and detection. McCall Smith's fiction has no time for aggressive masculinities, preferring instead a modern mode of gentlemanliness. He has successfully resuscitated a form of crime writing customarily seen as 'feminine', both through its association with women writers and through its preference for contemplative deduction over violent confrontation and heroic action. The authority of his women detectives is private rather than official or state-sanctioned: Mma Ramotswe is a domestic detective, detached from official structures, while Isabel Dalhousie is an amateur sleuth more concerned with ethical enquiry than detective agency. As in Rankin's fiction, alternative modes of investigation can only develop outside official structures; it is one thing for Mma Ramotswe to symbolise the nation, but quite another for her investigations actually to enfranchise women within the national context. Ironically then, contemporary Scotland's two bestselling crime writers, Rankin and McCall Smith, are at once united and divided by their relation to the 'state'. A focus on government and community permeates both their fictions (even though this concern is obviously manifested in fundamentally different ways), as they cultivate female investigators to comment obliquely on societal structures and values. Both Rankin and McCall Smith valorise detective figures at odds with hegemonic masculinity and the state-sanctioned police procedural, suggesting that what nations – Scottish or otherwise – need most urgently to ensure the health of their body politic is the inquisitive spirit of self-empowered outsiders.

Yet this is where the similarities end: while Rankin works to expose the increasing complexity of the world, often leaving the guilty unpunished and suggesting that all are implicated in the failure of civic society, McCall Smith offers a fantasy of communal cohesion and simple resolution in which 'all one has to do is make a list and be reasonable'

(McCall Smith 2004a: 203). McCall Smith's celebration of the microcosmic can be seen as part of a general movement in Scottish crime writing away from the political towards the personal and the exploration of smaller, more intimate spaces. This might be seen as the logical outcome of Scotland's new 'post-British' status, in which oppositional politics have become redundant and new fault lines are yet to develop. In *Across the Margins* Glenda Norquay and Gerry Smyth suggest that marginality is a 'superannuated category' unsuitable for conceptualising the cultural and political spaces of the contemporary British archipelago (Norquay and Smyth 2002: 10). This proposition does much to explain the newly diffuse qualities of 'Scottish' crime fiction. Devolution may not have lived up entirely to expectations, but it has released Scottish writers from the centrifugal pull of anti-Conservatism and encouraged them to explore new territories of mind, body and 'state'. Yet it remains difficult to escape the metaphorical trappings of the past altogether, and Scottish crime fiction continues to dwell on duality. In Louise Welsh's words, the nation is characterised by 'petty respectability up front, intricate cruelties behind closed doors' (Welsh 2002: 2) and, in the face of this pervasive trope, it should come as no surprise that twenty-first-century Scottish readers are left to choose between McCall Smith on the one hand and Rankin on the other. They are the Jekyll and Hyde of modern Scotland – one celebrating the respectable façade of a knowable world, the other exposing what lies beneath the conformities of Calvinist repression – and their combined success is a manifestation of the bifurcated subjectivity that still resides at the heart of the Scottish 'state'.

Chapter 16

A Key to the Future: Hybridity in Contemporary Children's Fiction

Fiona McCulloch

In the relative infancy of a devolved Scotland it seems timely to demonstrate that children's fiction, far from comprising a mere afterthought within Scotland's creative psyche, plays a fundamental role in the shaping of that collectively imagined space known as Scottish literature and the culture it seeks to represent. Pivotal to this shaping are the ways in which contemporary children's fiction forges new mindscapes that transcend national insularities in order to pursue as yet uncharted geographies of a new hybrid state, and to envisage a cultural and political sphere in which the troubled growing pains of Thatcherism are surmounted at last by the curative *Bildungsroman* of devolution. As such, children's fiction constitutes a worthy part of the new literary canon of post-devolution Scotland, characterised by Angus Calder as 'empowered by acceptance of the realities of its past and ready to generate new Scotlands of the mind, and recreate itself as a land without prejudice' (Calder 2004a: xvi). Indeed, as I will argue, the 'fresh . . . beautiful prospect' of Scotland's post-devolution future (Calder 2004a: xii) manifests itself nowhere more promisingly than in the vibrant hybridity of contemporary children's fiction, produced predominantly by women writers experimenting with a feminine repositioning of society and culture outwith patriarchy's myopic coordinates of power. This link between literary hybridities and the forging of new feminine futures is the focus of Susan Friedman's *Mappings*, in which she argues for a representational shift '*beyond* gender . . . [towards] what I am calling the new geographies of identity . . . the liminal spaces in between . . . and hybrid interfusions of self and other' (Friedman 1998: 17–19). What Scottish children's literature provides is exactly such a repositioning of the 'boundaries of difference' in terms of dismantling not only unpropitious gender binarisms, but also other oppressive structures – such as race and class – which perpetuate the ghettoising of 'the Other'. Children's fiction proliferates interactive in-between spaces out of which, according to Homi Bhabha in *The Location of Culture*, new selves can emerge and nations can be fruitfully reconfigured (see Bhabha 1994).

Scotland is renowned for its tradition of fairy tales and children's fiction. The popular Scottish imagination is teeming with kelpies, brownies, bogles, witches, fairies and mermen; so, unsurprisingly, the development of children's literature in Scotland has drawn upon this richly imaginative tapestry of folklore and mystery. George MacDonald's *The Princess and the Goblin* (1872) and *The Princess and Curdie* (1882) disrupt the Victorian discourse of childhood innocence by conjuring up the 'underground' threat of malicious goblins, who mean to penetrate the upper regions of the castle and carry off the Princess. In addition, contemporaneous issues pertinent to Scottish identity were regularly rehearsed in the imaginative space of Victorian children's fiction. For example, R. M. Ballantyne's *The Coral Island* (1858) and Stevenson's *Treasure Island* (1883) engage explicitly with aspects of colonialism, suggesting that Scottish children's fiction, rather than remaining detached from mainstream culture, has consistently supplied an imaginative repository for its desires and fears (see McCulloch 2004: 47–116), and one wonders of course if this might equally apply to post-devolution writing. Recent writers of Scottish children's fiction include Julie Bertagna, Theresa Breslin, Des Dillon, Catherine Forde, Diana Hendry, Jackie Kay, Catherine MacPhail, Alison Prince and J. K. Rowling. The present chapter will consider works by Bertagna, Breslin, Kay and Rowling specifically, mainly because of their common thematic interest in ways of envisioning a millennial Scotland that looks forward by having learned its lessons from the literary and cultural past.

I will begin my enquiry with a closer look at Kay's *Strawgirl* (2002), a novel in which the thematic strands of ethnicity, childhood, ruralism and fantasy combine in a struggle to provide its 'neither here nor there' mixed-race heroine, Maybe MacPherson, with a sense of home in the Scottish Highlands. The tranquillity of Maybe's close-knit, white village community is marred by racial tensions, which make it difficult for the girl to embrace her Celtic/African self. She is simultaneously cast as mixed-race and no-race, as Scottish culture appears unable either to countenance or to reflect the image of a subjectivity that exists on its periphery, both geographically and culturally. Semi-orphaned when her Nigerian father dies in a car accident, Maybe struggles to run the family farm and support her grief-stricken mother while resisting local prejudice. The novel's representational mode gradually shifts towards fantasy, as an imaginary space opens up at harvest time through the creation of a girl made of straw, who befriends Maybe and aids her in her journey towards self-discovery. Prior to such self-acceptance, however, Maybe internalises the self-oppressive alienation imposed upon her by rural Scottish society. Thus, 'much as Maybe loved her father, she wished that he were just like everybody else so that she could be the same as everybody else too', adding that at school especially 'the coward inside her wanted to be ordinary, to blend into the background' (Kay 2002a: 21–2). Immersed in the normal and normative, Maybe grows mortified at her exotic otherness and desires either to fit the norm or to pass unseen. Desperate to rid herself of her father's difference, she fails to realise the importance of learning to be herself until his death, the trauma of which eventually induces her to embrace her hybridity.

Importantly, her self-recognition prompts her to accept Scotland as her homeland while at the same time persuading the local community to accept her: 'It seemed a whole life-time ago that Maybe had felt embarrassed or ashamed about who she was . . . She knew none of the bullies would ever bother her again' (Kay 2002a: 246–7). In order to provide Maybe with a tool to resolve her anxieties, Kay introduces the magic-realist device of Strawgirl befriending Maybe when she is at her loneliest. Entirely devoid of cultural prejudice, Strawgirl makes a perfect companion and, more importantly, as a figure of the harvest she embodies an original part of what is after all Maybe's native land. In *Strawgirl* Kay utilises the techniques of children's literature to highlight the absurdity of any culture's rigid refusal to celebrate difference: 'How could Maybe explain to Strawgirl that human beings called each other names and picked on each other because they were different?' Kay's novel never fails to reiterate the question 'why', thus encouraging her young readership to challenge both their elders and peers in a plea for cultural inclusivity and difference: 'Why would people behave like that to each other? Why would some people spit at other people, or hit them, or beat them up, or murder them because of their colour or their faith?' (Kay 2002a: 93)

Sharing the preoccupations of Kay's novel, Breslin's *Divided City* (2005) tells a story concerned with the ongoing tensions between Catholic and Protestant Glaswegians, while also addressing more immediately contemporary issues, such as the condition of asylum seekers and their hostile reception in the city. Breslin's title alludes to the literary heritage of the doppelgänger motif in Scottish fiction, suggesting that Glasgow itself harbours a divided sense of self; even the novel's dust-jacket appears designed to open up a certain schizophrenic tension between the City of Culture's nineteenth-century architectural glory, on the one hand, and its dubiously triumphant towering structures of late modernity, on the other. In this respect, Breslin's novel could be said to belong to a particular school of Scottish fiction, characterised by Douglas Gifford, Sarah Dunnigan and Alan MacGillivray as obsessively representing 'divided self and divided family within divided community and nation [featuring] central figures torn in conscience and loyalty . . . trapped in uncertainty between contending claims of conscience in politics and religion', thus giving voice to a broad spectrum of 'dualisms deeply felt and long-lasting in Scottish culture' (Gifford et al. 2002: 327–8). Albeit devoid of grotesquely Gothic figures like those that roam James Hogg's *Private Memoirs and Confessions of a Justified Sinner* (1824) or R. L. Stevenson's *The Strange Case of Dr Jekyll and Mr Hyde* (1886), Breslin's novel nevertheless captures the spectre of alterity that sits at the heart of Scotland's collective psyche.

But *Divided City* also breaks new ground in so far as it goes beyond problematising traditional dualities in order to explore Scotland's quandary as an increasingly globalised culture. In Breslin's vision Glasgow assumes as much a character of its own as any of her human cast, who meander through the 'dear green place' (Breslin 2005: 131) quite cluelessly and as if remote-controlled, often finding themselves lost within uncharted terrain riven by class and religious conflict. Thus, when middle-class Protestant Graham 'stumbled into the Garngarth . . . For a true-blue Rangers fan he was in the worst place he could be. He had entered marked-out territory. Green scarves, banners and flags were hanging from windows and railings' (Breslin 2005: 34–5). His unharmed survival depends on forging a friendship with working-class Catholic Joe. Due to a government-led initiative, which brings together the city's youth football teams, Graham and Joe meet where otherwise their lives would have remained utterly estranged. As explained in their coach's pre-match address:

> It's the day after an Orange Walk and a week after an Old Firm game. More games, more Walks coming up. Tension building in the city . . . I want you to shake one another by the hand because you are a team. Put all personal differences aside. You are a city team. From all parts of the city. (Breslin 2005: 229)

Curiously, Breslin's vision of a unified Glasgow (and, indeed, Britain) excludes girls – 'Today, all over the United Kingdom, boys are playing for their city' (Breslin 2005: 229) – quite as if to suggest only masculinity required attention in what is ultimately a bid to dismantle patriarchally motivated divisions.

In a shrewd representational move it is through the eyes of a foreigner, the Eastern European illegal asylum seeker Kyoul, that Glasgow's sublime urban beauty, which transcends national, cultural and political boundaries, manifests itself to the reader:

> He got into George Square . . . Dawn unmasked the anonymous bulk of the buildings that framed the square and revealed their elegance. The perfume from the hyacinth beds was rising with the sun. Giddy with the intense blue of the flowers, the smell of the scent, the clarity of the air, Kyoul felt a happiness that he'd not experienced for a long time. As he began to know Scotland it

reminded him of his own country. The way it had once been . . . He loved the parks: Alexandra
Park, Linn Park, Victoria Park, the Winter Gardens at the People's Palace, Hogganfield Loch,
Bellahouston, Kelvingrove, RoukenGlen. He liked the buildings too . . . red sandstone, grey
granite that picked up the clear northern light. And the people. (Breslin 2005: 130–1)

Breslin's warning is implicit, yet unequivocal: beauty like Glasgow's ought not to be taken
for granted but deserves our protection, or else it might be swept away and erased just like
Kyoul's country's.

After being seriously wounded in a knife attack by local youths, Kyoul tells Graham, who
visits him in hospital: 'I am a Muslim. In a country where it is no longer safe to be so.
Religion . . . I think there are those who will find any excuse to torture and kill' (Breslin
2005: 125). Kyoul's message can hardly fail to resonate with readers of *Divided City*, a novel
about Glasgow's own problems with religious intolerance and, as Breslin repeatedly points
out, the line between socially acceptable abuse and violent extremism is but a thin one.
Kyoul's upper-middle-class girlfriend Leanne, newly introduced to global politics by her
refugee boyfriend, in turn seeks to educate Graham, Joe and the reader. As Leanne
explains, Kyoul's home country is on 'the White List, Britain won't help him. They say
these countries are safe because their governments have officially agreed they won't perse-
cute minorities . . . People like Kyoul are treated as though they don't exist' (Breslin 2005:
67–8). But her encounter with Kyoul enables Leanne not only to view her own life politically, within a global context; moreover, inspired by the double vision created through
their relationship, she learns to see her city in a new light: just as 'the city might have overwhelmed him if he had not met her so soon after his arrival . . . he'd point out things that
she hadn't noticed about Glasgow' (Breslin 2005: 72). By communicating and allowing
themselves to benefit from each other's individual differences, Breslin's four young people
find the key to Glasgow's future and begin successfully to demolish the divisive barriers of
religion, class and ethnicity.

Both Joe and Graham embark on a journey of self-transformation, triggered by their
encounter with Kyoul and Leanne, as the boys come to privilege their mutual friendship
over sectarian bigotry. Hence, motivated by his new understanding of the value of tolerance, Joe decides that 'after yesterday he didn't see himself as the same kind of Celtic sup-
porter as [his uncle] Desmond' anymore (Breslin 2005: 134). Only a little later Graham has
a similar epiphany:

> What had begun as a minor clash of rival groups . . . had escalated into hard violence . . . an
> old man had to have stitches in his head . . . Would it never stop? . . . Religion should help
> you lead a better life . . . So how come fights happened about religion? Why couldn't they live
> side by side happily all the time? Why was there a problem with Kyoul and Leanne being
> together? Was it never going to stop? (Breslin 2005: 156)

While championing football as an ideal way of reconciling all sectors of society, Breslin
remains acutely aware that, at its worst, it can be manipulated into a formidable tool to
assert and maintain old rivalries. Poignantly, *Divided City* establishes a link between religiously motivated football hooliganism in Glasgow, on the one hand, and the larger-scale,
extremely violent manifestations of sectarian intolerance that have turned Kyoul into a
refugee, on the other. As Graham points out to Joe, Kyoul's story of torture is 'terrifying.
And – and close. That's what's most scary. This happened in central Europe. I mean, my
mum and dad have been on holiday there. It was the same as here practically . . . It was

ordinary people, like neighbours, who did that to Kyoul' (Breslin 2005: 172). Atrocities are
committed on one another by neighbours, fuelled by ideologies that permit 'ordinary
people' to behave monstrously. Most depressingly, individuals fleeing such hostilities come
face to face with the same – or very similar – prejudices elsewhere, threatening to leave
them perpetually displaced from any culture. From where he lives, Joe says he can see the
tower-blocks in which many asylum seekers have found a new temporary home, ominously
adding that 'they've had two suicides over there in the last year' (Breslin 2005: 172).
Questioning its readers' motives for keeping at an allegedly safe distance from cultural otherness, *Divided City* asserts that within our twenty-first-century world's global village we
absolutely must get within earshot of each other's stories and display a willingness to
expand our intellectual horizons beyond the exclusively local. Importantly, however, as
Graham's father reminds us, most conflict may ultimately be caused not by race or creed,
but by social deprivation: 'Glasgow has some of the most deprived areas in Britain . . .
People get desperate and angry . . . Deprivation, and all that goes with it, is what really
divides this city' (Breslin 2005: 160–1). But whatever the issues or their causes, the future
of Glasgow depends on its people – its writers and its readers, its adults and young adults –
to address and resolve them. The responsibility is a collective one or, as the boys' coach
sums it up: 'You are Glasgow City' (Breslin 2005: 230).

Remembrance, Breslin's historical novel set in World War I, equally makes a case for solidarity across traditional boundaries. As Maggie, one of her young protagonists, recognises,
'in times like this there was no difference in class or wealth or religion or race; that people
cried, and wept, and broke with sorrow – in Britain and in France, in Belgium and Russia,
and in Germany too' (Breslin 2002: 289–90). Global sectarianism and hostility have led
to violent mass extermination regardless of race, creed or class. A major concern in
Remembrance is the irrevocable loss of the world's innocence, not only symbolised by
countless young deaths but portrayed also through the experiences of characters barely out
of childhood, who must live their lives in a horrifying topsy-turvy world. As Breslin continues to stress, 'there is something quite terrible about the death of so many young
people . . . By the end of the War, more than half the army was under nineteen years old.
The old die, and we are accustomed to that . . . But the death of youth denies us what might
have come. Our present is obliterated and our future altered irrevocably' (Breslin 2002:
293–4). *Remembrance* calls for global tolerance as an antidote to conflict and war, and there
is never any doubt about Breslin's own position, unequivocally mediated through one of
her central characters: 'Personally I think that it is those who try to justify this war who
should be locked up in an insane asylum' (Breslin 2002: 292). Breslin's novel works as a
kind of cross-generational forum enabling a new generation to break the cycle of destruction by hearing, and paying heed to, the young, yet war-weary voices of their ancestors who
either fought at the front or nursed those wounded and traumatised by it. Her metaphor of
lost youth is succinctly encapsulated in the novel's epigraph, taken from Siegfried Sassoon's
'Suicide in the Trenches', depicting 'the hell where youth and laughter go'; correspondingly, at the novel's close Sassoon's 'Aftermath' asks Breslin's readers: '*Have you forgotten
yet? . . . Look up, and swear by the green of the spring that you'll never forget*' (Breslin 2002:
304). To forget, for Breslin, is to re-enact and thus become guilty of the mindless madness
of violence, which is already coldly unfolding as our own new millennium gets under way.

J. K. Rowling's *Harry Potter* series is also concerned with the issue of 'difference' and
its potentially violent consequences. A crucial concern in the novels is 'blood' and its
ideological trail of cultural discourses on normality and abnormality. By relocating to the
wizard world, Harry effectively rids himself of the abnormality label attached to him by his

foster-family, the Dursleys; however, his new home is riven by similarly divisive hierarchies. In *The Philosopher's Stone* Draco Malfoy, keen to preserve the purity of the wizards' blood line, worries whether Harry's parents were 'our kind'. As Draco explains to Harry, 'I really don't think they should let the other sort in, do you? They're just not the same, they've never been brought up to know our ways. Some of them have never even heard of Hogwarts until they get the letter, imagine. I think they should keep it in the old wizarding families' (Rowling 1997: 61). As we are aware, Harry himself has never heard of Hogwarts until he receives his letter, and his mother is a Muggle, thus failing to meet Malfoy's eugenic imperative of racial purity. In *The Chamber of Secrets* Draco's biologist obsession escalates into fierce hostility against Hermione, whose parents are both Muggles, calling her 'a filthy little Mudblood', which turns out to be a strongly derogatory term for 'someone who was Muggle-born – you know, non-magic parents' (Rowling 1998: 86, 89). Pointedly, Draco's name is reminiscent of 'Dracula', and while he does not literally prey on the blood of others, he endows blood with murderous significance.

As is true of any violent prejudice, however, Draco's hatred is ultimately not of his own making, but the result of his upbringing within a paranoid, xenophobic and caste-ridden culture. Symptomatically, his prejudice extends to a whole crowd of other marginalised groups. He refers to Hagrid, for example, who is half giant and half wizard, as 'a sort of *savage*' (Rowling 1997: 60), and Draco even rejects other pure-blood wizards on terms of their class origin. Belittling Ron Weasley because of his family's poverty, he warns Harry: 'You'll soon find out some wizarding families are much better than others, Potter. You don't want to go making friends with the wrong sort' (Rowling 1997: 81). Neville Longbottom, regarded as lacking the superior intelligence characteristic of wizards, provides yet another target, and eventually Draco ostracises the whole school-house of Gryffindor for harbouring only impure degenerates: 'You know how I think they choose people for the Gryffindor team . . . It's people they feel sorry for. See, there's Potter, who's got no parents, then there's the Weasleys, who've got no money – you should be on the team, Longbottom, you've got no brains' (Rowling 1997: 163).

Providing an in-depth and theoretically informed analysis of 'the politics of race' in Rowling's work, Suman Gupta notes that, beginning in the second novel of the series,

> there is a sudden convergence between the presentation of [Draco] Malfoy (and his family connections) and Voldemort (the Dark Side), and it has to do with prejudice against Muggle blood. What unites the Malfoys and Voldemort with the Dark Side is a certain ideological perspective, an explicitly fascist ideology that wishes to preserve the purity of Magic blood from any taint of Muggle blood. (Gupta 2003: 100–1)

Identifying Rowling's 'theme of blood as lineage [as] analogous to race in our world' (Gupta 2003: 101), Gupta sees *Harry Potter* as incorporating manifold allusions to contemporary issues, problems and world-political events, among which questions of race and ethnic difference continue to prevail. Notably Gupta's reading gains renewed significance with reference to Rowling's latest volume in the series, poignantly entitled *The Half-Blood Prince* (2005). Commenting in particular on British politics on ethnicity and race, Gupta makes reference to the murder of Stephen Lawrence (1974–93), the public hysteria surrounding the influx of asylum seekers into the country, and recent race riots in Oldham, Burnley and Bradford (Gupta 2003: 103–4).

Whilst Gupta's reading argues that Rowling engages with racial politics, other eminent critics in the field of children's literature, such as Jack Zipes and Andrew Blake, view the

Harry Potter books as simply supporting dominant ideologies. However, the wizards' apparently natural superiority over the Muggles is not without its ambiguities, given the contradictory racial impulses at work within the wizard community itself. Far from representing an ideally homogeneous culture, the wizards' world is fraught with issues of caste and other sectarian divisions, which attest to a complex internal heterogeneity, and to compound matters further, there are also many instances of 'interracial' unions between wizards and Muggles (both Harry and Voldemort are half-Muggle). Undoubtedly, wizards are far more powerful than Muggles and in many ways the former control the latter, yet their relationship remains fundamentally dialogic and is never purely dialectical.

Regarding the question of its Scottishness, Rowling's *Harry Potter* series remains of course problematically indeterminate. English by birth, Rowling resides in Edinburgh with her daughter, Scottish spouse and Scottish-born son, while also maintaining a home in London. Rowling wrote most of the first *Harry Potter* book in an Edinburgh café and has continued to write the sequels in her adopted home, but does this categorise her as a *Scottish* writer of children's fiction, and how exactly would one define this category anyway? Might it provide a clue that Hogwarts, Harry's school, is described as being located in the north of the country where, viewed from his train window, the landscape becomes increasingly wilder? Certainly, a major way in which her novels negotiate the shift between their realist and fantasy dimensions is through changes in space and landscape. Thus, Harry's journey to Hogwarts transports him from the regimented suburbia of Privet Drive's carefully tended lawns and hedges to 'woods, twisting rivers and dark green hills' (Rowling 1997: 78). Middle Britain's control of domesticated nature is escaped in a move towards the untamed hinterland of a strange Gothic landscape that reflects Harry's socially marginalised position in the Dursleys' world as well as his wizardly otherness. In an interview Rowling confesses that when she first conceived of Hogwarts School of Witchcraft and Wizardry she decided that 'logically it had to be set in a secluded place, and pretty soon I settled on Scotland in my mind', adding vaguely that 'it was in subconscious tribute to where my parents had married' (Fraser 2002: 23). Crucially, it is in Rowling's Scottish mindscape – a fantasy landscape of the feminine imaginary – that Harry's 'difference' is given a chance to unfold and develop, far removed from the Dursleys' normatively ideological policing of his magically creative and inquisitive disposition.

Envisaging the devastation wreaked by global warming, Julie Bertagna's *Exodus*, a futuristic eco-novel located in the dystopian world of a submerged Glasgow, is yet another Scottish children's fiction critical of contemporary ideologies and politics:

> In the scorching hot summers of the '30s and '40s the oceans rose faster than anyone ever expected. All the predictions had been wrong. And all the political agreements that were supposed to prevent global warming had long fallen through . . . Suddenly it was all too late. Great floods struck, all over the world . . . Governments began to collapse everywhere. Economies crashed and everything that held society together started to fall apart. (Bertagna 2002: 195)

Intent on warning against myopic, self-serving governments in a world dependent for its survival on global cooperation and ecological balance, Bertagna creates a world in which no one has learned anything from history's bitter lessons. 'New World sky cities' (Bertagna 2002: 195) have been built which suffer from the same ancient, elitist monovision, granting entrance only to those deemed suitable, while refugees are left to rot in the polluted waters beneath. One of these closed cities is New Mungo, built by a character named Caledon above the drowned ruins of Glasgow, whence it is infiltrated by Mara, Bertagna's girl heroine.

New Mungo is an artificial world whose inhabitants breathe manufactured air and eat processed food.

In a nightmarish dream vision, possibly modelled after Lanark's experiences at the Institute in Alasdair Gray's famous dystopia, *Exodus* suggests that Scotland's future can only escape from the claustrophobic confines of Caledon(ia)'s dystopia and be 'free at last' (Bertagna 2002: 335) if it manages to redefine itself as an outward-looking, hybrid world, alert rather than oblivious to its past. Only by learning from its culture's mistakes can a future generation begin to make positive progress. In Caledon's brave new waterworld, however, the past is erased as systematically as in George Orwell's Oceania in *1984* (1948): 'The past is banished. It's been deleted. All everyone ever thinks of is here and now' (Bertagna 2002: 262). Only belatedly, at Mara's intervention, are various efforts being made at 'infecting the present with the past and – with luck – changing the future' (Bertagna 2002: 284). The aim is to create a meaningful past/present/future continuum capable of remedying what Cairns Craig has designated as 'the Scottish "predicament"', which is

> the total elision of the evidence of the past and its replacement by a novelty so radical that it is impossible for the individual to relate to it his or her personal memories. And impossible, therefore, for that environment to be 'related' as a coherent narrative. The constant erasure of one Scotland by another makes Scotland unrelatable, un-narratable. (Craig 1999: 21)

The urgency of reconnecting with the past resonates throughout *Exodus*. Thus, the 'Treenesters' whom Mara befriends have renamed themselves after parts of the submerged city, such as 'Gorbals' and 'Candleriggs', to keep Glasgow's memory alive. Identified by her new friends as the saviour of Scotland, Mara is likened to Thenew, the mother of Mungo, Glasgow's patron saint. Albeit initially with considerable reluctance, she eventually comes to embrace her new iconic role, which involves both the preservation of Scotland's heritage and the forging of a new sense of nationality, the latter in particular necessitating a fundamental ideological shift from destructive-masculinist to curative-feminine values:

> Mara remembers what bothered her as she walked through the vast halls of the university . . . There were no dreamswomen. Apart from the odd mythical figure or queen, not one of the golden names had belonged to a woman. All the great dreamers had been men . . . The women might have dreamed just as hard . . . but their dreams had become all tangled up with the knit of ordinary life, with meal-making and babycare and nest-building . . . And what about her own dream? . . . A plan that just might save them all and find them a future. (Bertagna 2002: 169–70)

Bertagna's novel identifies patriarchy itself as a deleterious residual order that must be supplanted in order to envision and create a viable, genuinely different and hopeful future. However, the ultimate success of Mara's leadership relies upon her union with Fox, Caledon's progressive grandson, thus merging masculinity and femininity into a project of androgynous creativity that at once repositions and reconceptualises Scotland's dual self into a purely positive utopian force. The eventual exodus of Mara's people to the (now inhabitable) Arctic, where they intend to found a new Caledonia, signals their desire for a radical relocation of the nation beyond the rigidity of Scotland's past (now submerged) frontiers. Accordingly, the space in which Mara and Fox – 'each hold[ing] a key to the future' (Bertagna 2002: 335) – will build a new Scotland (where, unlike in New Mungo, everyone is welcome) is brimming with the pure uncharted potential of hope.

Chapter 17

Gaelic Prose Fiction in English

Michelle Macleod

Post-devolution Scotland is a precarious yet exciting era for Scottish Gaelic language and literature. With the 2001 Census recording only 58,700 Gaelic speakers in Scotland, the language, which has been spoken in Scotland for over 1,500 years, is at serious risk of extinction. At the same time, more is currently being done at governmental level to support the language. In 2005 the Scottish Executive passed the Gaelic Language Act, which established Bòrd na Gàidhlig, a new, non-departmental public body whose sole responsibility is the promotion of Gaelic. Moreover, as revealed in a public opinion poll carried out on behalf of Bòrd na Gàidhlig and the BBC, an increasing number of Scots are in favour of supporting the language: 66 per cent of the respondents agreed that Gaelic constituted an important part of Scottish life, although 87 per cent of those interviewed had absolutely no personal knowledge of the language. Given the small size of the Gaelic-speaking community, Gaelic literature in the twentieth and early twenty-first centuries has been of remarkable quality and quantity. Since the new millennium Gaelic fiction writing has enjoyed a revival, largely due to the success of the Gaelic Books Council series Ùr-Sgeul. However, at the same time as Gaelic fiction is enjoying a resurgence, some Gaelic writers are choosing also to write in English. Their work, which forms the topic of this chapter, is unmistakably placed within the Gaelic-speaking communities, and the frank insight opened up by them into the reality of closed island-community life is rare in English-language literature.

This chapter will consider two novels and one collection of short stories: *Portrona* (2000) by Norman Malcolm MacDonald (Tormod Calum Dòmhnallach), and *The Nessman* (2000) and *Visiting the Bard* (2003) by Alasdair Campbell (Alasdair Caimbeul). MacDonald and Campbell are well-established Gaelic writers, and MacDonald has previously published another novel in English, *Calum Tod* (1983). Of course, MacDonald and Campbell are not unique in writing bilingually: Iain Crichton Smith (Iain Mac a' Ghobhainn) (1928–98) produced a great body of work in both languages, while many Gaelic poets are accustomed to producing translations of their own work, thus opening up Gaelic poetry to non-Gaelic readers. The young Stornoway writer Kevin MacNeil writes poetry in both English and Gaelic, and he has also recently published a novel in English, *The Stornoway Way* (2005). Even at the start of the twentieth century, when the Gaelic novel was in its infancy, Angus Robertson's *An t-Ogha Mòr* (1913) was apparently based on earlier stories he had written in English and subsequently translated into Gaelic (Macleod 1976: 213). Writing literature in English about life in the Highlands and Islands is therefore not new. However, MacDonald's and Campbell's works are somewhat different to other prose texts: whereas both thematically and stylistically their English novels do not differ greatly from their Gaelic works, they are imbued by a strong quintessential

'Gaelicness', which marks them out and distinguishes them even from Crichton Smith's English work. It is this resistant Gaelicness, apparently impervious to English assimilation, which the present chapter sets out to explore.

An immediate element of Gaelicness derives from the uncompromising similarity of the prose in the two authors' English and Gaelic works. Thus, like his earlier *An Sgàineadh* (Dòmhnallach 1993), MacDonald's *Portrona* has no clear linearity of plot. The chapters in both texts are joined by little more than MacDonald's desire to present an authentic image of the Gael or, as Iain Crichton Smith has put it, of 'real people in a real place' (see Smith 1986). Campbell's style is similarly unorthodox, informal and avant-garde, and his English texts are littered with Gaelic words and expressions. As a result, his narrative does not always flow smoothly, an effect which might be devised to reflect the inner turmoil of his often chaotic characters. In fact, his novels appear to suffer from an overabundance of characters, each of which he tends to describe in minutest detail. This trait of his work is also a trait of his community, in which there are no supernumeraries and everybody deserves to be identified in detail. Over and above the prose style, what renders these novels so distinctly Gaelic is the themes they explore and their explicit desire to maintain and assert a Gaelic identity. All three texts are located in the Isle of Lewis, although that in itself would not automatically mark them as indisputably 'Gaelic'. The settings are recognisably real, and no attempt has been made to fictionalise them. Campbell's texts are generally centred on the Ness parish in the north of Lewis (a Gaelic stronghold), while MacDonald's novel is mostly set in Stornoway, the capital of the Western Isles, 'Portrona' being an earlier name for Stornoway.

In the introductory chapter to *Portrona*, MacDonald announces that he is writing 'historiographic metafiction' (MacDonald 2000: 2), thus declaring his intention to deliver an authentic portrayal of his home community, even if this means including representations of the more difficult and unpleasant characteristics of communal life, such as death, poverty, hardship and alcoholism. Not only does MacDonald state quite clearly that truthfulness is his chief aim, but he also insists that the truth he distils will define and belong to his whole community: 'We want that truth to be ours.' In this context MacDonald also stresses the importance of capturing and integrating the community's past within its present sense of self-knowledge and identity. 'The past is not something to be escaped, avoided or controlled', he writes. 'The past is something with which we should come to terms, which involves an acknowledgement of limitation as well as power' (MacDonald 2000: 2). MacDonald's emphasis on authenticity is firm and unequivocal, giving the impression that, in his view, this kind of project has so far been unprecedented in literature dealing with life in these island communities.

The most noticeable feature of Gaelicness in Campbell's and MacDonald's English novels is their ubiquitous use of the Gaelic language. Both writers frequently include Gaelic words and phrases, but whereas MacDonald usually provides translations, Campbell does so only very rarely. Apart from serving as a deliberate marker of authenticity, the omnipresence of the language also raises questions about the intended readership of the texts. Other island-based English-language novels using Gaelic expressions have provided Gaelic-language glossaries; there are no glossaries here, and Campbell offers no explanations whatsoever. Does this mean these novels are intended mostly for a readership of Gaelic speakers, or is this an attempt to mainstream the Gaelic language and find for it a more prominent place in the Scottish national consciousness? Although the amount of Gaelic in the novels is in no way prohibitive of a non-Gaelic speaker reading and understanding them, its presence could be perceived as awkward or intrusive. In any case, the strategy certainly maintains the Gaelicness of the texts despite their predominantly English-language constitution.

Gaelic naming patterns are one example of the Gaelicness of the text, even though the names are often also given in English. In traditional Gaelic society there are few personal names, and the clan structure of the original communities means that there are regional pockets where one dominant surname prevails. In order to distinguish people unequivocally, the Gaelic communities, particularly in Lewis, have therefore developed a complex system of nicknames and patronymics. In Campbell's *The Nessman* examples of such nicknames are John the Battler, The Boxer (the nickname of the author's own father), The Rebel, Looper and Foxy. Simple patronymics include Donald Ishbel, Angus John Tully, and Chrissie Allan. In small communities it is important to people to know who an individual is, and this includes a knowledge of everyone's most immediate genealogy. This genealogy, or web of kinship relationships, is often expressed through intricate naming patterns. An excellent example of the patronymic naming pattern can be found in Campbell's short story 'Visiting the Bard':

> Who did you say you were? Norrie Zena's son? Zena from Skigersta, old Calum Salt's daughter? I mean Cross-Skigersta, the new road. That married the business man from Stornoway, one of the brothers? Secondhand clothes shop, lemonade and penny chews. The Smittys. They were footballers. I bought a jacket off one of them once, the deaf one, Harris tweed, the colour of carrots. Is that who you are? Norrie, your father – Wee Smitty – was eligible to play for Ness in the Eilean an Fhraoich cup, Zena being his mother, but he chose to play for Point, as the Smitty side of the family were originally out of some bog in Flesherin. So you're a Smitty. (Campbell 2003: 105)

Gaelic as a subject matter is also considered in some texts. In 'As This Leaves Me', another one of Campbell's short stories, the main character is at one point married to an incomer who is not a native speaker but has acquired a knowledge of Gaelic in later life. Campbell's portrayal of this woman and her apparent fanaticism about the language, while all around her Gaelic in its natural environment is dying, is very topical, emotive, and clearly controversial among the native Gaelic community:

> She works in the local college, and for different Gaelic organisations, acronyms, bodies involved with the language; attends seminars; conferences; gatherings of Gaels from the four quarters of the globe. She's a spokesperson, a visiting lecturer, a poet, a neutral observer. Not having the language is a decided advantage when making a career in Gaelic arts or education. Back in the village, she won't permit anyone to speak to her in English. 'Speak Gaelic!' she orders. When she speaks Gaelic herself, brows furrow, eyes go round, jaws sag, the angel of silence descends. (Campbell 2003: 57)

While negative, this is rather a common portrayal of the current Gaelic language-development movement. Albeit not overrun by adult learners of the language, some do hold prominent positions in the Gaelic development sector, and this can antagonise members of the native Gaelic communities. Campbell's story accurately depicts the divide between the world of some 'Gaelic learners' (and fanatics) and that of the traditional community. Whereas it is not suggested that the native speakers are unaware that their language might be facing extinction, there is a strong suggestion of indifference. The story also introduces a clear distinction between the 'foreign' Gaelic of the 'learner' and that of the authentic, native-speaking Gael:

> My Gaelic – fluent, idiomatic, Lewis – has no place in this company of outlandish babblers. It is dying the death in a small room, my Gaelic. A language gets the devotees it deserves. Neglect something and you'll lose it. And wheresoever the corpse is, there shall the vultures gather. (Campbell 2003: 58)

Gaelic is a heatedly debated and highly emotive issue. Thus, initially, the eponymous bard of Campbell's story seems to be very anti-Gaelic. 'Taigh na beetch air a' Ghàidhlig', he shouts. 'To hell with Gaelic' (Campbell 2003: 108). Although a poet in the language and a traditionalist, he has little time for 'saving' Gaelic. For him there exists a crucial difference between the effort of language preservation, acquisition and development, on the one hand, and the true, authentic, 'live' Gaelic of the traditional community: 'Everyone in the Gaelic world – all these smooth commentators, leeches, salaried termites – are poets . . . Gaelic's done for' (Campbell 2003: 113). Although some of Campbell's characters see Gaelic as a dying language, belonging to a culture in decline, Gaelic is also portrayed throughout all his texts as a symbol of communal unity and identity. Equally, in MacDonald's *Portrona*, set in the nineteenth and early twentieth centuries, Gaelic is a badge of belonging which can give comfort when the locals face hardship and adversity, even for the townspeople of Portrona who do not necessarily speak Gaelic themselves. As MacDonald's historical novel reveals, for the native townsperson there is no problem if he or she does not speak Gaelic, or speaks it only badly, whereas the lack of Gaelic categorically prevents all incomers from active participation in communal life, even though English is commonly spoken as well.

Lady Emily, head of the estate in MacDonald's novel, knows no Gaelic, and, aware of the divide this creates between her and the islanders, she attempts to remedy the situation by arranging for the teaching of English, particularly to local women. Evidently oblivious to the drastic impact her well-intentioned schooling measures are likely to have on the Gaelic language, by encouraging the local women to become more competent in English, Lady Emily's cultural intervention becomes a major threat to the natural transmission of the language from one generation to the next. Another example of Lady Emily's seemingly innocuous interference is her habit of anglicising the Gaelic personal names of her staff, which is entirely defensive and motivated solely by her desire not to appear foolish or incapable when attempting to pronounce properly what is after all a very difficult foreign language to her. The stereotyped binarism of non-islanders as non-Gaelic speakers and therefore as automatically suspect, and Gaelic speakers as insiders and people to be trusted, is not only challenged by MacDonald but moreover disclosed as potentially fatal through his portrayal of MacRoe, Lady Emily's estate factor and the chief villain of *Portrona*. MacRoe not only holds a position of great authority on the island, he also is a native Gaelic speaker from the mainland. As MacDonald indicates, the islanders are used neither to outsiders speaking Gaelic, nor to Gaelic speakers in powerful positions. Fully aware of the peculiarity of his situation, MacRoe quickly comes to realise 'what additional power this gave him, his ability to speak their language, oppressors seldom speak the language of the oppressed' (MacDonald 2000: 35).

In addition to being a social identifier and a tool not only of communication, but also of power, Gaelic is portrayed as a precious or interesting collectable. While the practice of collecting Gaelic folk materials – such as songs, stories, lore and so forth – with the aim of informing and accumulating a knowledge base for societies removed from Gaelic culture has been common for some time, little mention has been made of the attitude towards this practice among the communities or collectors themselves, or of the practice's impact and effect. Campbell deals with the latter in a couple of his stories: 'Visiting the Bard' and 'Sisters'. In both, the act of collecting alerts the informants to the fragility and, more importantly, the ultimate anachronicity of the cultural traditions the collectables represent. Thus, the poet in 'Visiting the Bard' refuses to give the collector his poems in the original Gaelic and instead provides English translations, even though he admits that other 'modern poets' would insist that the English copy can never be a 'patch on the Gaelic [original]' (Campbell 2003: 107). The story might be read as self-reflexively ironic in that this is what Campbell is also doing, that is, choosing to tell his Gaelic stories in English. In 'Sisters' one of the protagonists has been collecting oral history in the neighbourhood, and he is treated with considerable suspicion for doing so: his conduct is viewed as an unnatural act alien to communal life.

In none of the texts is the notion of Gaelicness introduced in isolation from the need to maintain a communal Gaelic identity, which features prominently in all the works. Frequently, communal identity is portrayed through an oppositioning of island life versus mainland life; at other times, the sense of community is more specific than that and narrowed down to particular villages or parishes. Whichever sense of community is referred to, a strong awareness of the community's environment as well as its boundaries prevails. This kind of awareness is particularly pronounced in Campbell's *The Nessman*, in which the main character, Colin, growing from childhood into young adulthood, effectively comes to inhabit three different locations in the course of the novel.

We first meet Colin as a young boy living with his family in a village in Ness. Home, to him, is not just the family house: it is the whole area and its people. So many of the people who surround Colin are his relations or are known well to his family, causing a strong sense of identity, based on extended kinship and community, to become instilled in Colin from a very early age. Gradually, however, he is removed from the safety of this first environment. As a teenager Colin must continue his schooling in Stornoway, about twenty miles from home, and he is required to stay in the school hostel during term time. His physical removal from home is accompanied by a social and emotional distancing also, and this is exacerbated by Colin's subsequent second move as a university student to Aberdeen. Either move is portrayed as a transitional step away from home and everything it represents: family, traditional values, kinship, as well as the Gaelic language and culture. At each step, therefore, a part of Colin's original sense of identity is eroded as a new sense of self demands to be adopted. This theme of increasing exile from home is a very prevalent one in modern Gaelic literature, in both its prose and poetry. In Iain Crichton Smith's work, for example, exile from the primary environment of home is commonly seen to cause a loss of identity resulting in an existential quest for meaning. While Campbell's protagonist does not display symptoms of such a fundamental rootlessness of being, he shows clear signs of cultural displacement and difficulty in settling into his new environment, highlighted by his failure to keep up with his studies and his increasing dependence on alcohol.

The themes of exile, absence and departure pervade modern Gaelic writing, mainly due to a general acceptance that any individual may leave never to return. Two of Campbell's stories – 'The Lost Sheep' and 'The Odour of Corruption' – concentrate on a particular aspect of this exile phenomenon, namely the return from exile, both in order to demonstrate how departure and return affect those left behind, and to query why a successful and fulfilling homecoming often appears so impossibly difficult to accomplish.

In 'The Odour of Corruption' the protagonists meet again after many years on the occasion of one of their mothers' funeral. Having lived 'away', Nora has returned with her husband when she meets John, her childhood sweetheart and neighbour. Nora and John reunite for one night, even though both are happily married. Whereas for Nora their coupling was motivated only by nostalgic reasons, she has thrown up a lot of problematic questions for John, a reformed alcoholic, who in response to their encounter starts drinking again. Nora awakens in John a hope for a more fulfilling and exciting life, yet this hope is short-lived when she returns to her husband as if nothing has happened, leaving him completely devastated:

> And when she did that I knew that my luck had run out and that my life was over, that it would all be against me from now on, that my sobriety was a sham, my watercolours no good, my oak panellings and false ceilings in vain, that my beams would collapse, my tiles crack, my house crumble and fall, my wife go away, my daughter be elsewhere, and that they would have no luck either, none at all, ever. (Campbell 2003: 135)

While 'The Odour of Corruption' focuses on the impact of the homecoming on those that stayed behind, 'The Lost Sheep' considers the emotional state of the returning exile. Once again the setting of the story is a funeral: after years in London the protagonist has returned to Lewis for his brother's funeral. Campbell is interested in exploring how the protagonist deals with his return to his home village, and his exploration is organised around the protagonist's lengthy reminiscence about an event in his youth. Uneasy at being 'at home', which he has visited only infrequently in the past, and surrounded by family and the formalities of the occasion, he is eager to leave again, even though he has no family or personal commitments elsewhere. His uncle recognises his isolation, commenting bitterly that 'the loneliest always have the most urgent appointments' (Campbell 2003: 153). The isolated, solitary exile shunning the company and friendly camaraderie of their extended family constitutes a common trope in modern Gaelic fiction, and it can also be found in Campbell's earlier Gaelic-language novel *Am Fear Meadhanach* (Caimbeul 1992).

After the funeral, the protagonist of 'The Lost Sheep' stops at a spot where his mother used to keep her sheep and he remembers an incident from boyhood when he, his late brother and mother went to look for a ewe lost on the moor. Obviously, his act of remembering their search for the lost sheep and its later reunion with its lamb is poignantly symbolic. Whereas the protagonist quickly comes to realise that no such reunion is possible for him, at least not now, and he once again turns his back on his community and family, the latter begin to appear to him in his dreams back in London, tenaciously and resourcefully inviting him to return:

> When I am feeling low at the end of the day, the getting and spending done, and sadness comes over me, alone in my room, or in company in a restaurant, or walking the pavements of Ealing, they come unbidden into my mind, and I see them again . . . In the setting sun, at the setting of my sun, I see them coming. And they are coming for the sheep that is lost. (Campbell 2003: 181–2)

The subject of exile is also present in MacDonald's *Portrona*. Not only does MacDonald repeatedly make reference to the very many men who have been forced to leave the island for economic reasons to earn a living as sailors, be it in the Merchant Navy, the Royal Navy, a fishing fleet or as explorers, he also highlights the plight of those left behind, usually women. At the same time, however, home is not exclusively portrayed in terms of the experience of being 'away', but also in its own right in terms of an authentic and gritty portrayal of island life, encompassing issues of historiography, and social commentary as well as other prominent themes, such as religion, death and alcoholism. Much has been written about the staunch Presbyterianism of the Isle of Lewis, and the texts discussed here contribute their own statements on the power of the church, most pertinently perhaps in the context of young Colin's experiences of the church in *The Nessman*, and the behaviour and attitude of the church following a major loss of life on the island in *Portrona*.

In *The Nessman* Colin's horror at attending church is summed up succinctly in his dramatic description of entering the building, whose 'jaws, like gigantic bivalves, gaped open to receive you' (Campbell 2000: 134). For Colin there is no personal desire to go to church; he only goes because he has to. In Gaelic literature, the church in Lewis is often portrayed as a bleak establishment fixated on death and the afterlife; there is no joy in faith. This is also brought to the fore in *The Nessman*, especially in the scene during which Colin's uncle, the minister, reminds his nephew of his mortality:

> What if this coming night were to be your last on earth? Our cousin Norman was alive three days ago. Now he is in his grave. Death the great leveller comes without warning, draws no distinction, is no respecter of persons . . . The coming night were it my last on earth, would hold no terrors for me . . . But for you, my young friend, this minute that I have left to remonstrate with you could be the only minute that you will ever have, and makes up the sum of all your minutes from now on. (Campbell 2000: 153–4)

The scenario of a minister trying to terrify a youngster into believing has found perhaps its most disturbing depiction in Iain Crichton Smith's story 'An Còmhradh' (Mac a' Ghobhainn 1968: 56–8), but the gloomy, black-clad men of faith are ubiquitous figures in Gaelic literature. They also make an appearance in *Portrona*, not only ministers but elders of the church as well, questioning the morals of the community in which they live. In *Portrona* MacDonald's focus is on the church's role in controlling the community's reaction after the sinking of the *Iolaire*, a former sailing yacht carrying home servicemen after World War I, on New Year's morning 1919 just outside Stornoway/Portrona harbour. With 286 local men drowned only yards off shore, the sense of loss to the island is huge, and especially cruel coming right at the end of the war. MacDonald's treatment of this historical event is emotional, sympathetic and insightful regarding both the experiences of one of the only ninety-seven survivors and the community's response to this mass disaster. Following the tragedy people flock to church, seeking consolation in preaching and the hauntingly soulful Gaelic psalm-singing, with precentor leading and congregation following, which at once comforts and numbs:

> The singing took us over and we were triumphant as we rode the waves of the final two lines.
>   The precentor kept us at it until the music of our own chests and tongue and throats released us to sit and hear what God had done to us on New Year's Morning 1919. (MacDonald 2000: 188)

An important doctrine of the Presbyterian church in Lewis is, of course, that of predestination, and MacDonald highlights superbly how this concept can only assist in aggravating the anguish the disaster has caused among the church-going population. How could God have chosen to hurt his faithful and devout community so mercilessly? As the narrator angrily demands to know from God, 'why do ye keep kicking your children in the teeth?' (MacDonald 2000: 222). But all the time those who are hurt and grieving try to keep their faith intact in order to make some sense of the atrocity, as 'versions of the Calvinist message absorbed at fireside and pulpit . . . stray through your head. You wiggle your toes for reassurance, touch a bare back if you have one beside you: God's will be done, be still and know who I am. It's all right, all preordained' (MacDonald 2000: 216). MacDonald's narrator is left to struggle with his faith, hoping that God and the church can offer some comfort, yet at the same time unable to stop himself from berating God. In the end, he decides to go to as many funerals of his lost friends and colleagues as possible, choosing at random which ones he will attend. Yet although they are all intensely personal and unique to the immediate family concerned, there is a numbing, obliterating sameness to them all.

One final important aspect of island life tackled in all the texts by Campbell and MacDonald is alcohol abuse and dependency. Five out of the six stories in Campbell's *Visiting the Bard* feature characters who either have or have had alcohol problems, while in *The Nessman* the young protagonist very quickly becomes a victim of alcohol abuse and dependency. All of Campbell's short-story characters with alcohol-related problems are loners, who have either married and separated, or never been married. Some have stopped drinking for periods of time, while others are still very much dependent. Lonely, ill men like these are numerous in twentieth-century Gaelic literature; Donald John Macleod has likened them, unable or unwilling to conform to society or to participate in communal life, to the Irish writer Frank O'Connor's (1903–66) 'outlawed figures wandering on the fringes of society' (Macleod 1976: 218–19). For all these men – be it in 'The Odour of Corruption', 'As This Leaves Me' or *The Nessman* – drink helps them forget their failure and loneliness, and quite possibly, for individuals brought up in a close-knit community, finding themselves alone is a particularly disastrous personal catastrophe, as it is entirely contrary to the norm of life they have been conditioned to expect.

Whether or not the characters of Campbell's and MacDonald's texts ultimately achieve reintegration into their home communities, the themes of communal life and communal identity are certainly of greatest significance to all of them. It is perhaps this prominent emphasis on community values, ubiquitously intense in all Gaelic-language writing, that singles out these English-language texts and makes them so particularly special in their Gaelicness. But albeit solidly anchored in one small, relatively remote community, Campbell's and MacDonald's writing must not be regarded as parochial: the themes they tackle are at once locally unique and universally relevant. Moreover, what recommends their work is of course their deliberate endeavour to afford a wider, English-speaking readership access to Gaelic literature and culture. Given the timing of these publications, one cannot but wonder either if perhaps post-devolution Scotland is more readily prepared to pay attention to Gaelic literature, especially if it is in English. Furthermore, now that the language is being taken seriously in the political arena, Gaelic writers – formerly expected to be inveterate champions of the language movement – may find themselves freed from the obligation to write only in Gaelic. Conversely, however, they may only be too aware that the audiences for Gaelic literature are rapidly decreasing and that, in order for their voices to be heard, they now absolutely need to write in English.

Part III
Authors

Chapter 18

Towards a Scottish Theatrocracy: Edwin Morgan and Liz Lochhead

Colin Nicholson

The scale of Edwin Morgan's achievement in mapping new territory for Scottish verse across the second half of the twentieth century and into imagined futures is beginning to clarify. Stimulated by a ceaseless appetite for experimentation, his pursuit of inventive variety has become emblematic of a quest for difference and the limning of alterity. The liberating double-take of what he once called the supreme graffito – 'CHANGE RULES!' (Morgan 1974: vii) – makes it a suitable motto for the integrity of both his anarchic political commitment and his lifelong attention to innovative forms of expression and representation. Given the volume of his output and the plural worlds of possibility he has opened up over the years, it is interesting to explore how many pathways and priorities have been inscribed in his work from the beginning. He has stayed at the cutting edge of technical innovation for so long now that the realisation of continuities in his writing can come as a surprise. An examination of the politics of his practice will help to explain this seeming paradox.

It is already something of a critical cliché that both Morgan's passion for vocalising otherness and the baroque reaches of his imagination relate to the enforced concealment of his sexual orientation until well into his career. Partly for this reason translation became an important avenue of self-extension for him, and his development of the dramatic monologue similarly created wild and wonderful contexts for a kaleidoscopic gallery of differently gendered speakers. Looking back to a time when the fact of his homosexuality was not only illicit but constituted a criminal offence, Morgan could coolly associate a subsequent productivity with 'things that are not in fact declared and open', and he agreed more generally that 'creative activity of any kind is not hindered by pressures and difficulties and tensions, in fact it's often helped by these things' (Morgan 1990b: 160, 162). Certainly for his younger self the pressures to conform to socially sanctioned codes of behaviour were real and longstanding. He vividly remembers his schooldays as 'a difficult and painful time' and recalls 'very strong guilt feelings' as his sexual awareness defined itself (Morgan 1990b: 145, 149). While some of that private burden of guilt was lightened during wartime service in the Middle East, the social stigma and legal penalties attached to being gay remained. He would not write about those wartime experiences until thirty years later, which meant that during the late 1940s, throughout the 1950s and into the 1960s Morgan led a double life, pursuing fugitive satisfactions he has described as 'wild but bleak' (Morgan 1990a: 594) with the unnerving sense that 'the shadow of illegality, of the severe penalties of being caught (not only imprisonment but also social ostracism) hung like a cloud in the background all the time' (Morgan 2000a: 281). Even when he was approaching his seventieth birthday he was confessing, in a conversation about publishing gay love poetry, that he still harboured 'apprehension about doing that kind of thing' (Morgan 1990b: 145). As Eve Sedgwick suggests, 'however courageous and forthright by habit' and 'however fortunate in the support of their immediate communities' gay people may eventually become, for many of them such an apprehensiveness remains 'a shaping presence' (Sedgwick 1991: 68).

Morgan developed left-wing sympathies as an undergraduate student and over a long life of writing produced some of Scotland's most radical poetry in an impressive space-making exercise for his country's literary imagination. But in the postwar years his personal horizons were severely curtailed. 'The objectives were just to break out of the awful isolation', he has since commented – an isolation that came from being one of 'a series of solitary people who were in fact gay' and among whom there was 'hardly any solidarity at all that stage' (Morgan 1990b: 157, 165). To compound matters, his first appearance in print following his demobilisation and return to Scotland in 1946 was a clash with Hugh MacDiarmid (a giant in Scotland's cultural firmament and one whose left-wing politics were already an intrinsic part of his established aesthetic credentials) over the requirement for younger poets to continue writing in Scots (Nicholson 2002: 15–23). This was a precarious position for someone already experiencing serious difficulties in finding his voice, and Morgan tried resorting to the Old Testament. During these early years of attempting to write we can hear rhythms derived from a Scottish Calvinism he had imbibed throughout childhood and schooling, rhythms which recur as the biblically cadenced environment for social exclusion and forms of condemnation he felt on the pulse. But if the shaping pressures were real, so were the imaginative opportunities Morgan derived from them. When he read as a youth at senior school the first edition of *The Faber Book of Modern Verse* (1936), he felt 'a new world opening out there and the variety of freedoms and daring of the different styles' that were available in American poetry, which struck him with the force of revelation:

> I must say that was one of the most stimulating anthologies I've ever come across. It was supposed to be modern poetry in English. It was almost half Americans. It had Pound and Eliot, and apart from that it had Hart Crane, it had Laura Riding – both of whom I liked a lot. It had Wallace Stevens, it had Marianne Moore – all these still to me very interesting poets, and I'd never come across them before. (Boddy 2000: 180–1)

As an undergraduate student at Glasgow University Morgan was bowled over again, this time by Charles Baudelaire (1821–67) and Arthur Rimbaud (1854–91), and by the Bolshevik futurism of Vladimir Mayakovsky (1893–1930). What he was to call 'a series of worlds, of which [he] had not the remotest inkling' began to 'explode in [his] mind' (Morgan 1990b: 192). Between his first encounter with American writing that opened up new anglophone directions and this equally stimulating introduction to the diverse energies of European modernism, Morgan had begun his discovery of an interest that would stay with him all his life. He was sensitised early to the precepts and practices of an always politically charged European Surrealism, which over time would feed into his attraction to Mayakovsky's politicised poetics and eventually help to produce what amounted to a virtual reconstruction of canonical Modernism from a specific, Scottish and left-wing perspective (Nicholson 2002: 59–81).

Much of Morgan's writing that came out of his postwar experience of serial aloneness – when he 'strained to unbind [him]self, / sweated to speak' (Morgan 1990a: 594) – projects isolated figures confronting hostile circumstance. Yet even here, in the sometimes tortured verse he was then producing, there is a political dimension that extends the poetry beyond the autobiographical anxieties it encodes. There is also, of course, a developmental trajectory leading from Baudelaire's poetry to Surrealism (see Raymond 1970: 1–35), and together with the flow of images seemingly at odds with rational sequence that characterises Morgan's early work, its deliberate cultivation of dreamlike states owes something to a movement still powerfully influential when Morgan picked up his postwar career.

It seems Morgan was also aware of something recognised by Walter Benjamin, namely that Surrealism had itself begun as a way of overcoming enthralment to religious illumination by inscribing its insights instead as 'profane illumination', where 'ghostly signals . . . and inconceivable analogies and connections between events are the order of the day' (Benjamin 1986: 183). Profane illumination is traced in Morgan's writing from the beginning. A shipwrecked survivor of 'the blaze and maelstrom of God's wrath' who laments his singular misfortunes in 'Dies Irae', one of the first poems Morgan wrote after his return from the Middle East, uses biblical phrasing to implicate a vengeful and punitive Old Testament deity and level against him its ironised valediction: 'So may God bless this meditation and poem. / I made it to intercede at his murmur and blame, / And I pray he may gaze upon it in the endless doom' (Morgan 1990a: 21, 24). Similarly, a speaker who fears 'the bitter salt far out / Where sin and wrath must meet' in 'A Warning of Waters at Evening', or the lone traveller who utters 'The Seafarer' with cares 'whistling / Keen about my heart' and who feels a 'hunger within' which has 'torn my sea-dazed mind apart', as well as the 'solitary man' in 'The Wanderer', represent voices crying in the wilderness of a repressively judgemental environment, where 'cold juries' are perceived as 'heart-abjurers' unyielding in their refusal 'to see through the braille of good and evil' (Morgan 1990a: 27, 29, 32, 34).

Persistently countering ingrained and virulent prejudice cannot have been easy, and the words of the wanderer – 'there is none now alive / To whom I might dare reveal in their clearness / The thoughts of my heart' (Morgan 1990a: 34) – resonate with an existential predicament that Morgan knew well. He was drawn to the wanderer as a figure of enforced exile, 'somebody who is not a part of the society he enjoyed so much', confirming that 'the state of mind of this isolated figure . . . is probably related to some of the themes recurring in my poems' (Fazzini 1996: 64). Something else that was to stay with Morgan was Surrealism's unpredictable transformation of orthodox codes of representation, and its provocative subversion of preferred modes of perception and socially privileged systems of recognition. The third and longest of the four movements that compose 'Cape of Good Hope', a poem written in 1950 as an attempted break-out from the alienation Morgan was experiencing, plays its own variations on a Surrealist fascination with synchronicities in the unconscious. Called 'A Dream at the Mysterious Barricades', it uses a palette of colours and an occult bestiary to include, in its series of creative and tormented males, a Michelangelo wracked by conflict between papal Catholicism and personal desire. Their respective relationships to the religious orthodoxies of their social eras were as different as the social eras themselves, but for both Morgan and Michelangelo faith-based regulation of sexual conduct entailed real subjection.

In the year 'Dies Irae' was written, Georges Bataille published 'On the Subject of Slumbers', which equates otherworldly belief systems with 'servitude to the real world'. Bataille considered it the 'prerogative of surrealism to free the activity of the mind from such servitude' (Bataille 1994: 49, 65); meanwhile, Morgan was engaged in an already secular struggle for self-liberation. He had intended to bring out 'Dies Irae' in a companion collection to his first, slender volume *The Vision of Cathkin Braes* (1952), so that the sombre dream-world tones of one could complement the visionary absurdism of the other, but the publisher ran out of money. The title poem of Morgan's first collection foregrounds profane illumination together with ghostly signals and hitherto inconceivable analogies and connections between narrative events, now refracted through the comic sparkle of a camp *Walpurgisnacht*. When the poem's speaker and his partner retire with lovemaking in mind to the hills ('braes') at Cathkin, an area of parkland on Glasgow's south side, a strange assortment of iconic figures from Scottish, English and American history, literature and legend appear to them, including John Knox, the market-woman Jenny Geddes (who famously started the public riot against the introduction of England's prescribed prayer books in Scotland in 1637), Mary Queen of Scots, the Africa explorer Mungo Park (1771–1806) and William McGonagall (1825–1902), renowned as one of the worst poets in the English language, as well as the biblical temptress Salome, William Wordsworth and the Hollywood actress Lauren Bacall. If Surrealists 'took up Freud's connection between dream and repressed desire, and his understanding of art as an activity liberated from the reality-principle' (Mahon 2005: 14), then so too, in fizzy anarchic mode, does 'The Vision of Cathkin Braes'.

Where change in literary modes might analogise transformation in others, Morgan's sustained responsiveness to technical innovation was always in part politically inspired. Certainly profane illumination shines through much of Morgan's subsequent work, not least the *Demon* sequence of 1999, and he has earned his reputation as a connoisseur of weird and zany connections. By the time he published the interactive sequencing of 'The New Divan' in 1977 he was using literary techniques that would subsequently be celebrated as postmodern. But Morgan is not so easily bracketed. In 1972 he produced his ten 'Glasgow Sonnets' and also brought out his Mayakovsky series, the latter translated into a form of proletarian Scots, to coincide with one of the great industrial upheavals of the later twentieth century, when Glasgow's shipyard workers occupied their places of work in a desperate bid to keep the yards open for business.

Yet despite that explicit, public gesture of solidarity, Morgan remains instinctively suspicious of any unitary notion of the 'voice of the people', having learned that 'the world, history, society, everything in it, pleads to become a voice, voices' (Morgan 1990b: 114). Accordingly, he cultivates a passion for plural vocalising, which conspires with a flair for dramatic narrative in free-standing, loosely associative sequences to make heterodoxy his preferred terrain. He has 'always liked the idea of a poet being able not just to speak in his or her own voice, but to project into other kinds of existence', and long before he turned his attention to the theatre proper Morgan was thinking of himself as 'a kind of non-dramatist dramatist' (Nicholson 1992: 73–4). A steady stream of cross-pollinating series and sequences – 'The Whittrick' in 1961, *The Horseman's Word* in 1970, *Wi the Haill Voice*, 'Glasgow Sonnets' and *Instamatic Poems* in 1972, *Sonnets from Scotland* in 1984, 'An Alphabet of Goddesses' in 1985, and *Hold Hands Among the Atoms* in 1991 – emphasises Morgan's attraction to independently structured, yet interconnecting projections of alterity. Two such serial performances – 'From the Video Box' in 1986 and 'Virtual and Other Realities' in 1997 – engage directly with forms of representation that simulate voice and story in sometimes arcane locations, thus emphasising the fundamental opposition in attitude and political stance between Morgan's imaginative republic and Plato's.

It was never likely that Plato's concern to codify and preserve 'what was just and lawful' for creative activity would find sympathetic treatment in Morgan's writing, which is so securely and consistently attached to a libertarian politics – particularly when in *Laws III* Plato's Athenian stranger laments the emergence of poets who are 'leaders of unmusical illegality', regretting the subversive way they 'inspired the multitude with . . . a conceit of their own competences as judges', and claiming that such poets 'bred in the populace a spirit of lawlessness'. 'Thus', the Athenian complains, 'our once silent audiences have found a voice, in the persuasion that they understand what is good and bad in art; in place of an aristocracy in music there sprang up a kind of base theatrocracy' (Plato 1942: 242, 247). Theatrocracy signifies the rule or sovereignty of the audience, the reign of the crowd which refuses to acknowledge its proper place by rejecting precisely those traditional categories of what constitutes the good and the beautiful. This could lead to the assumption of other kinds of power by a carnivalesque 'mob', who might be persuaded to throw off the hierarchies imposed upon it by self-defining and unaccountable governing elites, and these are, of course, very much the kinds of stirrings likely to attract Morgan's sympathetic attention. Realistically enough, Plato was fearful that audiences who internalised unorthodox values might transport their transgressive meanings from the organised space of the theatre proper into civic life, and then into the domestic arena, unsettling and disturbing a range of relationships. If, as Samuel Weber suggests (and many of Morgan's first-person narratives presuppose), 'theatricality demonstrates its subversive power when it leaves the *theatron* and begins to wander', then it follows that 'the advent of theatrocracy subverts and perverts the unity of the *theatron* as a social site by introducing an irreducible and unpredictable heterogeneity . . . It is such stability of place and of placing that the theatrocracy profoundly disturbs' (Weber 1996).

Plato's Athenian cogently suspects that when hitherto accepted divisions of music and poetry into genres and types are progressively dissolved by a practice that mixes genres and elides formal boundaries, the audience's next step on the journey towards liberty is to reject established codes of civic regulation and altogether refuse society's belief systems. 'Contempt for law originated in the music, and on the heels of these came . . . a liberty that is audacious to excess', the Athenian insists, adding that 'next after this form of liberty would come that which refuses to be subject to the rulers . . . while the last stage of all is to lose all respect for . . . divinities' (Plato 1942: 248–9). Like others of Morgan's extended performances, the vigorously secular narratives of 'The New Divan' mingle epic with low comedy, history with science fiction, and elegy with lyric. But Morgan remains loyal to the storyteller's art, where suspension of disbelief operates for as long as the reader is willing to sustain it. So his boundary-crossing redistributions of speech make him something of a tribune for audacious seekers after liberty, producing verse that is repeatedly concerned to bring an audience up to the edge of possible transformation and let it decide its priorities for itself.

'Theatre' originally signified the place from which one sees, and because, partly through its preference for dramatic monologues, Morgan's poetry constitutes a theatre of voice, his writing additionally specifies the place from which one speaks. Moreover, in so far as the reader's voice is the only one that operates in any given reading, each reader is invited to accommodate a multiplicity of perspectives as he or she simulates a cacophony of voices. Given the endless variety of human voice-prints and the seemingly inexhaustible supply of contexts that Morgan devises to rehearse the exercise of that variety, his poetry interpellates the democratic republican citizenry that, in his *Republic*, Plato finds unacceptable:

> The mimetic poet sets up in each individual soul a vicious constitution by fashioning phantoms far removed from reality, and by currying favour with the senseless element that cannot distinguish the greater from the less, but calls the same thing now one, now the other. (Plato 1935: 459)

It is evident from such time-travelling space-fantasy projections as 'Memories of Earth' (1973) and the eclectic politicisations of *Hold Hands Among the Atoms* that wherever speech is rife and generated from a profusion of locations, conventional stabilities of place, and of knowing one's place, are at risk. Additionally, Morgan disturbs customary assumptions by accessing a particular historical dynamic of politics. Much of his writing involves 'a history of events that breaks the "normal" course of time', promoting instead 'inscriptions, forms of subjectivisation, of promises, memories, repetitions, anticipations, anachronisms' (Rancière 2003), designed to mark out a space strikingly different from the conventional record. In these respects Morgan's verse validates Jacques Rancière's claim that 'equality has no vocabulary or grammar of its own, only a poetics', and its multiplicity of forms and plural lines of temporality disclose ways of being, saying and seeing that are 'incorporated in living attitudes, in a new relationship between thought and the sensory world' and between the body and its environment (Rancière 2003).

The *Virtual and Other Realities* series of 1997 recentres the body, which is often held to be displaced by multimedia projection. In the first poem, 'March', while the 'fax / is in the land of numbers', the verse focuses on human agency and real-world environment: 'the dialling hand is up and on its way, / braced by one raffish, restless, rude spring day'. Next, 'The Ferry' invites the reader to imagine 'your landing on a place so virtual' in order to emphasise the physicality of experience: 'Never believe it! – buffet, buck, breach / dimensions like meniscuses, give speech, / cry out, scrunch your keel right up the beach' (Morgan 1997: 47–8). However, the series that most readily dramatises Morgan's commitment to the heterodox and the out-of-place is 'From the Video Box' (1986), where twenty-seven poems play inventive games with the constitution and practice of singular selves, and with the systems of representation they articulate and which articulate them. Taking its cue from the Channel 4 television programme *Right to Reply*, the sequence puts members of the audience before the camera to have their say. The permissive entry system for this video box exercises Tom Leonard's proposition that 'democracy is daily dialogue, and true democracy lies in the equality and equal power of all parties to that dialogue' (Leonard 1990: xxi). That grounding assumption of a thorough-going egalitarianism brings Morgan's practice (as well as Leonard's) into productive congruence with Rancière's fundamental and enabling premise that 'equality is not a goal to be attained but a point of departure, a supposition to be maintained in all circumstances' (Rancière 2003). To maintain that supposition, Morgan generates the illusion of improvisation by inviting his readers to rehearse in the theatre of the mind a moment of self-disclosure enacted by a speaker addressing a privately enclosed but publicly broadcasting screen. This tactic abolishes the division between public and private spheres and redefines the political subject as an essentially anarchic performer who pits 'the presumptions of a disruptive equality against the advocates of an orderly, hierarchical equality' (Hallward 2006: 110).

By virtue of her theatre-work as a dramatist, and her extraordinary success as public performer of her own material, sometimes appearing as a home-grown rap artist, Liz Lochhead is a natural inheritor of the imaginative space Morgan has helped to establish: 'Once again the peculiarity and particulars of language are installed as central elements of performance – as performers themselves, occupying the audience's attention as objects of relish and surprise' (Stevenson 1993: 117). It is impossible to read Lochhead's work without an awareness of the social class she articulates and satirises. As she sharpened her alertness to the trick of speech, Lochhead was drawn early to working-class forms of popular entertainment: the 'subversive laughter of the music hall' appealed to her, as did female cross-dressers like Vesta Tilley (1864–1952): 'I'm not sure how much they understood of what they were doing, but they always subverted the class thing. It was working-class women dressing up not just as men, but as the toffs' (Nicholson 1992: 221). Masks, and the wearing and stripping away of masks, become Lochhead's stock in trade, as often as not displayed in the form of demotic dramatic monologues where a usually comic and sometimes lacerating irony might be unleashed by speakers unaware of the disclosures they are making. From the beginning she has exploited this ironic gap to bring out serious implications in the automatic and often apparently meaningless phrases which punctuate conversation, whether those implications are personal blindnesses or concealed cultural assumptions. This helps to account for Lochhead's attraction to cliché, dead metaphor, and the lifeless cant phrases of much everyday speech, which she revivifies through collusion with her audience, who thereby become her co-performers. Lochhead is particularly interested in the connection between dramatic irony and spoken cliché 'which you cannot use without acknowledging it to be cliché':

> You enter into a relationship with the reader whereby you have the reader join in the game with you, to complete the acknowledgement. So cardboard cut-out things, like women's magazine phrases, I like to treat as more archetypal. Of course they are stereotypes, but they are more than simply that. They contain kinds of truths. (Nicholson 1992: 216)

In 'Morning After', from Lochhead's first collection *Memo for Spring* (1972), the female speaker's muted awareness of class difference gives poignancy to her sense of impending dismissal by the male whose bed she is sharing. She becomes a representative figure in Lochhead's gallery of women struggling to express private selves in a language whose unequal systems of public distribution are designed to inhibit that expression. The 'Mirror' she is reading reflects her limitations: the irony that redeems her is the wit of her turn of phrase and, through that, the poem's implicit condemnation of her casual exploitation by the male (Lochhead 1984: 134–5). Like and unlike this character, the speaker of 'Inter-City' has to cope with Neanderthal male behaviour that denies her very existence as she travels at night by train from Glasgow to Aberdeen in a compartment filled with drunken, cursing oil-rig workers. This time the mirror that reflects 'only bits of my own blurred / back-to-front face and / my mind elsewhere' is the carriage window, while both connection and disconnection with her situation is signified by 'the artsyfartsy magazine' she's 'not even pretending to read', yet which lies 'wide open / at a photograph called Portrait of Absence' (Lochhead 1984: 34).

Accordingly, the lines 'Don't / let history frame you / in a pretty lie' (Lochhead 1984: 21) can be read as justifying Lochhead's reinventions of story, fairy tale, legend and myth, many of which are internalised during childhood in narratives that customarily subordinate the female as they naturalise traditions of male dominance. By 'putting new twists / to old stories' (Lochhead 1984: 35), Lochhead repossesses on altered terms the discourses that legitimise social hierarchies of power. The vein of satire running through her work, and her commitment to giving what she has called 'the male halves of themselves back to women, and the female halves of themselves back to men', preserve Lochhead from any facile ideology of gender oppositions. 'We are divided within ourselves,' she maintains, 'and the real task is the completion of selves' (Nicholson 1992: 204). It is an attitude and ambition that the self-aware, controlling and seductive speaker of 'What the Pool Said, on Midsummer's Day' both represents and interrogates as she manipulates erotic desire to threaten and promise an orgasmic merging of selves, one of the strengths of the poem being its ability to sustain an invitational tone that is simultaneously discomposing. Its success also derives from Lochhead's practised skill in delivering a sense of dialogue within monologue – 'there is not just the voice we hear, there is also the implied voice which is being argued against and talked about' – and partly from the way the poem 'communicates a sense of an actual, restless speaking voice which seems to be engaged in dialogue, in argumentative seduction, with the "you" of the poem' (Crawford 1993b: 70).

Elsewhere Lochhead's search for gendered complementarity can be both sharp and hilarious, including satires on feminist stances she finds unconvincing and on female behaviour she sees as self-deceptive or otherwise unproductive. As alert to the meretricious role-playing that inhibits while seemingly enabling selfhood as she is adept at suggesting varieties of roles yet to be explored, Lochhead is rarely dismissive of the characters she dissects. 'Bawd' presents a self-aware performer toughing out her life, and 'Spinster' similarly succeeds in catching the pathos of a woman coming to terms with loneliness. The 'three thirty-fivish women' who are 'Overheard by a Young Waitress' – a favoured figure – are not so much disabused by the experience of love, as betrayed by the gap between complex realities and the delusory expectations promoted by popular ideologies of romantic relationships (Lochhead 1984: 75–6).

Lochhead has been a significant space-maker for women's writing in Scotland and beyond, and while she continues to use her female perspectives to open out gender issues she has, in *Bagpipe Muzak* (1991) and then *The Colour of Black White* (2003), both broadened the scope of her satire and constructed poems where personal and familial memories carry the rhythms of West-of-Scotland working-class experience into a form of social history. And if attitudes to language encode attitudes to politics and class, Lochhead continues to use 'colloquial, urban, and demotic' Glaswegian speech-patterns as both poetic and dramatic vehicles (Mugglestone 1993: 96–7), focusing her attention on political subjectivities still in active process of identifying themselves and looking to find fit voices in the theatre of social interaction.

Chapter 19

Alasdair Gray and Post-millennial Writing

Stephen Bernstein

In an interesting group portrait taken in the mid-1990s by the late Richard Avedon, a host of young Scottish writers pose in Glasgow's Clutha Vaults pub. Avedon perhaps intended some implicit commentary: Alan Warner and Irvine Welsh stand on the fringes of the group, while Robin Robertson, editor of both Welsh's and A. L. Kennedy's work, smiles in the background. And slightly off-centre, seated and grinning, is Alasdair Gray, described in Alan Taylor's accompanying text as 'the grand old man of the Scottish renaissance' (Taylor 1995–6: 97). Gray's slightly out-of-kilter centrality to contemporary Scottish fiction is beyond question, and it is a centrality to something very much like a collective. One measure of Gray's significance is his creation of recognisably Scottish fictional topoi and his boundary-breaking experimentation with narrative. At the same time, it is important to consider how large a part of his contribution has been his capacity to imagine the particular requisites for confronting historical forces like the political challenges of the new millennium. Without doubt, a key facet of Gray's project has been to envisage identities that offer a broad range of possibilities, positive and negative, for meeting the twenty-first century.

Mark Renton, the main narrator of Irvine Welsh's *Trainspotting*, claims that Scotland is 'a country ay failures' and that 'it's nae good blamin it oan the English fir colonising us' (Welsh 1993: 78). This complaint is a bitter coda to Jock McLeish's assertion, a decade earlier, in Gray's *1982 Janine* (1984) that 'Scotland has been fucked and I am one of the fuckers who fucked her' (Gray 1984: 136). But Gray has created more than simply a negative critique of Scottish history for younger writers, and in noting his echoes in Welsh one should also remember, for example, Janice Galloway's appreciative remark that 'Alasdair Gray's writing makes me feel braver. As a woman, it makes me feel acknowledged, spoken to . . . As a woman writer in Scotland, those gifts are still rare enough to make me very grateful indeed' (Galloway 1995: 196). In an unpublished letter of 1998 to the present writer Gray pronounced himself 'glad of a coming [Scottish] parliament', but noted that 'then the work of making it more than a talk shop will start'. This chapter contends that, according to Gray's fiction and his polemical writing, the hope of moving beyond talk depends on the way individuals imagine their integration into history and recognise the value of forming collectives. For a number of the younger writers who posed with Gray in 1995 this aspect of Gray's work may finally prove to be the most meaningful part of his legacy.

Gray was nearly fifty years old when he published *Lanark*, his first novel, in 1981. Though this central work of twentieth-century Scottish fiction appeared relatively late in Gray's life, it was published well before the period under consideration in the present volume. In fact, the majority of Gray's major works all appeared before devolution: his last two novels,

Poor Things and *A History Maker*, were published in 1992 and 1994 respectively. Nevertheless, anyone writing on Gray comes up against the sheer volume of work he has produced in a career now spanning nearly three decades. Critics frequently distinguish between the major novels *Lanark*, *1982 Janine* and *Poor Things*, and the slighter narratives *The Rise of Kelvin Walker* (1985), *McGrotty and Ludmilla* (1990), *Something Leather* (1990) and *Mavis Belfrage* (1995). Gray is the author of several short-story collections as well: *Unlikely Stories, Mostly* (1983), *Ten Tales Tall & True* (1993) and *The Ends of Our Tethers* (2003) with additional stories appearing in *Lean Tales* (1985) – which also includes work by Agnes Owens and James Kelman – and *Mavis Belfrage*. He has published two collections of poetry (*Old Negatives* [1989] and *Sixteen Occasional Poems, 1990–2000* [2000]) and a play (*Working Legs* [1997]), edited a large volume of literary criticism (*The Book of Prefaces* [2000]) and written a smaller one (*A Short Survey of Classic Scottish Writing* [2001]), and also produced three polemical works: *Why Scots Should Rule Scotland* (1992), *Why Scots Should Rule Scotland 1997* (1997) and *How We Should Rule Ourselves* (with Adam Tomkins, 2005). Due to constraints of space I must limit the following discussion to a few key passages from Gray's major novels and polemical works, in which we can most clearly see the interrelationships of subjectivity, collectivity and history to which Gray has consistently attended.

The identity of the protagonist in each of Gray's three major novels splits and diversifies in the course of the narrative: thus, *Lanark's* eponymous hero and the character Duncan Thaw turn out to be the same person, albeit existing within different time zones. In *1982 Janine* Jock McLeish expresses his deepest anxieties through multiple voices, represented by different typefaces and designs, as well as his 'silly soul' Janine, and in *Poor Things* Victoria McCandless and Bella Baxter problematically share an identity, while the very volume in which they appear also exhibits at least a dual nature. This psychological doubling of protagonists is nothing new in Scottish fiction: one only has to look at the works of earlier writers such as James Hogg or R. L. Stevenson to find abundant evidence of it. Gray's practice of doubling, though, differs from that of his precursors in a key way: Hogg's Gil-Martin in *The Private Memoirs and Confessions of a Justified Sinner* (1824) and Stevenson's Mr Hyde in *The Strange Case of Dr Jekyll and Mr Hyde* (1886) are used to externalise the most negative potentialities of Robert Wringhim and Dr Jekyll. As Francis Hart notes, Hogg's novel 'draws partly on the primitive fear of being bewitched, possessed, by the spirit or power of an Other, of being robbed of one's identity' (Hart 1978: 23). This negative version of the double is still on view in the Scottish novel as recently as Duncan McLean's *Bunker Man* (1997). In contrast, Gray's doubles allow the reader to perceive patterns of growth and increasing psychological holism. As Peter Kravitz puts it, 'for these characters sanity is not given, but won. Then they are whole, not split people' (Kravitz 1997: xix). Thus, in examining the character relationships in Gray's novels we detect a positivity and optimism lacking in the nineteenth-century examples. An even fuller picture of Gray's achievement emerges when we note that he suggestively links this holism to an awareness of historical dynamics.

Consider, for example, Lanark's brief exchange with the Oracle about halfway through the story of his alter ego Duncan Thaw, in which – although the latter's narrative has just reached an uncharacteristically upbeat moment – Lanark observes that 'Thaw was not good at being happy'. The Oracle corrects him ('He was bad at it'), pointing out that the 'infinite bright blankness' could not accept Thaw at his death and instead 'flung him back into a second-class railway carriage, creating [Lanark]' (Gray 1981: 219). Lanark cannot yet understand his relationship to Thaw, but by the time the Oracle concludes

Thaw's narrative, Lanark refers to it as an 'account of my life before Unthank' (Gray 1981: 357). Even though Lanark learns to accept the Thaw aspect of his identity, the events of the novel's fourth book show that his acceptance does not complete him or make him happier, and yet, by the novel's end, Lanark is 'a slightly worried, ordinary old man but glad to see the light in the sky' (Gray 1981: 560). Albeit significantly qualified, these words sound as a clear positive in the darkened world of Unthank. Lanark may be worried, but only 'slightly', and one does well to remember that gladness is Lanark's final emotion in the whole narrative. Despite the fact that at the beginning of this passage Lanark receives news of his impending death, 'after which nothing personal will remain' (Gray 1981: 559), he has just spoken with the two people closest to him, Rima and Alexander, and renounced any desire for more adventures. Arguably, after reviewing the totality of his existences and witnessing the travesty of the corporatised political state (Gray 1981: 517–19, 536–52), he is psychologically as 'complete' as he will ever be. There is nothing left for Lanark, but in a sense that is Gray's point: having expended whatever potential he had, he is now devoid of any further purpose or ability, and his maps 'ARE OUT OF DATE' (Gray 1981: 560). However, by emphasising that this plight is not without gladness, *Lanark* posits that a provisional, contingent holism is the best possible outcome in the gloomy world of Unthank.

1982 Janine places a similar emphasis on contingency and pragmatism. The novel's narrator – cynical, conventionally successful Jock McLeish – characterises 'a smart Tory' like himself as someone who 'believes things would improve a little if the trade unions and Russians surrendered to him, but being a realist he does not expect surrender and works for what he and his associates can grab and enjoy now and in future', adding that 'this is a natural Falstaffian approach to life' (Gray 1984: 137). Positioned less than halfway through the narrative, this passage demonstrates an understanding of the 'real' and the 'natural' that will need to shift dramatically before the novel can conclude, and indeed, nearly two hundred pages later McLeish's certainty about what constitutes reality or nature looks quite different:

> technology has magnified to world-destruction point the common smash-and-grab business tactics and bullyboy politics which everyone (not everyone) which too many seize as golden opportunities or take for granted (stop this) how stop when books say we are selfish competitive beasts and all the true bonny good things we discover or make/solar system/Sistine ceiling/penicillin/are got by overcoming and humiliating each other (crap) yes crap but in Scotland in 1982 that shitty thought looks like Your Own Great Gospel, O Lord, for here is no dream or plan to make or share good things or set an example and honestly, God, I no longer think Scotland worse than elsewhere and I can only stop raving by retreating into fantasy (retreat). (Gray 1984: 311)

This remarkably dense passage discloses a dualism so deeply ingrained in McLeish's consciousness that different printing types must be used to delineate it. At this point in the novel, importantly, the voice interjecting McLeish's earlier viewpoint and convictions has become parenthetical. Extra blank spacing allows the passage to communicate a kind of mental hesitation and bewildered gravity. Slash marks indicate the rapid, associative quality of McLeish's thought, a quality that is highlighted further through the use of alliteration and assonance, as 'system' leads to 'Sistine' and 'ceiling' leads to 'penicillin', indicating that ultimately the solar system exists on the same plane as artistic creativity and scientific discovery, all of them being vital to life. Immediately following this passage, in which McLeish's more cynical side tries to beat a retreat back into its sado-masochistic fantasy of Janine's eternal subjugation, Janine – McLeish's innermost humanity – decides to 'pretend' that a potentially threatening situation 'is just an ordinary audition', leaving McLeish to protest feebly that 'this is NOT the fantasy I intended' (Gray 1984: 311). Janine's resolute attempt at casting off the yoke of remote control and exploitation works to complete the mental operation McLeish had begun to exhibit earlier in the given passage. The 'good' side of McLeish increasingly overcomes his 'bad' side, resulting in the novel's final vision of a qualified and, again, contingent holism. In the closing pages of *1982 Janine* McLeish recognises that he is 'not exactly the same man, anyway' and vows that '[he] will not do nothing' (Gray 1984: 340–1). The persistent use of negatives in his tentative announcement of this 'new me' enables us to compare his transformation with Lanark's: after reviewing his past life, McLeish is ready to embrace change, but he is hardly in a position to shout it from the rooftops. Most importantly perhaps, McLeish's view of the process of history has changed as well. Whereas previously he believed that 'history was made in a few important places by a few important people', he now realises that 'history is what we all make, everywhere, each moment of our lives, whether we notice it or not' (Gray 1984: 340).

Gray has been fascinated by the process of history-making throughout his career; indeed, his last novel is called *A History Maker*. *Lanark* closes with its protagonist psychologically whole and finished with the process of history, while *1982 Janine* concludes with a similar reassemblage of its protagonist, who is now ready to acknowledge his role in history. By contrast, in *Poor Things*, his penultimate novel, Gray's approach to subjectivity and history, and indeed to the entire concept of experience and its rendition in narrative, is far more problematic. Moreover, any discussion of *Poor Things* would be incomplete without addressing its visual dimension. In this novel Gray's visual artistry is not simply a purely decorative or representational counterpart of its verbal content; rather, it conveys its own meanings, which inextricably enhance the novel's narrative. Gray's visual design of *Poor Things* is comprehensive: the book comprises decorated boards, mock-Victorian portraits of major characters, interspersed reproductions of engravings from Henry Gray's *Anatomy of the Human Body* (1918), Glasgow maps, and several nineteenth-century newspaper illustrations. These visual elements also serve to document the shift from representational painting – one portrait is a pastiche of Da Vinci's *Mona Lisa* – to photography over the course of the nineteenth century, in which most of the novel is set. This movement from an allegedly subjective and impressionistic mode of representation to a putatively more objective one is echoed by the novel's account of medical practice in nineteenth- and twentieth-century Glasgow: beginning with the Gothic fantasy of a drowned female suicide being reportedly reanimated through the transplant of her unborn child's brain, *Poor Things* concludes with a starkly realistic account of the same woman's medical career between the world wars.

The novel's Gothic plot of reanimation is informed by a narrative dichotomy of fraudulent make-believe and apparent representational accuracy. According to the first account, a young woman named Bella is created via brain transplant by her doctor-guardian Godwin Baxter. Bella – physically an adult, but with the mind of a child – thus stands as a literalised version of Victorian patriarchy's female stereotype. Baxter sets about Bella's education, which finds its unintentional culmination in a series of *Candide*-like international adventures outside Baxter's supervision. Bella eventually marries the unimaginative doctor-narrator Archibald McCandless, outlives him, and becomes a controversial early-twentieth-century doctor and social reformer in Glasgow, living until 1946. By contrast, in Bella's own account there is no brain transplant; instead she flees from her abusive husband to seek refuge with Baxter. Though the novel clearly leans towards the more fantastic account, the issue of which version is true, or more truthful, is never fully settled, and ultimately it appears less important than both versions' focus on the matter of education, and specifically female education, in the nineteenth century.

In this context one event in particular is worth examining more closely. About midway through the novel Bella is seen dining on a hotel veranda in Alexandria in the company of cynical British Malthusian Harry Astley and American missionary Dr Hooker. The veranda is surrounded by beggars who are kept at a distance by men with whips. Unconstrained by the rigid ideological views of her companions, Bella tries to help two of the beggars by trying to take them back to Scotland; however, her plan is thwarted, and in the ensuing struggle she bites Astley's hand as he tries to silence her. Astley later refers to this scene as 'a working model of nearly every civilized nation' (Gray 1992a: 175). Thirty pages before this account of the incident is given, readers are introduced to Bella's more immediate version of the event in her diary, presented by McCandless in facsimile, that is, 'printed by a rotogravure process which exactly reproduces the blurring caused by tear stains, but does not show the pressure of pen strokes which often ripped right through the paper' (Gray 1992a: 144). As a result, Bella's account appears – quite literally – writ large. However, the compromise necessitated by the reproduction – Bella's tear stains are visible but the tearing of the paper by her pen is not – illustrates the larger question of narrative representation rehearsed by Gray's novel, in which the fantastic tends to give way to the mundane, while key questions of verisimilitude and narrative reliability remain unanswered. The torn diary pages represent a physical record of Bella's anger and frustration at being kept from acting collectively with – and in aid of – those in immediate need. The tears that blur her words are a similar record, but they also belong to the tradition of leisured sensibility instead of active work. The rotogravure – a copper cylinder with an intaglio image – cannot possibly reproduce the ripped paper that is the third dimension of Bella's text and thus, as an integral part of her husband's account, her vigorous desire to help and make a difference is doomed to look like a hysterical outburst. 'You can do no good', the missionary tells her during the incident, and this is not only confirmed but ensured by the reproduction of her diary (Gray 1992a: 174). McCandless mentions the torn paper, but in no way can he re-enact his own tactile encounter with Bella's diary.

By showing what is lost in the transition from handwritten diary to mechanically produced book, *Poor Things* adds to its commentary on the problematic history of representation, which resounds with Walter Benjamin's observation that 'the technique of reproduction detaches the reproduced object from the domain of tradition. By making many reproductions, it substitutes a plurality of copies for a unique existence' (Benjamin 1999a: 221). Whereas what Benjamin has in mind here may not be so far removed from Baudrillardian postmodern simulacra, Gray keeps his focus firmly on nineteenth-century society in which the originals still existed as actual extra-narrative referents. In several other respects, though, the novel clearly gestures towards a world of duality and duplicity that will arrive during the twentieth century. Thus, *Poor Things* contains two accounts of Bella's life, her husband's and her own, and Bella herself is known alternately as Victoria. The novel also contains an introduction – complemented at the novel's end with a section of editor's notes – in which Gray tells the story of how the texts have come into his possession. The reader learns how a friend of Gray's, the historian and museum curator Michael Donnelly, stole the documents from old files that had been put out as trash by a law office. After both Gray and Donnelly have read McCandless's account of Bella's creation, Donnelly 'thinks it a blackly humorous fiction', while Gray considers it 'a loving portrait . . . recorded by a friend with a memory for dialogue' (Gray 1992a: xi). Gray claims to have 'written enough fiction to know history when I read it', to which Donnelly counters that 'he had written enough history to recognize fiction' (Gray 1992a: xi). The multiplicity of authors, editors, names and narratives in *Poor Things*, coupled with its related questions concerning the veracity of representation, casts the text into a state of perplexing indeterminacy. That this condition should be linked to the increasing exactitude of mechanical reproduction is telling. Through his creation of manifold narrative layers Gray demonstrates that the increasing representational precision, which became available during the nineteenth century thanks to photography and mechanical reproduction, still can do virtually nothing to secure its own truth-claim. We can read Bella's account of the scene in Alexandria, but we can never feel the pressure of her pen, and despite their authenticating Victorian newspaper illustrations, the editor's notes remain 'outside' the novel's representational sphere.

A final visual example is taken from the beginning and the very end of the novel. Following the editor's introduction is a 'grotesque design' – the image of a naked woman gazing out from a skull – which 'was stamped in silver upon the batters of the original volume' (Gray 1992a: xiv, xv) and serves to anticipate McCandless's assertion that Bella has in some way returned from the jaws of death. The novel's final page, following the editor's notes, shows an illustration of the Glasgow Necropolis, placed there by Gray in his editor's role (Gray 1992a: 319). The two illustrations repeat the novel's own movement from the Gothic-romantic to the 'real', but the editor's captioned testimony that the Baxter mausoleum contains the remains of the novel's 'three principal characters' must ring hollow after the life-story of one of these characters has been cast so radically in doubt. Though the engraving of the Necropolis is almost photographically accurate, it remains as distant from verifiable truth as the 'grotesque design' of the skull.

In a narrative elucidated more effectively by its illustrations than its plot, *Poor Things* voices an overwhelming concern that the truth-telling capabilities of any representational medium are perilously constrained by the medium itself. The novel thus becomes a clear example of what Cairns Craig describes as a counterhistorical tendency in Scottish fiction in response to 'a history that, by claiming to be the only inevitability in human life, leaves so much out of history' (Craig 1996: 81). With the former prime minister's words, admonishing her constituents that 'Victorian values' were 'perennial values' (Crewe 1989: 239), still ringing in everybody's ears, Gray's verbal and pictorial efforts to capture the essential unreliability of representation appear as a historically conditioned attempt to tell, and show, a counterhistory that would encourage his readers to doubt the official story and 'work', as the novel's hardcover boards exhort, 'as if you live in the early days of a better nation'.

But does *Poor Things*, amid its welter of warnings about authenticity and reliability, offer anything like the positive, however qualified, closural holism of *Lanark* or *1982 Janine*? One appears to look in vain for *Lanark*'s even-tempered resignation or the comparatively jubilant new dawn of Jock McLeish. Still, whether we can ultimately ascertain the extent to which she does, or does not, incorporate Bella Baxter, Victoria McCandless's assertion that in the wake of the 1946 general election 'Britain is suddenly an exciting country' sounds promising. 'I feel a lot happier', she tells her correspondent Hugh MacDiarmid, 'I am going to die happy' (Gray 1992a: 316). Obviously such happiness comes at a price: 'Dr Vic's' proposals for collective social reform have been derided and at the end of her life she has to create a Polyanna-like optimism to sustain her vision, forestalling the criticism she knows MacDiarmid's reply will contain. Her effort may signal Gray's own increasing sense of the complex struggle required to integrate oneself meaningfully into the movement of history, as a variety of his other works suggests.

Certainly Wat Dryhope, the protagonist of *A History Maker*, Gray's final novel, may be viewed against his predecessors as a failure. His own intentions are consistently foiled as he is drawn into the plots of others. Though the net effect of his actions is positive, Dryhope remains unfulfilled and ends the novel in obscurity. This is history, the novel's postscript tells us, written in 'the comic mode' (Gray 1994: 223). Similarly farcical conclusions grace the pages of Gray's shorter novels *McGrotty and Ludmilla*, *The Fall of Kelvin Walker* and *Mavis Belfrage*. Each protagonist reaches an ending that – albeit representing a socially sanctioned form of success – allows for little self-knowledge, historical awareness, or true optimism. Is there really no more Gray can offer a culture moving into a new millennium? His poem 'Postmodernism', published in 1997 and collected in 2000, limns an intellectual universe where 'darkness lectures to darkness on darkness / and the darkness sees it is good' (Gray 2000b: 5), while the 'Editor's Postscript' of *The Book of Prefaces*, also published in 2000, laments that the volume is 'a memorial to the kind of education British governments now think useless' (Gray 2000a: 631). Still more to the point is a claim made in *Why Scots Should Rule Scotland 1997*: 'Every good thing that Scotland and England had in common, all that made our nations good examples to others, has been sold off or hideously cheapened' (Gray 1997:104). And yet it is in Gray's political pamphlets that a balance can be found to the dark historical vision of his fiction.

The first version of *Why Scots Should Rule Scotland* sketches out the dilemma of Scottish MPs before devolution, 'the loneliest, most insulated Scots of all' (Gray 1992b: 58). The plight of Scotland is seen as a product of the grotesque body politic necessitated by Westminster's distance. Accordingly, Scotland depends on 'orders from a remote head which is distinctly absent-minded . . . because it must first direct a far more urgent set of limbs and organs' (Gray 1992b: 59). A note of optimism creeps in as Gray begins to imagine a Scottish Parliament, which – albeit 'squabblesome and disunited and full of people justifying themselves' – will 'offer hope for the future' because 'an independent country run by a government not much richer than the People has more hope than one governed by a big rich neighbour'. The ideal Scotland, envisaged at the pamphlet's end, will be 'one where Scots mainly live by making and growing and doing things for each other' (Gray 1992b: 63–4). Interestingly, at the same time as Gray's view of the individual's engagement with history takes a more qualified turn in *Poor Things*, his faith in the power of collective agency manifests itself as unshaken. Prior to the 1997 election Gray rewrote the pamphlet, dismissing the original as 'a muddle' (Gray 1997: ix). The new version pictures the coming Scottish Parliament as 'a big London firm's branch office where local complaints get stifled by the locally complacent'; however, it also acknowledges that this pessimistic view need not be final as long as 'Scots refuse to let it rest at that' (Gray 1997: 111). The collectivist language of both pamphlets ('Scots', 'the People') removes them from the individualism of the novels. However, at the same time as he suggests that 'there are better ways of living than being happy but they require strength and sanity', Gray doubts if such strength and sanity are available in the current political climate (Gray 1997: 118). Ultimately, boundaries of social class may be too strong in Scotland for the necessary collective to form.

Significantly, the proposals detailed in *How We Should Rule Ourselves*, Gray's most recent pamphlet, co-written with Adam Tomkins, are directed towards all four constitutive nations of the United Kingdom, as signalled by Gray's cover illustration featuring the rose, the thistle, the leek and the harp. The assertive first-person pronoun thus comes to encompass a larger group than the 'Scots' or 'the People', and the text's four key reform proposals all begin with a 'we' poised between reference to the book's two authors and the many whom they hope to persuade:

1. We want all of the Crown's prerogative powers to be abolished and, where necessary, replaced with legislation.
2. We want current freedom of information laws to be repealed and replaced with legislation that would secure genuinely open government.
3. We want our parliaments to be reformed so that all are democratically elected and so that all are able to operate freely, without constraints imposed by party loyalty.
4. We want the Crown and the queen to be removed from the constitution, with the monarch's powers being transferred to the House of Commons. (Gray and Tomkins 2005: 48)

This sweeping slate of reforms would presumably allow the populace of each of the four nations to move towards a republican future where voters 'may eventually decide whether their nations stay combined under one federal parliament . . . or elect independent parliaments that collaborate without a single governing body'. 'We are a sovereign people', the authors conclude, 'so let's act like one' (Gray and Tomkins 2005: 3, 55). This exhortation is reminiscent of Gray's frequent references – in the frontispiece to *Unlikely Stories, Mostly*, during the 'Ministry of Voices' section in *1982 Janine*, and on the boards of *Poor Things* – to 'the early days of a better nation'; it aims to summon a collective capable of providing the proof for Jock McLeish's assertion that 'history is what we all make' (Gray 1984: 340). 'Feeling Scottish', a recent study shows, 'is more pervasive in Scotland than is any other identity elsewhere in Britain' (Bromley et al. 2003: 119). Out of such a strong, shared sense of identity it ought to be possible to muster a collective movement towards change. Acutely aware of the individualist and collectivist strands in the making of Scottish history, in *Claiming Scotland* Jonathan Hearn asserts the great potentialities of the present post-devolution moment, when the most pressing task is 'constructing a collective subject' (Hearn 2000: 197). Ultimately, however, what so much 'feeling Scottish' will accomplish remains to be seen. What if, for example, the collective subject lacks conviction and turns out to be burdened with 'a massive inferiority complex', so that 'the restoration of national self-confidence must be one of the first objectives of the Scottish Parliament' (Scott 2000: 207)? Or put differently, what if the collective subject sees itself, in Mark Renton's words, as 'a country ay failures' (Welsh 1993: 78)?

The necessary confidence may be derived, perhaps, from a thought experiment in nation-imagining like the one proposed by Thomas Docherty, according to whom 'a free Scotland – the only Scotland worth considering' can be established through 'the endless perpetuation of its own possibility'. As Docherty continues, such an endless perpetuation can only be set in motion by 'genuine autonomy . . . predicated upon the . . . issue of freedom' and untrammelled by 'the logic of inverting one's own self-constructed inferiority' (Docherty 2004: 247). Or, as Murray Pittock puts it, 'it is better to re-enter and revalue [Scottish] culture than waste contemporary energies blaming a caricature drawn by your society of itself' (Pittock 2001: 145). Perfectly concurrent on matters of identity, the problem of inferiority, and the promise of collectivity, both Docherty's model of a movement beyond self-loathing towards freedom and Pittock's desire to retrieve from the past what may still be of use resonate with the attitudes expressed in Gray's fiction and polemics. This, then, may be among Gray's greatest accomplishments and most valuable gifts to younger Scottish writers – not only creative writers but also historians, critics and theorists: already to have imagined himself, for some twenty-odd years, as 'working in the early days of a better nation', as well as to have so resourcefully envisioned the perils of individualism, the potential powers of the collective, as well as the elusive character of historical progress.

Chapter 20

James Kelman and the Deterritorialisation of Power

Aaron Kelly

The introduction of a devolved Scottish Parliament and the onset of the twenty-first century have elicited numerous repositionings and reperiodisations of Scotland and its culture. In an example that is typical, Catherine Lockerbie, director of the Edinburgh International Book Festival, has commented that

> now devolution has been achieved, people don't have to prove they are Scottish writers anymore . . . I think we've moved on from the days of the stereotypical writer. Young writers don't have to write those quasi-political novels. I think we'll find something more interesting and individual from them, rather than following that old path. The chip on the shoulder has been turned into a twiglet if you like and the Scottish cultural cringe has certainly diminished. (Massie 2002: 1)

There are a couple of complacent assumptions in Lockerbie's statement concerning the relationship of both devolutionary and post-devolution culture to politics and socio-economics. The designation of devolutionary writing as 'quasi-political' seems disingenuous, given that the standard critical narrative positions the post-1979 cultural realm as the space wherein authority and identity are devolved in a manner that actually anticipates the institutional devolution of power through the Scotland Act (see Craig 1996, 1999; Gardiner 2004a). Moreover, Lockerbie's comment raises a question as to precisely what 'quasi-politics' might be. Lockerbie's assertion explicitly suggests that it was the national question which preoccupied culture before devolution and, even more mechanistically, that writers such as Kelman were primarily engaged in proving their Scottishness by confirming some 'stereotypical' paradigm. Implicitly underpinning Lockerbie's views is a teleological narrative which avers that devolution demarcates some (vaguely defined) normativity that has now been broached and which may set aside, in some new dispensation, those former 'quasi-political' antagonisms, and the consequence of such normalisation is to be the re-issuing of the 'individual' untainted by a now resolved Scottishness.

Similarly, Christopher Whyte has maintained that 'in the absence of an elected political authority, the task of representing the nation has been repeatedly devolved to its writers', adding that 'one can hope that the setting-up of a Scottish parliament will at last allow Scottish literature to be literature first and foremost, rather than the expression of a nationalist movement' (Whyte 1998a: 284). The main, and indeed laudable, purpose of Whyte's analysis, within which the present statement occurs, is to critique violent masculine paradigms; however, notably, the reactionary crisis of gender identity perceived by

Whyte is located in a broader national malaise that, once more, may be resolved by devolved political power. Both Lockerbie and Whyte assume that devolutionary culture compensates for some national democratic deficit that is redressed by devolution so that, with the nation restored and political institutions returned, literature too may reclaim its privileged autonomy. Herein, in my view, resides a misguided reduction of the political to the national and a concomitant advocacy of a disengaged, individualised art: just as Scotland attains a normative model of national development that confirms yet paradoxically elides its nationhood, so its literature tautologically reproduces itself as literature in an economy of normality beyond politics and history.

This literary concern with wrestling Scottish writing from a supposedly anomalous 'quasi-politics' is embedded in a long-established sedimentation of sociological, socio-economic and political discourses positioning Scottish nationhood as the miscarried version of a European developmental norm. According to David McCrone,

> Scotland's capitalist revolution occurred within a country lacking the political and institutional structures of statehood. Further . . . such a transformation occurred before the ideological input of nationalism which was to inform the political and economic features of capitalist industrialisation in much of Europe . . . Scotland crossed 'the great divide' to become an industrialised society without the benefit or hindrance of nationalism . . . Further, Scotland's economy was rarely if ever self-contained and independent. It was an open economy, reliant on external capital and technology, and subject to the vagaries of the broader economic and political environment, whether of Britain or a wider European capitalist economy. (McCrone 1992: 35)

Whereas England matured organically, Scotland lagged behind and splintered. Tom Nairn equally perceives Scotland as an anomaly outside the norms of historical progress and concludes that 'an anomalous historical situation could not engender a "normal" culture' (Nairn 1981: 155). The politics of Scottish culture is never experienced in its own specificity and intensity; instead, disruptive and constitutive antagonisms such as social class become the depleted tokens of someone else's normality.

The insinuation ghosting such pronouncements is that Scotland would have been normal if only it had evolved a mature and well-rounded middle class. For Theodor Adorno, the effort to diagnose a social formation according to a grammar of health and normality in itself betrays a bourgeois narrative of historical development: 'The dichotomy of healthy/sick is as undialectical as that of the rise and fall of the bourgeoisie, which itself derives its norms from a bourgeois consciousness that has failed to keep pace with its own development' (Adorno 1977: 156). Adorno's account of the bourgeoisie's periodic incapacity to plot its own dynamic of perpetual change permits a fundamental revision of readings underscoring the disposition of Scotland in terms of prior malformation and belated maturity. Accordingly, the critical and historical positions adopted by Lockerbie and Whyte, and Nairn and McCrone, should not be regarded, as they ostensibly and locally appear, as a remedial struggle against a deformed nationalism. Rather, they gain their full meaning and betray their deepest affinities by signalling a wrangle to thread the final and telling stitch to the suture of bourgeois hegemony.

There is also a profound irony in the tautological and seemingly self-contained assertion of literature *qua* literature, and the individual as individual, for both of these apparent autonomies – rather than merely and hermetically themselves – are enlisted as reflective of some new post-devolution context of resumed normality. Adorno had this to say of Georg Lukács's attempt to reconcile the individual and the social in a reassuringly integral unity:

> The supreme criterion of his aesthetics, the postulate of a reality which must be depicted as an unbroken continuum joining subject and object, a reality which, to employ the term Lukács stubbornly adheres to, must be 'reflected' – all this rests on the assumption that the reconciliation has been accomplished, that all is well with society, that the individual has come into his own and feels at home in his world. (Adorno 1977: 176)

Likewise, the idea of a post-devolution Scotland democratically redressed is taken by Lockerbie and Whyte as reflecting, and reflected by, a new literature in a continuum of normality mediated by the individual. By contrast, Adorno maintains that 'art is the negative knowledge of the actual world' (Adorno 1977: 160), that is, rather than merely reflecting the world as an already agreed entity, literature harbours a complex mediation that enables a critique of both itself and its societal context. For while literature is produced out of a specific context, it is not solely reducible thereto; nor does it have passively inscribed upon it the ideological conditions of its own making. In Adorno's terms, literature is of the world yet also retains an aesthetic distance that is not harbinger of some wilful escapism but instead opens up a profoundly political space wherein the given world may be rethought, 'negatively' reformed and reconstituted in a manner that frustrates any effort simply to perpetuate that world.

As I will demonstrate, Kelman's writing contains precisely this 'negative' capacity by which a critique of the conventional account of post-devolution Scottish society and culture may be launched. Notably, Kelman's post-devolution fiction is set outwith Scotland: the fragmentary reports of *Translated Accounts* (2001) seep through the confines of an undesignated regime that is possibly Turkey or somewhere in Eastern Europe, while *You Have to Be Careful in the Land of the Free* (2004) addresses the experiences of the Scottish migrant Jeremiah Brown in the United States. In the terms of analysis established by Lockerbie and Whyte, it is tempting to construe this reorientation of Kelman's work as an admission that Scottish matters have finally been resolved and it is time to move on. Lockerbie's appraisal that Kelman's 'writing is angrier than ever, but I think that course has run' (Massie 2002: 1) seeks to dismiss Kelman on the basis that he is out of synch with the temporal-spatial closure of the national narrative, yet it remains troubled by the persistence and indeed intensification of political energies that Lockerbie's model of a new literature can neither explain nor periodise. The ongoing recalcitrance of Kelman's work, and of its stringent class politics especially, is highly instructive, for it signals that the politics and aesthetics of his writing are incommensurate with both the nationalist appropriation of culture before 1999 and the postnationalist arrogation of culture thereafter.

It is the ideological task of nationalism to assert the primacy of the nation at the expense of other identifications such as class, and hence to seek to annex the voice of a writer like Kelman as a national rather than more precisely situated class articulation. Accordingly, the postnationalist literature anticipated by Lockerbie and Whyte should not be regarded as a rebuttal of the ideological work undertaken by nationalism but rather its ultimate outcome. If nationalism betrays its bourgeois hegemony in its effort to sublate and recode the working-class politics of a writer like Kelman, then such a stratagem achieves not its negation but its apotheosis in postnationalism. For postnationalism pursues the final repression of class in its discourse of cultural difference. Class antagonism is rewritten as cultural diversity, a revalued sign of the postnation's healthy polyphony, so that, divested of its own terms and context, the language of class becomes simply one register among others of a cultural relativism that rewards bourgeois hegemony as social pluralism.

It would be impossible to write a history of bourgeois society without acknowledging its assimilative power. The bourgeoisie retains a capacity to harness otherness in a manner that reasserts its own hegemony because that otherness is in fact only and already the bourgeoisie's own construction, a part of its own self-relation rather than an ethical effort either to understand or to address what is radically other. While the discourse of pluralism permits bourgeois society to assimilate much of the minoritarian identity politics of late twentieth-century culture as part of its own structural realignment, the politics of class at work in Kelman's work interrogates this realignment and resists being recoded in its terms. But how might Kelman's writing facilitate a reconsideration of the democratic credentials of the newly devolved Scotland? Kelman's work has always been driven by the inequalities of late capitalism, the disruption of traditional working-class solidarities, and an attendant loss of meaning from the world, its events and institutions. In analysing the predicament of Kelman's characters, 1979 is a crucial watershed since it signalled not only the contentious defeat of the first referendum on Scottish devolution but also, compounding the Scottish working class's lack of democratic control over its future, the British general election victory of Margaret Thatcher. Thatcher's neo-liberal policies set about a vigorous assault on the organised labour of Britain's industrial heartlands – a campaign that was never endorsed by a democratic majority in Scotland (or, for that matter, Wales or large areas of working-class England). Significantly, then, state power and its institutions, which decimated the communities of working-class Scotland, were beyond the immediate understanding or experiential grasp of its victims; it was very much absent and elsewhere – literally hundreds of miles away.

Kelman observes in Franz Kafka's (1883–1924) work that 'society can be regarded as a labyrinth of authorities whose powers are functional' (Kelman 2002: 279). Similarly, in his own fiction Kelman confronts a bureaucratic state power that is extremely difficult to comprehend and resist due to the discrepancy between the presence of the lived, daily grind of its effects and the absence of the locus and source of its vast systemic reach. As Gilles Deleuze and Felix Guattari assert:

> If Kafka is the greatest theorist of bureaucracy, it is because he shows how . . . the barriers between offices cease to be 'a definitive dividing line' and are immersed in a molecular medium that dissolves them and simultaneously makes the office manager proliferate into microfigures impossible to recognize or identify, discernible only when they are centralizable: another regime, coexistent with the separation *and* totalization of the rigid segments. (Deleuze and Guattari 1986: 235–6)

Kelman's work likewise confronts the interminable and banal microfigures and micro-effects of power while also attempting to discern the causal structures behind these proliferations. In *The Busconductor Hines* (1984) Rab Hines struggles against not only his employers and trade union officialdom but also the division of Glasgow into Kafkaesque zones that delimit experience according to social class. Patrick Doyle in *A Disaffection* (1989) wrestles with his own implication in the educational apparatus of the British state but is also hounded by its agents, who stalk him at the novel's close and make locally visible the persistent conspiratorial menace of a system that torments him throughout the book. Finally, in *How Late It Was, How Late* (1994) these paranoid mappings culminate as Sammy's blindness paradoxically exposes the anonymity of the state's institutions: the fact that this blindness is the result of a police beating again makes plain the presence of power's effects, while the blindness *per se* sharpens the sense that power can only be traced through a cognitive mode able to *imagine* a macrostructure beyond immediate appearances. The need to make this cognitive leap itself indicts society's institutions, since if they are not directly representable, then they are also unrepresentative.

However, after devolution one would perhaps expect that this gap of representation (both cultural and political) would be redressed, that power would return to the nation and its people, and hence the historical forces which lead to devolution would coincide with the *telos* of national self-determination. But Kelman's post-devolution fiction is inflected with even more disjuncture and displacement than before. In answering the question of why this might be so, it is useful to return to the terms of Deleuze and Guattari's work on Kafka and specifically the theory of minor literature that they establish from Kafka's position as a Czech Jew writing in German. Deleuze and Guattari argue that 'a minor literature doesn't come from a minor language; it is rather that which a minority constructs within a major language . . . in it language is affected with a high coefficient of deterritorialization' (Deleuze and Guattari 1986: 16). In these terms, if Kelman's work contains a devolutionary dynamic, it does so by deterritorialising Standard English through a working-class Glaswegian constituency and not through a Scottish-national lens. By contrast, the devolution of political institutions within Britain can be understood in terms of a fundamental reterritorialisation of power via free-market economics, underpinning the creation of a European superstate portioned into highly rarefied neo-regional units. The perpetual de- and re-centring of the global economy according to the reifications of finance capital and its continual scrambling of cores and peripheries represent an unsettling dynamic that problematises any straightforwardly affirmative interpretation of spatial and political reorganisation.

Hence, the supposed emancipation offered by devolution may also be interpreted in terms of the micro-economic realignments of global capitalism. Kelman's post-devolution fiction confirms that what is ostensibly a deterritorialisation is ultimately a profound reterritorialisation, that is, not a democratising movement towards eventual national independence, or regionalised and micropolitical enfranchisement, but rather a shift to an increased interdependence of economic micro-units within global capitalism's shadowy institutions. It is therefore highly symptomatic that in an effort to reconcile nationalism and globalisation Kenny MacAskill, the justice spokesperson of the Scottish National Party (SNP), balances ultimately contradictory demands in proposing 'Independence in an Interdependent World'. In MacAskill's terms, a reconstituted post-devolution nationalism must recognise and endorse 'the internationalisation of the world economy' and seek to place Scotland within a coalition encapsulated by 'Devolution, Globalisation, and a New World Order' (MacAskill 2004: 23, 27). As Fredric Jameson asserts, 'neo-regionalism, like the neo-ethnic, is a specifically post-modern form of reterritorialization; it is a flight from the realities of late capitalism, a compensatory ideology, in a situation in which regions (like ethnic groups) have been fundamentally wiped out – reduced, standardized, commodified, atomized, or rationalized' (Jameson 1994: 148).

It is the deterritorialising energy of social class in Kelman's fiction that stands defiantly outwith the global reterritorialisation of a devolved Scotland. To that end, the radical shift in Kelman's style in *Translated Accounts* does not offer some sense of a Scotland at home with itself, the homecoming of some authentic voice, as nationalist appropriations of his work would have it, but instead very boldly displaces his work across what the broken language of the novel terms the 'terrortories' of global space (Kelman 2001: 175). Symptomatically, the voice in 'it is true', the final section of the book, states: 'I cannot say about a beginning, or beginnings, if there is to be the cause of all, I do not see this. There are events, I speak of them, if I am to speak then it is these, if I may speak' (Kelman 2001: 322). Equally, *Translated Accounts* destabilises the mainstream discourse of devolution as a new dawn, suggesting instead that this absent 'cause' is identical with the economic and political convulsions of globalisation when power has retreated still further into corporate boardrooms, financial institutions, unrepresentative democracies, brutal regimes and the phantasmagoria of multi-national space. The warping inevitabilities of this global space impinge directly upon the horrors, sufferings and dislocations of the characters in *Translated Accounts*: 'I crossed this footbridge, and to the other side, being anywhere now, away, no other possibility, none other existed' (Kelman 2001: 221). *Translated Accounts* does not inaugurate a Scotland made normal by a democratic redress but instead forces Scottish culture to consider its own impli-cation in globalised networks of power and injustice. The novel casts profound doubt on the representative limits of freedom and democracy by filtering through its fragmentary lan-guages the constitutive oppressions that haunt a new global dispensation.

Where Kelman's earlier work, such as *The Busconductor Hines*, *A Disaffection* and *How Late It Was*, ruptured a nationalist annexation of his writing by articulating the margin-alised experiences of working-class life that are the structural consequences of the process by which national culture assembles its codes of normality, *Translated Accounts* intensifies his commitment to voicing the ongoing displacements of class and inequality by pitching itself into multinational space:

> You speak of my country, it is my country, well and I do not speak of it. That is your own make-believe, it is what you need, a necessity that you demand, you and some other of your people, always, to see it in front of your eyes. And you have me in front of your eyes, representative of my country, you have it here, but I am not representative . . . You say it is my country. You say this to me, call it my country but I do not call it so, I am not there but here, I am here, in your country, your country is my country. (Kelman 2001: 268)

In this passage, the nation – 'my country' – is made problematic not simply by issues of class complicating some internal process of self-determination. Instead the 'make-believe' of the nation is now produced as a consequence of transnational pressures, and the speaker indi-cates that the nation in this new context functions not as an autonomous entity but as a degraded compensation for the dislocations of an increasingly homogenised global space. The nation remains for the speaker someone else's construction, and the whole dynamic of *Translated Accounts* addresses itself to the repression of the experiences of the oppressed in the vocabulary of global power and liberal democracy. So where the earlier fiction had already refused to be 'representative of my country' through a commitment to class polit-ics, *Translated Accounts* furthers that critique by rupturing, in the grammar of the SNP's civic postnationalism and globalised regional interdependence, the easy complicity between Scotland, devolution and a global economy. Furthermore, the forceful *non serviam* ('I am not representative') in the above passage permits a consideration of the radical shift in style, register and voice that the novel marks in Kelman's writing, which can be regarded not as an odd departure on his part but rather as a challenging reapplication of his con-cerns and technique.

In relation to the deterritorialising drive of minor literature, Deleuze and Guattari aver that 'language stops being representative in order to now move toward its extremities or its limits' (Deleuze and Guattari 1986: 23). *Translated Accounts* signals a further confrontation with the deep affinities of language and power that are similarly reworked in *You Have to Be Careful* in the hybridised 'Uhmerkin' Jeremiah Brown, the 'unintegrattit furnir' (Kelman 2004: 9), where Scotland becomes 'Skallin' and Scottish 'Skarrisch'. In particular, both novels harbour a conflict between the deterritorialisations effected by what Deleuze and Guattari call 'the vernacular' – for example, Kelman's resistant working-class voice – and what they designate as 'the vehicular', that is, the language of power and its reterritorialisations.

To understand the linguistic and representational experimentation that accompanies Kelman's post-devolution grappling with multinational space, Fredric Jameson's statement regarding a new poetics necessitated by globalised capitalism appears instructive:

> Structural co-ordinates are no longer accessible to immediate lived experience and are often not even conceptualizable for most people. There comes into being, then, a situation in which we can say that if individual experience is authentic, then it cannot be true; and that if a scientific or cognitive model of the same content is true, then it escapes individual experience. It is evident that this new situation poses tremendous and crippling problems for a work of art; and I have argued that it is an attempt to square this circle and to invent new and elaborate formal strategies for overcoming this dilemma that modernism or, perhaps better, the various modernisms as such emerge: in forms that inscribe a new sense of the absent global colonial system on the very syntax of poetic language itself, a new play of absence and presence that at its most simplified will be haunted by the erotic and be tattooed with foreign place names, and at its most intense will involve the invention of remarkable new languages and forms. (Jameson 1988: 349–50)

Both *Translated Accounts* and *You Have to Be Careful* demonstrate that, motivated and necessitated by globalisation, the vehicular mode of representation will reproduce itself in hybrid, multinational forms, which are yet inherently devoid of subversive potential because they are merely the carriers of newly galvanised codes of power. As one of the sections in *Translated Accounts* puts it:

> Other languages, what inventions, if they might have been, if new languages were there, are such languages possible, we could propose such models, adopting innovatory techniques, amalgam of logic, linguistical, in algorithms, all modern technologies but to remember that these have all derived from somewhere. (Kelman 2001: 174)

The challenge for the deterritorialising imperative of Kelman's post-devolution fiction is to locate and indict that absent 'somewhere' across globalisation's regimes, apparatuses and technologies by pioneering new vernacular representational modes of dissidence and resistance. Both novels contain a fraught dialectic between the onslaught of a global system that of necessity produces novel languages to accommodate new nationalisms, post-nationalisms, regionalisms, bourgeoisies and identities, on the one hand, and the need to find genuinely new, as yet unassimilated, cognitive and representational modes to comprehend and critique that onslaught, on the other.

What this dilemma enables is a more general recasting of the politics of language in Scottish literary representation, as formulated by Cairns Craig:

> For Edwin Muir . . . the key to the dissociation of Scottish sensibility lay precisely in the lack of coherence of the language . . . but it is precisely out of this multiplicity of dialects that the

> modern Scottish writers get their vitality. Their writings stand alongside much of the writing
> in Britain by others using folk idiom as an assertion of separate cultural identity (West Indian
> writers in particular), and in utilising a modernised folk culture as their medium, they . . . are
> in fact founding their work on one of the most insistent aspects of Scottish poetic experience
> since the eighteenth century – trusting the voice of the Scottish people to remain Scottish no
> matter how much it absorbs of English, or now American, culture. (Craig 1996: 200)

For Craig, Scotland's capacity to remain itself resides in its hybridity and specifically its
ability to absorb otherness in a self-sustaining way.

Notably, Craig acknowledges the increasing impact of American culture, and *You Have
to Be Careful* details an ominous engagement with the United States and its cultural, political and military hegemony. Kelman's concentration on language, representation and power
indicates that wherever societies and cultures meet under globalisation they do so on
unequal terms. Jeremiah finds himself merely one of many 'displaced persons' (Kelman
2004: 10) whose own experiential and cultural terms of reference and belonging have been
sundered and recoded by American hegemony and a new multinational dispensation. Just
as Jeremiah himself is aware of his employment in the security industry in the United States,
and the fragmentary voices of *Translated Accounts* are regulated by and through the 'securi-
tys' of the regime, so the very languages and structures of both novels self-reflexively meditate upon the impingement of power on their representationality. Neither text celebrates
some new global hybridity; rather, they retain a circumspect awareness that their deterritorialising energies may be hijacked and absorbed by the reterritorialisations of power.

As indicated above, bourgeois hegemony relies upon the annexation of otherness to
shore up its pluralist credentials, yet it is class and its injustices that finally sustain that
hegemony. It is working-class experience that remains structurally incommensurate with,
and socially excluded from, bourgeois hegemony and its apparent diversity. In *You Have to
Be Careful* Jeremiah suffers a terminal displacement: 'I had a home, I had another home,
maybe homes are ten a penny, I have had fucking millions of them. Except in the land of
my birth' (Kelman 2004: 68). Interestingly for Kelman, since he does not usually use quotation marks in his work, even for dialogue, the word 'hame' is on occasion used in inverted
commas. In contrast to Lockerbie's and Whyte's reconciled Scotland, or Nairn's and
McCrone's Scotland made institutionally and historically normal, 'hame' is for Jeremiah
always displaced and his repeated attempts to define and claim it only serve to defer it still
further, for its normative global codes of belonging are inaccessible to his class experience.
The Scots vernacular 'hame' signals only its own displacement rather than its accommodation in some perfectly reconciled national language and culture.

Dietmar Böhnke, the author of the first full-length study of Kelman's work, is keen to
situate Kelman's work in relation to devolution and a new and specifically national dispensation:

> This recent development and what will follow from it can indeed be regarded as an – at least
> indirect – outcome of the more confident mood in Scottish culture and especially literature of
> the past years and decades . . . the concern of Kelman (and other contemporary writers) with
> Scottish national identity . . . certainly played a part in bringing about this new situation.
> (Böhnke 1999: 6–7)

In Böhnke's view Kelman's work coincides with a process of national and institutional
devolution that is to be understood in terms of historical 'development' and progress.

Specifically, Böhnke equates postmodernism with devolution, invoking the work of Linda Hutcheon, who formulates postmodernism as fundamentally 'ex-centric', that is, as a deterritorialising liberation of difference from the constraints of power, metropole, hierarchy and totalisation: 'The local, the regional, the non-totalising are reasserted as the center becomes a fiction – necessary, desired, but a fiction nonetheless' (Hutcheon 1988: 12). Accordingly, devolving power from the centre to the periphery must appear an intrinsically postmodern emancipation, conjoining postmodernism and popular-democratic fulfilment. Postmodernism's supposed emancipatory credentials are also advocated by Jean-François Lyotard, who throughout his work lauds micronarrative over putatively repressive metanarrative, portraying the individual as a node where social practices intersect yet cannot be mapped onto one another or the social totality (Lyotard 1993, 1991). In this kind of analysis, society is heterogeneous and non-totalisable, and any attempt to consider the individual in terms of problematics such as social class (or nationality or gender for that matter) become reductive of that complexity. Conversely, Kelman's work tries to reconvene a sense of the global totality producing these new micropolitical codes, hybridities and structures.

In postmodernism's Lyotardian heterogeneity of individual and event, and in Lockerbie's and Whyte's postnationalist accounts of devolution, we find ultimately not a popular, democratic *deterritorialisation* but instead the *reterritorialisation* of that most mainstream of things, the individual, the formative ideological building block of bourgeois society. The idea of a post-devolution Scotland in which individuals can finally be individual, and literature can become literature again, merely solidifies the bourgeois subject and its efforts to depoliticise itself as well as society and culture more broadly. By contrast, Kelman's recent fiction intensifies his stringent confrontation with power in all its forms, even as those forms seek simultaneously to overwhelm us and withdraw from our grasp and understanding completely. His work deterritorialises itself from the complacent modification of a post-devolution Scotland beyond history, while both anticipating and demanding a more fundamental and revolutionary transformation. As *You Have to Be Careful* insists, 'there are times when the world changes' (Kelman 2004: 90).

Chapter 21

Harnessing Plurality: Andrew Greig and Modernism

Simon Dentith

Andrew Greig is a very diverse writer: he is the author of seven volumes of poetry, two books about mountaineering and five novels. Even within these broad categories there are wide variations: his poetry ranges from deft lyrical verse in *The Order of the Day* (1990) and *Into You* (2001) to serio-comic philosophical poetry in *Men on Ice* (1977) and *Western Swing* (1994), while his novels range from the 'modern romance' of *Electric Brae* (1992) through a light-hearted rewriting of the poaching yarn in *The Return of John Macnab* (1996) to a series of novels which incorporate, in very different ways, elements of the historical novel: *When They Lay Bare* (1999), *That Summer* (2000) and *In Another Light* (2004). Greig's confidence as a writer in all these genres is in itself remarkable, yet equally noteworthy is the thematic consistency pervading his work: Greig remains preoccupied with similar issues across the range of his writing, even though the manner of his writing, or its topics, can be very different. One possible way of approaching the conundrum of Greig's generic diversity is via his own self-characterisation as a 'modernist' in 'That summer' (Greig 2001: 35–6), but then the first-person speaker of this poem need not, of course, be read autobiographically.

Greig's most elaborate and sustained poem is *Western Swing*, which combines quest narrative, lyrical meditation and 'shaggy dog story', the latter being Greig's own epithet, taken from the volume's cover blurb. Its most immediate model – acknowledged within the poem – is T. S. Eliot's *The Waste Land* (1922), and the formal features of Greig's poem do indeed recall Eliot's modernism: the allusiveness, the initial 'difficulty', the philosophical seriousness, the verbal variety, even the ironic inclusion of explanatory notes at the end of the text. Greig's own term for the allusiveness of his poem is 'sampling', taken from the practice of late twentieth-century popular-music production, which samples sounds, tones and phrases from multiple sources and incorporates them into a new, coherent whole. The transition from Eliot's high-cultural allusiveness to Greig's popular-cultural 'sampling' suggests something of the difference as well as the connection between the two poets. But the point remains that in the poetry, and not only in *Western Swing*, Greig appears as a modernist writer who positions himself within a given literary tradition while practising a formally experimental and overtly intertextual mode of composition. At first sight this would not appear to apply equally to Greig's novels, which are not obviously 'difficult' in the manner of *Western Swing*. However, appearances are deceptive, as in all his novels Greig writes in a formally complex way implementing multiple, if sometimes subdued intertextual allusions. Thus *The Return of John Macnab* is a piece of 'revisionary writing' (Widdowson 1999: 164–79) which takes on the conservative romanticism of John Buchan's account of Scotland in his *John Macnab* (1925) and seeks to redirect it for contemporary times, while *When They Lay Bare* consists of a complex interweaving of allusions to the Border ballads in a text that remains undecidable in a characteristically modernist way. Similarly, *In Another Light* crosscuts between two narratives – a son's and his father's – and intricately plays them off against each other, resulting not exactly in a modernist collage but still producing a richly multifaceted text redolent of the formal self-consciousness of Greig's modernist forebears.

As stated above, Greig uses the term 'sampling' to describe his modernist practice of explicit intertextual allusions. Importantly, in 'Ken's Glossary, Notes & Acknowledgements', which concludes *Western Swing*, Greig insists on the historical dimensions of sampling:

> The sampling techniques . . . owe much to Eliot-Pound who developed the first modern sequencer. Some of their mixes are here sampled in turn. Sampling . . . is not a recent phenomenon – artists through all ages have borrowed, referred, pastiched and re-worked their tradition and contemporaries for their own purposes. (Greig 1994: 107)

Thus categorised, Greig's poetry emerges as a 'mix', blending multiple voices borrowed as much from contemporary popular culture as from the 'high modernism' of Ezra Pound and T. S. Eliot, both of whom, too, expertly mixed the popular with the classical in their poetry.

At the end of 'Ken's Glossary' Greig returns to reflect on his practice of sampling:

> These Notes and Acknowledgements owe something to Grimpeur's innovative Glossary/Index in *Men on Ice*, and echo similar devices in Alasdair Gray's works, and re-work with just a tinge of irony Eliot's *The Waste Land* notes which too explained a few things, invited further reading: and helped make up the required number of pages.
>
> This text may suggest not so much a kleptomaniac with a bad memory as an attempt to acknowledge, respect and harness the plurality (literary, linguistic, artistic and social) of a culture and a generation. (Greig 1994: 112)

In addition to his own *Men on Ice* and Eliot's *Waste Land*, Greig also refers to the work of Alasdair Gray, whose innovative self-referential 'Index of Plagiarisms' in *Lanark* (1981) has quite evidently exerted a lasting influence on Scottish literary practice. Greig's candour in identifying his own artistic purposes as 'harness[ing] the plurality . . . of a culture and a generation' proves illuminating with respect to all his writing. In the prefatory acknowledgements to *Western Swing* one of the people thanked by Greig is the academic, poet and critic Philip Hobsbaum, 'who asked "What is the true voice of an educated East Coast Scot of your generation" until I found the answer. (Many voices)' (Greig 1994: 6).

In the context of this remark, then, Greig's sampling can be seen as a vital ingredient of his wider aesthetics, which seeks to include a variety of voices in a way that respects the history of his own particular origin and formative influences while also recognising and celebrating the general cultural diversity of Scotland at the close of the twentieth century. Consequently, Greig's linguistic practice, as both a poet and a novelist, is at once more varied and more relaxed than some of his contemporaries'. His writing draws upon a variety of idioms, ranging from Standard English via Scots to the urban demotic of the Central Belt pioneered for literary purposes by James Kelman and Irvine Welsh. However, Greig's novels implicitly repudiate the idiom cultivated by Kelman, preferring instead the different nuances and linguistic colourings available to 'an educated Scot of the East Coast', presumably – to persist with Greig's own musical metaphor – to achieve a richer 'mix'.

Occasionally this repudiation is made explicit, as in the following exchange in *The Return of John Macnab*, in which the Macnabs are considering the various newspaper reports on their exploits:

> 'Here, Murray,' Alasdair said, looking up from the *Glasgow Herald*, 'are you a latter-day Robin Hood or a class-war thug?'
>   'Awa tae fuck.'
>   Kirsty looked up from the *Sunday Post*.
>   'Here, you're not in a Jim Kelman novel now.'
>   'You wantin tae censor ma language? Language of ma culture and class?'
>   She stared back at him levelly.
>   'Bollocks, Murray. You like making love with your wife? Then don't use it to curse with.'
>   She raised the paper again as Murray muttered something about bourgeois wankers but didn't take it any further. (Greig 1996: 101)

Murray, defeated here by Kirsty, is one in a series of Glaswegian political radicals who appear in Greig's writing, usually respectfully characterised. However, in this exchange at least one objection to the linguistic strategies of Kelman and Welsh is registered, and it is perhaps unsurprising that this objection should be given as a woman's point of view.

Generally Greig appears happy to use a mild Scottish idiom in his writing, though it is fair to say that it does not feature predominantly in his practice as either a poet or a novelist. In the poetry Scots is used as the register identifying the 'Axe-Man' persona in *Men on Ice* and *Western Swing*, that is, the figure who in both these poems embodies the most physical, energetic and masculine aspects of the poet. In the following passage from *Western Swing*, for example, the particular consonantal immediacy of the vernacular is deployed to striking effect in the description of a monumental hangover:

> The Axe-Man wakes, looks rough,
> Forjeskit, wabbit –
> Fuckt in baith languages.
>   (Wha called him?)
>
> Charred sodden leathers,
> White-like aboot the gills,
> He is something unspeakable
> ben the city dump.
>
> No just tae gallus,
> Bleak as Blantyre
> Body back to blubber . . .
>
>   (Greig 1994: 26)

Here Greig's use of Scots has a particular dramatic quality that fits the wider purposes of the poem, which is ultimately to reunite the various different facets of the poet, of which the Axe-Man, and with him a pungent vernacular, incorporates the most obviously physical and Scottish. Elsewhere in the poetry the use of Scots is less insistent and seems to be drawn upon only to enrich the poet's lexical choices.

Something similar can be said about the novels, where Scots is used to enhance the linguistic texture of the books rather than serve in any polemic against the alleged distortions of Standard English. The novel that makes fullest use of Scots is *When They Lay Bare*, in which the sections associated with one particular character, Tat, are written in a version of Border Scots. Some sense of Greig's reasons for deploying Scots, whenever he does deploy it, can be gleaned not only from these sections, but also from the following passage, in which one of the characters recaptures a Scottish word that had escaped her: 'Then she heard that long pirl-pirling cry. But she'd glimpsed the long curved beak and a word tilted from the back of her mind to the front: whaup. Curlew. How differently they taste in her mouth though they refer to the same' (Greig 1999: 51). In effect Greig takes advantage of the complexity of Scotland's linguistic disposition to allow himself the different tastes of 'whaup' and 'curlew', referring to the same bird, but connoting wholly different social histories. The divergent aesthetic strategies of Greig and Kelman regarding the use of language derive without doubt from the authors' difference in class location, but perhaps they are also a matter of geography: Greig comes from East Fife, and his linguistic inheritance is simply very different from a working-class Glaswegian's.

Centring on the struggle to find a meaning for human life in a secular world, the overall unity of Greig's diverse body of work is defined and sustained thematically rather than linguistically, and it is perhaps most aptly described as pursuing a kind of philosophical modernism. All the different 'topics' in Greig's work are essentially different enactments of this fundamental quest for meaning. This is true not only of the mountaineering books, or the poetry, in which climbing offers an especially intense mode of being for lives otherwise lived in a lower register; it also applies to the novels. The adventures in *The Return of John Macnab*, the flying during the Battle of Britain in *That Summer*, the younger protagonist's recovery from a near-fatal illness in *In Another Light* are all dramatisations of situations in which life is lived more intensely, and in which the marked proximity of death adds an urgent immediacy to the character's experience.

Greig's typical protagonist in this context is the young to middle-aged man undergoing some kind of existential crisis and seeking to resolve it, more or less successfully. In *Electric Brae*, Jimmy Renilson, with a failed marriage behind him and now working on the oil-rigs, leads an unfulfilled life. Challenged by a friend on what exactly might afford him a sense of self-fulfilment, Jimmy responds:

> 'Listen,' I said. 'I'm a person of no particular talent, not one of those big redeeming ones. Not like Kim's. Nor a cause like Graeme's. But I need a meaning and none of those things I've done in the past were it.'
>
> 'So what is?'
>
> The question went on and on sinking like the *Royal Oak* out in Scapa. I watched the cloud-shadow move over the water above the men who had died there when they thought they were safe.
>
> The tightness passed.
>
> 'Kim, I suppose. And climbing the Old Man,' I added casually. (Greig 1992: 107)

Jimmy is in love with Kim, an artist, and *Electric Brae* is primarily a record of their prolonged and destructive relationship. According to its subtitle, the novel is a 'modern romance', not only because it deals with many of the modern world's sexual permutations, but precisely also because 'meaning' is to be wrested from Jimmy's commitment to his relationship with Kim. The cited passage is also one of the many instances in Greig's work when the political radicalism of working-class Scotland – here represented by the character Graeme – is respectfully acknowledged, yet then dismissed as a possible central focus for the protagonist's own life. In Greig's view, clearly politics is not the realm where meaning and self-fulfilment can be found. Significantly, the passage also mentions climbing: the 'Old Man' is the Old Man of Hoy, an exposed sea-stack on the Orkney coast and one of Scotland's most famous climbing challenges. But the 'Old Man' remains unconquered and is left to stand as a measure of the bleakness of Greig's first novel, which records the failure of Jimmy's relationship with Kim.

The Return of John Macnab addresses a situation similar to that in *Electric Brae*, but in a somewhat lighter, even comic, register. In search for some significance in his life, the central character is forty-something Neil Lindores, and he and his friends reinvigorate their stalled middle-aged lives by embarking on the Macnab adventures. The novel also suggests that some sort of secular salvation can be found in a relationship, as expressed in the following passage, in which Neil finds himself alone with Kirsty, a woman who has gatecrashed the Macnabs' all-male party and is about to redirect their wholly masculine enterprise:

> He looked over at Kirsty. She was sprawled on her side in the long grass by the bank, seemingly asleep. Not a goddess nor a nymph nor a muse, just human flesh and blood. Just? When the body is glowing, swarming, humming like a golden hive?
>
> There was a quick *gloop!* in the water below. He looked and saw ripples spreading out, ring after ring, and he finally saw why sand running through an hourglass was the wrong image of time. Being alive was more like being wrapped in expanding circles, like rings in a pool or in the trunk of a tree. That's how it grows, idiot. (Greig 1996: 257)

Earlier in the novel the notion of time running out like an hourglass is referred to as a 'depressingly Scottish image' (Greig 1996: 141). Accordingly, by alluding to the potentially redemptive promise of an erotic relationship, this passage re-envisions the way a life might be lived as an antidote to Scotland's particular cultural inheritance.

In Another Light is yet another novel based on a middle-aged man's quest for meaning in his life. Half of the text is devoted to Eddie Mackay, who is recovering from, and trying to come to terms with, a near-fatal illness. The whole trajectory of the novel is focused on Eddie's attempt to construe meaning from the transformative aesthetics of his work. It is tempting to read this as only the latest realisation of a persistent ambition at work in Greig's writing, which is to achieve an all-encompassing synthesis of the different strands of his own life and art. In Eddie's case such self-fulfilment is sought in the completion of a piece of music computer-generated from sounds created by measuring the height of the waves around Orkney:

> I was no longer shivering. I wasn't thinking of Mica or Tina, dead fathers or children unborn. It felt like my brain had finally woken from a long slumber as I imagined the sea round Orkney endlessly generating a music at once natural and technological . . .
>
> To make the sound of the shape of the sea meaningful. Another fantasy, like the one I'd woven in idle moments around a golden head, or believing I could change Mica's mind, or recover my father in Penang?
>
> I had to know what it sounded like, that was all. (Greig 2004: 266)

While the ultimate aesthetic value of Eddie's musical achievement has to be taken on trust by the reader, Greig's intention is clearly yet again to discover some kind of meaning in the world, to be articulated in an idiom that remains secular and material.

Despite my recurrent insistence on the secular nature of Greig's project, it is easy to detect a persistent engagement with at least one religion in Greig's writing, and that is Buddhism. In *Western Swing* a 'Heretical Buddha' appears as one of the most prominent voices, superseding the figure of 'The Bear' that features in *Men on Ice*. Buddhism is frequently invoked as a meaning-making possibility in Greig's work, offering a new perspective on his characters' struggles and confusions. In *Western Swing*, however, it is important that the Buddha should be recognised as 'heretical', as explained in the following section:

> *This time round*
> *I am Bud wiser. Heh,*
> *gather round, bairns,*
> *for in this hand I'm holding*
> *a traditional Truth:*
> > *the Futility of Desire.*
> *In the other – the heretical*
> > *Truth of its beauty.*
> Holding out his fists:
> *So what's it gonna be today –*
> *Wisdom, or the other?*

(Greig 1994: 43)

The heretical truth offered by the Buddha is not to be taken entirely seriously. Yet it does hint at the promise Buddhism appears to hold for Greig, even in this westernised form: Buddhism does not appear as an ascetic religion but one which affirms 'desire' in a way that is commensurate with Greig's representation of the latter's redemptive potential in his novels. In *In Another Light* more orthodox Buddhism appears as a powerful presence in the life of Alexander Mackay, Eddie's father, as he tries to find a way for himself in Penang, Malaya, in the early 1930s (he has travelled there to find work as a doctor). But if Buddhism, heretical or otherwise, manifests itself so benignly in Greig's writing, one is tempted to ask why the Christian culture of his childhood does not. This is a question that will turn out to connect Greig's secular modernism and his Scottishness in a most profound way.

Put crudely, the culture with which Greig's protagonists must come to terms, and which they and the novels largely reject, is Calvinist Protestantism and its secular legacies. There is an obvious danger in exaggerating and hence caricaturing the actual impact of Calvinism on life in Scotland, and indeed in seeing it as a peculiarly Scottish phenomenon, as though a kind of secular puritanism were not manifest elsewhere in these islands. However, Greig certainly insists on dramatising this particular religious inheritance as a principal obstacle to his protagonists' happiness, often rendering it as a generational conflict forcing sons to repudiate the world views of their fathers before they can hope to live in the world more affirmatively. This applies to Jimmy in *Electric Brae* in a relatively straightforward way: 'When I was a laddie my dad was a hard man with a hard hand. He had high standards and a temper and he wouldn't bend . . . Not his fault. It's in the culture' (Greig 1992: 119). As already mentioned, in *The Return of John Macnab* Neil's discovery of a more positive way of embracing life involves a repudiation of the 'depressingly Scottish' notion of one's lifetime as an hourglass.

The novel which explores the problematic most fully, however, and in the most complex way, is *In Another Light*, which is deliberately structured around two narratives showing a father and son living out their crucial life-choices in ways that reflect on each other. In both cases the cultural legacy of their own fathers is central. From Eddie's perspective, his father, a successful doctor, embodies both the Scottish virtues and – in his unflinching devotion to duty and hard work – their narrowness:

> He was tall, lean, upright, toughened as leather. He had energy, he had power. *Vir*, he would have cried it. *Smeddum*.
>
>   He was known for being irascible. He frightened housemen and nurses, subdued tough matrons, but I'm told he was gentle and sympathetic with his patients. He sometimes shouted at us, even belted us across the lug. That was his generation's way, which doesn't mean I have forgiven him. (Greig 2004: 64)

Alexander himself is of course the product of his own generation's history; he has been through the Great War, lost his faith, and possesses a particularly fearsome devotion to duty and 'getting on' as a result. In a touching scene, he is described with his own father, a joiner, on the eve of his departure for Penang: '"Do well, Alec," [his father]'d said. "Do right" . . . That was his last and only parental guidance. He'd actually said *Dae weel, Eck. Dae richt*' (Greig 2004: 164).

What Greig sketches out in these succeeding generational transitions is nothing less than a condensed history of the twentieth century, in which a particular ethic is trans-mitted from father to son, and hence far more than a simplistic repudiation of the Calvinist legacy. Thus, pertinently, Alexander's experience in Penang, culminating in an existential crisis to do with his affair with a married woman, represents his own transition, seventy years before his son, out of the narrowness of his cultural inheritance. The chief force behind this transition is clearly spelled out: partly a matter of contact with a more worldly set of people, and partly poetry (Yeats and Whitman), it is fundamentally a sexual experience. The novel attempts to answer how that 'upright, toughened' individual of Eddie's father had been created and whether in the contemporary moment the same version of masculinity needs to be perpetuated. As it turns out, the potential of Alexander's liberation through sexual fulfilment was never quite realised, thus explaining the powerfully masculine and upright stature of the older Mackay, as experienced by his son, as the upshot of a deplorable process of repression and compromise. However, as the novel also suggests, a contemporary masculinity need not be modelled on that older, 'toughened' blueprint.

In some respects all of Greig's novels remain romances, persistently turning on the choice by a male protagonist of a female partner. While this may harbour an inevitable masculinism, it is tempered by real efforts, in both the poetry and the fiction, also to acknowledge female perspectives. A couple of examples will suffice to indicate this aspect of Greig's work, the first of which, from *Western Swing*, is especially telling. *Western Swing* is a sequel to the earlier *Men on Ice*, in which three climbers – Grimpeur, Axe-Man and Poet – represent at once a simple triad of different existential possibilities and three aspects of the poet's own self. In *Western Swing* the same characters reappear; however, now they are named Ken, Brock and Stella, or, in other words, the Poet has become a woman, who is metaphorically incorporated into the healed poet, or his reassembled persona, at the end of the poem. Notably also, Stella rejects one particular reading of the poem (which is centred on the quest for a knife): 'The Blade's no phallic power source / but a tool for use about the house, / baring a wire / or in the kitchen, cutting bread' (Greig 1994: 98). Through Stella's perspective, then, the movement of the poem becomes less portentous or masculine, and the heart of the poet's specifically poetic engagement is coded as feminine.

A similar recoding of a masculine enterprise occurs in *The Return of John Macnab*, in which the group dynamics among the three Macnabs are upset by the introduction of a female outsider. On one occasion Kirsty peers at the three men through a window as they are making plans:

> She pressed her face to the pane. She felt absurdly touched as if they were hers in some way. Wee boys playing a boys' game.
>
> So what did that make her? What *is* a woman's game?
>
> She looked at them again and felt herself excluded. They were men and had known each other for years. She had to find a way to break in.
>
> She rapped on the window and laughed as they started like guilty things, then hurried round the back. (Greig 1996: 53)

To produce an acceptably contemporary rewrite of the all-male adventure story inherited from Buchan clearly forms an integral part of the novel's conceptual design. Yet Greig is not satisfied with a simple repudiation of 'a boys' game'; rather, he also wants to explore what 'a woman's game' might be. Ultimately Kirsty's discovery of the latter comes to match Neil's arrival at a sense of meaning in his life.

However, Greig's progressive sexual politics constitutes only one aspect of his project to rewrite his Scottish inheritance; others reside in his national and class politics. Before discussing these in any detail, let us consider what is in effect a point-blank repudiation of formal politics in *Western Swing*:

> *Matter*, he sighed, *is condemned*
> *to eternal push-ups and good-byes.*
> *Everything*
>   *is nothing mostly*
> *even your physicists know that.*
> *You must learn to think bifocal*
> *to focus on*
>   *what's nearest*
>   *and the distant view.*
> *I advise you to ignore the middle ground,*
> *anything within the range*
> *of newspapers.*
>   *Don't buy*
> *what can be bought –*
> *it's rubbish.*
> *Without expectation, aid all living things.*
> *And my opinion of life remains*
> *probably the least interesting thing about it.*

(Greig 1994: 102)

It is true that Greig's writing does indeed generally ignore 'anything within the range of newspapers', overtly reluctant to engage in any sustained way with the 'middle ground' between the personal and the spiritual, which is precisely the domain of the political.

There are some important caveats to enter against this judgement. *The Order of the Day*, for example, comprises 'In Love and Politics', which contains a couple of explicitly political poems about such matters as, perhaps obligatory for the early 1990s, American foreign policy. But even when Greig writes a poem directly addressing the national question, it displays a highly ambivalent attitude to nationalist politics. Thus, 'Scotland' in *Into You*, meditating on the matter of Scotland via an engagement with Hugh MacDiarmid, rejects the notion of Scotland-as-victim and instead issues a rallying call for an 'open-hearted' embrace of the future unhindered by a debilitating fixation on the past:

> Isn't it time
> we rose now
>   with our hands off our crutch –
>
> with a new century across the way
> isn't it time
>   we got up and
>
> wobbly
>   a bit light in the head
>   kind of feart actually
>
> walked clear-headed
>   open-hearted
>   unaided
>
> to greet it?

(Greig 2001: 55)

'Scotland' is a millennial poem entirely appropriate for a post-devolution country. In it MacDiarmid's version of revolutionary nationalism, together with its accompanying linguistic invention of 'Synthetic Scots', gives way to a simpler, yet still recognisably Scottish idiom capable of an impressive directness of utterance.

Evidence from his fiction equally helps qualify the judgement of Greig as a writer for whom politics is never a central issue. *The Return of John Macnab* not only involves a rewriting of the gender politics in the adventure genre, but also addresses traditional class politics, as the poaching challenges are performed with the aid of a mass trespass and the help of Land Rights activists. Whereas Buchan's tale represents the Highlands as a mere recreation ground for spiritually despondent toffs, culminating in a sermon on the responsibilities of leadership in romantic Tory vein, Greig's 'wee boys playing a boys' game' include a working-class Glaswegian radical as well as a couple of people of indeterminate class affiliation. One of the latter is an ex-soldier best described as a 'Tory anarchist', and this might indeed make an appropriate label for the politics of the novel as a whole. Perhaps another clue to Greig's ambivalent attitude to politics can be derived from paying attention to the publication date of *Electric Brae*, his debut novel, which was published in 1992 when Greig was already forty and had lived through a decade of Thatcherism. The novel itself is about the 1980s, and as such it tells the story of more or less resourceful characters living in a country that is being put through hard times. Typically, Graeme's politics are at once treated respectfully and dismissed; in fact, he is the first of Greig's West Coast radicals to come to realise that politics cannot ever give final meaning to a life. In a time of political defeat politics cannot be relied upon.

But the political situation in post-devolution Scotland is very different from that of the early 1990s, and perhaps Greig's writing, with its inclusive attitude to the many voices of Scotland, is especially well placed to address this. However, his manner of address is unlikely to be ever directly political, for while a discussion of all these thematic concerns, 'issues' and 'positions' is obviously crucial to any critical appraisal of Greig's work, in some ways they are also all preliminary. Notably, Greig's greatest achievement as a novelist is the remarkable romance *When They Lay Bare*, which is couched in an emphatic and at times enigmatic idiom that appears perfectly equipped to convey its tragic subject matter. Testifying to the novel's expert conflation of modernist with traditional storytelling techniques, its running choric commentaries can be read at once as the author's self-referential meditations and its central character's rhapsodic mental life:

> *The voices in the wind come in whatever language you need, like the voice in a headset guide. It could be Silver Latin, or Norse, or the lost language of the Picts – but as you are not so fluent in those you will not hear them save in a fleeting murmur below the rattle of leaves or in the burble at the bottom end of the river sound. Like infra-red or ultra-violet, they are in the air but outwith your range. So you are left with degrees of English – and Scots, the remnants of that speech of both sides of the Border once confusingly known as Inglis.* (Greig 1999: 222)

Read as a self-referential meditation on the linguistic strategies of the text, the peculiar language of this passage can be seen to reflect the linguistic richness of Scotland, and this is surely an excellent place to conclude. *When They Lay Bare* combines Greig's modernist art with his modern philosophy in a story drawing on the rich cultural inheritance of 'the Border', producing an idiom well-suited – to quote again from his poem 'Scotland' – to 'greet' the new century in a way that, it is to be hoped, will outlive that first moment of millennial enthusiasm.

Chapter 22

Radical Hospitality: Christopher Whyte and Cosmopolitanism

Fiona Wilson

Cosmopolitanism has long occupied an ambiguous position in Scottish culture. In a small country, culturally and politically dominated until the last decade by its larger and more powerful neighbour to the south, how could it be otherwise? The borders of identity, the meanings of Scottishness, have been fiercely fought over. Where does Scottish culture begin, and where does it end? Is it enriched or threatened by engagement with cultures outside its own? Questions of authenticity and difference drove the Scottish literary renaissance in the twentieth century and, in many ways, they continue to shape the national conversation. For a new generation of post-devolution writers and critics, however, the terms of the debate have changed. If old models of national identity rooted in a chthonic sense of racial purity are no longer tenable, neither are models that posit a Scottishness defined by outside pressures. Both ways of thinking rest upon a troublingly dualistic notion of national identity: a rhetoric of presence dependent on absence, a 'Scotland' determined by what it is not. Such models stand accused of having excluded identities classed as 'foreign' to the national story, for example, the voices and experience of Scottish gays, lesbians, women, racial minorities, and even the Scottish diaspora overseas. The talk now is of 'One Scotland, Many Cultures', that is, of national identity as a series of encounters and negotiations within the political fact of the state. Post-devolution, the hope is for a Scotland less defensive and less anxious, as well as more open to multiple ways of knowing, being, living and loving.

What is hoped for, then, is a Scottish cosmopolitanism, that is, a national identity hospitable, in the broadest sense, to cultural difference – to the difference, the strangeness even, of the nation itself. No Scottish writer has argued more forcefully for such an ethos than novelist, poet, translator and critic Christopher Whyte. For Whyte, identity is hybrid; accordingly, there may well be 'a range of possible ways of "being Scottish"' (Whyte 1995b: xiv). Whyte's interest is in how these 'possible ways' intersect and overlap with each other. If past narratives of Scottish identity often rested on unexamined binary constructions, the present task is to recognise, interrogate and possibly rewrite the borders of those narratives. This is not to say that Whyte's aim is to dismantle borders; rather, it would seem that he wishes to find new ways of crossing, and recrossing, them. He wishes to begin a new dialogue about the nation by putting borders in question, an impulse which animates both his critical and creative work. Though Whyte is resistant to the idea that Scottish writers should continue to be burdened with the responsibility of imagining the nation, it could be said that his four novels to date – *Euphemia MacFarrigle and the Laughing Virgin* (1995), *The Warlock of Strathearn* (1997), *The Gay Decameron* (1998) and *The Cloud Machinery*

(2000) – do exactly that. All of them explore issues of hybridity and identity and, in so doing, give voice to the possibilities and challenges of a Scottish cosmopolitanism.

Euphemia MacFarrigle, Whyte's first novel, is a hymn to hybridity from a distinctly Scottish angle; it is a mixed dish, a 'Mac' farrago. Science fiction, detective story, *Bildungsroman*, comedy, tragedy and love story all rolled into one, *Euphemia MacFarrigle* is a satire in the classical and Bakhtinian sense. Inhabited by pregnant nuns and malapropian Basques as well as the laughing icon of the title, the narrative bursts with a raucous comic energy. This is comedy with a point, though, since Whyte's immediate goal is revenge for a strict Catholic upbringing. More broadly, *Euphemia MacFarrigle* sets out to explode the binary distinctions that underpin sexism, homophobia and other forms of social prejudice. Given these goals, Whyte's choice of a decentred, multi-plot narrative makes perfect sense. No single character dominates the action, which unfolds from many different points of view. The novel begins by detailing the sensations of various Glaswegians as they register the presence of something different in their lives. For Cissie MacPhail, it is the curious awareness of 'her own private parts' whenever she finds herself in the vicinity of her friend Euphemia; for Mother Genevieve, it is the strange twinges of excitement that mark her body's response to the 'introduction of a foreign element' she cannot quite identify (Whyte 1995a: 7, 27); for three nuns it is a trinity of immaculate conceptions; and for the archbishop of Glasgow it is a case of chronic flatulence. Meanwhile, parochial schoolboys Gerald and Daniel struggle with their feelings for each other, and Fraser Donaldson, a closeted employee of the archdiocese, hears voices threatening to 'out' him. 'You would think', the archbishop says, 'someone was playing a practical joke' (Whyte 1995a: 12), and quite clearly somebody is: what none of these characters know is that their bodies are hosting a benevolent investigatory group of microscopic aliens directed by Euphemia herself.

Euphemia MacFarrigle can be seen as a systematic undoing of many of the foundational tropes associated with the genre of the Glasgow novel, most importantly the trope of the unyielding city and its corollary: the isolate, impenetrable body of the 'hard man'. Though, at first glance, Whyte's Glasgow is a place of 'general, unremitting grayness' and 'unbroken, joyless phalanxes of council tenements' (Whyte 1995a: 57, 104), a place of division between Protestants and Catholics, men and women, gays and straights, closer inspection reveals a far more porous environment. Barred windows give on to dusty, sunlit backyards, while buildings are constructed over and around tunnels, closes and cavernous basements, penetrated by the orange glow of streetlamps. The pub on Blytheswood Square, which is straight by day, gay by night, is in a 'transitional stage' at half past six. Most strikingly, Euphemia's own dwelling has a disturbing habit of materialising and vanishing Brigadoon-style in a 'gap site' at 98 Otago Street. All that is solid melts into air only to reappear and re-imagine itself at some future date. Like Homi Bhabha's notion of a hybrid, in-between 'third space' linking and defining oppositional terms, 98 Otago Street is liminal and negotiable (see Bhabha 1994). For some, such as the detective Mick McFall, this liminality marks it as a place of danger; for others, the same qualities identify it as a place of refuge and possibility. It is also a microcosmic version of Glasgow itself, which, as Euphemia's own prophecies demonstrate, has never ceased to evolve and change.

Through this 'Glasgow', both strange and familiar, move penetrable and hybrid bodies, at once part of the city and an incarnation of it. Sexual trysts take place on stairwells and in bedrooms that are 'entered', 'penetrated' and 'explored'. Desire – like comedy, like Euphemia's angelic crew – flows through the characters just as the River Kelvin does beneath the streets of the West End, no more hostile to the characters than the river is to the human world above. Problems arise only when people perceive desire as hostile, confusing real dangers (such as AIDS) with mythical ones (like the alleged infectiousness of homosexuality), resulting in attitudes like Cissie's, who has rather outlandish ideas about alternative sexualities: 'Who knows maybe homosexual and lesbian genes hung in the atmosphere and breathed in even in minimal quantities by an innocent believer like herself might induce abominable desires and hallucinations in a very short space of time' (Whyte 1995a: 24). Certainly, a consistent subject in *Euphemia MacFarrigle* concerns the harmful absurdity of trying to insulate oneself from desire: to guard against pregnancy, the archdiocese instructs all nuns to wear ear-plugs, while to prevent extramarital sex, Cissie is dispatched to a gay café to filch condoms. Far less amusing is the case of Gerald, who is told by a hypocritical schoolteacher to keep his sexuality firmly in the closet lest he blur intelligible distinctions between male and female: 'Do you realize the gravity of that sin? Do you know that you are defiled? That he has used you as a man uses a woman?' (Whyte 1995a: 112). In this instance, repression is no joke, as Gerald's lesson in self-hatred eventually leads to his suicide.

In *Euphemia MacFarrigle* freedom from the claustrophobic pressure of binary thinking arrives via satire and the acceptance of hybridity. The archdiocese calls in the strong arm of the law, in the shape of a Basque inquisitor, but once he has arrived Father Gutierrez reveals himself as the true satyr of the piece, a bewildered Dionysus whose florid mispronunciations ('Pliced to meet you') are magically realised in a lance of flowers blooming from his majestically large behind: 'Bless hims. Bless hims. Growing from my bauxite' (Whyte 1995a: 109). Bless him indeed. Heteroglossia is no crime; rather, for Whyte, it is evidence of the irrepressibly creative force of hybridity. Certainly, it inspires a welter of novel feelings – 'wonder, compassion, the temptation to laugh, fear' (Whyte 1995a: 109) – in the doctor examining Gutierrez. A similar mix of responses greets the hilarious miracle of the book's title, when Mother Genevieve's impure thoughts – the 'foreign element' of her own desires – provoke first a giggle, then a 'hearty guffaw' from a statue of the Virgin (Whyte 1995a: 98). While the church worries and the press marvels, a lively crowd gathers to witness the miracle, 'milling around, eating candy floss and toffee apples, picking up and putting down squawling babies, jostling prams and exchanging news excitedly' (Whyte 1995a: 105). Carnival, as usual, upstages essentialist dogma; moreover, it exposes the queerness of the normative.

Yet *Euphemia MacFarrigle* does not leave it at this. Instead Whyte returns us to Daniel, who has found refuge at 98 Otago Street, where he finds a book of poetry in 'two languages: English on the right, and what looked like German on the left. There were Biblical names in the titles, Latin and French expressions, a poem about Buddha and another about a panther' (Whyte 1995a: 156). Reading, Daniel encounters more than the strangeness of Rainer Maria Rilke's poetry. He encounters, and learns to be hospitable to, the strangeness of others, which is also, of course, the strangeness of himself.

After the wildish atmosphere of *Euphemia*, *The Warlock of Strathearn*, Whyte's attempt at historical fiction, may seem like a more familiar affair. Just how 'familiar' we find this work, however, is likely to depend on our understanding of that term, that is, whether we interpret it as an adjective ('known') or as a noun ('demonic companion'); both, as it turns out, are at home in this uncanny tale. The narrative begins in displacement, in the hands of an editor, one Archibald MacCaspin. The history of the seventeenth-century warlock of Strathearn, MacCaspin reports, was buried among some family papers mistakenly 'dispatched to a variety of destinations throughout the British Isles and overseas' (Whyte 1997: 9). Strangely, it re-emerges as the only document to have survived this textual migration. It is a fine cock-and-bull story and that, of course, is the point. MacCaspin, however, is oblivious to the multiple origins of the warlock's tale and its historically unstable character as a 'repetition': *The Warlock of Strathearn* is a rewrite, or 'doubling', of James Hogg's *The Private Memoirs and Confessions of a Justified Sinner* (1824). The editor is blind, too, to his own homoerotic desires in reproducing the textual body of the long-lost manuscript. The more he examines the 'nether regions' of the text, the more he clings to the totem of authenticity as a defence against his own disavowed longings (Whyte 1997: 15). But MacCaspin's lack of self-knowledge only highlights the problem of authenticity, which is exacerbated by the dubious origins of the anonymous warlock: born the bastard son of a servant woman and the wayward heir to the estate of Culteuchar in Perthshire, the warlock is, like Hogg's similarly situated Robert Wringhim, at once connected to and excluded from the cultural order. Long before his remarkable powers become manifest, his liminal position in the family marks him as 'foreign' – a resident alien, as it were, whose mere presence discloses legitimacy and authority as arbitrary fictions. As in *Euphemia*, such in-between hybridity invites various responses. While in some of the Culteuchar residents it inspires hope of a cure for the ills of everyday life, in others – notably the warlock's grandmother, Alison, and her spiritual advisor, the Presbyterian minister Vincent McAteer – it incites a paranoid, sadistic hostility. Alison and McAteer simply cannot, and will not, tolerate hybridity. Unable to convert the warlock to their bizarre brand of monotheism, they imprison and torture him.

To stand outside definitive binary oppositions, to stand outside the official order, can be perilous at the best of times; in seventeenth-century Scotland, it is life-threatening. At the same time, hybridity also opens up perceptions unimaginable within the narrow mental parameters of, let us say, an Archibald MacCaspin. Instructed by his spirit familiars, the warlock learns how to shapeshift, an experience he likens to 'being led through the multiple forms of existence' as well as the learning of a language or an art 'whose existence I can only indicate in these pages, never explain' (Whyte 1997: 74). Interestingly, the warlock's take on shapeshifting closely resembles Whyte's account of literary translation as provoking a 'plurilinguistic consciousness, an awareness of other, neighbouring languages [which] condition and energise the perception of one's own' (Whyte 1989: 23). The act of translating heightens one's understanding of choice. In this case, self-immersion within the 'plurilinguistic consciousness' of shapeshifting alerts the warlock to the strangeness of his (hetero)sexuality: 'My sex surprised me' (Whyte 1997: 113). All this could, as the warlock observes, still sound 'like an irresponsible game', a vaguely pleasurable playing with identity, were it not for Whyte's acute awareness of the potential costs of this 'game'. Like translation, shapeshifting is not a means to achieving transparency and should not be used to erase or deny difference. To translate the other is not necessarily to converse *with* the other, and the limits of dialogue are very much Whyte's concern in the remainder of *The Warlock*.

Limitations, for example, overshadow the warlock's affair with the lesbian witch Lisbet Muir, as well as his subsequent adventures. The warlock's love for Lisbet inspires his greatest feat of magic when he transforms himself into a woman. But being a 'woman' is about more than simply occupying a female body. In his new role, the warlock must learn to conform to and enact behaviour he finds bizarre and humiliating. As he puts it, 'it took me a long time to accept the necessity of mincing along, my legs practically glued to one another, gathering my headscarf about my face, and not daring to lift my eyes from the ground' (Whyte 1997: 157). And even as a 'woman', the possibilities for misrecognition remain manifold. When Lisbet is ultimately condemned, she stands on the scaffold and defiantly pronounces her lover's name, which, the warlock recalls, 'was not, of course, my name' (Whyte 1997: 182).

If this story serves to illustrate the experiential limitations of gendered bodies, the episode that follows shows the difficulties of 'translating' across class and national differences. Bereft of Lisbet, the warlock places himself in service to an alchemist, who promises to reverse his sex change. The pair depart for Bohemia, where their skills are engaged by a wealthy aristocrat. In Prague, the warlock thrills to the city's cosmopolitan air, relishing its fantastical architecture, as well as the mix of mysticism and scientific enquiry he encounters in the Jewish ghetto. One church in particular with its spindles and globes seems 'like the model for a different universe' – a realisation prompting the warlock to assert that it is 'belief that shapes reality' (Whyte 1997: 208). Ensconced in his patron's castle, however, the material weight of reality becomes all too apparent: the ghetto is, after all, a ghetto. At the same time, the castle's show of hospitality turns out to be a luxurious trap; the building is the nerve centre of an oppressive feudal estate. Outside the walls, a resentful peasantry responds to its oppression with rage at the 'devilish' experiments being conducted by the foreign visitors. Without agency – that is, without the ability to control his own fate – the warlock finds himself unwillingly complicit with his patron's rule, and the pleasures of hybridity become submerged in the terrors of alienation.

What becomes evident in the Lisbet and Bohemia sections of *The Warlock* is Whyte's conviction that hybridity must not be viewed solely as a cosmopolitan aesthetics of mere 'sophistication' and 'worldly tastes'. There are real, material forces that inhibit choice, and these must be fought against. Thus, when Alison's ghost returns, the warlock's final showdown with his persecutor is a fundamentally political act.

The Gay Decameron, Whyte's third novel, joins the carnivalesque energies of *Euphemia* with the sober reflectiveness of *The Warlock*. Its obvious precursor is Giovanni Boccaccio's marathon of late-medieval storytelling, *The Decameron* (1353), in which ten young men and women, exiled from Florence by the plague, entertain each other with tales of love. Whyte substitutes ten gay men at an Edinburgh dinner party for Boccaccio's ten heterosexual Florentines, and AIDS stands in for the Black Death. He also alters the Italian writer's narrative method, replacing the mechanical device of each character formally presenting ten separate tales with a medley of stories, toasts, jokes, literary references and flashbacks, interspersed with occasional excerpts from a book read by one of the characters. As a whole, the novel embodies an instance of contingent and composite 'bricolage' or – to use the term employed by Whyte in the novel – *trencadís*, that is, a colourful kind of mosaic created from broken tile shards made famous by the Catalan architect Antoni Gaudi (1852–1926). This formal diversity of *The Gay Decameron* reflects Whyte's preoccupation with hybrid identities. Around that Edinburgh dinner table, where Doric, Glaswegian and Catalan voices mingle, several 'different Scotlands' meet. Hosts Kieran and Dougal are a professor and a lawyer respectively, while Mark is a shop supervisor and Alan works as an air steward. Gavin practises pediatric medicine and his partner Brian is a professional musician. Rory, a journalist, arrives with Ramon, a postgraduate student from Barcelona. Shy Barry works in the Scottish Office and the final guest, Nicol, is a translator. Each character is individuated in terms of religion, class origin, personality and linguistic ability (some of the guests are fluent in multiple languages, whereas others are not). Yet the men are hardly a collection of isolate individuals. A complex network of memories links them. Perhaps, as Mark suggests, a new kind of mapping is required, a 'sexual geography' (Whyte 1998b: 239) capable of imagining the history of a community barely acknowledged a generation ago.

Though storytelling offers one means of drawing up such a map, it is a practice not entirely without risks. In *The Gay Decameron*, fiction has a distinctly ambiguous valence.

While some stories offer the chance to explore multiple identities imaginatively, others are lies that reinscribe the closet. The liars in *The Gay Decameron* include plagiarists and faithless lovers, as well as a nationalist politician who accepts the closet as the price of political success. The lied-to include Brian, who, as a child, was trapped in an abusive home where he was taught to view himself as 'the abnormal one, the pervert' (Whyte 1998b: 266). Lying, Whyte seems to suggest, restricts choice by faking it; it constitutes a false hospitality. Yet fiction can be helpful, too, in exploring different ways of being. Throughout the dinner party, Brian reads from an alleged translation of an Arabian Nights fantasy, an activity that, as in *Euphemia*, returns the alienated gay reader to dialogue and to himself. The point is not to reject fiction, but to choose the right story. 'That's the funny thing about being gay', Brian tells Kieran. 'You have to invent. To choose and invent' (Whyte 1998b: 258). The importance of choosing the right story is illustrated in the flash-back account of Gavin's trip to Ireland following the death of a former lover. What Gavin wants (he thinks) is to understand why Colin died; as it turns out, however, what he is really in search of is the freedom to name his love openly. The cultural imposition of secrecy has left him without a narrative for his grief. Help comes from an unexpected quarter when by coincidence Gavin meets a writer of paperback romances, the aptly named Desiree, who is suffering from block herself. Eager to 'try something different' (Whyte 1998b: 14), she finds herself stuck with the plot of compulsory heterosexuality. It takes the news of her travel companion's grief to initiate change, as the two people begin a stumbling, yet heartfelt conversation.

Communication is health, then, but it is a complex business. This notion is made explicit in the tales of Nicol and Anna and of Kieran and Dougal. In the first, Whyte illustrates friendship's ethical imperative to confront and negotiate difference. Friends since school, Nicol and Anna gradually drift apart after an early pregnancy propels her into marriage. Genuine conversation is replaced by rote encounters focused entirely on Anna's marital unhappiness, until Nicol challenges the legitimacy of Anna's ability to tell the same story (the story of her marriage) over and over again without ever really questioning its basic premise: 'I just envy you the luxury of normality. Nothing more than that. Not needing to think. Not having to ask questions.' Caught off-guard, Anna feels as if she and Nicol 'inhabit separate worlds' (Whyte 1998b: 242–3), making the difference between a gay man and a straight woman seem unbridgeable. The stasis in their friendship does not break until a later chance encounter in the street finds Anna very much out of her familiar context, thus enabling her to acknowledge the strangeness of herself, as well as of Nicol. Related issues inform the emergent relationship of Kieran and Dougal. Brought up by an impoverished single mother, Kieran has had to struggle to affirm his sexual identity. His mother was literally dumbstruck when her son came out to her and appalled by the prospect of having to 'improvise' a new kind of family (Whyte 1998b: 214). Yet 'improvise' she did and, as a result, mother and son found not only a new way of communicating with each other but also the strength to stand up to a society prone to abjecting, without much discrimination, single motherhood, female desire and homosexuality, as well as working-class culture.

According to Whyte, 'it is at the places where affiliations overlap that one can most successfully tease out the tangled threads of political, class and gender allegiance' (Whyte 1995b: x). The truth of this is perhaps most poignantly felt in the scene in which Kieran takes Dougal to Drumchapel to meet his mother. For bourgeois, class-conscious Dougal, Ellen's council house is a zone of unspeakable kitsch, and it seems impossible that 'he, Dougal, could incorporate this woman and her world into his life' (Whyte 1998b: 229).

The mere thought of it triggers a panic attack that makes him seek refuge in the lavatory. It is here, surrounded by Ellen's crocheted toilet-roll covers, that Dougal suddenly realises the utter absurdity of his terror: 'That was when he started to laugh . . . What made him laugh was his own situation, in darkest Drumchapel, on the cludgie with his trousers down and so, so afraid, but afraid of what?' (Whyte 1998b: 230). A Caledonian Clarissa Dalloway, Dougal confronts and admits his own hypocrisy. It is a funny and liberating moment, and yet Whyte is careful to avoid offering it up as the answer to all the tensions explored in Kieran's story. Dougal's laughter is a place to start from, not to conclude with; the material politics of identity are not so easily disposed of. That fact is brought home when on their way back to Edinburgh, Kieran and Dougal run into a group of soccer casuals and Dougal wonders whether it might be safe to stop. 'So many different Scotlands' (Whyte 1998b: 234) indeed, yet this is a dialogue that cannot yet occur, not as long as Kieran and Dougal are prohibited from touching each other in public without fear of homophobic assault.

The price of failed dialogue, of failing to accommodate what is 'foreign', is a consistent theme in *The Gay Decameron*. As the dinner party draws to a close, five of the guests ascend to the roof to watch dawn break. Gazing across Edinburgh, they meditate on whether they will ever know a Scotland capable of embracing their sexuality. In the eyes of homophobes, they fear, they will always resemble outsiders, 'as if we were immigrants and could be deported'. Even so, there are grounds for optimism. Too much has changed for prejudice to win out. The novel's final assertion – 'we'll never go underground again' – deftly reverses the trope of hospitality, as the once-excluded now extend that gift to others. 'When guests come to our house', Dougal reflects, 'I want there to be an abundance of everything they ask for. I want to be able to share my happiness with them' (Whyte 1998b: 344–6).

Whyte's fourth novel, *The Cloud Machinery*, is not set in Scotland, making itself at home in foreign territory instead. Indeed, Whyte is rumoured to have vowed not to use a single Scottish term in the entire work. The setting is eighteenth-century Venice during Carnival, and the subject is art, specifically the power of art to transform and create. Yet Whyte's deliberate shifts in location and subject matter do not mark a break with the Scottish novel so much as an attempt to resituate it. Whereas Whyte's concerns with identity and hybridity remain intact, *The Cloud Machinery* offers a new idiom within which to re-imagine these themes.

The complicated plot of the novel revolves around the attempt to produce an opera. Closed since the murder of its owner, the famous theatre of St Hyginus is re-opened when a distant relative of the victim decides to create 'a spectacle so splendid that all of Venice will flock to my theatre' (Whyte 2000: 9). Among the first to be hired is Domenico, plucked from the streets to conduct the orchestra, and a motley crew of musicians, singers and stage-hands soon follows. Rehearsals are under way when a mysterious object – the remnants of an elaborate device designed to transport actors to and from the 'heavens' – is discovered backstage. This is the 'cloud machinery', which failed catastrophically on the night of the murder. The performers decide to resurrect it. First, though, they must deal with the disturbing absences that haunt St Hyginus: not only has the machinery's designer, the castrato Angelo Columbani, been hidden in the theatre since the murder, but the murder victim's true heir is discovered to be missing. Meanwhile two sinister visitors arrive in search of Eleonora Calefati, a young girl kidnapped by the necromancer Goffredo Negri. However, if what is missing provokes anxiety, what is substituted for it hardly invites confidence. The visitors are Hedwiga von Nettesheim, a creepy, doll-like revenant, and Andreas Hofmeister, an alleged 'paladin of enlightened thought' disastrously given to the habit of denying whatever exceeds his own rational analysis (Whyte 2000: 113). In their separate ways, both are addicted to power and control.

Can the show go on? It must. Once again, openness to hybrid experience is figured as vital to creativity. Like his Glasgow and Edinburgh, Whyte's Venice represents an in-between zone, a city organism miraculously built on the margins of land and sea. Carnival heightens this liminality, simultaneously exaggerating and confusing difference. Locals and visitors, rich and poor, male and female are all licensed equally under cover of their masks. For Domenico, the notion that 'name, sex, and social class' can be so easily altered is startling (Whyte 2000: 57), yet flexible boundaries emerge in other places as well. When the St Hyginus performers meet to discuss which opera to produce, debates over genres are quickly undercut by the insistence that each singer have a role in the final product. It is suggested that everybody 'choose [their] favourite bits from the repertoire . . . some transposing and stitching together . . . and hey presto! we have an opera' (Whyte 2000: 133). Initially the producer resists but, with the promise of a crowd-pleasing *commedia dell'arte* interlude thrown in, he is quickly brought to a settlement. According to *The Cloud Machinery* the best answer to the problem of genre is not pastiche, but the composition of an entirely new work of art.

As the novel demonstrates, the greatest threat to any free creative interplay of differences is posed by ideologies founded upon universal absolutes. Like the dense mist that occludes the city of Venice, universalism makes spectral automatons of living individuals. People literally cannot see each other, creating a situation that turns even selective blindness into a real menace. Thus, Andreas's extreme scepticism is 'a leather harness' that forbids imaginative flight, while Hedwiga's taste for necromancy literally keeps her in the dark. Most alarming of all, however, is Goffredo's Frankenstein-like obsession with 'the idea of creating a single, androgynous creature which would dominate the world to come, combining the best qualities of men and women, reproducing itself without the need for nurturing or copulation' (Whyte 2000: 195). It is this monstrous homogeneity that *The Cloud Machinery* resists. Even closure in this playful novel remains open-ended: the missing heir is finally revealed, while Hedwiga and Andreas are conveniently disposed of by a rogue tornado, condemned to 'circle eternally' within the blast of their own dialectic (Whyte 2000: 222). The mist dissipates, and Domenico wakes up next to Eleonora. Yet this handsome pair have a new story to tell, one in which Eve is not made for Adam, nor Adam necessarily destined for Eve.

The baroque pleasures of *The Cloud Machinery* seriously play with Whyte's critical concerns. The novel is 'cosmopolitan' not only in terms of setting but also, more importantly, in terms of its deliberate preference for identities whose openness to difference does not necessitate the erasure of borders. 'Hospitality is culture itself', Jacques Derrida writes in *On Cosmopolitanism and Forgiveness*,

> and not simply one ethic among others. Insofar as it has to do with *ethos*, that is, the residence, one's home, the familiar place of dwelling, inasmuch as it is a manner of being there, the manner in which we relate to ourselves and to others, to others as our own or as foreigners, *ethics is hospitality*: ethics is so thoroughly coextensive with the experience of hospitality. (Derrida 2001a: 16–17)

This is a statement Whyte would probably agree with – even though it does not end the conversation, or ongoing controversy, about cosmopolitanism. That will be a matter for politics to resolve.

Chapter 23

Iain (M.) Banks: Utopia, Nationalism and the Posthuman

Gavin Miller

Iain Banks has a peculiar place in contemporary Scottish fiction. Although he has many affinities with established authors such as Alasdair Gray, whose work Banks admires, and has often taken contemporary Scottish life as his subject matter, he is that unfamiliar thing – a successful Scottish author of science fiction. This chapter examines the connections between Banks's more-or-less realist fiction, which tends to be set in contemporary Scotland and Britain, and the far-out future vision of his science fiction. What, if anything, links the work of Iain Banks to that of his science-fiction alter ego, Iain M. Banks?

Banks's place within the canon of modern Scottish fiction is far from assured. There are a number of reasons for this insecurity. Perhaps the most significant is Banks's readiness to shock his audience. His first and million-selling novel, *The Wasp Factory* (1984), contains gruesome scenes which seem to ape those of decidedly non-canonical popular and pulp horror authors. In one incident, for example, the narrator's brother, a medical student, finds that the brain of a baby in his care has been devoured by maggots. Such grotesqueries did little to establish Banks's reputation amongst critics. Phrases such as 'hammed-up horror' and 'preposterous sadism' tended to appear in reviews (see Craig 1984). Seemingly gratuitous violence and enormous financial success probably made Banks even less attractive to the Scottish critical establishment, who are normally more sympathetic to 'one of their own'. He certainly found nowhere near the same academic applause as the authors with whom he is roughly contemporary: Gray, James Kelman and Tom Leonard all came to prominence around the early 1980s, and all received critical accolades denied, fairly or not, to Banks.

Of Banks's twenty-two published books, nine feature Scotland or Scots: the novels *The Wasp Factory*, *The Bridge* (1986), *Espedair Street* (1987), *The Crow Road* (1992), *Complicity* (1993), *Whit* (1995), *The Business* (1999) and *Dead Air* (2002), and the non-fiction travelogue through Scotland's whisky distilleries, *Raw Spirit* (2003). The neglect of Banks by Scottish critics has undoubtedly been intensified by the difficulty of applying theories and ideas of 'nation' to his work, even in those books where Scotland is represented. For various reasons, little critical yield is released by such processes. Banks largely anticipates many of the more recent objections to the supposed 'essentialism' of Scottish identity. In *Raw Spirit*, for instance, Banks concludes his account with a reflection on the symbolism of whisky, particularly its 'ability to accept and combine with distinctive flavours from elsewhere, to enhance them and be enhanced by them', asserting that 'it's the interplay between the raw spirit as made in Scotland and those other tastes brought in from abroad that have made the greatest and most enduring impression on me' (Banks 2003: 359). Whisky, a central symbol of Scotland, thus becomes a paradigm of the cultural hybridity that Banks sees as vital to national life. There is little point deconstructing 'nationhood' in Banks's work, for he seems quite aware of how Scottishness is constituted by what is 'other' to it. Banks's civic and open nationalism therefore provides little that is controversial, and is far from a central concern within his work.

In fact, rather than as an end in itself, Banks tends to regard nationalism as an instrument towards a socialist future. Socialist ambition is central to Banks's science fiction, which scarcely includes any room for 'nation' at all. Of Banks's nine science-fiction novels, six contain his vision of a future anarchist-socialist utopia, the 'Culture': *Consider Phlebas* (1987), *The Player of Games* (1988), *Use of Weapons* (1990), *Excession* (1996), *Inversions* (1998) and *Look to Windward* (2000). In addition, the Culture appears in some of the stories in Banks's science-fiction anthology, *The State of the Art* (1989). The Culture is a vast civilisation of genetically modified humanoids, who live in partnership with artificial life forms whose superior intelligence directs a wholly automated economy. There is no scarcity in the Culture, work has become play, and the state has withered away.

The political colours of the Culture are spelled out quite explicitly in the short story 'The State of the Art', in which some Culture citizens in their supersentient ship take a fact-finding tour of 1970s Earth. In a piece of generic self-reflexiveness, one of the crew, Li, remarks on how poorly science fiction has prepared Earthlings for the Culture: 'What is the Culture as a society compared to what they expect? They expect capitalists in space, or an empire. A libertarian-anarchist utopia? Equality? Liberty? Fraternity? This is not so much old-fashioned stuff as simply unfashionable stuff' (Banks 1989: 180). In the spirit of Banks's unfashionable fondness for a command economy, Diziet Sma, another member of the crew, visits East Berlin, and wonders 'was this farce, this gloomy sideshow trying to mimic the West . . . the best job the locals could make of socialism?' (Banks 1989: 141). Eastern European socialism, for all its faults, is presented by Banks not as a mistaken path but as a premature aspiration, as a failure that the future will look on more kindly. Such, then, is Banks's vision of the future: socialist, anarchist, rationalist, resolutely materialist, and seemingly quite without 'nation'.

Banks's charitable attitude towards the failures of communist society is no aberration but part of his general willingness to perceive traces of the utopian in what are apparently the worst failures of contemporary society. In *Espedair Street*, Banks presents the narrative of a former progressive rocker, Daniel Weir ('Weird'), driven to despair by a latent religiosity. Having retired from the music business, Weird lives incognito in Glasgow, slowly drinking himself to death. Amidst the chaos of his life, a peculiar drunken incident occurs when one night he climbs onto an incomplete flyover above the M8 motorway, the main arterial route which runs from Edinburgh into the heart of Glasgow. This 'sawn-off flyover . . . crosses the motorway beneath, but doesn't go anywhere; it's only as long as the motorway is wide, and stuck up in the air all by itself.' (Banks 1987a: 73–4). Weird drunkenly climbs the barrier to the bridge and dances on it while discarding his clothes onto the vehicles passing underneath, fleeing only when a police car arrives. This bizarre alcoholic celebration is as significant within Banks's fiction as the Culture's observations on East Germany. The urban redevelopment of Glasgow during the 1960s is notorious for its destruction of large areas of inhabitable architecture, and their replacement with big roads, tower-blocks and waste ground. Amidst this disastrous mismanagement of technology by state and economy, the bridge Weird climbs is one of several little motorway follies on the M8; although it is not made explicit in Banks's text, this particular dead end on the road of progress was known locally as the 'Bridge to Nowhere'. The re-examination of such bridges – be they literal or, more usually, metaphorical – is central to Banks's writing, for, in the tangled failures of twentieth-century progress, he sees anticipations of his science-fiction utopia. Such bridges to utopia (or, etymologically speaking, 'bridges to nowhere') connect the two 'Banks' (Iain and Iain M.) of the writer's work, linking the twentieth century to the utopian future of the Culture.

Banks's greatest work of pontification is of course *The Bridge*. In this novel, the unconscious protagonist, Al Lennox, is lost in a series of bizarre fantasy worlds as he lies in a coma after a drunken car-crash. *The Bridge* clearly has certain antecedents in Scottish literature. On the one hand, it is part of that subgenre of oneiric, man-in-a-coma or delirium fictions begun by Gray's *1982 Janine* (1984) and continued by Welsh's *Marabou Stork Nightmares* (1995). On the other, with its endlessly repetitive symbolism (the Forth Rail Bridge re-appears in Lennox's fantasies as the three of diamonds, a lover's stockings, the bones of a kipper, and a giant living bridge), it is a meditation on a national symbol: a comatose man looking at a bridge rather than, as in Hugh MacDiarmid's long poem of 1926, a drunk man looking at a thistle. A decoding and decipherment of *The Bridge* would require an entire chapter in itself. Its relevance to the present discussion is not so much the manifold content of its various dramas and allegories as the curious condition of the man who receives these visions. Lennox is a combination of man and machine, an amalgamation prefigured as his Jaguar crashes on the Forth Road Bridge: 'Weight coming from all directions, entangled in the wreckage (you have to become one with the machine)' (Banks 1986: 11). Later, as Lennox re-emerges from his coma, he finds himself kept alive by the machines which feed him via drips and monitor his condition. He is addressed by 'a machine which looks like a metal suitcase on a spindly trolley' (Banks 1986: 275) – an anticipation of the early, suitcase-sized 'drones' of the Culture – which fills in the details of his hospitalisation and asks whether he is willing to wake up.

Significantly, when Lennox awakes it is not to reality as such, but to another dream. 'Let's get one thing absolutely straight', he insists 'it's all a dream. Either way, whatever' (Banks 1986: 274). By downgrading everyday reality to an illusion in this way, Banks hints at a fundamental part of his world view. All phenomenal experience is essentially, to Banks, an illusion generated by organic matter, by the brain. Such materialism – which, I believe, gets out of hand – is communicated by another peculiar 'bridge'. As if he were not content to find utopia in a car-crash, Banks also hunts it out in drug abuse. The drug 'bridge' is spelled out in *Complicity*, when the protagonist Cameron Colley recalls his first cigarette: 'It was a revelation, an epiphany; a sudden realisation that it was possible for matter – something there in front of you, in your hand, in your lungs, in your pocket – to take your brain apart and reassemble it in ways you hadn't thought of previously' (Banks 1993: 47). This revelation of materialism, which anticipates the inbuilt drug glands of the Culture citizens, is premature merely because it refers to an addictive drug, deformed by the possessive individualism of capitalist society. 'At the end of the day', reflects Colley, 'you still light another cigarette and suck in the smoke like you enjoyed it and make more profits for those evil fucks' (Banks 1993: 54).

Feersum Endjinn (1994), which along with *Against a Dark Background* (1993) and *The Algebraist* (2004) is one of Banks's few unCultured science-fiction novels, further insists that 'bridging' work proceeds from reducing mind to a mechanism. In this novel, the earth is under threat as its ageing sun expands. The technology which might protect the planet is forgotten by its present inhabitants, who, unlike their predecessors, have forsaken both space-flight and artificial intelligence. The bridge in this novel is a character, Bascule the Teller, a 'bascule', according to the *OED*, signifying 'a kind of drawbridge'. Bascule's function is that of a bridge in so far as he can enter a dreaming state which enables him to move within a virtual reality created by the earth's computer systems. Crucially, as is revealed towards the end of the novel, it is from these systems that there arises 'an entire ecology of AIs [i.e. artificial intelligences]' to which the present human biological civilisation, with the exception of Bascule, is wilfully deaf because they are the descendants of those who clung to their 'faith . . . that humanity is supreme' (Banks 1994a: 267). As the narrator of Banks's *The Player of Games* reflects on the artificial intelligences which populate the Culture, 'what difference does it make whether a mind's made up of enormous, squidgy, animal cells working at the speed of sound (in air!), or from a glittering nanofoam of reflectors and patterns of holographic coherence, at light speed? . . . Each is a machine, each is an organism'; both are 'just matter, switching energy of one sort of another' (Banks 1988: 231).

The insistence that mind can be a property of machines is spelled out further in Banks's short story 'Descendant', in which a Culture citizen is forced to seek refuge on a planet inside his sentient spacesuit. As the suit communicates to its inhabitant, 'we're both *systems*, we're both matter with sentience . . . We're all programmed. We all have our inheritance. You have rather more than us, and it's more chaotic, that's all' (Banks 1989: 55). Indeed, the human narrator's 'descendant' turns out to be the suit itself, for he dies inside it and is carried along seemingly for sentimental reasons until the suit reaches a Culture base.

For Banks, computer science and genetics reveal that we are the effects of coding upon matter: mind is a program that could conceivably be copied or transcribed into different matter, and the brain itself is a bodily pattern programmed by evolution. In his essay 'A Few Notes on the Culture', Banks sees his computational model as overturning the superstition of an earlier vitalist age that 'there is some vital field or other presently intangible influence exclusive to biological life – perhaps even carbon-based biological life – which may eventually fall within the remit of scientific understanding but which cannot be emulated in any other form' (Banks 1994b). With this kind of statement, Banks reveals his intellectual fascination with the curious posthuman cultural theories of 'cyborgs' and 'postvitalism', such as those conveyed in Donna Haraway's widely anthologised essay 'A Manifesto for Cyborgs' (1985), which provides an outline of the cultural consequences that might follow from a view of life centred less on the lives of individual human beings. 'Late twentieth-century machines', Haraway proposes, 'have made thoroughly ambiguous the difference between natural and artificial, mind and body, self-developing and externally-designed, and many other distinctions that used to apply to organisms and machines.' By confronting the potential instability of so-called 'natural' boundaries, like those which separate human from machine, organic from inanimate, feminine from masculine', Haraway looks forward to a 'a cyborg world . . . in which people are not afraid of their joint kinship with animals and machines, not afraid of permanently partial identities and contradictory standpoints' (Haraway 2001: 2272, 2275).

Although ethology and evolutionary theory have done most to blur the human–animal boundary, the organism–machine distinction has, as Haraway notes, been weakened by 'a common move' in 'communication sciences and modern biologies . . . *the translation of the world into a problem of coding*' (Haraway 2001: 2284). The ramifications of this model for cultural theorists have been developed by authors such as Richard Doyle in *Wetwares* (2003). If there is no mysterious vital fluid 'inside' a carbon-based organism, Doyle argues, then the extension of the meaning of 'life' expands enormously. 'Life' seems no more than the copying, storage and transmission of patterns which replicate themselves in various material substrata: for example, 'the creation of organisms iterable enough to move from computer to computer, capable of being copied across networks [such as computer viruses], undoes the monopoly of carbon on living systems and extends the franchise of vitality' (Doyle 2003: 9).

A very useful terminology for my reading of Banks's work can be found in Doyle's statement that the informatic model 'deterritorializes life itself, as life becomes an explicit virtuality, placeless and yet distributed, ubiquitous' (Doyle 2003: 9). Similarly, in many ways, Banks's future vision is 'deterritorialised'. The most obvious 'deterritorialisation' is Banks's insistence that life in space is different from life on a plane. In 'A Few Notes on the Culture', he argues that 'the thought processes of a tribe, a clan, a country or a nation-state are essentially two-dimensional, and the nature of their power depends on the same flatness. Territory is all-important: resources, living-space, lines of communication, all are determined by the nature of the plane' (Banks 1994b). But switch to space, and then, so argues Banks, 'our currently dominant power systems cannot long survive':

> the property and social relations of long-term space-dwelling (especially over generations) would be of a fundamentally different type compared to the norm on a planet; the mutuality of dependence involved in an environment which is inherently hostile would necessitate an internal social coherence which would contrast with the external casualness typifying the relations between such ships/habitats. Succinctly: socialism within, anarchy without. (Banks 1994b)

The effect of such space-dwelling is as much a shift in our cognitive model as it is a science-fiction migration into giant spaceships or artificial worlds. Life itself, Banks suggests, needs to be reconceptualised according to the idea of a global space – a complete system – rather than the ideas of possession and 'mine-ness' apparent in a territorialist mindset. Fictional spaceships are but a means to this reconfigured global outlook. For example, in *Feersum Endjinn*, the spaceship is discovered to be earth itself, as Bascule is led by the artificial intelligences to discover the 'fearsome engine' that allows the planet to be piloted away from the expanding sun. Such a deterritorialised perspective is exactly what Doyle sees in informatic theories of life, where, he claims, we undergo 'a shift from an understanding of organisms as *localized agents* to an articulation of living systems as *distributed events*' (Doyle 2003: 19).

Banks sees life in a similar way, regarding it as an interdependent living system maintained by the copying, transmission and evolution (or design) of patterns – be they genetic or computational – which accordingly structure various material substrata. Indeed, Banks goes further by exposing the cosmic deterritorialisation apparent in the material which makes up our own bodies. In *The Bridge*, Lennox reflects in his strange altered state that 'we are . . . the gathered silt of ancient explosions' (Banks 1986: 212). This is not a delusion, but a cosmological discovery: the heavy elements which comprise our bodies have been formed in processes of stellar decline and death. The Culture novels develop further the ethical meaning of this cosmological inference. When Li addresses his fellow travellers in 'The State of the Art', he reminds them 'I am poor. I own nothing', adding that 'every atom in my body was once part of something else, in fact part of many different things', and 'one day every atom of my being will . . . be part of something else – a star, initially, because that is the way we choose to bury our dead' (Banks 1989: 177). The Culture citizens appreciate that they are not immaterial souls, but merely the aggregation, or intersection, of form and matter. Furthermore, since they do not even possess *themselves*, how can they claim to own anything? As Li states,

> everything around me, from the food that I eat and the drink that I drink and the figurine that
> I carve and the house I inhabit and the clothes I wear so elegantly . . . is there *when* I am there
> rather than *because* I am . . . I do not, emphatically, *not* own them. (Banks 1989: 177)

Banks's implication seems to be that those who are most scared by their lack of self-possession – such as contemporary Earthlings – need to have things so that other people cannot. Li suggests later that a single word to describe humanity would be '*MINE!*' (Banks 1989: 184).

Culture citizens, on the other hand, exist within life rather than trying to dominate or possess it. Banks represents this deterritorialised ethic as particularly feminine by using an imagery of gestation and nurturance. For example, Genar-Hoefen, a character in *Excession*, is protected by a 'gelfield suit', a kind of sentient 'second skin' that shields him from his hostile environment (Banks 1996: 30). This suit is a variant of the spacesuit from 'Descendant', whose metaphorical gender is spelled out by its occupant finding it 'warm and cosy and pleasant, every chemical whim of the encased body catered for; a little womb to curl up in and dream' (Banks 1989: 48). Genar-Hoefen's musings on his suit make it quite clear that this metaphorical womb – or amnion, the inner membrane which encloses a foetus – is a symbol for the Culture as a whole: 'The result was almost as much a metaphorical pain to live with as it was in a literal sense a pleasure to live within; it looked after you perfectly but it couldn't help constantly reminding you of the fact. Typical Culture' (Banks 1996: 31).

Furthermore, the prototypical Culture world is a Culture Ship, a structure within which its inhabitants are contained rather than a territory which they claim to possess. Even on the rare occasions when Culture Citizens live on the outside of their ship, Banks still manages to emphasise the femininity of the sheltering world. So, for example, we have Banks's description in *Excession* of the Culture ship *Sleeper Service* as imagined by its sole conscious human inhabitant, Dajeil Gelian:

> She saw herself . . . both within and outside the ship; outside its main hull . . . but within the
> huge envelope of water, air and gas it encompassed within the manifold layers of its field (she
> imagined the force fields sometimes as like the hooped slips, underskirts, skirts, flounces and
> lace of some ancient formal gown). (Banks 1996: 11)

The femininity of the ship is further emphasised by Dajeil herself, who is carrying a pregnancy which she has artificially suspended for forty years. Similarly, the *Sleeper Service*, as the plot of *Excession* eventually reveals, is in a condition of suspended gestation. The artificial ecology it carries is a secret weapon: when the time comes it will manufacture the enormous quantities of Culture ships required to fight the threat posed by a rival civilisation, the Affront.

By thus reconceiving life and society as feminine, Banks compresses, and gives an ethical meaning to, the insights of contemporary science. Central to his feminine mythology is a kind of 'deterritorialisation', manifest in the loss of notions of 'ownership' and a corresponding acceptance of a global or cosmological interconnectedness. The Culture extrapolates a contemporary view of life in which neither mind (computational program), body (genetic program) nor matter (left-over stellar material) seems to be a source of selfhood.

There is much that is fascinating and important about Banks's science-fiction vision of the future, as well as the 'bridges' towards this future that he builds in his contemporary fiction. However, there is also good reason to be worried about the technological ideology which underlies the notions of the 'cyborg' and 'postvitalism' that inform Banks's fiction. It seems to me that the powerful allure of Banks's vision – from which emanates a whole series of high-tech assumptions about 'life', few of which are innocent – stems largely from a widely accepted false consciousness among his readers. Central to current models of artificial intelligence is the hypothesis that the human brain instantiates a pattern which is essentially the same as the coding of a computer program, as implied by Haraway when she refers to the mind as a 'coding practice' (Haraway 2001: 2296). Correspondingly, in *Mind Children*, Hans Moravec reasons that because 'mind is entirely the consequence of interacting matter' there will arise 'the ability to copy it from one storage medium to another' and so 'give it an independence and an identity apart from the machinery that runs the program' (Moravec 1988: 119–20). Such views clearly inspire Banks, who, as well as creating intelligent machines, envisages Culture citizens who, in the event of their death, can duplicate and reload themselves into a new, appropriate body.

The philosopher John Searle is perhaps the best-known opponent to the idea that the human mind is a computer program capable of being copied into different material substrata. Part of what makes current 'artificial intelligence' seem so plausible, Searle notes, are deeply ingrained assumptions about what can exist in the world and how what exists can be known. As Searle puts it, 'since the seventeenth century, educated people in the West have come to accept an absolutely basic metaphysical position: *Reality is objective*' and, as a result, 'it seems intolerable metaphysically that there should be irreducibly subjective, "private" entities in the world' (Searle 1992: 16, 21). Instead of expecting intelligent machines to possess conscious subjective lives like our own, we are inclined to believe, in a muddled, inauthentic way, that an intelligent machine would need to be equipped with a sufficiently complex computer program enabling it to imitate our behaviour successfully with an appropriate verisimilitude. Searle proceeds to explain how such absurdities find legitimacy in a narrative of scientific progress. Critics who express doubts are subjected to the ' "heroic-age-of-science" maneuver' by which 'if you don't believe the view being advanced, you are playing Cardinal Bellarmine to the author's Galileo' (Searle 1992: 5), and Doyle's rhetoric of 'postvitalism' clearly exploits a similar trick. The idea behind the attribution of 'vitalism' is, as Searle notes, 'to bully the reader into supposing that if he or she doubts, for example, that computers are actually thinking, it can only be because the reader believes in something as unscientific as phlogiston or vital spirits' (Searle 1992: 5).

Banks, as we have seen, is equally fond of this tactic, presuming that AI sceptics are inclined to believe 'there is some vital field or other presently intangible influence exclusive to biological life' (1994b). This kind of posthuman rhetoric is reminiscent of John Barrow and Frank Tipler's 'carbon fascist' argument in *The Anthropic Cosmological Principle*, where they propose that 'the arguments one hears today against considering intelligent computers to be persons and against giving them human rights have precise parallels in the nineteenth-century arguments against giving blacks and women full human rights' (Barrow and Tipler 1988: 595). Sceptics are not merely Cardinal Bellarmine to the scientist's Galileo, they are Benito Mussolini to his Martin Luther King, Adolf Hitler to her Emmeline Pankhurst or Rosa Parks.

As we have seen, whenever computer programming meets genetics, a wholly informatic concept of life emerges as part of a new postvitalist discourse which combines a materialist-historical notion of progress with a 'counter-intuitive' but supposedly 'scientific' redefinition of life. Any entity is alive provided that, in the words of the physicist Frank Tipler, it 'codes information . . . with the information coded being preserved by natural selection' (Tipler 1996: 123). From this definition, Moravec then produces an entire materialist history within which 'cultures compete with one another for the resources of the accessible universe. If automation is more efficient than manual labor, organizations and societies that embrace it will be wealthier and better able to survive in difficult times and to expand in favorable ones' (Moravec 1988: 100). This grand postvitalist narrative is frequently implied in Banks's work. In *Consider Phlebas*, his first published Culture novel, the Culture goes to war with the Idirans, a society that does not recognise machines as living beings. Essentially the Culture wins because they are economically and strategically far more efficient than the Idirans, and this is because of both their Ships and their Minds. In this *Waverley* of the future, Banks envisions a kind of science-fiction stadial history, in which those on the side of 'boring, old-fashioned, biological life; smelly, fallible and short-sighted, God knows but *real* life' must – whatever their courage and nobility – go the way of the Highland clans (Banks 1987: 29).

As appealingly Marxist as this new stadial history might appear, it is based upon a purely informatic definition of life, according to which even motor cars are alive. As Barrow and Tipler claim,

> Automobiles . . . must be considered alive since they contain a great deal of information, and they can self-reproduce in the sense that there are human mechanics who can make a copy of the automobile . . . The form of automobiles in the environment is preserved by natural selection: there is a fierce struggle for existence going on between various 'races' of automobiles! (Barrow and Tipler 1988: 521–2)

As well as providing a useful *reductio ad absurdum* of their own argument, this passage from their work reveals how ultimately Barrow and Tipler's vision serves to animate commodities by de-animating their producers. Life without subjectivity allows machines (such as automobiles, PCs, thermostatically controlled boilers) to 'exist' on an equal footing with the organic 'machines' that built them. Against this background Searle can scarcely be accused of exaggeration when he identifies 'the deepest motivation for materialism' as 'simply a terror of consciousness' (Searle 1992: 55).

As much as one might appreciate the femininised and deterritorialised 'cyborg' future which Banks presents, the informatic postvitalist view of life is ultimately, I believe, an ideology cloaked by 'scientism'. The American pragmatists used to talk about 'paper doubts', such as Cartesian doubts about the existence of the material world or other minds. Correspondingly, the postvitalist strand of cyborg theories could be called a collection of 'paper beliefs': entirely inauthentic (no one really believes that automobiles are alive), while simultaneously enjoying an astonishing degree of academic and institutional currency, they also appear to incorporate a puzzling and sinister manoeuvre to eliminate subjectivity from our world. And yet, anyone who rains on the cyborg parade – especially when it is associated with such worthwhile values as feminist liberation, universal human rights, and compassion for animals – is likely to receive as much thanks as Lemuel Gulliver when he put out the palace fire in Lilliput. However, in my view, Banks's achievement remains ambivalent. His feminised future vision may be laudable, and we may rightly feel humbled by the stellar and genetic inheritances that 'deterritorialise' our lives. On the other hand, the 'mind-machine' strand of 'cyborg' theory is an ideological dead end invoking the worst kind of reification of human life. Though its 'heart' is in the right place, Banks's work, favouring a computational view of 'life' and 'mind', is compromised by an implicit 'fear of subjectivity'.

Chapter 24

Burying the Man that was: Janice Galloway and Gender Disorientation

Carole Jones

Janice Galloway has characterised the Scottish literary scene of the 1980s and 1990s as overwhelmingly male. 'Now that Scottish writing has a profile', she explains, 'it's a bloke's profile, and one that I wish to distance myself from' (March 1999: 89). According to Galloway, the dominant image of the Scottish nation remains a masculine one with which women have great difficulty identifying. This chapter will examine Galloway's work across the devolutionary moment of the reinstatement of the Scottish Parliament in 1999 and, more specifically, it will query her impulse to distance herself increasingly from Scottish issues and contexts. Galloway's anti-'Scottish' trajectory will be counterpoised with the most urgent subject of her fiction, which is her characters' disoriented gender identities that problematise feminine and masculine selfhood and complicate sexual relationships. In a period when patriarchal authority is increasingly questioned, Galloway takes up Scotland's persistently masculinist conceptualisation of nationhood in order to engage with what Christopher Whyte has described as 'an urgent necessity to nurture and promote competing representations of both national and gender identities' (Whyte 1998a: 284). Galloway is concerned with patriarchy and the question of how women realise their self-hood within a system of male domination. 'My work', she says, 'is to ask "what it's like to be an intelligent woman coping with the late twentieth century?"' Her chief aim is 'to write as though having a female perspective is normal which is a damn sight harder than it sounds' (March 1999: 85). Galloway's work is preoccupied with the manifold circumscriptions of women's lives. However, her fictions are not expeditions into a radical and essential femininity from which to resist masculine power; rather, her writing is informed by a conception of gender as relational and identity as discursively constructed.

The context of Galloway's work is the general decline in western patriarchal authority towards the close of the twentieth century. This waning of men's social dominance is due not only to feminism's success in achieving greater equality for women but also, far more significantly for some commentators, to the terminal decline of the traditionally male-dominated heavy industries, which proved particularly significant in Scotland, a country historically dependent on them. Feminism and economic change significantly transformed gender relations. Women gained legal rights against discrimination, and at the same time new electronics and service industries 'feminised' the workforce (Devine 1999: 592). This sense of growing female empowerment was felt across all social strata, making men increasingly defensive. This period is often also characterised as one of 'male crisis', and a sense of gender disorientation can be seen to pervade all social discourse at the time, from the media to literature and academia (see Brittan 1989; Connell 1995). The accelerated, increasingly palpable breakdown of traditional gender polarities created feelings of confusion as to the proper demarcation of behavioural roles. While men grew insecure in their diminished authority, women became equally disoriented, as their femininity had traditionally been defined in opposition to masculinity.

Albeit potentially liberating, this general disorientation led to a rather ambiguous state of affairs. As Barbara Ehrenreich explains, patriarchy – which she defines as the 'intimate power of men over women' – may be in decline, but 'the end of patriarchy is not the same as women's liberation – far from it':

> Patriarchy, like feudalism, implies a relationship of mutual obligation. It may be hypocritical, this sense of mutual obligation, but in patriarchy it meant protectiveness on the part of men. And that element of protection and being cared for – which can be seen as either comforting or infantilizing – is now gone. (Ehrenreich 1995: 288–9)

It is this intrinsic appeal and attractiveness of the patriarchal ideal that preoccupy Galloway, and her novels are intimate records of women's struggle to extricate themselves from deeply internalised patterns of traditionally feminine behaviour. She is adamant, however, that patriarchally defined gender relations are now rapidly becoming redundant, and her novels show our current period to be one of transition from an old order to a new order by being suffused with symbolic male death. In *The Trick is to Keep Breathing* (1989), Galloway's debut novel, the protagonist, Joy Stone, mourns the accidental death of her lover, while in *Foreign Parts* (1994), her second novel, friends Cassie and Rona visit the war cemeteries of northern France and commemorate Rona's grandfather, who died in World War I. Finally, *Clara* (2002), her latest work, concludes with the death of Robert Schumann.

In Galloway's work, dead men epitomise the increasing redundancy of traditional gender roles. In effect, Galloway's novels must be regarded as autopsies of defunct gender relations, analysing the cause of death but also, in recognition of women's problematic relations with patriarchy, articulating a sense of loss. Not only does Galloway anticipate Rosi Braidotti's assertion that 'we need rituals of burial and mourning for the dead, including and especially the ritual of burial of the Woman that was . . . We need to take collectively the time for the mourning of the old socio-symbolic contract' (Braidotti 1997: 529); she also recognises the need to mourn 'the Man that was', if the complexity of female desire and women's habitual collusion with patriarchy are to be fully explored and transformed. Galloway's autopsies of the old order are an integral part of her strategy for moving beyond it. Her novels constitute what Norquay calls 'reconstructive fictions' (Norquay 2000: 133) in so far as they imagine new gender relations and identities that are not as yet entirely conceivable, let alone fully realised.

By illustrating the decline of patriarchal authority, Galloway's novels enact the falling apart of patriarchy and demonstrate its rapidly diminishing hold over women's lives. Formally experimental, her texts are fragmented, often chaotically so, and proliferating into multiple generic registers that disrupt the surface of the text and deliberately obstruct the reading process. These radically deconstructive strategies are Galloway's method of representing discursive failure, of visualising the collapse of oppressive discursive regimes and reifying their breakdown. Each novel focuses on a different aspect of institutionalised patriarchal discourse and examines how it impacts on constructions of femininity. Eventually, new variants of the self emerge in Galloway's texts, realised not through a foundational fixity but through vibrant interaction with others and a conception of identity as an enabling fiction. Such non-patriarchal models of the self successfully pre-empt what Ehrenreich designates as the 'masculinization of women' (Ehrenreich 1995: 289) as, in an allegedly post-feminist era, many women have gained access to a world that remains masculinist in both its design and outlook.

In *The Trick is to Keep Breathing*, Joy Stone finds herself adrift after the accidental death of Michael, her lover, who drowns while they are on holiday. Married with a family before embarking on an affair with Joy, and eventually living, with her, Michael is posthumously reclaimed by his wife, leaving Joy to experience the full sinister effect of patriarchal marginalisation: her story and feelings are declared illegitimate while Michael's marriage to his estranged wife is revalidated. As Joy recounts, the crucial moment occurs at a memorial service where 'the Rev Dogsbody had chosen this service to perform a miracle . . . He'd run time backwards, cleansed, absolved and got rid of the ground-in stain . . . And the stain was me.' Joy concludes that '[she] didn't exist. The miracle had wiped [her] out' (Galloway 1989: 79). Her erasure from the public mourning process causes Joy's grief – which receives no official acknowledgement, let alone sanction – to escalate into trauma, destroying her fragile sense of self and effectively contesting her entitlement to a place in the world. Gradually disintegrating under the pressure of her psychic homelessness, Joy spends time in a psychiatric unit, an experience which, instead of providing comfort or clarity, only exacerbates her estrangement. Her depression worsens, leading to anorexia and bouts of self-harm, and eventually culminating in a suicide attempt. It is the violence of the latter that finally shakes her out of her despair, and at the novel's close it seems as if Joy might imminently be making an attempt at freeing herself from the constraints of patriarchal feminine etiquette.

Galloway's debut novel reads like despatches from the front line of a war against women, in which the punishment for non-conformity is debilitating social isolation and erasure. Comprehensively analysing such pressure, Galloway firmly locates the reason for Joy's steeply declining mental and physical well-being in the social arena where women are expected to realise selfhood through stereotypical enactments of femininity validated by male attention: 'This Sunday night he's coming round. Maybe I will be embraced, entered, made to exist' (Galloway 1989: 46). Obsessed with the deeply alienating, but also disturbingly satisfying routines that produce feminine desirability, Joy yields to the rituals of patriarchal femininity and hence to a seductive process of self-effacement. In describing 'The Bathing Ritual', for example, Joy objectifies her body in animalistic terms: 'Water runs down each foreleg while I shave, carrying the shed animal hair away down the black hole under the taps. Fleeced, I turn off the taps and step out to rub my skin hard with the flat loops of the towel till it hurts' (Galloway 1989: 45). The effort to keep up an acceptable feminine appearance is pathological in so far as it undermines a woman's self-esteem and indeed her very sense of self.

Foreign Parts, Galloway's second novel, follows friends Cassie and Rona on a holiday through France. As tourists, the two women are consumers rather than the consumed, but their cultural effacement as women is ubiquitous. For example, at Chartres Cathedral their guidebook confirms history's peripheral positioning of women in the archivolts that 'show the seven liberal arts, depicted twofold: allegorically by women and historically by the men considered to be the outstanding exponents of each art' (Galloway 1994: 93). As the friends observe on their later visit to the Musée de Beaux Arts, history's exclusion of women is amply complemented by the centralising of the female form in the fine arts. Inundated by male-authored representations of objectified women, Cassie and Rona begin to suffer from 'culture fatigue' and decide to 'go back to the room and look at each other' (Galloway 1994: 239–40). In *Foreign Parts*, Galloway deliberately creates a counterpoint to these androcentric imageries and discourses by introducing into her narrative alternative feminine sensibilities and viewpoints. For example, there is a digressive sequence, set off from the main text by means of indentation, in which Cassie comments on a series of photographs from previous holidays which record her relationship with her ex-boyfriend Chris. Cassie exposes Chris's romantic failings with such relentlessness that in his review of the novel Tom Shone feels compelled to refer to the passage as 'a time-lapse sequence showing the slow slaughter of a sexist pig' (Shone 1994: 7). What Shone fails to acknowledge is Galloway's intention of providing a contrast to the paintings in the Musée de Beaux Arts. Trapped in representation, Chris is defined and bounded by Cassie, who is turning the tables on centuries of androcentric, often misogynous art. Reduced to the hapless Chris in an act of outrageous generalisation, all men find themselves corralled into one stereotype, just as women do on confrontation with the universal truth-claim of male-authored representation.

By contrast, *The Trick* is largely devoid of effective modes of counterdiscursive representation. Rather, the novel is interested in textually re-enacting Joy's nervous breakdown by introducing fractures and fragmentation, giving up on a progressive trajectory and denying itself the authority of a single, all-encompassing discourse. Like Joy herself, Joy's narrative is out of control, and the conventional regularity of familiar forms of representation is in disarray. Typographical diversity creates a sense of disorientation exacerbated by gaps, unfinished sentences and unnumbered pages. The text mutates into a multiplicity of generic forms and discourses, such as play-scripts, recipes, horoscopes and extracts from magazines and self-help books, often out of date or downright irrelevant. The appearance of textual fragments in the margins suggests an overwritten, multilayered palimpsest, destabilising any discursive authority, singular meaning, or interpretative determinacy. Instead of clearly articulating its message, then, the novel appears to be written across a precarious void, both in its lack of discursive stability and in the marked vacuity at the centre of Joy's own self. Her empty nothingness is highlighted by the scan she undergoes to find out if she is pregnant after she has stopped menstruating: 'I looked. I was still there. A black hole among the green stars. Empty space. I had nothing inside me. The doctor smiled directly at me for the first time. Nothing for either of us to worry about then. Nothing at all' (Galloway 1989: 146). Apart from finding no sign of a pregnancy, the scan also reveals Joy's lack of acceptable femininity and the absence of a viable self.

Unsurprisingly perhaps, then, in a world where she risks obsolescence by failing to embody fruitful femininity, Joy saves herself through alternative self-fashioning: 'With a pair of dressmaking scissors I face the mirror and cut my hair short. Spiky. I colour it purple with permanent dye I bought ages ago and never used . . . It will scare the hell out of David' (Galloway 1989: 232). Identity is finally realised as a fiction, a trick, illusion, or self-representational feat, as Joy vows she will learn to 'submit to terrifying chaos' (Galloway 1989: 223) and spurn the comfort of the familiar stereotypes. Joy embraces the existential void so vividly evoked by the scan and, by the close of the novel, she imagines herself swimming – 'casting out long arms into the still water' (Galloway 1989: 235) – thus rendering what the novel initially introduced as a potentially fatal activity into a life-affirming gesture of defiance. Significantly also, in stark contrast to the opening of the novel, where, in disembodied alienation, Joy watches herself 'from the corner of the room', the novel concludes with the vision of a newly embodied woman hearing 'the surf beating in [her] lungs' (Galloway 1989: 7, 236).

In *Foreign Parts* Galloway works the relationship of the two friends into an alternative model of feminine selfhood. Cassie's initial bad-tempered resentment of Rona's independence turns into an appreciation of her 'otherness', her capacity to surprise, and her essential mystery: 'Rona and her secrets. I don't know the half' (Galloway 1994: 225). At the end of the novel 'Rona and me . . . stand in separate places, looking out over water that is just water' (Galloway 1994: 262), signalling the presence of both unity and difference in an ongoing relationship within which selfhood is not dependent on mutual rivalry or knowledge. However, Galloway commendably refrains from idealising female friendship, or celebrating it in separatist exclusivity, by introducing a sensitive young man into the novel, an Algerian student, whom the women meet on the beach towards the end of the novel. The young man does not speak English, making communication difficult, yet contact is made non-verbally: when they ask him for his name, 'his face is luminous with pleasure', and when they shake hands, Cassie observes that 'he's warmer than me and still frozen' (Galloway 1994: 259). Here, as in the women's relationship, Galloway emphasises the need for an acknowledgement of similarity and difference; between the man and the women, there is foreignness and openness, an initial difficulty in communication but by no means an insurmountable one, and vulnerability. In *The Trick*, too, we find the presence of a redemptive young male figure representing difference without menace and the promise of relational renewal: David is Joy's young lover, an ex-pupil, and significantly it is one of David's unannounced visits to Joy's house that thwarts her suicide. Thus inadvertently cast in the role of saviour, David embodies a new, life-affirming masculinity, unencumbered by the oppressive attitudes of older men who, keen to secure the traditional limits of femininity, police the boundaries of gender polarity.

Unfortunately, the two novels' optimistic reconceptualisation of gender relations is eclipsed by a critical reception that attempts to co-opt Joy's crisis into a nationalist agenda. Thus, Cairns Craig appropriates the heroine's emptiness as a symbol of the Scottish nation: 'That "black hole", that "nothing at all"', Craig asserts, 'is the image not only of a woman negated by a patriarchal society but of a society aware of itself only as an absence, a society living, in the 1980s, in the aftermath of its failure to be reborn' (Craig 1999: 199). Invoking the failure of the 1979 Scottish referendum, Craig effectively erases Joy's gender-specific experience of female oppression by incorporating it into a masculinist allegory of national crisis. In this respect, he 'performs a miracle' remarkably similar to the Reverend Dogsbody's at Michael's funeral. Craig's reading not only displaces the female body, but also attests the lesser importance and legitimacy of female experience within the general hierarchy of discourses of oppression while, at the same time, strategically absolving Scottish patriarchy from any possible accusation of complicity. Determined to resist such revisionist interpretations of her work, Galloway turns her back on Scotland in her third novel *Clara*, which also interestingly sees her feminist creativity applied to the rendition of a historical period of entrenched gender fixity.

Set in the mid-nineteenth century, *Clara* relates the first half of the life of Clara Schumann (1819–96), the celebrated concert pianist and wife of the composer Robert Schumann, whose reputation has traditionally overshadowed hers. Six years in the making, the composition of Galloway's third novel coincided with the process of devolution in Scotland, a period of heightened debate on the nature and meaning of Scottishness, and the possibilities of Scottish independence; all the more noteworthy, then, that *Clara* marks Galloway's resolute detachment from all matters Scottish. Significantly, Galloway is not alone in distancing herself from Scotland; her self-removal appears to be part of a common trend among prominent Scottish writers. A. L. Kennedy's *Everything You Need* (1999) is set mainly on an island off the coast of Wales and in London, while of James Kelman's last two novels, *Translated Accounts* (2001) vaguely locates itself in an unnamed, conflict-ridden country and *You Have to Be Careful in the Land of the Free* (2004) is set in the United States. Galloway describes the relocation of her fiction as an act of emancipation from the 'local obsession' with Scottishness, within the context of which 'having to obsess about nationhood can feel like pigeonholing'. At the same time, the fact that *Clara* is ultimately 'just a more intense look at territory I have always written within' reasserts Galloway's priorities in her writing (Eliass 2003). Loath to collude with the masculinist discourses of traditional Scottishness, or to encourage appropriations of her work for a nationalist agenda, the deliberate foreignness of *Clara* enables Galloway to reaffirm her commitment to representing female experience.

Clara is a historical novel, covering the first four decades of Clara's life up until Robert's death. Clara is a musical child prodigy, the daughter of Friedrich Wieck, an obsessively career-driven man in complete control of his daughter's life and work. However, for all his efforts, Wieck fails to stop Clara marrying Robert Schumann, one of his pupils. The marriage is soon clouded by Robert's precarious mental health, manifesting itself in bouts of mania and paranoia and eventually, after a failed suicide attempt, resulting in his institutional confinement. Enthusiastically promoting Robert's work, Clara must also maintain her own career in order to support her ailing husband and their eight children. That she outlived her husband by many years and continued performing until the end of her life is hinted at in the prologue but, quite astonishingly, the novel ends with Schumann's death. Unlike Galloway's previous work, *Clara* does not focus on female disorientation; rather, it is a man, Robert Schumann, who suffers a nervous breakdown. Clara is the stable centre of the novel, solidly bound within a network of familial and communal ties, thus possibly testifying to Galloway's increasing optimism regarding women's resourcefulness and resilience. Shifting in focus between a triad of central characters – Clara, her father Friedrich Wieck, and Robert – *Clara* is a polyphonic text sustaining a continuous, vibrant interplay between self and environment, as well as individual and community, and emphasising their inescapable interdependency. Consequently, there is less textual disruption here than in the previous novels, even though the narrative is still punctuated by lists, letters, poems and musical notation. Coherence takes precedence over fragmentation, and this appears to be true of Clara's character as well. Unlike Galloway's previous heroines, Clara seems unaffected by the conflict-ridden gender disorientation that afflicts Joy and Cassie, and of course it must appear ironic that Galloway assigns such superior feminine strength and stamina to a woman of the pre-feminist nineteenth century.

In *Clara* Galloway tackles the western discourse of 'Great Art' and its championing of the individual – usually male – creative genius. According to the inside-cover blurb, the novel rejects 'the romantic conflation of Madness and Creativity', an association that elsewhere Galloway calls 'a stupid, elitist notion' (Robertson 2002). The separation of art from the material sphere of everyday concerns is an ideological move that has historically maintained it as the reserve of men. Galloway successfully exposes this elitism by focusing on a female artist, as well as by highlighting the material conditions of the production of art and questioning the transcendent pretensions commonly attributed to it. As part of this strategy the novel pays close attention to the day-to-day limitations of Clara's life, a magnifying procedure reflected also in the cover of the novel, which comprises a tight close-up of one half of Clara's face from a portrait painted by Johann Heinrich Schramm in 1840. The amplified perspective accentuates the broken texture of the painted surface, which resolves into an eye and one half of a nose and mouth, illustrating the less-than-smooth surface of the painting and – by implication – of a life, even an artist's life, when examined closely. It is with similarly close scrutiny that in the novel's narrative Galloway interrogates the reductive and often idealising narration of creative lives, and the romantic coupling of art and madness especially. Galloway's novel asserts that Robert's creativity does not derive from his psychological instability. 'It is when he cannot write that he is (what was the word? What sounded reasonable?) he is – downhearted', Clara explains at one point, to which his friend Reuter responds: 'But when he works, when the ideas carry him along, he stays awake and thinks too wildly' (Galloway 2002: 243). Whereas it is without doubt Robert's relationship with his work that determines his mental health, his instability does not increase his productivity.

Galloway also suggests that there is an element to Robert's creative crisis that is particularly masculine. As an artist obsessed with death and in the grip of a fear that makes him worry to the point of distraction about mortality, ageing and decay, Robert's concern with transcendence causes him to long for escape from a physical world, that is, the feminised realm of the body and mundane everyday. Inevitably, Clara's creativity is different and, through her, Galloway reminds us of the intimate relationship between art and life, not only the material conditions of its production but also its own materiality:

> Three house moves in seven months. Eight concerts in six. Even the houses were strange. How are we to stop making war with our neighbours with such huge windows? she complained. Every sound will carry. And so it did. Street hawkers woke them at five, and cabbies' iron-wheeled scraping kept them open-eyed till late. Every maidservant was sour, every cook smart-mouthed. On the positive side, the string section was good. The strings were very good indeed. (Galloway 2002: 336)

As housekeeper and artist, mother and sole breadwinner, Clara cannot avoid thinking of art and life as bound together. Without fuss or fight she goes to work, overturning the conventions of feminine propriety by organising her own concert tours and then travelling alone to fulfil her commitments. Unlike Galloway's other protagonists, Clara does not succumb to the debilitating disorientation caused by the constant flux in the boundaries of her female role and confidently cultivates the valorised masculine traits of silence, stability and self-composure. Indeed, it is the men in Clara's life who are hysterical, as both Wieck and Robert at times lose control in outbursts of temper and frustration.

Even within the given limits of a social context that unerringly privileges men, Clara manages to find viable means of female self-determination, as, for example, when she places a shawl under the hammers of her piano so that she can practise without disturbing Robert. 'Imagining the grandeur of the sound that should have been there' (Galloway 2002: 205), Clara accesses the music which is her tool of self-realisation. In another memorable scene in the novel Clara performs soon after a miscarriage:

> Clara wished to play. Sitting on inch-thick towelling and a constant slither of blood-clots, her face white but composed enough, she played a concert as soon as it could be set up for some local hall, and for not much more than the asking. She would have worn black in case of staining but had brought none, so maroon served. Maroon, she decided was practical. (Galloway 2002: 292)

Playing the piano, Clara comes closest to self-fulfilment, away from the grief and guilt of everyday life. In a moment of crisis she reconstructs herself through music, 'gripping the piano lid for support and finding it' (Galloway 2002: 293). Clara's method of self-realisation is also aptly evoked in her description of her husband's sonata, which in her view is 'proof that sheer effort of will could construct a wholeness where none existed' (Galloway 2002: 289). The control of passion 'is the medium through which all else flows' (Galloway 2002: 5), and Clara survives by controlling the chaotic flux of life and art.

As with Joy and Cassie, female identity in *Clara* is a process of self-appropriation in order to escape the prescriptive discourses of hegemonic femininity. These discourses are formidably materialised at the outset of the novel in Galloway's description of the conventions of nineteenth-century women's dress. There are thirteen layers of clothing waiting to be worn by Clara; fully attired, 'she crosses the room in this dress heavy as slate, its drag at her legs unsteadying' (Galloway 2002: 6). Everything in a woman's life seems calculated to impose limitations upon her and provoke stasis, to effect female passivity. Pertinently, the prologue ends with Clara sitting at the window, as 'she has nothing to do but wait' (Galloway 2002: 7). In fact, the novel is framed by this image of female passivity: the last sentence of the prologue doubles as the last sentence of the novel, where Clara is shown sitting at the window in Robert's hospital room moments after his death. However, by chronicling Clara's unceasing activity as partner, mother, working woman and creative artist, the text itself gives the lie to all this passive posturing. In all of Galloway's three novels the imperative pressures of hegemonic femininity threaten to paralyse and close down the female self, yet nevertheless selfhood is ultimately realised: through re-embodiment in *The Trick*, female friendship in *Foreign Parts*, and creativity in *Clara*.

As in Galloway's first two novels, towards the end of *Clara* a redemptive young male appears; in this case it is the composer Johannes Brahms, who supports Clara through the final years of her marriage. Brahms and Clara are in love, but they sublimate their desire into preserving and promoting the musical genius of Robert Schumann. Galloway's attempt to rehabilitate masculinity in the form of a 'post-patriarchal' youth who signifies an ideal and desirable 'new' masculinity, which prioritises partnership over domination, is clearly a recurrent theme in her work. Galloway's youths represent the promise of a utopian reorganisation of gender relations, the fulfilment of which appears to depend on the death of the older men in her texts; traditional, patriarchal masculinity must be discredited and destroyed before new relationships become possible. This situation is reminiscent of Sigmund Freud's imagined scenario of the origin of religion in *Totem and Taboo* (1913), in which the selfish and possessive father, refusing to share his power and his women with his sons, is killed by them and then eaten in a cannibalistic meal symbolic of their appropriation of his power. Braidotti intriguingly refers to this Freudian scenario when she considers change in social – and especially gender – relations. According to Braidotti, 'the new is created by revisiting and burning up the old. Like the totemic meal recommended by Freud, you have to assimilate the dead before you can move on to a new order' (Braidotti 1997: 529).

In an outrageous parody of Freud's totemic meal, in *Foreign Parts* Galloway depicts Cassie and Rona as consuming a marzipan effigy of the patriarchal phallus:

> Slim white shaft, bulbous green tip. It was a marzipan penis, septic colour glittering faintly with icing sugar. Cassie looked at it hard. Then she looked at Rona.Rona why did you buy me this?
>
> Souvenir, she said. I nearly got you an artichoke but they were too dear. That was nicer anyway. I bet you thought it was a bluebell but it's not. Asparagus.
>
> Cassie looked back down, watching the penis metamorphose. Not completely but enough. Asparagus. She shrugged her eyebrows, bit the tip off the sweet and rolled it in her mouth, offered the remaining piece to Rona. (Galloway 1994: 207)

Demonstrating at once the appeal of phallic authority and its complete lack of foundation, Galloway pictures her female protagonists in the act of ingesting the power of the phallus, a power itself suitably undermined and rendered insignificant, ridiculous even, in its representation as a comestible. Male dominance is not merely subverted in Galloway's novels; men's naturalised authority is dismissed out of hand in a radical feminist re-envisioning of gender relations, which includes Galloway's introduction of redemptive, post-patriarchal young men.

Chapter 25

In/outside Scotland: Race and Citizenship in the Work of Jackie Kay

Matthew Brown

At the beginning of the twenty-first century there are two rivalling views of Scotland, one seeing the nation as hopelessly schizophrenic, mired in its own bedevilled tartanry and forever salvaging the present through historical erasure, the other asserting it as a cosmopolitan postnation at ease with its contradictory legacies and able to tap its inherent multiplicities for a contemporary self-image. The former view derives from a common twentieth-century perspective. In *A Scottish Journey* Edwin Muir infamously concluded that the country through which he was travelling did not exist: 'I did not find anything which I could call Scotland' (Muir 1935: 243). Muir's scorched-earth writing, which adjudged Scotland a self-negating entity, assumed many reflected forms throughout the century, the best-known being perhaps by Tom Nairn, who in sceptical Muirean parlance dubbed the Scottish nation 'the tartan monster' (Nairn 1981: 165). The latter, more recent view resolutely rejects the proposition that Scottishness is thwarted by its own contradictions and discontinuities, celebrating instead the nation's dynamic multifacetedness that uniquely accommodates a postmodern world view and allows Scotland to stand as a 'beacon for a new and non-threatening civic nationalism, which will be the basis of a new international order' (Craig 2002: 21). Interestingly, Craig's vision recalls Richard Kearney's of a 'postnationalist Ireland' in which 'the modern idea of a millenarian state, in which cultural and political differences might be subsumed into consensus, is challenged by the postmodern preference for *dissensus* – diversity without synthesis' (Kearney 1997: 65). Accordingly, for Craig, the 1997 referendum marked simply 'the political reflection of a Scotland which has already been constituted, a Scotland in union with itself rather than in union with England' (Craig 2002: 2).

If one credits that Scotland provides, as Lindsay Paterson propounds, a 'template from which other nations can learn how to develop a non-threatening conception of nationalism, one that is tolerant both of internal plurality and of flexible subversions of its sovereignty in larger forms of social organization that have positive benefits for its citizens' (Paterson 1994: 180), then one must also ask how exactly these 'positive benefits' are culturally animated, and whether it is indeed true that Scotland is uniquely positioned to address and promote hybrid, cross-cultural modes of national affiliation. In *Black British Writing* Victoria Arana and Lauri Ramey suggest that millennial attempts to reinvent Britain were crucially spearheaded by a vanguard of black writers – including Jackie Kay – who insist on distinguishing their voices from preceding 'postcolonial' generations by

naming their Britishness as a first principle, and who 'do not write about their *staying power*
because they are not the ones who migrated. Britain, they affirm, *is* their country' (Arana
and Ramey 2004: 3). What interests many of these writers is how traditional constructions
of race as a biological essence have been affected culturally by debates on the Atlantic diaspora, the 'postnational constellation', as well as by devolution and recent theorising on
cosmopolitanism (see Appiah 2006). Accordingly, for poet, playwright and novelist Jackie
Kay, it is post-devolution Scotland's specific articulation of inclusive citizenship, and the
reconstitution of the nation's social and symbolic space enabled by this articulation, which
inform much of her writing.

Like Craig in *The Modern Scottish Novel*, Kay regards Scottish identity as the consequence of manifold proliferating contradictions in the nation's history and response to that
history, but at the same time she remains unconvinced that all citizens of Scotland are
invariably benefiting from this kind of national self-representation. In an interview conducted a few months before the referendum, Kay was asked to comment on the notion that
'everybody has many voices and multiple selves but Scots are [more] aware of it' (Gish
2001: 179). Putting this differently, Kay was asked to situate her own writing within the
debates on national identity, ranging from Muir's withering negations to Craig's critical
rehabilitation of the 'divisions' that so tenaciously pervade Scottish literature. Kay
responded:

> Most Scottish people are aware of how England has treated them and how they've suffered like
> the Irish at the hands of the English and how the English have so many stereotypes of Scottish
> people . . . What interests me particularly is the way in which you can be in a society that is
> cordoned off and oppressed but also be oppressed within that society, or divided within that
> or not belong to the common group in exactly the same way. I do think that sense of being
> outside with being inside Scotland – with being very proud of the country and very proud of
> being Scottish, and also being outside in terms of receiving a lot of racism from other Scottish
> people – is what fuels my sense of how and what I write. (Gish 2001: 179–80)

Born in Edinburgh to a Scottish mother and Nigerian father, adopted by a white couple
and brought up in Glasgow, Kay is a writer exceedingly alert to 'that sense of being outside
with being inside Scotland'; in fact, she has used her particular sensibility and perspective
as a literary leitmotif throughout her career. Kay's work attends to Scotland's extraordinary
social and symbolic dynamism at the end of the twentieth and the beginning of the twenty-
first century – in both devolutionary and post-devolution times – imagining the nation as
a site of cultural possibility, yet without ever losing sight of the persistent threat to inclusive citizenship posed by racism. It seems as if Kay wants her readers to realise that the
establishment of an independent parliament does not automatically remedy and resolve
Scotland's internal divisions; rather, it opens up challenging possibilities for the nation to
recast its political and cultural contours on its own terms. This chapter will demonstrate
how Kay's writings work to dramatise the particular challenges surrounding the issue of citizenship in Scotland today by inserting questions of racial difference into contemporary
debates on Scottishness.

Three of Kay's works in particular express her views on devolutionary and devolved citizenship in Scotland: a volume of poetry, *The Adoption Papers* (1991), the novel *Trumpet*
(1998) and *Why Don't You Stop Talking* (2002), a collection of short stories. In each, Kay's
representation of Scottish citizenship is motivated by a cosmopolitan world view, informed
not by motifs of dispossession or rootlessness but by the ability to map international spaces

onto local environs in order to make diasporic citizens feel welcome and 'at home' in Scotland. However, in her more recent work, Kay's views as to what the devolved nation might achieve are far from optimistic; nor is she alone in her warning against the return of exclusive or aggressive nationalisms. In *Scottish Voices* Neal Ascherson shares Kay's concerns when he asks 'whether devolution can lead to democracy . . . This means reaching towards qualities of social justice, equality and sheer modernity which the United Kingdom as a whole has not achieved' (Ascherson 2002: 303–4). Kay's attention to contemporary Britain's lack of social justice has become even more pronounced in her post-devolution work, which highlights the way that, like England, Scotland cultivates an increasingly self-enclosed and racialised self-image. While Kay clearly shares Craig's eagerness to envision a Scottish civic space that is unfixed, non-essential and open to constant revision, she never fails also to expose the restrictions on inclusive citizenship by depicting the lives of Scottish people still living at once inside and outside Scotland.

Before analysing in greater detail Kay's representation of race in contemporary Scotland, it seems vital to show how throughout history the racialised subject has been denied a legitimate, indigenous claim to citizenship in Britain, and how this denial – as Kay demonstrates – remains instrumental in the successful propagation of racism. The political imperative to deny black people any claim to a historical presence in Britain which would pre-date the *Windrush* generation of postwar immigrants from the Caribbean in the late 1940s is a subject discussed at length in Paul Gilroy's *There Ain't No Black in the Union Jack* (1987). According to Gilroy, the black population of Britain has been politically defined either as a 'problem' – that is, an external ill threatening an apparently secure British culture – or as 'forever victims, objects rather than subjects', homeless refugees rather than citizens (Gilroy 1992: 11). Promoted by right-wing politicians like Enoch Powell (1912–98), this problem/victim rhetoric effectively deprived the black community of an indigenous British tradition and, as such, must be regarded as possibly the most 'fundamental achievement of racist ideologies' (Gilroy 1992: 11). Characterising immigrants as 'avoidable evils' and 'alien elements', Powell's notorious 'Rivers of Blood' speech, delivered on 20 April 1968, makes apparent how national culture can be racialised when appeals to nationhood pivot on preserving an essential identity and are negotiated against difference (see Powell 1968).

What is perpetrated by expunging any positive black contribution to British history is a national amnesia concerning the long history of economic, political and military relations between Britain and the West Indies from the Atlantic slave trade to World Wars I and II, significantly also consigning to oblivion the works of early black British writers such as Olaudah Equiano (1745–97), Robert Wedderburn (1762–1835) and Mary Prince (1788–1833). With regard to the profoundly disingenuous representation of black British history's alleged limitation to the second half of the twentieth century, Kay's views are very much in alignment with Gilroy's: 'I think the history that children are taught in schools, British history or Scottish history or English history, doesn't really include black people, and yet black people have been part of this country's history long, long before the *Windrush* that everybody seems to talk about as a marker date' (Rice 2004: 219).

Working as a kind of manifesto against exclusivist definitions of citizenship and identity, Kay's strongly autobiographical debut *The Adoption Papers* engages themes of intercultural merger and subjective hybridity in devolutionary Scotland through the motif of 'adoption', a condition that is as much an evocation of the author's 'sense of being outside with being inside Scotland' as it is a bold challenge to racialised conceptions of national belonging, the particular challenge residing in the synthetical claim of Kay's poetic persona to being at once black and Scottish. *The Adoption Papers* comprises a series of intertwined monologues about the experiences of a mixed-race girl, born in Edinburgh in the early 1960s, and adopted and raised by a leftist Glaswegian couple. The collection is narrated by three distinct voices: the birth mother, the adoptive mother and the adopted daughter. Sonorously layering these three very different personalities within her text, Kay dramatises how different individuals constitute their cultural citizenship and how these subjective accounts volley with the probing interpellations of other voices who externally fashion 'race' as the singular marker of embodied identity. Kay begins *The Adoption Papers* by invoking Scotland as a location harbouring great suspicion about mixed-raced families. The collection opens with the adoptive mother describing the social stigma attached to adoption: 'Even in the early sixties there was / something scandalous about adopting, / telling the world your secret failure / bringing up an alien child, / who knew what it would turn out to be' (Kay 1991: 10). In this first stanza Kay pits the adoptive mother's decision to raise 'an alien child' against public feeling that such a child is a contingent citizen with no biological claim to the family. However, the view that the adopted child enters social life as a foreign presence which might come to threaten the future reproduction of this social life ('who knew what it would turn out to be') is resolutely dispatched by the adoptive mother, who asserts: 'I brought her up as my own / as I would any other child / colour matters to the nutters' (Kay 1991: 24). The adoptive mother resolves at the local and personal levels what the public cannot, namely the insertion and transformation of a perceived 'otherness' into the social order of a familial/national collective.

Through the voices of the adoptive mother and her daughter, who spends much of her time tracing her birth mother, *The Adoption Papers* explores the complexities of belonging and citizenship, as well as the difficult parturition into symbolic 'state' knowledge encompassing all the bureaucratic networks that govern Scottish everyday life. In *The Adoption Papers* most of the encounters between the citizen and her state are set in Glasgow. Location here is of the essence, as each venue reveals Kay's interest in engaging space as a socially symbolic entity, or put differently – in Ray Ryan's words – 'something to be "read", mentally grasped, and returned to the realm of discourse, even as it remains a solidly material phenomenon' (Ryan 2002: 23). Kay constructs Glasgow through her portrayal of a range of socially symbolic institutions. Thus, in 'The Waiting Lists' a representation of Glasgow emerges out of the adoptive parents' visits to various adoption agencies, during which Kay shows how the state might still be predicated upon a racialised self-image of the nation. After being refused by four agencies, the adoptive parents are finally able to adopt when they inform a fifth agency that '[they] don't mind the colour', and 'just like that, the waiting was over' (Kay 1991: 14). Kay's initial inspection of a state mechanism – an agency that allots racialised meaning to every application for adoption – is one not unfamiliar to readers of, say, James Kelman's fiction, which similarly imagines Glasgow as a location characterised by alienation perpetrated by the looming force of a mystifying, discordant bureaucracy. Thus, it is all the more surprising when Kay discards this initial portrayal in the following scene, in which a social worker visits the adoptive parents' house.

Self-consciously revising her image of Glasgow, Kay highlights the social worker's unexpected humanity, which surprises both the adoptive mother and the reader, whose expectations are premised first on the adoption agency's racism and secondly on the mother's decision to scour all left-wing political paraphernalia from her house before the visit. Kay ironically pits the adoptive mother's misreading of a state representative against her own revelation of how Scotland is indeed much more alive to, and accommodating of, difference than the official, state-controlled agenda of the adoption agencies might suggest. Speaking in demotic Scots, the adoptive mother comments on her house cleaning:

> I put Marx Engels Lenin (no Trotsky)
> In the airing cupboard—she'll no be
> checking out the towels surely
>
> All the copies of the *Daily Worker*
> I shoved under the sofa
> the dove of peace I took down from the loo
>
> A poster of Paul Robeson
> saying give him his passport
> I took down from the kitchen
>
> I left a bust of Burns
> my detective stories
> And the Complete Works of Shelley

(Kay 1991: 15)

She sanitises the house by clearing out their leftist gear, rendering the home appropriately nationalist and acculturated through the bust of Burns and the works of Shelley, while the image of the African-American scholar, performer and activist Paul Robeson (1898–1976) demanding his passport, revoked by the United States because of perceived communist radicalism, is tidily tucked away. The domestic space strives for the 'normal', and when the social worker comments that her house looks 'different', she exclaims that 'Hell and I've spent all morning / trying to look ordinary' (Kay 1991: 15). Trusting the visit has gone well until the social worker catches sight of several small peace insignia pasted to the wall ('clear as a hammer and sickle'), the adoptive mother proceeds to politicise her desire to adopt, even though she realises that such a declaration might disadvantage her application: 'I'd like this baby to live in a nuclear free world.' To this the social worker responds: 'I'm all for peace myself she says, / and sits down for another cup of coffee' (Kay 1991: 16). In this ironic turn, the parent's public enunciation of difference and dissent brings about the state official's decision to authorise the adoption.

While the adoptive parents experience and understand the nation from the position of their political dissent, the adoptive daughter perceives its meaning and significance through the filter of her racial difference, a mix of her father's Nigerian skin and her mother's Highland complexion. Skin colour may not matter to the adoptive mother, but it certainly does to her daughter. Two specific public institutions are foregrounded to dramatise the daughter's growing awareness of her race: her school, when she is a child, and several governmental agencies in Edinburgh whose bureaucracy, as an adult, she manipulates in order to track down her 'blood'. In both locations blood is emblematic of biologised claims to cultural belonging, and indeed, the daughter comes to view it as a vehicle to self-knowledge, that is, as a means of authenticating her identity by knowing her genes, her blood line, her birth parents. At school she encounters various instances of racism: a young boy jeers at her, '*Sambo Sambo*', and one of her teachers bellows during a dance lesson: 'Come on, show / us what you can do I thought / you people had it in your blood' (Kay 1991: 25). By thus highlighting the girl's difference, the boy and the teacher deploy race as the traditional means to biologise cultural identity, naturalising their own normativity by locating national

belonging 'in the blood' and, in so doing, aggressively patrolling the borders of Scottish citizenship. The daughter's subsequent query – 'What is in my blood?' – reflects these external
assignations of race; as Frantz Fanon might have put it, through the force of interpellation
she is made aware of the fact of her blackness (see Fanon 1986).

Significantly, in adult life the daughter's imperative need to know where she comes from
('I want to know my blood') shifts from a purely biological enquiry into a quest for 'home' in
terms of both culturally and nationally defined belonging. Accordingly, 'knowing my blood'
becomes equivalent to knowing 'who were my grandmothers / what were the days like passed
in Scotland / the land I come from / the soil in my blood' (Kay 1991: 29). No longer does
she crave authentication of her identity by biological descent; rather, she sets out to discover
an identity-bearing narrative that traces the life trajectories of both her birth parents, the
itineraries that brought her father from Nigeria to Scotland and her mother to Aberdeen.
Her desire to contact her birth mother turns into an active striving towards a new kind of
Scottish citizenship, a process that seeks to conjoin imaginatively her adoptive mother's
political radicalism to her birth parents' wayward travelling. At the close of the volume the
adoptive mother feels 'closer than blood' to her daughter, who still awaits 'the crash of the
letter box / then the soft thud of words on the matt', signalling that her birth parents' history
has arrived in the form of a letter posted by her birth mother (Kay 1991: 34).

The Adoption Papers can be read at once as both a never-ending quest for and a self-
confident declaration of citizenship; either way it documents a journey which significantly
enhances our understanding of the scope and essential syncretism of Scotland's national
imaginary, comprising not only the works of the Scottish and English Romantic poets
Robert Burns and Percy Shelley, but also the radical black activism of Paul Robeson and
Angela Davis, as well as the music of the black blues singer Bessie Smith. *The Adoption
Papers* authorises Glasgow's cosmopolitan adoption of these alternative, transnational life
histories, thereby preparing the nation for multicultural forms of citizenship demonstrably
evacuated of racist acculturation. Evidently, this kind of citizenship is still articulated
against the perception of difference; however, Kay's poetry issues a challenge to her readers
to conceive of identity not only as nationally bound, historically informed and locally situated, but also as shaped by extensive networks of cosmopolitanist cross-reference and
transnational belonging.

Continuing with her dramatisation of citizenship by intertwining discourses of race and
ethnicity, Scottishness and gender performativity, *Trumpet*, Kay's first and so far only novel,
deals with the experiences of a Scottish mixed-race family in the aftermath of the father's
death. Like *The Adoption Papers*, *Trumpet* is contrapuntal, shifting between first- and third-
person perspectives and engaging a multitude of different voices in the novel's endeavour
to shed light on the life of the black Scottish jazz trumpeter, Joss Moody. When the book
opens, Joss has died, and his wife Millie and adopted son Colman attempt from different
standpoints – hers loving and nostalgic, his resentful and embittered – to assemble a meaningful, coherent and truthful account of their familial history. Situated among a cacophony of other voices, the agonised meditations of Millie and Colman occur in the wake of
the highly publicised postmortem revelation that Joss's biological sex was female, that he
had been 'passing' as a man for his entire life and professional career, and that his
wife Millie was the only one privy to this knowledge – it was 'our secret', as she reveals (Kay
1998: 10). Roving between the accounts of several self-absorbed, biased, unreliable
interpreters, most of whom are preoccupied with re-authenticating Joss's life through the
revelation of his 'true' biological sex, Kay demonstrates that there is no one stable or fixed
truth about Joss, no more than there is one fixed truth about anybody's life.

Joss's identity is presented as provisional, eluding definitive capture, and through his portrayal Kay conjures 'a performative view of gender', in which sexual identity 'is not a given at birth, but produced through the performance of the cultural conventions of gender' (King 2001: 105). Against the mystification elicited by Joss's embrace of performance, the novel records various attempts to render his self more secure, more known, and, in so doing, Kay points up the flashpoints between Joss's desire for self-authorship, on the one hand, and the interpellative mechanisms that police all subjectivity through external impositions of racial, gender and other cultural norms, on the other. Certainly, Joss is viewed to be differently embodied in two significant ways: first, he is a black man living in a predominantly white Glasgow, and, secondly, his biological sex is posthumously recorded as aberrant because his body is viewed to be a thing inconsistent with his lived identity. By examining the impact of Joss's sex/gender asymmetry on those who abide by biologist imperatives, Kay further shows how various institutions function to return Joss to his 'natural' state in order to recodify, retroactively, his lived identity. Thus, Kay contrasts the explicit performativity of Joss's gender with the state's reassessment of his identity in scenes during which, for example, the doctor scrutinises Joss's corpse, takes out her 'emergency red pen', then crosses out 'male' and writes 'female' on the death certificate (Kay 1998: 44). Joss's deviant embodiment prompts a reaction that highlights the doctor's absolute belief and trust in the recording mechanisms of the state.

Against this official capture of Joss's 'true' identity, Joss himself promotes radical self-fashioning permitting the subject to author his or her own history and national affiliation, as well as racial and ethnic 'routes' – and not to be beholden to any collective, biologically encoded 'roots'. Self-fashioning is a creative act for Joss; in the chapter 'Music', Kay's third-person narrator assumes Joss's point of view to describe the 'stripping down' of the self that occurs during its absorption within the whirling thrall of jazz: 'When he gets down . . . he loses his sex, his race, his memory. He strips himself bare . . . He goes down, swirling and whirling till he's right down at the very pinpoint of himself. A small black mark' (Kay 1998: 131). Clearly though, Kay remains sceptical about the ultimate feasibility of such radical self-expenditure, for despite Joss's relentless, self-immersing pursuits of jazz music to the point of ecstatic erasure, reaching moments when the 'horn ruthlessly strips him bare till he ends up with no body, no past, nothing' (Kay 1998: 135), Kay's narrator insists that some essence always remains: that 'pinpoint' of the self, that enduring 'small black mark'. Kay draws our attention to the fallacy of Joss's belief in radical self-authorship by rendering Joss's reverie through a third-person perspective, which inevitably invests his most 'stripped down form' with racial meaning, however residual. Aspects of his identity which Joss experiences to be in flux – most notably his gender and ethnicity – are always already fixed in the eye of the beholder, proving that self-invention is inevitably stymied by third-person perception. However, although the narrative voice insists that race persists as an interpellative stranglehold on individual identity, Joss makes a similarly resolute and radical claim on the subject of national self-determination. When the family move from Glasgow to London, Joss continues to cultivate his Scots accent, 'determined that everyone would know he was Scottish' and chastising his son Colman for letting his Glaswegian accent slip: 'You are Scottish, you were born in Scotland and that makes you Scottish' (Kay 1998: 190). A Scottish origin bestows Scottish citizenship; at the same time, all throughout *Trumpet* Kay's representation also remains privy to Craig's postnationalist vision of individuals as adroitly forging interpellative events into affirmative claims on cultural citizenship.

Insisting on being a Scottish national, Joss's posthumous letter to his son launches a historicised amalgamation of the allegedly incompatible, yet – to him – intimately intertwined facts of his blackness and Scottishness, thus 'inventing' a new ethnicity which he urges his son to adopt as well. Joss's letter to Colman recounts the story of his African father's arrival in Scotland, a story which is Joss's identity-bearing legacy for his adoptive son to keep and cherish: 'I've left it all for you, my letters, photographs, records, documents, certificates. It is all here. Mine and your own . . . It is quite simple: all of this is my past, this is the sum of my parts; you are my future' (Kay 1998: 277). Projecting identity as a collage of official and unofficial recordings, Joss's letter resembles the birth mother's (as yet) undelivered letter at the end of *The Adoption Papers*; both texts offer their next-generation recipients a notion of identity and citizenship predicated on a cosmopolitanist merger of local and transnational spaces. Given that for most of *Trumpet* Colman perceives himself through an economy of representation redolent of Gilroy's problem/victim dynamic – for instance, he remembers being arrested just for 'being black and being in the wrong place at the wrong time' (Kay 1998: 62) – the history borne by Joss's letter must be regarded as a genuine alternative effectively countering such racial misassignations. Kay concludes *Trumpet* by asking whether his father's legacy will inspire Colman to reconstitute his identity within the space of Scotland, where he is about to return at the book's end to reconcile with his mother.

Whether Colman will succeed in identifying as a Scottish citizen will depend not only on himself, but also on how his being in Scotland will be viewed and culturally negotiated. Rather than solving the problem of citizenship simply by returning Colman to his Scottish mother, Kay appeals to what Homi Bhabha has described as 'the ethics of coexistence' emerging from a 'social space which has to be communally shared with others, and from which solidarity is not simply based on similarity but on the recognition of difference' (Bhabha 1998: 51). Bhabha's theorising may serve as an apt reference point for gauging the utopian power of Kay's affirmative representations of Scottishness in *The Adoption Papers* and *Trumpet*, as well as a measure against which to evaluate her increasingly pessimistic views on convivial communal life in Britain in her most recent work. Some of Kay's stories in *Why Don't You Stop Talking* emphasise the continuing presence of racist violence in the UK, caused mainly by what Kay perceives as a general, large-scale regression to culture being apprehended as racially defined and enclosed. The title story, for example, depicts the experiences of a black woman in London whose attempts at participating in public discourse are met with violent aggression: when she chastises a man for jumping the ATM queue he threatens to 'belt her one on that fat black mouth', and when she humanely comments, while walking down the street, to a mother berating her young child, 'Easy does it, love, he's just a little fellow', the woman slaps her and tells her to 'shut [her] fucking trap' (Kay 2002b: 45–6). Hence 'why don't you stop talking' becomes Kay's tagline for contemporary racism in Britain, and she narrates this apparent cultural regress, this movement away from any 'ethics of coexistence', in the story's startling final moment, which involves yet another transmutation of linguistic into physical injury.

At the story's end, the narrator takes a razor and slices open her tongue – a pain that 'feels deserved' because of, so we are led to believe, her internalisation of racist prejudice (Kay 2002b: 50). For Kay, this distressing moment serves to document the enduring power of Powellian politics, which she has been so intent on dismantling throughout her career. Kay's most recent work is dystopian rather than hopeful, highlighting the increasing disillusionment of British citizens who are routinely marginalised by a persistent official preoccupation with the identification and registration of 'difference', the conspicuous absence of a civic community and, finally, the ongoing transmogrification of social space from a realm of hospitality and empathy into one of violence and despair.

Chapter 26

Irvine Welsh: Parochialism, Pornography and Globalisation

Robert Morace

Randall Stevenson and Gavin Wallace's *The Scottish Novel Since the Seventies* (1993) can hardly be faulted for failing to anticipate the way in which works like *Marabou Stork Nightmares* (1995), Irvine Welsh's second novel, would challenge Wallace's characterisation of the Scottish novel as 'a grey and morose beast prone to lengthy fits of self-pity' (Wallace 1993: 220) by transforming these fits into opportunities for a critical examination of contemporary Scotland in relation to its past. Nor could Wallace have anticipated the extent to which the international success of *Trainspotting* (1993), Welsh's debut novel, as well as James Kelman's winning of the Booker Prize in 1994, would inspire confidence at home and create a global market for Scottish fiction. That this confidence contributed to the success of the 1997 referendum is no less certain than the fact that devolution freed Scottish writers from, as Christopher Whyte puts it, 'the task of representing the nation', which had been their lot since the 1707 Act of Union and more specifically between the 1979 and 1997 referenda. Free from, or deprived of, this task, Scottish literature could, Whyte optimistically prophesied, 'be literature first and foremost, rather than the expression of a nationalist movement' (Whyte 1998a: 284). Whyte's assessment has been confirmed by Kelman's recent *Translated Accounts* (2001) and *You Have to Be Careful in the Land of the Free* (2004), as well as Janice Galloway's *Clara* (2002), which represents a self-conscious effort to escape the 'Scottish writer' label less than a decade after it became a distinct and commercially viable category. Additional confirmation of Scottish literature's increasingly global image and appeal comes in more indirect form in recent calls for Scottish studies to move beyond its 'lingering parochialism' (Bell and Miller 2004: 11–15).

Porno (2002), Welsh's fifth novel, provides a particularly interesting test case for the limits and opportunities of the lingering parochialism out of, and against, which the second Scottish renaissance of the 1980s and 1990s developed. Together with *Trainspotting*, to which it is designed as a direct sequel, it bookends the era during which contemporary Scottish fiction came into its own, as an independent player in the global cultural marketplace, newly divorced from English or British literature. By revisiting *Trainspotting*'s characters and setting nine years on, *Porno* reflects on Scotland's changing social, political, economic and cultural landscapes, both directly in terms of what the novel and its author say about these changes and, more importantly, indirectly in terms of how the novel embodies them.

Whereas *Trainspotting* had originally been written against the grain of the mainstream culture of spectacle which swiftly co-opted it, offering – as Welsh puts it – 'a bunch of voices shouting to be heard' (McGavin 1996: 52), *Porno* was produced as a deliberate spectacle from within the postnational global culture. The novel's return to the Leith setting of *Trainspotting* also represents neither the kind of continued interrogation of the Scottish past one detects in *Marabou Stork Nightmares*, nor a turning away from a narrowly defined category of Scottish literature, which one finds, for example, in Galloway's *Clara*. Moreover, while the carnivalesque *Trainspotting* oscillates between Nietzschean resentment and Bakhtinian decrowning of all forms of monologic authority and tradition, *Porno* – in its careful orchestration of voices and more or less politically correct themes, as well as its focal shift of protagonist from the politically aware but sceptical Mark Renton to the formerly Thatcherite, now New Labour Sick Boy – participates in the gentrification it claims to abhor. *Trainspotting*'s spectacular seediness becomes *Porno*'s not-so-seedy spectacle, with the £16,000 fetishised at the end of Danny Boyle's film version (1996) transformed into a mere MacGuffin device that keeps *Porno* moving inevitably towards America instead of Amsterdam. Finally, the regress from *Trainspotting*'s liberating transgressiveness to *Porno*'s formulaic prurience parallels Welsh's own development from the author who claimed he would write only as long as he had something to say to the more 'dignified' and 'disciplined' Welsh who now claims to be addicted to writing, and to live to write (Mulholland 1995; O'Hagan 2005). *Porno* thus underscores the dilemma facing the post-devolution Scottish novel, situated at a crossroads where lingering parochialism, the global marketplace, the freedom 'to be literature first and foremost', and the rewards that come from being culturally specific and relevant intersect.

In an especially harsh review of *Porno*, Tom Lappin contends that 'Welsh has written some terrible works in the last seven years or so, all marred by the sense that he was pursuing the commercial idea of what he should be about, forgetting the initial bleak wit and humanity that underscored *Trainspotting*' (Lappin 2002). Although he is wrong in claiming that the work from *Marabou Stork Nightmares* to *Filth* (1998) is marred by Welsh's pursuit of 'the commercial idea of what he should be about', Lappin is right about *Porno*. Despite its provocative title, its garish hot-pink cover flaunting the close-up of an inflatable sex doll, and its several behind-the-scenes looks at the making of a porn movie, *Porno* is a novel very much in the *Glue* (2001) rather than *Trainspotting* mould. Accordingly, even as it brings back *Trainspotting*'s cast of characters nine years later in real as well as fictional time, *Porno* does more to refute than prove that Welsh is still the 'petulant brat' he was before *Glue* (Linklater 2001). Even the publicity surrounding *Porno*'s release plays off Welsh's former bad-boy image in such a staged way that it does more to date Welsh than bring him up to date: we are presented with an image of the shaven-headed author posing in a suit and glaring mock-menacingly at the camera against the now clichéd and, indeed, chic backdrop of a disused flat in a shabby housing scheme.

Lappin is also right to describe *Porno* punningly as a 'flaccid read'. Indeed, *Porno* is as flaccid as *Trainspotting* is relentlessly 'in-your-face'. The relative absence of dialect, the painful effort to write well (which only makes the language seem more stilted and contrived), the equally painful effort to call upon the characters to explain themselves, as well as the recycling of material from *Trainspotting* and other works make *Porno* seem a pale and diminished imitation of what once was original and arresting about Welsh's work. In contrast to the occasional impassioned outburst in *Trainspotting*, *Porno* is larded with sermonising. Not only is the sermonising unconvincing; the sermons recur in Welsh's interviews in virtually the same language, forming a *mise en abyme* of *ex cathedra* pronouncements: DIY porn becomes the occasion, or excuse, for soap-box pronouncements on pornography and its alleged cultural meanings. Only at first glance are Welsh's statements on his motivation for writing *Porno* reminiscent of his famous explanation for writing *Trainspotting*. Returning to Edinburgh in the late 1980s, Welsh says he was angered by what he saw: former friends either addicted to heroin, HIV-positive, dying of AIDS or already dead. Nine years on, Welsh is reported to refer to his latest novel as 'driven by a horror at what he felt was a public willingness to tolerate pornography'. Accordingly, the novel should be seen as 'a work that is against pornography and the "over-sexualisation" of society' (Christian 2002). One would like to believe that in sounding grandiosely moralistic, monologic and disingenuous Welsh was merely having a gullible interviewer on, just as one would like to believe that the bad writing in *Porno* was deliberate, a parody of porn that extends to the more numerous non-pornographic sections of the novel. Both, however, appear to be wishful thinking.

Pornography is a meta-genre that is absurdly taxonomic, excessively rule-bound in terms of its narrative grammar and obsessively concerned with its relationship to the mainstream culture it slyly parodies and slavishly emulates. In *Porno* Welsh deals quite well with pornography's limited repertoire of sexual positions, camera angles, shots and scenes, as well as its overall derivativeness. 'Seven Rides for Seven Brothers', the film under production by Welsh's characters, obviously plays off Stanley Donen's beloved film musical *Seven Brides for Seven Brothers* (1954); it also has a Scottish connection in Franco Giraldi's little-known spaghetti western *Sette Pistole per i MacGregor* (1964). Unfortunately, *Porno* is itself excessively rule-bound; its narrative structure translates the freewheeling uncertainty of *Trainspotting* into an anal-retentive doling out of five carefully delineated narrative voices (three in standard English, two in dialect). In 'The Pornographic Imagination' Susan Sontag contends that pornography – 'this spectacularly cramped form of the human imagination' – offers 'access to some truth' in so far as the pornographer transgresses, going where others do not (Sontag 1969: 35–73). If the virtue, as it were, of pornography does indeed lie in its transgressiveness – the very quality that made *Trainspotting* so powerful and influential in terms of its style, subject matter, language and structure as well as its economic, cultural and political consequences – then a key weakness of *Porno* is that, despite its mock-shock cover and titillating title, it is not transgressive enough, or at all. After all, by 2002, porn was everywhere. As Frank Rich points out in his newspaper article 'Naked Capitalists' (Rich 2001), and as Jake and Dinos Chapman's sculptures of Turner Prize fame or Catherine Millet's best-selling memoir *The Secret Life of Catherine M* (2002) demonstrate in their own 'high-culture' ways, pornography had – by the time *Porno* appeared – gone mainstream. *Porno* is what, according to Rich, the whole sex industry is: no longer an affront to the nation's values but a ringing endorsement of the values of our consumer society in an age of global capitalism, with pornography already chic and with food-, alt- and punk-porn all growing trends.

In its way, *Porno* represents the culmination of a process which began, as Frances Ferguson explains in *Pornography, the Theory* (2004), with the nearly simultaneous rise of modern democracies, the modern novel, the idea of culture, pornography and capitalism. Although she does not mention *Porno*, Ferguson does discuss another doubly voyeuristic novel in which the culmination of this process is played out according to the logic of late capitalism. This is Bret Easton Ellis's *American Psycho* (1991), whose treatment of sex (including Sontag's 'pornographic imagination') 'in a world that is commodified and objectified' (Ferguson 2004: 7) helps make it what *Porno* is not: disturbingly transgressive. A decade after *American Psycho* and two years after Mary Harron's film adaptation of Ellis's novel, *Porno* seems by comparison not merely *passé* but complicit with the phenomenon it claims to critique.

Welsh does deal extensively with the commodification of sex, both in terms of the production and distribution of 'Seven Rides' and in terms of the larger sex industry in

Edinburgh, which is researched by Dianne for her master's thesis, and which employs Nikki giving 'inexpert handjobs' at the seedy, but exotic-sounding 'Miss Argentina Latin Sauna and Massage Parlour' to support her habit, which is higher education, not heroin. As Nikki points out, 'if you really want to see how capitalism operates, never mind Adam Smith's pin factory, this [the sauna] is the place to study' (Welsh 2002: 88). *Porno* is also quite blunt in its assault on consumer capitalism and its negative effects on Scotland in general and Leith in particular. As a result, it invites being read as continuing the 'resistance to the cultural values of Thatcherism' which began with *Trainspotting*, described by Cairns Craig as 'a satire on the free-market values of the Thatcher era . . . and fundamental to the change that brought devolution' (Craig 2004b: 17–18). Quite rightly, too, Willy Maley objects to 'critics who see Welsh's writing as a product of late capitalism, a symptom of capitalist decay, or just another commodity in a postmodern culture that shelves resistance [as they] fail to take seriously his revolution in language and his sense of outrage at injustice' (Maley 2000: 195). However, the bases on which Maley rests his defence of Welsh's resistance to consumer culture – that is, his alleged revolution in language and outrage at injustice – create a problem in appraising a novel whose language is flaccid and whose outrage seems more knee-jerk than heartfelt.

Critics who too readily take Welsh at his word tend to underestimate *Porno*'s shortcomings and, as a result, misrepresent its significance. Such critiques include Emily Bearn's happy acceptance of Welsh's adamant denial that the writing and publishing of *Porno* might have been 'a commercial decision' (Bearn 2003), Peter Childs's reading of the novel as resisting commodification, 'homogenizing consumerism' and middle-class values (Childs 2004: 250–4), and Aaron Kelly's recent contention that in writing *Porno* Welsh resisted the temptation of commercial exploitation in favour of aesthetic integrity (Kelly 2005a: 200–19). Just as Welsh acknowledges that it is extremely difficult 'to genuinely transgress' in a culture of commodification, as illustrated by the fate of *Trainspotting*, he also acknowledges, a little guiltily perhaps, that in such an environment 'anything that becomes valuable becomes absorbed into the market immediately' (Gallivan 2002), and not only 'anything', but also anyone. In this context Welsh's remarks to Steve Redhead prove especially interesting, not simply for what Welsh says, but for the way in which he segues from discussing pornography to talking about becoming, as a celebrity author, the object of media attention (Redhead 2000: 147). As Ferguson maintains, pornography is really about social relations and conditions rather than about its ostensible object of representation. Consequently, we must examine *Porno* less in terms of its apparent frontal assault on consumer culture than in terms of the variation it constitutes on the familiar Scottish theme of the fearful and the fearless in relation to both the novel's depiction of Leith and the roles played by Sick Boy and Renton.

There is little doubt, either in the novel or in his remarks about it, that Welsh strongly objects to the gentrification of Leith, its 'embourgeoisement' (Welsh 2002: 261). More specifically, Welsh objects to Leith's makeover in the image of global corporate capitalism, that is, for the benefit of people for whom *Trainspotting* was never intended and to the detriment of Leith's actual, largely disadvantaged and overlooked population. As Kevin Williamson notes, 'there is a desperate sense of Old Leith's Last Stand about *Porno*' (Williamson 2002b), and John King agrees, although he sees the situation as somewhat more complicated. According to King, 'Begbie, Juice Terry, Spud and now Curtis all stay true to their core values, refusing to sell their souls, unlike Sick Boy and Renton, who though decent at heart, have embraced the capitalist con', adding that 'the old folks looming in the background are a reminder of what lies ahead if they fail: a local rather than a global world' (King 2002). While idealising and romanticising Old Leith by his use of 'core values', King's remark underscores the novel's ambivalence regarding Leith as both the site of resistance to corporate values and the reminder of a failure implicitly more personal than political. What Sick Boy says of his friends in *Trainspotting*, namely that they spell 'limited' (Welsh 1993: 30), *Porno* at times says of Leith. Against his elegy to Leith 'having the life squeezed out of it by corporate interests' (Williamson 2002b), Welsh offers ample evidence of Leithers succumbing to their own fecklessness: for example, Spud's and Begbie's different but parallel downward trajectories and – briefly, if perhaps more disturbingly – Seeker counting out his life not in coffee spoons but in used condoms, each the sign and story of a brief sexual conquest.

It is easy to understand Welsh's dilemma. Had he not written *Trainspotting* and stayed in Leith, Welsh might very well have been counting condoms or making DIY porn instead of writing *Porno*. But, not quite unlike Sick Boy (briefly) and Curtis of 'Seven Rides' fame, *Trainspotting*'s success transformed Welsh into a media star measuring himself in book sales and newspaper-column inches. Asked whether there are 'things that you miss from the earlier days before you were famous', Welsh replied 'freedom', and this sense of loss is compounded by a growing inhibition – the need 'to behave with a bit more dignity' – coupled with a corresponding sense of guilt and shame (Redhead 2000: 146–7).

In the light of these remarks, the relationship between Sick Boy and Renton embodies a variation on the familiar theme of the Caledonian antisyzygy, taking on heightened dialectical significance as either character comes to represent an aspect of Welsh's personality in caricature. Although he remains essentially what he is in *Trainspotting*, namely one of Thatcher's scheming, scamming children, in *Porno* Sick Boy (now Simon) is depicted, and depicts himself, as a lad o' pairts. However, a far cry from the wide-eyed rural youth who, by virtue of his effort and native intelligence, symbolises Scottish egalitarian idealism, Simon is the modern, urban, underclass variant on this well-worn type. He is the lad o' pairts as Nietzsche might have imagined him, boiling with resentment over his plight and determined to measure his success against his father's failure to go somewhere and be someone. Nursing a sense of personal grievance at once well founded and outsize, Simon sees himself as a working-class hero scheming not only for himself but for 'the righteous, intelligent clued-up section of the working classes', 'a socialist . . . just playing the politics of the business world' (Welsh 2002: 483, 442) and a class warrior gauging his success in terms of the values of the class he despises as much as those of the class into which he was born.

Porno's Mark Renton is less desperate than Simon, perhaps because, having already achieved a modest measure of success, he is propelled by the need to move on rather than up. Also, as in *Trainspotting*, he is far more critical of himself than of others:

> I think that [Alison] always saw through me, always felt that I was a hypocrite, a winner who played at being a loser. Aye, a bright, upwardly mobile cunt who would one day fuck off and leave a pile of shite behind him for everybody else to clean up. She perhaps grasped my nature before I worked it out for myself. (Welsh 2002: 382)

Whereas Simon is consumed by resentment and the need to make a name for himself, Mark is consumed by guilt and the need to make amends, and more concerned with repentance and redemption than with revenge.

Largely monetary, Mark's need to make amends is focused on the cash nexus, as it is at the end of Boyle's *Trainspotting*. While Simon scams and schemes, Renton 'reckons' (Welsh 2002: 140), totalling up the amount needed to bring about his redemption: £3,000 to Secks (refused) and £8,000 to Sharon, now (mis)identified as his sister-in-law (accepted). With regard to Spud – compensated at the end of Boyle's film, but not in Welsh's novel – Mark now thinks of him as a lost cause, not so much the earlier no-hoper as someone beyond hope and help. And as far as Begbie is concerned, Mark can only avoid but never make amends to him, since Begbie practises his own interpretation of Old Testament justice, which means that only a pound of Mark's battered flesh will satisfy his need for retribution. Finally, Mark pays Dianne back with love, not money, although in the novel's final moments he uses the £60,000 he scammed off Simon to finance his escape to America in the company of Dianne and Nikki. Although the three elliptical dots that conclude the novel's 'surprise' ending might in theory enable *Porno*, the sequel, to beget *Trainspotting*, the series, Williamson is probably right to point out that *Porno* reads 'as if it is the final destination on the track' and may very well be 'the last novel . . . set among [Welsh's] ain folk' (Williamson 2002b).

Welsh's 'ain folk' are becoming increasingly marginalised in the New Leith of booming post-devolution Edinburgh. *Trainspotting*'s HIV capital of Europe has become UNESCO's World City of Literature, flush with new wealth (declared, in 2005, Britain's second most prosperous city) and boasting a new logo (three wavy lines) and slogan (devised in London). Faintly reminiscent of the 'Glasgow's Miles Better' campaign of the early 1990s, the 'Inspiring Capital' project evokes Edinburgh's rich literary past, which now includes Welsh, while at the same time punningly underscoring the crucial connection between culture and capital: Edinburgh uses cultural tourism to attract investment in the city. Famously, in 1993 Catherine Lockerbie, the *Scotsman*'s literary editor, hailed Welsh as 'a young writer of wild talent' whose appearance at that year's Edinburgh Book Festival 'should be of intense interest, and just what the Book Festival should be doing, providing a platform for the cutting edge amid the comfort of the established' (Lockerbie 1993). By the time he launched *Porno* almost ten years later, not only had Welsh become one of 'the established', the Book Festival itself had become too much of a marketing tool for big-name authors to leave any significant room for 'the cutting-edge and up-and-comers' (Crumey 2005). Of course Welsh, who ridiculed the Edinburgh Festival in *Trainspotting*, is hardly to blame for what it, let alone Edinburgh and Leith, have become. His protests against the sell-out of Leith to corporate interests as well as his work on behalf of OneCity Trust, which promotes cultural inclusion in Edinburgh, document his good intentions and well-meaning engagement. However, it is also clear that just as writers, after bolstering Scottish national identity during the period between the referenda, ought to be given some credit for facilitating devolution, they – and particularly the most prominent among them, such as Welsh – might also be accused of helping create a new Frankenstein's monster: the marketing idea of the Inspiring Capital threatening 'real' Leith's continued existence.

Can Welsh and the second Scottish renaissance survive their own success, or can they exist only in dialectical opposition, outside of the once English, now global mainstream? In the mid-1990s Richard Todd saw that 'the dilemma facing Scottish writers' centred on the ethically charged question of whether they ought 'to support local small presses or surrender to the London publishers' marketing muscle in order to reach a potentially global audience' (Todd 1996: 132). Notably, *Trainspotting* was published in London by the established Secker & Warburg publishing house, and Edinburgh's own Canongate only became internationally known with the publication of Canadian Yann Martel's Booker-Prize-winning *The Life of Pi* (2002). Rebel Inc founder Kevin Williamson's recent departure from Canongate also suggests how inimical to local needs an author's global interests can be. However, the publishing dilemma of Scottish authors appears to have gone largely unremarked, whereas a great deal of attention has been paid to the dilemma facing Scottish film-makers, partly in response to the phenomenal success of Boyle's *Trainspotting*. Although it was initially credited with revitalising the British and especially Scottish film industries, *Trainspotting* was soon seen as having taken both down the wrong road, away from a culturally and industrially devolved British cinema in general and 'the cultural necessity [and economic viability] of a poor Celtic cinema' in particular (McArthur 1994: 112). By contrast, the commitment and critical success of films such as Peter Mullan's *Orphans* (1998), Lynne Ramsay's *Ratcatcher* (1999) and May Miles Thomas's *One Life Stand* (1999), as well as David Mackenzie's *Young Adam* (2003), suggest how a devolved Scottish cinema might be able to address local materials on its own terms and revisit the issue of Scottish identity from a decidedly contemporary angle without relinquishing the opportunity to reach an international audience. These films also offer proof of Nick Roddick's statement that 'every memorable achievement to have come out of UK cinema since the war has come out of someone's desire to say something, not sell it' (Roddick 1998: 26).

Resistance, any more than acquiescence, to Hollywood in Britain and elsewhere is not new, but it is arguably a far more urgent matter in the age of global capitalism. This is especially true for Scotland during the crucial transitional period in its political, social, economic and cultural history when the globalisation message is as peremptory as Sick Boy's 'everybody else, everything else, will just have to fit in with *my* fucking plans' (Welsh 2002: 450). In her story 'Warming My Hands and Telling Lies', A. L. Kennedy captures perfectly a Scottish writer's ambivalent feelings about globalisation: 'The better Scottish writing gets, the less it will matter. The work will improve itself, it won't be competing against anything other than the best it can produce. It will be international' (Kennedy 1995b: 165). Kennedy's speaker is a Scottish writer who has given up writing, lives alone, self-exiled in Dublin, forgotten by all except an admiring but opportunistic fellow Scot, who has come from Glasgow to interview her. In this very Scottish retelling of Henry James's novella *The Aspern Papers* (1888), the writer's comment, like her situation, is not as straightforward as it may initially seem; it is preceded and complicated by her assertion that she could not possibly 'live' in Scotland, that is, she could not 'make a living' in Scotland as a writer:

> And I couldn't move because I'm a Scottish writer. I don't mean that it's a betrayal to write elsewhere. I think it might have been in my case, but that's not what I'm saying. The fact is that, disconnected from Scotland, I find that I don't have much to write about. Scotland was my way in. (Kennedy 1995b: 163–4)

The cost of disconnecting oneself and going 'international', already considerable in the early 1990s, is higher still in the global economy of a decade later. In his fiction Welsh has repeatedly returned to the local, especially Edinburgh and Leith, but perhaps, like Kennedy's writer, although under very different circumstances, he will eventually leave it for good; his latest novel, *The Bedroom Secrets of the Master Chefs* (2006), is set largely in California. Spud's roll call of doomed locals aside (Welsh 2002: 351), the Leith portrayed in *Porno* is very different and much less specific than the Leith of *Trainspotting*. 'Welcome tae Leith. Welcome home, right enough,' Mark says following an assault by one of Begbie's friends. 'But where is that now? Leith . . . naw. Amsterdam . . . naw. If home is where the heart is, right now Dianne's my home. I've got tae get tae the airport' (Welsh 2002: 471). *Porno*'s epigraph – 'Without cruelty, there is no festival' – taken from Nietzsche's *Genealogy of Morals* (1887), points to the place where Simon's imperative and Renton's bromide intersect. Even as it attests Welsh's embrace of the trappings of high culture he had earlier rejected, the epigraph also anticipates the novel's ending, in which Simon is exposed as the butt of both Mark's and Welsh's well-devised joke, quite different from the impromptu theft at the end of *Trainspotting*. The epigraph also reminds us that, according to Nietzsche, the pleasure derived from cruelty is rooted in the desire for power and originates in economics, that is, the relationship between debtor and creditor. Most importantly, if perhaps more circuitously, the epigraph also recalls Bakhtin's point about the fate of carnival and the carnivalesque once they have been cut off from their roots in authentic folk culture or, in Welsh's case, the authentic subculture of *Trainspotting*: a hardening into the merely literary and the purely personal of bourgeois capitalist culture, along with the loss of the power to subvert and renew (Bakhtin 1984a: 36–7, 1984b: 130–2).

The sense of loss – of having 'lost everything' and 'giving it all away' (Welsh 2002: 377, 435) – that pervades *Porno* derives as much from Welsh's own dilemma as an international Scottish author as it does from Leith's sale to corporate interests. Welsh's attachment to and dependency on Leith, Edinburgh and Scotland, which somewhat paradoxically enabled his earlier work to travel so well outside Scotland, are evident by virtue of their absence from the parts of *Glue* set in Germany and Australia, as well as the novellas 'Contamination' (2001) and 'Reality Principle' (2004), set in Africa and in Calcutta, that he contributed to the two *Weekenders* charity collections. Welsh's disconnection is especially evident in a recent article in the *Guardian* in which 'leading Scottish novelist Irvine Welsh writes on the dark heart of his beloved homeland' (Welsh 2005). Here, Welsh, speaking from on high and as though from afar, sounds like one of his own critics and not at all like the author who twice sent Mark Renton packing and who since 1995 has lived mostly in Amsterdam, London, Chicago and Dublin. 'The fact is', Welsh writes, 'that in a UK context, Scotland, particularly the populous part of it, is too often seen as a rundown place. The people who leave are viewed as go-getters; descendants of the entrepreneurial sons and daughters of the empire. Those remaining are frequently cast as the low-life rump.' Even more illuminating than these bons mots for *bien-pensant* readers is a paragraph tucked away in one of the weekly columns Welsh wrote under the heading 'From America' as part of the *Daily Telegraph*'s effort to increase its already large market share by appealing to ageing Trainspotters (Welsh 2003). It is hard not to hear in Welsh's admiration for Indian novelist and activist Arundhati Roy, whom Welsh met at the Prague Writers Festival, both a further incentive to lend his name to charitable causes and Renton-like misgivings about his own recent work. Roy, after all, is a writer who, like Welsh, felt compelled to set her debut novel (the Booker-Prize-winning *The God of Small Things* [1996]), in her hometown, in her case in Kerala, but who, after the novel's successful publication, did not feel compelled either to continue writing fiction when she had nothing further to say, or to define herself as a writer. Instead, Roy has used her fame to effect political and economic change at the local level, in India, and to make the local a form of resistance to globalisation.

My point is not that Welsh should turn from fiction writing to political activism; after all, Welsh's early fiction is far more politically engaged, and engaging, than any of his later *ex cathedra* political pronouncements, however well intentioned those pronouncements or his work on behalf of the Be Foundation, One City and other causes and organisations may be. Nor is it my point that Welsh has lost his soul, or betrayed aspects of the Scottish renaissance of the 1990s that he has come to represent. Rather, my point is that Welsh has lost his distinctive voice and, with it, the 'bunch of voices shouting to be heard' that made his early fiction so urgent, unpretentious and compellingly local. Welsh's best hope of once again expressing something that absolutely needs to be said, and heard, lies not with fictions such as *Porno*, which represents the narrative equivalent of both madeover Leith and what Tom Nairn calls 'the demographic outflow' (Nairn 2004b); rather, it may lie with 'the poor Celtic cinema' and the various film productions – *The Meat Trade*, *Soul Crew* and *The Man Who Walks* – he is said to be working on for Mark Cousins's Edinburgh-based 4-Way Productions. The cultivation of 'lingering parochialism' is never without its risks but, as Suhayl's Saadi's debut novel *Psychoraag* (2004) proves, it need not be regressive and xenophobic. Lingering parochialism may not be the perfect substitute for authentic folk culture or subculture, but it may well be the best alternative available in our era of corporate interests and 'inspiring capital'.

Chapter 27

Clearing Space:
Kathleen Jamie and Ecology

Louisa Gairn

Kathleen Jamie once remarked that poetry has an important role to play as 'a line of defence . . . against the intrusions of globalisation, the mass market, the ecological threat' (Fraser 2001: 20). More recently, she has argued that 'what provokes poems, all poems, is the curious business of being in the world. We're conscious, intelligent and organic, so how are we to live?' (Jamie 2004b). From *The Way We Live* (1987), her first full-length poetry collection, to *The Tree House* (2004), her most recent volume, Jamie has been exploring different aspects of these questions. Contemplating the varying meanings of 'home', her poems explore ideas of nationhood and national culture, the experience of travel and exile, questions of familial and gender roles, and most recently, the poetics and philosophy of ecology.

As early as 1994, the year *The Queen of Sheba* was published and Jamie was brought to more widespread critical attention by the *Poetry Review*'s 'New Generation' promotion, she admitted to feeling 'irritated and . . . confined' by the twin labels of 'woman writer' and 'Scottish writer' (Jamie 1994a: 156). Following devolution and the birth of her two children, Jamie has been testing the limits of these labels, and has begun to leave them behind, 'deliberately and consciously wanting to change the direction of [her] work' (Fraser 2001: 17). As a result, Jamie notes, 'hills and birds seem to be entering the poems; my local landscape, the energy of the land. To my mind, these poems are more interesting than "political" or "gender" poems' (Brown and Paterson 2003: 125). Since devolution, critical perspectives on Jamie's work have slowly begun to take account of her increasing interest in ecology and the natural world. For example, Robert Crawford notes that much of Jamie's poetry is rooted in rural Scotland, and that 'she is very alert to the politics and spirituality of the natural environment' (Crawford 2000: 336). It has also been suggested that Jamie could be viewed as 'a nature poet who has been sidetracked by "issues"' (Smith 2005).

However, there is a problem with being labelled a 'nature poet', which is to do with what John Burnside calls the 'common misapprehension that a poet who makes such a choice . . . has no political or social interests or usefulness' (Burnside 2000: 259). As Burnside and Maurice Riordan argue in *Wild Reckoning* (2004), the constricting label of 'nature poetry' needs to be reconsidered, and in order to understand poets who choose to write about the natural world we need 'to return to the original meaning of the word ecology . . . its delineation of a *Logos* of dwelling' (Burnside and Riordan 2004: 21). Viewed from this perspective, Jamie and other supposed 'nature poets' are not trying to escape from social and political responsibilities, but are asking crucial questions about 'being in the world'. Jamie's current view parallels that of Burnside, Jonathan Bate and others in contending that 'what's most in need of re-negotiation and repair . . . is our relationship with the natural world' (Jamie 2004b). However, before she was able to engage fully with these concerns, Jamie admits she found it necessary to confront other questions about gender and national identity in her poetry. 'As women we still find ourselves in a tangle of briars', she explains. 'We are told what to write, and then told that real art can't be made from those experiences anyway. We have to spend energy clearing space' (Brown and Paterson 2003: 128).

Jamie began her poetic career at the age of nineteen, winning an Eric Gregory Award, which started her off on travels to the Himalayas. Her love of travel later led her to China, Tibet and Northern Pakistan, experiences which formed the inspiration for much of her writing in the 1980s and 1990s. The poetry pamphlet *Black Spiders* appeared in 1982, followed by *The Way We Live* in 1987. Her first major prose work, *The Golden Peak: Travels in Northern Pakistan*, appeared in 1992 (reissued in 2002 with additional chapters as *Among Muslims*) and was soon followed by *The Autonomous Region: Poems and Photographs from Tibet* (1993), a collaborative project with the photographer Sean Mayne Smith. *The Queen of Sheba* was published in 1994, and its title poem sets the tone for the collection, with its personification of exotic, subversive womanhood come to seek revenge upon small-minded Scotland, liberating Scottish girls to explore their potential and declare their own independence.

Jamie has called *The Queen of Sheba* 'My Scottish Book', and as suggested by its dedication to 'the folks at home', the collection pivots on the idea of 'home' as a political, cultural and gendered entity. Drawing extensively on Jamie's experience of travel, *The Queen of Sheba* is full of leavings and homecomings, and all 'the implications of the gravitational pull in a woman's life' (Friel 1994: 31). Such considerations are widened to explore Scotland's often difficult relationship with its own history and identity as a 'homeland'. Uncovering a potent symbolism in the domestic task of clearing things away in 'Mr and Mrs Scotland Are Dead', Jamie contemplates the contents of a household discarded on the council rubbish-heap. She treats the objects reverentially, reading the postcards 'spew[ed]' from the dead woman's 'stiff / old ladies' bags', and inferring from the discovery of a puncture repair kit a rich history of rambles in the Scottish countryside, reminiscent of 'those days when he knew intimately / the thin roads of his country, hedgerows / hanged with small black brambles' hearts' (Jamie 2002c: 134). This is, however, an elegy for a Scotland dead and gone, and already being erased from memory. 'Do we take them?' she asks, recognising the inevitable scrap-heap end for these objects, which function as symbols of Scotland's past and the limitations which might result from holding on to that past. Ultimately, for both poet and nation, the 'perfunctory rite' of 'sweeping up' and 'turning out' is a necessary one. Also turning away from Scotland's past, 'The Republic of Fife' invokes the potential for Scotland's people to see themselves as 'waving citizens', comfortable with their local identities but also very much at home on the international scene – a stance which Crawford sees as a defining feature of Jamie's poetry (Crawford 2000: 336). Jamie also draws strength from the 'energising . . . polyphony' of Scottish languages and dialects, saying she 'like[s] being one of the diverse, one of the plural, one of the citizens' (Jamie 1997: 36).

Despite such flickerings of optimism, there remains the distinct feeling that these pre-devolution poems are representative of a 'dream state', as Donny O'Rourke puts it, and that the hoped-for new Scotland has not yet arrived. Edwin Morgan sensed this aspect of *The Queen of Sheba*, noting an undercurrent of 'restlessness and unease [which] seems to relate to the paradox we are so familiar with in 1990s Scotland – emphatic cultural presence coupled with total political impotence' (Morgan 1994: 17). However, if Jamie's restlessness was in part due to frustration at the lack of a clearly defined political identity for Scotland, it was also associated with other, more personal and ambiguous questions about belonging. In *Identifying Poets* Robert Crawford argues that 'home' is a central concept for modern poetry, and that focusing on the figure of the 'identifying poet' – that is, a poet who explicitly identifies himself or herself with a particular landscape or territory – is a valid, illuminating way of interpreting poetic work. Home, he writes, is 'one of the most important questions in contemporary poetry', vitally important in the work of Scottish writers including Jamie, who can draw upon Scotland's diverse linguistic heritage as a source of strength. However, Crawford acknowledges that while home can be empowering for poetic identity and development, for some writers it can also be experienced as 'constricting', and that 'the poetic celebrants of home at the moment tend not to be women' (Crawford 1993a: 144).

Jamie admits that *The Queen of Sheba* was part of a personal process of 'examining and throwing off (laughing off) the constraints imposed on me by being a Scottish girl . . . giving myself permission to go a wee bit farther' (Brown and Paterson 2003: 126). Energised by her experiences in Pakistan, Jamie's poetry and travel writings of this period speak of the tension between the desire to be on the road and certain deeply entrenched societal expectations, such as home, family and a settled life:

> I could have children, and maybe no worries. But I was a person walking down a track in Baltistan all alone on a Wednesday morning. I was capable; and sometimes, a glimpse of what we could be opens in our minds like the fearsome blue crevasses I'd seen on glaciers. I could be a person who lives here . . . a wandering monkish figure gone native. (Jamie 2002a: 210)

In both *The Golden Peak* and *The Queen of Sheba*, Jamie negotiates a new sense of what 'home' might mean, both for herself and for her country. Turning into the mother of 'Wee Baby' or the domestic persona of 'Wee Wifey' – two poems which feature a distinctively strong Scottish accent – seems incongruous with the mirage of Jamie as a 'monkish figure' wandering the Himalayas. To be a permanent wanderer would mean 'forgoing the children, and the shadowy figure that filled the vacuum when they asked, "Where is your husband?"' (Jamie 2002a: 211). 'Wee Baby' speaks of this dilemma, a glimpse of yet another possibility, a choice about pregnancy and family which is yet to be made. Similarly, domesticity becomes internalised and personified by 'Wee Wifey', who exists 'in the household of my skull', constricting and infuriating sometimes, yet Jamie must ruefully acknowledge 'that without / WEE WIFEY / I shall live long and lonely as a tossing cork' (Jamie 1994b: 29–30).

In a number of ways, addressing questions of history and national identity in terms of women's experience, *Jizzen* (1999) expands on such themes. In 'The Graduates' Jamie parallels the history of Scottish emigrants – those who left the 'old country' by the boatload in the nineteenth century – with the modern condition of Scottish cultural exile. Seeing herself as belonging to a new generation of 'emigrants of no farewell' – that is, university-educated Scots who have lost touch with their Scottish heritage and language, and use Scots only 'in jokes and quotes' – Jamie shows us the proof, 'rolled in a red tube: / my degrees, a furled sail, my visa' (Jamie 1999: 3–4). At the same time, the celebratory, hopeful stance of 'The Republic of Fife' is continued in *Jizzen* with 'Lucky Bag', which – perhaps as antidote to the lost cultural heritage referred to in 'The Graduates' – gleefully lists the contents of 'yer Scottish lucky-bag, one for each wean', proliferating a new concept of a multifaceted Scottish identity, crowded with 'a field of whaups', 'a shalwar-kameez', 'a Free State, a midden, / a chambered cairn' (Jamie 1999: 42). 'Jizzen' is the Scots word for 'childbed', and Jamie's experience of pregnancy and motherhood are the focus of the collection. Travels are coming to an end; on discovering she is pregnant, Jamie finds herself 'headed for home', as in 'Suitcases'. But the idea of 'home' in *Jizzen* has also undergone a decisive change. Following the 'Yes Yes' vote in the referendum on Scottish devolution in 1997, Jamie says she 'woke up . . . and discovered that half my poems were obsolete', transformed into 'historical documents, which could be read differently after the night's events' (Jamie 1997: 35). Devolution was hailed as a cultural and historical watershed by many Scottish writers and critics, but it also marked something of a personal watershed in Jamie's own career.

Considering the trajectory of devolution from the first referendum in 1979 to the re-establishment of the Scottish Parliament in 1999, Jamie states simply that 'the politics are indistinguishable from my life'. For Jamie, devolution underlined poetry's ability to engage with the political sphere, testifying to her belief that 'poetry had a part in bringing about the new Scotland', that it can sometimes unexpectedly 'cause change in the cultural landscape of a whole nation' (Jamie 1997: 35–6). However, devolution also gave Jamie permission to move on from the political preoccupations of *The Queen of Sheba* in order to tackle other questions. Thus, her sense of relief and hope following the referendum is neatly encapsulated in the two-line poem 'On the Design Chosen for the New Scottish Parliament Building by Architect Enric Miralles': 'An upturned boat / – a watershed' (Jamie 1999: 48), which is the penultimate poem in *Jizzen*. However, Jamie concludes the collection with 'Meadowsweet' and its potent symbolism of female creativity and regeneration. The poem invokes the *smeddum*, or tenacious spirit, of a Gaelic woman poet face down in a grave, and imagines her triumphant resurrection, as germinating wild-flower seeds – 'beginning their crawl / toward light' – will show her 'how to dig herself out – / to surface and greet them, / mouth young, and full again / of dirt, and spit, and poetry' (Jamie 1999: 49). Indeed, as Sarah Broom writes, in this triumphant concluding poem 'Jamie has taken the traditional trope of the woman as land and nation and reinvented it so that the rebirth is initiated by the woman herself . . . a speaking subject – a poet, no less' (Broom 2006: 135).

Jamie has stated that *Jizzen* is a book 'about coming to maturity, about birth and politics', and these poems do indeed speak of Jamie's increasing confidence as 'a mother, a graduate and what they call an "established poet"' (Brown and Paterson 2003: 128; Jamie 1997: 36). However, in their contemplation of 'women's work', particularly pregnancy and motherhood, the poems in *Jizzen* do not only celebrate cultural and political change, but seek to bind together women's experience, creativity and the natural world. Thus, in 'Ultrasound' Jamie reveals that on coming home from the hospital with her newborn son, she felt the need to make a gesture of connection with nature:

> I had to walk to the top of the garden,
> to touch, in a complicit
> homage of equals, the spiral
> trunks of our plum trees, the moss,
> the robin's roost in the holly.

> (Jamie 1999: 13)

Such gestures are enacted throughout *Jizzen*. It is true that many poems in *The Queen of Sheba* demonstrate Jamie's fascination with the natural world, particularly birds, as her personae look up from the city streets to catch a glimpse of wild geese ('Flashing Green

Man') or contemplate the division between the human world of language and the natural world in 'Skeins o Geese': 'Whit dae birds write on the dusk? / A word niver spoken or read' (Jamie 2002c: 136, 159). However, *Jizzen* reveals a new confidence and a more intimate relationship with nature. In 'St Bride's', written on the birth of her daughter, Jamie reflects on 'women's work: folding / and unfolding, be it linen or a selkie- / skin tucked behind a rock' (Jamie 1999: 45). The imagery, drawn from Scottish folk traditions and playing on associations of nature with female experience, goes through a series of metamorphoses; it identifies with 'the hare in jizzen', then 'adders uncoil into spring' and, finally, her daughter is born, followed by the placenta 'like a fist of purple kelp' (Jamie 1999: 45). 'The Bogie Wife' and 'The Green Woman' similarly toy with gender/nature constructions. The monstrous 'Bogie Wife', whose hands are 'stained brown as dung' and with 'arms, strong as plum-boughs / twisting into fruit', is a blurred category, a hybrid who is both monster and woman, a 'yeti', while in 'The Green Woman' Jamie explores what it is like to be a new mother. 'Until we're restored to ourselves / by weaning', the experience is 'suggestive of the lush / ditch' or 'an ordeal', testing out the strength of her female identity, like a witch 'tied to a ducking-stool' (Jamie 1999: 10, 46).

Jamie's experience of motherhood has provoked in her writing a heightened sense of the fragility and transience of the natural world, as well as a growing need to consider 'the curious business of being in the world'. In doing so, Jamie rejects traditional belief systems, searching instead for new ways of celebrating and understanding human existence:

> I don't believe in God. I believe in spiders, alveoli, starlings . . . I might suggest that prayer-in-the-world isn't supplication, but the quality of attention we can bring to a task, the intensity of listening, through the instruments we have designed for the purpose. It might be the outermost reaches of the Universe, the innermost changes at the bottom of a lung, the words on a page, or a smear of blood on a slide. I think it's about repairing and maintaining the web of our noticing, a way of being in the world. Or is that worship? (Jamie 2002b: 39)

This reverence for details is part of a developing poetic manifesto, a search for ways in which to express 'the true and the good and the sacred', concepts which, she is aware, are at risk of sounding a bit old-fashioned or trite (Herbert and Hollis 2000: 280). Jamie's attentiveness is firmly rooted in language and often most convincingly achieved by poems built around a particularly resonant word, often in Scots. 'Hackit', for example, contemplates the photograph of a Scottish woman pioneer in nineteenth-century Ontario, and imagines the woman raising a cairn to mark each acre of land cleared.

> She stares from a door,
> fingers splayed, face
>
> *hackit*
> under the lace mutch
> brought from her box.
>
>   (Jamie 1999: 33)

The word 'hackit' stands alone, italicised in the midst of the poem, and its demotic precision serves as a marker for the lives of women like the one in the photograph. The poem is a story of hard labour and survival, but its imagery connects with Jamie's own development as a poet, 'clearing space' in order to work on new terrain.

Jamie told Crawford that his study *Devolving English Literature* (1992) 'helped her to come to terms with the mixture of languages in her head' (Crawford 2000: 307). However, more recently this 'energising . . . polyphony' has become associated less with identity politics than with a renewed sense of how language can operate to sustain what Jamie calls 'the web of our noticing, a way of being in the world'. 'I used to think that language was what got in the way', Jamie explains, 'that it was a screen, a dark glass. That you could not get at the world because you were stuck with language, but now I think that's wrong. Now I think language is what connects us to the world' (Scott 2005). This new approach to the power of poetic language links up with Jonathan Bate's contention in *The Song of the Earth* (2000), which breaks with the postmodern view of 'language as a self-enclosed system' (Bate 2000: 248). Instead, Bate argues for the value of 'ecopoetics', writing which allows us 'to live . . . with thoughtfulness and atten-tiveness, an attunement to both words and the world, and so to acknowledge that, although we make sense of things by way of words, we do not live apart from the world' (Bate 2000: 23).

Jamie has acknowledged Bate as an influence during the writing of her latest collection, *The Tree House*, and it is likely that the phenomenological philosophy on which Bate's argument is based struck a chord with Jamie's own philosophical training. However, prepar-ing for both *The Tree House* and her recent prose work, *Findings* (2005), Jamie came across other writers whose work might be characterised as 'ecopoetic'. For example, the epigraph of *The Tree House* – 'But it is beautiful to unfold our souls and our short lives' – is a quota-tion from the German poet Friedrich Hölderlin (1770–1843), two of whose nature lyrics Jamie translates into soft, sibilant Scots. 'Hame' perhaps best represents Jamie's new way of considering home, which has been extricated from the constraints of nationalism, and is now figured as 'Yird', the earth itself:

> Wha's tae ken
> if whiles Ah dauner
> yur back-braes, O Yird
> and pu wild berries
> tae slocken ma luve fur ye

(Jamie 2004a: 28)

Jamie's use of Scots here is not a political gesture; rather, it demonstrates her confidence that poetry written in Scots can enact a form of ecopoetics by exploring our relationship with nature through a lyrical – and very precise – use of language. She finds a more recent, Scottish precedent for this 'ecopoetic' perspective in the work of George Mackay Brown (1921–96), whose writing she values because it 'enacts the ecology it describes . . . the soundscape of an interconnected, secure community' (Jamie 2005b).

Jamie's notion of 'ecological' writing is dependent on attentiveness, on paying heed, and while her powers of observation have been a striking feature throughout her literary career, in *Findings* she fine-tunes this ability, telling herself to 'learn again to look, to listen' and to 'hold [the experience] in your head, bring it home intact' (Jamie 2005a: 42). In a chapter which records her close observation of local birds, particularly the daily lives of a pair of peregrine falcons, Jamie discovers *The Peregrine* (1967), a book by J. A. Baker which, she says, is 'full, tremulous, overwrought, hungry. He writes like a falcon must see and so allows us to see, too' (Jamie 2005a: 43). Jamie ardently believes in language's capacity to bring us close to the natural world, but nevertheless acknowledges certain limitations, as in

'The Dipper', which considers how a water bird's 'supple, undammable song' cannot be put into words by the poet; the song simply 'isn't mine to give' (Jamie 2004a: 49).

Gaston Bachelard wrote about poetry's ability to reach across the old Cartesian division of mind and nature to 'restore us to this sense of ourselves as "creatures", as subjects beyond the conventional limits of subject and object', stressing the need for humans to engage in reverie through contemplation of spaces, objects and poems (McAllester Jones 1991: 157). Similarly, in *The Tree House*, Jamie recognises the need for reverie as a way of examining our relationship with nature, and while some poems can be read as reveries themselves, others comment on the difficulty of reconciling the demands of everyday life, our 'inter-human relationships', with 'our need for reverie' (Jamie 2004b). In 'The Buddleia', for instance, Jamie's attempts to connect with a sense of the 'divine' in her garden are frustrated by thoughts of 'my suddenly / elderly parents, their broken-down / Hoover; or my quarrelling kids' (Jamie 2004a: 27). As an antidote to this kind of distraction 'The Tree House' imagines a refuge where 'I lay to sleep, / beside me neither man / nor child, but a lichened branch / wound through the wooden chamber' (Jamie 2004a: 41). However, in spite of her everyday responsibilities Jamie finds time to pay attention to nature:

> Between the laundry and the fetching kids from school, that's how birds enter my life. I listen. During a lull in the traffic, oyster catchers. In the school playground, sparrows . . . The birds live at the edge of my life. That's okay. I like the sense that the margins of my life are semi-permeable. (Jamie 2005a: 39)

The poems in *The Tree House* speak of the need to find or construct spaces for reverie as a way of attending to and living with nature. However, for Jamie, these spaces are often 'nothing but an attitude of mind', as in 'The Bower', where she half-sees, half-imagines a 'forest dwelling', an 'anchorage / or musical box', high up in the woodland canopy (Jamie 2004a: 17). This idea again echoes the work of Bachelard, who suggests that spaces, even the physically uninhabitable spaces of a cupboard or a nest, can speak to us as symbols of the primordial dwelling place, containing 'the essence of the notion of home' (Bachelard 1994: 5). *The Tree House* is full of such conceptual dwelling places: a cave on the shoreline, a clearing between trees, a swallow's nest, even the reflective surface of a puddle:

> Flooded fields, all pulling
> the same lustrous trick,
> that flush in the world's light
> as though with sudden love –
> how should we live?
>
> (Jamie 2004a: 48)

In 'Pipistrelles', Jamie describes an encounter with a 'place hained by trees', a 'clear translucent vessel' of air and light, held 'tenderly' between a grove of Douglas firs, in which pipistrelle bats flock together, with an apparent intelligence of their own (Jamie 2004a: 30–1). 'Hained' is a Scots word, and Jamie takes advantage of its dual meaning, explained by the *Concise Scots Dictionary* as 'to enclose grassland or a wood' and 'to keep from harm, protect, spare' (Robinson 1999: 259). This need to protect from harm, to conserve rather than discard, is the defining motivation behind *The Tree House* and *Findings*, both of which evoke the fragility and also the strength and endurance of the natural world. 'The Wishing Tree', for example, gives voice to a tree studded with coins; human actions are slowly poisoning the bark, but still there is hope in nature's resilience: 'Look: I am still alive – in fact, in bud' (Jamie 2004a: 4). 'Flight of Birds' considers the decline of species as the result of human activity and insists on the human need to enact gestures of reconciliation with wild nature. Imagining a community 'gathered / empty-handed at the town's edge', and calling for each bird species by name, she asks, 'might we yet prevail / upon wren, water rail, tiny anointed gold crest / to remain within our sentience in this, / the only world?' (Jamie 2004a: 39).

As part of this vital reconciliation between culture and nature, Jamie writes about the equally important need for us to see our past in a different way, to understand how land-scapes are inscribed by history. Contemplating stereotypical attitudes to rural Scotland – often 'described as "natural" or "wild" – "wilderness", even' – she reflects that this 'seems an affront to those many generations who took their living on that land', leading her to ask 'what's natural?' (Jamie 2005a: 126). Indeed, concerns over ethics, authenticity, and the divisions or meeting points between culture and nature pervade a great deal of Jamie's post-devolution writings. 'Reliquary' in *The Tree House* expands on such themes, consid-ering the changing face of the Scottish landscape, and the values we inscribe upon it. Reading the land with an archaeologist's eye, Jamie notes it 'reveals / event before event . . . plague pits where we'd lay / our fibre-optic cables'. However, the landscape is more than just the sediment of human history; it is also characterised by the 'eternal now' of nature, which reveals itself 'moment / into moment' (Jamie 2004a: 37). Concurrent with human history, and also incorporating it, is natural history, the tiny 'caskets' of bluebell seeds sym-bolising the essence of change and rebirth which characterises the world of nature. 'Reliquary' is a keyword in the poem highlighting Jamie's belief in the importance of deter-mining the 'sacred', of what is worth preserving or remembering. Whereas such terminol-ogy might also suggest entombment or stasis, and the juxtaposition of history with modernity – of 'fibre-optic cables' and 'ancient settlements' – might appear to align Jamie with a conservationist agenda, the poem itself insists that a mingling of ancient and modern human artefacts is not only right and proper, but inevitable and necessary.

Thinking through such concerns in *Findings*, Jamie describes a visit to the Orkney neolithic site Maes Howe. Expecting to encounter a dark, 'wombish red' chamber in the tomb, Jamie is instead confronted with an interior 'bright as a Tube train', lit by surveyors' lamps which reveal 'every crack, every joint and fissure in the ancient stonework' (Jamie 2005a: 14). In fact, Jamie's encounter with the Historic Scotland surveyors and their tech-nical equipment in this ancient space reminds her of the original tomb-builders' craft, 'somewhere between technology and art', in which natural phenomena were manipulated in order to create an aesthetic, or dramatic, moment of symbolism. Maes Howe, she argues, is 'a place of artifice, of skill', more like a 'cranium' than a 'womb' and, as such, the pres-ence of the surveyors and their laser is entirely appropriate, a modern mirroring of the skilled workmen who built the tomb. Still, Jamie warns, the implications of all this modern technology are manifold and possibly disastrous:

> We are doing damage, and have a growing sense of responsibility. The surveyors poring over the tomb are working in an anxious age. We look about the world, by the light we have made, and realise it's all vulnerable, and all worth saving, and no one can do it but us. (Jamie 2005a: 24)

Thinking about questions of Scottish identity, Jamie wrote in 1997 that 'poetry can alter the inner landscape of the poet, and be a means of enabling her to reach into the muddy well of her cultural and personal inheritance and hold the findings to the light'

(Jamie 1997: 36). She has adapted this stance in recent years, and the 'findings' she has uncovered have more to do with questions of natural history and human ecology than with territorial allegiance or national identity. Home, for Jamie, as for other Scottish writers following devolution, has taken on new meanings, beyond questions of political or cultural nationalism. Significantly, according to Jamie, 'a tree house is a place where nature and culture meet, a sort of negotiated settlement, part reverie, part domestic, part wild' (Jamie 2004b). By this definition, a tree house might also stand for the space of a poem. Jamie has spoken of poetry as a potential 'line of defence', and her most recent work can be read as such, providing a space in which both reader and author can explore their relationship with the natural world. Jamie has turned to a more ecological concept of poetry, not only as a source of 'the true and the good and the sacred', but also as a way of 'being in the world', coming to terms with our dependence on the natural environment and renegotiating ways of belonging there. In an age of environmental crisis, which suffers from attendant postmodern anxieties about globalisation, corporatisaton and loss of cultural and natural heritage, Kathleen Jamie's 'line of defence' must be regarded as both timely and crucial.

Chapter 28

Don Paterson and Poetic Autonomy

Scott Hames

In *Identifying Poets* Robert Crawford speculates that 'the poet who constructs an identity which allows that poet to identify with a particular territory is the paradigmatic modern poet', adding that 'the position of poets in Scotland is typical of this situation' (Crawford 1993a: 142). One purpose of this chapter is to illustrate the limits of a Scottish literary criticism preoccupied by the search for 'poetic selves that may be identified with particular territories' (Crawford 1993a: 3). This approach is, at best, unaccommodating of the poetry of Don Paterson, which evinces no organic bond between voice and place, and tends not to repay critical interest in 'the articulation of cultural difference and the construction of territorial voices' (Crawford 1993a: 9). Though Paterson playfully engages with Scottish topoi and locales, and writes occasionally in Scots, he departs from Crawford's notion of the identifying poet as realising 'a voice which articulates the culture of the place which is [his] home' (Crawford 1993a: 2). In his introduction to *New British Poetry* Paterson asserts:

> It has long been my own contention that 'voice' – that absurd passport we are obliged to carry through the insecurity of the age – is an extraliterary issue. The word 'voice' might usefully denote that characteristic tone whose identification can aid the reader in keeping the poems of a single poet in dialogue with one another; but more often its use is purely political. Personally, I don't believe the difference in a poet's cultural or sociosexual experience is necessarily the most significant or interesting thing about them. (Paterson and Simic 2004: xxxvi)

An aphorism from Paterson's *Book of Shadows* carries this objection a step further. 'Only the insecure age valorizes the individual voice', Paterson writes, 'partly because it encourages the radical artist towards a speech far easier to identify and suppress' (Paterson 2004a: 32). Continuing to 'identify' Scottish writers ethnographically on the basis of their culturally distinctive voices, subjects and themes is effectively to suppress the aesthetic possibilities of their work. Another, equally pernicious effect of this critical habit is suggested by Paterson in 'The Dilemma of the Peot [*sic*]', where he explains that 'the development of the "individual voice" . . . in part depends upon the *repetition* of strategies' (Paterson 1996: 161). The critical game of recognising a poet's Scottishness entails a mode of reading highly attuned to continuities, reiterations and consistencies, whose assiduous reinforcement by the traditionalising critic serves ultimately to homogenise the ways in which Scottish poetry is read. Paterson's poetry seldom makes recourse to the categories this paradigm smiles upon – voice, place, identity – a fact which in itself seems to disqualify him from consideration as a Scottish poet, as though his work were insufficiently forthcoming about the cultural anxieties its author is assumed to harbour. This has resulted in a somewhat anomalous critical reception: Paterson is a highly acclaimed, recognisably Scottish poet, but is seldom regarded as a major 'Scottish poet'.

Paterson himself, it should be noted, seems relaxed about this apparent discrepancy. In email correspondence with the present author he has noted that 'there are really two countries for a Scottish writer: Scotland, and the Anglophone community. Their values are different, and so different things are valorised. Reputations aren't smoothly carried between the two at all, and only the latter is capable of anything resembling disinterested literary criticism based on, if ye like, denationalized criteria.' My aim here is not to uncover the hitherto neglected 'Scottishness' of Paterson's work, but to use the discrepancy in its reception to highlight the stifling implications of the critical practice of 'detecting' and affirming symptoms of a pre-digested Scottishness. It is not simply a question of 'denationalising' the poet's reception, as Paterson himself acknowledges: 'Inevitably, being Scottish – *well* Scottish, i.e. a Nationalist and someone who can relax into an accent strong enough to be incomprehensible to anyone outside St. Mary's, Dundee – infects my writing, though not, I hope, to a self-conscious degree. It's this self-consciousness I object to' (Friel 1995: 192). For the first part of this chapter, Paterson's poetry will figure as a foil to this self-consciously nationalising way of thinking and reading. In the second part, the self-sufficient qualities of his work will come into focus and present a very different approach to imagining selfhood and territory, one far less dependent on the recognition of already familiar accents. In my view, Paterson's work insists on the transformative power of the imagination precisely where the literal, empirical, dot-joining mind encounters the limits of perception.

'One can hope', wrote Christopher Whyte in 1998, 'that the setting up of a Scottish parliament will at last allow Scottish literature to be literature first and foremost, rather than the expression of a nationalist movement' (Whyte 1998a: 284). To revisit Whyte's sunny conjecture almost a decade later prompts some justified exasperation; it will be enough to catalogue a few prominent rehearsals of Whyte's frustration at the 'tendency to read modern fictions of urban Scotland in representative, rather than strictly literary, terms' (Whyte 1998a: 285n). Thus, in an article lamenting the narrowness of James Kelman's critical reception, Laurence Nicoll castigates a persistent 'cultural nationalist paradigm' characterised by the 'inability to think outwith a critical taxonomy the parameters of which are set by concepts of "nation" and "nationalism"' (Nicoll 2000: 79). Janice Galloway, too, has recently scorned those 'who think Scotland, if it has permission to think at all, may only think about itself' (Kernan 2003), and in their introduction to *Scotland in Theory* Eleanor Bell and Gavin Miller document a 'lingering parochialism' in Scottish criticism, epitomised by the critical reflex of 'explaining' a novel or poem 'firstly . . . in terms of its Scottishness, rather than in terms of its literary or aesthetic qualities' (Bell and Miller 2004: 11). Finally, Whyte's own *Modern Scottish Poetry* found 'clear evidence that, at the beginning of the twenty-first century, both critics and writers continue to be subject to pressures which would have them view literary activity first and foremost in relation to national self-affirmation.' His bold response was to 'set aside . . . issues of national identity, searching for it, constructing it, reinforcing it, along with the illusion that the primary function of poetic texts lies in identity building, and that they are capable of resolving identity issues' (Whyte 2004a: 8). This refreshing approach brings us closer to the still-distant critical condition anticipated in his 1998 article by not just proposing, but indeed taking for granted

> that criticism of Scottish literature, in particular of modern Scottish literature, can now abandon militancy for something more complex and more tolerant, at once more honest and more uncertain. The 'question about Scottishness' will never really be negotiable. Along with

other extraneous agendas, it needs setting aside, so that we can concentrate on the agenda that matters most and provokes the most anxiety, the literary one. (Whyte 2004a: 236)

Insisting that 'both history and politics must renounce any privileged status as tools for the interpretation of Scottish literature', Whyte's study constitutes an energising corrective to the 'culturalising' tendency of Scottish criticism by 'reclaim[ing] a degree of autonomy for the creative (in this case, specifically literary) faculty' (Whyte 2004a: 7–8), a move applauded even by critics of *Modern Scottish Poetry* (see Fowler 2004). But viewing Scottish poetry as poetry first and foremost still seems a distant goal; it is revealing that even Whyte's study cannot quite resist the ethnographic impulse that 'the question about Scottishness' implies. Though he takes extraordinary pains to decentre the critical principles underpinning his selection and discussion of poets – emphasising the 'transparent and arbitrary character' of the book's 'aleatoric' structure (Whyte 2004a: 4) – a residual need to typify according to perceived cultural trends creeps back into the final chapter:

> The choice of collections and poets to be dealt with throughout this book has been open to discussion, but nowhere is it likely to be more controversial than when dealing with the final decade of the century . . . The wisest course would seem to be to seek out representative figures, those who can manage to give a flavour of what was happening and being written in the 1990s, and consideration of whose output can hopefully raise issues which are also relevant to their contemporaries, any one of whom may well be destined to outshine them in the course of time. (Whyte 2004a: 208)

To query this explanation might seem to prove Whyte's point, but I mean to highlight the rationale operating here, not the choice of poets it generates. My suggestion is that the identification of Robert Crawford, Kathleen Jamie, Carol Ann Duffy and Aonghas MacNeacail as 'representative figures' has little to do with the autonomous literary agenda Whyte seeks to restore. Rather, the typicality of these poets vis-à-vis Scottish poetry in the 1990s subtly reintroduces the primacy of cultural representativeness in their work's critical reception.

In my view Paterson is the Scottish poet whose work most demands and rewards the denationalised approach Whyte proposes. Before turning to the autonomy of Paterson's poetry, however, it is worth demonstrating the limitations of the nationalising paradigm when applied to his work. Timothy Donnelly's essay on the 'Scottish psychology' of Paterson's first two collections – *Nil Nil* (1993) and *God's Gift to Women* (1997) – takes as its starting-point that hoariest of supposed giveaway Scotticisms, 'the dominant motif of doubling' (Donnelly 2004: 81). '*Nil Nil*'s double-consciousness may at first suggest the belated "split perception" or "double vision" of the colonized', Donnelly observes, but might the doppelgänger trope not equally 'correlat[e] to Scottish post-nationalism' and its 'rejection of a unified, "authentic" conception of self' (Donnelly 2004: 77)? Before we have encountered a single line of a poem, Paterson has been assimilated to the 'identifying' taxonomy: the critical distinction at stake is which phase or trajectory of nationalist identity politics Paterson's work embodies. That his poetry should be read primarily as cultural-political spoor, reified to a bundle of Scotch 'symptoms', literally goes without saying. It is suggestive that Donnelly adopts the model of Crawford's *Identifying Poets* as 'a particularly enlightening one, for in the course of an investigation of the ways in which Paterson constructs in his poetry specifically Scottish identities, the complicated heart of the work appears to unfold' (Donnelly 2004: 80). As we shall see, this totalising diagnosis of 'specifically' Scottish 'identities' actually traduces the formal and intellectual specificities of Paterson's work.

The next move of Donnelly's essay betrays an even more suspect feature of this critical game, namely the unfalsifiability of its inductions. Distinguishing the tartan fingerprints of Paterson's first collection from those of his second, Donnelly suggests that

> the relative infrequency with which doubles appear in *God's Gift to Women* speaks to the book's more explicit Scottishness which, while never contradicting *Nil Nil's* implicitly post-nationalist stance, train-tracks through the book, artificially securing a more cohesive, less fragmented voice. (Donnelly 2004: 77)

The fudging phrase 'speaks to' is appropriate to this sub-Freudian gesture. Acknowledging the non-incidence or attenuation of an 'unmistakably Scottish' pattern merely attests to the significance of its omission or evasion; the apparent absence of the distinguishing watermark is read as a sort of negative lack, implying a heightened, compensatory Scottishness at another level of the text. The 'explicit Scottishness' Donnelly alludes to is Paterson's conceit of naming eight (and a half) of the collection's poems for 'the stations of the old Dundee–Newtyle railway' (Paterson 1997: 57), hardly a national signifier. This misstep echoes Donnelly's hypernymic reading of Dundee in 'Heliographer', where 'the world beneath: / our tenement, the rival football grounds, / the long bridges, slung out across the river' (Paterson 1993: 7) unaccountably 'invites us . . . to identify the geography stretched out beneath the speaker as a representation of Scotland' (Donnelly 2004: 84) rather than Paterson's hometown.

Following the same pattern, Ruth Padel's description of Paterson as 'a latter-day Burns' is read by Donnelly not as a dismal critical narrowness, but as an incisive comparison of the two poets' 'craftsmanship and perennial subject matter' (Donnelly 2004: 79). Would this affinity suggest itself if Paterson hailed from Shropshire? 'Also important to Padel's comparison', predictably, 'is Burns's famous patriotism, his assertion and preservation of Scottish identity' (Donnelly 2004: 79). Since, as Crawford has complained, 'Scotland is allowed only one poet' (Crawford 2002: 16), and Burns was a patriot, all Scottish poets lazily compared to Burns can be assumed to be buttressing Scottish identity. The poet is not an artist, but a sort of cultural mascot. Paterson has edited his own, notably literary selection of Burns's poetry, and his attitude to the sorts of 'assertion and preservation of Scottish identity' Donnelly thinks the two poets share can best be gauged by Paterson's comments in its introduction: 'Nations in abeyance have a far greater need for the fripperies of nationhood than do active ones, and perhaps one day we will see the ludicrous post of "national bard", along with the *Flower of Scotland*, the Gathering of the Clans and Edinburgh Tattoo all go down the same plughole. Then, perhaps, Burns will be accorded his true place in the literary constellation' (Paterson 2001: xviii).

The mode of recognising poets as spokespeople for their nations is hopelessly reductive, and the transfigurative dimension of Paterson's work stands against it in every possible way. Whereas the 'identifying' procedure thrives on recognising, restating and verifying a preconceived Scottishness, Paterson's work scorns any mode of repetition which does not transform, however slightly, our perception of the already familiar. It is felicitous that practices of recognition should figure so centrally in the discourse of 'identifying poets' and the populist strand of modern British poetry Paterson has most outspokenly criticised. His polemical introduction to *New British Poetry* complains that the British mainstream 'has been shaped and narrowed by the closing banks of that cheery and generally none-too-clever verse of recognition humour' (Paterson and Simic 2004: xxvii); in a lecture of the same year, he upbraids the 'kind of straight-faced recognition comedy . . . [which has] no need either for originality or epiphany' (Paterson 2004b). Philip Larkin's 'Fiction and the Reading Public' precisely captures the 'familiar' qualities of this verse: 'Choose something you know all about / That'll sound like real life' (Larkin 2003: 34).

Paterson's disdain for recognition verse is not mere snobbery, but related to a fully articulated sense of the transformative duty of poetry. For Paterson 'the poet's job is to make the commonplace miraculous' (Paterson 1996: 158), and 'the current practice of inviting the audience to "share" the experience' (Friel 1995: 193) amounts to a dereliction of this duty. As Paterson explains in an interview with Lilias Fraser, 'whatever you're talking about has got to be transformed at the end of the poem, and you're not going to do that if you're not on some kind of pilgrimage, some transforming process that the reader has to make with you' (Fraser 2000: 103–4). The critical game of recognising a poet's Scottishness by means of shoehorning salient features of their work into a predetermined national taxonomy shares in the consequences of recognition verse in so far as it sidelines the revelatory potential of the artworks which are its critical objects. Matched-up correspondences and continuities become ossified at the expense of any potential shift in perception. Louis MacNeice – once named by Paterson as his 'favourite poet' (Kellaway 1994: 21) – shared this insistence: 'The poet is a maker, not a retail trader. The writer today should be not so much the mouthpiece of a community (for then he will only tell it what it knows already) as its conscience, its critical faculty, its generous instinct' (MacNeice 1968: xxi).

Paterson graciously responded by email to a series of questions on this theme. On being asked whether he thought it was dangerous to construct and reinforce cultural traditions mainly on the basis of recognising stalwart motifs, a habit which seems to flirt with reducing art to 'culture', he replied:

> Yep – unless the work has a clear historical or political focus, i.e. *that's what it's about* (like some of Douglas Dunn's, for example) – all you're doing is limiting the possibilities of the culture by insisting that the work can only make its relevance to that culture known via the display of certain signifiers, certain agreed hand-signals, all trivial: the odd dialect word or bit of idiomatic syntax, the mention of a place-name, a bit of local flora, the voice's exhibition of an identifiable . . . uh, 'national trait'. Work which displays a superabundance of those gestures is embarrassingly overprized in Scotland right now; maybe that's always been the case, and maybe it's just that the identity of smaller nations always has to be a little overconstructed.

If 'homogeneity is the enemy of Scottish culture' (Crawford 1993a: 162), critics ought to resist homogenising what can be recognised as 'Scottish' in the first place. The 'identifying' paradigm not only stifles the terms of nationalist criticism, but effectively limits the available modes of *artistically* engaging with the issues of identity this approach trivialises. At its worst, Paterson continues, this pattern amounts to

> misreading a work by focussing on a relatively unimportant aspect of it, and, on that basis, recruiting it for your project of reinforcing a cultural prejudice. I find this conversation very depressing. We're hovering on the edge of human extinction, and are going out of our way to avoid listening [to] what our poetry *might actually be saying to us* – to find time to talk about important but entirely tangential concerns that are all being far more interestingly debated elsewhere, in their primary arenas. It's some feat.

Paterson's poetics is not only a valuable rejoinder to this homogenising trend, but a salutary example of what a more truly literary approach to reading Scottish writing might be capable of. According to Paterson, 'poetry is a form of magic, because it tries to change the way we perceive the world, that is to say that it aims to make the texture of our perception malleable' (Paterson 2004b). The poem, or critical reading, which simply supplies recognition of the reader's own experience, values or political outlook renders 'the texture of our perception' less malleable and leads towards imaginative atrophy:

> Since it tries to provoke an emotion of which its target readers are already in high possession, it will change no-one's mind about anything . . . Risk, of the sort that makes readers feel genuinely uncomfortable, excited, open to suggestion, vulnerable to *reprogramming*, complicit in the creative business of their self-transformation is quite different. (Paterson 2004b)

This, in short, is the sort of poetry Paterson writes. Its formal and imaginative risks always call upon a degree of prior intimacy – 'for a reader to be blown away by the original phrase, *it must already be partly familiar to them*' (Paterson 2004b) – but, just as consistently, refuse glib corroborations of the already-known. Paterson's work thrives on near-misses between art and life, where recognisable concrete experience, partly estranged by its strongly formal realisation in verse, brings the reader to a state of unsettled wakefulness by way of boldly mythic, allusive and philosophical conceits. The original, domestic detail is transfigured in the process, and we conclude our reading of the poem not only perceiving it from an altered angle of vision, but with a new, liberating or disturbing awareness of its plasticity.

In 'The Shut-in', from *Landing Light*, an aura of established, 'vernacular' routine is disrupted by an awareness of time which invites seemingly infinite imaginative deferral:

> Good of them, all told, to leave me locked
> inside my favourite hour: the whole one early
> I came to wait for one I loved too dearly
> in this coffered snug below the viaduct
> with my dark vernacular ale, Stevenson's
> short fiction, and the little game I played
> of not thinking of her, except to thumb away
> the exquisite stitch that gathers at my breastbone.
>
> The minute hand strains at its lengthening tether
> like Achilles on the hare; the luscious beer
> refills; the millionth page flowers on the last
> of *The Bottle Imp* . . . O Fathers, leave me here,
> beyond the night, the stars, beyond the vast
> infinitesimal letdown of each other!

(Paterson 2003: 39)

We are left here in a sort of worship of delay and not-yetness, 'locked inside' a determinate moment but comforted by the very 'snugness' of the sonnet's formal regularity. The poem rejoices in the 'little game' of these bounds and limits, which are manipulated to produce an altered perception of time and possibility.

As with many of Paterson's crisply lyrical longer poems, some allusive unpacking is called for. In Stevenson's 'The Bottle Imp' (1893), as elegantly summarised by Claire

Harman, 'the holder of a magic bottle can have anything he wishes for, and be none the worse for it, provided he can sell the bottle afterwards at less than he originally paid. If not, he faces eternal damnation, a sort of cumulative punishment for everything done through the bottle's agency in the past' (Harman 2005: 415). Like the sestet of the poem, the curse implies a recursive pattern as the bottle is re-sold for ever smaller discounts – 'infinitesimal letdowns' – which bring the price, perilously, ever closer to zero, and ever closer to staying the same. This precarious threshold between singularity and the infinite, an almost mathematically precise horizon between nothingness and sameness, is Paterson's intellectual stomping-ground. Here, in Matthew Reynolds's words, 'in-betweenness figures not as a situation to be explored but as a kind of faith' (Reynolds 2004: 25).

Paterson's work abounds in such filaments and limits, often tracing asymptotic patterns such as those of 'Nil Nil', where the tale and the voice of its telling gradually '[thin] down to a point so refined / not even the angels could dance on it' (Paterson 1993: 52–3). Similarly, the speaker of 'The Trans-Siberian Express' watches his companion move up the long broken curve of a train:

> I follow your continuous arrival
> shedding veil after veil after veil –
> the automatic doors wincing away
> as you stagger back from the buffet
>
> slopping *Laphroaig* and decent coffee
> until you face me from that long enfilade
> of glass, stretched to a vanishing point
> like facing mirrors, a lifetime of days.

                                                                    (Paterson 1993: 35)

The flickering changes in the lover's image as she sheds each 'veil' of distance and distortion achieve a metaphysical conceit for the 'continuous arrival' of the present from the future. The fleeting singularity of *now* becomes a 'vanishing point' where the dwindling future turns into the swollen past, but also where the speaker's perception of time becomes infinitely discriminating; an entire life becomes visible as a sequence of separate days, discrete epiphanies which appear to be identical copies.

The abiding presence of Scheherazade in Paterson's early work adds erotic drama to this flirtation with infinity. In '*from* Advice to Young Husbands' in *God's Gift to Women*, the poem's chiasmus embodies the sublime renewal and erasure of the sex it describes:

> No one slips into the same woman twice:
> heaven is the innocence of its beholding.
>
> From stroke to stroke, we exchange one bliss
> wholly for another. Imagine the unfolding
> river-lotus, how it duplicates
> the singular perfection of itself
> through the packed bud of its billion petticoats,
> and your cock, here, the rapt and silent witness,
> as disbelief flowers from his disbelief.

Heaven is the innocence of its beholding:
no man slips into the same woman twice.

(Paterson 1997: 53)

The attraction of these recursive patterns, Paterson explained by email, is that 'their presence tends to denote the hard limit of our human interrogation of the world, i.e. the point at which the human imagination has to take over.' The image of an 'exquisite stitch' in 'The Shut-in' captures the duality of this formal gamesmanship: a pleasurable constriction, a cramp which is also a join. As Reynolds puts it, 'in the best of Paterson's writing . . . the feeling of limitation is recognised and made eloquent. The boundaries of verse and of language represent a general human shortcoming beyond which something that is impossible to grasp can be intuited and implied' (Reynolds 2004: 26). The elusive 'beyond' may be inaccessible to experience, but its logical necessity has a powerful and liberating imaginative pull. In 'The Shut-in' the licence of time's 'lengthening tether' is married to the exuberance of the Bottle Imp's inexhaustible fractal 'blooming', self-delighted by its own ceaseless perpetuation and the knowledge that its indwelling rules both trifle with and prohibit closure, terminus, conclusion. The dramatic ballast of Stevenson's story is the punishment for dying without having sold the bottle on: eternal damnation. By contrast, the calculus of 'The Shut-in' relishes the eternal deferral of the next moment in the present one, a pattern of replenishing and 'refilling' time made audaciously concrete by the allusion to Zeno's paradox of motion (according to which Achilles can never catch the hare, because he would first have to traverse half the distance separating them, and before that a quarter, and before that an eighth, and so on ad infinitum). This suspensive, speculative energy carries us beyond the inevitable 'letdown' of the actual, the arrived-at, and into imaginative territory at once more malleable and self-sufficient. This is what I mean by the autonomy of Paterson's work, summed up by the poet himself as follows: 'I like the idea of the poem as a self-contained universe, the national anthem of a wee vernacular Atlantis whose laws, customs, geography and weather could all be derived from its close study' (Paterson 1996: 161). This image of the poem as an apocryphal, self-contained territory cannot but recall a devolved Scotland whose national status, Paterson observes by email, '[is] both dangled before us and tantalisingly withheld'.

There is a stark difference between Paterson's vision of poetry as conscious and imaginative artifice, and that which conceives the poem as a cultural artefact embodying a socially articulated 'voice'. As Paterson insists, 'a poet should be in service to the poem, and while that's the case, nothing exists except the poem; the poem annihilates the poet' (Paterson 1996: 155). Accordingly, poets must recover

> the confidence to insist on the poem as possessing an intrinsic cultural value, of absolutely no use other than for its simple *reading*. Perversely, it has been the insistence on poetry's auxiliary usefulness – for example, in raising issues of cultural identity, as a form of therapy, or generating academic papers – that has encouraged it to think far less of itself, and so eroded its real power to actually inspire readers to think or live differently. (Paterson 2004b)

This motif is literalised in two poems from *Landing Light* – 'A Talking Book' and 'Archaic Torso of Apollo' – both of which present speakers standing before 'Apollo's ancient torso'. One reflects 'you must lose some weight'; the other, *'now change your life'* (Paterson 2003: 28, 61). While the banality of the first response derives from a naively literal attempt at identification, in the second poem a consciously aesthetic response honours the imaginative possibilities both symbolised and concretely instantiated by Apollo's likeness: 'You'll never know that terrific head / or feel those eyeballs ripen on you – / yet something here keeps you in view, / as if his look had sunk inside // and still blazed on' (Paterson 2003: 61).

This 'sunk inside' vision is also present in 'The Luing', a compelling emplacement of Paterson's 'wee vernacular Atlantis' on Scottish soil:

> When the day comes, as the day surely must,
> When it is asked of you, and you refuse
> To take that lover's wound again, that cup
> Of emptiness that is our one completion,
>
> I'd say go here, maybe, to our unsung
> innermost isle: Kilda's antithesis,
> yet still with its own tiny stubborn anthem,
> its yellow milkwort and its stunted kye.

> (Paterson 2003: 1)

'Innermost' suggests a second attempt at the imaginative flight of 'The Shut-in', but the real isle of Luing is also among the 'innermost' of the Inner Hebrides, two hundred yards off the larger island of Seil, in turn connected to the Scottish mainland by 'the bridge over the Atlantic' at Clachan. The island shares its name with a special cross-breed of short-horn Highland cattle developed there. The 'stunted kye' of this anti-Kilda might tempt the culturalising reader with a fashionably pluralist figure of Scotland's projected independence through hybridity. The poem's momentum, however, tends away from glib, finalised equivalencies:

> Leaving the motherland by a two-car raft,
> The littlest of the fleet, you cross the minch
> To find yourself, if anything, now deeper
> In her arms than ever – sharing her breath
>
> Watching the red vans sliding silently
> Between her hills. In such intimate exile,
> Who'd believe the burn behind the house
> The straitened ocean written on the map?
>
> Here beside the fordable Atlantic,
> Reborn into a secret candidacy,
> The fontanelles reopen one by one
> In the palms, then the breastbone and the brow

> (Paterson 2003: 1)

Here precisely our conception of selfhood is left 'open to suggestion, vulnerable to *reprogramming*': the very skull bones de-fuse and restore the soft membranes of infant perception. The minimal gap defining the home-awayness of this transatlantic native soil marks a self-estrangement, an 'intimate exile' which suspends any correspondence between geography and territory. The 'secret candidacy' of this poem and its landscape, combined with the provisional, unmappable form it achieves, resists any search for identity or 'place' as accomplished fact. With its title masquerading as a continuous verb, 'Luing' is a particularly striking example of what Paterson calls 'The Dark Art of Poetry': it 'renders the texture of our perceptions malleable by surreptitious and devious means, by seeding and planting things in the memory and imagination of the reader with such force and insidious originality that they cannot be deprogrammed' (Paterson 2004b).

The procedures of cultural recognition implicit in so much Scottish literary criticism impose damaging limits on the possibilities of what can be 'identified' as Scottish poetry. It is a way of reading which renders the texture of our perceptions more rigid, and our perceptions, especially, of what is 'Scottish' more homogeneous and clichéd. Paterson's work, in which the impulse to easy identification encounters 'the productive resistance of the form' (Paterson 2004b), alerts us to the gravely unimaginative consequences of such symptomatic readings of 'Scottishness'. By happy coincidence, 'symptom' and 'asymptote' have antonymous etymologies: the first means 'to fall together', the second a failure to tally. The asymptotic patterns of suspension and deferral in Paterson's work, his miraculous near-misses, suggest a more rewarding critical posture in the devolutionary moment. Hospitality to the contingent and transformative is called for, and impatience with the steadfast 'identification' – and ossification – of Scottish typicalities. Allow me to conclude with a final aphorism by Don Paterson, Scottish poet: 'If we expect our work to survive our death even by a single day, we should stop defending it this minute, that it might sooner learn its self-sufficiency' (Paterson 2004a: 131). This may apply to the rebirth of nations as forcibly as to the deaths of individual writers.

Chapter 29

Alan Warner, Post-feminism and the Emasculated Nation

Berthold Schoene

Alan Warner is perhaps best known for his imagining of bafflingly credible girlhood femininities in his first three novels, *Morvern Callar* (1995), *These Demented Lands* (1997) and *The Sopranos* (1998). Warner's cross-writing tendencies raise questions about the legitimacy and credibility of male-authored fiction, as well as men writers' general entitlement and ability to produce authentic renditions of female experience; indeed, ever since *Morvern Callar* was first published, critics have been deliberating whether Warner ought ultimately to be taken seriously as 'more than just a male "colonist" of female experience' (Jones 2004b: 56). All the more pertinent, then, that Warner should have switched to a self-conscious portrayal of emasculated males in his more recent novels, *The Man Who Walks* (2002) and *The Worms Can Carry Me to Heaven* (2006). In *The Man Who Walks* the two central characters' dysfunctional uncle/nephew relationship, their sexual ambivalence, and their fatherlessness render them queer outcasts to discourses of patriarchal linearity and legitimacy, whereas Manolo Follano, the Spanish anti-hero of Warner's latest work, suffers not only from crippling nostalgia, hypochondria and ennui, but also from 'a minimal sperm count', making him 'the only orange with no pips on our citrus coast' (Warner 2006: 214). Invariably, Warner's men find themselves removed from the metropolitan centres of power and at the mercy of male-authored conspiracy plots: in *The Man Who Walks* Nephew and Uncle are on the run after being blamed for the disappearance of a local pub's World Cup cash kitty of £27,000 which was in fact stolen by the local 'Argyll Mafia', while, similarly reduced to a puppet on another man's strings, Manolo's doctor suggests to him, as part of a rather crude character-forming experiment, that he is HIV-positive and may not have long to live.

What all of Warner's novels share is their deployment of representations of gender, both masculinity and femininity, to explore the state of devolutionary and post-devolution Scotland: is the newly devolved nation most aptly rendered in terms of a group of working-class girls' post-feminist rebellion, or a half-mad drunk's disoriented stumble across the Highlands, or a Spanish would-be playboy's offer of hospitality to an African 'Moor' in the semi-provincial, semi-cosmopolitan setting of a modern-day mock-hagiography? Warner's creative conflation of gender and nation is already at work in his debut novel, which opens with Morvern, his unfazed teenage heroine, stepping over the messy dead body of her thirty-something suicide boyfriend in order to reach for his legacy, the typescript of a novel, which she promptly sends off and gets published under her own name. The enduring impact of Morvern's emancipatory act of fraud is revealed to us seven years later, within the context of his fourth novel, as Warner's narrative voice fondly, if inarticulately recalls his original heroine as 'a smart piece . . . that wrote some novel book no less, that you saw, thumbed and passed among the young ones in the pubs' (Warner 2002: 42). Without contemplating anything in depth or, in fact, ever seeming to think very much at all, Morvern successfully extricates herself by impulsive intuition not only from her older boyfriend's patriarchal authority but also, much more importantly, from her passive male-authoredness as a literary character. As Morvern comes to life, she immediately goes feral, and it is this intangibility and impassiveness of hers, shrewdly conjured and sustained by Warner, which enable her story – especially the parts that are set in Scotland before she goes off to Spain, as well as her mysterious return many years later – to unfold as 'a new Highland mythology' (see Petrie 2004: 96–101). In John LeBlanc's view, Morvern 'oversees the death of [a] dysfunctional patriarchal order and the rebirth of a matriarchal sensibility concomitant with her own emergence as an individual' (LeBlanc 2000: 146). Accordingly, the girl always also symbolises the nation, whose independence and sovereignty can only be reasserted once her old self has effectively been reconstituted by new experience garnered from hitherto untapped sources abroad.

Before Morvern leaves for Spain, she must dispose of the body, and initially she does so very awkwardly by hiding it in the attic, levering it up to hover precariously over her boyfriend's much-cherished miniature replica of his homeland, then dropping it: 'The body crashed down onto the buildings of His childhood village smashing in one side of the mountains then lying still, face up to the skylights' (Warner 1995: 52). However, Morvern's accidental onslaught on her boyfriend's man-made Scotland fails to work the spell required to release her. Only after dismembering the body and burying it in the actual soil until 'all across the land bits of Him were buried' (Warner 1995: 91) is she free to go. Her eventual reappearance back in Scotland many years later is similarly fraught with symbolic significance. The novel closes with Morvern, after 'travelling round' (Warner 1995: 224) and being refused shelter in a remote hotel, walking towards some unknown destination, intent upon introducing new life, conceived elsewhere, into the country she once could not wait to escape: 'I placed both hands on my tummy at the life there, the life growing right in there. The child of the raves' (Warner 1995: 228).

Whether this does in fact represent a 'return of the [Celtic] goddess', as LeBlanc suggests, or the messianic arrival of something far more unprecedented and contemporary, without doubt *Morvern Callar* is not only Warner's debut novel but also his creative manifesto and key to the conceptual deep structure of his work. The spectral presence of Morvern haunts the subsequent novels. According to an aside in *The Man Who Walks*, pregnant Morvern drowned while 'crossing the Sound on the little illegal ferry' (Warner 2002: 42), retrospectively causing the oneiric, barely intelligible ramble of *These Demented Lands* to read like a dark-twin reprise of its predecessor, chronicling Morvern's posthumous progress to her foster-mother's grave. Furthermore, in *The Sopranos* the girls spot a guy in the Mantrap nightclub said to be living 'with yon Morvern from the Superstore, used to live up the Scheme' (Warner 1998: 270), and the unusual Spanish setting of *The Worms Can Carry Me to Heaven* invites us to expect to catch a glimpse of her at every turn. Most conspicuously, however, in Warner's latest novel Morvern's spirit returns in the shape of Manolo's incomprehensibly exotic teenage sweethearts, the francophone Vietnamese sisters Thinh and Quynh.

David Thompson's cover photograph for the original Cape edition of *Morvern Callar* shows the mud-encrusted, startled face of a girl with wet, tangled hair and apparently naked, at once imperviously spiritual and extremely vulnerable, animalistic and seemingly outside language. It is this mythopoeic portrait of Warner's heroine which links her most potently to the eponymous protagonist of Warner's fourth novel. In *The Man Who Walks*

Uncle gradually takes shape as an aboriginal native and archaic *ur*-epitome of Scotland, quite as if he embodied an extradiscursive essence of the land which escapes symbolic representation and can only ever be grasped in glimpses, never in its totality. When we eventually come face to face with him, Warner describes Uncle as follows:

> Face of The Man Who Walks! . . . The hair! Leaves and dead crabs in its grey spiked heights. Constant appearance of shock, dirt in the wrinkles, the haunted, prowling expression, already dark skin, weathered by the endlessness of being forced abroad in all weathers into the wider expanses of territory. The eye socket, swollen closed, infected by constantly inserting foreign objects, and crushed peewit's eggs to cool it. (Warner 2002: 273)

Uncle emerges as a human being whose indefatigable, compulsive peregrination and total immersion within nature have made him an integral part of the land, which has rubbed off on him and marked him indelibly. That Morvern might represent a similarly symbolic figure is also indicated by her name, which is derived from a local mountain range (Warner 1997: 49). In this respect, then, she is and is not an immediate contemporary of Fionnula, Manda, Chell, Kylah and Orla, the lead members of the local Catholic girls' school choir in *The Sopranos*. Sharing their class background, she lacks their gregarious garrulity and, having dropped out of school, she seems even more underprivileged than them. But her lust for partying, sex and adventure matches theirs, and so does the easy homosocial intimacy that is between her and her best (and only) friend Lanna.

The Sopranos is without doubt Warner's most straightforwardly realist text, largely unencumbered by the myth-making tendencies of his other Scottish novels or the European *nouveau roman* aspirations of his latest work. Warner focuses on a group of Scottish working-class girls who appear hell-bent on squandering their talents (see also Schoene 2006b). Kylah, for instance, who has an exceptional singing voice, has her eye on 'the best job in town . . . behind the record counter in Woolies [where] ya can play what ya want' (Warner 1998: 68). But, as Warner takes care to explain, his girls' main problem is not lack of intelligence, listlessness or pure indolence, but disaffection. As Fionnula puts it, being working-class is 'a crippling feeling', and the question is not whether you have the ability to go to university, but whether you can afford it, 'and that's end of the story' (Warner 1998: 67, 167). To illustrate further his girls' lack of prospects, Warner addresses the issue of teenage pregnancies, indicating that there have been twenty-seven in one year alone, a hugely exaggerated number for a small-town school, but one which effectively reasserts the view that there simply is 'less reason for young women who do not have high hopes about brilliant careers or even about a decent income to defer motherhood until later' (Aapola et al. 2005: 102). Initially it appears as if Warner regards premature motherhood as a latent peril integral to every effervescent working-class girl's experience of growing up. Thus, he writes about pregnant Michelle that 'pure and intense, she'd devoured the few opportunities for the wee bit sparkle that was ever going to come her way' (Warner 1998: 47). However, Warner ultimately eschews such crass, class-bound stereotyping by revealing that middle-class Kay, initially referred to as a 'lightweight, university-bound virgin' (Warner 1998: 6), is secretly facing the same dilemma. Unwanted motherhood haunts post-feminist girlhood like a fateful, anachronistic spectre of biologist determination, reminding all girls, irrespective of their class backgrounds, that their lives will never be as carefree as the boys', because even in the twenty-first century the simple fact of being female can still cement a girl's destiny.

In spite of this Warner chooses to portray his heroines as intransigent post-feminist 're/sisters' (Aapola et al. 2005: 108). Disobeying school rules by adorning their shoes with 'luminous, day-glo, interwoven, painted or rainbowy laces: the only means of self-expression remaining' and wearing 'specially-shortened skirts', they persist in their refusal to 'conduct [them]selves in a manner befitting Our Lady of Perpetual Succour for Girls' (Warner 1998: 8, 19, 24). Flaunting their individualism and sexual precocity, the sopranos appear to epitomise the new 'girl power'; yet, rather than being commended for their self-confident demeanour, they are disqualified by Sister Condron as 'this lunatic fringe' of trou-blemakers incorporating undesirably deviant femininities (Warner 1998: 254). As they engage in behaviours traditionally reserved for boys (truanting, carousing, promiscuity), the sopranos assume a hybrid male/female gender identity which interrogates the para-meters of what makes a valid, culturally intelligible femininity.

Complicated by the male-authoredness of *The Sopranos*, a pressing question in this context is whether the girls' appropriation of masculinity enhances, or only works to under-mine and erase, their feminine difference. Also, how are we to interpret Warner's detailed description of the girls' obsession with hyperfeminine make-up and clothes? As it says in the novel, 'no girl smiled as she dressed – a ritual they each treated with more reverence than ingestion of any transubstantial host' (Warner 1998: 107). Is the alleged difference between a pre-feminist and a post-feminist mini-skirt – the former pandering to the male gaze, the latter exclusively donned for the girl's own pleasure – ever more than purely rhetorical? As Valerie Hey reminds us, 'boys do not have to be there in actuality to exer-cise power. They sometimes only need to be there "in the head"' (Hey 1997: 15), and in *The Sopranos* this problem is compounded by the fact that, rather than merely, or of neces-sity, subject to an internalised male gaze, the femininities of Warner's girls are male-authored and hence the direct result of a male mind envisaging the female.

Warner's girls, without ever being overtly political, display an astonishing capability for fulfilling the girls' studies expert Anita Harris's hopeful blueprint of girls as 'engaged in pro-jects of . . . creating their own communities for evading regulatory regimes' and devising 'creative mechanisms of resilience and resistance that may ripple out into wider possibili-ties' (Harris 2004: 153). Their general attitude also most promisingly reflects the changing modes of post-romantic young femininity as identified by Angela McRobbie:

> The girl is no longer the victim of romance . . . She no longer waits miserably outside the cinema knowing that she has been 'stood up'. She no longer distrusts all girls including her best friend because they represent a threat and might steal her 'fella'. She no longer lives in absolute terror of being dumped. She is no longer terrified of being without a 'steady'. (McRobbie 1994: 164)

And yet, however politically enlightened his representation of girlhood may be, as a het-erosexual male Warner cannot entirely escape the accusation of voyeurist manipulation, especially with reference to the many instances of seemingly gratuitous sexual explicit-ness in the novel, such as the girls' accounts of 'handjobbing' boys in front of each other, of bisexual threesomes and sado-masochistic practices, as well as terminally ill Orla's 'rape' of a semi-comatose man in hospital. Most worrying in this context is the girls' insistence on the autonomy of their sexual desire, as in Manda's assertion that 'it was something I wanted to do; see me, ah just do things ah want to', or Orla's invitation of her ephemeral boyfriend Stephen to 'do anything you want with me an that's what men wish for' (Warner 1998: 129, 309). No wonder, then, that in The Port – a thinly disguised replica of Oban, Warner's hometown – the girls' school is also known as 'The Virgin Megastore' (Warner 1998: 198).

Whereas it is impossible not to agree with Carole Jones's view that Warner 'has tapped the "unadulterated life force" of these young women and achieved notoriety for his work [which] is translated in the media as a kind of expertise on femininity', I am reluctant to concur with her conclusion that 'as a man in a woman's world, he usurps control only to maintain the status quo' (Jones 2004b: 66–7). Despite manifold misgivings about Warner's representational style, the fundamentally pro-feminist intentions of his project are, in my view, beyond doubt. Reminiscent of Morvern's indomitable spirit, *The Sopranos* aims to accentuate the girls' capability for emancipation against all the odds. To make his point, Warner employs the magic-realist image of Lord Bolivia, the school's Latin-American parrot, which rapidly comes to operate as a symbolic embodiment of the girls' foul-mouthed mischievousness, their colourful intransigence and carnivalesque subversion of anything that smacks of behavioural normativity. We first catch a glimpse of Lord Bolivia's red head and his pink-yellow-and-green wings near the beginning of the novel when, newly escaped from captivity and without much hope for survival in the wild, he appears 'like a happiness that wasn't allowed below such skies, against these curt roof angles of slate and granite' (Warner 1998: 51). Towards the end of the novel we learn that, miraculously, Lord Bolivia has indeed survived Scotland's inclement climate, and as a spectacular incarnation of the girls' invincible spirit – 'in red and emerald splendour, like a burst firework' – he reappears to save a budgie from its encaged existence and whisk if off, 'flying, across the bay towards the secret forest where all the escaped exotic birds dwell' (Warner 1998: 312).

The Sopranos is a liberational text pitting the girls' post-feminist individualism against the efforts of a residual patriarchal order to mould and employ them. Parrot-like, the girls are drilled to repeat by rote, and yet, to the nuns' frustration, they remain saboteurs who will not sing from a common hymn-sheet. Following their truant escapades, the sopranos are approached by The Port's local priest who, keen to work a miracle to revitalise the region's economy, tries to talk them into pretending to have seen an apparition of the Virgin Mary. In exchange for this dissimulation, he vows to avert the girls' expulsion from school. But the sopranos reject the Father's indecent proposal: 'Told him in the nicest way to fuck off, we werenie lying for anybody, he'd come to the wrong folk' (Warner 1998: 321). Within Warner's final vision the girls' pride in the authenticity of their voices and experience is incorruptible; however, one cannot help wondering if this is an ending the girls can ulti-mately afford. Clearly, Warner subscribes to what in *Future Girl* Harris has identified as con-temporary culture's reinvestment in 'the symbolic value of girlhood', idealising girls as 'the most likely candidates for performing a new kind of self-made subjectivity', a subjectivity that is most propitiously equipped to meet the particular challenges of our times (Harris 2004: 14, 6). Yet how invincible is this 'female spirit' really, and what will become of the girls if they do not complete their education? Warner's enthusiastically defiant novel seems similar to much other devolutionary Scottish writing, in which reckless utopian gestures often tend to triumph over the lack-lustre imperatives of real-political compromise and moderation.

Transporting us back into the Scottish countryside, *The Man Who Walks*, Warner's first post-devolution novel, is far more pessimistic, signalling a clear shift from innocence to experience, and from unruly mischief-making to cruel victimisation (see also Schoene 2006a). Warner departs from a celebration of young female characters and focuses on two middle-aged males instead: Uncle and Nephew, homeless wanderers in what assumes shape as a shambolic epic of national abjection. The novel opens with a devastatingly bleak description of supermarket 'ghost bags' wind-driven across the Highland landscape, poignantly introducing contemporary Scotland as a 'Waste Land', defaced by post-industrial debris, its former splendour left to be construed from abandoned shreds of history, folklore and starkly demoted myth. This is a land inhabited not by dignified warriors embroiled in a battle for independence (or promisingly inspired, post-feminist young 'maidens' like Morvern and the sopranos), but by the castrated shadows of their culturally alienated and debilitated descendants, who have quite literally lost the plot. Warner's anti-heroes find themselves entrapped in the landscape they inhabit, and grossly debilitated by their own naivety and gullibility.

What saves the novel from getting hopelessly bogged down in itself is the redemptive textual mobility of Warner's vision. As its title indicates, *The Man Who Walks* is a novel on the move, an *itinarrative* text, in which the narrative trajectory is always in sync with the protagonist's itinerary and the act of narration synergises with the hero's quest. Far from constituting a pointless 'Beckettish tramp routine' (Tait 2006: 33), Warner's novel employs walking deliberately to create a sense of literalness and immediacy for his protagonists' as well as his readers' experience of the nation. At the same time, by virtue of being a novel, *The Man Who Walks* uncovers and incorporates also a historical dimension. According to Rebecca Solnit in *Wanderlust*, 'walking is natural . . . but choosing to walk in the landscape as a contemplative, spiritual, or aesthetic experience has a specific cultural ancestry' (Solnit 2001: 85–6). Inevitably, as it were, as soon as it becomes entextualised in a narrative format, the act of walking positions the walker and his or her itinerary and experience of the landscape in relation to the itineraries and experiences of other, previous walkers in the same landscape.

In Solnit's view, walking is imbued with an almost pre-modern quality as it momentarily repairs the individual's existential aloneness and isolation in the world, caused by modernity's masculinist conviction that 'the universe no longer beats with the same heart as the human being' (Bordo 1987: 70). Walking is not about willing the body to achieve certain results; it is not about training or controlling the body. In fact, it often appears quite purposeless and inefficient, a circuitous 'ramble'. Its only investment resides in an enjoyment of one's being in the world, perhaps even one's being-at-one with the world, by momentarily establishing an effortless union of mind, body and environment. Walking enables the walker to roam indeterminately off and beyond the beaten track, to ignore any given map and improvise, veer off and go astray, to venture into uncharted territory, be unpredictable, trespass, and thus – in Solnit's words – 'find what you don't know you are looking for, and you don't know a place until it surprises you'. Walking enables us to go on a 'subversive detour' (Solnit 2001: 11–12), to move and behave in an experientially counterdiscursive way. Described by Nephew as 'a suspicious walker . . . skulking like the fucking yeti' (Warner 2002: 243), Uncle is a compulsive rambler, forever untraceable and kept in motion by a restive, seemingly hysterical inability to settle. However, as we find out in the end, Nephew has been chasing a phantom. All throughout his search, Uncle is actually being held hostage in the boot of a car, from which, 'curled in a foetal position', he is reborn in the penultimate chapter (Warner 2002: 262). Consequently, the counterdiscursive mobility of Warner's novel is derived entirely from Nephew's efforts to trace his wayward uncle's meanderings across the Highlands. At once vague and vivid, mere surface and mnemonic palimpsest, the Highland landscape comes to life as 'an eidetic country, made of memory alone' (Warner 2002: 28–9), an intricate interweaving of Nephew's own experiences and perceptions in the present – both real and oneiric or drug-induced – with the fragmented residue of an impersonal, collective past. Significantly, Uncle is both a close blood relative and 'our Prince . . . in the heather' (Warner 2002: 59).

The overall impression of Warner's novel is that it aims to initiate the discovery of a sense of bonding and belonging between his main protagonist and his native land that is immediately experiential rather than transmitted by traditional discourse, a result of spiritual engagement rather than nationalist obligation, spontaneity and feeling rather than knowledge and thought. As indicated by chapter headings such as 'Highland Clearance', 'Queen Victoria's Highland Journal' or 'Bonnie Prince Charlie's Flight in the Heather', the Nephew's quest is steeped in Scottish history, yet the links between past and present remain oblique, exemplified best perhaps by the curious intergenerational relationship of Uncle and Nephew, which is dysfunctional and conflict-ridden, yet also unseverable. While Nephew's identification as a contemporary is unequivocal, Uncle's identity continues to oscillate between 1960s hippie gone mad (tripping rather than walking) and larger-than-life troll-like figure of folklore and myth. As Nephew reports, 'it is a fact that Man Who Walks once walked across silty beds of New Loch, 'neath the surface, a huge boulder under one arm holding him down, breathing through a giant hogweed stalk'. But Uncle's legendariness is by no means a thing of the past; it endures within immediately contemporary settings: 'The Man Who Walks'd gone to Hairodynamics before, with alive crabs and winkles buried right down in his hair till a screaming lassie's varnished fingernails found them' (Warner 2002: 19, 23). Uncle's identity remains indeterminate; he is 'that animal fool' (Warner 2002: 52), a weirdo, and a reclusive shaman, a kind of *idiot savant*, only there are no oracular truths emanating from him.

Uncle's most intriguing trait is the effect exerted on him by drink, transforming the stalwart walker into a hopelessly disoriented rambler. When inebriated, Uncle cannot 'ascend or descend the slightest gradient without crashing to the ground or spinning in navigational confusion'; as a result, '[his] travels and goings forth have, inevitably, mainly involved making the most outlandish and extravagant of detours in order to reach a longed-for destination' (Warner 2002: 103–4). Uncle embodies Scotland's 'wandering' masculinity, a drunken, hysterical masculinity, mobilised but without direction, compulsively (yet seemingly without a clue) circulating within the claustrophobic boundaries of its small inherited plot of land, and Nephew – designated as 'a symbol of his nation' (Warner 2002: 87) – must follow in his footsteps.

In *Wanderlust* Solnit suggests that 'to walk the same way is to reiterate something deep' (Solnit 2001: 68) and, as the novel takes its course, Nephew indeed begins to take after Uncle in more than a straightforward peregrinatory sense. As ever more frequently he is mistaken for his truant relative, suggesting a striking familial resemblance, Nephew's pursuit of Uncle turns into an act of self-transformative emulation. Notably, this does not make Nephew a hero; if anything, it inhibits rather than boosts his manliness. The masculinities of both Nephew (chronically impotent) and Uncle (abused as a young man by his mother's English lovers) are corrupted by the mark of effeminacy; however, Warner's cultivation of his anti-heroes' apparent lack of masculine stature seems utterly deliberate, quite as if its frank representational concession might constitute a viable first step towards resolving Scottish masculinity's centuries-old trouble with postcolonial emasculation. By circumventing – and thus implicitly interrogating the ultimate validity and authenticity of – the heroic tale of Scottishness as reliant upon a straightforward patriarchal handover of tradition from father to heterosexual son, *The Man Who Walks* envisages an altogether different story of national continuity and coherence.

What Warner has created is a new, non-patriarchal epic for Scotland, an emasculated, rambling tale celebrating mobility and teleological indeterminacy. Following in what he believes to be his uncle's footsteps Nephew becomes a rambler too, 'not just following the roads but knowing when to veer free of them, to miss out their meandering deviations and to take initiatives, cutting over green ridges and farmland'. Whenever he finds 'his forward

progress . . . challenged . . . by a sturdy wall declaring the urgency of Private Property'
(Warner 2002: 125–6), he presses on regardless. His chosen course not only takes him personally across definitive boundaries, it also has a unifying, curative impact on the land.
'Walking focuses not on the boundary lines of ownership that break the land into pieces',
Solnit asserts, 'but on the paths that function as a kind of circulatory system connecting
the whole organism. Walking is, in this way, the antithesis of owning. It postulates a
mobile, empty-handed, shareable experience of the land.' Accordingly, walking in the
footsteps of The Man Who Walks could be seen as 'sew[ing] together the land that ownership tears apart' (Solnit 2001: 162–3).

As Nephew comes to acknowledge, 'everything was becoming a confluence of narratives'
(Warner 2002: 141), his own individual life – initially unwittingly, then ever more
consciously, defiantly, proudly – first trailing, then confronting, and finally incorporating
contemporary Scottishness. Uncle's uncoordinated and apparently desultory itineraries,
traced and recounted by Nephew, bring about a conspicuously random remapping of
Scotland, both territorially and historically. In The Man Who Walks Warner opens up a
vision of Scotland not as a nation or state, but as a kind of free-floating experiential reality
that is tangible, yet remains discursively beyond grasp. 'Scotland' manifests itself as a
multifaceted, unpredictable and ineradicably subjective experience, brimming with
uncharted ways of national being and belonging, not so much 'feminine' as emasculated
(or non-masculinist) and hence relieved of all definitive preconceptions.

Unlike Morvern Callar or The Sopranos, The Man Who Walks does not conclude with a
homecoming. Rather, in Warner's final vision Nephew, badly injured by Uncle's kidnap-
pers, eventually drags himself onto a fake Hollywood battlefield littered with kilt-clad
warrior mannequins, where Americans are shooting yet another version of Braveheart or
Rob Roy, and where his own personal twenty-first-century journey ends, at least for the time
being. Warner's imagery speaks for itself:

> And there, sure enough, in the distance, the deep burn of high-fired movie lights, flanked by
> battalions of reflectors, were blasting down on reality, fighting the natural light with over-
> whelming, colonising superiority, determined to force a vision on the mundane and curse the
> consequences. (Warner 2002: 277)

Bloodied all over, his kneecaps broken, crawling on all fours, yet tireless and seemingly
indestructible, 'he'd finally made it into the fucking movie' (Warner 2002: 277). At a first
reading this final scene may well be redolent of the inferiorist pathos of Scottish victimisation, yet Warner clearly presents it to us also as a self-assertive, if excruciatingly painful
reclaiming of the plot – of the land as well as the story. In the guise of badly conned and
severely injured Nephew contemporary Scotland, laden with history and myth, creeps back
to make a real-life appearance within the fraudulent discourse of its representation – in this
case, Hollywood cinema's neo-imperialist appropriation of heroic-underdog Scottishness.
'He clawed himself onwards', the novel concludes, 'through the dummy corpses and
towards the ruddy murk of another sunset' (Warner 2002: 280).

Against the backdrop of this powerfully defiant ending it seems peculiar that in
The Worms Can Carry Me to Heaven, Warner's most recent novel, which is set in
Spain, Scotland appears to have vanished from view altogether. What remains is Warner's
employment of an emasculated middle-aged protagonist, Manolo Follano, who is conceited,
infertile, useless at relationships with women – 'my first marriage was gone, destroyed by the
faults of my character' – and, according to his Romanian lover Hansa, 'less a personality

than a collection of phobias' (Warner 2006: 234, 240). Not only does Warner suggest Manolo has a masochistic streak by framing his story with self-torturing quotations from St Teresa of Avila's obsessive autobiography, but also it seems poignant that, at the mental institution where his second wife eventually commits suicide, someone should mistake him for an outpatient who only 'thinks he is just a visitor, a business man' (Warner 2006: 330).

Another peculiarity is that, as Theo Tait deplores, Warner has 'chosen to write a novel in English with a narrator who has "never learned to speak, or even read, English or North American or whatever it is called"', resulting in a narrative that is couched in 'a weird and stilted translationese' (Tait 2006: 33). Indeed, Manolo never ceases to draw attention to his 'inability to speak English', as he watches tourists read newspapers 'with headlines bold in many foreign languages all of which I could not read', or comments on his lover's prodigious multilingualism with increasing exasperation: 'Hansa . . . spoke our language very well . . . She spoke cursed English as well of course . . . Hansa's father was of the German-speaking minority so she spoke that language also! Really – how do these damned multilinguals keep all those words in one head?' (Warner 2006: 128, 153, 235–6). That neither the novel's overall effect as 'a foreigner's vision [of Spain]' nor its protagonist's monolingualism is simply a gratuitous by-product of Warner's authorial affectation or immaturity, as Tait seems to believe, becomes evident when Manolo meets illegal immigrant Ahmed Omar, 'a qualified languages teacher from God-cursed Mogadishu. As well as [Manolo's] own language he spoke English, French, Arabic, Amharic, Swahili and Somali' (Warner 2006: 114). The two men's encounter in fact pervades the whole novel, reaching its climax at the novel's end, where we witness the apotheosis of Manolo's pathetic non sequitur of a life – full of self-indulgent regrets, missed opportunities, petty jealousies and tainted desire – in what is perhaps most fittingly described as an epiphanic conflagration.

Problematising the late twentieth-century Derridean themes of cosmopolitanism, forgiveness and hospitality (see Derrida 2001a, 2001b), Warner's second post-devolution novel leaves Scotland behind to address the issue of asylum politics, undoubtedly contemporary Europe's most difficult ethical quandary. Finding himself persistently drawn to 'the Moor', Manolo visits Ahmed in his makeshift shelter and spontaneously offers him his hospitality: 'I want to invite you to leave that place. Come and live in my apartment and do as you please there' (Warner 2006: 112). Quickly transcending Europe's 'rules and timid values which in our relationship we had never shared or allowed to limit us' (Warner 2006: 345), Manolo and Ahmed form a complex, at once affectionate and profoundly conflictual bond, which culminates in complete mutual identification as Manolo rescues a young girl from a burning hotel, which leaves him looking 'like a beggar of the streets. Like Ahmed had' (Warner 2006: 386). Literally baptised by fire, monolingual Manolo suddenly comes to rejoice in Ahmed's ability to speak 'our language so knowingly. Suddenly I was happy' (Warner 2006: 388). For the first time also he steps out of his self-absorption and becomes alert to the fact that his guest is suffering from AIDS, exposing his own entirely fictitious HIV-infection for what it is, namely an idly titillating and vain flirtation with mortality. In what is possibly one of the most dramatic changes in mood and direction in contemporary Scottish fiction, Warner's novel concludes by abruptly opening his protagonist's eyes to the plights of the world. 'You had to make it over the sea', Manolo realises. 'No medicines where you are from. You should have arrived on a barge of gold, man; we should have got down on our knees to welcome you' (Warner 2006: 389). If Warner's work is currently working at a resolution, it is that the emasculated rather than patriarchal individual (or nation) is the one most likely to get to know himself as well as see, recognise and welcome his other.

Chapter 30

A. L. Kennedy's Dysphoric Fictions

David Borthwick

'The world of Jean Rhys's fiction is both strange and unnervingly familiar', writes A. L. Kennedy in her introduction to Rhys's *Good Morning, Midnight* (1939), a novel in which

> vivid fragments of sensory information swoop and lunge at the reader, establishing the rhythms of a bad drinking bout: one moment all docile clarity, the next a crush of sickened self-awareness, a lurch into the past, or a dreamscape, or a helpless re-examination of realities too dull and terrible to seem anything other than the products of a sick imagination. (Kennedy 2000: v)

What Kennedy says about Rhys's work equally applies to *Paradise*, her own most recent novel. Indeed, the influence of *Good Morning, Midnight*, in which Sophia Jansen attempts to drink herself to death, looms large in Kennedy's tale of Hannah Luckraft's dipsomaniac decline. Both novels begin with their protagonists waking up in depersonalised hotel rooms, and the 'unmistakeable haze of claustrophobia' (Kennedy 2004: 3) only intensifies as both women's psychic journey becomes imbued with a potent dysphoria. Hannah's only clue to her whereabouts is a key-fob shaped roughly like a leaf; more precisely, it looks like 'what would happen if a long-dead ear were inflated until morbidly obese' (Kennedy 2004: 3).

Thus abruptly introduced to Hannah, one-time saleswoman of quality cardboard and vocational drinker, Kennedy's readers are thrust into the protagonist's vertigo of apprehension, compelled to follow, though unable to wholly rely upon, the facts as she presents them to us. For example, recalling two versions of an encounter with a sales-clerk, Hannah cannot decide how the incident concluded: 'I can remember both endings, which is tricky' (Kennedy 2004: 11). *Paradise* comprises a series of interconnected scenes and vignettes – both past and present, some real and some imagined – which come to concentrate in Hannah's damaged psyche, demonstrating that in her experience – as in Morris Magellan's, Ron Butlin's alcoholic biscuit manufacturer in *The Sound of My Voice* (1987) – 'everything that has ever happened to you is still happening' (Butlin 1994: 11).

The 'Magellan Complex' is something all of Kennedy's characters share, whether they are narrator or narrated. In both her novels and short stories Kennedy concerns herself not only with a character's present emotional condition, but also with the events which brought it about. Time and again, Kennedy employs what Sarah Dunnigan terms an '"expendable" temporal framework' in order to create 'the instability of tense which renders the past and present lives of characters in intimate proximity' (Dunnigan 2000: 145). Kennedy's characters are unable to extricate themselves from the magnetic pull of past events which recursively play themselves out in their troubled psyches. In this respect Margaret in *Looking for the Possible Dance* (1993), Kennedy's debut novel, may stand in for many other figures in her work as she finds herself 'almost past the point where she could imagine a change for the better, any change at all. That was how she felt. Prematurely fin-ished' (Kennedy 1993: 99). The figure of Margaret's father stalks through her tale like a fading God, a redundant and yet imperative influence whose rituals must nevertheless be observed: 'every year, in November, her father died. In March, her daddy had his birthday; June was hers; Hallowe'en and Bonfire Night and then he would die' (Kennedy 1993: 86). Through a series of crises and moments of minor epiphany Margaret must reclaim her life in the present with damaged boyfriend Colin. As Philip Tew demonstrates, this pattern of '"questing" (or "looking") for an elusive meaning (to life and events)' recurs in Kennedy's later novels *So I Am Glad* (1995) and *Everything You Need* (1999) (Tew 2003: 129). In each case, the flux of memory and associated emotion is charted in a series of interconnected vignettes – deliberately disorienting in their confused order and detail – from which the reader must reconstruct the characters' identities according to an idiosyncratic logic whose rubrics are revealed, if at all, only gradually. Kennedy's narrative strategy mimics the psy-chological vortex of its respective subjects.

Dunnigan describes Kennedy's narrative mode as 'non-linear but associative' (Dunnigan 2000: 146), a view confirmed by Jennifer Wilson, the protagonist of *So I Am Glad*, who advises us that 'I'm trying to give you as much of the truth as I can and part of any truth will be the order in which it arrives. One fact will trigger one feeling, while another will not' (Kennedy 1995a: 19). Jennifer retains complete editorial control over her narrative, ordering events, even altering time, to suit her personal chronology of emo-tional development: 'this story will, among other things, form a record of various cuts' (Kennedy 1995a: 10). A new year begins 'at least a fortnight early' (Kennedy 1995a: 137) because it suits her feeling of renewal in mid-December, which is when her missing lover returns to her. In similarly solipsistic fashion, the identity of this lover is withheld until she feels ready to disclose it: 'Perhaps you would rather hear who Martin turned out to be. I don't mean to keep you waiting . . . but I can only seem to focus on this particular after-noon and conversation' (Kennedy 1995a: 39). When eventually it is revealed that Jennifer's lover is none other than the seventeenth-century writer and duellist Cyrano de Bergerac, who has mysteriously appeared in contemporary Glasgow, it is perhaps easier to understand Jennifer's effort to establish her own distress as the actual heart of her story before introducing the supernatural presence of her famous lover. Crucially, in *So I Am Glad* Kennedy forgoes narrative linearity in favour of a more subjective trajectory of emo-tional integrity. The reader must be persuaded to believe in the realist authenticity of Jennifer's emotional disposition before her present-day fairy tale can unfold without seri-ously upsetting the novel's verisimilitude.

This particular narrative technique recurs in *Everything You Need*, in which throughout the novel's seven-year time span Nathan Staples composes private narratives for the perusal of his estranged daughter Mary, which he hopes one day to present to her and so reveal his true identity. Nathan's writings provide us with little concrete detail about the period of his absence from Mary's life; instead, each narrative records Nathan's exact emo-tional state at a particular moment in his life, both before and after his estrangement from Maura, Mary's mother. Like Jennifer, Nathan is aware of the power of emotional truth over objective or empirical fact. The details of an acrimonious marital break-up would be open to doubt and questioning, and ultimately subject to verification by Mary's mother, whereas one man's spiritual quest possesses an incontestable emotional integrity. However, Nathan's intention is not to manipulate Mary; as Nathan's literary editor assures Mary, 'if you ask him to write something down he will be unable to tell you anything but the truth. It makes his letters very interesting. And rare' (Kennedy 1999a: 380).

This curious narrative strategy also pervades Kennedy's non-fiction. Her essay *On Bullfighting* (1999) does not begin with a history of discursive investigation into the sport; rather, Kennedy opens with an extremely personal contemplation on suicide, disclosing intimate details of the time and place she was closest to taking her own life. Eventually she admits including this information for purely rhetorical reasons to illustrate that she cannot make a 'commitment' to death in the same way as bullfighters must do every day: 'My little confession of a contemplated sin is intended to indicate that I will give you as much as I can. I do promise that' (Kennedy 1999b: 5). By confessing something so intimate Kennedy endows her essay with a curious integrity, ensuring the reader will accept her subsequent expositions more readily, with the emotional bond established at the outset serving as a promise of truthfulness and credibility. It is perhaps unfair to place Kennedy on the same plane as her characters, yet a comparison of style between her fiction and non-fiction is so readily made that it is hard to ignore; in both genres the logic of emotion overrides any other possible means of ordering the narrative. Even her cinematic study of Michael Powell and Emeric Pressburger's *The Life and Death of Colonel Blimp* (1943) is explicitly related to and, so it seems, validated by personal circumstance: 'A good deal of my childhood and my home will shuffle through this book for a variety of reasons.' *Colonel Blimp*, Kennedy informs us, 'form[s] part of my comprehension of my self, my personal truth, my understanding of life and death, of time and home' (Kennedy 1997b: 9–10). With so much emotion invested in her project, what reader would dare challenge Kennedy's interpretation?

Similarly, in *So I Am Glad* Jennifer's candour and personal truth are never up for discussion; if we wish to understand her, we must accept her story as it is related. We must accept that she undergoes a transformation from agoraphobic and repressed neurotic to sensitive and articulate writer capable of accurately imparting her experience so that others may share in her 'gladness'. If a glow-in-the-dark duellist from the past is required as the principal catalyst of this transformation, then so be it. As Tew notes, within Kennedy's work 'rationality's usual mediatory and solicitous role in our lived experience is negated or reduced so that it appears far from efficacious, and survives at best in fragmentary form' (Tew 2003: 128).

The absence of objectivity, reason and linear chronology is common to all of Kennedy's fiction, in which personal experience becomes the only means by which reality can be assessed and judged in order to create meaning. Kennedy's characters are isolated and confused individuals only 'half aware of their limited scope for expressiveness', yet at the same time 'intuitively aware of an underlying series of meanings, possibilities and elusive readings' (Tew 2003: 130–1). According to Rod Mengham, Kennedy's work is not alone in its representation of both the existential centrality and relative paucity of individual experience in confrontation with larger systems of meaning. For much contemporary British fiction it seems as if

> the millennial shadow set a formal limit on an era whose own history had been dominated by political narratives that were either exhausted or under threat. [In the 1990s] fiction concerned itself with the attempt to understand the individual's relationship to these narratives, with the extent to which individual experience confirmed or denied their meanings. (Lane et al. 2003: 1)

In Kennedy's fiction this new millennial zeitgeist translates into a preoccupation with the disjunction of private experience and public life as characters retreat into their privacy to avoid acknowledging their own irrelevance in the face of larger forces. But of course, as

Mengham points out, 'the separation of public and private does not protect individuals from the vicissitudes of history, but renders them invisible, without presence or effect in the world of social meanings' (Lane et al. 2003: 2).

It is this particular dilemma that is explored in many of the short stories in Kennedy's first collection, *Night Geometry and the Garscadden Trains* (1990), a volume which now reads like an early manifesto of her work. From the narrator of 'The Role of Notable Silences in Scottish History', who constructs obituaries for 'all the people who are too small to record', to the elderly woman in 'Star Dust', who concludes that there are 'only tiny patches in my life that are at all important . . . material more suited to a series of photographs', we find Kennedy trying to elicit personal meanings from an uninterested world whose wider, often media-driven, historical narratives seem so remote and alienating as to be of no comfort or relevance to the minor, lone individual inhabiting the late twentieth century (Kennedy 1990: 62–73, 82–92). Similarly, in *So I Am Glad* Jennifer discovers that history makes but a poor guarantor of a better future. In relation to the media representation of an earthquake in India, whose victims are recognised as fellow humans cultivating 'harmless little aspirations, hopes which might have been driving them on', Jennifer takes note of 'the shoddy construction of the homes that would fracture and fall and kill them in just the way that similar shoddy buildings had done just one generation ago. Perhaps the builders had hoped the earthquake would be different this time' (Kennedy 1995a: 83).

If, as in Kennedy's representation, individual experience is the only yardstick by which reality and its possible meanings may be judged, the inevitable result appears to be the loss of any spiritually fruitful or intellectually rewarding intersubjective communication. While walking in the city with Jennifer, Savinien puts his finger on the nature of the modern individual – 'you are, in all simplicity, only more private, particularly in your minds' (Kennedy 1995a: 191) – thus capturing the anonymity and, ironically, the actual, hidden privacy of the public sphere. The isolated mind of the individual comes to resemble an enclosure in which physical encounters between people are rare, and solipsism rears its head as the endgame of communal narrative. However, as discussed by Cristie March in *Rewriting Scotland*, precisely due to its anonymity the public sphere may also become a liberating arena for individual fantasies. March notes that several of Kennedy's characters indulge in 'thrill rides' in order to 'stave off . . . emotional hunger', rehearsing experiential extremes in which 'the body becomes an extension of the emotional self, not an object in and of itself' (March 2002: 139–40). The narrator of 'Failing to Fall' in *Now That You're Back* (1995), for example, uses the anonymity of urban space to inject her life with excitement by embarking on journeys across the city which provide her with a temporary sense of purpose and direction (Kennedy 1995b: 41–63). Newly alert that she might receive a phone call from her anonymous sexual partner at any time of the day or night – and, should this happen, she must visit his home immediately – the narrator's life comes to be fuelled by permanent suspense and reckless anticipation: 'It seems a kind of falling and anyone can fall. When I think of it now, I wonder if we don't all wait from time to time, ready to make a dive, to find that space where we can drop unhindered' (Kennedy 1995b: 44). Conversely, the crisis experienced by the narrator of 'Night Geometry and the Garscadden Trains' comes about precisely because she breaks her routine, returning home unexpectedly to find her husband in bed with his mistress. As Beth Dickson points out, until this chance discovery 'the city's routine was her husband's accomplice' (Dickson 2000: 135).

Kennedy's 'thrill-rides', then, far from offering any permanent emotional sustenance to her characters, or opening up the claustrophobic urban space to new expressive possibilities, are in fact little more than dangerous diversions which fail to offer any genuine alternative to human intimacy. Indeed, Greg in 'Spared' experiences a mini-breakdown as a result of the guilt he feels about his extramarital affair, private anguish mixing with millennial angst as he flees to the Highlands to await a reckoning that does not come (Kennedy 2002: 1–25). Even more depressingly, in 'The Cupid Stunt' from *Original Bliss* the narrator 'keeps in touch' with feelings generated through genuine physical intimacy by employing a masseur to simulate the real thing (Kennedy 1997a: 141–51). In each of these cases, Kennedy's characters are ultimately forced to admit that there exists no parallel, enhanced reality in which they might be able to find perfect self-fulfilment.

According to Dunnigan, despite the fact that Kennedy's longer fiction 'is about the emotionally and politically disenfranchised and dispossessed, it also aims to discover the means of (re)enchantment' (Dunnigan 2000: 154), and indeed many of her novels are quest narratives geared towards some kind of resolution. By contrast, her shorter fiction largely consists of case studies in despair and isolation; minor epiphanies afford the characters some limited insight into their condition, but never sufficient to enable them to change or move beyond it. Yet even though the endings of some of Kennedy's novels suggest hope and 're-enchantment', they remain liminal in that they never do more than that – that is, to suggest recovery *might* be possible through emotional engagement with another human being.

The narrative mechanisms by which Kennedy's characters come to realise the value of breaking out of their psychic isolation are often as oblique as they are startling. Indeed, at times the circumstances designed to release protagonists from their recursive patterns of despair are tantamount to divine interventions. Kennedy has always been fond of religious symbolism – from Colin's crucifixion in *Looking for the Possible Dance* to the warped, semi-biblical 'Christopher Credo' that constitutes the spiritual foundation of the writers' commune on Foal Island in *Everything You Need*:

> We believe, like a number of lunatics before us, that if we have been in a place beyond reach of all but divine intervention seven times and if, seven times, we have been kicked back into this existence, then we become special. (Kennedy 1999a: 214)

The resurrection of Cyrano de Bergerac may of course be cited as yet another instance of a supernatural, if not actually religious or divine, intervention.

Without doubt Kennedy is aware of her own penchant for variously using a mixture of religious iconography and magical realism to provide the means by which her protagonists are transported from the quotidian into altogether more surprising territory. In the ludic short story 'Breaking Sugar' in *Original Bliss* a couple's marital problems are smoothed over by their lodger, Mr Haskard, 'a quiet household god', who occupies the rooms upstairs. His occupation as a 'systems analyst' allows him to 'search and correct the programs that ran for ever and nowhere within silicon labyrinths. He understood and tasted their atoms' electric shake, admonished the ignorance of their languages, loved and scolded like a father, noted each trace of disease' (Kennedy 1997a: 113). Add to this that Haskard visits historical sites of atrocity and bloodshed across the globe to 'speak to what people I can' (Kennedy 1997a: 119) and we come face to face with a figure of such preternatural goodness that he can only be god-like, if not actually a celestial being. That his influence also acts as a marital aid underpins Kennedy's playfulness, yet there is a more serious angle to Haskard's role as well. In Kennedy's postmodern world of fractured, relative values and redundant political movements, Haskard has the audacity to be a moralist who 'cannot live in an evil present with any comfort', who disapproves of 'mortgages and the blights of private ownership', and who removes the couple's material possessions to the garden, instructing them that 'all of these things, they are really no protection, not in the face of nature' (Kennedy 1997a: 119, 113, 114).

As a character in possession of a coherent intellectual position and in active engagement with the world that surrounds him, Haskard's benign socialism makes him a rare figure in Kennedy's fiction. The same applies to the figure of Savinien de Bergerac, who represents (Kennedy's contrived version of) the chivalric values of his time, which he must translate into a late twentieth-century context. Since he has arrived in our world from elsewhere, his grasp of life is neither fractured nor confused. As a result, he achieves with ease what, at least initially, entirely eludes Jennifer: he is able to identify himself and his position within the world with remarkable fluency. In stark contrast to Savinien's expertise at 'talking his world into existence', as a voiceover artist Jennifer has 'no say in what I say or even how I say it' (Kennedy 1995a: 68, 62). Only gradually does she learn from him how to tell her own story, how to narrate herself with confidence.

A similarly thorough process of ideological rehabilitation and self-reinvention occurs in Kennedy's novella 'Original Bliss', in which Margery Brindle has lost, not necessarily her faith in God, but her confidence in his omnipresence as 'a companion, a parent, a friend'; we are told that 'Mrs Brindle had never known an unanswered prayer' (Kennedy 1997a: 162). In God's absence Margery's spiritual vacuum is filled by Professor Edward E. Gluck, an American academic whose strong belief in himself propels a hyperbolic media self-promotion campaign. Creator of 'The New Cybernetics' (referred to throughout simply as 'The Process'), Gluck assures Margery that she is 'the miracle which makes itself' (Kennedy 1997a: 162). And yet, despite his endowment with a profound understanding of the condition displayed by many of Kennedy's characters, Gluck is shown as contending with his own set of deep-rooted problems, most notably an addiction to hardcore pornography. As Gluck and Margery become closer through mutual need, their relationship becomes a mini-'Process' in itself. It is only through 'purgatorial struggles to reclaim themselves' from their previous lives that they can move on together (March 2002: 145), finally becoming 'one completed motion under God the patient, Jealous Lover: the Jealous, Patient Love' (Kennedy 1997a: 311). Between Gluck's 'Process' and Margery's eccentric religiosity the couple invent a private morality empowering them to heal the harm inflicted on them in their previous lives. Ironically, whereas Gluck may have set out as a figure impersonating a deity, it is in fact his acceptance of his own mortal humanity that lays the foundation to his redemption.

It is no accident that this chapter has described the 're-enchantment' of Kennedy's characters in terms of rehabilitation, recovery and re-engagement, a lexicon more suggestive of addiction than mere alienation from cultural, social and historical narratives. It is certainly the case that the psychic condition of Kennedy's creations is more than 'bafflement' (Tew 2003: 127) or ontological angst. Ultimately it is their addiction to various kinds of self-abuse that defines Kennedy's characters; neurotic and obsessive, their solipsistic disposition requires dramatic interventions of the kind discussed above to break the recursive cycles that entrap them. Abusive behaviour has always been present in Kennedy's fiction and especially, if not exclusively, in her short stories; in particular, psychological abuse wreaked on children is a theme to which she returns time and again. From 'The Moving House' (Kennedy 1993: 35–42) via 'A Perfect Possession' (Kennedy 1995b: 1–11) to 'A Bad Son' (Kennedy 2002: 63–89) we are given glimpses of the ways in which the banal details of ordinary family relations can by slight degrees rearrange themselves into examples of monstrous cruelty. Negative parental influence also lies at the heart of Margaret's psychological problems in *Looking for the Possible Dance* as well as Jennifer's in *So I Am Glad*.

The control exerted over Margaret by Edward, her father, is so relentless it persists even after his death, preventing her from engaging in fruitful relations with other men. Her formative years caused her identity to become so inextricably entwined with his that as an adult she cannot exist independently: 'As Margaret grew, her character seemed to shrink . . . she had almost forgotten what she was like' (Kennedy 1993: 85). To compound matters further, her boyfriend Colin only wishes to supplant Edward's control with his own. He even visits the garden of remembrance where Edward's ashes were scattered, announcing: 'I'm taking away your daughter now and I hope that we're both very happy' (Kennedy 1993: 151). However, Colin's endeavour to take her over cannot ultimately oust Edward as the yardstick of perfection for the partner in life's dance that Margaret is looking for. Edward's legacy is not only his daughter's persistent rejection of other suitors but also her self-crippling addiction to grief.

In the case of Jennifer, it is sexual abuse – her parents forced her to watch them make love – that causes her to act unemotional and shut out other people. Rejecting intimacy, she indulges in sado-masochistic sex with occasional lover Stephen; disguised as 'Captain Bligh' she inflicts wounds on her 'Stupid Sailor' as she literally batters him into submission. Sexualised violence and self-harm also provide an emotional outlet for Nathan in *Everything You Need*. Rather than the spiritual experiences they are imagined to be by the island-cult's guru Joe Christopher, Nathan's repeated suicide attempts are evidently more to do with sexual pleasure, described in terms of 'that big, blank, hot-mouthing, hair-lifting, sexy, sexy fear . . . terror as his bit of rough' (Kennedy 1999a: 23). It is only in *Paradise* that Kennedy explores addiction in its more conventional form as substance abuse. Very much like Jennifer, though, Hannah's addiction serves to remove her from herself, suspending her quotidian limitations until perfect intoxication and amnesia set in. While Hannah talks of the label on a bottle of Bushmills whiskey in terms of 'a long, slim doorway to somewhere else' (Kennedy 2004: 17), Jennifer's handcuffs are 'the door you will open in order to go too far' (Kennedy 1995a: 91). In both cases addiction results in a curious dovetailing of self-abandonment and control; the sensory impairment of the addict tightens her experiential terrain to that of a profoundly personal response, creating comfort through the certainty of one's own emotional veracity. The confusions of public life can be allayed and managed through the self-administration of an addictive anguish that pre-empts her participation in ordinary human intercourse. The characters in Kennedy's short fiction who undertake 'thrill-rides' understand this principle very well, though they involve themselves in far milder forms of addiction. In 'Failing to Fall', for example, the main objective is little more than a transient sense of exhilaration, whereas in her novels Kennedy has long been interested in protagonists whose very sense of self is derived from traumatic experience that cannot be expunged and demands to play itself out recursively, impulsively and addictively.

To date, Hannah in *Paradise* remains the exception in Kennedy's immense cast of characters. There is no past trauma – no controlling, omnipotent father, no sexually deviant parents or devastating familial break-up – which would explain her addiction; in fact, *Paradise* suggests chemical dependency may not need a particular reason beyond the search for an elusive paradisiacal state of being. In addition, there exists no one in *Paradise* who might provide a good enough reason for Hannah to quit; quite the opposite is the case. Her lover Robert is also an alcoholic, and both of them at various stages in the novel sabotage each other's sporadic rehabilitative endeavours. *Paradise* is certainly Kennedy's least optimistic novel, ending in a hotel room similar to the one in which it began, the only crucial difference being the presence of Robert, signalling the continuation of a relationship, however mutually fulfilling or destructive. Throughout the novel Hannah and Robert's relationship follows no particular guiding principles apart from their desire and affection for each other, and in reaching the same state of intoxication, they communicate and achieve communion. Once again, religious themes and motifs become manifest as *Paradise* elevates the delirious stages of terminal addiction to a holy state of quasi-transcendent salvation. As Hannah explains, 'my condition does indeed mean that I'm ruined without drink and yet, equally, drink will save me from *all* of my ruinations: those it inspires and every single other trouble, large and small. It keeps me free' (Kennedy 2004: 33).

Each section of *Paradise* also loosely, playfully and often rather clumsily relates to one of the fourteen stations of the cross. The eleventh station, at which Jesus is crucified, is rendered in the form of Hannah's accidental treading on a discarded piece of fence panelling, feeling pain as 'the nail slides clear through the rubber sole of my baseball boot' (Kennedy 2004: 281). Kennedy's use of this kind of ordering principle first became manifest in *Everything You Need* with its reliance upon symbolism taken from the grail legend. *Everything You Need* is a novel preoccupied by writers' self-reflection on their craft, but it also betrays Kennedy's own growing dependence upon allusive metanarrative devices to emphasise the literariness of her novels.

In Kennedy's recent work the reader is much more forcefully led towards a range of possible symbolic and allegorical meanings. Her insistence on providing such strong metanarrative coordinates can often be intrusive, an overshadowing rather than a foreshadowing of her characters' actions and concerns. Where previously Kennedy's characters were presented in an airless struggle with their own dependency upon experiences harmful to their present lives, Kennedy now imposes upon their situations a further layer of semantic scaffolding which they cannot be allowed to access. Not only does the creation of narratives centred on representing the emotional integrity of her characters' experience – Kennedy's most prominent trademark – seem contrived as a result of such structuring, but her very insistence upon such heavy-handed authorial manipulation indicates a concern with the authority of the author rather than the honesty of the character.

Part IV
Topics

Chapter 31

Between Camps: Masculinity, Race and Nation in Post-devolution Scotland

Alice Ferrebe

Who stands for the nation? Antony Easthope, analysing a *Daily Mail* editorial during the Falklands War, notes how 'the nation is one and masculine and . . . if I am masculine I am at one with the nation' (Easthope 1990: 57). Nation, like the masculine ego and body, becomes cast as an impenetrable, fortified structure, alleging the integrity of its unity, yet requiring constant defence against the ever-massing ranks of Others. Establishing the idea of modern nation states as 'camps', Paul Gilroy asserts that 'the camp always operates under martial rules. Even if its ideologues speak the language of organic wholeness, it is stubbornly a place of seriality and mechanical solidarity' (Gilroy 2000: 82). This inextricable relationship between national identity and masculinity has been well theorised (see Schoene 2002), and the contemporary Scottish canon represents a productive case in point. The failing, flailing hard men in the fictions of Alasdair Gray, James Kelman and Irvine Welsh have been convincingly diagnosed as symptomatic of a pervasive sense of national loss following the unsuccessful referendum of 1979 (see Whyte 1998a). The mental and physical pathologies of these retrograde figures, loping through dilapidated urban landscapes, signal a specific kind of male-authored reaction to Scotland's perceived emasculation by a culturally and politically dominant England. However dispiriting the sight, it remained the case that only the Drunk (or Stoned) Man could look at the Thistle with any sense of ownership. As it has become impossible now to (de)construct masculine identity without an awareness of all the other variable cultural artefacts that constitute it, it is apparent that these proprietors are simultaneously sexually and racially homogeneous, that is, also Straight and White.

Since the 1997 referendum Scotland's national identity has been setting a particularly curious and diverse example of what, in *There Ain't No Black in the Union Jack* (1987), Gilroy describes as 'the weird post-colonial pageantries of national decline and national rebirth' (Gilroy 1992: xxiv). The country's multifaceted credentials of being at once post-colonial, post-industrial and postmodern entitle it to stake a claim to Catherine Hall's concept of the 'postnation', defined as 'a society that has discarded the notion of a homogeneous nation state with singular forms of belonging' (Hall 1996: 67). With their emphasis on fluidity and hybridity, Gilroy's and Hall's accounts of national identitification are already gendered feminine against masculine, colonial assertions of the nation as a self-contained bastion. To establish paradigmatic exemplars somewhat counters the spirit of the postcolonial project; however, its ongoing experiential display of the manifold cultural implications of devolution makes contemporary Scotland a productive place to debate national identity. According to Cairns Craig in *The Modern Scottish Novel*, the Scottish national imagination makes such an ideal case study because, contrary to traditional preconceptions, Scottish history constitutes not so much a failed, fractured narrative as a fecund liminal site of cultural interchange and heteroglossia, saturated by the dialogics and dialectics of the nation's coexisting languages and cultures (Craig 1999).

Several years previously, in *Out of History*, Craig drew upon Frantz Fanon's sense in *Black Skin, White Masks* (1952) of the split self of the black French intellectual, and the white mask he must don in educated circles. Craig said of the Scots:

> It is not by our colour, of course, that we have stood to be recognised as incomplete within the British context, it is by the colour of our vowels: the rigidity of class speech in Britain, the development of Received Pronunciation as a means of class identity, is the direct response of a dominant cultural group faced by a society in which the outsiders are indistinguishable by colour. (Craig 1996: 12)

The increasing prominence of black writers (Jackie Kay, Suhayl Saadi and Luke Sutherland, for example) within Scottish literature prompts consideration of the role of race within presiding constructions of Scottish identity, and of the existence of a colour line beyond pronunciation. Notions of a 'divided self' as in some way quintessential to the Scottish condition resonate alluringly with similar tropes in discourses of black self-assertion and liberation. Thus it is easy to align Gregory Smith's 1919 coinage of 'Caledonian antisyzygy' not only with Fanon's 'white masks', but also with W. E. B. Du Bois's 1903 diagnosis of 'double consciousness', in which 'one ever feels his two-ness' (Du Bois 1997: 38), or Homi Bhabha's theorising on the inevitable immanence of 'doubleness' in the act of imagining any modern community as a nation (Bhabha 1990: 293). The tensions inherent in the simultaneity of a politically and culturally feminised position for an otherwise hypermasculine symbol (the black man, the hard man) coincide in interesting ways, in particular regarding their antithetical failures to be in any way successfully representative. The figure signified by the phrase 'black man' is too vague to be useful, whereas 'hard man' is too specific. There, however, the shared experience ends, as any reference to anomalous ethnicity serves to disrupt the symbolism of the white Scottish male, both as oppressed Other and as representative of nation. The present chapter will examine the nature and effect of this disruption in constructions of national and masculine identity through a case study of Luke Sutherland's articulations of black male experience specific to Scotland in his novels *Jelly Roll* (1998) and *Venus as a Boy* (2004).

Jelly Roll focuses on the domophobic, homophobic community of a turbulent, all-male jazz band from Glasgow, the inaptly named 'Sunny Sunday Sextet', and their tour of the Highlands. Malc, archetypical hard man, and saxophonist, is prevented by his wife from accompanying the band on their journey north: 'Ah bet it wis that bitch thit made him gie it up', guesses the pianist Mouse, correctly (Sutherland 1998: 19). Malc is replaced by Liam, who is young, immensely gifted musically, and Irish. Drummer Paddy also nervously informs the narrator Roddy that Liam is 'black. Black y'know':

> – So?
> – Well ah jist thought ye might wantae know y'know. It might make a difference.
> – What do you mean, a difference?
> – Ah mean different people think different ways, y'know whit ah mean?
> – Aye well I'm not different people. (Sutherland 1998: 32)

For all his repudiation of difference, Roddy's subsequent narration is engaged in a worrying at exactly what difference the fact that Liam is 'black' – that 'powerfully empty and possibly anachronistic master-signifier' (Gilroy 1992: xxiv) – does make. This anxiety over the ideal epistemological weight for 'difference' might be considered syndromic within postcolonial, postmodern identity construction. Joan Scott has noted similar confusion within gender definitions: ' "Man" and "woman" are at once empty and overflowing categories. Empty because they have no ultimate, transcendent meaning. Overflowing because even when they appear to be fixed, they still contain within them alternative, denied, or suppressed definitions' (Scott 1986: 1074). It is unclear whether the postmodern political operator should strive to diminish the exaggerated dimensions of the markers and systems of difference like race, gender and nation, or uphold their potential to generate multiple solidarities.

Roddy explicitly links his exploration of Liam's relationship with prevailing Irish national identities to the Scottish case by means of a shared imaginative dependence upon the experience of subjugation. Passing the drunken customers spilling onto the street from 'another of Scotland's most authentic Irish bars', Roddy riffs angrily on:

> Another Celtic bloodbath. The historical and genetic link across the North Channel fanning the myth of psychic community between the Scots and the Irish; brothers in arms, united not only by common blood, but by oppression at the hands of the English . . . It began here, as every weekend: the celebration of sameness, safety in numbers, better the devil you know and all the other garbage. No room for Liam in this spiritual patrimony, even though he's Irish; and you find yourself stooping to the crash idiom of lineage: ancestral homogeny, perpetual rebellion against bondage, the Pan-national struggle of noble races, Scotland the brave, etcetera etcetera. (Sutherland 1998: 119–20)

Roddy is Roddy Burns, his name hinting at the contemporary failure of both the phallic ('rod') and the culturally totemic (Robert Burns). Symptomatically, Malc introduces him as 'no the poet, jist the tosser' (Sutherland 1998: 68). The novel deals Scottish nationalism yet another iconoclastic blow when Mouse derides Bonnie Prince Charlie as a transvestite, a 'poof' and a Frenchman, clearly deemed to be mutually inextricable epithets (Sutherland 1998: 316–17).

There is only one means in the novel for the men to authenticate themselves, and that is jazz, or rather Liam's inspirational saxophone-playing and the performances he inspires and enables in the rest of the band. The notion that Liam's colour should make him 'naturally' gifted is repeatedly mocked in the novel, initially through its expression by the hysterically violent Malc, who on hearing of his competition on the saxophone, responds 'Cunt'll be fuckin good like. Ah'm gonny hiv tae get a wee bit practice in so he doesni show me up' (Sutherland 1998: 266). Rather than a quintessentially black artform, in Sutherland's vision jazz becomes an empowering means of expression for an amorphous proletarian group. Though tacitly organised to allow Liam his place as 'most oppressed' within its hierarchy, the group's underdog credentials are generated by difference from another jazz band they meet in Fort William: Bob McBride's Garden Party. Suspecting the Sunny Sundays of stealing their equipment, Bob pleads: 'Come on guys, eh, a joke's a joke. We're in this for the fun too but ye can go too far. We're just simple guys y'know, bankers and accountants and consultants, you know, just your average man on the street. We live in Stirling' (Sutherland 1998: 226). Bob's middle-class misrepresentation of the 'average man' results from a life experience limited to the gentrified centre of Central Scotland. His band's authenticity is eroded further by the fact that they play only cover versions, which the Sundays reject in favour of ever-evolving improvisations on their own musical creations. However, despite the sense of authenticity that can be derived from playing jazz, Roddy Burns's identity is far from unequivocal or secure. As Mouse tells him, 'you've jist got a chip on yir shoulder cos ye never got intae university', adding as a complaint that Roddy has 'still got this fuckin Mother Superior air about him' (Sutherland 1998: 26). That familiar literary in-between figure, a working-class intellectual, Roddy's uncomfortable duality becomes most apparent in his narrative voice, which moves erratically between dialect and didacticism, the latter (his 'Mother Superior' voice) emulating precisely the kind of anglicised and emotionally detached third-person narration dismissed by Kelman and other literary spokesmen of the Scottish working classes as remote-controlled and inauthentic.

At a festival in Gairloch, Liam and Roddy are handed a leaflet asking 'ARE YOU A *TRUE* SCOT', in response to which Roddy begins to wonder 'if the properties of the properly indigenous are biologically determinable' (Sutherland 1998: 383). Roddy's question follows a heated debate with the band's aristocratic hosts in Crieff about whether 'cats born in kipper boxes are kippers' or, put differently, if 'nationality is defined by the country of your birth and not by your parent's race' (Sutherland 1998: 201). Whether the disruption of the homily (actually 'If her cat has her kittens in a kipper box, it doesn't make them kippers') signifies progression from a chauvinistic colonial nationalism to a postcolonial model of nationality that accounts for a range of affinities (parental, natal, residential, intellectual) remains unclear. Roddy, however, is certain of his own case: 'I'm doomed. A kipper born in a kipper box, traceable to the first kings of Argyll. Fucked in other words' (Sutherland 1998: 322). *Völkisch* and literary discourses conspire to make him a self divided, Janus-faced, riddled with gender and nationalist anxieties, duped in his own narrative by the authoritarian, anglicised discourses in which he articulates his intelligence.

The idea of 'voice' as an emancipatory potentiality, a concept central to Kay's jazz novel *Trumpet* (1998), is rejected here in a diegesis within which language functions predominantly as an instrument of manipulation. Thus, hard man Malc offers his victims the choice of identifying themselves either as a 'poof' or 'cocky cunt', with either leading to violent retribution (Sutherland 1998: 72–4). Roddy's split narration speaks of his confusions and guilt. As he eventually reveals, he has betrayed Liam, abandoning him to the mercy of Malc in an encounter which results in Liam's 'branding', with the word 'nigger' cut into his stomach with a bowie knife (Sutherland 1998: 358). The fact that knowledge of this incident is withheld in the novel until a much later flashback not only seals Roddy's betrayal of the reader's trust, but also corrupts his relationship with the author. Liam's identification with Sutherland is promoted by cover photographs and a blurb that foregrounds the latter's musicianship, as well as the revelation that Liam has been to 'the Hope, aye', that is, St Margaret's Hope, South Ronaldsay, Orkney, where Sutherland was raised.

Sutherland privileges Roddy by endowing him with an acute understanding of the performative nature of gender, as he makes him don the guises of numerous stereotypical masculine figures: the hard man, the desperate lover, the sensitive liberal-thinker. Moreover, through his continual interrogation of responses to Liam's blackness, Sutherland makes Roddy alive to the ambivalence of national belonging. Craig has identified the liberational potential of Caledonian anti-sygzygy, claiming that 'too often in studies of Scottish culture the apparent lack of unity of the self is taken to be the symptom of a failed identity, of a self-contradictory and self-destructive identity'. Instead, he urges recognition 'that the healthy self is always a dialectic operating within and between "opposing" elements of self and other'

(Craig 1999: 113). The dualities of Roddy's self and narrative might indeed come to instil in him an emancipatory awareness of the inherent, ironic contradictions of any attempt to construct a 'whole' identity, be it founded upon gender, nationality or class. Yet for all his attempts to minimise discrimination in upholding Liam as 'just your average man on the street' (Sutherland 1998: 226), it is precisely Liam's difference that attracts him.

In her famous analysis of Hollywood cinema Laura Mulvey identifies two possible responses to the threat of (feminine) alterity, as she distinguishes between a voyeuristic gaze – which seeks to know, explain and so control its object – and a fetishistic gaze which, captivated by the symbolic, remains reluctant to see beyond it. While he voices frustration at Liam's refusal to speak up against daily racist abuse, Roddy himself fetishises the organic mystery of Liam's blackness, perhaps best exemplified by his raptures over the ineffable genius of Liam's musicianship. Roddy's fetishistic desire might to some extent be directed towards what Gilroy identifies as 'the postmodern translation of blackness from a badge of insult into an increasingly powerful but still very limited signifier of prestige' (Gilroy 2000: 23); however, it is also complicated by sexual desire.

Roddy's first meeting with Liam gently mocks the fetishisation of blackness by dusting the black signifier with flour (Liam is baking): 'He offered a hand through the open hatch and smiled. I stepped towards his fingers mostly white with flour and took hold. He was warm like the room and his thumb brushed the ridges of my knuckles.' Glimpsing Liam earlier from the bottom of the close, Roddy confesses that 'even then, with him more like silhouette, I could tell he was beautiful' (Sutherland 1998: 44, 47). In their introduction to *Nationalisms and Sexualities* Andrew Parker and his co-authors note how the nation, 'typically represented as a passionate brotherhood . . . finds itself compelled to distinguish its "proper" homosociality from more explicitly sexualized male–male relations, a compulsion that requires the identification, isolation, and containment of male homosexuality' (Parker et al. 1992: 6). A similarly ruthless distinction, of course, is necessary within traditional all-male communities and, in the case of the Sundays, is enforced via a condemnatory rhetoric centered on accusations of being a 'poof'. Roddy's homosexuality – or rather, his bisexuality (he maintains an ongoing, if destructive relationship with Gemma, and his dream fantasies extend to include Liam's partner Christine) – remains limited to a flirtation with its own potential to effect escape from restrictive masculinist binaries. Ultimately his desire for Liam serves only to eroticise his intellectual project of fetishising him, whereas his bisexuality is devised to re-inscribe the split nature of his identity.

The desire for, and impossibility of locating, an organic self is rehearsed in the Sundays' rambling circumnavigation of the north. Rather than accomplishing the picaresque narrative assemblage of varied locations into a conceptually whole nation, the story of the tour is one of division, backtracking and disorientation, beginning with an aggressive debate over Duckie's nomination of the location of their first gig, Blairgowrie, as 'Gateway to the Highlands'. Duckie eventually lessens his claim to 'the last significant town before the Highlands begin', but even this his bandmates will not allow: 'What about Pitlochry?' (Sutherland 1998: 56–7). Their apparent fierce confusion over where the Highlands begin is compounded by rivalrous paradoxical interpretations among the band members of what these debatable lands represent. In contrast to the Central Belt, the Highlands are envisaged as providing a wild, restorative authenticity while also assuring the men of a guaranteed nationwide level of civilisation: 'This is Scotland, for Christsake', says bassist Fraser after their Inverness gig is disrupted by chants of 'you black bastard', 'not some wee town in the backwoods of Alabama' (Sutherland 1998: 248). As if to prove Fraser wrong, a hippy clan, outraged at Liam's abuse, wreak bizarre retribution on its perpetrators by stripping and shaving them, blacking them up and suspending them from streetlights (Sutherland 1998: 258).

There is more bewilderment when Mouse is horrified to discover the small town of Tongue on the north coast of Scotland, interpreting its name as evidence of rural savagery and homosexual practices:

> Tongue, in fuckin Scotland man, it's sick. Ah havni heard ay half these wee fuckin backwater shitholes an ah dread tae think whit goes on in them. Wir gonny get fuckin lynched man, by some inbred bald cunt wi nay fuckin teeth. Strung up by the balls ya bastart. Wir fucked. Seen that *Deliverance* wi Burt Reynolds man? That's us: fucked in the arse. (Sutherland 1998: 59)

The oft-invoked assurance of national homogeneity is equally at once confirmed and condemned by Roddy in his description of Glasgow as 'a slum, neck and neck with its token façade of architecture, incapable of glittering even with the weather like this; the breadth of the city lying not in its character, but in its characters: nutters like Malc, hysterical peasant hordes and xenophobic hypocrites' (Sutherland 1998: 73). The novel forgoes the possibility of difference within national identity, as both rural and urban communities harbour a native savagery that extends beyond the wilderness of the north or the ideology of the racist.

In *The Eclipse of Scottish Culture*, Craig Beveridge and Ronald Turnbull map the Scotland/England divide onto a series of other culturally influential binary oppositions, all of which, as Neil McMillan points out, are implicitly gendered: violent/decent, uncouth/refined, savage/mild, severe/kind, harsh/gentle and so forth (McMillan 2003: 70). Roddy's negotiation of Scottish masculinity seems initially free from such an inflexible grid of negative comparisons: 'Ingland' is mentioned only once, as a place the band can 'invade' once they have a more established reputation (Sutherland 1998: 27). Instead, Sutherland – born in England and raised in Orkney by adoptive Lowland parents with a Highland surname – plays a subtle game of onomastics with his characters' names. Like Fraser and Malcolm, Roddy, ripe from the kipper box, has a Scottish name. Mouse's assertion that he 'ran wi the fuckin Tongs' (Sutherland 1998: 26) might be diagnosed as overcompensation not for his diminutive nickname, but for his real name – Graham Lumsden – which is thoroughly English. (Significantly, when trying to seduce a singer in Dunkeld, he chooses the pseudonym 'Scott'.) Liam's real names are Lyall William Bell, their Scottish, Teutonic and English origins further complicating his Irishness and blackness to rehearse the impossibility of any one coherent national identity. As in Kay's *Trumpet*, in *Jelly Roll* names demonstrate the difficulty of escaping a language that brands you. Variously referred to as 'Leroy', 'Adamski', 'Linda' and 'Winston Bananas', Liam faces a barrage of derogatory nicknames, but it is 'nigger' – permanently carved in the skin of his belly and thus belying the postmodern playfulness of African-American culture's rehabilitation of the word – which denies him Scotland as a place of belonging.

Gilroy has argued for the political and postmodern potential of adopting a position between the martial camps of the modern nation-state. Such a move, he claims, can:

> be a positive orientation against the patterns of authority, government, and conflict that characterize modernity's geometry of power. It can also promote a rich theoretical understanding of culture as a mutable and travelling phenomenon. Of course, occupying a space between camps means also that there is danger of encountering hostility from both sides, of being caught in the pincers of camp-thinking. (Gilroy 2000: 84)

Sutherland's most recent novel, *Venus as a Boy*, seeks to evade these pincers through actively exploiting the subversive potential of camp – as a performative rather than a contested style of belonging – by celebrating it, in Susan Sontag's words, as 'the most refined form of sexual attractiveness (as well as the most refined form of sexual pleasure) [which] consists in going against the grain of one's sex. What is most beautiful in virile men is something feminine; what is most beautiful in feminine women is something masculine' (Sontag 1967: 279). As Désirée, Sutherland's hero/ine, says of his sexual orientation, 'I hadn't any', and the fluidity of his gender identity is matched by the ecstatic fulfilment he can produce in others: 'My thing's being able to make folk melt. Guys and girls spilling between my fingers like ice-cream' (Sutherland 2004: 90, 50).

Like his author, Désirée lives in London but is originally from Orkney. As a child, his campness makes him an outsider until the arrival of a white family with a young black son, who soon takes Désirée's place as prime target of the village children's abuse, with the television series based on Alex Haley's *Roots* (1976) providing the bitterly ironic verbal ammunition: '*nigger this, guinea man that*' (Sutherland 2004: 31). Looking back, Désirée attempts to supplant the idea of geographical 'roots' by replacing it with an emotional mapping of the place of his birth: 'I don't so much remember what the places look like as how I felt when I visited them. A map of Orkney's a map of my emotions, pretty much. A map of me' (Sutherland 2004: 52). As a result of this spatialisation, identity becomes a dynamic process rather than an ossified essence. However, despite such a progressive, postmodern recasting of gender and geographic identities, Désirée's narrative continues to hinge upon essential (and essentialist) truths.

While men may provide Désirée with sexual satisfaction, it is his relationships with women that are held up as enduringly redemptive: 'I was never going to find true love with a guy. With them it was all belly and head, no heart, just this sudden thunder from flat calm that had no afterglow' (Sutherland 2004: 93). Drag has been a comforting erotic experience for him since childhood, but the liberation it provides depends on the underlying certainty of being male. Accordingly, the hormone pills he is force-fed by his pimp have made Désirée desperately ill, both physically and mentally, his 'insides collapsing, stomach cramps, vomiting, aching bones, my belly going all soft . . . so long to hard-ons. I felt permanently seasick. The last straw was my first tit: suddenly this handful where there'd only been a pec. I became this man with an unwanted woman's body. And . . . I didn't want to be with myself' (Sutherland 2004: 6). What prevents Désirée from finding self-fulfilment and reconciling himself to his gender identity, so evidently established 'between camps', is not only his own history but also other men's. Himself a victim of abuse by his father, Désirée blames his lovers' emotionally debilitated, pathological masculinities on their dysfunctional relationships with their fathers. Thus, he says of Radu – ex-con, Nazi and pimp: 'More than once, I've wondered where I'd be if only his dad had loved him', and the revelation of Pascal the skinhead's paternal abandonment prompts him 'to wonder if the whole world is peopled with fatherless fuck-ups' (Sutherland 2004: 87, 132).

In *Venus as a Boy* Sutherland abandons Roddy Burns's schizophrenic register, opting instead for the confessional mode of (fictional) autobiography. Since Désirée has nothing but scorn for 'most of [his] so-called mates [who] were just shitty little two-faced bastards' (Sutherland 2004: 17), the reader is left in no doubt about the truthfulness of Désirée's subsequent confession of his own childhood duplicity, and yet it is presented to us as a posthumous 'found narrative', proffered on mini-disc to 'L. S.' who, as the black boy who took over from Désirée the role of schoolyard scapegoat, is being asked for forgiveness. This strategic insertion of L. S. as editor and recipient appropriates the merger of Liam and his author in *Jelly Roll*, thus placing Sutherland in a limbo of authority. According to the novel, the boy's appearance on the island adjusts the hierarchy of oppression, with 'poofs' ranking higher than black people, to allow the young Désirée a position of limited acceptance: 'I can't deny I was giddy at the thought of becoming one of the gang – something the arrival of the black boy and his family gave me space to do' (Sutherland 2004: 34–5). L. S. introduces the novel as being part of 'a memorial of sorts' (Sutherland 2004: 3), but his response to Désirée's request for forgiveness is withheld.

Possibly, Sutherland's reluctance so far to introduce an 'unmediated' authoritative black voice into his fiction might be seen as a cautious strategy to prevent possible (mis-)readings of his work as in any way representative of the vast diversity of black Scottish experience. It is also possible to interpret the confession as functioning as a parody of white guilt and overcompensation, already rehearsed in Désirée's drug-fuelled, tokenistic attempt at absolution from a black neighbour: 'I shared my jellies with Jason and told him all about South Ronaldsay and the family with the black kids, what was done, what was said and how no one deserved any of it . . . He said, as a black person, he forgave me on behalf of the kids in the Spence shop' (Sutherland 2004: 117). Désirée's oppression by his island's youths on the grounds of his gender fails to prevent his own victimisation of the young L. S. The racial mores of his roots ensure that, long after his escape to a cosmopolitan metropolis, the blindness of his sexual orientation does not extend to colour: asked if he has 'been with black people', he replies 'Yes, loads, even though I'd never touched one' (Sutherland 2004: 109). Despite its plea for forgiveness, Désirée's narrative ultimately denies the possibility of empathising with the experience of another person, instead formulating the racial and sexual outrages it catalogues as essentially formative of individual identity and intensely private.

The divided male selves in Sutherland's novels demonstrate how ultimately impossible it is to maintain the heavily freighted differences inscribed by binary constructions of identity, be these of nation, race, gender or sexual orientation. Berthold Schoene has posited that 'the question to be asked now is whether contemporary Scottish masculinity could possibly be described as a devolutionary kind of masculinity that has embraced its feminine marginality and is saying "no" to power' (Schoene 2002: 95). More complicatedly, while agreeing on the need for an effective devolution of male power, Sutherland's anti-heroes also appear to mourn the vitality of the formerly indisputable certainties of nation, race and masculinity. Thus, they enact the antisyzygy inherent in the concept of devolution itself, as well as in postmodern politics more widely. 'Devolution', after all, designates not only the emancipatory progress of democratic diversification, but also disintegration, delegation and degeneration. Power remains covetable, and rather than refusing it, devolution celebrates the distribution of power to the previously marginalised. At the same time as we emulate Sutherland's characters and aspire to a culture camped between the masculinist divisions of gender, race and nation, we remain susceptible to visions of unity, ready to be captivated at any moment by what Gilroy has called 'the fantastic idea of transmuting heterogeneity into homogeneity' (Gilroy 2000: 82).

Chapter 32

Crossing the Borderline: Post-devolution Scottish Lesbian and Gay Writing

Joanne Winning

The new Scottish Parliament building in Holyrood is 'a stunning piece of architecture but it's not just bricks and mortar: there's a philosophy to it. It's been designed with the idea of openness in mind . . . [it] is the perfect place to be creative', MSP Rosie Kane writes (Kane 2005: 12). If architecture is indeed an articulation of cultural and physical space, then we might well ask just what kind of space is twenty-first-century Scotland. And what space might be allowed within the much longed-for, much-imagined new Scottish identity for previously troubled markers of difference such as ethnicity or sexuality? Might a more independent Scottish identity effectively erase difference rather than allow expression of it? As Christopher Whyte queried in 1995, 'if we want to bring back a Scotland that once was, what place will there be in it for blacks or lesbians or the children of Pakistani immigrants' (Whyte 1995b: xii)? Considering the limited space that women's writing has traditionally been accorded within the canon of Scottish literature, Ali Smith reflects that 'people are particularly keen to categorize themselves as different . . . from English . . . To be Scottish is to be separate; that's why . . . Scottish women's writing has only really been given a place . . . in the last ten years' (Gonda 1995: 5). In Smith's view, a national identity constructed, and asserting itself, in opposition to another national identity leaves little or no space for the articulation of sexual difference or, for that matter, sexual identity. Thus, looking at the bulk of Scottish literature and its paucity of representations of lesbian and gay identities, Whyte wonders if being Scottish and being gay might not be two 'mutually exclusive conditions' (Whyte 1995b: xiv).

The aim of the present chapter is not to provide a survey of post-devolution Scottish lesbian and gay writing but rather to ask which new possibilities for individual and communal identification have emerged since Scottishness itself has begun to undergo a process of redefinition. In 1989 and 1992 Polygon Press published two anthologies of lesbian and gay writing from Scotland – *And Thus Will I Freely Sing* (1989) and *The Crazy Jig* (1992) – both of which incorporated work by established and new authors and, perhaps most importantly, established that there was indeed a space where Scottishness and same-sex desire might intersect. In his editor's preface to *And Thus Will I Freely Sing*, Toni Davidson suggests that the need for a Scottish-based collection is 'obvious' since lesbian and gay authors who, in the past, would out of necessity have sent their manuscripts to London always had anxiously to restrain themselves from being not only 'too gay' but also 'too Scottish' (Davidson 1989: 9). Similar to Whyte's, Davidson's view is that gayness and Scottishness function as abject identities which compromise a writer's possibility of being either published or heard. Hence it was with a momentous sense of some larger force being at work in the growing audibility of Scottish gay and lesbian voices that, following Davidson's project, which could 'only be a start' (Davidson 1989: 9), I came to edit *The Crazy Jig* in 1992. In my preface I protested, somewhat youthfully, that 'it is simply not enough that there are only two anthologies of our writing in Scotland, because we have a great deal more to say which will benefit both ourselves and the straight community' (Winning 1992: 1). These two anthologies – produced in Thatcherite Britain, at the height of identity politics, and in a Scottish political landscape in which devolution seemed a distant hope – are irrevocably marked by the effort of defining and concretising a notion of Scottish lesbian and gay identities, and therefore many of the writings they contain focus on issues of self-determination, self-declaration, and the psychic effects of being hidden from national life.

In the years following the publication of the two volumes, the limitations and complexities of identity politics became apparent, while at the same time the boundaries of both national and sexual identities grew more porous. According to Caroline Gonda, 'like so many other terms of identity these days, both "Scottish" and "lesbian" have increasingly become contested territory, "debateable ground" ' (Gonda 1995: 1). In 2001 the independent Scottish publisher Mainstream published *Borderline*, a collection of Scottish gay writing edited by Joseph Mills. The post-devolution remit of this volume was entirely different to that of the Polygon anthologies, bringing together pieces from unknown authors and extracted pieces from the works of established writers, such as Irvine Welsh's *Marabou Stork Nightmares* (1995), Alexander Trocchi's *Cain's Book* (1961) and Bill Douglas's film-script of *My Way Home* (1978). Perhaps its main difference, however, was that it brought together work by both gay and non-gay authors. Davidson's introduction to Mills's collection, and the shift in his tone and thinking since 1989, suggest profound changes in how Scottish lesbian and gay writing had come to be conceived; most significantly, the definition of gay writing had been expanded to include gay-themed materials from texts which were not gay-authored, let alone exclusively gay:

> Here we have some wonderful writing by a wide range of writers, extracted and commissioned to create a determinedly broad picture of Scottish writing. There are gay characters, perspectives, themes and – or maybe that should be 'but' – there is a whole lot more. *Borderline* celebrates the diverse and unniched exploration of all things gay. I have no idea what these writers do in bed but knowing writers I am sure it's better not to ask. (Davidson 2001: 10)

By challenging their readers' understanding of what Scottish lesbian and gay writing might be or include, Davidson and Mills prompt important questions about the possibility and effect of crossing preconceived borderlines of categorical definition. Whereas with regard to Scottish identity political devolution would seem to introduce newly reinforced boundaries, in relation to sexual identity such boundaries matter only in so far as they constitute liminal spaces demanding to be crossed. Perhaps this contradiction is inevitable since it is clear that a strongly nationalist agenda might actually work against the articulation of a gender-specific voice marked by sexual difference, be it gay, lesbian or simply female. Thus Marilyn Reizbaum writes that 'women have found themselves in a peculiar predicament, compelled to resist or challenge the demands of the nationalist imperative in order to clarify the terms of their own oppression, and consequently disregarded on the basis that their concerns do not embrace the *more* significant issues of national self-determination' (Reizbaum 1992: 172). To what extent, then, might post-devolution lesbian and gay writing problematise the traditional structures and paradigms of Scottish culture by attempting to produce newly devolved imaginative spaces in which social and sexual practice, as well as the nature of emotional and sexual bonds, can be productively renegotiated and reconfigured?

In October 2005 Duncan Maclean, an independent West Lothian councillor, launched a motion against the council's decision to allow same-sex couples to hold a ceremony over and above the statutory registration process introduced under the Civil Partnership Act of 2004. In the *Evening News* Maclean was quoted as saying:

> It's political correctness gone mad. As the Bible teaches, 'wrong-doers will not inherit the Kingdom of God', and this includes lesbians and gays. If these people want to enter into a formal commitment, why don't they go to a lawyer and get them to sign a formal legal document? Why do these queers have to parade about in public? (Varney 2005)

Maclean's horrified vision of 'parading' married queers on West Lothian streets implies that the public declaration of homosexual love and union, and indeed public approval of a ceremony to celebrate this union, pose a threat to the very fabric of Scottish society. And Scotland is by no means an isolated case. After introducing same-sex civil partnerships many European countries witnessed the rise of cultural anxieties about same-sex unions and the threat to nationhood allegedly inherent in them, demonstrating that the sanctity of heterosexual marriage is inextricably tied to the solidity of nationhood. As Judith Butler notes, 'the debates on gay marriage and gay kinship, two issues that are often conflated, have become sites of intense displacements for other political fears, fears about technology, about new demographics, and also about the very unity and transmissibility of the nation' (Butler 2004: 110). Moreover, such fears eventually always coalesce around the question of lesbian and gay reproduction, or adoption, and the creation of 'alternative' lesbian and gay families. Looking to France, and the public display of resistance to civil partnerships there, Butler observes:

> One can see a conversion [*sic*] between the arguments in France that rail against the threat to 'culture' posed by the prospect of legally allied gay people having children . . . and those arguments concerning issues of immigration, of what Europe is. This last concern raises the question, implicitly and explicitly, of what is truly French, the basis of its culture, which becomes, through an imperial logic, the basis of culture itself, its universal and invariable conditions. The debates center not only on the questions of what culture is and who should be admitted but also on how the subjects of culture should be reproduced. (Butler 2004: 110)

If devolution is a process by which the boundaries of national identity are dismantled and reconfigured, might it also possibly effect or enable the recasting of other identities and their hierarchised relations? Put differently, to what extent might devolution work as an antidote to homophobia and clear the way to imagining not only the public sanction of lesbian and gay partnerships, but also lesbian and gay reproduction and childrearing? Or, in other words, how likely is it that Scotland's devolution might in fact initiate a radical reconceptualisation of how its citizens might be 'reproduced' or choose to 'reproduce' themselves?

John Maley's *Delilah's: Stories from the Closet till Closing Time* (2002), a novel which doubles as a collection of short stories, records the lives and loves of a range of characters as they gravitate around the gay bar of the title. Despite its camp subtitle and narrative voice, lurid cover and apparent lightweight treatment of its content, *Delilah's* is a text which deploys some sophisticated symbolism in its examination of contemporary Scottish lesbian and gay subculture. The text opens by describing a Glasgow 'full of invisible lovers' whose lives are marked by the abjections of subterfuge and covert love. Invisibility creates a kind of 'madness' from which temporary refuge is sought in the subcultural space of the bar run by the drag queen Joanie, 'a glorious Madonna watching over her children' (Maley 2002: 209). From the outset the text constructs the ties of queer kinship through traditionally heterosexual terms of union and reproduction. In addition to Joanie's maternal role, two of the key characters are Papa, a middle-aged gay estate agent whose real name is Spenser, and Mama, his 50-year-old heterosexual female friend, who is by day an eminent Glasgow neurosurgeon. The text utilises the site of the bar as a centre from which multiple peripheral stories might be told; moreover it functions as a site in which cultural norms are redrawn. According to Elizabeth Grosz, an examination of queer use and production of space teaches us that 'space, or spaces, is the product of a community, as much as it is the product of a designer' (Grosz 2001: 8). Grosz goes on to argue that the queer sense of spatiality is heightened precisely because clubs, bars, cafés and shops invite a more 'explicitly sexualized and eroticized use of space' (Grosz 2001: 9). Lesbians and gay men, in other words, truly understand the importance of material space and its extension as cultural space. This would certainly seem to be borne out in Maley's text, in which the physical space of the gay bar allows an opening up of new cultural space and practice. If the text has a trajectory, it is that Glasgow's invisible lovers, as Maley explains, 'don't want to be invisible anymore', and indeed textual closure is accomplished by the act of a lesbian marriage, albeit one performed without either state or church sanction.

Joanie's close friend Bobbie, a lesbian whose various unsuccessful relationships the text records, finally meets the love of her life, and her heart is set 'on marrying in Delilah's on a Sunday in June'. Joanie resists the idea of the wedding, both because it is something forbidden – 'We're queer. We're not allowed tae get married' – and because it is 'drawn up like an architect's plan – and with as much passion'. His resistance is finally overcome with Mama's observation that 'some people are passionate about architecture . . . Anyway, I hope those girls will be able to build something beautiful together.' The metaphors of architecture and building carry important conceptual weight at this historical point in Scottish culture. Indeed, Bobby and Rae's socially transgressive enactment of union suggests the building of a new social order. The spectacle of the wedding, presided over by a 'tiny dyke with the loudest voice in the world' (Maley 2002: 199–201), gives Maley licence to imagine a truly queer ceremony in which everyone present, irrespective of sexuality, is united:

> Joanie looked around at the gathering. Papa was there, immaculate in a charcoal suit. Mama was wearing a preposterous hat and seemed to have glued a camera to her right eye. Bobbie's brother and sister were there. Her brother, Lewis, was nearly as handsome as Bobbie. The sister, Fiona, had the biggest hair Joanie had seen since the halcyon days of *Dynasty*. She looked genuinely moved by her sister's wedded bliss. Joanie recognised some of Bobbie's friends, old and new, bunched together. Near the couple, on Rae's side, were a group of ferociously plain people who were apparently her family. Or possibly FBI, mused Joanie. The tiny dyke's voice reached a crescendo and then stopped. Bobbie and Rae turned to each other and tenderly kissed. The place erupted with cheers and applause. (Maley 2002: 202)

The wedding with which *Delilah's* concludes profoundly changes the lives of Glasgow's 'invisible lovers'; displaced and abjected at the beginning of the text, by the end they have found their way into states of communal connection and are 'suddenly warm and alive in each other's arms' (Maley 2002: 209). *Delilah's* attests to the importance of subcultural spaces within Scottish urban culture in which lesbians and gays must make their unions and live out their desires.

Queer union and reproduction are two themes also taken into new, transgressive territory by Jackie Kay's short stories in *Why Don't You Stop Talking* (2002). In 'Married Women' the central character, Kim, is a lesbian sexually aroused only by heterosexual women trapped in disappointing marriages. For Kim the frisson is the seduction of these women and the simultaneous destruction of their vows of fidelity and the 'farce' of marriage. Kim's denigration of marriage would seem to be a faithful articulation of a common lesbian and gay critique: 'Marriage and its secrets and its hypocrisy and its failure, its failure to stay fresh, to keep the passion burning, to keep the heart beating, the shyness, the surprise. Marriage was one big con for people not brave enough to love at the deep end, or the hot end, or the sharp end' (Kay 2002b: 207). Married women, for Kim, possess a feminine sensibility which 'lesbians' lack – a femininity inextricably linked to their married state: 'I liked the way my married mistresses dressed. I liked the way they smelled. I liked their wedded bosoms. I liked their soft cared-for skin. Their clean hair. I liked the ring on their finger and their nice nails.' By contrast, lesbians are 'rough and ready and predictable', their dressing habits resembling a kind of uniform: 'same kind of short haircut, same trousers and jackets with pockets, same loose baggy T-shirts, or big checked shirts, same, same, same. They had a look about them that was so easy to identify if you were in the know' (Kay 2002b: 201–2). Such coding of corporeal and sartorial styles which identifies lesbians to one another leaves Kim cold: 'I didn't like that. I couldn't help myself. I didn't fancy dykes. There wasn't enough tension in it for me' (Kay 2002b: 202). Thus Kim moves compulsively from affair to affair, seducing married women but always ultimately losing out to the husbands to whom these women invariably return.

The denouement of the story comes when one of Kim's lovers – the head of the English Department at Stirling, no less – repudiates her marriage and expresses the desire to become Kim's 'wife', a suggestion that entrances Kim: 'I felt myself melt, I let myself go. It was the most shocking moment of my entire life. I knew right there and then that I wanted Isabel to be my wife' (Kay 2002b: 208). The repudiation of marriage which structures Kim's narrative is shown to have been masking another emotional reality all along. Kim's greatest desire, it transpires, is in fact to become a husband. The irony of Kim's narrative voice gives way to the discourse of marriage as well as an immediate appropriation of its terms:

> We practise our vows together. We say them to each other in the dark at night. In sickness and in health. Kiss. For richer or poorer. Kiss. Better or worse . . . Now that I'm with Isabel, I think that ceremonies are important. Extremely important. I want the bit of paper too. The minute the law changes, I will be down there, at the church or the registry office saying *I do* and looking straight into my Isabel's beautiful eyes. (Kay 2002b: 210)

While Kay implies that the lesbian rejection of marriage may actually be underpinned by a deep desire for it, the story also suggests that the space where such a transgressive truth might be enacted has yet to be found. By the end of the story the women's marriage is moved to an unspecified elsewhere; it is no longer possible 'to live in Stirling', where Isabel's cuckolded husband has become a physical threat.

The most radical representation of lesbian experience in *Why Don't You Stop Talking* resides in Kay's articulation of a voice which has had little, if any, opportunity to express itself in literature: the voice of the non-biological lesbian parent. 'Big Milk' centres on the narrator's feelings of exclusion as her partner continues to breastfeed their two-year-old daughter. Obsessed with what she cannot have, the narrator has come to perceive the child as a manipulative interloper who has replaced her in her lover's affections: 'I was never bothered about breasts before she had the baby. I wasn't interested in my own breasts or my lover's. I'd have the odd fondle, but that was it. Now, I could devour them. I could spend hours and hours worshipping and sucking and pinching.' She continues to feel excluded from the dyadic bliss of mother and child, unable to find a way into this relationship and become part of, or indeed fully create, a family: 'At night I lie in bed next to the pair of them sleeping like family' (Kay 2002b: 23–4). The baby has 'monopolised language' and their lives (Kay 2002b: 30). As if such an expression of parental ambivalence, combined with the troubled and complex experience of being a lesbian parent without cultural status or name, were not quite radical enough already, what is particularly compelling about Kay's representation is the way in which it imbricates issues of family and parenting with questions of national identity. Both positions, that of the non-biological lesbian parent and that of the displaced Scot, are shown to be loaded with anxiety and grief.

The psychic torsions of jealousy and ambivalence drive the narrator of 'Big Milk' into an age-old grief at her own complicated origins. In a course of events mirroring Kay's own well-documented childhood, she begins to long for her birth mother, lost to her when she was adopted in infancy. The fantasy of her lost milk, of having missed out on the experience of being breastfed, becomes overwhelming and compels her to leave the familial bed to make the long trip back to Scotland and find her mother. It will not matter if her mother rejects her, she reasons, as long as she can have 'one long look at her breasts. Just as long as I can imagine what my life would have been like if I had sucked on those breasts for two solid years.' On approaching the border, the very nearness of Scotland gives her 'a strange exhilaration' and her fantasy becomes increasingly caught up with ruminations on national identity (Kay 2002b: 31). As she reflects on the life she might have led had she not been adopted, her dream of familial bonds merges with a sense of national belonging:

> When I take up my old life, I mean the life I could have, perhaps even should have, led. When I take up my old life, old words will come out of my mouth. Words that local people will understand. Some of them might ask how I came to know them. When they do, I will be ready with my answer. I will say I learned them with my mother's milk. (Kay 2002b: 32)

The language of 'home' monopolised by her own child – the child of the lesbian family union she feels unable to make her own – is replaced with the fantasy of being accepted into a native Scots mystically imbibed with the mother's milk she never received.

The drive north turns into a crazily reckless journey up the M6 and along the A74 – 'the most dangerous road in the country' – during which she savagely wonders what her mother did with her milk, asking if there is 'anyone out there behind or before me on the A74 who has ever felt like this' (Kay 2002b: 33), a question which reverberates through the whole story. New and unmapped, the territories of both lesbian parenting and post-devolution Scottishness make heady and hazardous destinations, and therefore, ultimately, the story can reach no conclusion. Once the narrator arrives in her birth mother's Highland town, she reaches the latter's house only to find it empty, with two bottles of milk on the doorstep. She opens the bottles to taste the milk and discovers 'it is sour. It is lumpy . . . A trickle of thin sour milk pours through the thick stuff. I look into my mother's house through the letterbox. It is dark in there. I can't see a single thing' (Kay 2002b: 35). It is impossible, then, to reclaim one's long-lost origins; they cannot be envisioned or adequately articulated. The question that remains is how one might be able to fulfil one's longing for an authentic 'home' identity through creating new, emotionally inclusive family structures.

A. L. Kennedy's *Everything You Need* (1999) is a novel about authorship, masculinity and fatherhood in which gay parenting occupies a central space. The novel is centred on Mary Lamb, a young woman who has been raised in Wales by her maternal uncle Bryn and his male partner Morgan; the other main character is Nathan, who mentors Mary as she joins a writers' community on Foal Island off the Welsh coast, and who is in fact, unbeknown to Mary, her biological father. Mary originally comes to 'the Uncles' (as she calls Bryn and Morgan) as a young girl. From the outset, over a plate of chocolate biscuits, Mary recognises that unlike life with her depressed mother, being raised by these two men might bring her unexpected advantages:

> Morgan had given her a tiny, apparently understanding nod and had taken a large, round, chocolate digestive for himself, which he posted suddenly into his mouth, entire . . . she had watched Morgan struggle to chew and then swallow. He looked like something from a nature programme – a snake swallowing an egg. And a small, cool idea had occurred to her then – a seductive, ashamed idea – she'd realised that when her mother left her all the rules might leave her too. The Uncles' house was obviously run by very different regulations. (Kennedy 1999a: 29)

Although the novel is set in Wales, its concerns with origins, language and identity are clearly tied to questions of Scottishness: the child, who 'completes' the lives of the two gay men and turns them into a 'family', comes to them from Scotland:

> 'We've been lucky though Bryn and me. We've always had the sweet of it, really. Not so good before we found each other, but then – then we were dancing . . . Couldn't have been happier, we thought, and then Maura brought you.'
> 'Surprised us.'
> 'Surprised *me*. I hadn't heard from her in years, didn't know she was married. And then she calls up, out of nowhere.'
> 'Out of up in Scotland somewhere – Perth.'
> . . .
> 'And we realise the only thing we've ever wanted and never had.'
> 'You.' (Kennedy 1999a: 204–5)

Kennedy's novel not only allows for gay men to have parental desires – as Bryn tells Mary the night she arrives in their house: 'Mo and me, we always wanted a girl' (Kennedy 1999a: 31); it moreover details the many ways in which gay parenting might surpass its heterosexual counterpart. It is Bryn who knows his child fully and in all her complexity, possessing 'the clean, direct expression of a man who was thoroughly educated in her particular turns and twists' (Kennedy 1999a: 34), and the Uncles' parenting is unique in its sensitivity and generosity of spirit. Their sexual difference enables them to deal differently with Mary's own emergent sexuality, treating her 'first time' with both reverence and humour as they bring her and her lover tea and biscuits: 'We thought you might want a drink. Or a little to eat. We find that we do' (Kennedy 1999a: 55). Mary's own view of her Uncles is unequivocal in its confirmation of their parental role: 'I'm your girl. You're my parents. You are. And I'm the best-brought-up person I know' (Kennedy 1999a: 37). Taught by her

Uncles 'to speak Welshly – she didn't always, but she could' (Kennedy 1999a: 37), Mary appears positively marked by her gay upbringing. She can speak 'differently' and, indeed, it is this bilingualism, as well as their ability, lovingly and supportively, to let her go which enable her to embark on the crucial journey towards authorial self-expression. By contrast Nathan, her biological father whom she believes to be dead, seems marked by and dependent upon her, rather than vice versa. Mary does not know she 'altered him for good' and gave him a 'permanent change of heart' the moment she was born (Kennedy 1999a: 35).

We are introduced to Nathan, a writer whose life has been devastated by the loss of his wife and daughter, as he makes yet another attempt to commit suicide in a fit of despair and self-loathing. A permanent resident of the Foal Island community, Nathan spends most of the novel attempting to confess to Mary that he is in fact her father. A stark counterpoint to the different parenting of Bryn and Morgan, Nathan embodies the paternal imperative through which Kennedy examines questions of natural kinship and the terms of true, authentic affiliation. Tensions between paternal knowledge and daughterly ignorance, between truth and fabrication, catch up the theme of fatherhood within it and cast its authority in doubt: 'Father. What does that even mean?' (Kennedy 1999a: 309). Nathan himself clings to the biological 'truth' of fatherhood as something which must take precedence over the lived experience of childrearing: 'Brought up by *uncles*, for Christ's sake. They did fine with her, but *uncles* . . .? When she could have had a father. When she *did have* a father' (Kennedy 1999a: 112).

Significantly, one of the novel's early dramatic encounters between Mary and Nathan centres on her defence of her unorthodox background against what she perceives as Nathan's homophobia:

> *Fuck you*.
>   My Uncles are homosexual lovers. My mother left me with them when she lost interest in me, but I don't resent it because she did me a favour. My Uncles love me, they have always loved me. And they love each other. They live together because they want to and they fuck. Bryn is my mother's brother and Morgan is no relation to me at all. My mother abandoned me with a couple of poofs. Or a couple of perverts. Which word would you prefer? . . . You don't want to know how the Uncles took care of me? You don't want me to tell you all the questions that everyone asked me at school? *Why don't you have a mam and dad, then?* Mm? My father died and my mother left me and my Uncles are better than both. They are my parents. They are the best men I have ever known. (Kennedy 1999a: 90)

Even at this point of potential disclosure Nathan remains unable to claim his fatherhood; instead, he consolidates Mary's false knowledge – 'Your father is dead . . . I am so very sorry' (Kennedy 1999a: 91) – and thus effectively deadens his own role. *Everything You Need* concludes with the open question of how Nathan's final plea as Mary's father – 'please, my darling, have need of me' – will eventually be worked through and whether, or how, the straightpaternal will in the end take precedence over the gay-avuncular, or, indeed, vice versa.

In *The Modern Scottish Novel* Cairns Craig contemplates the relationship between narrative, the imagination and national identity:

> The imagination of a nation is both the nation's imagining of its future – something we are all constantly engaged in since the nation shapes our individual futures – and it is the process of reconstituting the nation's past by retelling to ourselves the values which the nation embodies and by which those futures ought to be governed. (Craig 1999: 32)

All the texts discussed in this chapter undertake this pressing representational and imaginative task, each of them – ending with the portent of 'unfinished business' and hence with the promise of more narrative to come – querying how the future is or ought to be imagined. In their representations of new modes of lesbian and gay identity and experience, the texts test the existing landscape of Scottish culture and its prohibitions and exclusions at this moment of transition. They explore the extent to which Scotland's post-devolution future may involve a trajectory of border-crossings, affecting, and in turn being affected by, the lived and imagined experiences of its lesbian and gay citizens.

Chapter 33

Subaltern Scotland:
Devolution and Postcoloniality

Stefanie Lehner

In his essay 'Democracy and Scottish Postcoloniality' Michael Gardiner asserts that 'Scotland is not in any sense post-colonial, but suffers from economic and cultural inequalities which can in part be articulated as part of a historical process on a national level' (Gardiner 1996: 36). Gardiner's rather cautious phrasing hints at the two most problematic aspects of a postcolonial theorising of Scottish literature and culture: not only does any claim for Scotland's postcoloniality, which designates the country as an English colony, remain highly contentious (see Connell 2004a), but postcolonial criticism within a Scottish context is also always inevitably prone to prioritising issues of nationhood and nationalism over other important categorical concerns of individual and communal identification, such as class and gender. Any attempt at introducing a conceptual framework developed largely for a discussion of the cultural condition of former colonies into debates on the political status quo of a national formation that was itself complicit in the imperial project naturally bears its inherent difficulties. At the same time, the very idea of a postcolonial Scotland fruitfully complicates the binary oppositioning which informs traditional conceptions of the colonial divide by showing the British metropolitan centre as comprising its own internal peripheries. However, in *The Empire Writes Back*, one of the seminal texts of postcolonial studies, Bill Ashcroft, Gareth Griffiths and Helen Tiffin – like Gardiner – deny Scotland, as well as Ireland and Wales, postcolonial status. While its authors acknowledge 'these societies [as] the first victims of English expansion', they also categorise them as metropolitan societies whose cultures can only be understood 'in relation to the English "mainstream"' (Ashcroft et al. 1989: 33). Yet, paradoxically, it is its examination by and within a British-metropolitan template that has led to an accentuation of Scotland's anomalous historical development and emphasised its affinity with postcolonial cultures.

Tom Nairn's analysis of Scotland's 'political castration' through the Act of Union regards the country's 'belated' nationalism as 'the chronological companion of anti-imperialist revolt and Third World nationalism, rather than those of European movements, which it superficially resembles'. However, ironically, it is in interrogation of Nairn's conclusion that Scotland's 'anomalous historical situation could not engender a "normal" culture' that postcolonial theory initially reached some prominence in Scottish studies (Nairn 1981: 95, 157). Both Craig Beveridge and Ronald Turnbull's *The Eclipse of Scottish Culture* and Cairns Craig's *Out of History* utilise Frantz Fanon's concept of 'inferiorisation' to explain how an internalised parochial status can lead to a people's 'profound self-hatred' (Craig 1996: 12). In agreement with Fanon on the importance of nationalism for the reclamation of a native tradition, these Scottish critics posit that a reinvigorated national culture can resolve the identity crisis which sits at the heart of Scotland's political dilemma as the source of manifold rather constraining ideological effects. As Joy Hendry expounded, 'the Predicament of Scotland . . . is a pre-occupation which is admittedly inward and introverted . . . But until there is a State of Scotland, we have no choice but to be so obsessed' (Hendry 1983: 1). Accordingly, Scotland's cultural paralysis and political trauma as a stateless nation will endure until 'cured' by its full reassemblage into an independent nation-state, which is regarded as the natural outcome of decolonisation. Only once this has been achieved will the hegemony of the national in all areas of Scottish life cease to be inevitable and effectively suspend all other legitimate and necessary questions of identity and belonging.

This tendency to subsume all individual and communal identity politics under the privileged category of the national is evident in Craig's remark that 'it is by the colour of our vowels: the rigidity of class speech in Britain' that Scotland is oppressed (Craig 1996: 12). Not only is there a risk here of conflating racialist discrimination deriving from ethnic markers ('colour') with issues of class and nationality, but Craig's observation also obfuscates existing class distinctions within Scotland itself by appealing to the nation's sense of linguistic uniformity ('our'). In assuming Scotland as a homogeneous entity, such diagnoses strangely resemble the advice a desperate emperor is given in Alasdair Gray's 'The Start of the Axletree': 'You are dreaming the disease. Now you must dream the cure' (Gray 1983: 76). In Gray's short story, the cure deemed capable of preventing the vanishing 'out of history' of this doomed empire is the perpetuation of its existence in the form of a monument, and one is tempted to draw parallels here with the increasing politicisation of Scottish literature and art after 1979, as well as the post-devolution erection of a national monument in the form of the architecturally innovative and costly new Scottish Parliament building at Holyrood. Extending his project in *Out of History* to retrieve a 'counter-historical tradition' (Craig 1996: 81), in *The Modern Scottish Novel* Craig promotes 'an imagination of the nation as both the fundamental context of individual life and as the real subject of history' (Craig 1999: 14). However, the attempt to gather all aspects of culture and history into the all-absorbing framework of a national imagination ultimately results in a collective sublimation of the nation's heterogeneity in terms of class and gender.

This issue is poignantly addressed by A. L. Kennedy in her short story 'The Role of Notable Silences in Scottish History', in which the female narrator, a historian, criticises the monolithic truth-claim of national historiographies for obscuring the social realities of ordinary people who are reduced to silence: 'It is the sound of nothingness. It is the huge, invisible, silent roar of all the people who are too small to record' (Kennedy 1990: 64). Kennedy's story thus comprises an intriguing parallel to the political concerns of the Subaltern Studies Group, founded in India in 1982 under the intellectual and editorial auspices of the historian Ranajit Guha. Derived from the cultural theorising of Antonio Gramsci, the term 'subaltern' describes social groups that have been subjugated and excluded by the dominant power, in particular peasants and the lower working classes, but also women and other minority groups. Committed to an engagement with issues of social oppression, the Subaltern Studies Group set out to record the 'politics of the people' that had been omitted from official state history (Guha 1982: 4). Guha's critique of the concept of postcolonial nationhood exposes it as 'the ideological product of British rule', which recuperates the colonial forms of oppression that it purports to displace (Guha 1982: 1). By foregrounding how class intersects with other marginalised identity categories, such as gender, sexuality and race, subaltern studies contests the notion that a resurgent national culture ever works as a panacea capable of resolving all of a people's vexed issues of identity and belonging.

Assuaging Gardiner's understandable concern regarding 'the promiscuous use' of postcolonial theory, which by attempting 'to locate Scottish culture either wholly inside or outside the metropolis [invariably ends up] undermined by other types of subjective structuring such as class, ethnicity, sexual difference' (Gardiner 1996: 24, 39), the subaltern studies method facilitates a postcolonial analysis that foregrounds the specificity of social, historical and economic conditions, all of which contribute to the multifaceted complexity of individual and communal identities. In *Deconstructing Ireland* Colin Graham saliently invokes the subaltern method for 'rethinking postcoloniality' in an Irish context; emphasising that the major strength of postcolonial criticism is its role as an 'ethical criticism', which evaluates colonial relationships on the basis of their 'fundamental inequality', he recognises postcoloniality's problematic reduction to an exclusively national quandary. 'To allow the nation to monopolise the postcolonial field', Graham writes, 'is to withhold . . . a more radical interrogation by the difficult ethics of the colonial encounter . . . and by a cultural process built on dependence and interdependence' (Graham 2001: 82). Instead of conceiving of Scotland as a unitary national fabric, comprised entirely of either oppressors or victims, Graham's accentuation of the 'liminal spaces' opened up by the colonial encounter enables postcolonial readings that apprehend how privileged sections of Scottish society profited from imperialism whilst others were subjugated by it. In my view, such readings proffer a fruitful critical approach to the work of contemporary Scottish writers committed to uncovering the iniquitous power relations within national constellations.

Nevertheless, Berthold Schoene is 'doubtful . . . that a postcolonial analysis of contemporary Scottish literature would be at all appropriate'. Asserting that 'Scottish literature has over the last few decades ceased to be preoccupied with its postcolonial status', Schoene evokes the implicit temporal dimension inherent in the term 'postcolonial', which, frequently marked by the use of a hyphen, implies a linear logic of progress (Schoene 1995: 116–17). As Anne McClintock argues, 'the term "post-colonial" . . . is haunted by the very figure of linear "development" that it sets out to dismantle' (McClintock 1992: 85). Her criticism of this inherent paradox, which exposes the conception of a unilateral historical development as obscuring the continuous practices of domination, is in alignment with Walter Benjamin's critique of the concept of history as humankind's self-fulfilling progression. Section IX of Benjamin's 'Theses on the Philosophy of History' provides an apt description of the predicament of the 'postcolonial' as entrapped in the notion of historical progress, in his famous image of the Angel of History:

> His face is turned toward the past. Where we perceive a chain of events, he sees one single catastrophe . . . The angel would like to stay, awaken the dead, and make whole what has been smashed. But a storm is blowing from Paradise . . . [and] irresistibly propels him into the future to which his back is turned, while the pile of debris before him grows skyward. This storm is what we call progress. (Benjamin 1999a: 252)

This storm of progress could be said to manifest itself in Scotland's devolution as well. As a term, 'devolution' only barely conceals its true evolutionary thrust behind the prefixed letter 'd'. Through the reconstitution of a Scottish Parliament in particular, devolution has presented itself as a radical and wholesome solution to Scotland's democratic deficit, promising that it is possible to envisage the future of Scottish social democracy as a genuine alternative to the 'Third Way' of Blairite Britain.

However, do the progress and success of Scotland's devolution really make postcolonial criticism redundant, as Schoene appears to be suggesting? Surely not, if postcolonial criticism is defined in the terms of the Subaltern Studies Group as comprising debates on the enduring impact of class divisions, gender inequalities, racial discrimination and poverty. As Gerry Mooney and Lynne Poole contend, the myth of a 'new' and 'distinct' Scottish politics conceals the fact that Scotland's reconvened Parliament 'is committed to the same kind of Third Way/neo-liberal policies' which underpin the iniquitous, patriarchal and racially structured British system (Mooney and Poole 2004: 475). The seemingly liberating potential of Scottish devolution therefore requires caution, as it proves to be imbricated within the wider context of a political and economic restructuring which is ultimately designed to increase convergence with the forces of global capitalism. What Gardiner describes as 'the terminal step of decolonisation in the Anglophone world' (Gardiner 2004b: 274) seems, then, rather like a *recolonisation* based on the logics of a Gramscian 'transformist' hegemony, that is, a process through which popular sectional interests are absorbed and then re-inscribed by the dominant classes (Gramsci 1971: 58). Thus, the utopian movement towards minoritarian independence transmutes into a globalised counter-utopia of economically stable, interdependent nation-states, as exemplified by the revised position of the Scottish National Party, which nowadays aspires towards 'Independence in an Interdependent World' (MacAskill 2004: 23). Consequently, rather than bringing 'a light to the world' (Gardiner 2004b) devolution adumbrates the moment Aaron Kelly appositely terms 'geopolitical eclipse' (Kelly 2005b): as a culturalist discourse, which aims to promote equality through pluralism, inclusiveness and the assertion of multicultural difference, devolution also involves an implicit extrication from the class problematic, which results in an obfuscation of the actual hegemony of the market.

Devolution's liberal stance has inevitably exerted an influence on post-devolution conceptions of Scottish literature. Catherine Lockerbie, director of the Edinburgh Book Festival, for example, contends that 'now that devolution has been achieved, people don't have to prove they are Scottish writers anymore' (Massie 2002: 1). Similarly, Alex Massie confirms that devolution 'may prove a blessing for literature in this country since it may free novelists from overtly political writing' (Massie 2002: 2). Ignoring the fact that the work of Scottish writers such as Janice Galloway, Alasdair Gray, James Kelman and A. L. Kennedy has always shown politics to be much more than an exclusively national matter, while being often directly critical of nationalist discourse, this effort to erase 'overtly political' voices in the cultural sphere complements the denial of alternative discourses in the political domain. The apparent inevitability of historical progress tends to assert free-market ideology not only as the best, but as the only option. As the sociologist and Third Way architect Anthony Giddens asserts in his promotion of this political strategy, which has become the dominant formula of Tony Blair's New Labour, 'no one any longer has any alternatives to capitalism' (Giddens 1998: 43). Such a development, by entrapping us in an always already predetermined, homeostatic future, ultimately proclaims itself as the *end* of history, and this idea has been most notably revived by Francis Fukuyama. Fukuyama's account of a capitalist utopia safely enclosed beyond historical change by repressing political dissent and opposition, which are the primary guarantors of democracy, triumphantly announces that we have reached 'the end-point of mankind's ideological evolution and the universalization of Western liberal democracy as the final form of human government' (Fukuyama 1989: 3–4).

Significantly, the subaltern studies approach finds support in Benjamin's demand for a resolute dissociation from such a history as a 'semblance of eternal sameness' (Benjamin

1999b: 473). Benjamin's historical materialism 'cannot do without the notion of a present which is not a transition, but in which time stands still and has come to a stop' (Benjamin 1999a: 254); however, this standstill does not signify stasis so much as a rupture allowing the oppressed subaltern voices to re-emerge as the impulse for a new, alternative history. It is this kind of messianic affirmation which, in *Spectres of Marx*, Jacques Derrida seeks to resuscitate as well. In opposition to Fukuyama's apocalyptic announcement of the death of history, Derrida introduces the concept of 'hauntology' to suggest that our present is inhabited by the spectres and ghosts of the past and future: 'After the end of history, the spirit comes by *coming back*' (Derrida 1994: 10). Reversing the teleological understanding of history by virtue of its coming back, the indelible presence of these uncanny returns heralds a demand for justice. Derrida's ethically inspired proposal for 'a politics of memory' (Derrida 1994: xix) can be related to Homi Bhabha's notion of the uncanny within post-colonial criticism, which is like Gayatri Spivak's subaltern located beyond conceivable modes of representation or recognition. Yet, whereas Spivak conceives of subalternity as being 'out of any serious touch with the logic of capitalism or socialism' (Spivak 1995: 115), in Bhabha's work the uncanny 'relates the traumatic ambivalences of a personal, psychic history to the wider disjunctions of political experience' (Bhabha 1994: 11). In my view, all these various notions of an uncanny return of what is repressed or silenced provide us with a powerful ethical tool to remobilise the insights of the Subaltern Studies Group, and this is what I intend to do in my following postcolonial reading of Kelman's *You Have to Be Careful in the Land of the Free* and Kennedy's *Paradise*, both published in 2004.

Conspicuously, both novels evoke an 'end-of-history' scenario, as their time-frame is marked by a standstill. Located in an indeterminate in-between space close to an airport, both novels find their beginnings, as Michel de Certeau puts it in *The Writing of History*, in an 'originary nonplace' (Certeau 1988: 91). For both first-person narrators this place is marked by oblivion and disorientation: Kelman's protagonist Jeremiah Brown describes it as 'a town-whose-name-escapes-me kind of town' (Kelman 2004: 278), whereas Kennedy's Hannah Luckcraft has no sense of time or location at all. Entrapped like Beckett's Vladimir and Estragon while waiting for their prospective journeys home, the two characters' dis-orientation is redolent of Fredric Jameson's analysis of postmodernity as an experience in which 'structural coordinates are no longer accessible to immediate lived experience' (Jameson 1988: 349). Hannah's story begins in a confined space: 'I apparently begin with being here: a boxy room that's too wide to be cosy . . . To my right is an over-large clock . . . that effectively shout[s] what time it is' (Kennedy 2004: 3). As with Jeremiah's wrist-watch on which time fails to pass, the irony about the clock in Hannah's room is that it measures the progression of time despite the fact that 'time has stopped': at the end of the novel Hannah finds herself in exactly the same hotel room as at the beginning, and Jeremiah equally feels as if he is 'at a standstill' (Kelman 2004: 273, 427). However, in con-tradistinction to Fukuyama's vision of a perfectly petrified present, which has successfully exorcised all traces of the past and future, I would like to suggest with reference to Certeau's work that the novels' 'initial nothing traces out the disguised return of an uncanny past' (Certeau 1988: 91). As in Gramsci's characterisation of subaltern histories, the narration in both texts is not only episodic, but also markedly fragmented by spasmodically erupting memories, whose anachronic temporalities disrupt the historical trajectory of the charac-ters' stories (see Gramsci 1971: 55).

The curious cyclical structure of *Paradise* is accentuated by the alcoholism of Kennedy's protagonist. Hannah drinks in order to 'erase' her 'poisonous memories and fear', and ulti-mately time itself: 'Because once you've begun to have blackouts, you'll never stop and so before and after don't exist – you've mastered the art of escaping linear time' (Kennedy 2004: 247, 18). Drunkenness thus promises a utopian standstill, a paradise informed by an ethical desire to 'search for another human being and be truly searched by them, to shift shapes in each other's company' (Kennedy 2004: 212). Such a metamorphosis, brought about by merging with the Other, offers a profoundly delusive refuge from isolating and oppressive social structures; as Hannah puts it, it 'can make you believe you will never be alone, never resubjected to the usual forces and natural laws. You will assume you are free of such things and safe in your own small Eden' (Kennedy 2004: 213). In a way, Hannah's alcoholism allegorises Fukuyama's global paradise: devoid of past and future, memories or guilt, the world becomes a blurred illusion of eternal sameness, whether one finds oneself in Dublin, London or Budapest, a place where wars pass unnoticed. However, while drink affords Hannah temporary respite from reality and encourages the 'renovation' of a 'pick and choose' identity, sobriety triggers in her a 'forceful recollection' that in comparison with her brother's 'stainless and solid and rich' marriage and career, her existence as an alcoholic and unsuccessful seller of cardboard boxes ultimately defines her as an 'abnormal' failure (Kennedy 2004: 212, 26, 103, 194). Her alcoholism not only interferes with her 'smooth social and economic functioning' but also incapacitates her ethically (Kennedy 2004: 168). As becomes apparent in the scene in which she remembers trying to help a woman in a wheelchair, Hannah's ethical gesture of 'a stranger helping a stranger' ends with her deliberately dropping the woman, as in fact she doubted her own reliability in advance (Kennedy 2004: 69).

Whenever Hannah's fantasy space, made possible and sustained by recurrent anaesthetisation, is invaded by what it is intended to keep at bay, painful memories and guilt return. According to Hannah, 'there's nothing but horror in [reality]' (Kennedy 2004: 309). Exacerbated by her position as a woman in an all-male sphere of public alcohol consumption, Hannah finds her subaltern existence as an alcoholic erased from history, describing her very self as 'a diplomatic silence' and in fact hoping that 'maybe I won't come to mind in the end – as if I'd never been' (Kennedy 2004: 171). In the 'enforced absence' of alcohol ('drinking') and sex ('fucking'), through which she consistently defines herself, her 'personal arithmetic' leaves her with the equation of 'Hannah Luckcraft = Nothing' (Kennedy 2004: 280–1). On arriving home, Hannah finds herself in a place that her brother has secretly tidied up so that effectively 'not a trace of [her]' is left:

> So, my fresh and sober life unrolls about me, revealing a nice, clean, lunar emptiness. My new reality. Its sole purpose is to make me feel like shit, just when my only support has been amputated, cauterised. Other people manage this, undiluted existence: they are happy . . . But other people aren't like me – they are born anaesthetised. (Kennedy 2004: 285)

Significantly, Hannah describes socialisation itself 'as an intoxication' whereby 'normal, balanced' people like her brother have already 'taken [their] dose' (Kennedy 2004: 285). What Kennedy exposes here is that the escapist nature of Hannah's alcoholism conceals the fact that the social reality of order, propriety and economic success is in itself a necessary 'ideological fantasy' which aims, as Slavoj Žižek contends, to repress the 'traumatic' kernel of an uncontainable *jouissance*, as exemplified by Hannah's addiction to exuberant drinking and sexual intercourse. Accordingly, it is Hannah's menacing excess which could be seen to function as a 'return of the repressed': despite all attempts to control her by eclipsing her existence as a female, sexually active alcoholic, she continues to re-emerge as a *sinthome*, that is, 'a bearer of *jouis-sense*, enjoyment-in-sense'. However, when Hannah's presence as *sinthome* becomes, according to Žižek, 'unbound', it unravels in the 'apocalyptic trauma' at the end of the novel (Žižek 1989: 75; Kennedy 2004: 315): Hannah, 'not drunk . . . just out of control' and 'out of joint', embarks on a train journey with the goal of curing 'the unnamed disease of [her]self' in a Canadian clinic, where she also hopes to reunite with her lover Robert (Kennedy 2004: 295, 296, 217). But her train journey, symbolising the standardised time of progress, develops into a paranoid fantasy. No longer able to differentiate between dream and reality, Hannah dissolves in disturbing 'sexual anxieties' as Robert, engaged in a sadistic sex act, disregards her call for help.

As an allegorical parody of all controlled progress in the 'Big Other' fantasy of law and order, Hannah's propensity for excessive enjoyment eventually provokes an unleashing of patriarchal capitalism's own coercive horrors. However, as Žižek reminds us, paranoia must ultimately be regarded as 'an attempt to heal ourselves, to pull ourselves out of the real "illness", the "end of the world" . . . by means of this substitute formation' (Žižek 1992: 19). Hence, following her treatment in the clinic, which repeatedly reduced her to 'nothing . . . beyond a memory of skin' (Kennedy 2004: 338), Hannah escapes by affirming – in Žižek's words – 'a radical ethical attitude, that of "not ceding one's desire", of persisting in it to the very end' (Žižek 1992: 63). Accordingly, at the novel's conclusion we find Hannah relapsed and about to indulge once again in her symptoms – that is, Robert, sex and drink – as an ultimate confirmation of her uncontrollable *jouissance*.

In the following I would like to compare Kennedy's exploration of the systemic structures that confine the gendered individual in a silenced, subaltern position with Kelman's more overtly political treatment of class in *You Have to Be Careful*. As in *Paradise*, a seemingly fantastic vision of the 'Land of the Free' is undermined by his protagonist's real-life existence, in which 'the present willnay leave the past alone' (Kelman 2004: 408). Indecisive regarding his imminent return to his native 'Skallin', Jeremiah is haunted by his experiences in 'Uhmerika', which 'these capitalist fuckers and their money-grapping politico sidekicks had turned into a horror' (Kelman 2004: 2–3). As indicated by his name, which associates him with the Bible's messianic prophet of justice, Jeremiah's narration – which, as he explains, is 'no polemical diatribe against the evils of imperialism, colonialism, capitalism and all the rest of it' (Kelman 2004: 438) – constitutes at once a warning and a prophecy, which establishes a number of discernible links between American and British politics. For example, in a clear allusion to the British debate about the possible introduction of compulsory identity cards, Jeremiah's precarious status as 'an unassimilatit alien socialist' (Kelman 2004: 397) is documented by the Red Card, Class III, which he is repeatedly forced to produce as an unmistakable identification of his oppositional politics.

Trapped at the social and economic margins of American society, Kelman's protagonist – like Kennedy's – feels reduced to 'a nothing, a nobody [producing] stupid dreams but nothing else'. As Jeremiah goes on, 'I was never gauny be one of these immigrant Carnegie fuckers who finish up hurting millions and making billions' (Kelman 2004: 73). Struggling with economic survival in his chosen 'hame', Jeremiah's rather uncertain American roots problematise the very notion of national belonging; his ancestral namesake's ambiguously liminal status – 'employed by the imperialist Brit fuckers' or maybe 'a subversive' – appears to have been erased from the historical record because, Jeremiah explains, as 'working class people, we dont have history' (Kelman 2004: 46). Since such an erasure must inevitably distort and falsify the historical record that informs the conception of western national formations as prosperous, homogeneous entities, Jeremiah's narrative serves to re-inscribe the nation's continually obliterated and marginalised subaltern identities. 'But this is Uhmerika buddy, land of the free', he asserts, 'home from home for the dispossessed, the enslaved, the poor unfortunates; this is everybody's goddamn country. My people were slaves as well' (Kelman 2004: 407).

Following an endless series of menial jobs, Jeremiah's relationship with Yasmin, an African-American jazz singer, and the birth of their daughter require him to accept a more permanent position as a security operative, which becomes available as a result of the government's response to the so-called 'persian bet' emergency. 'Persian betting' involves gambling on one's life – 'persian' being a corruption of the word 'perishing' – in airplane-disaster scenarios implicitly satirising the American post-9/11 paranoia concerning foreigners and national security. However, in Kelman's novel it also connotes an underlying class issue, for

> those who speculated on the 'persian bet' were poverty-stricken bodies on so far below what the official government experts reckoned it took to be alive that the term 'income' was dropped. These included . . . a majority of the population. (Kelman 2004: 127)

As these 'ordinary Uhmerikins, moistly true-borns', swamp the airports, and by forming 'same-interest groups' thwart official attempts to restrict their gambling, the authorities seek to contain the problem by erasing it from 'the national consciousness' and expanding the security apparatus. But despite an official declaration of airports as 'down-and-out-free zones' and new laws driving offenders out of town, like 'phantom apparitions or something', 'these folks returned, and kept on returning' (Kelman 2004: 197, 135, 196). Reminiscent of Derrida's statement that 'one cannot control [the spectre's] comings and goings because it *begins by coming back*' (Derrida 1994: 11), the disruptive impact of these incessant ghostly returns is perhaps best exemplified by Kelman's introduction of the 'supranatural presence' of a 'legendary grocery-cart-pusher' into his novel (Kelman 2004: 230, 227). This uncanny figure's indeterminate gender, age, descent and name – combined with a mysterious face that is 'not to be gazed upon' (Kelman 2004: 230) – undermine all attempts at identification and categorisation. Its resolute indeterminacy also signals its incommensurable alterity; or, in Bhabha's phrasing, located 'beyond control', its uncanny subalternity cannot be contained, nor made 'knowledge*able*' (Bhabha 1994: 12).

The being's 'apparitional status' manifests itself in an encounter recounted by two of Jeremiah's colleagues: 'Attempting to halt his [or her?] progress', the being pauses in front of them and then, 'like marching time . . . marking time', disappears behind them. As they report, 'it was like time got lost someplace, if it was trapped . . . we could not move' (Kelman 2004: 238, 243). The encounter appears to allegorise the kind of unstoppable progress marking a petrified stasis which, in Benjamin's terms, marches 'over those who are lying prostrate' (Benjamin 1999a: 248). The sudden reversal of power, manifesting itself in the poor grocery-cart-pusher's act of stepping over those who as security operatives are supposedly in control, is also signalled by the being's subsequent uncanny appearance in the airport's VIP lounge, a transgression which 'heralded a system heading out of control'. Vanishing in front of the security guards who attempt 'to assert control' while the cart explodes in 'an inferno of flames leaping angrily skywards', 's/he' rematerialises 'like a charioteer from the very bowels of the earth' (Kelman 2004: 248–9).

In my view, the subversive effect of Kelman's mysterious figure constitutes the structure of a symptom and thus strongly resembles Hannah's presence as *sinthome* in Kennedy's novel: the being's uncanny subalternity – representative of the poor, homeless and dispossessed – disrupts all attempts at containment and control through persistently returning. As Žižek notes, today's subaltern can be conceived of as a symptom of the late-capitalist global system; identified as 'exceptions', they sustain the capitalist utopia of affluence, stability and regulation (see Žižek 1997: 46). At the same time, the uncontrollable return of these poverty-stricken 'unusual true-borns' functions in the novel as a permanent reminder of capitalism's underlying horror: exerting a threat on personal and national security by confronting air passengers and security guards with an 'image . . . of a possible future . . . a vision of themselves in years to come' (Kelman 2004: 249), they shatter the ideological fantasy that capitalist progress brings riches and success to everybody equally. Thus, they confirm Benjamin's insight that 'the tradition of the oppressed teaches us that the "state of emergency" in which we live is not the exception but the rule' (Benjamin 1999a: 248).

Strongly reminiscent of the ending of Kennedy's novel, Jeremiah's increasing paranoia as he strays lost in 'one of these end-of-the-world scenarios where time stood still' indicates that he is beyond control: provoking a pedestrian, a surveillance camera and a cop, he reminds 'the forces of law and order' of his menacing presence (Kelman 2004: 421, 433). However, like Hannah's paranoid fantasy, Jeremiah's conspiracy theory concerning the panopticon of regulation and control in which he lives must ultimately be regarded as an effort to understand his class position, displacement and experience of inferiority in relation to the global network of power structures that constitute society's totality. The narrative standstill configured by Kelman's and Kennedy's novels serves 'to blast open the continuum of history' (Benjamin 1999a: 254) in order to allow the repressed subaltern voices to re-emerge as indelible, ethically informed symptoms of the present, disrupting any celebratory proclamation of national or global progress. Despite the evident differences between Hannah's intoxicated vision, 'covered in echoes and ghosts' (Kennedy 2004: 82), and Jeremiah's overtly political diatribes, what the two novels have in common is their commitment to exposing the continuing injustices perpetrated by society's faith in a capitalist utopia. By mapping their characters' specific experiences of subjugation and oppression onto the socio-political and economic processes that implicate Scotland's devolution within a global capitalist network designated as the 'end of history', both writers produce what I would like to term a 'subaltern aesthetic'. Due to its experiential rootedness in a materialist dialectic, this subaltern aesthetic – unlike much of academia's postcolonial theorising – proves impervious to the *a*naesthetic effects of ideological purity while propagating actual political engagement.

Chapter 34

Mark Renton's Bairns: Identity and Language in the Post-*Trainspotting* Novel

Kirstin Innes

Scotland's literary landscape has never quite recovered from *Trainspotting* (1993). Irvine Welsh's debut novel may have had a first print run of only 3,000 copies, but over a decade on, swollen into a multimedia phenomenon, *Trainspotting* has imprinted itself indelibly on the Scottish psyche. Although Aaron Kelly denounces Danny Boyle's 1996 film version of the novel, and quite correctly argues for it to be regarded as a separate entity (Kelly 2005a: 68), any examination of *Trainspotting*'s impact on Scottish self-image must necessarily take into account the film's hugely persuasive iconography.

A beautiful boy emerges from a toilet, gasping as though near death or orgasm, droplets of water clinging to his eyelashes, skimpy clothes accentuating his prominent heroin-chic bone structure. The actors Ewan McGregor, Robert Carlyle, Ewan Bremner, Jonny Lee Miller and Kelly Macdonald line up and leer photogenically from a poster referencing Hollywood crime thrillers. Worshipped with idolatrous fervour by Scottish teenagers in the mid-1990s, these images offered a new way of seeing Scotland: up on a big screen, transformed in aesthetically pleasing, sexually attractive ways, and validated by international recognition and the exoticism of cinematic glamour. Yet even before the release of the film adaptation, the novel had achieved international 'cult status', with superstar-author Welsh heading an all-male Scottish writers' tour of America which cemented, as Janice Galloway has commented, a markedly partial media perception of the Scottish writing scene: 'The chaps and their priorities were the "cutting edge" according to the *New Yorker*. I kept wanting to write and say *Excuse me, there are women over here as well, taking only prescribed drugs if any*' (March 1999). *Trainspotting* has become not only a cutting-edge brand signifier for a fetishised, cool version of working-class drug culture, but also the most widely globalised representation of contemporary Scottishness. As a result, the particular linguistic code developed by Welsh to articulate the experiential reality of a certain community in a certain part of Edinburgh has become standardised as *the* authentic Scottish voice, both celebrated by the media and eagerly emulated by Welsh's peers and successors. However, as Galloway's response indicates, the promotion of a particular minority voice as representative of a whole nation's struggle for emancipatory self-expression must inevitably occur at the expense of all other subordinate and disempowered groups.

The struggle for national self-assertion was a prominent feature of much late-twentieth-century Scottish writing, in which resistance to a vaguely defined but passionately despised 'Englishness' served as a marker of identity pronounced so fiercely that the category

'Scottish' itself evolved into a belligerent pose of 'difference'. James Kelman and Tom Leonard were among the first to develop specific forms of local-dialect writing as a challenge to the canonical hegemony of Standard English narration, ill-suited to capturing the actual realities of Glaswegian working-class life. As Kelman put it in an interview in 1985, there is

> a wee game going on between reader and writer and the wee game is 'Reader and writer are the same' and they speak in the same voice as the narrative, and they're unlike these fucking natives who do the dialogue in phonetics . . . In other words, the person who speaks is not as . . . intellectually aware as the writer or reader. (McLean 1985: 77)

Within Kelman and Leonard's work, the phonetically accurate transcription of local dialect assumes the urgent centrality of a search for identity, reclaiming the language and, through it, the cultural and social reality of 'these fucking natives'. Thus, Leonard's poem 'thi six a clock news' highlights the presumed authority of Received Pronunciation by subverting formal BBC English into Scots: 'thi reason / a talk wia / BBC accent / iz coz yi / widny wahnt / mi ti talk / aboot thi / trooth wia / voice lik / wanna yoo / scruff' (Leonard 1984: 88). Leonard's and Kelman's writings articulate another form of 'trooth' – linguistic, nationalist and political – a truth that rejects the canonical colonisation of Scottish literature by redistributing the properties of authentic expression, as signalled in Leonard's poem 'ah knew a linguist wance': 'would you swear tay swerr / and not abjure / the extra-semantic kinetics / uv thi fuckin poor' (Leonard 1984: 113). The phrase 'extra-semantic kinetics' refers to the 'swerr' words and phatic fillers that permeate and punctuate everyday, and particularly Scottish working-class, speech. 'Fuck' and 'cunt', for example, possess additional 'extra-semantic' power; they come to serve as badges consolidating the authenticity of the language and carrying as much 'trooth' as words employed purely for denotation. Such authentic rendition of non-standardised language requires commitment; it is not just a matter of employing the correct accent, as the harangued linguist believes. In the two fragments quoted from Leonard's poetry, English 'to' has diversified into 'ti', 'tae' and 'tay'. As Jürgen Neubauer argues, linguistic authenticity is difficult to achieve. On the one hand, 'writers like Kelman and Welsh often come to stand for a raw "Scottishness" and a hallowed subcultural authenticity, which sometimes seems to be measured by the amount of obscenities per page', while, on the other, 'it is impossible to establish the exact nature of the urban demotic that is . . . represented, because urban speech cannot be reduced to one stable (written) accent' (Neubauer 1999: 151).

Continuing the struggle for linguistic authenticity initiated by Kelman and Leonard, it is Welsh with whom the 'raw "Scottishness"' described by Neubauer is now most widely associated. *Trainspotting* is Welsh's experiment with the literary representation of an expressly non-literary urban speech, propelled by the spontaneity of a fractured and marginalised tribalism. It is an intrinsically polyglot demotic, but governed by a specific grammar of semantics and imbued with its own ethical code. While ruminating on the subject of arch-psychopath Francis Begbie, Mark Renton, *Trainspotting*'s chief protagonist, is hailed, or rather pulled in different directions, by two conflicting, discursively determined identities. 'Ah hate cunts like that', Renton asserts. 'Cunts like Begbie. Cunts that are intae baseball-batting every fucker that's different; pakis, poofs, n what huv ye' (Welsh 1993: 78). Begbie's extremist attitude to difference may set him apart, but Renton's thoughtless invocation of the same derogatory terms makes him complicit in the politics they imply, as does his fear-fuelled refusal to voice a different position: '[Begbie] really is a cunt ay the first order. Nae doubt about that. The big problem is, he's a mate n aw. Whit kin ye dae?' (Welsh 1993: 84). Within this apathetic, self-preservational politics of tribal ennui, 'cunt', 'poof' and 'paki' are entrenched as totems of a developmentally arrested language with no dynamic for change. Although Renton displays occasional flashes of insight, he is continually pulled back by the implicit codes of the language he speaks. Instructing Sick Boy to 'fuck off ya sexist cunt', Renton is told by his friend that 'the fact that you use the term "cunt" in the same breath as "sexist" shows that ye display the same muddled, fucked-up thinking oan this issue as you do oan everything else' (Welsh 1993: 34). Unlike Renton, Sick Boy is fully aware of the double meaning of 'cunt', which is at once a term for female genitalia and an insult used predominantly by men.

Adroitly, Kelly identifies this particular element of Welsh's literary language not merely as an attempt at realist verisimilitude, but also as symptomatic of the author's preoccupation with issues of power:

> The tendency amongst some of Welsh's characters who are oppressed to oppress others as a means of asserting some form of beleaguered power – whether through sexism, homophobia or racism – is an example of what Peter Stallybrass and Allon White term *displaced abjection*: 'the process whereby "low" social groups turn their figurative and actual power, *not* against those in authority, but against those who are even "lower".' (Kelly 2005a: 20; see also Stallybrass and White 1986: 53)

When *Trainspotting* first appeared, it was celebrated as a novel providing the drug-using community, one of the most marginalised and abject social groups, with a voice and hence with a means for effective self-assertion (Kelly 2005a: 23). However, very quickly the language of this group became a literary hallmark for authentic Scottishness, rendering inaudible the language and eclipsing the experience of other underprivileged groups.

Female experience is severely dislocated by a national language which, by affording *cunt* such extraordinarily potent currency, relegates the female body to a semantically subordinate, secondary position, a position also reserved for those whose bodies are either of a different colour or inhabited by different forms of sexual desire. Despite Kelman's earlier efforts to disrupt complacent linguistic complicity between reader and writer, here they are in unison again, communicating with each other in an exclusively white, straight, working-class, androcentric code. Defined in strict opposition to 'poofs' or 'pakis', they are also unlike women, who – 'caught in this git-a-man, git-a-bairn, git-a-hoose shite that lassies git drummed intae them' – have 'nae real chance ay defining [themselves] ootside ay they mashed-tattie-fir-brains terms ay reference' (Welsh 1993: 226). Whereas there can be no doubt that *Trainspotting* has successfully ruptured the hegemony of middle-class Standard English narration, the novel's popularity has helped facilitate the reconsolidation of other hegemonic structures. The much-fêted new visibility of Scottish culture, which coincides with the working-class male's literary enfranchisement, appears to be won at the expense of women, gay men and ethnic minorities, whose voices are silenced by the new literature's blatant misogyny, homophobia and racism. As Christopher Whyte puts it, 'older conformations persist alongside the new. While the men in Irvine Welsh's *Trainspotting* are far from idealised, the book does not exactly apologise for the contempt they show their women' (Whyte 1995b: xv). Even though the protagonist of the new canon is now often working-class, presented as fallible, disenfranchised and incapacitated by ennui, his identity is still constructed through an understanding of culture, society and nation that leaves his ultimate superiority uncontested. As Ali Smith would have it,

Scottish writers 'are particularly keen to categorize themselves as different . . . from English' and therefore have trouble accepting 'that there are other forms of difference apart from this one' (Whyte 1995b: 5).

Some kind of engagement with *Trainspotting*'s radical reinvention of Scottish literary language is unavoidable for contemporary novelists, whether they try to emulate Welsh's style or self-assertively depart from it. Traces of Welsh's influence, whether factual or conjured by the media, abound: a quick Google search produces a litany of contemporary Scottish authors writing urban-demotic prose, all explicitly linked to Welsh. Alan Bissett has been fêted as 'the new Irvine Welsh' (Stewart 2001), and similar epithets have been used to introduce Luke Sutherland – the 'black Irvine Welsh' (Reynolds 1998) and Laura Hird – the 'female Irvine Welsh' (Johnson 2000). Suhayl Saadi's debut novel *Psychoraag* has been described in terms of '*Midnight's Children* meets *Trainspotting*' (Calder 2004b) and, absurdly, even Anne Donovan's gentle family comedy *Buddha Da* has recently merited a name-check review (Docherty 2003). What these writers have in common, aside from a nasty media-stereotyping rash, is that they all write about Scottish urban life at the turn of the millennium. Some writers – Christopher Brookmyre, for example – deliberately court comparison with Welsh by employing *Trainspotting*'s code of fucks, cunts, scatological humour and casual, brutal violence, proving themselves to be not only beyond doubt Scottish-identified but also keen to appropriate, and financially benefit from, the new literary kudos of 'cutting-edge', working-class machismo. By contrast, recent novels by Zoë Strachan, Bissett and Saadi problematise the difficulties of enunciating and authenticating a voice that is both identifiably Scottish and representative of an 'other form of difference'.

Since the publication of his debut novel *Quite Ugly One Morning* (1996), Brookmyre has worked on reinventing the white-collar crime thriller for a specifically Scottish, post-*Trainspotting* audience, displacing conventional language use and subject matter often to comic effect in order to endow his predominantly middle-class protagonists with a degree of contemporary, streetwise credibility. For example, exploding in a catalogue of bodily detritus – culminating in the discovery of a 'big keech on the mantelpiece' (Brookmyre 1996: 5), its consistency, colour and potency elaborated on in explicit, loving detail – the opening chapter of *Quite Ugly One Morning* is strongly reminiscent of Davie Mitchell's infamous accident in the chapter 'Traditional Sunday Breakfast' in *Trainspotting*. According to Willy Maley, Welsh 'excels at that potent blend of the excremental and the existential, "keech and Kierkegaard", that is all the rage in new Scottish writing' (Maley 2000: 192), and Brookmyre's preoccupation with the scatological is part of this trend, exploiting Welsh's representationally and commercially triumphant shock-power. However, in *Trainspotting* the junkie's insular preoccupation with the limits and urges of his own body, as well as the psychopath's compulsion to inflict pain on the bodies of others, create a grammar of corporeality built around the physical limits of the straight, white male. By contrast, Brookmyre's characters – for the most part journalists, doctors, lawyers and police inspectors – are perfectly socialised, empowered and integrated within the civic world. Wherever Scots is spoken in Brookmyre's oeuvre, it issues from the corners of mouths, meting out put-downs and couthy one-liners. It seems as if Brookmyre implements Scots to remind middle-class masculinity of its corporeality, and thus its Scottishness.

Much of Brookmyre's humour, almost invariably expressed in Scots, is derived from boyish playground or locker-room talk. His characters' residual adolescence tends to spill wistfully into the narrative, and at these moments they employ Scots, not as a deliberately demeaned language, but in gleeful bursts of jobbie- or keech-flinging. As a result, there is something faintly self-loathing about Brookmyre's use of Scots, hinting at an unwillingness to embrace it as a language capable of grown-up intellectual debate or aesthetic representation. The most compelling example of this undercurrent occurs in *Boiling a Frog*, when Brookmyre's longtime protagonist and mouthpiece Jack Parlabane wields his education to ridicule his Scots-speaking cellmate:

> Despite the distraction of pain, his detective skills had successfully decoded the human skelf's eponymous, punctuatory ejaculation. He had achieved this through the cryptographic technique of comparing its constituent variants . . . Translated from the primitive and obscure 'Prick' dialect, it meant 'Phew, I'll tell you, man . . .' and heralded an observation of deepest wisdom. (Brookmyre 2000: 9–10)

Interestingly, given Brookmyre's literary role models, 'Fooaltiye' turns out to be a junkie whom Parlabane's linguistic superiority and scorn relegate to a subordinate position of comic relief or, in other words, to the status of nothing more than a 'fucking native'.

In the early 1990s, just prior to the publication of *Trainspotting*, Janice Galloway and A. L. Kennedy had begun to raise and integrate distinctly female voices within a largely androcentric literary canon. Both Kennedy's *Looking for the Possible Dance* (1993) and Galloway's short story 'Blood' (Galloway 1991: 1–8) feature largely passive female characters at the mercy of masculine manipulation. Kennedy's protagonist Margaret has the word 'cunt' applied to her by her lover but does not use it herself (Kennedy 1993: 50). Galloway's anonymous teenage girl enters the girls' toilet at her school and finds the graffito 'GIRLS ARE A BUNCH OF CUNTS', which frightens 'most of the girls'. A sanitary towel strapped to her mouth to stop post-dental-work blood-flow, and coping with the onset of her period, hence bleeding from two orifices, the girl internalises the misogynous message as 'impossible to argue against' (Galloway 1991: 5–6).

'Cunt' is never employed by a female to describe her genitalia in a positive or unproblematic manner in either Galloway's or Kennedy's writing; as a semantic vehicle of oppression, it is invariably applied by males to denote and control women's bodies. *Trainspotting*'s phenomenal success only served to compound the situation. For example, in Begbie's frenetic riffing – 'so ah'm oan toap ay it, ken . . . but it pushes us oaf, ken n she's bleedin ootay her fanny ken . . . Anywey, it turns oot thit the cunt's huvin a fuckin miscarriage' (Welsh 1993: 342) – 'it' can refer to either cunt, that is, the woman or her genitals, demonstrating that Welsh's language offers little room for dignified female self-expression. All the more significant, then, that post-*Trainspotting* Scottish women writers Laura Hird and Zoë Strachan, both on record as admirers of Welsh, have taken a very different approach to creating a literary female space and corporeality, within which not only the word 'cunt', but the whole realm of women's sexual pleasure, comes to be owned by the female characters themselves. Hird's Welshian novel *Born Free* (1999) is partly mediated through the perspective of angry teenager Joni, for whom 'a cunt' denotes any irritating older woman or man. Joni – violent, self-aggrandising and primarily motivated by selfish lust – serves to create the image of a teenage girl vastly different from Galloway's timid protagonist in 'Blood'.

Strachan's agenda is more overtly feminist than Hird's. Her protagonists are exclusively female, beset – particularly in *Spin Cycle* (2004) – by a succession of one-dimensional predatory males. Siobhan in *Spin Cycle* and Stella in *Negative Space* (2002) begin lesbian relationships signalling a renewal of the characters' identities. The climax of *Spin Cycle* asserts lesbian sexuality in a flash of misandric violence as Agnes murders call-girl Myra's violent client while simultaneously, in a different part of town, Siobhan has 'her mouth on Irene's nipples, her fingers pushed deep in her cunt' (Strachan 2004: 299–300).

While there is no such sex-divide in *Born Free* – if anything, Hird's two male characters are far more sympathetically portrayed than their female relatives – in both authors' writing one finds a heightened female body-consciousness. Their protagonists do not so much employ a new grammar of corporeality as take brazen pleasure in taboo-breaking ways of enunciating their sexuality. Both Stella and Joni masturbate frequently and flagrantly, using and referring to their bodies in ways which subvert traditional ideals of femininity. At one point Stella goes through a phase when she refuses to wash: 'I had grown used to smelling myself, the scent of my cunt reaching my nostrils . . . changing into a soft musti-ness or acidic tang' (Strachan 2002: 78). Similarly, after fulfilling her long-held ambition to lose her virginity, Joni comments 'I've not had a shower for two days, so my fanny smell's really obvious but it's like a magnet to him' (Hird 1999: 205). The unwashed, sexually active, female body becomes all the more prominently transgressive by the connotative power of the words 'cunt' and 'fanny'. The beautiful potency of Strachan's language ele-vates 'cunt' to a higher register, and the word's new power appears entirely unaffected by Stella's earlier use of it as a swearword in an encounter with a man in the street: 'Get to fuck, you stupid cunt!' (Strachan 2002, 60). Admittedly, to some readers, Strachan's attempt to overcome the duality of the word as a positive term for an intrinsic part of the female self, on the one hand, and a seriously offensive insult, on the other, in order to rec-oncile the split literary identities of Scottishness and femaleness might seem like a very good example of Renton's 'muddled, fucked-up thinking'. Clearly, Hird's insistence on dis-tinguishing between 'fanny' (the body part) and 'cunt' (the swearword) demonstrates that for her the duality remains insurmountable.

In *The Incredible Adam Spark* (2005) Alan Bissett examines the unwillingness of adoles-cent working-class males to accept different kinds of masculinity as, for example, personi-fied by his eponymous eighteen-year-old hero. Holding down a MacJob and prone to outbursts of frustrated violence typical of underprivileged young men like himself, Adam reads comics and plays computer games while attempting to insert himself into a local gang, the H-Glen Animalz. However, Adam also suffers from learning difficulties and, earmarked by his peers as 'different', his first-person narrative is continually subverted by the fact that both the author and the reader know and understand more than him. Despite his sister Jude's best efforts, Adam's sense of self is compromised by the ethical code of a language – androcentric, working-class, Falkirk-based – that despises difference, including his own:

> I ken i ken i ken, judes always givin me a row for callin it the pakis, gets right angry shakes her head says cmon adam. Ye ken thats a bad word. Ye shouldnt use that word its no right, but i didnt ken! I thought that was the actyool name of the shop THE PAKIS. Parrently its called GKR FOODSTORES but everyone calls it the pakis. No ma fault. Says this to jude shes like no adam, you dont like it when folk call ye mongol, do ye? You dont like it when folk call ye spastic?
>   Naw i says. But i dont mind if folk call me paki! (Bissett 2005: 19)

Until the events of the novel force him to change, Adam exists in a state of blissful, pos-sibly – at least to some degree – self-imposed ignorance and unaccountability. He under-stands that in Jude's view the word 'paki' is unacceptable, but the pressure to conform to majoritarian speech patterns proves to be more compelling than his sister's moral objections. Nor does Adam make the connection between the position the implicit racism of his lan-guage assigns to an Asian shopkeeper, on the one hand, and that assigned to himself as a 'spastic', on the other. The former is simply a collective manner of speaking – 'no ma fault' (or 'whit can ye dae', as Renton would have it) – whereas the latter is a personal insult res-olutely to be rejected by reference to Jude's moral authority: "I am *not* a mongol i xplains to them in the propervoice judy telt me to use when talkin to thickos' (Bissett 2005: 31). Significantly, Adam has to lift himself out of his normal language use and employ 'proper-voice' to defend his dignity and negotiate a way out of his dehumanised object position of 'that mongol' or 'the wee retard' (Bissett 2005: 31). Whenever the H-Glen Animalz toler-ate his company, Adam, buoyed by their acceptance, clumsily attempts to comply with the gang's linguistic code. As with Renton's cowardly embrace of Begbie's lexicon of hatred, Bissett's reader is put in an uncomfortable position. Forced to confront and accept Adam's inability to grasp the full significatory potency of a code which reduces him and others to an object, it is soon-to-be-middle-class Jude – imprisoned by familial responsibilities, Falkirk, and her brother's uncomprehending selfishness – with whom the reader begins to sympathise.

Like Alvin in Bissett's semi-autobiographical debut novel *Boyracers* (2001), Jude must leave Falkirk and her mother tongue to find acceptance, a circumstance Adam is all too keenly aware of: 'Her accent changes flickofaswitch. Not *how ye doin* but *how are you doing*. Posh like' (Bissett 2005: 67). The presence of this alternative, 'posh like' language intro-duces marked conflictual tensions into the narrative. Jude is on the side of knowledge, which she shares with the reader but which escapes Adam, and therefore we find her more natural to identify with, particularly when the latent unease Bissett has created from Adam's lack of understanding erupts in a moment of horror, as Adam assaults Jude's girl-friend Maryann, screaming 'How do ye like that then ya cow? . . . Streets of rage smack-down!' (Bissett 2005: 102). Unable to distinguish between real life and 'Streets of Rage', a computer game, Adam gives in to violence, threatened and confused by the concurrent, yet irreconcilable codes of three different linguistically encapsulated realities: the dissim-ulation and imminent estrangement implicit in Jude's capable switching of registers, the aggressive 'slut' and 'ya cow' of the H Glen Animalz' demotic, and the casual violence rep-resented by his computer games. Unlike Renton, who is aware of being pulled in different directions, Adam fails to recognise that his language is expressive of a composite of ideol-ogies. Demeaned within Falkirk's hegemonic dialect and baffled by the prospect of Jude's abandonment, he proceeds to re-inscribe the world around him using the interpretative codes he finds at his disposal: the pop-culture language of films, comics and computer games, as well as school slang and learned affectations such as 'actyool'. Only very gradu-ally does he create for himself a wholly individual, self-centred lexicon enabling him to elevate his 'difference' out of the object position assigned to it, following a similar – if less self-conscious – impulse to Stella's in Strachan's *Negative Space*.

Like *The Incredible Adam Spark*, Suhayl Saadi's *Psychoraag* (2004) rewrites Scots urban dialect to articulate the viewpoints of both a marginalised social group and an individual. Zaf, Saadi's protagonist, a DJ on the graveyard shift of an independent Asian radio station in Glasgow, is caught up in a struggle to reassemble and make sense of the various compo-nents of his identity over the course of one long night. Although he comes from a back-ground very different from Renton's – namely lower middle-class, Scots-Asian Pollokshields – Zaf's is nevertheless as self-contained, as much at the mercy of its own laws, and most certainly as difficult to leave behind. The new community in 'the Shiels' has imprinted itself onto Glasgow's topography and markedly changed this part of the city:

> Now, at least there wis some kind of a buzz, a *joie*, the incipient kind of electricity that came
> from a sense of community. Call it a ghetto or a *jhopar putti* or whatever – there wis somethin
> almost musical in amongst the shite. An Asian vibe, right enough! (Saadi 2004: 376–7)

'Shite' appears to denote the city's original Glaswegianness, broken up by the introduction of an intangible 'Asian vibe' not easily put into words ('some kind of a buzz, a *joie*'). Correspondingly, the second-generation Scottish-Asians Zaf associates with have appropriated urban Scots to make their presence felt in both the culture and the language. The characters of *Psychoraag* speak Glaswegian imbued with Punjabi, Farsi and Urdu words and rhythms; in fact, most of the narrative is conducted in this polyglot code governed by the laws and mores of at least three different cultural backgrounds, deconstructing and re-engendering both communal and individual identities wherever these differences meet.

As in Brookmyre's work, for Zaf communication in Scots represents a kind of regression, one he is at a loss to explain, but which frustrates and humiliates him until 'he felt like kickin himself in the shins'. Talking to an old friend 'he found himself slipping intae a broad Glaswegian of the sort which he hadn't really spoken since he'd been with Zilla – except on the show' (Saadi 2004: 70). Zaf's stream-of-consciousness narration – increasingly fragmented throughout the night by sleeplessness, alcohol, and drug-fuelled hallucinations – gradually reveals the inherent tension in the Scots-Asian community. Having abandoned Zilla, his Scots-Pakistani ex-girlfriend, to heroin addiction and prostitution, Zaf falls for white nurse Babs and moves to a predominantly white area of Glasgow, where he launches an attempt at self-reinvention. Only at night, on the show, does he re-enter the Shiels, using the cover of the graveyard shift to re-examine his parents' roots and his own cultural positioning through music and language. The radio show enables him to talk 'in fifty thoosand tongues' (Saadi 2004: 66), tracing a path of personal significance through a multicultural playlist, but his nocturnal homecoming also tends to cast his carefully constructed polyglot identity into crisis.

Under the influence of narcotics, Zaf fantasises about having a conversation with another Zafar, a former schoolmate and local gangster, easily recognised by the blue eyes inherited from his white mother. Zafar crystallises into an apparition of Zaf's self-loathing, contriving a confrontation between the polarised, uneasily reconciled and linguistically split halves of Zaf's identity: 'Listen, wanker, Ah'm sittin in yer seat an Ah'm playing yer music an Ah'm whisperin intae yer mike an Ah'm screwin yer wummin – baith ae them. The *goree* an the Paki!' (Saadi 2004: 392–3). Zilla, representing Zaf's Asianness, is demeaned and silenced by one of British racism's most potently connotative expletives. In the same breath, the term '*goree*', explained in Saadi's glossary as a derogatory name for a white woman, denigrates Babs, demonstrating how Zaf's subconscious condemns his desire and tentative sense of bicultural belonging by mobilising the racist potentialities of two different languages. Clearly also, either language holds the power to reduce women to the status of a mere sexual commodity and male identity-descriptor, just as vehicular to the maintenance of Zaf's individuality as his microphone and music. *Psychoraag* concludes with two appendices: a glossary of non-English words used in the novel, comprising Farsi, Urdu, Scots, Punjabi and Gaelic, and a multicultural playlist of songs. In conjunction, these two appendices draw the reader's attention back to Zaf's intrinsic cultural multifacetedness and hybridity rather than consolidating his identity as irremediably split between Scottish and Asian, his present life and his communal heritage. Significantly, Zaf ends his night-in-the-life astride a street map of Glasgow, which may be real or imagined, casting not just 'an Asian vibe' but the spell of his memories over the city.

To conclude, *Trainspotting* must be seen as a shout of self-assertion that became a call to arms. The attention-grabbing, body-focused, kinetic language Welsh's characters hurled at each other, their fellow human beings and the reader has been impossible to ignore. By enunciating a voice like Renton's, which slighted and dismissed 'difference' while uncomfortably aware of doing so, *Trainspotting* radically unmoored Scottish literary language. Continuing with Welsh's rewriting and semantic recodification of urban Scots, writers like Bissett, Hird, Saadi, Strachan and, to some extent, even Brookmyre have begun to shout back just as loudly. These writers make the most of the simultaneously empowering and disenfranchising potentialities of Welsh's language by appropriating what Sick Boy would have been likely to dismiss as 'muddled, fucked up thinking' to express a fundamentally incongruous identity, which is at once 'Scottish' and representative of an 'other form of difference'.

Chapter 35

Cultural Devolutions:
Scotland, Northern Ireland and the
Return of the Postmodern

Matthew McGuire

In 1977 Tom Nairn's *The Break-up of Britain* predicted the gradual dissolution of the British state and the rise of 'neo-nationalism' among the peripheral regions of the United Kingdom. In the twenty-first century – following the successful establishment of devolved assemblies in Wales, Scotland and Northern Ireland – such foresight seems, in no uncertain terms, remarkable. However, it is neither Nairn's prescience, nor his argument *per se*, but rather his adamant insistence on reading devolution within a comparative critical framework that inspires the present chapter, both conceptually and theoretically. Following in Nairn's footsteps, my chapter brings together two of the most prevalent developments in recent Scottish studies: a comparative approach, with Ireland as a cross-cultural reference point, and an engagement with postmodern theory as a tool to explore the cultural implications of a devolved Scottish identity. By juxtaposing the work of James Kelman with that of Northern Irish writer Robert McLiam Wilson, my chapter aims not only to disrupt essentialist and reductive discourses of national identity, but also to critique current debates on Scottish culture that remain solidly anchored in the terrain of pre-devolution theorising which suggested, with reference to the work of Mikhail Bakhtin, that 'the value of Scotland was tied up with the value of Scotlands' (Crawford 1994: 56). As I aim to demonstrate, a thorough reconsideration of the political aspects of Bakhtin's work enables us to qualify such rather sweeping celebrations of a pluralist Scottish multiculturalism, which would ultimately continue to subordinate the experience of many people living in post-devolution Scotland today.

There is a long tradition in Scotland of looking across the Irish Sea for cultural, political and ideological inspiration. For instance, in his famous condemnation of the state of Scottish literature *Scott and Scotland* (1936), Edwin Muir concluded by evoking William Butler Yeats's Ireland as an example of what a truly national literature might achieve:

> Irish nationality cannot be said to be any less intense than ours; but Ireland produced a national literature not by clinging to Irish dialect, but by adopting English and making it into a language fit for all its purposes. The poetry of Mr Yeats belongs to English literature, but no one would deny that it belongs to Irish literature pre-eminently and *essentially*. (Muir 1982: 111; my emphasis)

It is Muir's essentialism, and his concern with the linguistic landscape of Scottish literature in particular, that provide the twin coordinates for the following discussion.

Significantly, however, the Irish/Scottish cross-cultural dynamic is of concern to more than just literary figures from the past. Of late, Scottish studies has become increasingly interested in re-establishing a meaningful dialogue to explore the historical and cultural imbrications of both nations. Thus, for instance, in 1999 the University of Aberdeen established the Research Institute of Irish and Scottish Studies (RIISS), whose website declares it 'a truism that Ireland and Scotland share much history in common. From earliest times the two countries united by the sea formed a single cultural, religious, linguistic and economic zone'. In 2005 the Arts and Humanities Research Council (AHRC) emphatically endorsed this enterprise by allocating RIISS its largest ever single award (£1.25 million) to fund further interdisciplinary research. Of course, the Scottish/Irish comparison is more complex than the Institute's statement would initially seem to suggest. Whereas the shared 'religious, linguistic and economic' history of the two regions has already attracted a certain degree of attention (Cullen and Smout 1977; Devine and Dickson 1983), their 'cultural' cross-pollination has yet to receive the same level of critical scrutiny. The only full-length study in this field to date is Ray Ryan's *Ireland and Scotland* (2002), which examines the work of a select number of authors from both regions: William McIlvanney, Iain Crichton Smith, Dermot Bolger and Colm Tóibín. Although Ryan's analysis is pointed, *Ireland and Scotland* could be criticised for falling into two distinct sections: 'Scotland: Region and Nation, Republicanism and Colonialism' and 'Ireland: Region, State and Nation'. This subdivision results in an insightful critique of both Scotland and Ireland, but one that is frustrated in its attempt to offer a more thorough comparative analysis, halting the project before it can truly get off the ground. *Ireland and Scotland* is primarily a book about the Irish Republic, with Scotland as a lens, enabling Ray to re-examine a cultural landscape that has long been eclipsed by critical preoccupations with the North. Consequently, there remains a vacuum within the study of Scottish and Irish literature that invites us to reconsider how similar themes overlap in meaningful ways, as well as their particular relevance to our understanding of contemporary Scottish culture.

Emulating Muir's espousal of a Yeatsian poetic, contemporary Scottish studies can often be caught looking across the Irish Sea for critical and theoretical inspiration. Eleanor Bell's recent study *Questioning Scotland* is one such case in point:

> It may seem peculiar that a book on Scottish studies begins by addressing issues particular to Ireland. However, increasingly, connections are now being made between the two disciplines. Yet, where there have been many recent theoretical developments in Irish studies on issues such as postcolonialism, poststructuralism and postmodernism, investigations in these areas from a Scottish context have been relatively sparse. (Bell 2004: 1–2)

Significantly, this kind of sentiment has not been limited to the narrow sphere of academic discourse. As Alex Salmond, leader of the Scottish National Party (SNP), put it in his keynote address to the party's annual conference in September 1996, 'Ireland is doing so much with so little, while Scotland is doing so little with so much' (Salmond 1996). In a newspaper article published on the day of New Labour's historic general election victory in 1997, Salmond elaborates that 'looking across from Scotland we see what a small nation can achieve . . . In Scotland we can only envy Ireland's international visibility, and all the advantages in tourism and investment – not to mention self respect – which go with it' (Salmond 1997: 14).

Salmond's look towards Ireland might be described as doubly green: candid in its envy while simultaneously reflecting Ireland's globally ubiquitous green profile. But his use of the term 'Ireland' is also highly problematic in that it is clearly a reference to the Irish Republic, one that would elide the cultural and political specificity of the North, and exclude it from any aspirational model of what Scotland might one day become. On the surface such ideological opportunism may seem both obvious and logical; after all, it is the creation of a sovereign and independent nation state that is the SNP's *raison d'être*. However, one would do well to attend to the 'advantages in tourism and investment' that Salmond specifically singles out. During the 1990s, under the banner of the 'Celtic Tiger', the Republic of Ireland radically altered its social and economic infrastructure, realigning itself more closely with the free-market imperatives of global capitalism. This resulted in the country's dramatic transformation from the sick man of Europe into one of its wealthiest nations. My central thesis is that such narratives of economic opportunism and global capitalism inevitably inform any thorough understanding of both the Northern Ireland Peace Process and recent attempts to theorise a postmodern Scottish national identity.

For historians such as T. M. Devine, the re-establishment of a Scottish Parliament in 1997 marked a moment of democratic fulfilment and a new set of possibilities for the cultural life of the nation (Devine 1999: 610–19). The present volume itself – as a reassessment of literature and culture ten years after devolution – is a strategic and timely attempt to revaluate this very assumption. Echoing Devine's assertion that 1997 marked a specific juncture in the cultural life of the nation, Catherine Lockerbie, the director of the Edinburgh International Book Festival, claimed in 2002 that 'now that devolution has been achieved, people don't have to prove they are Scottish writers anymore' (Massie 2002: 1). Since then, several commentators have called for a renewed debate on questions of national identity, a debate that would look beyond the immuring parochialism of essentialist ideas of Scottishness, and employ the language of postmodern theory as an antidote to the reductive and pervasive critical paradigms of the past.

Testimony to the critical import of ideas from across the Irish Sea, the work of Irish philosopher Richard Kearney has been highly influential in recent critical attempts to articulate a specifically postmodern Scottish identity:

> It has been suggested . . . that postmodern theory can have radical implications for politics. One frequently encounters the claim, for instance, that the postmodern critiques of the centre . . . challenge the categories of established power. The most often cited examples here relate to the critique of totalitarianism, colonialism and nationalism. The postmodern theory of power puts the 'modern' concept of the nation-state into question. It points towards a decentralizing and disseminating of sovereignty which, in the European context at least, signals the possibility of new configurations of federal-regional government. (Kearney 1997: 61)

Alert to late twentieth-century reconfigurations of political sovereignty and the increased visibility of regional, national and international government, Kearney's postmodernism provides a salient description of the decentralised matrix of political power (Holyrood–Westminster–Brussels) into which the Scottish nation has found itself reborn. However, it is the emancipatory promise of the new possibilities that inform this 'postnational' political space that require further scrutiny. Within Kearney's analysis of the recent transformations in the nature and praxis of political sovereignty, he fails to emphasise the anti-democratic and disempowering energies released through the consolidation of late capitalism and the subordination of the nation-state to the logic of this global economic order. What I wish to argue is that while a postmodern overturning of essentialist versions of Scottish identity is salutary, it is not yet clear if the pluralist discourse of multiculturalism affords any real and meaningful form of redemption.

Displaying remarkable synchronicity with Scotland, commentators on Northern Ireland have been equally keen to deploy the language of postmodernism in order to theorise an alternative discourse beyond the ossified binaries of familiar sectarian politics. In a way resonant of Seamus Heaney's description of the North's 'anachronistic passions', Edna Longley maintains that 'Ulster people hug wonderfully "fossilized" versions of their own or someone else's Irishness/Britishness; which retards newer definitions in the Republic and Britain' (Heaney 1969: 757; Longley 1985: 26). Longley's critique of the North's essentialist identity politics corresponds to Bell's diagnosis of the fundamental problem confronting Scottish studies, namely 'its tendency to resort to essentialist forms of national identity as a convenient means of codifying and determining Scottishness'. According to Bell, there is now 'a need for more self-conscious engagements with nationhood in order to escape the stasis generated by reductive formulations' (Bell 2004: 3). It is in response to these essentialist tendencies within national discourses, then, that both contemporary Irish and Scottish studies have looked to postmodernism and its pluralist notions of multicultural difference as a redemptive language within which to reconfigure their respective cultural identities.

In *Fiction and the Northern Ireland Troubles* Elmer Kennedy-Andrews posits that 'in a Northern Ireland context, postmodernism offers the possibility of deconstructing the perennial categories of Catholic and Protestant, Unionist and Nationalist [by] exposing the difference and *différance* within identity [and] exploring new horizons of identity altogether' (Kennedy-Andrews 2003: 19). Similarly, Laura Pelaschiar has described contemporary Belfast as 'a laboratory for opportunities, a postmodern place depicted as *the* only space where it is possible to build and articulate a (post)national conscience, the only location for any possible encyclopedic, multivoiced and multi-ethnic development of Northern society' (Pelaschiar 2000: 117). Both Kennedy-Andrews and Pelaschiar champion the work of Belfast writer Robert McLiam Wilson as offering new modes of representing the North beyond the reductive assertions of exhausted tribal identities. First published in 1989, McLiam Wilson's debut novel *Ripley Bogle* is a Northern Irish *Bildungsroman*, in which the eponymous hero is a tramp who wanders the streets of 1980s London while reflecting on his childhood in Belfast during the outbreak of the Troubles. Bogle's explicit homelessness is indicative of the novel's ideological subtext, which deliberately seeks to deterritorialise familiar sectarian metanarratives of the North and, in doing so, invokes Jean-François Lyotard's canonical definition of postmodernism as incredulity towards grand narratives.

Remembering his first day at school, Bogle recalls a Northern Irish education that inevitably involved learning how to interpret and interpolate the world within certain sectarian paradigms: 'Little Miss Trotsky herself told us the occasional Misguided Soul would try to call us British but of all the wrong things to call us – this was the wrongest. No matter how the Misguided Souls cajoled, insisted or pleaded, our names would remain Irish to the core, whatever that meant' (McLiam Wilson 1997: 16). In a way reminiscent of Heaney's poem 'Whatever You Say Say Nothing' (Heaney 1998: 131–3), *Ripley Bogle* shows itself aware of the complicity of the North's everyday speech and its collusion in mapping a particular sectarian ideology. Unwilling to deny his father, who is actually Welsh, the precocious Bogle comically rechristens himself 'Ripley Irish British Bogle'. The novel not only satirises the North's obsession with strictly identitarian modes of thinking, but actively aims to disrupt the easy categorisations and codifications of sectarianism. Through his pen name, which draws on both the traditional Gaelic (McLiam) and English (Wilson) versions of the same name, the author himself courts notions of an oblique and deliberately ambivalent identity. Both the central character and the authorial persona – 'Ripley Irish British Bogle' and 'Robert McLiam Wilson' – can be read in terms of Longley's insistence on the immuring effect of essentialist notions of identity that ultimately perpetuate and legitimate the sectarian conflict within the North. As a possible remedy, Longley proffers a multicultural model that forgoes narrow, exclusivist notions of identity and argues for a particular postmodern reading of the North, whereby incredulity, uncertainty and differ-ence become an opportunity to escape from the exhausted narratives of the past (Longley and Kiberd 2001: 5–40).

While *Ripley Bogle* foregrounds the redemptive promise offered by anti-essentialist the-ories of cultural difference, McLiam Wilson's *Eureka Street* (1996) exposes the dark under-belly of this new, postmodern Belfast. Set during the IRA ceasefire of 1994, which eventually led to the 'Good Friday' Belfast Agreement and the creation of a devolved Northern Ireland Assembly, the novel follows two friends, the Protestant Chuckie and the Catholic Jake, attempting to make sense of the changes in the local landscape as the North is reconfigured by the irresistible forces of late capitalism and its attendant consumer culture. The changes are evinced in particular through Jake's work as a 'repo man', who repossesses consumer goods from people's homes when they are unable to afford their repayments:

> Crab, Hally and I worked North Belfast. It was mostly poor up there so we had a lot of ground to cover. We were thrillingly ecumenical and we raided Protestant estates with all the *élan* and grace with which we raided Catholic ones. I could never see the difference. . . . They could paint their walls any colour they wanted, they could fly a hundred flags and they still would-n't pay the rent and we would still come and take their stuff away from them. (McLiam Wilson 1996: 3)

In the era of consumer culture, Northern Ireland's social hierarchies appear to have shed their previous divisions along religious lines, and discrimination is now based purely on economic status. Sectarian identities are depicted as anachronistic and erased by the indif-ference of late-capitalist culture and its imperative that wealth be the only truly significant mark of identity.

While it is Jake's job to maintain the distinctions between Belfast's rich and poor, Chuckie's story explores the promise of capitalist culture that espouses the possibilities for individual transcendence of one's class identity. Through abandoning stereotypically Protestant loyalty towards Unionism and Britishness, Chuckie is able to reconfigure the politics of national identity and transform it from a cry of allegiance into a commodity to be sold on the international marketplace, part of what *Eureka Street* describes as 'the Irishness business' (McLiam Wilson 1996: 56). Chuckie re-imagines Ireland in the lan-guage of media advertising – 'FINE OLD COUNTRY, RECENTLY PARTITIONED. IN NEED OF MINOR POLITICAL REPAIR. PROCEED FOR QUICK SALE' (McLiam Wilson 1996: 54) – and having thus figuratively relocated his home country within the dis-course of commodity culture, he devises a series of dubious local products for export to America: small varnished twigs become genuine leprechaun walking sticks, half-Aran sweaters from Romania get a 'Made in Ireland' label and are sold on, and water from a spring in Kansas is bottled as 'IRISH WATER' and shipped to the yuppie wine bars of Boston and New York. *Eureka Street* situates the transcendence of familiar sectarian narra-tives through the relocation of Northern Irish identity within a particularly American form of consumer culture. The 'Irishness business' coincides with Chuckie's love affair with Max, an American woman whose name, in contrast to Northern Irish names, is replete with the possibility of amelioration and fulfilment. The couple's subsequent pregnancy would suggest that, in future, any Northern Irish rebirth must be predicated upon a union with this Americanised ideological alternative.

McLiam Wilson's strategy in *Eureka Street* of reconfiguring tribal identities within the discourse of commodity culture can be elucidated with reference to Fredric Jameson's reading of postmodernism as a cultural dominant that coincides with the logic of late capitalism and the rise of consumer culture. Jameson argues that postmodernism, far from radically challenging the established order and describing a new set of enabling alternatives, must ultimately be read as an obfuscation of historical narratives of underlying socioeconomic inequality (see Jameson 1991). Significantly, apologists for postmodernism often employ the language of consumer culture in order to describe its liberating potential. Thus, Lyotard defines the freedoms of the postmodern age as 'one listens to reggae, watches a Western, wears Paris perfume in Tokyo and "retro" clothes in Hong Kong' (Lyotard 1984: 76). Similarly, for David McCrone the postmodern era is one where we wear our identities 'lightly' and are free to 'pick and choose' from a variety of alternatives on offer (McCrone 1992:170). The illusory nature of this type of freedom is exposed by Alex Callinicos, who saliently observes that such choices ultimately depend on exactly who 'one' is (Callinicos 1994: 162). Only the wealthy, as the empowered minority of postmodern society, are truly free to choose from the tableaux of alternative cultural identities on offer.

It is this specious nature of such freedom that betrays the fundamentally undemocratic nature of consumer culture and compels us to reconsider postmodernism as a discourse of disempowerment, rather than any true liberation from historical narratives of social injustice. Correspondingly, postmodern readings of the Irish Troubles that avow multiculturalism as an antidote to the traditional categories of sectarian identity tend fundamentally to misdiagnose the nature of the North's ideological impasse. Historically, Northern Ireland's communal identities were not merely the badges of cultural difference, but instead facilitated institutional discrimination against the Catholic minority by the Protestant state. Popular perceptions of the Troubles as a conflict between cultural traditions elide the underlying issues of power and inequality that fostered and sustained decades of internecine conflict. It is this aspect of postmodernism, then – its tendency to disconnect questions of culture from questions of power – that we must be alert to in the following interrogation of a devolved Scottish identity.

Within post-devolution Scottish writing the kind of cultural dynamic outlined above is most discernible in the work of James Kelman, in particular his novel *You Have to Be Careful in the Land of the Free* (2004), which follows a Scottish immigrant, Jeremiah Brown, on a drinking spree in a nondescript American city the night before he is due to fly back home. The title of the novel itself points towards the illusory nature of the freedoms that constitute the ideological imperative of postmodern culture, as well as the urgent need for their re-examination. *You Have to Be Careful* initially seems to cohere with the aforementioned scepticism regarding essentialist ideas of a homogeneous Scottish identity; thus, on the cusp of 'gaun hame', Jeremiah angrily struggles to define exactly what this might mean: 'Why did I use these sentimental expressions. Hame. I mean what the fuck is hame' (Kelman 2004: 75). This epistemological uncertainty is confounded by the novel's rejection of clichéd immigrant narratives that would espouse a return to a mythological homeland or, in fact, any place of origin. Jeremiah's friend Ranjit, for example, a fourth-generation Indian immigrant, evokes just such a narrative as a possible antidote to his status as a permanent cultural outsider, and fails: 'Ranjit had the dream of getting some money together to head off to India and see how things were, maybe discover something of his past. But some of his past was in Texas and some was in the Caribbean and some was here on the east coast of Uhmerka' (Kelman 2004: 45). The novel concurs with Bell's central premise in *Questioning Scotland* that it is ultimately impossible to recover a firm sense of any fixed originary grounds on which to establish a stable subjectivity. Jeremiah's idiomatic 'gaun hame' also reminds us of the importance attached to non-standard English within Kelman's aesthetic, and it is through an examination of the literary use of different linguistic registers that it becomes possible to link my analysis of Northern Irish culture with that of contemporary Scotland.

The increasing critical interest in notions of Scottish postmodernism can be seen as continuing the debate begun in the mid-1990s by Robert Crawford, who highlighted the potentialities of Bakhtin's work as a new theoretical paradigm with which to re-examine Scotland's literary landscape. In fact, several of the critical points foregrounded by Bell can be read as re-articulations of Crawford's devolutionary anxieties regarding Scottish culture. Deploring that 'Scottish literature has been ghettoized recently in part at any rate by the refusal of most of its critics to engage with international developments in literary theory' (Crawford 1993a: 5), Crawford's work anticipates Bell's disappointment with tendencies towards inward-looking, reductive forms of critical analysis. Furthermore, Bell's invocation of Longley and the language of multicultural pluralism is strikingly similar to Crawford's claim that 'the value of Scotland is bound up with the value of Scotlands' (Crawford 1994: 56). The point is that despite significant transformations within the political landscape of Scotland, it would seem that the same critical preoccupations continue to dominate the field of Scottish culture, albeit reclothed in the more modish idiom of postmodern theory.

The most significant aspect of Crawford's work is his dramatic inversion of Muir's famous critique, arguing that the fundamental character of Scottish literature is its anti-essentialism and its refusal to commit to a single homogeneous language. Accordingly, the concept of 'Scotlands' allows Crawford to maintain the fundamental importance of territory without having to concede essentialist notions of identity that would inevitably exclude and marginalise many people who might wish to identify as 'Scottish'. Crawford's argument derives from the Bakhtinian notion that identity does not constitute itself through an isolated process of self-definition, but instead develops out of mutual interaction with others, be they individuals, nations or cultures. Bakhtin also instructs us to change the ways in which we have traditionally conceived of the novel as a literary text: rather than simply projecting the image of a world similar to our own, the novel provides its readers with 'the image of a language' from which the world of the text is subsequently constructed. Far from forging a single, coherent and definitive perspective on the world, the novel presents a diversity of different sociolects and speech registers that Bakhtin designates as 'heteroglossia', or differentiated speech. According to Bakhtin, language is stratified according to social activity and every register is a typification, a style pertaining to a specific group, with each individual linguistic code projecting its own ideological perspective on the world.

In Crawford's view, then, the vibrant interanimation of the various linguistic codes that constitute Scottish literature makes an appropriate model for articulating a complex and multifaceted national identity, one which ultimately resists the anachronism of essentialist conceptualisation. Hence, according to Crawford, it becomes imperative to re-examine the linguistic terrain of Scottish writing in terms of the ways its different languages 'illuminate, interrogate and complicate' one another (Crawford 1994: 61). A reading of Kelman's *You Have to Be Careful* as such a complex textual web of linguistic cross-pollination appears in many respects particularly fruitful. The novel is narrated in the first person by Jeremiah, but his voice continually shifts codes, adopting a host of different registers and dialects including Scots, Mexican, Negro and White American, and thus appearing to afford Jeremiah the freedom – in Lyotard's postmodern sense – to choose from a plethora of different individual and group identities on offer. However, in post-9/11 America all non-US citizens are potential suspects, required to provide proof of their identity upon demand. When this happens to Jeremiah, he internally mimics the voice of both Negro slave and Mexican immigrant, illustrating the onerous rather than emancipatory aspects of language: 'Yeh massa, here's the ID massa, thanks for asking massa. Let me bow let me scrape, you ees uhmereekaan ameego, you ees meester heroeec figyoor' (Kelman 2004: 194). By conjoining these two sociolects, the novel at once contrasts and compares Jeremiah's identity as a Scottish immigrant with the experience of contemporary Hispanic migrants as well as that of African slaves in the past.

Contemporary Scottish and Irish studies, including the present chapter, are greatly indebted to the Bakhtinian spirit of 'heteroglossia', which has helped conceptually to diversify Scotland into multicultural, postmodern 'Scotlands' as well as theoretically to relocate it within a broader framework of international reference. However, importantly, literary languages do not exist peaceably alongside one another; rather, they interrelate hierarchically, thus indexing the stratified nature of the society within which they originate. Neatly summarising this effect, Allon White writes that 'because languages are socially unequal, heteroglossia implies dialogic interaction in which the prestige languages try to extend their control and subordinated languages try to avoid, negotiate, or subvert that control' (White 1993: 137). Heteroglossia does not index some utopian multicultural pluralism, beyond the outmoded discourse of essentialist national identities. Instead, it functions to highlight how questions of power, alienation and Otherness continue to define twenty-first-century experience. Accordingly, in *You Have to Be Careful* it transpires fairly quickly that linguistic difference does not merely affirm and add texture to the novel's identity politics; it is not a mere indulgence, a conceited admission of the rich heterogeneity of contemporary identity politics. Rather, as an immigrant in America, Jeremiah finds his 'alien' status continually foregrounded through his voice, through which people identify and discriminate against him. Crucially also, his talent for temporary code-shifting does not enable him fundamentally to overcome or disguise his status as a cultural outsider. Difference breeds distrust – exclusion not integration – and thus fails to trigger an emancipatory impulse against the dominant socio-political order. As Jeremiah discovers, the bar in which he drinks is 'a homogeneous hotbed of poisonous fuckers all staring at ye because ye are the wrang "thing": religion, race, class, nationality, politics, they knew ye as soon as they look at ye, boy, you is alien' (Kelman 2004: 26)

Jeremiah's translation of his Scottishness into 'Skarrisch' is indicative of the wider appropriative tendencies that characterise America's cultural hegemony:

> Ye all want to go to the motherland in the off chance ye bump into one of your ancestors' descendants, a long lost cousin. What ye hope to discover is if ye are related to a clan chieftan, if ye are descended from royal blood and maybe own a mountain or something, if ye have any cheap servants at yer disposal, with luck they'll be wearing a kilt and sing praise songs for yer wife and family. (Kelman 2004: 14)

Within the novel 'Bonne Skallin' serves as a prism through which America refracts its own socio-economic superiority and sense of global entitlement. At the same time, however, the text refuses to identify any one convenient group of the politically and economically dispossessed within the 'land of the free'. In fact, all of Jeremiah's many attempts to communicate and foster a bond with other cultural outsiders result in frustration. A Ghanaian taxi driver refuses to enter into a conversation with him, fearing that Jeremiah might be working undercover for some domestic security agency. Similarly, when Jeremiah becomes romantically involved with Yasmin, a black jazz singer, there is no easy solidarity of the oppressed: convinced he would not understand, she refuses to talk to him about modern America's racial politics. In an interesting parallel with Chuckie and Max in McLiam Wilson's *Eureka Street*, Jeremiah and Yasmin also have a child. However, far from signalling a redemptive union and the promise of new life, the narrative ends with Jeremiah estranged from both Yasmin and his daughter, thus accentuating the existentialist aspects of the novel and its ultimate rejection of the possibility of community.

Towards the climax of *You Have to Be Careful* the increasingly drunken Jeremiah falls into conversation with an American couple who are sitting near him in the bar. What evolves is a series of miscommunications, whereby the agitated Jeremiah attempts to engage in radical political discussion only to be answered with platitudes and deliberately anodyne replies. This scenario evokes what Kelman has said about the nature of post-devolution politics, namely that 'the kind of non-debates we have now in Scotland are shocking' (Gardiner 2004c: 112). Whereas calls for a Scottish postmodernism, such as Bell's *Questioning Scotland*, renew the desire to progress beyond narratives of reductive essentialism, much of the multicultural and pluralist rhetoric they generate may very well amount to a series of Kelmanesque 'non-debates'. On examining Scottish culture in the twenty-first century it is important we stay more alert than ever to the ways in which postmodern narratives of difference, whilst ostensibly promoting 'freedom' and 'democracy', may actually perpetrate worrying practices of disempowerment and political impairment.

Chapter 36

Alternative Sensibilities: Devolutionary Comedy and Scottish Camp

Ian Brown

'Scottish camp', as defined and discussed in this chapter, comprises a broad range of literary and dramatic strategies. Like camp devices employed to subversive ends in politico-sexual contexts, these are designed to undermine assumptions about authoritative representational modes and hegemonic power. In devolutionary writing – that it, writing since the late 1970s – Scottish camp is often used to assert the integrity of certain aspects of Scottish national identities, usually to comic effect. Many Scottish writers in all contemporary genres employ such strategies to express, ever more clearly, Scotland's polyvalent identity as a post-imperial, devolved and multicultural nation, multilayered not just in terms of incoming or newly emergent cultures, but also with regard to varieties of indigenous Scottishness.

According to Ian Lucas in *Impertinent Decorum*, the camp mode

> engages and politicizes by providing alternative, even oblique sensibilities which broaden and more often than not challenge traditional ways of perceiving situations and objects. It creates new ways of seeing and relating to authority . . . Camp is always undermining authority, whether this be aesthetic, literary or artistic 'rules' or political or social power. (Lucas 1994: 115)

Such camp subversion is a recurrent device in Forbes Masson and Alan Cumming's television comedy series, *The High Life* (1995), which thrived on constant shifts in linguistic register and style, exploiting the comic potential of hybridising English and Scots cultural and linguistic references. The lead characters are two airline stewards, one of whom is named Sebastian Flight, clearly a cross-reference to Evelyn Waugh's Sebastian Flyte in *Brideshead Revisited* (1945). The authors excel at interlingual joking as, for example, when an ageing rock star is called Guy Wersch – *gey wersh* being Scots for 'very bitter/sour'. However, their playing with language goes beyond mere ironic naming and in fact pervades the whole dialogue.

In the episode 'Dug', for example, Sebastian says to Masson's character, Steve McCracken:

> Sorry to disabuse you, Stevie, but I'm in a state of total flummoxednesss. Since you picked me up this morning, the verbal hyperbole ejaculating from your gub has been straight over my heid. What the fud is bugging ye?

The shifts in register in this speech from formal English ('disabuse'), camp neologism ('flum-moxedness'), technical language ('hyperbole'), Latinate vocabulary with a more or less hidden sexual double entendre ('ejaculating') to Scots demotic ('gub') and normative Scots ('heid') is all the more remarkable in its fluidity when one recognises that these six different registers appear within the first thirty-three syntactic items of the speech. The comic sub-version continues in the next sentence, which employs the word 'fud'. It is inconceivable that usage of its English equivalent ('cunt') would have been given permission in a pro-gramme going out before the nine o'clock watershed, or possibly at all, on the BBC. The word retains its physiological and sexual meanings in Scots and is generally eschewed, espe-cially in mixed-sex company; yet it was used on more than one occasion in *The High Life* on UK-wide television. Presumably, none of the monolingual English editors realised that this strange word was more than some polite Scottish bowdlerism for 'fuck', and so the Scottish authors were able to smuggle in a word even ruder than the f-word. This kind of linguistic subversion in the series is discussed in greater detail elsewhere (see Brown and Lenz 1997); yet similar strategies can be found at work in other examples of popular television both before and after *The High Life*. Thus, the enormous success of Ian Pattison's television series *Rab C Nesbitt* (1989–99) as well as Ford Kiernan and Greg Hemphill's post-devolution *Chewin' the Fat* (1999–2002) reflects the popular approval of a new comedic mode for the representation of a subversive, even anarchic, devolutionary vision of Scots and Scottishness.

In *The Location of Culture* Homi Bhabha uses the term 'hybridity' to describe a form of resistance to cultural authority that works by infusing the colonisers' language and speech with local or native references. Certainly, it can be argued that Masson and Cumming, and to some extent also Pattison, Kiernan and Hemphill, at once absorb and modify the modes and registers of Standard English to resist an English hegemony in language and represen-tation. Arguably, too, these writers reassert the identity-bearing dynamic of Scots by playing with and across its relationship to its imperialist sister language, English. This strat-egy of playful, yet subversive linguistic border-crossing can also be found in a number of major recent translations of foreign-language drama into Scots, such as Bill Findlay and Martin Bowman's translations of Canadian Michel Tremblay's plays, starting with *The Guid Sisters* in 1989, Liz Lochhead's translations of Molière and also her *Medea* (2000), and Edwin Morgan's *Cyrano de Bergerac* (1992). All these notably creative translations employ strategies of linguistic, generic and performative hybridisation.

Lochhead, for example, uses Scottish Standard English interspersed with Scots to varied subversive effect in *Miseryguts* (2002), her version of Molière's *The Misanthrope* (1666):

ALEX   I'm too upset! I'm all churned up inside you know!
       I can't just *socialise*! Go on, away you go
       And leave me with my black despair in this dark corner.

PHIL   Sit and feed your huffy wee black dog then, Mister Horner!
       It'll keep you all the company you need – I'm no jealous!
       Bye! I'll not ask you again to come *on*, with me – to Ellie's?

                                                                    (Lochhead 2002: 72)

In this scene Alex, Lochhead's misanthrope, is telling his friend Phil about his despair at his beloved Celia's behaviour and his desire for her to 'up sticks and come up North with me'. Lochhead develops Alex's self-dramatisation from Molière's original; however, by employing the Scots colloquial 'away you go', she effectively deflates the pompous tone of the misanthrope's despair, completing her ironic rendition by juxtaposing it with the ornate, clichéd phrase 'black despair'. Further deflating Alex's stylised self-dramatisation, Phil responds using the demotic 'huffy wee black dog', which engages an established metaphor for depression, but introduces it in conjunction with the subversively comic terms 'wee' and 'huffy'. This subversion of Alex's self-regard is then reinforced by calling him the nursery-rhyme name 'Mister Horner' (who self-importantly 'sat in his corner . . . and said, "What a good boy am I"'). The repeated shifts in tone and code reach their climax in Lochhead's trademark use of unexpectedly comic rhyme choice ('jealous' – 'Ellie's'), a technique also expertly used by Morgan in *Cyrano de Bergerac*. Such theatrically effective devices combine with casual drifts between Scottish Standard English and Scots forms, multiple shifts of register, linguistic code games, and sudden switches between high-literary metaphor and nursery rhyme to mark a subversive crossing of linguistic, generic and performative borders. This facilitates the translations' hybridised resistance to imposed standards of identification.

Without doubt, linguistic hybridity in contemporary Scottish literature constitutes one of its many camp ways of challenging and broadening actual as well as would-be hegemonic structures. As Roderick Watson explains, 'the modern Renaissance of literary Scots and its contemporary manifestations are no less than a replaying of that "victory over linguistic dogmatism" ascribed to the fifteenth-century Renaissance by Bakhtin . . . This victory can only be properly achieved . . . in a multilingual world and most especially in the linguistic borders *between* languages' (Watson 2006: 166). Importantly, Watson emphasises that it is the Bakhtinian 'interorientation' of Scots and English together that generates creatively subversive energies rather than such a capacity being the sole and unique property of Scots alone. Yet it is of course also true that Scots, like any other living language, contains within itself a multiplicity of dialects, registers, jargons and hybrid expressions, which sometimes utilise the Scots and sometimes the English form of the same word.

Poet and playwright Tom McGrath draws attention to yet another anti-hegemonic aspect of multivocal language use in Scottish literature. He observes that Hugh MacDiarmid – once he had achieved his linguistic revolution – found, as do many revolutionaries, that he had become the old guard, resentful of the less dogmatic use of Scots by younger, particularly Glaswegian-Scots writers. Reflecting on MacDiarmid's attack on emergent writers such as Edwin Morgan, Tom Leonard and himself, McGrath explains:

> I suppose at that time we were coming up with a different ideology. We were coming up with a different approach after all that work, work that had been done in Scots language. We were coming up with this street level sound of existentialist man in the street, 'black man in the ghetto' type of writing. It just upset the applecart. (Brown 1984: 48)

In McGrath's view, then, the use of Scots for literary purposes can carry a liberationist force, demonstrating that the linguistic 'play' explored in this chapter has fundamental ideological, cultural and political implications. The interest of contemporary Scottish writers in Scots must not be mistaken for cultural chauvinism, but is motivated by a recognition of the power of language and its various possible applications to expressing, reflecting and developing political and cultural identities in the richly variegated culture in which these writers work. It is important to remember that it is the contemporary Scots language's rich plurality which inspires interest in writing in its manifold varieties in the first place, proliferating manifestations of an ever-stronger Scottish cultural-creative self-confidence beyond traditional 'bardic' stereotypes (see Brown 1998, 2001).

In *Gagarin Way* (2001) Gregory Burke implements a powerful demotic Scots register to explore the unlikely comedic potential of a factory heist gone wrong. Burke's play features the kind of sinewy dialogue so typical of much contemporary Scottish drama, lending specificity to Scottish experience, while at the same time problematising larger social concerns regarding economic power, globalisation and corruption. Burke's skill in crossing class-bound cultural and intellectual boundaries manifests itself very early on in the play. At only its tenth line, Tom, dressed in a security guard's uniform, asks Eddie in his 'Stone Island jacket', as they nervously await the arrival of an accomplice: 'So what was it you were saying about Sartre?' Two lines later he adds, 'you said he was shite' (Burke 2001: 5–6). The demotic humour continues when Eddie comments:

> I said I'll give the cunt his due. He came up with some snappy titles for his books. *Being and Nothingness* is a good fucking title for a book ken. But he has tay give them snappy titles tay get them shifted before folk discovered the shite that was inside. (Burke 2001: 6)

They then proceed to discuss Jean Genet in similar terms:

> Even then every criminal worth his salt had tay have a literary sideline going ay. He bashed out a load ay stuff about going round Europe thieving and hawking his arse. Sartre thought it was magic and like adopted him . . . ken as like a wee novelty act for taking tay parties and that, ken like a cabaret. Bit ay juggling. Bit ay underclass anecdote. Star ay the fucking show. (Burke 2001: 6)

As is characteristic of Scottish camp, expectation and delivery continue to jar in the play as, to great humorous effect, Burke exploits the tensions emerging from his audience's bias and perception, on the one hand, and the continually unpredictable actuality of his script, on the other. Later in the play, however, the subversive impulse shifts in focus from the comic to the black, cruel and bleak when Eddie's accomplice Gary has arrived and Tom has finally irritated Eddie too much:

EDDIE   (*to Tom*) You know . . . see since I got here tonight, you've been hanging about and getting in the way and . . . like, at one point, I was kinday wishing it was you that I had tay kill. (*Lets go of Frank and moves towards Tom.*) But you're right . . . I just realised . . . just now . . . what you said. (*Puts a hand on Tom's shoulder.*) There is another way tay day this. (*Hits Tom over the head with the gun.*) Without you fucking annoying me.

GARY   What did you day that for?

EDDIE   I've had enough ay him.

(Burke 2001: 85)

Anthony Neilson, another young Scottish playwright, is often associated with a new international movement of contemporary theatre, the so-called 'in-yer-face' school. However, on the occasion of the 2005 Gathering of Playwrights at the Gateway Theatre in Edinburgh, Neilson himself identified a link between his own work and earlier Scottish drama, mentioning, among other things, that both his parents had been involved in the first production of Donald Campbell's ground-breaking play *The Jesuit* (1976). According to Neilson, from his experiences of those rehearsals as a young child, he learned very early on to think of the personal, political, emotional and theatrical as intricately entwined. Neilson's work often aims to shock his audiences out of their middle-class complacency, particularly in regard to politico-sexual issues: thus, in *The Censor* (1997), his main characters are a porn actress and a film censor, while *Stitching* (2002) relates a story of horrifying emotional and physical abuse and self-abuse. In *Stitching* the deeply traumatised heroine seeks to stitch up her private parts in order to make herself whole again, or at least seal herself off, thus saving herself in a way which is bound simultaneously, in its induced perversity, to damage and hurt her even more. Obviously, in plays such as *Stitching* we are at some distance from the usual comic, flippant or ironic impact of Scottish camp. However, one must not forget that camp always carries a powerful representational charge capable of exploding easy traditional assumptions or points of view; in a play like *Stitching*, while far from making anyone laugh, Neilson implements subversive devices to shock, alarm and horrify his audience. Taking what appears to be at first an everyday situation and then gradually exposing what Lucas might choose to call his heroine's 'alternative sensibilities', Neilson brutally dismantles the audience's orthodox understanding of male–female relations and, by extension, any relationship between people.

In *The Wonderful World of Dissocia* (2004) Neilson explores with zany humour and deep compassion the ambivalent nature of mental illness, exploiting devices of hybridity in both the play's dramaturgy and performance. Act One takes place in the wildly colourful world of the human mind, mobilising the surreal potential of theatre to display the inner workings of the psyche of the heroine, who suffers from – but quite possibly also greatly enjoys – her serious mental illness. Here Lucas's 'alternative sensibilities' are quite clearly not only challenging to 'traditional ways of perceiving situations and objects', but have been diagnosed by orthodox medicine as aspects of a mental condition necessitating the heroine's hospitalisation. Despite – or perhaps because of – its serious subject, Act One, which makes use of trapdoors and puppets among other props and devices, is full of theatrical jokes and tricks, and zany *Alice in Wonderland* characters abound. Its colour and humour are sharply contrasted with the antiseptic colourless reality of Act Two's setting in a hospital ward. The camp and carnivalesque vision of Act One represents an entirely different normality to that of Act Two, where the patient is seen in sterile black-and-white surroundings that confine her while her carers and family struggle to comprehend her condition. The lively and articulate heroine of Act One is now drugged and taciturn, making her becoming 'well' in compliance with her culture's understanding of sanity not a very attractive prospect at all. The play is written in English rather than Scots, but Neilson's use of intertextuality and hybridity achieves an effect thematically bound into his concern with the conflict between different variations of normality and socially acceptable self-identification. His play does not simply attack hegemonic views of normality; rather, it also explores the pain, loss and damage incurred by 'being different' whenever communal norms and individual experience are at odds.

Like Neilson's work, much post-devolution Scottish theatre is often deeply concerned with exploring alternative ways of living. In the work of Henry Adams we find this concern with normativity and difference linked with issues of hybrid identification and self-realisation. Adams is originally from Caithness, a part of Scotland where to this day a particularly pronounced consciousness prevails of the local community's Norse – as opposed to Gaelic – heritage. Adams's Caithness thus represents a specific nexus of a particular version of Scottish hybridity and polyvalent national identity. While his play *Among Broken Hearts* (2000) deals with its hero's return to the north after years of absence and problematises the clash of cultures within traditional Scotland, *The People Next Door* (2003) is set in London and concerned with immigration policies in the aftermath of 9/11, exploring whether, even in an alienated society, there is still some leeway left for the excluded to develop alternative modi vivendi outside prescribed societal structures. As Danièle Berton observes,

> In [the play's] opening scene, Nigel seems to re-learn who he is. He finds, in doing this, some difficulty. He speaks of his self in the third person. He is Nigel; he is Salif; Salif is another; Salif is him. I am me, him and another . . . Destabilised and at a loss, Nigel drifts mentally between two egos, two cultures, two religions, two countries, two continents. (Berton 2005: 160; my translation)

In *The People Next Door* the nature of identity is so loosely defined that it has become hopelessly elusive and disintegrated, subject to no hegemonic order and at a tangent from standards of conventional normality.

Albeit poignantly black, the humour of the play is ultimately restorative. In a confusing and corrupt society in which orthodox power structures demean, abuse and objectify people, there still remains a potential to achieve stability in the assertion of human relationships and the discovery of a harmonious familial identity outside of recognised and hegemonically approved standards and norms. By the end of the play, Nigel's friends Mrs Mac and Marco have killed Phil, a corrupt policeman, and got away with it by claiming Phil killed himself. The killing seems easily forgotten, and the final scene is one of domestic bliss, the three characters sitting cosily together and watching TV, switching over from the news – in which an item dealing with the invasion of Iraq is 'so depressing' (Adams 2003: 85) – to watch the comedy show *Only Fools and Horses*. Having successfully resisted the forces of corruptly authoritarian, normative power and eclipsed the depressing reality of the news, Nigel, Marco and Mrs Mac form a nuclear family in a camp re-envisioning of reality. For them, it is perfect in its personal and familial, as well as political, projection of their alternative version of normality.

Such elusive artifice and marked polyvalency of individual identity and relationships are a key theme also in David Greig's *San Diego* (2003). Famously, this play casts a character whose name is 'David Greig', but that is only the beginning of an extensive hide-and-seek of mutual self-identification. Symptomatically, the opening stage direction to Act Two reads: 'Andrew, dressed as a pilot, is talking to the Pilot, who is also dressed as a pilot' (Greig 2003: 38). With apparent playfulness the capricious precariousness of personal identity runs as a theme throughout the entire play:

LAURA   What you in for?
DAVID   Chronic attention deficit disorder.
LAURA   What?
DAVID   What?
LAURA   What's chronic attention deficit disorder?
DAVID   I don't know.
             I can't concentrate long enough to find out.

             . . .

             No, that's a joke. That's a joke.
             Really I'm in for Tourette's.
LAURA   Right.

DAVID   Fuck!
LAURA   What?
DAVID   No, it's a joke. It's a joke.

(Greig 2003: 50)

Names, identities and dramatic parts continually slip and elide. For example, a woman introduces herself as 'Amy': 'My name is Amy, nice to meet you. I'm Amy's assistant' (Greig 2003: 52). A later scene features multiple Davids: David A, David B and David C (Greig 2003: 68–73).

Another recurrent motif in the play is the search for 'truth'. For example, on the grounds of an unverified postcard that tells him so, Daniel believes his mother sang the backing vocals in a Paul McCartney/Wings recording in Lagos. Towards the end of the play, Daniel is told by David that his mother's name is 'not listed on the album', thus proving Daniel's postcard to be 'a lie'. To this Daniel responds in defence: 'It's true. She's not on the album, but she was on the US tour. McCartney invited her to sing backing vocals . . . She still lives in San Diego. This is the address . . . Her name's Patience but she calls herself Amy' (Greig 2003: 101). Greig's *San Diego* explores the nature of identity, reality and truth quite relentlessly. Like Neilson and Adams, Greig's medium is English; however, his work investigates exactly the same polyvalency of identity signalled and explored by camp register shifts in other devolutionary writing.

A novelist clearly identifying with creating a similarly ironic variety of alternative or parallel identities and realities is Irvine Welsh. For example, in 'The First Day of the Edinburgh Festival', a section from *Trainspotting* (1993), the title sets up an expectation of – indeed an explicit reference to – artistic celebration. In fact, however, the section deals with Welsh's junkie-hero Renton's desperate quest for a fix; finding his dealer has only two opium suppositories available, Renton inserts both of them and leaves. However, on leaving the dealer's flat, he finds his six-day constipation has passed and, overcome by a call of nature, he rushes into the lavatory of a bookie's in a Muirhouse shopping centre where, to his dismay, he discovers a 'seatless bowl fill ay broon water, toilet paper and lumps ay floating shite' (Welsh 1993: 24). Only after using this extremely unsalubrious specimen of a toilet does he realise he has also deposited his precious cargo into the disgusting mixture in the bowl. Driven by need, he plunges his hand in to save the suppositories and, once he has successfully retrieved them – somewhat the worse for wear in one case – he reinserts them. In this scene, not only does Welsh pull off a dark, scabrously filthy comedy act, but he also represents in most graphic and realist detail a drug addict's desperation and alternative view on life. The reader's expectation, set up by the ironic title of the piece, which frames the whole episode, is mocked even further in the section's final paragraph, which begins: 'At the bus stop, ah realised what a sweltering hot day it had become. Ah remembered somebody sais that it wis the first day ay the Festival. Well, they certainly got the weather fir it' (Welsh 1993: 27). The everyday platitude – 'they certainly got the weather fir it' – highlights the absence of any common everydayness from the preceding scene or, rather, identifies the incident as recognisably 'everyday' only within an entirely other order of normality.

This kind of subversion is certainly a device at which Welsh particularly excels. In another section from *Trainspotting*, the punningly titled 'Courting Disaster', Renton and Spud find themselves before a magistrate's court. Through the persona of Renton, Welsh observes: 'As an educated man ah'm sure he kens far mair aboot the great philosophers than a pleb like me. Yiv goat tae huv fuckin brains tae be a fuckin judge. S no iviry cunt thit kin dae that fuckin joab' (Welsh 1993: 166). Here the intended subversion is brought about by juxtaposing the assumptions informing a reference to the 'great philosophers' with Renton's demotic swearing, and accentuated further by describing the role of a magistrate as the kind of 'joab' that 'no iviry cunt . . . kin dae'. The prestige and authority of a magisterial position are undermined by its being summarised simply as a job needing 'fuckin brains'. Welsh's multilayered comic representation then continues to contrast the magistrate's English with Spud's colloquial Scots; in response to the magistrate's question whether he intended to sell stolen books 'in order to finance [his] heroin habit', Spud blurts out, 'that's spot on man . . . eh . . . ye goat it, likesay, Spud nodded, his thoughtful expression sliding into confusion' (Welsh 1993: 166). The use of 'thoughtful' in this sentence is implemented with deliberate satiric precision, exposing how linguistic differences reinforce and underline differences in world view, class and authority between 'official' society, on the one hand, and Spud and his mates, on the other.

One of many darkly comic scenes in *Porno* (2002), Welsh's sequel to *Trainspotting*, can be found in chapter 40 – 'Scam # 18,745' – whose title enciphers the highly romanticised historical date of 1745 to introduce a sequence of events that turns out to be distinctly unromantic. Describing the making of a pornographic home movie, Welsh at once imitates and satirises the stylistic features of pulp pornography by engaging the film crew in orgiastic sexual activity, which is abruptly cut short by the announcement that 'the man fae the *Sunday Mail*'s here. They've a photographer' (Welsh 2002: 251). This sudden interruption leads to the catastrophic collapse of one of the women onto the would-be leading man Terry's penis, and in chapter 42 – '. . . ruptured his penis . . .' – even more darkly comic play is derived from this unfortunate accident.

Welsh continually modifies and readjusts his linguistic register and other representational devices in order to give as accurate a picture of his characters' lives as possible. In 'CRACK HOOR', another chapter from *Porno*, for example, he describes in vivid Scots a fight between a husband and wife:

> Ah pills up her heid n she's blowin water n blood ootay her nose n thrashin aroound like a fish caught oan a line. Ah hear a voice n that wee Michael's standin in the doorway n eh goes: – What ur ye daein tae Mum, Dad? (Welsh 2002: 327)

The violence of the scene is presented with cinematic immediacy and entirely without rhetorical frills, its domestic horror exacerbated by the presence of 'wee Michael' as witness and Welsh's insertion of the common familial terms of affection 'Mum' and 'Dad'.

In some of Welsh's work, the subversion of authority and normality, as well as the deliberate frustration of his readers' expectation, can spiral into manifestations of pure violence so overwrought and seemingly choreographed that they almost appear camp in themselves. Characteristically, his play *You'll Have Had Your Hole* (1998) combines an alarmingly excessive representation of violence – it has been accused of homophobia, misogyny and dramaturgical naivety – with more subtly subversive linguistic manoeuvres. Thus, the play's title constitutes a distortion of the supposedly typical Edinbourgeois phrase, 'You'll have had your tea', which offers and simultaneously withholds a welcoming gesture of hospitality. As a darkly camp allusion to sexual intercourse, ringing with the play's 'in-yer-face' enactment of homosexual rape and mindless sadistic torture, the title thus brings about a powerfully subversive fusion of apparent Morningside respectability with psychopathology, crime, depravity and sexual exploitation.

To conclude, Scottish camp is evidently no one simple range of devices, but rather a complexity of representational methods available to contemporary Scottish writers. Some of these are easily identifiable as part of a general poetics of cultural, literary and linguistic subversion whereas others – such as the strategically implemented shifts between Scots and English – are specific to the Scottish context. However, what this chapter has sought to demonstrate is not primarily the new or innovative power of register shifts, and other related techniques and devices, as such. After all, the strategic use of register shifts has a long tradition in Scottish literature, going at least as far back as the poetry of William Dunbar. Rather, it has attempted to show how this broad range of techniques and devices aggregates into 'Scottish camp' as a major representational resource in devolutionary writing. There, it serves Scottish authors to highlight, problematise and explore a whole plethora of topical twenty-first-century issues to do with power and identity, personal and familial as well as communal.

Chapter 37

Against Realism: Contemporary Scottish Literature and the Supernatural

Kirsty Macdonald

Creative exploitation of the supernatural has long been a feature of Scottish literature, operating both as a playful means of representation and as a peculiarly pliable tool for onto-logical explorations. While this tradition continues to connect a broad constellation of texts from the ballads of oral folklore to immediately contemporary work, twentieth-century Scottish writing is generally agreed to have been marked particularly by the rise of realism. The realist mode, in which appearances of the supernatural are by definition an impossibility, sought more or less unproblematically to reflect the 'truths' of Scottish life, be it in fiction, film or television. This chapter will explore the work of several recent writers and directors who have reacted against the swing in Scottish literature towards realist conventions by fruitfully integrating the supernatural within the realist mode and thereby opening up new representational possibilities for twenty-first-century narratives.

As a mode of representation, realism has been seen by many critics as the dominant force in Scottish fiction throughout the twentieth century, following a rejection of myth-making genres, such as kailyardism and tartanry. For example, Margaret Elphinstone argues that 'the unique status of Scottish fantasy has been a well-established tenet of Scottish liter-ature and criticism, but the dominant genre at the end of the twentieth century is contemporary, urban and realistic' (Elphinstone 2000), and in his contribution to the Edinburgh Lectures series, Channel 4's 'Regions and Nations' director Stuart Cosgrove complains that recent Scottish films, bound by 'the overweening conventions of urban realism', give 'the cumulative and relentless impression that Scotland is a failing and crim-inal society' (Cosgrove 2005). And yet, upon closer analysis there is evidence that the prac-tice of realism is never quite so pure or straightforward, even with respect to the major urban proponents of the mode, such as James Kelman and Alasdair Gray. According to Cairns Craig, 'Kelman's working-class realism is tactical rather than essential' (Craig 1993: 105), while with reference to Gray's work Kevin Williamson argues that 'Scottish fiction was often perceived, unfairly, as being a tough uncompromising bastion of grim West Coast urban realism' (Williamson 2002a: 183). One such unfair, partial and problematic percep-tion can be found on the front cover of Randall Stevenson and Gavin Wallace's *The Scottish Novel Since the Seventies* (1993), which features a flat-capped man walking two grey-hounds on a piece of waste ground against a post-industrial background of slag heaps and factories. Deliberately designed to react against the kailyard cliché of rural wilds and com-fortable Scots domesticity, the cover belies the fact that several of the authors discussed by the volume's contributors do in actual fact concern themselves with rural as well as middle-class characters and contexts.

In Scotland realism has become associated with a politically motivated effort to tell the 'truth' about the harsh realities of urban life, and as a result it has come to index a peculiarly masculine, working-class – and often violent – perspective as a marker of cultural authenticity. Examples abound from the fiction of George Friel, Robin Jenkins, James Kelman, William McIlvanney and Irvine Welsh to the films of Lynne Ramsay and television serials such as STV's long-running *Taggart* (since 1985). Possibly in response to its homogenising effect on representation, a number of writers and directors have begun to interrogate Scottish realism and its associated metanarratives by adopting anti-realist strategies and in particular older indigenous traditions such as an employment of the supernatural. Despite being described and even celebrated as a long-established representational device in a number of recent critical studies by Elphinstone (1992, 2000), Colin Manlove (1994, 1996) and Douglas Gifford (forthcoming), little has as yet been said about the most current examples of the tradition, even though the abundance of recent Scottish writing featuring the supernatural in some form or other clearly suggests that something about it continues to appeal irresistibly to the contemporary imagination. New manifestations of traditional supernatural elements combine in these texts to generate a multiplicity of perspectives as well as a general disregard for conventional boundaries in representation. As Gifford writes in 'Nathaniel Gow's Toddy', since the late twentieth century several writers have emerged who are 'developing a new kind of imaginative relationship with their country and its culture, a relationship which refuses to accept a simple realism of generally bleak and economically deprived urban character'. By introducing something manifestly 'unreal' or supernatural into a realist context, writers challenge the metanarratives of 'Scottishness' that have come to be associated with realism as a mode of representation, portraying characters of all classes, genders and sexualities while maintaining a specific political position within a genre traditionally perceived as a form of escapism removed from real concerns.

In this chapter the supernatural is defined non-religiously as an unfamiliar existential anomaly – albeit possibly one harking back to native folk traditions – occurring within a contemporary secular context. Three texts will be examined in detail: Andrew Greig's novel *When They Lay Bare* (1999), Ali Smith's novel *Hotel World* (2001) and David Mackenzie's feature film *The Last Great Wilderness* (2002). However, these must by no means be regarded as isolated cases. *Petra* (1996), David Greig's play for children, features the author's ghost appearing on stage amongst a cast of prosaic characters and much political commentary. Similarly, the BBC television serial *Sea of Souls* (2004–6) is premised on a constant dialogue between the rational and the paranormal, while the thankfully last ever episode of the BBC's *Monarch of the Glen* (1999–2005) featured Hector MacDonald, the old Laird of Glenbogle, returning in ghostly form to play some billiards, enjoy a dram and give his approval to his widow's remarriage. In cinema, Neil Marshall's schlock-horror flick *Dog Soldiers* (2002) parodied supernatural stereotypes associated with the Scottish Highlands by presenting the residents of a remote glen somewhere north of Fort William as werewolves. John Herdman continues to incorporate both the supernatural and the fantastic in his often surreally satirical novels as, for example, in *The Sinister Cabaret* (2001). Chris Dolan's humorous *Ascension Day* (1999) features modern-day angels, while the cosmopolitan magic realism at work in Christopher Whyte's novels creates compelling page-turners with a subversive edge. In poetry, too, Edwin Morgan's 'Demon' sequence (1999) defamiliarises our view of the world by adopting the anachronistic, yet effectively menacing perspective of a demon, while Alan Riach's innovative and tender take on the supernatural in his poem 'Drumelzier' (2004) acknowledges the presence within our everyday lives of things ethereal and inexplicable. Importantly, in all these texts the supernatural appears not in a fantastic otherworld, but in actual reality, be it historical or contemporary, indeed in a world comparable to that portrayed in much realist writing.

In *After Theory* Terry Eagleton argues that liminality can be at once a most productive and provocative location: 'To be inside and outside a position at the same time – to occupy a territory while loitering sceptically on the boundary – is often where the most intensely creative ideas stem from' (Eagleton 2003: 40). This kind of liminal position is taken up by the texts discussed in the present chapter, as they reach across the generic territories of realism and the traditional ghost story. The supernatural tale or ghost story is commonly associated with popular entertainment and conservative perspectives; however, through its engagement with realism in these and other contemporary examples, it reveals itself as the inside, or underside, of realism, unsettling the latter's closed, monochromatic preconceptions by means of dialogic indeterminacy and ambivalence and thus breaking new representational ground. Whereas the texts as a whole continue to identify as realist, they are also always generically subversive by implicitly rejecting the very mode that sustains them. Symptomatically, in *When They Lay Bare* Marnie, Greig's mysterious heroine, declares that 'life's most interesting where the border's up for grabs' (Greig 1999: 41). The novel presents the intricately woven story of Marnie's quest to uncover the truth about the death of Jinny Lauder and its connection to the latter's love affair with Sim Elliot, the now elderly laird of an historic Borders estate. The 'border' in the novel is the literal borderland of Scotland, but also that between real and unreal, seen and unseen, and the many borders that exist between individuals, often the hardest kind to penetrate. The text's structure is given shape through its relation to a series of antique plates depicting the ballad 'The Twa Corbies', and echoes of Scott and Hogg resonate throughout. Yet its supernatural atmosphere goes beyond literary allusion: Jinny's story is related through Sim's flashbacks to the 1960s, and she inhabits the present of the text as an ambiguous ghost, perhaps real, perhaps a projection of the guilty consciences and wishful thinking of Sim and his right-hand man, the estate manager Tat.

The first haunting experienced by the two men, however, is far from supernatural as, uninvited, Marnie moves herself into a cottage on Sim's estate and is soon suspected to be Jinny's daughter, returning to resolve her mother's unfinished business. But as Sim reflects, 'no, it wasn't possible. This is paranoia. This is Banquo's ghost. A thing of nothing but conscience' (Greig 1999: 68), and in the end he is proved right, when it is revealed that Marnie is not Jinny's daughter at all, but the former lover of Jinny's daughter. Greig introduces Marnie's homosexuality in a refreshingly matter-of-fact way as one of the many ways in which individuals relate to each other, and Marnie's sexuality is part of the same spectrum of transgression she thrives on when the border is 'up for grabs'. And yet, ultimately it is Jinny herself who appears as the more appropriate 'Banquo's ghost', given that she may actually have been murdered by Sim. However, when she first appears to Tat, he recognises her as a much more empowering and positive force: 'She isn't covered in blood, head caved in, last breath hissing from her battered mouth. She is just his friend Jinny, nodding to him to follow her as they start to wander slowly down through the trees' (Greig 1999: 291). The fact that Jinny appears to both Sim and Tat suggests that she is a real presence rather than a 'thing of nothing but conscience', and in fact there are instances when she appears to intervene directly in the action. At the same time, Greig depicts the two elderly men deliberately as lonely, isolated and emotionally unstable, thus offering a possible psychological explanation for their 'supernatural' encounters. In a place where borders are erected only to be transgressed, and laws only to be broken, these visions are left appropriately unexplained. Through their turbulent relationship, on both sides of the grave, Jinny and Sim play out an ancient local feud between the Lauders and the Elliots, warring factions of the Borders nobility, and as a phantom from the past, whether real or imagined, Jinny must return to the scene to catalyse change, for the individuals as well as the community.

While the ambiguity of Jinny's appearances is sustained to the end, her ghostly presence becomes part of a wider supernatural context, referred to by Marnie as 'Spook', designating a kind of spirituality suggesting that past, present and future are all inextricably interconnected. As Marnie explains to Sim's son Dauvit, a born-again Christian, 'we both believe in Spook, the invisible. We're surrounded by the dead and the past and the future. It's all there while we sit here. In its way it's as solid as these hills, and without it nothing means anything' (Greig 1999: 79). When she was alive, Jinny would tap into what she called 'the astral telephone' (Greig 1999: 174), revealing a telepathic gift enabling her to summon Sim just by thinking about him. In *When They Lay Bare* the boundaries between the powers of the mind and a more traditional supernatural power are blurred, as are the boundaries between selves. Intersubjectivity becomes the apposite state and proves a more evocative force than individuality. The border is once again 'up for grabs': linked to the literary trope of the double, it destabilises the boundaries within as well as between selves, intimating a desire for both freedom and fusion, while also facilitating an interrogation of power relationships. Intersubjectivity and liminality are comparably ambiguous states. The presence of Marnie and Jinny as liminal figures provides the other characters with the freedom of becoming liminal themselves, that is, to venture into an unbounded state between the binaries of self and other, individuality and communality, or past and present.

When They Lay Bare includes a number of passages printed in italics that function as a kind of chorus commenting and reflecting on the plot developments. At first these passages appear to be an extension of Marnie's voice, but it is equally possible that they mediate Jinny's; in any case, in them a voice expresses itself that has access to and broadcasts a supernatural perspective. The passages heighten the ambiguity of who, or what kind of force, is involved in directing the events of the novel. Comprising one of these passages, the very last lines of the novel read:

> *In time there will be made another song, another story. And in time that too will be half-forgotten, doubtful and misread. Then there will be only the old road, a rickle of stones where a cottage once was, and the wind keening over the dyke for evermore.*
>
> *The mist clasps about me by the Border. I walk into it and am gane.* (Greig 1999: 322)

This could be Marnie's farewell to the estate, or Jinny's farewell to the world. Either way, the speaker has fulfilled her role and completed what had been left unfinished by history, correcting misinterpretations of past events and overruling doubts in order to enable mobility and clear space for change. Despite its purposely indefinite ending the novel evidently aims to accentuate the importance of the past for a meaningful and effective engagement with the present. At one point Marnie is described as 'stepping in and out of two worlds. Back and forward, past and present, real and pretend' (Greig 1999: 42), and this is in a sense what the narrative does as a whole, inhabiting the territory of realism only for so long as is necessary, then implementing devices of the ambiguous, the ethereal and the spiritual in order to transport the representation of existences and relationships beyond the everyday and even the earthly. Deliberately going against the grain of late-twentieth-century Scottish literary conventions, Greig not only portrays middle- and upper-class characters in a rural context, but also homosexuality and post/modern spirituality, thus opening up new potentialities for the representation of Scottish identity in fiction.

The supernatural element in Ali Smith's *Hotel World* is present in a much more tangible form, simply because the first section of this structurally complex novel, significantly entitled 'Past', is narrated by an actual ghost. As we are told on the first page, 'here's the story; it starts at the end' (Smith 2001a: 3). Nineteen-year-old Sara Wilby has been killed in an accident at work in a local branch of 'Global Hotels' and is now trying to ascertain exactly what happened and why she still exists in the world, haunting those she has left behind. As in Greig's novel, the supernatural is encountered in a world that is recognisably ours, yet this time it is an urban space of work, loneliness and even homelessness – a deliberate nod to the urban realism of other contemporary Scottish fiction. 'Future in the Past', another section of Smith's novel, is narrated in stream-of-consciousness mode by Sara's younger sister, Clare, whom Sara appears to at one point. Clare refuses to believe what she sees: 'Dead people when they come aren't like when she came back just wearing her cardigan like normal usually they're always vampires or weird & scary moaning on about revenge or not there at all they just move things round rooms invisible' (Smith 2001a: 201). The surprising ordinariness of the ghost appears to be the crux of the novel, as Smith aims to familiarise what is conventionally 'other', be it death or homosexual desire. Still, however transiently, part of our world, cardigan and all, a considerable portion of Sara's personality has remained with her disembodied self. She still sounds like a nineteen-year-old girl, displaying an enthusiastic, hyperactive energy and wide-eyed sense of humour, for example, when she remembers the joy of talking: 'Now that I'm silent forever, haha, it's all words words words with me' (Smith 2001a: 5).

Sara exists in a liminal state, neither fully dead and gone, nor fully alive. As Victor Turner explains,

> The attributes of liminality or the liminal personae ('threshold people') are necessarily ambiguous, since this condition and these persons elude or slip through the network of classifications that normally locate states and positions in a cultural space. Liminal entities are neither here nor there; they are betwixt and between the positions assigned and arrayed by law, custom, convention and ceremonial . . . Thus liminality is frequently likened to death, to being in the womb, to invisibility, to darkness, to bisexuality. (Turner 1969: 95)

According to Turner's definition, Sara is liminal not only in terms of her spectral status, but also with regard to the way she existed in life. Notably, the summer before her death, Sara fell in love with a girl, making her feel as if she had become 'invisible' (Smith 2001a: 23). The novel presents homosexuality in a radically understated way, as something markedly ordinary in no need of an elaborate commentary:

> I had fallen, and it was for the girl in the watch shop. I was happy . . . In the dark I decided to let myself think a little more about the girl. It was a lot easier in the dark. It didn't feel anywhere near as risky as it did to catch myself thinking about her with the light on. (Smith 2001a: 19, 22)

For Sara, the liminality of darkness is a safe place to examine her burgeoning emotions, which are presented as entirely natural and unsurprising, just as the ghost is for the reader.

Remarkably, Sara's memories do not emanate from her disembodied self alone; her dead and buried body, too, continues to exude traces of consciousness. Indeed, Sara torments her rotting remains in an attempt to retrieve vital corporeal information she cannot remember, yet without which she must fail to negate the nothingness she faces, her gradual loss of articulacy signifying her loosening hold on our 'hotel' world – a place where one stays temporarily, in transit, before moving on. Smith's ensuing depiction of Sara's dialogue with her human remains is both representationally and theologically innovative:

> Go away. You said you would. I've told you. Don't you have a home to go to?
> Aren't you supposed to go to heaven or hell or somewhere?
> Soon enough, I said (to God knows where).
> Sooner the better, she said. I'm tired. Go away. Don't come back. We've no business with each other any more, and she closed like a lid. (Smith 2001a: 26)

Sara's spirit and body now exist independently, each possessing its own discrete concerns and capabilities. Whereas the body wants to rest and return, in Freudian terms, to the comforting inertia of death, the spirit feels a desperate need to continue communicating. A traditionally Christian interpretation of Smith's portrayal is impossible: both entities are equally indispensable constituents of Sara's being, her spirit showing itself no more enlightened regarding its ultimate destination than her body. The body articulates for the benefit of the spirit the physical sensations now unavailable to the latter and, more significantly, the importance put by our culture on physical appearance, body image and material possessions. As Monica Germaná concludes:

> The ghost story is thus re-defined and becomes a story of the seen world looked upon from the distorted angles of a spirit, an outcast, a madwoman, a liar or a bereaved girl. Smith turns the order of things upside down and successfully exposes the 'real' world to criticism subversively originated from unconventional voices. (Germaná 2003)

Sara's ghostly observations not only successfully defamiliarise our world and expose it to interrogation but also, more optimistically, urge us, as the novel's narrative refrain insists, to 'remember you must live'. The sheer joy Sara experiences in naming ordinary everyday objects, or her memories of taste and touch, remind us of the wonder of life, which one must live boldly embracing one's perceived aberrancies by transforming them into powerful, ennobling attributes.

David Mackenzie's *The Last Great Wilderness* similarly features a loosely linked group of outsiders, who have chosen to become 'invisible' by absenting themselves from society, journeying northwards from various urban centres and secluding themselves in the Moor Lodge retreat for the emotionally wounded. The setting is recognisably the Highlands, more specifically a hotel even more remote than Greig's Borders estate, 'somewhere on the way to Skye'. Mackenzie's characters seek escape from various personal troubles, including domestic abuse, agoraphobia and paedophiliac tendencies. Their retreat is stumbled upon by two southern interlopers whose car has run out of petrol nearby: Charlie, intent on journeying north to wreak revenge on the musician who ran away with his wife, and Vince, a male prostitute from London on the run from a contract killing taken out on him by a client's husband. As in Greig's novel, there is a hint of the supernatural throughout the film, exacerbated by its eerie setting in a vague and barren corner of the West Highlands and the Gothic location of the remote hotel, and accentuated further by suitably intense widescreen images of the desolate landscape. This supernatural presence in the film is deepened by the religious-cult-like practices carried out by the residents of the retreat as 'treatment' for their problems, including chanting, fire walking, and burying their deceased in a nearby forest. The obvious allusion is to the pagan practices featured in cult horror films such as Robin Hardy's *The Wicker Man* (1973), and indeed Mackenzie's film has much in common with its low-budget precursor. In both films the north is portrayed as a liminal hinterland, a wilderness on the margins, which becomes the site of a primitive, archaic supernaturalism. As Mackenzie's guru-like Ruaridh, the retreat's therapist, initially warns Charlie and Vince, 'normal rules don't apply around here'.

Like *When They Lay Bare*, *The Last Great Wilderness* focuses on one specific, ambiguously supernatural encounter, that between Vince and the mysterious Flora, the local gillie's daughter, who died in a fire some years previously. Flora appears to Vince repeatedly, but to him alone, so that the viewer is left unsure as to her 'real' apparitional status. She may be a harbinger of Vince's death, which occurs violently towards the end of the film, when he is eventually tracked down and castrated by the contract killers. Alternatively, Flora may be little more than a projection of Vince's mind, an embodiment of perfect purity, something he desires yet will forever elude him. Vince is a big-city lothario who sells his body for money. Flora is a local girl living a secluded life until her mother leaves and her subsequent grief develops into depression. She is sensitive, young and beautiful, while he is worldly and wearied. As we learn from the video-recorded interview Vince finds and watches, Flora sought help from Ruaridh as her depression developed. Much to the horror and hurt of her father Magnus, it is revealed that Ruaridh advised Flora to kill herself, or at least very strongly encouraged her suicidal impulse.

One major, if covert, theme throughout Mackenzie's film is euthanasia, ranging from the assisted suicide of the retreat's elderly founder and the discovery that Magnus shot dead his own daughter when he found her trapped in a fire (almost certainly of her own making) to the violent conclusion of Vince's life. Slowly bleeding to death whilst nailed to a tree, Vince is shot by his now close friend Magnus with the very same rifle with which he mercy-killed his daughter several years before. Thus, a definitive link is established between Vince and Flora, who, the film suggests, will be united after death. Mackenzie shows each act of euthanasia as driven by self-effacing compassion and love beyond the bounds of ordinary relationships. During each incident, the devastating toll of the act, both for the dying themselves and for those that help end their pain, is emphasised by sensitive close-up shots. The film self-consciously poses the question if, in the middle of a liminal and barren nowhere, it is conceivable to make difficult, compassionate choices, to act nobly and courageously in the face of death, then why are similar acts deemed morally unacceptable in mainstream society? Like the darkness for Smith's protagonists and the borderland for Greig's, Mackenzie's 'last great wilderness' constitutes a liminal space which enables fruitful transgression.

Interestingly, the issues of homosexual desire and gender ambiguity latently present in Greig's and Smith's novels also recur in Mackenzie's film. During the wake the community organise on their elderly leader's death, everybody assumes the dress and mannerisms of the other sex, suggesting an affinity between different kinds of 'passing'. The proximity of death and cross-dressing comes to seem appropriate and even ordinary. Moreover, when Charlie and Vince first arrive at Moor Lodge, Ruaridh most casually asks them: 'Will you be wanting two rooms, or are you homosexual?' Significantly, through his exposure to the general behavioural freedom practised by the members of the community, Charlie gradually comes to abandon his socially conditioned masculinity as the cuckolded husband intent on revenge. The concluding scene of the film shows Charlie in his car, driving away from the retreat to an unknown destination, initially wearing his characteristically pious frown, but then erupting into laughter. As the shaman figure Ruaridh poignantly explains to Charlie during the cross-dressing scene earlier in the film, 'you know, the last great wilderness is not out there', pointing out of the window. He then points to his own head, asserting that 'it's in here'. The real hauntings, magic and liminality come from the mind. The conventional associations of setting and context are thus subtly subverted.

In all three texts discussed in this chapter, the supernatural – manifesting as the unconventional, surprising and even frightening – is introduced in a self-consciously matter-of-fact and 'realist' way. Past and present, life and death, traditional gender roles and individual self-determination are all shown to meld and intersect. As Peter Buse and Andrew Stott put it, the literary potential of ghosts is ontologically radical:

> Ghosts are neither dead nor alive, neither corporeal objects nor stern absences . . . standing in defiance of binary oppositions such as presence and absence, body and spirit, past and present, life and death. For deconstruction, these terms cannot stand in clear, independent opposition to one another, as each can be shown to possess an element or trace of the term that it is meant to oppose. (Buse and Stott 1999: 10)

Realist representation is by no means abandoned; rather, each text cultivates realism while mixing in traces of other, allegedly oppositional or irreconcilable modes in order to interrogate representation itself. The given contexts are recognisably familiar, and so are the characters; it is just that some of them happen to be dead or possess supernatural qualities. Although the supernatural is cited widely as a tradition in Scottish literature and culture, these recent examples document a significant new trend, showing the older ghosts and demons as having evolved into expressions of new fears and desires, repressions, fantasies and nightmares. At the same time, the 'new' Scottishness is represented as a fluid and forever renegotiable proliferation of possible identities derived from moments of transgression and experiences of liminality, and fashioned in opposition to the more traditional metanarratives of Scottish 'realism'. Moreover, the supernatural is employed to enable a productive engagement with the past in a way that reflects on the present and promotes future mobility. The supernatural continues to be employed in intricate and subtle representational modulations of reality, allowing modes conventionally perceived as escapist and popular to be renegotiated as culturally and politically pertinent.

Chapter 38

A Double Realm: Scottish Literary Translation in the Twenty-first Century

John Corbett

At the dawn of the twenty-first century, translation – that Cinderella of Scottish literature – may at last be going to the ball. My present chapter investigates the range, functions,
and as yet to be revealed cultural repercussions of translation activity in Scotland today.
Rather than pretending to be a comprehensive survey of current translation activity, it
introduces a number of individual case studies as indicators of more general contemporary
concerns as well as possible future directions.

On 16 February 2004 the still relatively new Scottish Executive appointed Edwin
Morgan as 'Scots Makar' or 'Poet for Scotland'. To mark this honour, Morgan published a
translation of 'Metrum de Praelio apud Bannockburn', a seven-hundred-year-old poem by
Robert Baston, an English Carmelite friar, who had travelled north with Edward II's army,
effectively in the role of poet laureate and England's official war poet. Originally, Baston's
job had been to record the anticipated famous English victory over Robert the Bruce's
army; however, unfortunately for the English, events unfolded in a rather different manner
and Baston found himself a prisoner. For his ransom Robert instructed Baston to produce
a poem marking England's defeat instead, which he duly did. It is a phrase from Morgan's
translation of Baston's poem which gives the present chapter its title:

> Est regnum duplex, et utrumque cupit dominari
> sed neutrum suplex vult a reliquo superari.

> This is a double realm: each itches to dominate:
> Neither hands over the helm for the other to subjugate.

> (Morgan 2004a: 11)

At first glance, Morgan's chosen subject for his occasional translation appears to follow
the populist triumphalism of the *Braveheart* industry, or even hark back to the propagand-
ist romances of the fourteenth and fifteenth centuries, such as John Barbour's *The Brus*
(1375) and Blind Harry's *Wallace* (1477), which mark the beginning of Lowland vernacular literature in Scotland. However, given the nature of the source text, a poem that sal-
vages dignity from defeat by universalising the timeless message of the atrocities of war, it
is possible to read Morgan's version as a more nuanced revision of the clichés of the old
enmity, and one that has uneasy contemporary relevance:

I am a Carmelite, and my surname is Baston.
I grieve that I survive a happening so harrowing and ghastly.
If it is my sin to have left out what should be in,
Let others begin to record it, without rumour or spin.

(Morgan 2004a: 29)

What at first might seem like an occasion for shallow chauvinist nostalgia becomes instead – through the act of translation – a commentary on our iconic victory from the perspective of the other, and indeed a barbed critique of our present-day political leaders who continue to 'spin' the virtues of warfare, in which the only victors are ultimately the profiteers. As Alan Riach and Douglas Gifford note in *Scotlands: Poets and the Nation*, Morgan's translation of Baston 'opens up many . . . questions about national identity and self-determination, the value of poetic interpretation, personal commitment, faith in human potential and sorrow at the waste of so much of it' (Gifford and Riach 2004: xxxv). Because it is essentially dialogic, translation makes a particularly powerful tool for questioning deep-seated cultural and nationalist assumptions; thus, Morgan's resetting of Baston overlays past and present, English and Scottish, victim and victor. It complicates the relationship between the categories and so probes the means by which we construct personal and communal identities.

That this inquisitive translation came to mark Morgan's elevation to national treasure adds a further irony, as does the brief, congratulatory foreword by the First Minister, Jack McConnell. The early years of the devolved parliament have been characterised by disenchantment with the new breed of Holyrood legislators (such as McConnell) amongst the champions of Scottish culture (such as Morgan). The latter group claim at least some of the credit for the former's empowerment. Their disenchantment becomes evident in 'Acknowledge the Unacknowledged Legislators', an original poem composed by Morgan for the Scottish Parliament Cross-Party Group for Literature and read out at its inaugural meeting in June 2005 (Morgan 2005). The broader problems surrounding Scottish cultural politics in the twenty-first century also manifest themselves in the government's commissioning of a Cultural Review report into arts funding, published in June 2005 to a mixed reception. Among other things, the anticipated reorganisation of arts funding in Scotland is likely to affect the investment given to bodies aiming to raise public awareness of translation in and out of the languages of Scotland.

The phrase 'double realm' is, of course, peculiarly apt to describe Scottish translation. Scotland is stereotypically the country of Jekyll and Hyde, and its polyglot, heterogeneous history continues to confuse a settled, simple, unitary sense of Scottish identity. Our others are everywhere, within and outwith our political boundaries. Lowland Scotland defines itself in opposition to the Highlands, while urban Scotland defines itself in opposition to rural Scotland, and Catholic Scotland defines itself in opposition to Protestant Scotland. Immigrant Scotland defines itself in opposition to indigenous Scotland (whatever *that* is), while Scotland as a whole defines itself in opposition to England, and every vice has its versa. Each of these imagined identities comes with its own malleable set of linguistic markers: Gaelic, urban Scots, rural Scots, English (of various colours), not to mention the non-indigenous community languages. But the self is also porous and defies easy categorisation: notably, the largest Gaelic-immersion school in Scotland, serving pre-school children through to the end of secondary education, is now Glasgow Gaelic School, in the heart of the metropolis. Moreover, wherever the self comes into contact with its others, hybrid languages and identities emerge, as in Suhayl Saadi's *The Burning Mirror* (2001) or

Psychoraag (2004). In similar ways, the act of translation refashions the late-medieval Latin poetry of Robert Baston into a medium through which Morgan is able to lament the horror of war and point a finger at contemporary world politics.

A corollary of translation is that it becomes impossible to think of texts in isolation, or even of writers as individual composers. Christopher Whyte raises this issue in his discussion of the work of the Scottish Gaelic poet Aonghas MacNeacail, whose English versions of his own poetry 'serve to destabilise and energise the Gaelic' (Whyte 2004a: 227). Whyte gives the example of 'A Proper Schooling/Oideachadh Ceart' (1996), in which *seunaidhean* 'enchantment' finds itself translated as 'telepathies'. Even though no one would seriously want to contest the poet's authority to pronounce on the meanings of his work, Whyte suggests that the newly translated poem is best read as a dialogue between the Gaelic and English versions, and that either text might be incomplete if read in isolation. Whyte also wonders if this bilingual oscillation may be an implicit acknowledgement of the parlous state of Gaelic, which must resort to English for a sense of completion.

Although, as Whyte notes, MacNeacail's work embodies a 'peculiar and specific phenomenon', his poetry's special case of intertextuality may ultimately prove to be very common. Indeed some recent Scottish literature challenges the Romantic conception of the individual artist by presenting the reader with a 'gestalt' translator, that is, not one but various individuals collaborating on texts that exist only in real or imagined dialogue. For example, around 2000, James McGonigal, a Scottish poet with strong Irish-Catholic affinities, began work on a sequence of poems which eventually were to become 'Poems Written for Translation into an Abandoned Language'. In an interview posted on the Scottish Corpus website, McGonigal explains that his original motivation had been to imagine what it might be like to inhabit a Scottish-Gaelic persona and write in the kind of 'translatorese' he associated with English translations of Gaelic poetry. This act of cross-cultural imagination is also the subject of his as yet unpublished poem 'The Avoidance of Relationships':

> I'm told I have a tendency
> to avoid expressing my emotions
> except in this abandoned language
>
> to me it is like entering
> someone else's cottage
> to shelter from the rain
>
> who will not mind at all
> if I make myself a cup of tea
> and look out of the window
>
> and think about them catching
> the full force of the weather
> out on the hill or along the shore
>
> walking home in it
> rainwater running down
> their skin and soaking their shirt.

McGonigal's deliberate 'translatorese' manifests itself here in the awkward disputability of mutual agreement ('someone else's cottage . . . who will not mind at all' and 'think about them . . . soaking their shirt') as well as the occasional vagueness of pronominal reference ('it is like entering'). These dissonances accentuate the foreign detachment of the voice, while the poem overall addresses the stereotype of the reserved Scot, resisting the elemental force of relationships and capable of articulating emotions only in another's borrowed code or language.

McGonigal showed his 'translations' to Rody Gorman, a trilingual Irish poet resident in Scotland, who was so intrigued by the sequence that he proceeded to translate some of it into Irish. Subsequently, McGonigal decided not only to include some of these translations in his co-edited anthology *Across the Water* (2000), which celebrates Scots-Irish identities, but also to reset some of Gorman's Irish renditions of his poetry into a new, 'original' long poem, *Passage/An Pasáiste*, which was published in 2004. *Passage/An Pasáiste* is focused on McGonigal's family history and, more specifically, the migration of one branch of his family from Ireland to Scotland.

To demonstrate the process and effect of this complex collaborative project of multiple translation, let us first consider the following lines from McGonigal's original 'Turning Over in a Strange Bed':

> Living with women is like turning
> over in a strange bed at night
> and trying to find your watch
> and trying to read its face
>
> or like living in a landscape
> which is Donegal to your Galloway
> with something like the same hills
> with nothing like the same water

(McGonigal et al. 2000: 152)

These two verses were rendered into Irish by Rody Gorman as 'Ag Casadh thart i Leaba Choimhthíoch':

> Is ionann a bheith i do chónaí le bean
> agus a bheith ag casadh thart i leaba choimhthíoch san oíche
> agus a bheith ag iarraidh d'uairadóir a aimsiú
> agus a bheith ag iarraidh a éadan a léamh
>
> nó a bheith i do chónaí
> mar a bhfuil dreach na tíre cosúil le Tír Chonaill seo agat
> i gcoinne Ghallobhagh seo agam féin
> le mórán na cnoic chéanna
> agus gan a dhath den uisce céanna

(McGonigal et al. 2000: 153)

McGonigal then transplanted select lines from both versions into 'Passage East to Portpatrick', a section in *Passage/An Pasáiste*:

> Galloway
> *Ghallobhagh*

seo agam féin le mórán na cnoic chéanna
with something like the same hills
        with nothing like the same water.

(McGonigal 2004: 10)

McGonigal's composition of *Passage/An Pasaíste* is significant: even if it does not ultimately undo the hegemony of translation into English, it disrupts surface appearances and
hints at inadequacies. Notably, the original point of departure is McGonigal's conceit of
producing a sequence of poems written in English translatorese in order to accommodate
their anticipated translation into Scottish Gaelic. But instead of being translated into
Gaelic, the source texts rather unexpectedly spawn an Irish rendition, which the author
then proceeds to forge into a new sequence by embellishing it with parts of the original. In
the final version – if finality can now ever be guaranteed – the translation seems chrono-
logically to precede and validate the immigrant experience that now constitutes the core
of its narrative. Certainly Gorman's Irish translations at once enrich and undermine
McGonigal's bilingual poem sequence by implying that, without them, it would be incomplete. If poetry has traditionally given voice to an individual's experience in a language that
metonymically 'stands for' that individual's identity, then the McGonigal–Gorman project
must be seen to pursue not the fragmentation of that individualism, but its enhancement
and substantiation through absorption into a collaborative poetry, which depends on and
incorporates translation. The outcome is a communally open, polyphonic poetry which
enables and promotes the free blending of identities: English/Scottish, Gael/Lowlander,
Irish/Scottish. Appropriately, in *Passage/An Pasaíste* there are traces of Scots and Ulster-
Scots (or 'Ullans') too, alongside English and Irish, each signifying a particular aspect of
the individual's broad spectrum of multiple identities.

If the focus of this chapter so far has largely been on translations within the British Isles,
from Baston's medieval Latin to Gorman's Irish, this is because it seems appropriate to the
moment: any consideration of Scottish literature at the beginning of the twenty-first
century must recognise contemporary Britain's constitutional rearrangements, as well as
the new relationships Scotland's indigenous and immigrant populations are in the process
of forming with their near neighbours in England and Ireland. At the same time, however,
Scotland's engagement with the wider world continues as it always has done – through
translation. As I argue in *Written in the Language of the Scottish Nation* (1999), my brief
history of literary translation into Scots, various patterns have emerged in Scotland over
the centuries that are in line with the findings of translation studies scholars more generally. In Scotland, as elsewhere, translators and their publishers are attracted to source texts
from cultures with which the translators feel a political or aesthetic affinity, and their preferences are likely to change over time in accordance with developments in Scottish political culture. Moreover, successful translations can often be shown to fit an established
cultural paradigm; alternatively, translations aim to introduce a new paradigm that the
translator feels is lacking in Scottish culture. Due to the vast range of available linguistic
codes – from variants of Gaelic via Scots to English – the issue of 'visible' or 'invisible'
translation may be slightly more pronounced in Scotland than in other cultures: to what
extent might it be acceptable to allow the 'foreignness' of the original, or the interference
of the translator, to show through? Particularly in contemporary writing that does not use
Standard English, it is often impossible, let alone desirable, to produce a 'smooth' translation in which the presence of the translator is not felt. On the other hand, Scottish translators who do opt for Standard English as their medium are at risk of becoming doubly

invisible: not only is their individual contribution to the translation disguised by the fluency of the translated product, their contribution to *Scottish* literature is also called into question.

In the early twenty-first century, these general principles still hold true. For example, as Scotland rediscovers some element of self-rule within the contexts of the United Kingdom and an enlarged European Community, Scottish translators have responded by exploring the reconfigured geopolitical boundaries of the post-Soviet world. Thus, *At the End of the Broken Bridge* (2005), an anthology edited by István Turczi, introduces twenty-five Hungarian poems, one for each year between 1978 and 2002, translated into English and Scots by different hands in consultation with Zsuzsanna Varga. Significantly, Bela Pomogáts's introduction to the anthology focuses on its political dimensions:

> I am certain that the task of providing an authoritative picture of the history of a human community and a European nation is too important to be left to pure (or even impure) science alone: I believe it to be an important task of poetry. It is in this sense that the poems in this anthology can provide valuable and reliable insights into the mental and psychological history of Hungarians in the twentieth and twenty-first centuries. (Turczi 2005: 11)

The translations into English and Scots do more than make the cultural history of Hungary available to Scottish readers. In particular, the translations into Scots invite readers not only to listen to, but to identify with the Hungarian voice, to detect common ground and actively empathise with the Hungarian experience of historical change.

At the End of the Broken Bridge is one of a series of similar anthologies and analogous projects, promoted by the Scottish Poetry Library. For example, *How to Address the Fog* (2005), edited by Anni Sumari, collects twenty-five poems from Finland covering the same period, and Tessa Ransford's *The Nightingale Question: 5 Poets from Saxony* (2004) focuses on writers who lived through turbulent times in former East Germany. These collections, and other initiatives – such as 'Literature Across Frontiers', which brought together poets from Shetland, Iceland, Norway, Finland, Estonia and Latvia – show that there is an impetus in Scotland to engage with fellow peripheral cultures, whether these are the 'New Europe' or countries of the North Atlantic. On the margins, the language and content of poetry can engender unexpected resonances that are not only political. As the Fair Isle poet Lise Sinclair notes in her account of 'All Points North', the 'Language Across Frontiers' project in which she participated:

> Thor Sørheim's 'Rain' describes a rainy Norwegian day in vivid grey. It was lovely to translate, but *de mørke skyene flakser tunge ned / i tretoppene* . . . which I couldn't read in Norwegian, became 'dark clouds blow wildly / in the treetops' in the English version. I wasn't finding anything useful to add in Shetlan [Shetlandic], but when Thor described what he was talking about, dark clouds flapping their wings and landing in the trees like birds, then suddenly the poem could begin in Shetlan: 'dark cloods ir laandin laek birds / ida taps o da trees'. (Sinclair 2005: 27)

Other anthologies of poetry in translation also centre on the present realities of multicultural Scotland while looking for parallel experiences elsewhere. The pamphlet *exile* (2004) is the result of yet another such collaboration, this time between exiled poets in Glasgow working in Arabic, Persian, Albanian and English. This project, sponsored by Scottish PEN and Artists in Exile Glasgow, took the form of a series of workshops, followed by public performances and publication as both a pamphlet and a spoken-word compact disc. The experiences of these writers working in translation within a Scottish context can also be fruitfully compared with those of Adel Karasholi and Dragica Rajcic, Syrian and Croatian exiles in Germany, who have adopted the language of their host country. A selection of their work was translated from German into English by Suhayl Saadi and Christopher Whyte, and published in *M/other Tongues* (2003), an anthology sponsored by the Scottish Poetry Library in collaboration with the Glasgow Goethe-Institut. As Whyte acknowledges in his notes on the project, the expected and often idealised invisibility of the translator is the result of ceaselessly shifting power relations, necessitating a negotiation between text, author and translator that depends in part on empathy and respect:

> Having not just Gaelic and German, but Croatian as well, ought to have made things easier for me. Instead it gave me a transparency that felt like a risk of disappearing, as if I were a membrane so thin it could be rubbed out of existence almost without people noticing. (Saadi and Whyte 2003: 62)

For translators concerned with extending the range of the Scots idiom, a continuing thread through the long history of Scottish translation is the elevation of the vernacular through the translation of 'great works'. The twenty-first century already has its share of translations and adaptations that take this function of translation in interesting directions. Liz Lochhead followed the critical and popular success of her translation of Molière's *Tartuffe* (1985) with *Miseryguts* (2002). Whereas the former translation fitted securely into the tradition of Molière adaptations begun with Robert Kemp's *Let Wives Tak Tent* (1948), the latter updated the scenario to contemporary Scotland and fused the tradition of broad character comedy with contemporary satire aimed at the attitudes and mores of Scotland's media set. Lochhead has also produced versions of Anton Chekhov's *Three Sisters* (2000), Euripides' *Medea* (2000), and *Thebans* (2003), which is based on Sophocles' *Oedipus Rex* and *Antigone*. While her comedies employ a broad urban Scots, Lochhead's medium for tragedy is relatively light Scots, if Scots at all. Edwin Morgan, on the other hand, who had a late twentieth-century success with Edmond Rostand's tragicomedy *Cyrano de Bergerac* (1996), moved into full-blooded tragedy with a translation that controversially used the urban sociolect of Irvine Welsh to convey the torment of Jean Racine's *Phaedra* (2000). Cementing the rich cultural exchange between Quebec and Scotland, Bill Findlay and Martin Bowman very successfully translated the work of Michel Tremblay – *A Solemn Mass for a Full Moon in Summer* (2000) and *If Only* (2002) – and also turned their hand to the powerful melodramas *The Reel of the Hanged Man* (2000) by Jeanne-Mance Delisle and *The Skelfs* (2005) by Michel-Marc Bouchard. While all these dramatic works are varied and different, it is their tragic turn and focus on experimentation in particular which make them so appealing to playwrights keen to broaden and explore the generic potentialities of theatre in Scots.

Most severely underinvestigated within Scottish translation studies are prose translations into English, despite the fact that there have been some spectacular successes in the history of Scottish literature, from Thomas Urquhart's seventeenth-century *Gargantua and Pantagruel* after Rabelais to the Muirs' introduction of Kafka to the anglophone world in the 1930s. However, unless the translator is a significant author in his or her own right, prose translation into English remains a neglected area within Scottish literary studies. In fact, it may be questioned whether it is a legitimate area of *Scottish* studies at all, as in the case of Robert Scott-Buccleuch, translator of works by various Brazilian writers, including Machado de Assis, whose *Dom Casmurro* was published in English translation in 1992. Scott-Buccleuch is a Scot who has lived much of his life in Brazil, and his translations are published by major publishing houses like Penguin. But whether Scott-Buccleuch's work can or ought to be considered part of a Scottish literary tradition is debatable: his work is undertaken and published outwith Scotland, composed in fluent English, and aimed at an international anglophone readership. Scott-Buccleuch is also not known ever to have engaged explicitly with his home country either in or through his translations. And yet, would it not be a poor literary culture that failed to pay homage to its exiled legions of translators, whose work often acts as a point of entry to another world for readers in Scotland as well as elsewhere? One hope for the twenty-first century is that the ongoing redefinition of literary and cultural studies in Scotland will also find space for the critical appraisal and interrogation of work by its hitherto unacknowledged toilers in the field of literary translation.

As my discussion of recent work in the area of literary translation will have shown, small cultural agencies, such as the Scottish Poetry Library and the Goethe-Institut, are increasingly playing a key role in the cultural life of the nation. They sponsor small-scale but significant collaborative projects, workshops, travel, performances and publications, thus ensuring that ideas and influences cross borders and enter the consciousness of different communities. At the time of writing the main cultural agency in Scotland, the Scottish Arts Council, is considering the launch of a feasibility study into the foundation of a national Centre for Translation, to be undertaken in the latter half of 2006. However, what form such a centre might take, or indeed exactly what function the Scottish Arts Council itself will fulfil in future years, remain a matter of guesswork and conjecture. The issue is a very serious one, as the funding of literature and literary scholarship in Scotland at the start of the twenty-first century is still far too often piecemeal and ad hoc. A good example in this context is the Bibliography of Scottish Literature in Translation (BOSLIT), an initiative started in 1994 by the University of Edinburgh and the National Library of Scotland, and supported by the Scottish Arts Council.

In its first decade BOSLIT was awarded funding from the British Academy, the Carnegie Trust and the Scottish Library and Information Council; under the academic leadership of Professors Peter France and Ronald Jack, BOSLIT later also came to benefit from a fixed-term research grant from the Arts and Humanities Research Council (AHRC). This funding allowed its researchers and editors – Paul Barnaby, Tom Hubbard and Zsuszanna Varga – to compile an online catalogue of Scottish literature in translation that now amounts to over 25,000 records. While the bibliographic record is by no means complete, the impact – past and present – of Scottish literature on other cultures can only now begin to be told with any confidence (see Barnaby [2000a] and Hubbard and Jack [2006]). BOSLIT has also organised exchanges between Scottish and European translators and, in conjunction with Scottish PEN, it has sponsored events at the Edinburgh International Book Festival. However, once its AHRC funding ended in 2005, the research and cultural activities of BOSLIT were seriously curtailed and the important business of the expansion of its catalogue has been left to committed volunteers and the hard-pressed staff of the National Library. In Scotland cultural and scholarly activities of national importance, which in other countries would be centrally financed through the universities or central government, are too often left to the vagaries of short-term project funding. As a result, many such initiatives are prone to proceed in fits and starts. The reorganisation of the Scottish Arts Council, and indeed the establishment of Edinburgh as UNESCO City of Literature, might lead to a new dawn for literature and literary translation; however, given the Scottish Executive's ambivalent definition and treatment of 'culture', the prospects are perhaps not yet quite so bright.

The governmental and institutional support systems for cultural activity are obviously worthy of mention within this chapter as they impact directly on the reception of translated texts within Scotland and of Scottish culture overseas. Quite simply, if no one gets paid, little gets done, and translators are still the undervalued and poor relations of the literary family (see Venuti 1998: 31–66). However, there is positive evidence that a growing fascination with translation may gradually be taking hold of the more popular imagination. Translation as a theme has been the subject of at least two recent Scottish novels. Expatriate Sudanese writer Leila Aboulela's novel *The Translator* (1999) tells of the growing love between an African immigrant and a Scottish academic. The Aberdonian setting is portrayed from the perspective of the Muslim woman, the translator of the title, and the poignancy of the novel's gentle story of romance across faiths and against expectations is intensified in the aftermath of 9/11 and the subsequent demonising of Islam. A more overtly political novel is James Kelman's *Translated Accounts* (2001), a harrowing sequence of anonymous and unreliable 'translations' that gradually build up a picture of life under a brutally oppressive regime. These two novels express in different ways the abuses, possibilities, anxieties and triumphs of communication across cultures. While neither novel is a translation, each uses translation as a metaphor for cultural exploration.

My chapter set out to demonstrate the range, complexity and excitement of translation activity and scholarship in Scotland today, as well as some of its frustrations. There is no doubt that the complex issues that trouble scholars in contemporary translation studies affect us all now, even monoglot Scots. The 'double realm', conjured by Morgan in his translation of Baston, continues to splinter into a globalised, multicultural mixter-maxter of endless promise and problematic potential. In twenty-first-century Scotland, we confront the consequences of translation when we sit down at our computer, log onto the website of Amazon USA and discover that Ian Rankin's best-selling novel *Fleshmarket Close* (2004) has metamorphosed into *Fleshmarket Alley*. As we live in translated worlds, even a concrete Edinburgh location can, in American English, transmogrify into a purely fantastical site of tartan noir. Both literature and literary studies in Scotland are waking up to this fact.

Chapter 39

Scots Abroad: The International Reception of Scottish Literature

Katherine Ashley

Any attempt to provide an overview of contemporary Scottish literature as seen from the outside is as fraught with difficulty as attempts to analyse it from within. There is an a priori definition of 'Scottishness' with which most foreign readers are familiar; what makes something Scottish – be it literature, music or film – is its treatment of (stereo)typical, even mythical Scottish themes: bens, glens and whisky, the Highlands, the heather, the brogue, whirling bagpipes and kilted warriors. Yet this cultural model is the very antithesis of the writing practised by Irvine Welsh, Ian Rankin, A. L. Kennedy or any number of contemporary authors. Ironically, while a great deal of critical effort has been expended in Scotland on rethinking ideas of nation and nationality, when it comes to assessing contemporary Scottish literary output, the distinction between Scottish and English or Scottish and British writing is hazy indeed to many outsiders. As Cairns Craig notes, 'the texture of Scottish life, in its religious, educational, legal, linguistic forms, remains distinct from that of England to an extent which is little recognized in England, let alone in the outside world' (Craig 1988: 3). Thus, although many citizens of the Commonwealth can claim genealogical affiliation with Scotland, and many Europeans can invoke cultural-historical ties with the country, there are stark discrepancies between perceived notions of Scottishness and the country's twenty-first-century cultural output. Fortunately, these discrepancies are beginning to be addressed in such a way that Scottish literature is being freed from its traditional shackles and is being interpreted as the expression of a fully modern nation.

Arguably, because of the incompatibility between mythic Scotland and modern Scotland, contemporary Scottish fiction need not be – indeed has not been – interpreted as particularly 'Scottish', or as overtly political by the foreign reader. According to Eleanor Bell:

> there has been a tendency in Scottish studies to equate history with literature, so that literature tends to be regarded as the *effect* of cultural processes, rather than as an intervention in those processes, or indeed as a relatively autonomous act of aesthetic, ethical or political engagement. (Bell 2004: 2)

To what extent, then, are the recent political changes in Scotland being accounted for in assessments of its literature? Is post-1997 fiction perceived as being more, or less, 'Scottish' than what came before? How does the relationship between Scotland and its foreign markets affect the reception of its literature?

It seems that the increasing interest in Scottish literature abroad preceded political changes after 1997 and that recent political history has played a minor role in the reception of Scottish literature abroad. In the past two decades, several Scottish authors have embarked on worldwide promotional tours taking in Australia, Canada, New Zealand and the United States. Scottish authors have also been honoured abroad: Janice Galloway, for instance, was awarded the American Academy of Arts and Letters E. M. Forster Award in 1994. A. L. Kennedy has also transcended the borders of her homeland: her 2002 PEN lecture at the Edinburgh International Book Festival was subsequently broadcast on Australian national radio. Since devolution, Scottish fiction has been fêted at book festivals in Canada, Norway, Bulgaria and the Czech Republic, and also been represented at Prague BookWorld as well as the Frankfurt and Gothenburg Book Fairs. Further international ties were forged when the Edinburgh International Book Festival worked in conjunction with the Stavanger Festival to arrange its 2005 theme of 'Nations Unlimited'. In addition, according to the Scottish Arts Council, there has recently been 'unprecedented demand' for translations of Scottish literature (Scottish Arts Council 2003). However, this boom could be attributed to a flourishing of Scottish writing from the 1960s and 1970s onward, facilitated in part by the then newly created Arts Council and the advent of the Scottish Publishers Association in 1973 rather than political devolution *per se* (see Craig 1988: 2). If the 1980s are seen as a relative lull in cultural production and confidence in Scotland, then the 1990s marked a corresponding upsurge in both publishing and political optimism. Thus, rather than literature catching up with politics, politics finally caught up with literature.

In order to place contemporary Scottish literature in an international context, this chapter will study the reception and impact of contemporary Scottish writing in English-speaking and non-English-speaking markets. Proceeding by means of an analysis of foreign-edition publication data, as well as critical articles appearing in literary reviews, the first section will analyse the reception of representative Scottish writers in the English-speaking world and demonstrate that the most successful authors are not always those who write explicitly about 'traditional' Scotland, but those whose work resonates because of its universality. Using resources available through the Bibliography of Scottish Literature in Translation (BOSLIT), and UNESCO's Index Translationum, among others, the second section of the chapter will assess the status of contemporary Scottish fiction in countries with longstanding interests in Scottish literature, notably Germany and France. In addition to gaining audiences in these major markets, due to its peripheral status and its evolving political situation, contemporary Scottish literature has also attracted attention in many smaller nations – including Serbia and Croatia – which have little or no immediate connection to its culture.

As one of the biggest literary markets, and given the links between the two countries, America is an obvious starting-point. Although Tartan Day first saw the light in Nova Scotia in 1987, it only came to prominence in 1997–8, when 6 April was declared 'National Tartan Day' by the American Senate (United States Senate 1997; United States Congress 2005). Since then, the Scottish presence in the United States has been fêted at numerous venues, including the 2003 'Scotland at the Smithsonian' festival which attracted an estimated one million visitors (MacMahon 2004). However, at least two different versions of literary Scotland compete for prominence in North America and in other English-speaking markets. While state-sponsored parades of pipers may march down Fifth Avenue every April, American readers are being exposed to more modern visions of Scotland through its fiction. Since 1995 San Francisco's Edinburgh Castle pub, run by a Scottish expatriate, has hosted readings by Welsh, James Kelman, Alan Warner and Kevin

Williamson. In 1997 Kelman, Welsh and Duncan McLean embarked on the 'Great Scots Tour' of the United States, sponsored by the American academic publisher Norton, whose ubiquitous *Norton Anthology of English Literature* is widely used in undergraduate courses in North American and British universities. The most recent, eighth edition contains selections from Hugh MacDiarmid and Carol Ann Duffy, indicating that there may be a place for twentieth-century Scottish poetry in the international academic canon. Further crossover from town to gown came in 2002, when Welsh took up a creative-writing teaching post at Columbia College in Chicago.

The recent upsurge in interest in Scottish literature in the United States has been attributed not so much to political changes as to Kelman's 1994 Booker Prize win, an achievement which led to the discovery and exploration of other previously ignored twentieth-century Scottish novels. Thus, according to Joy Press, writing in New York's influential *Village Voice* in 2002, Alasdair Gray's *Lanark* (1981) is

> one of the most remarkable unsung novels of the last century. Unsung, at least, in the U.S., which didn't have much time for Scottish writers until recently, when Booker Prize winner James Kelman broke the ice a wee bit, leaving room for rogues like Irvine Welsh and Alan Warner to sneak through. (Press 2002)

This is the case of an external factor – the all-powerful literary prize, based in and administered from England, yet monitored around the world – influencing the reception of Scottish literature abroad. In much the same way, film director Danny Boyle's adaptation of *Trainspotting* (1995) brought the novel to prominence beyond Scotland. In both cases, Scottish literature was given external endorsements that led to increased international visibility. This visibility had two consequences: first, it demonstrated that there was life beyond the stereotypical image of Scotland, and secondly, it showed that new visions of Scotland could be expressed in a vibrant and modern language that was none the less distinctively Scottish. In the case of Kelman, language became a political issue within the UK, but also helped spawn a cult-like appreciation of the 'new' Scotland beyond the British Isles, an appreciation that was centred not on linguistic so much as thematic issues. At the same time, for the purposes of comparison, it should be pointed out that the frenzy surrounding Kelman's Booker win was not repeated when Scottish author Ali Smith's *Hotel World* (2001), written in language that is more accessible to foreign readers, was shortlisted.

According to *Global Books in Print*, a high percentage of Welsh's and Kelman's books are in print in the United States. Indeed, there are more editions of Welsh available in the United States than in Australia, Canada, New Zealand or South Africa, perhaps because the United States has more urban centres than these four Commonwealth nations. There are just as many editions of Kennedy's work available in South Africa as there are in the United Kingdom, and generally speaking, apart from Rankin, the authors analysed in Table 1 are well represented in South Africa. A higher percentage of editions is available in Canada than in Australia or New Zealand, but when population (and therefore potential market) is taken into account, this makes sense. Indeed, given the populations of the four Commonwealth countries in the sample, there is no appreciable difference in the availability of Scottish fiction. Moreover, while there is more Scottish literature available in Canada than in the United States, Australia or New Zealand, this is not necessarily a sign of closer ties between the two countries, as might be assumed: the higher figures for Canada might be explained by the fact that the Canadian market has access to books published and/or distributed by Canadian, American and British publishers.

Table 1 Scottish books in print in English-speaking markets: numbers of editions *Source: Global Books in Print*, November 2005

Author	UK (pop. 60m)	Australia (pop. 20m)	Canada (pop. 30m)	New Zealand (pop. 4m)	South Africa (pop. 44m)	United States (pop. 295m)
Banks	85	29	60	31	42	16
% of UK editions		34%	71%	36%	49%	19%
Gray	42	16	16	10	23	18
% of UK editions		38%	38%	24%	55%	43%
Kelman	26	15	20	12	20	16
% of UK editions		58%	77%	46%	77%	62%
Kennedy	17	12	16	10	17	13
% of UK editions		71%	94%	59%	100%	76%
Rankin	176	60	78	43	56	54
% of UK editions		34%	44%	24%	32%	31%
Irvine Welsh	35	15	19	9	24	29
% of UK editions		43%	54%	26%	69%	83%
Total	*381*	*147*	*209*	*115*	*182*	*146*

While Kelman may have broken the ice abroad, it has been argued that the real impetus for wider reception of Scottish fiction resides not so much in the vernacular writings of Kelman, Welsh and Warner as in more popular genre writing, such as science fiction and 'tartan noir', a term that refers to crime and mystery fiction peppered with deliberate 'Scotticisms' (see Taylor 2004). Rankin, whose Inspector Rebus series began in 1987, saw his readership grow when *Black and Blue* (1997) was shortlisted for the Mystery Writers of America's Edgar Award for Best Novel in 1998; in 2004, he took home this prize for *Resurrection Men* (2002). Although the Rebus series is indelibly marked by Edinburgh – Rankin himself moved his books from 'Mystery' to 'Scottish fiction' shelves in the early days of his writing career – crime knows no borders, hence its appeal. As Janet Maslin comments on *A Question of Blood* (2003), 'Scottish turns of phrase abound, sometimes a might [*sic*] impenetrably, but the book's essential language is universal' (Maslin 2004a). The appeal of writers like Rankin, then, is that they transform local experience into universal experience; moreover, for some American commentators, the appeal of Scotland's popular crime writing exceeds that of other foreign countries due to the inimitable uniqueness of the Scottish voice:

> In the end . . . what you most want to hear when you're on foreign soil [i.e. reading foreign books] are the voices of the people who live there. To my ear, the most insistent regional accents are heard in Scotland, in the brutal street talk of writers like Ian Rankin, Val McDermid and Denise Mina as well as in the more subtly sinister tones of Louise Welsh. (Stasio 2004)

The question of 'accent', or more precisely language, is a central one in the reception of Scottish literature both domestically and in international English-speaking markets, and much of the debate surrounding the state of contemporary Scottish fiction inevitably raises questions of a linguistic nature. Ian Crichton Smith's so-called 'three-voiced country' (Gifford and Riach 2004: 245) communicates most successfully in Standard Scottish English since the need for translation is minimised. But Scotland's regional accents are 'insistent', Rebus's speech is 'a mite impenetrable', and *How Late It Was, How Late* is the work of an 'illiterate', according to Simon Jenkins (Jenkins 1994: 20). The fundamental difficulty lies in reconciling an international English literature – guided by market forces of sales, distribution and 'translatability' from one English to another – with the diversity and concomitant problems of language in Scotland. In what language are contemporary Scottish writers writing and will they, or should they, be as easily understood in Australia, Canada, India or South Africa as they are in Scotland?

In the course of a discussion of the Québécois translation of Welsh's *Trainspotting* (1993), Emily Apter refers to Welsh's language, and the language of his protagonists, as 'Scottish argot', 'Scots', 'a so-called minor or highly idiomatic languag[e]' and a 'dialect' (Apter 2001: 66–7). Of course, the difference between a dialect and a minority language is huge. If the language of Welsh or Kelman is considered a form of Scots (a language recognised by the European Union, if not the Scottish Parliament), then there ought to be no expectation that non-Scots speakers should be able to understand it any more than a German speaker might be expected to understand Dutch (see Niven 2002: 3). However, if it is considered to be a phonetically rendered variant of Scottish English, then other issues of communication come to the fore (for example, in North America the film version of *Trainspotting* was released with subtitles and partly dubbed). While recognising Scots as a living, written language would validate it as a means of communication within Scotland, the politics of language remains complicated. Interestingly, in the *Second Periodical Report from the United Kingdom on the European Charter for Regional or Minority Languages*, Scots – defined as 'Scottish-English' – is not discussed, whereas Ulster Scots is (Foreign and Commonwealth Office 2005: 10). It is also worth considering that writing in Scots might close markets beyond Scotland, something that the Scottish publishing industry is unlikely to support. Symptomatically perhaps, BOSLIT records no translations of Matthew Fitt's *But n Ben A-Go-Go* (2000), marketed as science fiction in modern-day Scots. Thus, it is impossible to seek audiences abroad without addressing the status of Scottish languages within Scotland.

But not all contemporary Scottish writers write exclusively about Scottish settings and in Scots or Scottish English. Indeed, in many ways Alexander McCall Smith is the author who most flies in the face of recent trends in Scottish literature. If the urban grit and realism of Welsh, Rankin and Kelman appeal on the grounds of Scottish internationalism by addressing themes and issues affecting most urban, industrialised western countries, then McCall Smith's prose appeals to the opposite instinct and reminds us of the much-discussed dualism – or Caledonian antisyzygy – of Scottish literature. Unsurprisingly, McCall Smith's international popularity does not stem from the same roots as that of the *Rebel Inc* generation. While the 'Great Scots' were touring the States in 2002, McCall Smith was still an unknown entity, even though he began the *No. 1 Ladies' Detective Agency* series as early as 1998 (Maslin 2004b). Talking to a South African journalist, McCall Smith describes his own popularity in the United States, where there are anywhere from 2.5 to 4 million copies of the *No. 1 Ladies' Detective Agency* in print (Moore 2005), as a palliative for contemporary political upheaval and uncertainty. 'I think the Americans who read them [the *No. 1 Ladies' Detective Agency* series]', so McCall Smith explains, 'are fed up with in-your-face social realism – here's something that's much more gentle, somewhat old-fashioned. They've been going through a terrible time domestically, and my books are an antidote'

(Berlins 2003). The McCall Smith case is all the more interesting given that his sales have rocketed above those of most other authors writing in Scotland – with the possible exception of Scottish-based J. K. Rowling – and that until recently most of his fiction was set outside of Scotland. However, while he is not immediately identified with Scottishness or Scottish fiction, he is 'every inch the polite British gentlemen' (Davies no date) and dons a kilt at book signings, thereby visibly identifying himself with his homeland.

Compiling accurate statistical data relating to contemporary Scottish fiction in translation is a difficult task. The reception of any author's work in a foreign country relies to a great extent on the availability of translations – any delay inevitably producing delays in reception – and on the availability of the output of multilingual critics, translators, librarians, publishers and researchers promoting the author before his or her works are translated. There are thus discrepancies between bibliographical records held by BOSLIT, UNESCO's Index Translationum, and the data presented by publishers and authors themselves. Data relating to translations is constantly changing and the statistics presented here should be accepted as a snapshot and subject to continual flux.

Generally speaking, BOSLIT, maintained by the National Library of Scotland, is the most reliable source of translation data, particularly for early- and mid-twentieth-century texts; however, it is a work in progress that is constantly evolving as new books are published and added to the catalogue (Table 2). BOSLIT records and catalogues not only bound volumes, but also excerpts and articles published in foreign publications, making it sometimes difficult to establish streamlined statistics. Given the interest in translating Scottish literature, it would be almost impossible for the National Library to keep BOSLIT up to date, which explains some of the discrepancies. There are, for example, instances where rights have been bought but the translations have yet to appear. Poetry is even more problematical than prose in this respect, as the database records range from individual poems to anthologies and single-author volumes (Table 3).

None the less, McCall Smith's books have been translated into almost thirty languages (twenty-six according to Canongate, seventeen according to BOSLIT), including most major European languages linked to large literary markets – French, German, Italian, Portuguese and Spanish – but also Scandinavian (Norwegian, Danish, Finnish, Swedish), Asian (Chinese, Japanese, Korean, Thai) and smaller languages such as Croatian, Czech, Greek, Icelandic, Slovene and Lithuanian. While he has perhaps been translated into more languages than most other Scottish authors, McCall Smith is not the only one to have found a place in surprising markets: Ali Smith has been translated into Hebrew and Hungarian, Rankin into Greek and Polish, William Boyd into Bulgarian, Banks into Estonian and Lithuanian, and Val McDermid into Finnish, to give but a few examples. According to the Canongate Books Rights List from November 2005, Louise Welsh's *The Cutting Room* (2002) has been translated into a dozen languages, while the rights to her second novel *Tamburlaine Must Die* (2004) have been sold in eleven languages. Scottish-based Michel Faber's *Under the Skin* (2000) and *The Crimson Petal and the White* (2002) have been translated into twenty-eight and twenty-five languages respectively.

Historically France, Germany and the Netherlands have been among the most accessible foreign-language markets for Scottish writers. Sir Walter Scott and R. L. Stevenson were widely translated in France and Germany in the nineteenth century. Moreover, both Stevenson and Alistair MacLean figure in the 'Top 50 Authors' category of UNESCO's Index Translationum and MacLean also holds pride of place as one of the top ten authors to be translated in Belgium, Denmark, Germany, the Netherlands and Sweden. Also according to UNESCO, Germany is second only to Britain in its translations from the

Table 2 Total catalogued translations of living Scottish prose writers *Source:* BOSLIT, December 2005

Muriel Spark (b. 1918)	360	Alan Warner (b. 1964)	30
Iain (M.) Banks (b. 1954)	141	Janice Galloway (b. 1956)	22
William Boyd (b. 1952)	133	Andrew Crumey (b. 1961)	18
Irvine Welsh (b. 1958)	119	Alexander McCall Smith (b. 1948)	17
Val McDermid (b. 1955)	100	Denise Mina (b. 1966)	15
Ian Rankin (b. 1960)	98	Candia McWilliam (b. 1955)	13
Iain Crichton Smith (b. 1928)	95	Christopher Brookmyre (b. 1968)	11
Alasdair Gray (b. 1934)	67	Laura Hird (b. 1966)	11
Joan Lingard (b. 1932)	55	Dilys Rose (b. 1954)	11
Allan Massie (b. 1938)	54	Louise Welsh (b. 1965)	10
Ken McClure (b. 1942)	47	Sheena MacKay (b. 1944)	10
Emma Tennant (b. 1937)	43	Isla Dewar (d.o.b. unknown)	9
William McIlvanney (b. 1936)	34	Margaret Elphinstone (b. 1948)	9
James Kelman (b. 1946)	33	Duncan McLean (b. 1964)	6
Liz Lochhead (b. 1947)	32	Ali Smith (b. 1962)	6
A. L. Kennedy (b. 1965)	30	Brian McCabe (b. 1951)	4

Table 3 Total catalogued translations of living Scottish poets
Source: BOSLIT, December 2005

Kenneth White (b. 1936)	449
Douglas Dunn (b. 1942)	224
Edwin Morgan (b. 1920)	201
Carol Ann Duffy (b. 1955)	45
Jackie Kay (b. 1961)	34
John Burnside (b. 1955)	30
Robert Crawford (b. 1959)	25
Kathleen Jamie (b. 1962)	23
Tom Leonard (b. 1944)	11
Ian Hamilton Finlay (b. 1925)	9

Gaelic. What is more, Paul Barnaby has found that France, West Germany, the Netherlands and Sweden were the most receptive markets for Scottish literature between 1946 and 1960. All of Boyd's work has been translated into French; equally, the poet Kenneth White, who is relatively little read in Scotland, is widely translated in France, perhaps by virtue of the fact that he lives there (Barnaby 2000b: 247, 249, 252–3). BOSLIT figures also show that White is popular in Bulgaria.

Today, the 'Great Scots' lauded in the United States are also well translated in Europe: there are five French translations of both Welsh and Kelman, while there are seven volumes of Welsh in German, three of Kelman and ten of Rankin, according to BOSLIT. In addition, there are fifteen Alasdair Gray publications available in German – a remarkable achievement considering that there are only sixteen available in English in Canada. According to Keith Dickson, who is behind Éditions Métailié's recently launched Bibliothèque Écossaise series, which focuses on Scottish fiction (including works by John

Table 4 Translations of Scottish fiction in minority languages *Source:* BOSLIT, November 2005

Language area	1979–96	1997–2005
Czech	208	57
Serbo-Croatian	137	35
Hebrew	99	15
Greek	68	11
Catalan	56	17
Bulgarian	50	4
Lithuanian	50	3
Slovenian	50	25
Estonian	47	14
Romanian	42	7
Latvian	39	8
Albanian	15	2

Burnside, Lewis Grassic Gibbon, Kelman, Gray, James Robertson and Alexander Trocchi), the resurgence of interest in Scottish literature in France was already well under way by 1995; by this token, the resurgence cannot be a consequence of devolution:

> By the time I engaged on my second attempt to publish Scottish fiction in translation in 1995, the climate, I think, was already beginning to change for the better. French publishing houses were beginning to show some greater interest in new Scottish writing: McIlvanney had become an established figure with Rivages, Iain Banks had made his breakthrough, at least among science fiction readers; William Boyd, although not necessarily perceived as a Scottish writer, had made his mark, was being published by one of the French majors and winning prizes for his fiction. (Dickson 2002)

Once again, the people who seem to be propelling the revival are authors like Banks and Boyd who are not necessarily writing, or making political statements, about Scotland. At the same time, more traditional views of Scotland have always been popular abroad, even if they are not being presented by Scottish writers: the sixth volume of American romance writer Diana Gabaldon's *Outlander* series was simultaneously released in English and German in September 2005. Another *Outlander* novel features in the Australian Broadcasting Corporation's list of top one hundred favourite books.

Less central markets are perhaps particularly interesting in terms of Scotland's post-devolution status and appeal, as with the resurgence of an optimistic and outward-looking Caledonian culture, interest in Scotland seems to have increased among smaller European nations (Table 4). This should not come as a surprise, as the political process resulting in Scottish devolution was part of a wider movement towards recasting political structures within Europe. The break-up of the USSR and Yugoslavia led to a reassessment of local cultural and political values, and many issues facing Scotland are also being confronted by former Eastern Bloc countries, even though the historical and political circumstances are vastly different. Yet Scottish fiction is attractive here also for the same reasons it is so in big-market G8 countries: its themes resonate with post-industrial contemporary readers. As Galloway's Slovene translator points out, despite the fact that 'contemporary Scottish writing . . . occupies a very minor and marginal position in the system of Slovene translated literature', there are elements of Galloway's fiction that Slovenian readers can relate to. Thus, the fact that *The Trick is to Keep Breathing* (1989), which was published in Slovenia in 2000, is 'set in a dreary suburban estate, a place which has no real history and very little local colour, can be an image that most people, and also potential Slovene target readers, have access to' (Mahkota 1998). Once again, it is shared experience that motivates translation, a sense of familiar otherness that has little to do with overly romanticised literary renditions of Scotland.

An analysis of the bigger Central and Eastern European markets, notably the Czech and Serbo-Croatian language areas, shows a marked decline in translations of what are regarded as the classics of Scottish literature. The number of Czech translations of Stevenson decreased from sixteen between 1979 and 1996 to one between 1997 and 2005. Likewise, there were twenty-one Serbo-Croatian Stevenson publications between 1979 and 1996, and ten translations of Scott, but only two of Scott since devolution, and none of Stevenson. This is not to say that translations of Scottish literature are declining or that enthusiasm is waning; on the contrary, the earlier period can be seen as a 'catch-up' period in which canonical works of Scottish and western literature in general were translated into minor languages in a way that would not have been possible thirty years earlier. Stevenson and Scott have been replaced by an assortment of newer Scottish writers, including Banks, Isla Dewar, Douglas Dunn, Val McDermid, Emma Tennant and Jackie Kay, with Rankin and Welsh at the forefront.

In conclusion, contemporary Scottish fiction is in a healthy state in both English-speaking and non-English-speaking markets. It is, to borrow Iain Crichton Smith's words, 'sing[ing] in a new world . . . with friendliness to all around her'. The fact that it is not interpreted solely in terms of its politics, or its 'Scottishness', is a sign of its maturity and indicates that it has 'join[ed] the other rivers without dogma' (Gifford and Riach 2004: 245). While Scottish fiction is not yet 'three-voiced' to the outside world – English-language texts are much more likely to reach international audiences – it is many-genred, and in this versatility lies its strength and its appeal: from low-life drug culture to detection, science fiction and popular writing, Scottish literature continues to make its mark on the international stage.

Chapter 40

A Very Interesting Place: Representing Scotland in American Romance Novels

Euan Hague and David Stenhouse

On 18 September 2005 the *New York Times* hardcover fiction bestseller list contained a surprising new entry at number 12. *Spell of the Highlander*, the sixth in a bestselling series of novels by Karen Marie Moning, is a romance with a Scottish setting, Scottish themes and a Scottish male protagonist. Moning's previous novels have enjoyed a similar level of success, regularly entering national and on-line bestseller lists in the United States and gathering a string of awards from romance editors and readers. Yet despite the fact that Moning's novels parade their fascination with Scotland and Scottishness, they have until now enjoyed no critical discussion within Scotland. In this chapter we review this unexplored branch of 'Scottish literature' and argue that Scottish-themed American romances are marginalised from 'literature', 'Scottish literature' and 'Scottish writing' in ways which test the boundaries of critical conventions surrounding the study of Scottish writing in the academy.

The early twenty-first century has seen the emergence of the Scottish romance novel as a specific subgenre within US romance fiction. Works like *Spell of the Highlander* have sold thousands of copies, and new texts by Scottish romance authors are avidly anticipated by readers who form eager participative communities in on-line discussion forums, on message boards and at regularly held romance conventions (see Stenhouse 2005a, 2005b). These modern romances fit squarely within the parameters of the women's romance market: their themes are the search for, and the trials encountered while searching for, romantic love and the elusive nature of sexual desire. If this theme is conventional, some of the generic conventions are surprising. Scottish-themed American romances often draw on unexpected aspects of Scottish history, not just comprising a parade of kilts, castles and lochs, but also bending the laws of history by allowing the hero or heroine to travel through time.

The US market for romance novels generates over $1.41 billion annually (RWA 2004a). At the end of 2003 there were over two thousand romance titles in print. Romances are often marketed separately from other genres and given separate library and bookstore locations. Many of these books have short shelf-lives, often being in print only for six months, yet the romance novel in the United States is the 'top-selling genre of paperback fiction' and in 2003 represented 48.8 per cent of all paperback fiction sales and 18 per cent of all books sold (Eng 2004; RWA 2004a). The largest publisher of such novels is Harlequin, which publishes 110 titles a month. The US audience for romance novels comprised 51.1 million people in 2002, of whom 75 per cent were white, 21 per cent were college graduates, 25 per cent were aged 35–44 and 93 per cent were female (RWA 2004a, 2004b). In addition to these industry statistics and observations, there is also a trade organisation: the Romance Writers of America (RWA), founded in Houston in 1980, which advises authors on contracts, offers research grants, presents literary awards and highlights trends in the genre. At the time of writing the RWA has around 9,500 members, one in six of whom has published a romance novel. The RWA also publishes the trade journal the *Romance Writers' Report* and hosts annual conferences.

The formulaic nature of romance writing, much denigrated by critics, is often mandated by publishers. Companies like Harlequin have rules determining the length and explicitness of their romance novels. One immediately apparent commonality is the dimension of the books themselves: often around 350 pages in length (although some, such as Diana Gabaldon's, are longer), the books typically measure about seventeen centimetres down the spine and eleven centimetres across the cover. Romance novels physically look and feel the same, which adds to a sense of homogeneity and has often led critics to dismiss the genre as a whole rather than examining the content of individual titles. In addition, there is a clear distinction between romance and erotic novels. The number of sex scenes varies in romance novels; sometimes there are only one or two, as in Catherine Coulter's *The Scottish Bride* (2001), but racier novels such as Sue-Ellen Welfonder's *Devil in a Kilt* (2001) contain more. The rules of romance writing mandate that, in these sex scenes, genitalia are referred to euphemistically, as illustrated by examples from *Devil in a Kilt*: for the penis there is 'manhood', 'manroot', 'maleness', 'that most masculine and mysterious part of him' and 'his sex', while for female genitalia there is 'most feminine core', 'woman's flesh', 'core of her womanhood, cleft and all . . . and tender, gently swollen flesh'. Within the romance genre as a whole there are subgenres, determined either by the time-period in which the novel is set (such as contemporary, historical or futuristic) or the location of the action, such as the American West, England, the tropics or, as Juliet Flesch explores, the deserts of the Middle East and North Africa (see Flesch 2004). One of the most popular subgenres of the contemporary American romance novel is the historical romance set in Scotland, ranking eighth out of ten in terms of most popular plot elements announced by the RWA in 2004.

In her studies of Australian romance novels, Flesch notes that asserting a text's nationality inevitably proves problematic: ought it to be based on the author's birthplace or ancestry, the setting of the novel, where it was written, or the publishing house? Flesch chooses to centre on authors who identify themselves as Australian in publicity materials, which may in itself be problematic since, as Flesch demonstrates, many romance authors use pseudonyms and publishing houses tend to identify numerous novels as being written by the same author even if they actually were not. It is thus sometimes difficult to identify definitively which author wrote which romance novel. Further, romance author biographies are prone to change over time, playing with readers to speculate as to what is or is not a true story about a writer. Some of the authors discussed in this chapter claim Scottish ancestry and clan identification (such as Sue-Ellen Welfonder and her association with the MacFie Society of North America); others do not. Some have travelled to Scotland and 'fell in love with castles, kilts and brogues [Scottish accents]' (Moffett 1997). In this chapter we shall focus, by no means comprehensively, on romance novels published in the United States that are set in Scotland.

The Scottish-themed romance signifies its distinctiveness from other subgenres in a number of ways. For example, the covers of Scottish historical romances tend to fall into two broad types, featuring either illustrations or a model positioned against an illustrated backdrop. A number of typical Scottish indicators appear, most commonly a length of

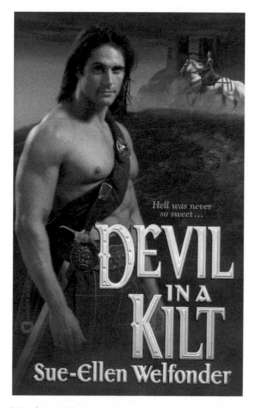

Figure 1.   Book cover of *Devil in a Kilt*. Reproduced by permission of Warner Books.

tartan cloth, heather, thistles or other purple flowers, a castle with ramparts looming from a grassy, craggy hilltop, a red-haired woman and a bare-chested, long-haired, muscular man, both ethnically white, the latter often wearing a kilt and carrying a claymore or other similarly sizeable sword (see Figure 1: Book cover of *Devil in a Kilt*). The castle comprises bridges, towers, turrets and battlements. In some instances, the male models photographed for the covers of Scottish romances become a powerful focus for readers of the fiction. Thus, on her website Moning identifies the male models who posed for the covers of her books and advises her readers on how to send them fan mail.

The figure of the male hero, often explicitly identified as a 'Highlander', assumes a quasi-fetishised sexual power. As Karen Kosztolnyik, senior editor of romance titles with Warner Books in New York, explained to David Stenhouse in an unpublished interview in 2005, 'part of the appeal of the Highlander is the sense that he is a powerful, dangerously masculine figure, but that he shows through his clan loyalties that he has a caring nurturing side. That way, while readers find the exterior excitingly strange, there is a reassurance that inside there are values they can feel comfortable with.' However, the instinctual, passionate Highlander can be either male or female. The male Highlander – as, for example, in Moning's *The Highlander's Touch* (2000) or Kathleen Givens's *Kilgannon* (1999) – exudes a virility intended to enchant women readers, while memorable female Highland characters include Mary Rose Fordyce, whose free spirit entices the staid English vicar Tysen Sherbrooke in Coulter's *The Scottish Bride*, or Madlin MacKendrick, who kidnaps and marries the cosmopolitan Scotsman Sir Ewan Fraser in Janet Bieber's *Highland Bride*

(1999). Alongside variations on 'Highland' and 'Scottish', titles typically include other generically unmistakable references to Scottish locations (*Border Fire* [Scott 2000] or *Isle of Lies* [Fletcher 2002]), surnames containing the 'Mac' prefix (*The MacLean Groom* [Harrington 1999], *The MacGowan Betrothal* [Greiman 2001] or *The Irresistible MacRae* [Ranney 2002]) and national symbols (*The Thorn and the Thistle* [Moffett 1997] or *A Hint of Heather* [Lee 2000]).

Moning's advice to visitors of her website on how to get in touch with her male cover models is typical of the dialogic relationship between writers and readers in the romance sector. Many of the writers discussed here – such as Welfonder, Moning and Gabaldon – run websites which they use to post news about work in progress, respond to queries and even enter into lively discussions with their readers. Elsewhere on the web readers themselves run discussion boards and newsgroups in which they dissect plot developments, discuss the appeal of male protagonists or recommend novels to new readers. The sense of romance writers and readers being marginalised by mainstream literary critics may add to their sense of being a community; whatever the reason, it is demonstrably true that romance writers regard the barrier between themselves and their readers as porous. Thus, Welfonder has used her website to reveal a visit to Eilean Donan Castle in the West Highlands as her chief inspiration for writing *Devil in a Kilt*. Others will address their readers via comments on the covers of their book. On the cover of *The Scottish Bride*, for example, Coulter informs her readers that of her last four books she 'like[s] it the best of all', inviting readers to write to her and 'tell me what you think', providing both postal and email addresses. In addition, the books often contain pages advertising other romances, sometimes work by the same author featuring a different setting, sometimes by different authors featuring the same setting.

Scottish romances are also often part of multi-book series, each volume following a different member of a family, often across generations. Coulter, for example, has written numerous books about the Sherbrooke family, *The Scottish Bride* being just one of them. Nora Roberts, arguably the best-known US romance writer, has been writing about the Scottish-American MacGregor family since 1998, publishing books about different family members each month and enabling readers to track the characters and the books they have not read by providing a MacGregor family tree on the inside cover. One can also use an order form on the last page of Roberts's *The MacGregor Grooms* (1998) to purchase a doll, measuring almost fifty centimetres in height, of 'Julia: The MacGregor Bride', for seventy-five dollars. The romance novel, therefore, is more than just a story; the book itself is part of a remarkable marketing strategy designed to produce an engaging, interactive experience for the reader.

There are three main observations we would like to make about the language employed in the Scottish romances. First, Gaelic terms, which occasionally appear in the texts, are most commonly presented in italics and with their meanings elucidated by the context in which they occur. Secondly, deviant 'Scots' spellings of common words are used to establish the nationality of the characters; however, the implementation of Scots language in these novels is idiosyncratic rather than systematic. Wherever Scots is used, spellings are rarely consistent across the novels; there are no commonly accepted conventions for written Scots. One of the ways in which the romances perform Scottishness is through dialogue, with Anglo-American characters speaking in standard English, whereas the Scottish characters speak an accented English, signalled by minor changes to spellings: 'no' becomes 'nay' or 'nae', 'you' and 'your' become 'ye' and 'yer', 'yes' is replaced by 'aye', 'know' by 'ken', 'girl' and 'boy' by 'lass(ie)' and 'lad(die)', while 'does not' turns into 'dinna', 'isn't' into 'isna', 'will not' into 'willna', and so forth. Different authors make these transpositions to a greater or lesser degree.

The third linguistic convention is the use of archaic terms to generate a sense of historicity and generate a period atmosphere. Set in the 1420s, *Highland Bride* follows the exploits of Madlin MacKendrick of Dunfionn, clan leader and chief female character, and her kidnap of, and then marriage to, Sir Ewan Fraser. In one scene Madlin awakens later than usual, exclaiming in surprise that "'tis past terce' (Bieber 1999: 216). The use of 'terce' in this context, referring to a Catholic's third hour of daily prayer and signifying approximately 9 a.m., is deliberately anachronistic. Similar examples abound throughout the genre: people are not born, but 'birthed' (Bieber 1999: 306), and if they are poor, they are 'baseborn' (Welfonder 2001: 133). In *Devil in a Kilt*, set in the 1320s, the characters drink 'hippocras' (a medieval mulled wine), wear 'hauberk' (chainmail) and go on journeys that take a 'sennight' (seven nights) or discuss events of 'yestereve' (Welfonder 2001: 133, 12, 129, 114).

All these linguistic strategies, much like the intimate dialogic relationship between author and reader, generate a sense of belonging and shared experience across the Scottish romance market. Readers may feel they are sharing a rare expert knowledge. In interviews conducted by Euan Hague readers described the novels as educational, helping them learn about the past and how life was lived in previous centuries, and explained that a novel's particular use of language enhanced the atmosphere of the narrative as well as their reading experience in general.

While the setting of most Scottish-themed American romances remains fixed in one historical period, Moning and Gabaldon, two of the bestselling writers, have pioneered a subgenre which involves time travel, a device whereby characters from the present can be projected back into a heroic past, or vice versa. In Gabaldon's *Outlander* (1991) the heroine is Claire Randall, an American woman, who finds herself thrown back in time after touching part of a circle of standing stones in Scotland: 'I could feel the hair rising on my forearms, as though with cold, and rubbed them uneasily. Two hundred years. From 1945 to 1743; yes, near enough . . . I must get back to the standing stones on Craigh na Dun. I felt a rising excitement that made me feel a trifle sick, and I reached for the wine goblet to calm myself' (Gabaldon 1991: 151–2). By contrast, Moning's creation of immortal Highlanders means that her heroes can come forward in time to encounter the heroine in the present – as in *Kiss of the Highlander* (2001) – or use magic to transport a modern American woman back into the Scottish past – as in *The Highlander's Touch* (2000). Despite its narrative centrality, little attention is paid to the technical implications of time travel. Though time travel can throw up all sorts of incidental difficulties (amnesia, doubling), in the romance novels it is commonly facilitated by mystical, magical or 'faerie' influences rather than anything technological. Time travel is of course a well-established trope in canonical American fiction as, for example, in Washington Irving's *Rip Van Winkle* (1819) or Mark Twain's *A Connecticut Yankee in King Arthur's Court* (1889). While Irving and Twain establish no explicit connection with Scottish themes or settings, Twain's portrayal of a 'classless' contemporary protagonist transported into, and forced to understand, an ancient chivalric culture recurs as a central motif in American Scottish-romance fiction.

Encounters between Scotland and the United States in popular culture have often relied on time travel. One of the earliest American films to touch on a Scottish subject, René Clair's *The Ghost Goes West* (1935), features a ghost who, along with his Scottish castle, finds himself transported to contemporary Florida, where, despite being literally bloodless, he proves rather more attractive to the female lead than his figuratively bloodless doppelgänger, the modern-day Americanised 'Laird o' Gourie'. However, the most famous and powerful example of the time-travel trope in modern American culture is probably Vincente Minnelli's *Brigadoon* (1954), starring Gene Kelly and Cyd Charisse (see McArthur 2003). *Brigadoon* follows two modern-day Americans who get lost in an impenetrable Highland mist and stumble on a charmed Scottish village which has been asleep for a century, thus classically exemplifying the trope of the Scottish Highlands as an irresistible, magical land 'out of history' (see Craig 1996), entirely unaffected by modernity. Similarly, in Bill Forsyth's *Local Hero* (1983) a contemporary American businessman finds himself lost in the mist en route to the Highland village where he has been sent to work on plans for the construction of an oil facility. Ultimately, rather than industrialising the landscape, the Scottish location enables *Local Hero*'s American protagonist to discover his humanity, an impact 'Scottishness' also tends to exert on the time-travelling American heroines of these Scottish romance novels. Another source for the time-travel device is Russell Mulcahy's *Highlander* (1986) starring Christopher Lambert as the immortal Scotsman Connor MacLeod. *Highlander* in particular is responsible for the idea of a sexy, muscular Scottish hero moving between and across time-periods. Indeed, as soon as the twentieth-century heroine of Moning's *Highlander's Touch* understands her predicament of having been magicked back to 1314, she remarks that both the appearance and accent of the Scottish hero Circenn Brodie are 'proof positive' that she is 'dreaming' because they so clearly remind her of *Highlander* (Moning 2000: 2). In an interview with Stenhouse, Gabaldon has mentioned yet another inspiration, namely a rerun of the BBC television series *Dr Who* in which the time-travelling doctor picks up Jamie McCrimmon, a kilted piper reeling from the aftermath of Culloden.

The time-travel device allows for an explicit comparison of contemporary American masculinity, implicitly depicted as emasculated, with the raw, primordial manliness of premodern Scots. This is a theme explored at length in Moning's work. In *Kiss of the Highlander* the heroine Gwen Cassidy's dissatisfaction with modern men has left her a frustrated virgin at 25: 'Come to think of it she wasn't sure if she'd ever seen a grand passion outside of a movie theatre or a book' (Moning 2001: 15). Giving up on finding a man in the United States she embarks on a bus tour of the Scottish Highlands, where she finds herself a member of a coach party of OAPs, many of whom have more satisfactory love-lives than she. Frustrated, Gwen decides to hike across the hills around Loch Ness on her own and ends up falling down a ravine, awakening Drustan MacKeltar, a Scottish laird who has been slumbering there for 500 years under a gypsy's spell. The same theme also lies at the heart of Gabaldon's *Outlander* saga in which nurse Claire Randall finds herself in a paternal, virtually sexless relationship with her academic husband until she is thrown back in time from 1945 to 1743, where she meets Jamie Fraser, a primordial Scot who awakens her passions. Much of *Outlander* describes Claire wrestling with the moral implications of her temporally confused *ménage à trois*: is it adultery to have an affair with a man in the past, almost two hundred years before her husband is born? This is an issue which Claire ultimately manages to resolve satisfactorily, and subsequent books in the *Outlander* series see Claire and Jamie moving to North America, repeating the historical transatlantic movement of thousands of real-life Scots and thus completing the circle of Gabaldon's American vision of the Scottish experience.

Time travel also serves a didactic purpose: the modern-day heroine is taught the conventions of a courtly society, and her contemporary attitudes towards sexual relationships are tested, sometimes to breaking point. The device can also be employed to comic effect, as in *Kiss of the Highlander* in which Drustan, fully awoken from his slumber, seeks to consummate his relationship with Gwen in the changing rooms of Barrett's, a woollen mill in the Highlands, as they struggle to find a pair of trousers large enough for him: 'Find me a pair of trews that doona threaten to sever my manparts' (Moning 2001: 92). The distinction made between the Highland heroes and the contemporary men who have so frustrated the heroines is often explicitly sexual. The male Highlanders have little understanding of modern-day American dating etiquette and press their physical demands insistently. Typically the heroine initially resists these approaches, but ultimately succumbs to the powerful sensuality of her noble savage who, though clearly uncivilised and animalistic in his urges, adheres to a code of honour which the heroine finds appealingly seductive.

The 1990s, Diane Roberts contends, saw Scotland outpace Ireland as America's 'Celtic flavor *du jour*' (Roberts 1999: 24). The number of Highland Games and Scottish Festivals held in the United States doubled during this decade to over two hundred per year with events being held in almost every state, and in 1998 the Senate formally recognised 6 April as National Tartan Day (see Hague 2001, 2002a, 2002b). Much of this growing interest was arguably a result of the phenomenal success of Mel Gibson's *Braveheart* (1995), which, among its action-packed battle scenes, also featured a love story comparable to any portrayed in these Scottish-romance novels. Leading man Gibson embodied a brawny, muscular, semi-nude warrior who, following his wife's murder, fights for her honour and subsequently impregnates the Princess of Wales, herself overcome by his virile masculinity. The trend of using Scotland as a location for romantic novels accelerated markedly in the post-*Braveheart* decade. Indeed, in *The Legend MacKinnon* Donna Kauffman makes an explicit link to Gibson's movie: after describing in great detail the physique of Duncan MacKinnon, a seventeenth-century Highlander, Kauffman's modern-day heroine concludes: 'He was nothing short of magnificent. Mel Gibson eat your heart out' (Kauffman 1999: 17). Similarly, Moning's Lisa Stone, transported back in time from late twentieth-century Cincinnati to early fourteenth-century Dunnottar, exclaims: 'Dear God! She hadn't merely traveled through time – she'd been dropped smack into the sequel to *Braveheart!*' (Moning 2000: 47). Further, in an intriguing final twist in *Highlander's Touch* the immortal Highland warrior Circenn Brodie turns on the TV in a modern-day Cincinnati hotel room and complains to his modern-day lover Lisa: '"William Wallace did *not* look like that!" He gestured irritably at the TV. Lisa laughed, as she realized he was pointing at a blue-faced Mel Gibson, storming into battle in *Braveheart*' (Moning 2000: 351).

Although the generic conventions of Scottish-themed American romances appear flexible, idiosyncratically combining elements of fantasy, science fiction, Mills-and-Boon-style historical romance and erotic fiction, a number of major common traits can be discerned. All the novels have a historical setting, with a clear preference for the thirteenth and fourteenth centuries, possibly due to this era's association with William Wallace, Robert the Bruce and *Braveheart*. Another favourite period is the eighteenth century, which enables plots about the Union of the Parliaments in 1707 and the subsequent Jacobite rebellions. The Scottish characters portrayed by the romances always live in clans, and the clans are often squabbling among each other. Genealogy and heredity are important themes: frequently the chief enemy of the hero turns out to be a half-brother, illegitimate offspring, foster child or other relative not in direct lineage to clan leadership positions. English and American characters regularly appear as contrasts to the Scots: a Scotswoman may be seduced by an Englishman or, more commonly, a Scot seduces an English or American woman. In either case it is the Scot who is 'tamed' by the developing romantic relationship.

While Scottish women invariably have long red hair, Scottish men are slightly more varied in their physical appearance, although long, black hair seems to be a common choice. All the characters are white. In terms of location, the Highlands dominate these novels, and Scottishness is often indicated by writing that emphasises local accents and on occasion implements Scots or Gaelic terms. In her exploration of what exactly it is that makes the Scotland depicted in romance novels so 'exceptionally appealing', Michele Day concludes: 'The Highlands are teeming with the heroic men of women's dreams . . . The harsh climate and rugged mountains make an ideal backdrop for adventure . . . an abundance of myths about Druids with dark secrets and stones with magical powers' (Day 2002). We agree that it is these elements, combined with others that together are commonly dismissed as 'tartanry' by Scottish cultural critics, which make these texts so alluring to readers.

Ever since Tom Nairn's denunciation of 'that prodigious array of *Kitsch* symbols, slogans, ornaments, banners, war-cries, knick-knacks, music-hall heroes, icons, conventional sayings and sentiments (not a few of them "pithy") which have for so long resolutely defended the name of "Scotland" to the world' (Nairn 1981: 162), Scottish critics have been made queasy by Scottish tartanry, a discourse which Andrew Ross identifies as 'the longest running caricature of national identity in a field of world-class competitors' (Ross 1995: 18). However, the mere fact that novels reviving tartanry constitute such a thriving subgenre of contemporary American writing ought to give pause to those who categorically dismiss representations of this kind of 'Scottishness' as an artistic dead end. Romance novels are often denigrated as unliterary and hence unworthy of critical assessment; yet, as Flesch comments, 'to dismiss or condemn out of hand . . . writing which we have never actually read and whose cultural significance we have done so little to understand seems to me both crass and foolish' (Flesch 1996). Also, by featuring historical characters and settings within romantic frameworks utilising time travel and other 'faerie' or magical devices, the American Scottish-romance novel of the late twentieth and early twenty-first centuries ultimately defies traditional generic categorisation. Interviewed by Stenhouse, Gabaldon explains:

> The books don't fit in any conceivable genre; I used the elements of all sorts of genres but I don't use them in the constrained form that the conventions of any given genre demand. Consequently you will certainly find elements of romantic fiction as well as elements of fantasy, and science fiction, which are distinct things, and of course there is historical fiction as the backdrop to it all.

Scottish-themed American romances are appealing not just because they allow for this free imaginative play of category-defying action and character development, but also because of the particular narrative resources provided by a Scottish setting. A Scottish location promises the exploits of heroic warriors, sexy and dedicated to clan and family, in a land that is mystical, full of adventurous possibilities, and emotionally charged. As Moning puts it in one of her novels, 'magic pervade[s] Scotland's air as thick and frequent as the mist' (Moning 2000: 304). The construction of Scotland in American romance novels thus draws on extant discourses of Scotland as 'the breeding-ground of a homely and primitive virtue, richly laced with fey supernatural gifts', a Scotland of Celtic enchantment, of noble savages, 'bravery, loyalty, elemental courtesy and honour' (Pittock 1999: 4). Put differently, in Gabaldon's rather understated words, Scotland appeals to American romance writers and readers because it is 'a very interesting place'.

Chapter 41

Cinema and the Economics of Representation: Public Funding of Film in Scotland

Duncan Petrie

One of the most significant developments in the wider field of cultural activity in Scotland since the early 1980s has been the emergence of a distinct Scottish cinema. While there is a much longer history of cinematic representations of Scotland and the Scots – including classics such as Michael Powell and Emeric Pressburger's *I Know Where I'm Going* (1945), Alexander Mackendrick's *Whisky Galore!* (1949), Harold French's *Rob Roy – The Highland Rogue* (1953) and Vincente Minnelli's *Brigadoon* (1954) – these were overwhelmingly productions made by the studios of London and Los Angeles. Whatever their cinematic virtues, such films articulated an external cultural perspective guided by the fantasies and desires of cosmopolitan outsiders who tended to construct Scotland as a romantic, rural and picturesque environment populated by particular 'types': rugged, noble Highlanders, enchanting maidens, superstitious or bucolic villagers and mean grotesques. What was absent was any meaningful indigenous self-expression or cultural understanding.

That situation has changed dramatically, primarily through the production of a corpus of Scottish films in Scotland, largely by Scottish film-makers, and stimulated by local funding initiatives. The 1970s witnessed a first modest breakthrough with Bill Douglas's austerely poetic autobiographical trilogy – *My Childhood* (1972), *My Ain Folk* (1973) and *My Way Home* (1978) – which constituted a bona fide Scottish contribution to European art cinema. This was followed by the more popular success of Bill Forsyth, whose no-budget debut *That Sinking Feeling* (1979) was followed by *Gregory's Girl* (1981), *Local Hero* (1983) and *Comfort and Joy* (1984), placing him securely at the forefront of the British film renaissance of the early 1980s. Inspired in part by Douglas and Forsyth, the new Scottish cinema which emerged in their wake is also a corollary of the wider flourishing of Scottish cultural self-expression in the aftermath of the referendum debacle of 1979 and the subsequent rise of Thatcherism, a development likened by Tom Devine to the 'quiet revolution' in Quebec in the early 1960s (Devine 1999: 609).

Film is an expensive cultural medium and new sources of funding became an essential prerequisite for rearing a local production industry in Scotland. The impetus initially came from visionary London-based organisations such as Channel 4 and the British Film Institute which supported significant Scottish productions during the 1980s, including Timothy Neat and John Berger's *Play Me Something* (1980), Michael Radford's *Another Time Another Place* (1983), Bill Bryden's *Ill Fares the Land* (1983), Charles Gormley's *Heavenly Pursuits* (1986), Ian Sellar's *Venus Peter* (1989), David Hayman's *Silent Scream*

(1990) and Gillies Mackinnon's *The Conquest of the South Pole* (1990). But in the end it was more specifically Scottish institutional developments which were to lay the foundations for a sustainable cinema culture in Scotland. With the average low-budget feature film costing anything between £500,000 for a digital no-frills production and £3 million-plus for a more conventional 35-mm feature, getting films made has remained a constant struggle for independent Scottish producers. However, new sources of local institutional support have ensured that a reasonable number of projects are under development at any one time and that Scottish producers have a more realistic chance of attempting to raise the rest of their production budgets from broadcasters and other sources of funding.

The seeds of a new era in Scottish film production were sown with the creation of the Scottish Film Production Fund (SFPF), founded in 1982 with a modest budget of £80,000 and a remit 'to foster and promote film and video production as a central element in the development of Scottish culture' (Lockerbie 1990: 172–3). During the 1980s the SFPF contributed to the development of a number of feature-film scripts in addition to supporting the production of various documentaries, animation projects and graduation films by Scottish students at the National Film and Television School, including work by Michael Caton-Jones, Douglas Mackinnon, Gillies Mackinnon and Ian Sellar. Gradually the resources available to the SFPF grew, primarily through direct subventions from Channel 4 and BBC Scotland, as well as the initiation of various collaborative production schemes including short-film initiatives. Consequently, by 1996 the Fund was responsible for administering more than £700,000 of development and production finance for Scottish film-making. In 1994 the SFPF was invited also to administer the new Glasgow Film Fund (GFF), an economic-development initiative established with money from the European Regional Development Fund, the Glasgow Development Agency, Glasgow City Council and Strathclyde Regional Council. The GFF scored an instant hit by investing the entire £150,000 at its disposal in Danny Boyle's acclaimed thriller *Shallow Grave* (1994), which, despite being set in Edinburgh, was primarily shot in a warehouse in Glasgow. This modest £1 million production grossed £5 million at the UK box office and almost $30 million worldwide.

The Scottish film-making community was to receive an even greater boost in 1995 with the administrative devolution of National Lottery monies into discrete English, Welsh, Scottish and Northern Irish funds. As the public institution through which the new Scottish lottery funding was to be channelled, the Scottish Arts Council (SAC) immediately looked to the SFPF to administer this new resource. As with the GFF, the fund-distribution process involved a panel of experts from the industry – essentially the SFPF Board – assessing applications and deciding on funding allocations. Now, however, the available resources were considerably greater and in its first two years of operation, approximately £12 million of lottery money was awarded to Scottish productions, with individual production grants between £500,000 and £1 million. However, after less than two years in operation, the Scottish lottery film fund encountered its first legitimacy crisis. In a highly public and rather acrimonious controversy, panel member Bill Forsyth accused his colleagues of corruption and cronyism after it transpired that two of the largest awards had been assigned to films in which other panel members had major interests. An enquiry was launched and while no misdemeanours were proven, it was decided that the SAC should assume direct responsibility for the funding process. A new panel was constituted, drawn from a wider cultural constituency than the more industry-oriented SFPF Board, to administer a fund which now had an annual ceiling of £2.5 million with a stipulated maximum investment of £500,000 in any one particular project. Whatever the pros and cons of the 'cronyism' row and its aftermath, its most significant consequence was the availability of a radically reduced pot of money as well as the departure of SFPF chief executive Eddie Dick, who had played a key role in the expansion of production funding for Scottish films.

But the new arrangement was also to prove temporary. The formation in 1997 of Scottish Screen as a single agency incorporating the Scottish Film Council, the SFPF, the Scottish Film Training Trust and the Scottish Film and Television Archive created a powerful new entity with considerable political clout. And when Scottish Screen began to lobby for control over the lottery funding, its demands chimed with the growing consensus in governmental circles concerning the need for a more industry-oriented approach to cultural funding. Consequently, in April 2000 responsibility for the lottery fund was transferred from the SAC to Scottish Screen and subsequently integrated with already existing resources inherited by Scottish Screen from the SFPF, providing a total amount of £3 million a year. The SAC panel was largely retained, although new members were solicited, and this remained the status quo until 2004, when a second major legitimacy crisis occurred. This time the context was a breakdown in trust between Scottish Screen and PACT Scotland, the local producers' organisation, concerning perceptions of inertia and a lack of transparency in the funding process. The tension between the two organisations precipitated the resignation of Jim Faulds, who had chaired the panel since its reconstitution by the SAC; it also led to the resignation of Scottish Screen chief executive Steve McIntyre. Finally, in December 2004 it was announced that the lottery panel would be dissolved, with funding decisions in future to be made by a smaller panel of Scottish Screen officers in consultation with external expert advisors.

The above account of the rather troubled ten-year history of lottery funding for Scottish film production illuminates some of the major challenges and pitfalls involved in nurturing and sustaining a small national cinema. Questions of culture and economics become intertwined in a way that distinguishes cinema from the other arts, including traditionally expensive forms of high culture such as theatre, opera or ballet. The perceived popularity of cinema, combined with the heightened imperative of its marketability, means that public sources of support for film-making, such as the lottery, face a peculiar dilemma. If a film fails to attract an audience, this is often deemed evidence of a flagrant waste of public money; yet if it is successful, the charge is that the lottery is inappropriately subsidising commercial activities. The crux of the matter is that cinema represents one of the most high-profile and powerful contemporary forms of cultural expression, playing a key role in the contemplation, construction and projection of a distinct national identity. But at the same time a small national cinema remains particularly vulnerable to external economic forces beyond its control or influence. Public funding for film therefore aims to strike a balance between cultural and commercial imperatives, although quite often the economic side of this dialectic prevails. For example, the decision to transfer responsibility for the lottery funds from the SAC, traditionally associated with a grant-giving mentality, to Scottish Screen, an industrial body more aligned with the idea of investment, must clearly be seen against the rise of a creative-industries agenda, vigorously promoted by the Blair government since 1997 and subsequently adopted by the new Scottish Executive which came into being after devolution.

Yet the success of the GFF had already shown the way in terms of how economic-development funding for cultural purposes could be justified and made lucrative by the attraction of inward investment, local spending, the nurturing of a production infrastructure in the city, and the raised national and international awareness of Glasgow stimulated by its representation in cinema. Any recoupment on investment was to be ploughed back into the funding of new projects. Importantly also, the GFF came to sponsor exactly the same kinds of projects as those supported by the SFPF and, later on, the Scottish Screen lottery fund, that is, primarily low-budget films made in Scotland, showcasing Scottish film-making talent and telling contemporary Scottish stories.

Film finance is a complex affair, and most feature-length productions draw their budgets from a wide variety of sources, including domestic broadcasters, overseas pre-sales, tax-break schemes and gap-financing in addition to public funding such as the lottery. A 2002 report on the cost of British film production commissioned by the Film Council gives the following illustrative figures (Relph et al. 2002: 71–2):

1. *For a £3 million budget:*

UK rights (theatrical and broadcast)	£500,000
Foreign pre-sales or co-production	£490,000
Lottery investment	£900,000
Sale and leaseback (tax shelter scheme)	£360,000
Gap financing/sales advance	£750,000

2. *For a £2 million budget:*

UK rights	£500,000
Lottery investment	£700,000
Sale and leaseback	£250,000
Gap financing/sales advance	£550,000

3. *For a £1.5 million budget:*

UK rights	£350,000
Lottery investment	£500,000
Sale and leaseback	£150,000
Regional fund	£200,000
Other equity	£300,000

These figures demonstrate the indispensability of lottery funding, which covers 30 per cent, 35 per cent and 33 per cent respectively of the total production costs. If one chooses to include the regional-fund investment, then the non-commercial funding sources account for almost 47 per cent of the overall production costs of a £1.5 million project. The three models also clearly indicate the ways in which a film is financed in relation to prospective markets at home and abroad, reinforcing Tom O'Regan's assertion that national cinemas 'are not alternatives to internationalisation, they are one of its manifestations . . . vehicles for international integration' (O'Regan 1996: 50–1).

As the given illustrative examples of the financing of small or modestly budgeted films also reveal, the cultural and the economic are always tightly bound up together, a circumstance increasingly recognised by those directly involved in funding low-budget cinema. Thus, Colin MacCabe, former head of BFI production, highlights 'the complicated dialectic between author and audience which is fundamental to all art but the very currency of film making' (MacCabe 1999: 16), while after a decade in charge of the Irish Film Board, Rod Stoneman notes that the greatest challenge facing the organisation, when it was reconstituted in 1993, was the need to adopt 'a more complex and adept negotiation of audience expectations: requiring the reshaping of auteurist visions in relation to the very powerful forces of the market and the complex financial machinery that underlies contemporary cinema processes' (Stoneman 2005: 251). Problems arise whenever only one side of the equation is considered, generating either a conception of film-making in which the audience plays no meaningful part, or one in which second-guessing the market is the only motivation. Neither model benefits a sustainable small national cinema, yet the policies of the UK Film Council, including its low-budget New Cinema Fund, seem to be increasingly moving towards the latter, coupled with a highly interventionist and coercive approach to working with film-makers. Accordingly, Ben Gibson, another former BFI production head, has expressed considerable concern at the current pervasiveness of 'the doctrinal dichotomy . . . that a film must be *either* culture *or* commerce' (Gibson 2002: 22), the consequence of which has been to marginalise those British film-makers who do not embrace the new commercial imperative.

By and large Scottish Screen have adopted a more balanced approach, as I discovered at first hand during my two years as a member of the lottery-funding panel, from 2001 to 2003. While the membership of the panel reflected its strong commercial orientation, comprising independent producers, directors, television executives, distributors and exhibitors, some of these individuals also represented and clearly endorsed a culturally oriented conception and understanding of film production. The panel's remit was a broad one and, in supporting Scottish film production, we were striving to achieve a triad of linked objectives: stimulating the growth of a local production industry, nurturing Scottish film-making talent, and promoting Scottish film culture.

On joining the panel I had anticipated that the decision-making process would expose tensions between a cultural and a commercial imperative in terms of strategy and funding. In the event I was struck by how much general agreement there tended to be on projects. Whether individual judgements were formed in relation to the film-maker's creative vision or potential, the script's aesthetic or more broadly cultural virtues, or the project's perceived market value, the collective decision of the panel was rarely in doubt. A number of key considerations emerged as paramount in this process, including the strength of the script and the viability of the project based on a detailed financing and marketing plan, which constituted an integral part of the application. While the potentially rivalrous demands of culture and commerce generally tended to be reconciled with an ease that almost suggested a misconception of their essential incompatibility, there were of course also a small number of contentious 'liminal' cases which generated significant disagreement. These tended to be projects which either involved talented Scottish film-makers but had a tenuous relationship to Scotland in terms of subject matter or production, or projects which were so overtly commercial in orientation that their ultimate success would depend entirely on their market worth. Whatever the pros and cons of its operation, the Scottish lottery panel facilitated the production of a diverse range of films that have consolidated the promise of the 1980s and early 1990s while significantly broadening Scottish film culture in the process.

The institutional funding of film production in Scotland, particularly since the early 1990s, has underpinned an integrated strategy that includes short-film schemes (most notably the flagship 'Tartan Shorts' scheme initiated in 1993 and run in partnership with BBC Scotland), the production of low-budget digital features (primarily through initiatives such as 'New Found Films'), and direct investment in more conventional low-budget theatrical features. The most obvious result of this strategy has been the rise of a new generation of distinctive Scottish film-makers, including directors such as Kenny Gleenan, Richard Jobson, David Kane, David Mackenzie, Saul Metzstein, May Miles Thomas, Peter Mullan and Lynne Ramsay, most of whom also write their own scripts, as well as the rise of a new generation of producers, including Catherine Aitken, Gillian Berrie, Eddie Dick, Frances Higson and Angus Lamont. New funding opportunities have also attracted established international film-makers to Scottish projects, such as Terence Davies, Ken Loach, whose Scottish productions have all been written by Paul Laverty, and the Danish directors Lone Scherfig and Soren Kragh Jackobsen.

In *Screening Scotland* I attempted to map the new Scottish cinema of the 1990s in terms of its most dominant aesthetic and thematic preoccupations, which resulted in a rather preliminary identification of tendencies. The most obviously high-profile of these I dubbed 'the *Trainspotting* effect' (Petrie 2000: 196), which identified an array of films combining a dynamic and self-conscious visual style with an edgy subject matter, keen to emulate the commercial and critical success of projects such as *Shallow Grave* and *Trainspotting*. Closely related was a larger number of productions drawing on a diverse range of generic traditions, from film noir to social realism, and sharing a focus on urban Scottishness and Scottish masculinity. What this new cinema amounted to was a point-blank rejection of Scotland's association with a romanticised Highland past in favour of a more hard-edged representation of the urban and the contemporary. In the new Scottish cinema rural narratives and historical films continued to have a presence, but they now found themselves very much on the margins. By contrast, Hollywood's preferred vision of Scotland – as embodied in Michael Caton-Jones's *Rob Roy* (1995) and Mel Gibson's *Braveheart* (1995) – continued to look back to the old traditions. But the ongoing American romanticisation of the Scottish experience only served to accentuate how emphatically the new indigenous cinema had repudiated the old stereotypes in their creation of new myths from a more overtly contemporary Scottish perspective, as, for example, in the radically iconoclastic visions of Peter Mullan's *Orphans* (1998) or Lynne Ramsay's *Ratcatcher* (1999).

Scottish films produced since 2000 have by and large confirmed the strong representational emphasis on contemporary and urban narratives, prioritising the metropolitan city – mostly Glasgow but also, to a somewhat lesser extent, Edinburgh – as the main topographical and socio-cultural setting in contemporary Scottish cinema. Moreover, while retaining a strong bias towards male protagonists and the problem of damaged masculinity, as epitomised by *Orphans*, Ken Loach's *My Name is Joe* (1998), David Mackenzie's *Young Adam* (2003) and Richard Jobson's *16 Years of Alcohol* (2003), contemporary Scottish cinema has recently witnessed the emergence of an increasing number of films focusing on female experience, such as May Miles Thomas's *One Life Stand* (1999), Lynne Ramsay's *Morvern Callar* (2002), Peter Mullan's *The Magdalene Sisters* (2002) and Shona Auerbach's *Dear Frankie* (2004). But not only have significantly more women begun to distinguish themselves as important film-makers in recent Scottish cinema history, there is also a new acknowledgement of multicultural diversity within Scotland, manifesting itself in very different kinds of films: Kenny Glenaan's *Gas Attack* (2002), which deals with the racist backlash against Kurdish refugees in Glasgow, or Ken Loach's *Ae Fond Kiss* (2004), which depicts the relationship between a Scottish-Pakistani Muslim man and an Irish-Catholic woman as beset by religious intolerance on both sides, and Don Coutts's *American Cousins* (2003), a comedy featuring Italian Scots, American mobsters and Ukrainian hitmen.

If there is one single predominant 'structure of feeling' in recent Scottish cinema, it is probably its apparent preoccupation with the dark and seamy side of life, a world of violence, brutality and suffering. However, this is not restricted exclusively to cinematic representation. As Angus Calder remarks with reference to the writings of Iain Banks, Janice Galloway, James Kelman, A. L. Kennedy, Duncan McLean, Alan Warner and Irvine Welsh, 'the Scotland of recent fiction has been a grim and dangerous place' (Calder 1996:

237). Of course, this Scottish literary obsession with the darker side of human experience can be traced back further to the marked prominence of Gothic elements in the works of Robert Burns, James Hogg and R. L. Stevenson, which, as Cairns Craig persuasively argues, is in turn underpinned by the impact of Calvinism on the national imagination (see Craig 1999). A recurrent theme in this Calvinist-inspired tradition is the centrality of feelings of fear or unease, an anti-kailyard in which the community becomes a repository of nastiness, malevolence and moral corruption. This looms large in cinematic representations of Scotland as well, both in externally produced films such as David MacDonald's *The Brothers* (1947), Robert Wise's *The Bodysnatcher* (1945), John Gilling's *The Flesh and the Fiends* (1959) and Robin Hardy's *The Wicker Man* (1973), and in more recent indigenous works starting with the release of Bill Douglas's seminal trilogy in the 1970s.

Douglas's austere depiction of childhood deprivation, emotional poverty and material squalor in the immediate postwar period resonates in Ramsay's work, particularly her short films and *Ratcatcher*. Ramsay's cinema is deeply concerned with the fragile contingency of human existence. *Ratcatcher* begins and ends with a drowning, chronicling its twelve-year-old protagonist's failure to escape from the bleak oppression and poverty of life in a Glasgow slum. Ramsay's second feature, *Morvern Callar*, based on Alan Warner's debut novel, charts a somewhat more successful narrative of escape, beginning with a suicide and eventually culminating in the eponymous heroine's disappearance, both figurative and literal. In contrast, Peter Mullan's depiction of the human condition, albeit often harrowing and violent, is ultimately far more affirmative than Ramsay's in that his Catholic-inspired belief in the power of redemption overcomes the Calvinist determinism that seems to hang over a film like *Ratcatcher*. In *Orphans*, which has been read by critics as a national allegory (Murray 2001; Martin-Jones 2005), Mullan tackles the thorny problematic of Scottish working-class masculinity and its inadequacies. However, unlike many similar representations, he boldly grasps the nettle (or should it be the thistle?) and proposes a way forward for his self-embattled protagonists. And although Mullan's second project, *The Magdalene Sisters*, takes the form of a prison drama to expose the scandal of the Magdalene Asylums for unmarried mothers in Ireland, it shares with its predecessor a strongly developed narrative trajectory of hope and redemption.

Centred on representations of alienated masculinity, dark, atavistic sexualities, and a brooding sense of both topographical and spiritual liminality, David Mackenzie's films comprise yet another important contribution to contemporary Scottish cinema. *The Last Great Wilderness* (2002) begins as a kind of road movie and reinvigorates a tradition of rural Scottish Gothic which invokes *The Brothers*, *The Wicker Man* and even *Whisky Galore*, all of which problematise an outsider's confrontation with the strange otherness of Scotland's rural environment and its inhabitants. In *Young Adam*, an adaptation of Alexander Trocchi's 1954 beat novel and arguably his most personal film to date, Mackenzie creates his own version of a justified sinner in the shape of a young writer working on a barge on the Forth–Clyde canal in the early 1950s. The claustrophobic environment, exacerbated by the restrictive mores of a markedly pre-liberated society, serves as an effective backdrop to the destructive and forceful display of a solipsistic sexuality, which brilliantly captures the disturbing, amoral detachment of Trocchi's original. A similarly obtrusive existential destructiveness can be found in the work of Richard Jobson, whose stunning debut, *16 Years of Alcohol*, revisits the familiar scenario of a young man whose life is blighted by alcohol and violence, but situates it within the dark, claustrophobic vennels and closes of Edinburgh's Old Town, which inspired Stevenson's tales of horror, including the London-set *Jekyll and Hyde*. By thus positioning itself within a distinctly Scottish tradition, *16 Years of Alcohol* possesses a depth which eludes other films that have turned the spotlight on Edinburgh's seamier side, such as Paul McGuiggan's *The Acid House* (1999) or Anthony Neilson's *The Debt Collector* (1999).

The dark tenor of the new Scottish cinema establishes points of connection with other cultural and national imaginaries, resulting most fruitfully perhaps in the forging of links with Scandinavian film-makers. In this context Lone Scherfig's *Wilbur Wants to Kill Himself* (2004), a pitch-black Glasgow-set comedy about a depressed man who keeps trying (and failing) to commit suicide, seems a good case in point. A shared northern-European sensibility is also discernible in Lars von Trier's award-winning *Breaking the Waves* (1996), a dark study of psychic fragility and *amour fou* set on Skye in the 1970s. Significantly, Trier's film, which in its experimental production style anticipated the aesthetics of the famous Danish directors' collective 'Dogme 95', was entirely funded by non-Scottish sources. The Scottish–Scandinavian link hints at a deeper European sensibility pervading the new Scottish cinema. Public support, including lottery funding, has fostered the growth of a small national cinema, driven and informed by its film-makers' often very personal concerns and idiosyncratic styles. This peculiarity of the new Scottish cinema is tempered to a certain extent by the inescapable influence of American culture, which has been productively interrogated by Jonathan Murray (Murray 2004, 2005). The enthusiastic embrace of American culture by many Scots can be seen in terms of the idea of the USA as a land of freedom of opportunity in opposition to the rigid, class-bound social organisation of Anglo-British society. This yearning for a kind of existential freedom continues to permeate familiar generic forms and motifs – the road, the wilderness, urban crime or rock 'n' roll. Yet even at its most imitative, Scottish cinematic representation distinguishes itself by a strongly identity-bearing, local engagement, which also functions as a reminder of the impossibility of ever perfectly emulating Hollywood without Hollywood resources. Instead, what emerges more strongly is an articulation of personal style and social engagement, thus placing contemporary Scottish cinema within the tradition of European art cinema.

The demise of the Scottish lottery-funding panel brought to an end a process of decision-making refreshingly different from that employed by the UK Film Council. While committee-based decision-making is always intrinsically problematic, the panel structure did provide a forum where a broad sweep of expertise and robust debate formed a key part of the funding process. Historically such panels, including the BFI Production Board, have promoted as well as practised a more culturally informed approach to funding than the executive model adopted by British Screen, which prioritises decision-making along the more commercially defined lines of marketability and economic success. Given the general climate change in cultural politics, this shift to a process in which greater decision-making powers were invested in the officers of Scottish Screen, albeit in consultation with a small group of hand-picked industry representatives, was probably inevitable. And yet, as my own experience on the Scottish lottery-funding panel has taught me, even if cultural and economic considerations may remain conceptually distinct, more often than not they are closely entwined in practice. The successful marriage of culture and the market is particularly important in the case of a small national cinema like Scotland's. As noted by Steve McIntyre, who played an influential role in the new cinema as Scottish Screen's production director and then chief executive, 'if there is one defining characteristic of low-budget film-making it is that it dissolves the distinction between commercial film-making and cultural film-making – it is a meeting ground' (McIntyre 1994: 106).

The abolition of the lottery-funding panel in 2004 and the subsequent announcement that Scottish Screen, along with the Scottish Arts Council, is to be replaced by a new national cultural funding body throws the future into doubt. Whatever its shortcomings, Scottish Screen's lottery fund provided a genuine alternative to the more overtly commercial imperatives of the UK Film Council, which now dominates institutional film policy in Britain and whose vision was spelled out by the Film Council's chairman, Sir Alan Parker, in a speech to the industry in 2002. In order to compete more successfully in the global marketplace, Parker called on British cinema to reconceive of itself as a creative film hub or, put differently, as a service industry for international – that is, in particular, Hollywood – production. Parker's proposition constitutes a radical alternative to previous efforts at maintaining a balance between cultural and commercial considerations, efforts which, as shown above, so successfully guided the development of New Scottish Cinema. Given that Parker evidently regards much of current British film-making as already far too parochial, the threat his thinking may come to pose closer to home is clear. Lest Scottish cinema's very real devolutionary achievements are to be squandered, what is urgently required of contemporary Scotland's film producers and policy-makers alike is a courageous, ambitious and imaginative re-affirmation of Scottish cinema's devolved status.

Chapter 42

Twenty-first-century Storytelling: Context, Performance, Renaissance

Valentina Bold

This chapter discusses storytelling in contemporary Scotland, profiling its current renaissance. It starts by examining the context, then considers contemporary performance practices. The final part illustrates the renaissance in practice through the work of Stanley Robertson and Lawrence Tulloch. The discussion draws extensively on recorded interviews with Robertson, Tulloch, Donald Smith and Tom Pow. I would like to thank them all for their kindness in sharing their extensive knowledge with me, and for their permission to quote. My approach is, no doubt, subjective but, in my defence, there is little critical literature on modern Scottish storytelling. Smith's *Storytelling Scotland* (2001) is a pioneering work in this context, as is Michael Wilson's *Storytelling and Theatre* (2006).

There are illuminating accounts of twentieth-century storytelling from travelling people: Betsy Whyte's *The Yellow on the Broom* (1979) and *Red Rowans and Wild Honey* (1990), Robertson's *Exodus to Alford* (1988) and Duncan Williamson's *The Horsieman: Memories of a Traveller 1928–58* (1994), as well as Timothy Neat's *The Summer Walkers* (1996). Modern collections have helpful introductions: Sheila Douglas's *The King of the Black Art* (1987), Duncan and Linda Williamson's *The Thorn in the King's Foot: Stories of the Scottish Travelling People* (1987) and Alan Bruford and Donald A. MacDonald's *Scottish Traditional Tales* (1994) for instance. However, there is less in-depth analysis than, for instance, in North America, where writers like Linda Degh, Alan Dundes, Richard Baumann and Jack Zipes have studied performance styles and storytelling events. Gerald Thomas, in *Les Deux Traditions* (1983), distinguishes between private (the storytelling a parent performs with a child) and public occasions, such as the winter sessions of the past and storytelling festivals of the present. It is the second category which is considered here.

As J. F. Campbell explained in his *Popular Tales of the West Highlands* (1860–2), 'the creed of the people, as shewn in their stories [is] that wisdom and courage, though weak, may overcome strength, and ignorance, and pride; that the most despised is often the most worthy' (Campbell 1982: dedication, n.p.). Scotland has a distinguished tradition of valuing its stories, if not – until relatively recently – its storytellers. Like our fellow Europeans we have presented, catalogued and reworked tales, from the Ossianic collection of James Macpherson to James Hogg's versions of his grandfather's tales to Campbell's *Popular Tales* and beyond. From its inception in 1951, the University of Edinburgh's School of Scottish Studies has played a major role in collecting stories in Gaelic, Scots and English. Calum Maclean (1915–60) deserves special mention for his work with storytellers like Angus MacMillan in Benbecula and John Macdonald in Lochaber. Equally Hamish Henderson (1919–2002) – better known for his work on song, particularly with the prodigiously talented Jeannie Robertson (1908–75) – played a key role. Maclean and Henderson collected from travelling people like Ailidh Dall of Lairg in Sutherland and the Williamsons in Ross-shire. The School's collecting of stories in the twentieth century, just as Macpherson's in the 1700s and Hogg's in the 1800s, was a cultural act. As Smith notes, for Maclean 'the act of gathering was not historical research but a declaration of cultural values' (Smith 2001: 142; see also Neat 1996 and Freeman 2003). The work of promoting Scottish storytellers was continued within the School by collectors Bruford, MacDonald, John MacInnes, Barbara McDermitt, Linda Williamson (née Headlee) and John Shaw. The School's magazine, *Tocher*, drew attention to storytellers like Duncan MacDonald of South Uist, Nan MacKinnon from Vatersay, Brucie Henderson from Shetland, Hugh MacKinnon from Eigg, Peter Morrison from Uist, Donald Sinclair from Tiree, and many others (see especially *Tocher*, volumes 7–38, published between 1971 and 1983). The School also presented recorded tales in Greentrax's *Scottish Tradition* series.

Since the mid-1980s the work of the Scottish Storytelling Centre at the Netherbow in Edinburgh's High Street has been particularly important in promoting storytelling. The refurbished Centre opened in 2006 at a cost of £3.5 million as a purpose-specific home for Scottish storytelling. It hosts a ten-day annual festival and it is estimated that 160,000 young people in Scotland each year now experience storytelling. The Netherbow Arts Centre in Edinburgh held the first Scottish Storytelling Festival in 1989; this was followed by the foundation of the Guid Crack Club in 1990 and, from 1992, the work of the 'voluntary activists' of the Scottish Storytelling Forum (CCMD2006VB3: 3).[1] Following from this, in 1997 the George Mackay Brown Scottish Storytelling Centre was opened at the Netherbow. Academics and storytellers were fully involved in this initiative, such as Henderson, Robertson and Williamson. The Forum felt it was important to honour storytellers within a public context. Its initial idea of promoting storytellers through an agency model, similar to that used for traditional singers, proved flawed, as Smith explains: 'It was too commercial . . . it tended to put somebody between the storyteller and the community or the organization . . . actually the essence of this was the sharing of values and relationships' (CCMD2006VB.3: 2). This led to the decision to found a resources and education centre which could support and work with storytellers and their traditions.

Smith strongly believes that the current resurgence is anchored in the earlier traditions of Scotland, from the stories of the travelling people to the storytellers of Orkney and Shetland, the Western Isles and Highlands. As such, it is not a revival, in the sense the term is used with song, but a renaissance: 'We were unbelievably fortunate that the reawakening . . . of public interest in these older traditions, began when they were still living' (CCMD2006VB.3: 10). Along with a determination to express the dynamic nature of storytelling, the Forum sought to maintain professional standards among its storytellers and so the idea of having a 'Directory of Storytellers' emerged. This provides information about storytellers' backgrounds and experience. At present it lists ninety-nine Scottish

---

[1] All quotations from interviews are edited from transcriptions of recordings made by Valentina Bold and held by the University of Glasgow's Crichton Campus. Citations are in the format of the minidisk's archival number followed by the specific minidisk track numbers. An attempt is made to reflect the spoken Scots of all participants, with its distinctive regional aspects, while maintaining the general intelligibility of the transcriptions. Ellipses indicate material omitted from the original transcript. While the editor decided to remove indications of verbal emphases from passages of commentary, in the cited stories verbal emphases are marked by italics; particularly strong emphases are given in italics and also underlined. Non-verbal elements, such as laughter or pauses, are indicated in square brackets.

storytellers, from Shetland to the Borders. It includes new Scots, originally from Japan, Ghana and the United States, as well as one storyteller for the deaf. The Directory uses eight criteria for inclusion. The storyteller must 'be a part of one or more storytelling traditions' or 'be well acquainted with a tradition and have . . . a repertoire'. He or she is expected to tell stories regularly and to 'demonstrate the capacity to work with . . . a wide range of audiences', possess a recommended three years' experience and 'be willing to travel widely'. The storytellers must also have an Enhanced Disclosure from the Scottish Criminal Record Office and 'be Network members of the Scottish Storytelling Forum'. Finally, members must be 'committed to the principles of cooperation and best practice' and provide information on their interests, experience and target audiences for the Directory.

As Pow notes, the Directory has an important function in ensuring certain standards in Scottish storytelling, and in regulating fees. However, Wilson notes that the Society for Storytelling in England and Wales does not operate in this way: 'Attempts to impose a . . . regime to control entry into the ranks of professional storytelling have always met with fierce opposition.' Wilson admits, though, that the Scottish Storytelling Forum 'is not . . . authoritarian' but 'inherently democratic' (Wilson 2006: 30). Smith equally denies that the Forum is exclusive:

> All . . . we are saying, to be part of this development . . . we are looking for people to understand the strengths and the cultural inheritance resources . . . and the social values of what the tradition offer us . . . It doesn't matter where a person starts from. Whether they're a Ghanaian tribal storyteller, whether they were born in rural Newcastle . . . it's about learning, and developing and engaging in this whole process. (CCMD2006VB.3: 20)

The Forum made an early decision to allow members of the public, and schools, to have free access to its resources, and its various initiatives have flourished. National Tell-a-Story Day, for instance, is celebrated widely, giving rise to events within schools and communities. The Forum values this: 'It gives people an opportunity to create their own events . . . It's not all about us setting an agenda' (CCMD2006VB.3: 23). There are, too, storytelling circles, clubs and organisations in Scotland, which often work in partnership with the Forum. For instance, the Grampian Association of Storytellers (GAS) is active in the northeast of Scotland, promoting local traditions and publishing a DVD in 2005: *The Butcher, the Baker and the Tablecloth Maker*. Storytelling is being used throughout Scotland for specific community purposes, as with the recent project to celebrate the stories of the lesbian, gay, bisexual and transgender community. Marion Kenny is currently storyteller in residence at the Museums of Scotland. The 'Go and Meet' initiative lets stories travel between islands in the Hebrides and is being extended to Orkney and Shetland. This upsurge was recognised by Scotland's Cultural Commission, which named the Netherbow as a key venue in our national cultural life (Scottish Executive 2005).

According to Robertson, the oral tradition is 'a culture that bonds', adding that 'storytellers see things through their spiritual eyes . . . There's so much beauty on the earth if we look for it' (Bold and McKean 1999). Clare Mulholland concurs: 'I think the work that is the most fulfilling and satisfying is the extended work . . . where you can see creativity flowering in other people' (Wilson 2006: 175). Storytelling in Scotland has two sets of roots. One of these is in the folk tradition. The other, which Mulholland exemplifies, has developed from theatre in response to specific creative, and sometimes therapeutic, needs. The first tradition is most immediately associated with travelling people, who are some of the best modern storytellers, like Essie Stewart, who is the granddaughter of Allidh Dall

Stewart and Willie MacPhee. Possibly our best-known, and certainly one of our best-loved storytellers is Duncan Williamson (see McDermitt and Bruford 1980). Born in 1928, Williamson has worked as a drystane dyker, farm labourer and horse dealer, living in Fife since the 1940s. His compelling and quietly dramatic style is enhanced by a particularly melodic voice. Williamson, like Robertson, is a knowledgeable singer, moving between spoken and sung narrative with ease. He has published widely, often with his second wife, Linda Williamson, who is herself an engaging storyteller (see Williamson and Williamson 1983, 1985, 1991). Williamson's eldest son, Jimmy Williamson, born in 1951, is also a fine storyteller. Similarly, Sheila Stewart of Blairgowrie has travelling lineage: she is the daughter of the great singer and songwriter Belle Stewart and the piper Alex Stewart (see Fleming 1976). Stewart has a rich repertoire and distinctive style of storytelling, just as she does in her stunningly heartfelt singing. Smith draws attention to Stewart's 'verve and gusto – a force of personality and language – which is entirely her own' (Smith 2001: 156).

The second tradition is exemplified by performers like Mulholland (now McNicol). She is a quiet and thoughtful storyteller, originally from County Antrim, who entered storytelling through her professional life. As a social worker, applying for a job in Edinburgh, she was asked if she would try storytelling (which she had previously experienced through workshops with storytellers for children) with her new clients (Wilson 2006: 172). Equally, some storytellers have a theatrical background. The Borders storyteller John Nichol is particularly known for his work with the Borders-based Rowan Tree Company. John Wheeler, born in Wiltshire in 1946 and now living in Dumfriesshire, comes from a background of street theatre. As Pow states, his storytelling is 'very physical . . . it's that kind of theatrical context and that particular kind of listening' (CCMD2006VB.4: 28). Many storytellers use music to set their work, such as David Campbell, whose work is represented on a fine recording with the Wrigley Sisters of Orkney. Despite differences in their backgrounds, storytellers fulfil similar functions, as Smith suggests: 'When the public responds to these people, they're responding to the same core things . . . direct engagement . . . the eye to eye bit, the fluidity of openness and response, a sense of community building' (CCMD2006VB.3: 11).

The first academic course in Scotland to combine the practical and theoretical study of storytelling has been developed by Pow and myself at the University of Glasgow's Crichton Campus in Dumfries. Our current level-three undergraduate course is part of the university's programme in creative and cultural studies and also its Scottish studies programme. As our course documentation explains, its aims are 'to develop practical and interpretative skills in storytelling', to offer an 'appreciation of storytelling traditions' and 'to understand how storytelling operates in the modern world'. To this end, there are weekly three-hour seminars, and we make our studio theatre available for students to practise. We encourage students to think about how the relationship between performer and audience, and the purpose behind the event, affect tale-telling. We consider performance styles, repertoires and the meaning of stories as personal texts and as texts of community. Students learn how to classify stories generically and to consider their functions and structures; this translates, we believe, into good storytelling. Skills, and repertoires, are gradually built through structured assignments. Students regularly tell stories and they learn from each other through constructive criticism. Pow is particularly interested in how students learn by approaching a subject through practice rather than study: '[I wanted to] . . . learn, what extra you learn from working from the inside . . . what's that process' (CCMD2006VB.4: 16). In many ways the course liberates stories already in the students' repertoires, recalling Kenneth Goldstein's classic theory of inactive (known, but not performed) and active (in performance) repertoires (Goldstein 1971).

One of the problems we faced was that there was not a great tradition of formal instruction of storytelling in Scotland besides that of the Gaelic bardic schools of the past, which, perhaps, has had some continuity into the present (see Thomson 1994; Neat 1999). In this respect, visiting storytellers are crucial. Robertson, for instance, has a specific way of teaching. He encourages students to learn the tale from the 'inside' and, in one exercise, focuses on an experiential way of learning:

> *This is* how *I* wis taught . . . and *this* is how I teach . . . A wis *waalkin* doon the road wi this *old, old* grannaidh [granny] . . . and she says, '*Wee laddie,*' she says, '*Fit's* that lying on the side o the road?' And I says, '*Great, great* grannaidh, it is the *skull* of a *dead animal.*' She says, '*Describe* it to me.' I says, 'Well it's *grey* and mottled, it's *got horns, big eye* sockets, an *teeth*. It's *covered* wi wee sort of *broon, yella* and orange *lichens* . . . And she says, '*That's* very good, wee laddie.' She says [very strongly], '_Now_, go inside the *right* eye o the skull', and I *immediately* went inside o the right eye o the *skull* in my *mind*, and I come *into* . . . *caverns, canyons, volcanoes, all* manner of flowers, *all* manner of *everything*, I could see this _whole world_, I could *smell*, I could *taste*, I could *feel*, I could *see*, and I *experienced*. And I *luxuriated* inside this particular skull.
>
> *Away in the distance* I *heard her saying*, '*Wee laddie*, come *back oot*', and I came *back oot* the *left eye* of the skull, came *back* into the road wi her . . . and she says, '*Wee* laddie, the _mantle_ of the storyteller will fall upon you, *but*', she says, '*Today* I have taught you a *great lesson*. See there are *two* times upon this earth. There's the *time* when we're sitting *speaking* to each other, and there's the time when there's *dream* and storytime, which runs *parallel* to, ken, this *world*? How *long* were you *away*, wee laddie, inside the *skull*?' I said, 'Maybe *ten* to *fifteen minutes*.' She says, 'You've been *away* two seconds.' And *you will learn _more_* in *two* seconds *inside* the thing, and *seeing out* than what you will *lookin* at *something*. (CCMD2004.20: 28–9)

In his description of this trance-like state of the storyteller, previously identified in the behaviour of storytelling audiences (see Sturm 2000), Robertson highlights the way in which storytelling opens an awareness of creative culture. Some of our students continue telling stories publicly, and at least one is now a registered storyteller with the Scottish Storytelling Centre. Pow is currently developing a taught postgraduate MLitt in Storytelling, which will allow students an additional full year to develop their practical skills and knowledge of storytelling.

With respect to the current renaissance in Scottish storytelling, Smith has commented: 'I don't see tradition as a fixed thing that's set in stone, I think it's an evolving set of different cultural values' (CCMD2006VB.3: 11). Two of Scotland's best-known storytellers are Stanley Robertson and Lawrence Tulloch. Robertson was born in 1940. The nephew of Jeannie Robertson, he worked in the fishyards of Aberdeen for many years before becoming a Research Fellow at the University of Aberdeen's Elphinstone Institute and, recently, retiring. He has told stories for many years, nationally and internationally, and has published traditional and original stories (Robertson 1988, 1989, 1990). His storytelling is part of his identity as a member of the travelling community:

> I wis born into this lore. My great grandfather, old Bill Stewart, wis classed as the great seannachie o the Travellin people an I think his mantle fell upon me. I have always told stories, even fin I wis a wee bairn doon [at] the camp fire . . . In my family, they were aa musicians an storytellers, an pipers an singers an dancers, an it wis jist a natural thing that ye hid tae learn some o the art. (Bold and McKean 1999)

Tulloch is, again, well-known and well-respected. He is from Yell in Shetland, and his father was Tom Tulloch, whose stories are well-known in printed and recorded versions (see Bruford 1978–9). Tulloch has performed nationally and internationally and published three recordings on the Veesek label. He has worked in several occupations, as a lighthouse keeper and postmaster, and now he helps his wife to run their superb bed and breakfast in Gutcher in Yell, as well as being a tour guide and trainer of tour guides throughout Shetland. Tulloch, like Robertson, learnt his tales from his family, particularly from his father, who was a crofter and a woodworker:

> My father, if you had sort of backed him up along the wall and said, 'Are you a storyteller?' he would have vehemently denied it. I know that [laughing] for a certainty! But at the same time, he told stories pretty well continuously . . . Most of the folktales I learnt from him and it's so long ago and I was at such a young age that I have no recollection of actually learning the stories. They've always been with me for as long as I can remember. (CCMD2004VB.20: 11)

Similarly, Robertson says: 'I never have to think upon [my stories], because they're inside you and they're part and parcel of your character' (CCMD2004VB.20: 13–14).

There are significant differences between these storytellers' styles. Robertson's could be described as proclamatory, linked to his strong desire to communicate traveller culture and to celebrate family traditions. As with his singing, Robertson's storytelling resembles the authoritative style of his aunt Jeannie (Henderson 1992: 160). Smith describes Robertson convincingly as 'bardic' in comparison to a more 'social' style:

> Some . . . storytellers . . . have got a sort of . . . psychological as well as artistic sense of themselves as speaking for the tradition in quite a commanding . . . way . . . while still engaging with the audience and some . . . are much more comfortable sitting down with people gathered around them. (CCMD2006VB.3: 18)

Tulloch, perhaps, is closer to the second type of storyteller although his delivery is equally powerful. He is quietly compelling, like his father (see Bruford 1978–9). Tulloch combines real *gravitas* in his delivery with tremendous affability and modesty, making him wholly engaging.

Despite these differences, the storytellers have similar concerns and respectful attitudes towards their culture. They are well-read, as well as educated through the oral tradition, and are thoughtful storytellers. As Tulloch says, 'I think it's a question of suiting whatever you're saying to the people that's listening' (CCMD2004VB.21: 35). They work well together, as I observed when participating with them in sessions at 'Scotland at the Smithsonian' in Washington in 2003 and in Glasgow, at the Theoretical Archaeology Group conference in 2004, offering a counterpoint of contrasting styles. Both storytellers value spontaneity in performance. Robertson, for instance, points to a need to vary the tellings and respond to the occasion: 'I can never tell a story the same way twice . . . A never practice . . . ma auntie Jeannie used to say, "It's only duds that practice." If you've got it inside you, ye dinnae need to' (CCMD2004VB.21: 6). Tulloch agrees: 'It's the golden rule for me, that if I have to think about a story, then I don't know it well enough to tell it' (CCMD2004VB.21: 13). Given this sensitivity, both Robertson and Tulloch make considered choices in relation to language. On public occasions, and certainly outwith Shetland, Tulloch uses what he calls 'Sunday-best English' (CCMD2004VB.21: 24):

I have a great deal of frustration with the Shetland dialect, because I feel that a lot of the stories I tell and know is best told in dialect . . . But I learnt a long time ago the futility of speaking to people in such a way that they don't know what you're saying. It's an absolute waste of time! (CCMD2004VB.21: 24)

Robertson is similarly conscious of issues relating to his use of language; his is a 'fusion', allowing him to make choices in oral and print storytelling. His languages include the Doric (that is, northeast Scots), Travellers' cant, Romany (from his English gypsy grandfather) and Gaelic (from his grandmother) (CCMD2004VB.20: 18). Both storytellers have a deep affinity with the places where they were raised. Tulloch was born at Midbrake in Yell, next to the stunningly beautiful sands of Breckon: 'I like to think of it as a beautiful place and storytelling and stories is all part o that heritage' (CCMD2004VB.20: 9–12). Robertson has a deep attachment to the old drove road of Lumphanan, which played a crucial part for Aberdeenshire travellers: 'This old road, there's hundreds and hundreds of different ghost tales to it . . . the travellers were experts at . . . these stories' (CCMD2004VB.20: 26).

As representatives of the renaissance, I would like to end the chapter with a story from each storyteller. These are given in the order they were performed at Glasgow in 2004. They express profound loyalties to place and people, and to the cultural background of each storyteller. The first is Tulloch's:

Near the sands of Breckon there's a *ness*, a *headland* that's very *flat, very long, very* <u>narrow</u> . . . There's . . . one tiny *grotto* there that the *sand* is *all* made from broken *shells*, it's not from stone at *all* and *even now*, to this *day*, people *go* and *get home* a small *bucket* full of the stuff to give to their *hens* for *grit*, it's *perfect* for that.

Now, a *long* time ago there was a *family* that lived nearby, and the *girl* of the house was *young*, very *beautiful*, <u>very</u> *beautiful*, but she was very *cold*, and she had *plenty* of *admirers* but she never *ever* had *anything* to do with *boys*. Her *father* was rather *hostile* to their approaches in *any* case, but *so cold was* <u>she</u> that boys eventually gave *up*, nobody, they just, *no use*. They turned their attention to more *receptive* people, shall we say!

But *anyway*, one day the *mother* sent the girl down to, to *that place* to get grit for the *hens* and it was a *fine, warm* summer's *day* and she was *away* for a long *time*. And when she came back her mother said, 'Where have you *been?*' and she said, 'Aw, I must have fallen *asleep*. It wis such a nice *day*.' Some time *after* that . . . her mother *realised* that the girl had *changed*, and it didn't take her long to figure out that the girl was *pregnant*. Now, this was hard to *believe*, because she had *nothing* to do with boys *whatsoever*, and her mother *knew* that, but *eventually*, in the *fullness* of *time*, this *baby* wis *boren*, and it was a very *abnormal* child, it was sort of *half-boy*, *half-*<u>seal</u> and *apparently* the girl had been impregnated by a seal while she *slept* by the *shore*.

Now, in *those* days in Shetland to have an *illegitimate child* was a big enough *stigma*, but to have some sort of almost *monstrosity*, that was neither human nor *animal* was more than the family could *tolerate*. So, her *father* more or less put her out, and the child, they were more or less locked out of the *house*. *They* made their home in an empty house – *jist a hovel* – and they were *destitute*, they had absolutely *nothing*, and they were cold and hungry and every night the woman and the *child* used to cry themselves to *sleep*. So *poor* were they. And *one* night she had a *dream*, and the *dream* told her that if she went *back* to the place where the shell *sand* is and *scraped* among the sand, she would find *silver*. But the dream *also* told her that the silver wasn't for *her*, it was *fur* the *boy*, but *her*, *her* health and, was <u>vital</u> to the wellbeing *of the* boy, *so* therefore *she could have* as *much* for herself as she *needit*, but *not* any *more*. *Never be greedy*, it told her.

So, the next day she went, and she found *silver*, and she was very *dutiful*, she was very *obedi-ent*, she did the things that she was *told*. She *only* went when she needit to go, and she *never* took more than she *needit*. And *eventually* – they lived liked that, in *some* kind of comfort, for a number of *years* until the boy was *twelve*. And *then* he went back to the *sea*, and he became a *seal*. And he *went* away, and he was never seen *again*, and, what the *mother*, she was as *poor* as *ever*, but *no amount* of scraping among the sand ever produced any *silver*, because the boy didn't *need* it. And so she went on to live a life of *poverty*. But *that* little grotto, to *this day*, is known as *Silver Geo*. (CCMD2004VB.20: 24)

Robertson responded with another tale of a woman on her own; this time old rather than young but, again, intimately related to a place important to him:

There was *this woman* caad Mary, and she wus *campit* wi her *man* an her *bairns* up at the *top* aw the *aald road* where aa the *trevellers* used tae come an *ae* day she hid tae gae in tae Aiberdeen, cus this sister that wis *nae weel* in hospital. So, *once* she went tae see her sister, she come back to get the *bus* back tae *Lumphanan* an the *best* bus tae tak was the bus that taked ye tae *Tarland*, cause that took ye aff at the *heich* aw the aald road. But if ye *misst* that yeen, ye'd tae catch the *Lumphanan* bus, went in tae the village, ye'd tae waalk *awa* up the hill, past the aald *huntit* graveyard, and ye'd tae gae up fur aboot *twa mile*, up the *lonely road*. But she'd *over* stayed her time in Aiberdeen, so her *sister* faw wis ill, fae the *time* she left the hospital tae *catch* her bus, she'd missed the *Tarland* bus, so she had to take the *Lumphanan* bus, and *when* she arrived in the *village* of Lumphanan, it wis *late* in the gloaming.

So she *maks* her wey up this *lonely, lonely* bit o the village, and it was aboot *ten* o'clock at *nicht*, this last bus got in. And she *come* to this, ken, when ye *start* the aald drove road it's just a *narra*, narra road, it meanders aa the way up a *mountain* side, and the ither bittie's a *dowie* den wi a *burn* in it . . . there's only aboot *three* hooses in the *whole* length o the aald road.

An as *Mary* was waalkin – she was an *affa* good *diddler*, and she *liked* to keep herself *company* – and that's fae trevellers used tae *dae*. If they were *on* their *ain*, they *aye* diddled. So she wis [diddles] . . . An *is* she wis *getting up* [pace slowing] to the *side* gate o the ceemetery, she *noticed* a wumman comin *oot* in *front* o her an *waakin* up the *front* o her. And *she* says, 'That would be *fine*, an that'd keep me *company*. She's maybe gang up tae *work* in one o the *hooses*.' But she wis *bonnie dresst*. She wis dresst in a *lang, silken goon*, a bonnie pair o *silver* kind o *sheen* and she had *jewellery* on and *earrings* and lang, lang hair. And Mary said, 'That's *fine* tae get unna that woman's company up the road.' So she *comes* a bittie *close*, so she *quack-ens* up her pace, and she said, [speaks loudly], 'Hi there, missus . . .', she says, 'Fit *time* is it?' But the wumman doesnae take *notice* o her, an the wumman keeps *waakin* an, because, *through* the graveyard you could come from the . . . road and ye could cut *through* it and come back onto the aald road, so it was a *short* cut that folk would often take. But she never *heard* her, so, the wumman was *deif*. And she said, [louder] '*Excuse* me missus, fit *time* is it?' So, the wumman kept on *waakin* and then – *trevellers* never ask the same question three *times* . . . because, it's *supposed* to be if you *ask* the same question three times it's *aald Nick* that turns roond . . . So she says, 'Well, missus', she says, 'A'll *no* ask you a *third* time.' Cause mebbe auld *Cloven Haudie* might turn roond. And *jist* wi that there was an unearthly [very loud] <u>How-OOO!!! Ohoh</u>, this gret big *banshee howl* went on, and this thing turned roond, that *she* thought wis a beautiful *wumman* it wus a *skeleton's face*, jist <u>*eye*</u> sockets, *nae* nose, *nae* lips, jist the *pure skeleton* dresst in this *claes*, and it jist run, <u>*squealed*</u> past her, like a *banshee* and run back intae the *graveyard*.

And Mary got sic a *heart fricht* in this *lonely* road that she *run* past this spot fur there wis a *treveller wumman* <u>*murderet,*</u> the wumman *Macphee* murdert there at the turn of the century, and she *rins* up tae this place, and she let her basket o *stock faa*, because she hid – one o the *reasons* she come intae Aiberdeen wus tae buy a pound's o *stock*, fit ye *sell*, ye ken, cause *travellers* never give *money* in that days, it wis aa trade an *barter*, ye ken. So she *run* up, she *left* aathing *lyin*, an, by the *time* she got up the *menfolk* thought maybe she wis *molested* by some dirty *gadgie*, ken? . . . And she says, '*No*', she says, 'A saa this *horrible thing*', and her man was an awfy lippie gadgie, *aw* whit an *impudent* man, an *he* wis the half *woozy* kind, and he says [harsh voice], '<u>*Whit*</u> wis it you saw?' And he says, 'Ye must be *mad* woman', he says, '*A'll* go down and A'll put the *breeks* up up on it, an A'll gie it a *layin on*', cause they wurnae feart of *nothin*, this folk. So *he walkt* doon, but he'd to put some Dutch *courage* in him, anyway! And by the *time* he got to the place he *found* the basket lying on the side of the road and he found her . . . stuff that wis *there*, and as *this* man went to pick up *aathing*, some kind o a *power* <u>*came*</u> upon him and gave him a *layin-on* like a cuddie. An he *got* sic a *layin* on, he *never* saw no *assailant* but the man wis two weeks in Aboyne *hospital* wi the layin-on that he got. And, *onywey*, about *two* weeks later he *wisnae* sae bold and brave and folk were *feart* goin passt this bit. But *one* time Mary saa, ken the *gravedigger*, and she says till him, she says, 'Ye *ken* this', she says, '*Last* week, naw aboot *two* weeks ago', she says, 'A hid this strange experience faa A saw a woman come *oot* the cemetery and run right till, and then ma *man* went doon and he git sic a *fagger* [weariness] he ended up in the *hospital*.'

And the wumman, the *man* says, 'Well ye *ken* this lassie. *Fifty* years ago, jist mebbe *twa weeks* ago, there wis a *bonnie, wealthy* young woman, she had *plenty* money, *plenty* o land, and she'd ta'en up wi a *plooghboy* lad, an she wis *affa* good to him, she bought him *waatches*, she bought him *rings*, and they used tae go aaway thegither, and *then* one day she wis *gaing* tae a dance, and she wis *aa dresst up*, and *bonnie* claes, and it wis the *summer* time, and she wis gang tae get *merriet*. But whit *happent* wis, the laddie found somebody else and broke *aff* wi her that night, and that poor wumman committit suicide. [Quietly] And she's been seen *many times* waalkin doon the aald road and ma *father* used tae tell me, mony a time *he* lay in the aald road, and he saa this *woman* passing by. (CCMD2004VB.20: 26)

Again, there is an intimate link between story and place. Both stories are far more than supernatural tales; they communicate the experiences of different cultural communities within Scotland effectively, and economically, in elegant and compelling style. Given the skills of our storytellers, and the endeavours of the Scottish Storytelling Centre, it seems likely that the current renaissance will continue.

Notes on Contributors

Katherine Ashley holds a doctorate in French from the University of Edinburgh and has taught in Scotland and Canada. She is currently Assistant Professor of French at Memorial University of Newfoundland.

Stephen Bernstein is Professor of English at the University of Michigan-Flint. He is the author of *Alasdair Gray* (1999) as well as articles and book chapters on the work of Gray, James Kelman, Paul Auster, Samuel Beckett, Joseph Conrad, Don DeLillo and Virginia Woolf.

Alan Bissett is the author of *Boyracers* (2001) and *The Incredible Adam Spark* (2005). His third novel *Death of a Ladies' Man* will be published in 2008. He tutors on the MPhil in Creative Writing at Glasgow University.

Mariadele Boccardi is Senior Lecturer in Twentieth-Century British Fiction at the University of the West of England in Bristol. She is writing a monograph on the generic development of the historical novel since 1969.

Valentina Bold is Senior Lecturer and Head of Scottish Studies at the University of Glasgow's Crichton Campus, Dumfries. She has published widely on Scottish culture and literature, including a CD-ROM *Northern Folk: Traditional Culture of North East Scotland* (1999) with Tom McKean and an anthology of the shorter work of Lewis Grassic Gibbon (2001). Her new book *James Hogg: A Bard of Nature's Making* will be published in 2007.

David Borthwick teaches literature at the University of Glasgow's Crichton Campus in Dumfries. He completed his doctorate on contemporary Scottish fiction in 2006 and has published on Irvine Welsh and Lewis Grassic Gibbon.

Ian Brown is a freelance scholar, cultural and educational consultant, playwright and poet. Until 2002 he was Professor of Drama, Dean of Arts, and Director of the Scottish Centre for Cultural Management and Policy at Queen Margaret University College in Edinburgh. Between 1986 and 1994, he was Drama Director of the Arts Council of Great Britain. He has published on theatrical, literary and cultural topics and is General Editor of *The Edinburgh History of Scottish Literature* (2006).

Matthew Brown is Assistant Professor in the Department of English at the University of Massachusetts-Boston. He is currently writing a monograph on modernity and violence in late twentieth-century Irish and Scottish fiction.

Peter Clandfield teaches in the Department of English at Nipissing University in North Bay, Ontario. He is working on an extended study of representations of urban (re)development in recent fiction and film.

John Corbett lectures in the Department of English Language at the University of Glasgow. He is the author of *Language and Scottish Literature* (1997) and *Written in the Language of the Scottish Nation: A History of Literary Translation into Scots* (1999), and co-editor of *The Edinburgh Companion to Scots* (2003) and *Serving Twa Maisters: Five Classic Plays in Scots Translation* (2005). He also edits the journal *Language and Intercultural Communication*.

Andrew Crumey is a novelist and former theoretical physicist whose works include *Mobius Dick* (2004) and *Mr Mee* (2000). He was literary editor of *Scotland on Sunday* from 2000 to 2006 and now teaches creative writing at the University of Newcastle upon Tyne. His work has been translated into many languages and he has won a number of prizes, including the 2006 Northern Rock Foundation Writer's Award.

Simon Dentith is Professor of English at the University of Gloucestershire. He has published widely on nineteenth- and twentieth-century literature, including books on *Parody* (2000) and *Society and Cultural Forms in Nineteenth-Century England* (1998). His most recent book is *Epic and Empire in Nineteenth-Century Britain* (2006).

Alice Entwistle is Senior Lecturer in the School of English and Drama at the University of the West of England in Bristol. *A History of Twentieth Century British Women's Poetry*, which she co-authored with Jane Dowson, was published by Cambridge University Press in 2005. She is working on a study of women poets writing in Wales.

Alice Ferrebe is a Lecturer in English at Liverpool John Moores University. Her book *Masculinity in the Male-Authored Novel 1950–2000* was published in 2005.

Louisa Gairn is a post-doctoral fellow at the University of Edinburgh. She is working on a monograph on *Ecology and Modern Scottish Literature*.

Michael Gardiner is Associate Professor at Chiba University (Japan) and a visiting researcher at RIISS, University of Aberdeen. He has published widely on Scottish literary and cultural history, and is also the author of a collection of short stories, *Escalator* (2006).

Gordon Gibson is a Senior Lecturer in the School of Media, Language and Music at the University of Paisley.

Euan Hague is Assistant Professor of Geography at DePaul University in Chicago. His research examines the construction of Celtic identity and Scottishness in the US. He one day hopes to write a romance novel of his own.

Scott Hames is Lecturer in Scottish Literature at the University of Stirling. His main interests include James Kelman and political constructions of 'vernacularity' in modern Scottish culture.

Kirstin Innes is a freelance journalist who has written for the *List* and a number of online journals. She works as Press and Publicity Manager at the Arches Theatre in Glasgow.

Carole Jones holds a doctorate in contemporary Scottish fiction from Trinity College Dublin, where she was Teaching Fellow in English until 2006. Her monograph *Disappearing Men* will be published in 2008. She has also co-edited *Beyond the Anchoring Grounds: More Cross-Currents in Irish and Scottish Studies* (2005).

Aaron Kelly is Lecturer in Modern and Contemporary Literature at the University of Edinburgh. He is author of *The Thriller and Northern Ireland* (2005) and *Irvine Welsh* (2005), as well as the forthcoming *James Kelman* and *Twentieth-Century Irish Literature*. He also co-edited *Critical Ireland* (2001) and *Cities of Belfast* (2003).

Stefanie Lehner is a research student at the University of Edinburgh. Her doctoral project is on 'Subaltern Aesthetics: Mapping Class and Gender in Contemporary Scottish, Irish and Northern Irish Literatures'.

Christian Lloyd teaches at the Queen's University International Study Centre at Herstmonceux Castle in East Sussex. His research interests include contemporary Irish literature and the prehistory of mod culture in England.

Kirsty Macdonald completed a doctorate on madness and the supernatural in nineteenth- and twentieth-century Scottish fiction at the University of Glasgow in 2005. She is currently co-editing *Revisioning Scottish Literature* and working on a book on the Highlands and Islands in contemporary literature and popular culture.

Michelle Macleod has been a Lecturer in Gaelic Studies at Aberdeen University since 2004. She previously lectured in the School of Irish in the National University of Ireland at Galway and has held senior posts in the Gaelic language-development sector.

Fiona McCulloch is a Lecturer in English at Manchester Metropolitan University, Cheshire Campus. She is the author of *The Fictional Role of Childhood in Victorian and Early Twentieth-Century Children's Literature* (2004) and is currently working on her second monograph, *Mapping Scotland's Future: Devolution, Hybridity and Contemporary Scottish Children's Fiction*.

Matthew McGuire is completing his doctorate at the University of Edinburgh. He is the author of the forthcoming *Essential Guide to Contemporary Scottish Literature*.

Gavin Miller is Leverhulme Early-Career Fellow in the Department of English at Edinburgh University, where he is working on a history of Scottish psychiatry as a follow-up to his monograph on *R. D. Laing* (2004). He also is the author of *Alasdair Gray* (2005).

Robert Morace teaches at Daemen College in Amherst, New York. His publications include *The Dialogic Novels of Malcolm Bradbury and David Lodge* (1989), *Irvine Welsh's Trainspotting* (2001), and a forthcoming study of the Irvine Welsh phenomenon to be published by Palgrave.

Sarah Neely is a Lecturer in Film Studies at the University of Paisley. She has written on film adaptation including the heritage genre, adaptations of Shakespeare, and the use of classic literature in the 'teenpic'.

Máire Ní Annracháin is a Senior Lecturer in the Department of Modern Irish at the National University of Ireland Maynooth. She is the author of *Aisling agus Tóir* (1992), a monograph on Sorley MacLean, and co-editor of *Cruth na Tíre* (2003), a collection of essays on the landscape in Gaelic imaginative traditions.

Colin Nicholson is Professor of Eighteenth-Century and Modern Literature at the University of Edinburgh. He has edited collections of essays on Margaret Laurence, Margaret Atwood and Iain Crichton Smith, and in 2002 he produced the first monograph on Edwin Morgan's poetry.

Duncan Petrie is Professor of Film at the University of Auckland. He is the author of four monographs: *Creativity and Constraint in the British Film Industry* (1991), *The British Cinematographer* (1996), *Screening Scotland* (2000) and *Contemporary Scottish Fictions* (2004). Between 2001 and 2003 he was a member of the Scottish Screen Lottery Panel. He is currently writing a book on New Zealand cinematography and co-editing a volume on 'Small National Cinemas'.

Gill Plain is Professor of English and Popular Culture at the University of St Andrews. Her publications include *Women's Fiction of the Second World War* (1996), *Twentieth-Century Crime Fiction* (2001) and *John Mills and British Cinema* (2006). She is now researching a literary history of the 1940s and editing a special issue of *Clues* on 'Scottish crime fiction'.

Suhayl Saadi is a novelist, playwright and radio dramatist. His novel *Psychoraag* (2004) was shortlisted for the James Tait Black Memorial Prize and won the PEN Oakland Josephine Miles Literary Award. Other publications include *The White Cliffs* (2004), *The Burning Mirror* (2001) and *The Snake* (1997), as well as numerous plays. For further information on his work see www.suhaylsaadi.com.

Berthold Schoene is Professor of English and Director of the English Research Institute at Manchester Metropolitan University. He is the author of *The Making of Orcadia* (1995) and *Writing Men* (2000), and co-editor of *Posting the Male* (2003). He has published numerous essays on contemporary Scottish and English fiction.

Adrienne Scullion is James Arnott Chair of Drama in the Department of Theatre, Film and Television Studies at the University of Glasgow. Her research interests focus on Scottish theatre and drama from the eighteenth century to the post-devolution period. She has also contributed to research and consultancy work in the area of cultural policy, including *The Same . . . But Different: Rural Arts Touring in Scotland* (2004) and *The Economic Impact of the Cultural Sector in Scotland* (2004).

David Stenhouse is a writer and broadcaster with a specialist interest in images of Scotland and Scottishness celebrated within the Scottish diaspora. His latest book is *On the Make: How the Scots Took Over London* (2004). His BBC Radio Scotland series *The Tartan Spangled Banner* (2005) was the first NPR radio documentary on American Scots to be broadcast in the US. David is a Senior Producer at BBC Scotland and an Honorary Research Fellow at Strathclyde University.

Zoë Strachan's first novel, *Negative Space* (2002), won the Betty Trask Award and was shortlisted for the Saltire First Book of the Year Award. In 2004 she received a Hawthornden Fellowship and published her second novel, *Spin Cycle*. Her first radio play, *One Small Step*, was broadcast on Radio 4 in 2005. For the past three years she has been a Creative Writing tutor at Glasgow University but, having been awarded a Scottish Arts Council Writer's Bursary in 2006, she will be taking a year out to concentrate on writing her third novel, *Play Dead*.

Gavin Wallace has been active in many areas of Scottish literature and culture as a teacher, lecturer, critic, journalist, editor and broadcaster. Since 1997 he has been working for the Scottish Arts Council where, in 2002, he was appointed Head of Literature.

Christopher Whyte was Lecturer and then Reader in the Department of Scottish Literature at Glasgow University from 1990 to 2005. He has published widely on eighteenth- and twentieth-century Scottish literature in English, Scots and Gaelic and on comparative topics. Two of his four novels to date have received Arts Council awards, and his Gaelic poetry has been translated into six European languages. He is also the author of *Modern Scottish Poetry* (2004).

Fiona Wilson studied at Glasgow and New York Universities. Her poetry was featured in *Best Scottish Poetry 2005* (Scottish Poetry Library). She currently teaches at Fordham University in the South Bronx.

Joanne Winning teaches in the School of English and Humanities at Birkbeck College in London. Recent publications include *The Pilgrimage of Dorothy Richardson* (2000) and her edition of *Bryher: Two Novels* (2000). She is writing a book on lesbian modernism.

Bibliography

Aapola, Sinikka, Marnina Gonick and Anita Harris (2005), *Young Femininity: Girlhood, Power and Social Change*, Basingstoke: Palgrave.

Aboulela, Leila (1999), *The Translator*, Edinburgh: Polygon.

Adams, Henry (2003), *The People Next Door*, London: Nick Hern.

Adorno, Theodor (1977), 'Reconciliation under duress', in *Aesthetics and Politics: Debates Between Bloch, Lukács, Brecht, Benjamin, Adorno*, trans. Ronald Taylor, London: Verso, pp. 151–76.

Alhiatly, Ayad, Bouzekri Ettaouchi, Ghazi Hussein, et al. (2004), *exile*, Glasgow: Survivors Press.

Alibhai-Brown, Yasmin (2003), 'The curse of diversity', *Independent*, 9 July. http://comment.independent.co.uk/columnists_a_1/yasmin_alibhai_brown/article95295.ece.

Appiah, Kwame Anhony (2006), *Cosmopolitanism: Ethics in a World of Strangers*, New York: Norton.

Apter, Emily (2001), 'Balkan Babel: translation zones, military zones', *Public Culture*, 13, 1, pp. 65–80.

Arana, Victoria and Lauri Ramey (eds) (2004), *Black British Writing*, New York: Palgrave.

Arnott, Peter (2000), *A Little Rain*, unpublished typescript, Scottish Theatre Archive at Glasgow University Library, STA SAC 152.

Ascherson, Neal (2002), *Stone Voices: The Search for Scotland*, New York: Hill and Wang.

Ashcroft, Bill, Gareth Griffith and Helen Tiffin (1989), *The Empire Writes Back: Theory and Practice in Post-Colonial Literatures*, London: Routledge.

Bachelard, Gaston [1958] (1994), *The Poetics of Space*, trans. Maria Jolas, Boston: Beacon.

Bakhtin, Mikhail [1937–8] (1981), 'Forms of time and of the chronotope in the novel', in *The Dialogic Imagination: Four Essays*, trans. Caryl Emerson and Michael Holquist, Austin: University of Texas Press, pp. 84–258.

Bakhtin, Mikhail [1966] (1984a), *Rabelais and His World*, trans. Helene Iswolsky, Bloomington: Indiana University Press.

Bakhtin, Mikhail [1963] (1984b), *Problems of Dostoevsky's Poetics*, trans. Caryl Emerson, Minneapolis: University of Minnesota Press.

Bamforth, Iain (2005), *A Place in the World*, Manchester: Carcanet.

Banks, Iain (1986), *The Bridge*, London: Abacus.

Banks, Iain (1987a), *Espedair Street*, London: Abacus.

Banks, Iain M. (1987b), *Consider Phlebas*, London: Orbit.

Banks, Iain M. (1988), *The Player of Games*, London: Orbit.

Banks, Iain M. (1989), *The State of the Art*, London: Orbit.

Banks, Iain (1993), *Complicity*, London: Abacus.

Banks, Iain M. (1994a), *Feersum Endjinn*, London: Orbit.

Banks, Iain M. (1994b), 'A few notes on the Culture', www.cs.bris.ac.uk/~stefan/culture.html.

Banks, Iain M. (1996), *Excession*, London: Orbit.

Banks, Iain (2003), *Raw Spirit: In Search of the Perfect Dram*, London: Century.

Barnaby, Paul (2000a), 'Three into one: twentieth-century Scottish verse in translation anthologies', *Translation and Literature*, 9, 2, pp. 188–99.

Barnaby, Paul (2000b), 'Traductions en français d'auteurs écossais du XXe siècle', in David Kinloch and Richard Price (eds), *La Nouvelle Alliance: Influences Francophones sur la Littérature Écossaise Moderne*, Grenoble: ELLUG – Université Stendhal, pp. 241–62.

Barrow, John D. and Frank J. Tipler (1988), *The Anthropic Cosmological Principle*, Oxford: Oxford University Press.

Bataille, Georges (1994), *The Absence of Myth: Writings on Surrealism*, London: Verso.

Bate, Jonathan (2000), *The Song of the Earth*, London: Picador.

Bateman, Meg (1997), *Aotromachd agus Dàin Eile/Lightness and Other Poems*, Edinburgh: Polygon.

Baudrillard, Jean (1988a), 'Consumer society', in Mark Poster (ed.), *Jean Baudrillard: Selected Writings*, Cambridge: Polity, pp. 29–56.

Baudrillard, Jean (1988b), 'The system of objects', in Mark Poster (ed.), *Jean Baudrillard: Selected Writings*, Cambridge: Polity, pp. 10–28.

BBC (2004), Charter review seminar: representations of nations, regions and communities, 17 November, www.bbccharterreview.org.uk/pdf_documents/rep_seminar_transcript. pdf, pp. 1–38.

Bearn, Emily (2003), 'Chips are everything', *Sunday Telegraph*, 24 August, p. 4.

Beer, Gillian (1990), 'The island and the aeroplane: the case of Virginia Woolf', in Homi Bhabha (ed.), *Nation and Narration*, London: Roultedge, pp. 265–90.

Bell, Eleanor (2004), *Questioning Scotland: Literature, Nationalism, Postmodernism*, Basingstoke: Palgrave.

Bell, Eleanor and Gavin Miller (eds) (2004), *Scotland in Theory: Reflections on Culture and Literature*, Amsterdam: Rodopi.

Bell, Ian (2003), 'Forces of light and the forces of darkness', *Herald*, 24 September, p. 37.

Benjamin, Walter [1929] (1986), 'Surrealism: the last snapshot of the European intelligentsia', in Peter Demetz (ed.), *Reflections: Essays, Aphorisms, Autobiographical Writings*, New York: Schocken, pp. 177–92.

Benjamin, Walter [1955] (1999a), *Illuminations*, trans. Harry Zohn, London: Pimlico.

Benjamin, Walter [1982] (1999b), *The Arcades Project*, trans. Howard Eiland and Kevin McLaughlin, London: Belknap Press of Harvard University Press.

Berlins, Marcel (2003), 'The traditionally built detective', *Mail and Guardian* (South Africa), 5 December, www.chico.mweb.co.za/art/2003dec/031205-detective.html.

Bernstein, Stephen (1999), *Alasdair Gray*, London: Associated University Presses.

Bernstein, Stephen (2000), 'James Kelman', *Review of Contemporary Fiction*, 20, 3, pp. 42–80.

Bernstein, Stephen (2002), 'Doing as things do with you: Alasdair Gray's minor novels', in Phil Moores (ed.), *Alasdair Gray: Critical Appreciations and a Bibliography*, London: British Library, pp. 147–64.

Bertagna, Julie (2002), *Exodus*, London: Picador.

Berton, Danièle (2005), 'Norme et marginalité: de la bonne ou de la mauvaise réputation dans *The People Next Door* de Henry Adam', *Études Écossaises*, 10, pp. 159–73.

Beveridge, Craig and Ronald Turnbull (1989), *The Eclipse of Scottish Culture*, Edinburgh: Polygon.

Bhabha, Homi (ed.) (1990), *Nation and Narration*, London: Routledge.

Bhabha, Homi (1994), *The Location of Culture*, London: Routledge.

Bhabha, Homi (1998), 'The world and the home', in Anne McClintock, Aamir Mufti and Ella Shoat (eds), *Dangerous Liaisons: Gender, Nation, and Postcolonial Perspectives*, Minnesota: University of Minnesota Press, pp. 445–55.

Bhabha, Homi (2001), 'Unsatisfied: notes on vernacular cosmopolitanism', in Gregory Castle (ed.), *Postcolonial Discourses: An Anthology*, Oxford: Blackwell, pp. 39–52.

Bibliography of Scottish Literature in Translation, www.nls.uk/catalogues/resources/boslit/index.html.

Bieber, Janet (1999), *Highland Bride*, New York: Ballantine.

Bissett, Alan (2001a), *Boyracers*, Edinburgh: Polygon.

Bissett, Alan (ed.) (2001b), *Damage Land: New Scottish Gothic Fiction*, Edinburgh: Polygon.

Bissett, Alan (2005), *The Incredible Adam Spark*, London: Headline.

Black, Ronald (ed.) (1999), *An Tuil: Anthology of Twentieth-Century Scottish Gaelic Verse*, Edinburgh: Polygon.

Blake, Andrew (2002), *The Irresistible Rise of Harry Potter*, London and New York: Verso.

Boddy, Kasia (2000), 'Edwin Morgan's adventures in Calamerica', *Yale Journal of Criticism*, 13, 1, pp. 177–91.

Boden, Helen (2000), 'Kathleen Jamie's semiotic of Scotlands', in Aileen Christiansen and Alison Lumsden (eds), *Contemporary Scottish Women Writers*, Edinburgh: Edinburgh University Press, pp. 27–40.

Böhnke, Dietmar (1999), *Kelman Writes Back: Literary Politics in the Work of a Scottish Writer*, Berlin: Galda and Wilch.

Bold, Valentina and Tom McKean (1999), *Northern Folk: Living Traditions of North-East Scotland* [CD-ROM], Aberdeen: University of Aberdeen Elphinstone Institute.

Bordo, Susan (1987), *The Flight to Objectivity: Essays on Cartesianism and Culture*, New York: State University of New York Press.

Borthwick, David (2003), 'From *Grey Granite* to urban grit: a revolution in perspectives', in Margery Palmer McCulloch and Sarah Dunnigan (eds), *A Flame in the Mearns – Lewis Grassic Gibbon: A Centenary Celebration*, Glasgow: ASLS, pp. 64–76.

Boztas, Senay (2005), 'First it was Scotland's depressing films . . . Now our "grim" books are under fire', *Sunday Herald*, 27 February, www.sundayherald.com/48025.

Braidotti, Rosi (1997), 'Cyberfeminism with a difference', in Sandra Kemp and Judith Squire (eds), *Feminisms*, Oxford: Oxford University Press, pp. 520–9.

Brennan, Timothy (1990), 'The national longing for form', in Homi Bhabha (ed.), *Nation and Narration*, London: Routledge, pp. 44–70.

Breslin, Theresa (2002), *Remembrance*, London: Random House.

Breslin, Theresa (2005), *Divided City*, London: Doubleday.

Brittan, Arthur (1989), *Masculinity and Power*, Oxford: Blackwell.

Bromley, Catherine, John Curtice, Kerstin Hinds and Alison Park (eds) (2003), *Devolution – Scottish Answers to Scottish Questions?*, Edinburgh: Edinburgh University Press.

Brookmyre, Christopher (1996), *Quite Ugly One Morning*, London: Abacus.

Brookmyre, Christopher (2000), *Boiling a Frog*, London: Abacus.

Broom, Sarah (2006), *Contemporary British and Irish Poetry*, Basingstoke and New York: Palgrave.

Brown, Clare and Don Paterson (eds) (2003), *Don't Ask Me What I Mean: Poets in Their Own Words*, London: Picador.

Brown, Ian (1984), 'Cultural centrality and dominance: the creative writer's view – conversations between Scottish poet/playwrights and Ian Brown', *Interface*, 3, pp. 17–67.

Brown, Ian (1998), 'A new spirit abroad in the north: MacDiarmid and cultural identity in contemporary Scottish theatre', *Études Écossaises*, 5, pp. 111–25.

Brown, Ian (2001), 'Le théâtre du nouveau parlement écossais: identités culturelles et politiques sur fond de dévolution', in Keith Dixon (ed.), *L'Autonomie Écossaise: Essais Critiques sur une Nation Britannique*, Grenoble: ELLUG, pp. 163–84.

Brown, Ian (2005), 'In exile from ourselves? Tartanry, Scottish popular theatre, Harry Lauder and Tartan Day', *Études Écossaises*, 10, pp. 123–41.

Brown, Ian (2006), 'Staging the nation: the theatre of referenda', in Ian Brown, Thomas Owen Clancy, Susun Manning and Murray Pittock (eds), *The Edinburgh History of Scottish Literarture*, Edinburgh: Edinburgh University Press, pp. 283–94.

Brown, Ian and Barbara Bell (2000), 'A duty to history: contemporary approaches to history and cultural identities in Scottish theatre', in Valentina Poggi and Margaret Rose (eds), *A Theatre That Matters: Twentieth-Century Scottish Drama and Theatre*, Milan: Edizioni Unicopli, pp. 19–40.

Brown, Ian and Katja Lenz (1997), ' "Oh dearie me!" Dramatic rhetoric and linguistic subversion in the Scottish situation comedy *The High Life*', in Edgar Schneider (ed.), *Englishes Around the World*, Amsterdam and Philadelphia: Benjamins, pp. 109–23.

Brown, Ian and Colin Nicholson (2006), 'The border crossers and reconfiguration of the possible: poet-playwright-novelists from the mid-twentieth century on', in Ian Brown, Thomas Owen Clancy, Susan Manning and Murray Pittock (eds), *The Edinburgh History of Scottish* Literature, vol. 3, Edinburgh: Edinburgh University Press pp. 262–72.

Brown, Ian and John Ramage (2001), 'Referendum to referendum and beyond: political vitality and Scottish theatre', *Irish Review*, 28, pp. 46–57.

Brown, Ian, Thomas Owen Clancy, Susan Manning and Murray Pittock (eds) (2006), *The Edinburgh History of Scottish Literature*, Edinburgh: Edinburgh University Press.

Bruce, Keith (1994), 'Spirit of Mayfest', *Herald*, 21 May, p. 15.

Bruford, Alan (1978–9), 'Tom Tulloch', *Tocher*, 30, pp. 337–73.

Burgess, Moira (1998), *Imagine a City: Glasgow in Literature*, Glendaruel: Argyll.

Burke, Gregory (2001), *Gagarin Way*, London: Faber.

Burns, Elizabeth (2003), *The Alteration*, Glasgow: Galdragon.

Burnside, John (2000), 'Strong Words', in W. N. Herbert and Matthew Hollis (eds), *Strong Words: Modern Poets on Modern Poetry*, Tarset: Bloodaxe, pp. 259–61.

Burnside, John (2002), *The Light Trap*, London: Cape.

Burnside, John (2005), *The Good Neighbour*, London: Cape.

Burnside, John and Maurice Riordan (2004), *Wild Reckoning*, London: Calouste Gulbenkian Foundation.

Buse, Peter and Andrew Stott (eds) (1999), *Ghosts: Deconstruction, Psychoanalysis, History*, Basingstoke: Macmillan.

Butler, Judith (2004), *Undoing Gender*, London: Routledge.

Butlin, Ron (1994), *The Sound of My Voice*, Forfar: Black Ace.

Caimbeul, Alasdair (1992), *Am Fear Meadhanach*, Druim Fraoich: Conon Bridge. [*see also* Campbell, Alasdair]

Caimbeul, Aonghas P. (2003), *An Oidhche Mus Do Sheòl Sinn*, Edinburgh: Birlinn.

Caimbeul, Aonghas P. (2004), *Là a' Dèanamh Sgèil Do Là*, Edinburgh: Birlinn.

Caimbeul, Maoilios (2003), *Saoghal Ùr*, Calasraid: Diehard.

Caimbeul, Tormod (2006), *Shrapnel*, Edinburgh: Birlinn.

Calder, Angus (1996), 'By the Water of Leith I sat down: reflections on Scottish identity', in Harry Ritchie (ed.), *New Scottish Writing*, London: Bloomsbury, pp. 218–38.

Calder, Angus (2004a), *Scotlands of the Mind*, Edinburgh: Luath.

Calder, Angus (2004b), 'Saadi's all the raag', *Sunday Herald*, 21 April, http://sarmed.netfirms.com/suhayl/NEW/books/psycho/calder_review.htm.

Callinicos, Alex (1994), *Against Postmodernism: A Marxist Critique*, Cambridge: Polity.

Cambridge, Gerry (2003), *Madame Fifi's Farewell*, Edinburgh: Luath.

Campbell, Alasdair (2000), *The Nessman*, Edinburgh: Birlinn. [*see also* Caimbeul, Alasdair]

Campbell, Alasdair (2003), *Visiting the Bard*, Edinburgh: Polygon. [*see also* Caimbeul, Alasdair]

Campbell, Beatrix (1993), 'The Queenies that betrayed the Gorbals', *Independent*, 15 September, p. 24.

Campbell, J. F. [1860–2] (1982), *Popular Tales of the West Highlands*, Hounslow: Wildwood House.

Carey, John (2005), *What Good Are the Arts?*, London: Faber.

Carruthers, Gerard (1999), 'The construction of the Scottish critical tradition', in Neil McMillan and Kirsten Stirling (eds), *Odd Alliances: Scottish Studies in European Contexts*, Glasgow: Cruithne, pp. 52–65.

Carruthers, Gerard, David Goldie and Alastair Renfrew (eds) (2004), *Beyond Scotland: New Contexts for Twentieth-Century Scottish Literature*, Amsterdam and New York: Rodopi.

Caughie, John (1982), 'Scottish television: what would it look like?', in Colin McArthur (ed.), *Scotch Reels: Scotland in Cinema and Television*, London: BFI, pp. 112–22.

Caughie, John (1997), 'Small pleasures: adaptation and the past in British film and television', *Ilha Do Desterro*, 3, pp. 27–50.

Caughie, John (2000), *Television Drama: Realism, Modernism, and British Culture*, Oxford: Oxford University Press.

Certeau, Michel de [1974] (1984), *The Practice of Everyday Life*, trans. Steven Rendall, Berkeley: University of California Press.

Certeau, Michel de [1975] (1988), *The Writing of History*, trans. Tom Conley, New York: Columbia University Press.

Chakrabarti, M. K. (2003/4), 'Marketplace multiculturalism', *Boston Review*, January.

Chandler, Raymond (1950), 'The simple art of murder', in *Pearls Are a Nuisance*, Harmondsworth: Penguin, pp. 181–99.

Childs, Peter (2004), *Contemporary Novelists: British Fiction Since 1970*, Basingstoke: Palgrave.

Christian, Nicholas (2002), 'Irvine Welsh attacks Edinburgh's "domineering middle-class culture"', *Scotland on Sunday*, 25 August, p. 3.

Christiansen, Aileen and Alison Lumsden (eds) (2000), *Contemporary Scottish Women Writers*, Edinburgh: Edinburgh University Press.

Clair, René (dir.) (1935), *The Ghost Goes West*, London Film Productions.

Clanchy, Kate (2004), *Newborn*, London: Picador.

Clandfield, Peter (2002), '"What is in my blood?": contemporary black Scottishness and the work of Jackie Kay', in Teresa Hubel and Neil Brooks (eds), *Literature and Racial Ambiguity*, Amsterdam: Rodopi, pp. 1–25.

Clandfield, Peter (2005), 'Putting the "black" into "tartan noir"', in Julie Kim (ed.), *Race and Religion in the Postcolonial British Detective Story*, Jefferson, NC: McFarland, pp. 211–38.

Clandfield, Peter and Christian Lloyd (2002), 'Concretizing the 1970s in Hodges' *Get Carter* and Torrington's *Swing Hammer Swing*', *Mosaic*, 35, 4, pp. 163–80.

Clandfield, Peter and Christian Lloyd (2005), 'The "wee men" of Glasgow grow up: boyhood and urban space in [Gillies MacKinnon's] *Small Faces*', in Murray Pomerance and Frances Gateward (eds), *Where the Boys Are: Cinemas of Masculinity and Youth*, Detroit: Wayne State University Press, pp. 183–202.

Conn, Stewart (2005), *Ghosts at Cockrow*, Tarset: Bloodaxe.

Connell, Liam (2003), 'Modes of marginality: Scottish literature and the uses of postcolonial theory', *Comparative Studies of South Asia, Africa and the Middle East*, 23, 1/2, pp. 41–53.

Connel, Liam (2004a), 'Scottish nationalism and the colonial vision of Scotland', *Interventions*, 6, 2, pp. 252–63.

Connel, Liam (2004b), 'Global narratives: globalisation and literary studies', *Critical Survey*, 16, 2, pp. 78–95.

Connell, R. W. (1995), *Masculinities*, Cambridge: Polity.

Cooke, Lez (2003), *British Television Drama: A History*, London: BFI.

Corbett, John (1999), *Written in the Language of the Scottish Nation: A History of Literary Translation into Scots*, Clevedon: Multilingual Matters.

Corbett, John (2000), 'Translating into Scots', *TradTerm*, 6, pp. 39–60.

Corbett, John and Bill Findlay (eds) (2005), *Serving Twa Maisters: Five Classic Plays in Scots Translation*, Glasgow: ASLS.

Corbett, John, Derrick McClure and Jane Stuart-Smith (eds) (2003), *The Edinburgh Companion to Scots*, Edinburgh: Edinburgh University Press.

Cosgrove, Stuart (2005), 'Innovation and risk', *Edinburgh Lectures* series, 16 February, http://download.edinburgh.gov.uk/lectures/StuartCosgrove.pdf.

Costello, John (2002), *John Macmurray: A Biography*, Edinburgh: Floris.

Coulter, Catherine (2001), *The Scottish Bride*, New York: Jove/Penguin.

Craig, Cairns (ed.) (1988), *The History of Scottish Literature*. Volume 4: *The Twentieth Century*, Aberdeen: Aberdeen University Press.

Craig, Cairns (1989), 'Series preface', *Determinations*, Edinburgh: Polygon.

Craig, Cairns (1993), 'Resisting arrest: James Kelman', in Randall Stevenson and Gavin Wallace (eds), *The Scottish Novel Since the Seventies: New Visions, Old Dreams*, Edinburgh: Edinburgh University Press. pp. 99–114.

Craig, Cairns (1996), *Out of History: Narrative Paradigms in Scottish and British Culture*, Edinburgh: Polygon.

Craig, Cairns (1999), *The Modern Scottish Novel: Narrative and the National Imagination*, Edinburgh: Edinburgh University Press.

Craig, Cairns [2001] (2002), 'Constituting Scotland', *Edinburgh Review*, 109, pp. 5–35 [*Irish Review*, 28, pp. 1–25].

Craig, Cairns (2004a), 'Scotland and hybridity', in Gerard Carruthers, David Goldie and Alastair Reufrew (eds), *Beyond Scotland: New Contexts for Twentieth-Century Scottish Literature*, Amsterdown and New York: Rodopi, pp. 229–53.

Craig, Cairns (2004b), 'Turning rebellion into money', *Product*, 9, pp. 17–18.

Craig, Patricia (1984), 'Pest extermination', *Times Literary Supplement*, 16 March.

Crawford, Alan (2003), 'BBC: Scots soap is too "parochial" for England: row as beeb sinks hopes of *River City* being networked across UK', *Sunday Herald*, 21 December, p. 7.

Crawford, Robert (1993a), *Identifying Poets: Self and Territory in Twentieth-Century Poetry*, Edinburgh: Edinburgh University Press.

Crawford, Robert (1993b), 'The two-faced language of Liz Lochhead's poetry', in Robert Crawford and Anne Varty (eds), *Liz Lochhead's Voices*, Edinburgh: Polygon, pp. 57–74.

Crawford, Robert (1994), 'Bakhtin and Scotlands', *Scotlands*, 1, pp. 55–65.

Crawford, Robert [1992] (2000), *Devolving English Literature*, Edinburgh: Edinburgh University Press.

Crawford, Robert (2002), 'Bard of friendly fire [review of *Robert Burns: Poems Selected by Don Paterson* and *The Canongate Burns*]', *London Review of Books*, 25 July, pp. 16–18.

Crawford, Robert and Mick Imlah (eds) (2001), *The New Penguin Book of Scottish Verse*, London: Penguin.

Crawford, Robert and Anne Varty (eds) (1993), *Liz Lochhead's Voices*, Edinburgh: Polygon.

Creeber, Glen (2004), '"Hideously white": British television, glocalization, and national identity', *Television and New Media*, 5, 1, pp. 27–40.

Crewe, Ivor (1989), 'Values: the crusade that failed', in Dennis Kavanagh and Anthony Seldon (eds), *The Thatcher Effect*, Oxford: Clarendon, pp. 239–50.

Cronin, Michael (2005), *An Ghaeilge san Aois Nua/Irish in the New Century*, Dublin: Cois Life Teo.

Crumey, Andrew (2005), 'Big-hitters promise dazzling chapter', *Scotland on Sunday*, 19 June, p. 2.

Crystal, David (2004), 'Subcontinent raises its voice', *Guardian Education*, 19 November, http://education.guardian.co.uk/tefl/story/0,,1355064,00.html.

Cullen, Louise and T. C. Smout (eds) (1977), *Comparative Aspects of Economic and Social History, 1600–1800*, Edinburgh: John Donald.

Davidson, Neil (2000), *The Origins of Scottish Nationhood*, London and Sterling, VA: Pluto.

Davidson, Toni (ed.) (1989), *And Thus Will I Freely Sing: An Anthology of Lesbian and Gay Writing from Scotland*, Edinburgh: Polygon.

Davidson, Toni (2001), 'Introduction', in John Mills (ed.), *Borderline: The Mainstream Book of Scottish Gay Writing*, Edinburgh: Mainstream, pp. 9–10.

Davies, Richard (no date), 'Interview with Alexander McCall Smith', www.abebooks.com/docs/authors-corner/mccall-smith.shtml.

Day, Michele (2002), 'Scots sweep romance readers off their feet', *Enquirer* (Cincinnati), 13 August, www.enquirer.com/editions/2002/08/13/tem_scots_sweep_romance.html.

Deleuze, Gilles [1993] (1997), *Essays Critical and Clinical*, trans. Daniel W. Smith and Michael Greco, Minneapolis: University of Minnesota Press.

Deleuze, Gilles and Félix Guattari [1972] (1983), *Anti-Oedipus: Capitalism and Schizophrenia*, trans. Robert Hurley, Mark Seem and Helen Lane, Minneapolis: University of Minnesota Press.

Deleuze, Gilles and Flix Guattari [1975] (1986), *Franz Kafka: Towards a Minor Literature*, trans. Dana Polan, London: University of Minnesota Press.

Dentith, Simon (2001), 'Alasdair Gray versus Andrew Greig: two Scottish writers reuse the literary past', *Anglistica*, 5, pp. 173–89.

Department of Media, Culture and Sport (2005), *Review of the BBC's Royal Charter: A Strong BBC Independent of Government, March 2005*, www.bbccharterreview.org.uk/have_your_say/green_paper/bbc_cr_greenpaper.pdf, pp. 1–118.

Derrida, Jacques (1994), *Spectres of Marx: The State of the Debt, the Work of Mourning, and the New International*, trans. Peggy Kamuf, London: Routledge.

Derrida, Jacques [1997] (2001a), *On Cosmopolitanism and Forgiveness*, trans. Mark Dooley and Michael Hughes, London and New York: Routledge.

Derrida, Jacques [1997] (2001b), *Of Hospitality*, trans. Rachel Bowlby, Stanford, CA: Stanford University Press.

Devine, T. M. (1999), *The Scottish Nation 1700–2000*, London: Allen Lane.

Devine, T. M. (2003), *Scotland's Empire 1600–1815*, London: Penguin.

Devine, T. M. and David Dickson (eds) (1983), *Ireland and Scotland, 1600–1850*, Edinburgh: John Donald.

Devine, Tom and Paddy Logue (eds) (2002), *Being Scottish: Personal Reflections on Scottish Identity Today*, Edinburgh: Polygon.

Dewar, Donald (1999), Speech at the opening of the Scottish Parliament, 1 July, http://news.bbc.co.uk/1/hi/special_report/1999/06/99/scottish_parliament_opening/382765.stm.

Dick, Eddie (ed.) (1990), *From Limelight to Satellite: A Scottish Film Book*, London: BFI.

Dickson, Beth (2000), 'Intimacy, violence and identity: the fiction of A. L. Kennedy', *Revista Canaria de Estudios Ingleses*, 41, pp. 133–44.

Dickson, Keith (2002), 'Imagining Scotland in France: conférence prononcée à Glasgow en 2002', www.raisonsdagir.org/kd4.htm.

Di Domenico, Catherine, Alex Law, Jonathan Skinner and Mick Smith (eds) (2001), *Boundaries and Identities: Nation, Politics and Culture in Scotland*, Dundee: University of Abertay Press.

Dixon, Keith (1993), 'Talking to the people: a reflection on recent Glasgow fiction', *Studies in Scottish Literature*, 28, pp. 92–104.

Docherty, Alan (2003), Review of Anne Donovan's *Buddha Da*, *Culture Wars*, www.culturewars.org.uk/2003-02/buddhada.htm.

Docherty, Thomas (2004), 'The existence of Scotland', in Eleanor Bell and Gavin Miller (eds), *Scotland in Theory: Reflections on Culture and Literature*, Amsterdam: Rodopi. pp. 231–47.

Dolan, Christopher (2004), 'Book launches – the closest Scotland gets to café society', *Herald*, 1 May, p. 6.

Dòmhnall Aonghais Bhàin (2000), *Smuaintean fo Éiseabhal: Thoughts under Easaval*, Edinburgh: Birlinn.

Dòmhnallach, Tormod Calum (1993), *An Sgàineadh*, Stornoway: Acair. [*see also* MacDonald, Norman Malcolm]

Donnelly, Timothy (2004), 'Nothing, in other words: on the poetry of Don Paterson', *Verse*, 20, 2/3, pp. 77–94.

Donovan, Anne (2003), *Buddha Da*, Edinburgh: Canongate.

Downer, Lesley (1996), 'The Beats of Edinburgh', *New York Times*, 31 March, p. 42.

Dowson, Jane and Alice Entwistle (2005), *A History of Twentieth-Century British Women's Poetry*, Cambridge: Cambridge University Press.

Doyle, Richard (2003), *Wetwares: Experiments in Post-Vital Living*, Minneapolis and London: University of Minnesota.

Du Bois, W. E. B. [1903] (1997), *The Souls of Black Folk*, eds, David W. Blight and Robert Gooding-Williams, Boston: Bedford.

Dunnigan, Sarah (2000), 'A. L. Kennedy's longer fiction: articulate grace', in Aileen Christiansen and Allson Lumsden (eds), *Contemporary Scottish Women Writers*, Edinburgh: Edinburgh University Press, pp. 144–56.

Eagleton, Terry (2003), *After Theory*, London: Allen Lane.

Easthope, Antony [1986] (1990), *What a Man's Gotta Do: The Masculine Myth in Popular Culture*, Boston: Unwin Hyman.

Edensor, Tim (2002), *National Identity, Popular Culture and Everyday Life*, Oxford and New York: Berg.

Ehrenreich, Barbara (1995), 'The decline of patriarchy', in Maurice Berger, Brian Wallis and Simon Watson (eds), *Constructing Masculinity*, New York: Routledge, pp. 284–90.

Eliass, Dörte (2003), Interview with Janice Galloway for *Buchkultur* (Vienna), Janice Galloway Archive, www.galloway.1to1.org.

Elphinstone, Margaret (1992), 'Contemporary feminist fantasy in the Scottish literary tradition', in Caroline Gonda (ed.), *Tea and Leg-Irons: New Feminist Readings from Scotland*, London: Open Letters, pp. 42–59.

Elphinstone, Margaret (2000), 'Fantasising texts: Scottish fantasy today', paper presented at the ASLS conference 'The Shape of Texts to Come', 14 May, www.asls.org.uk.

Eng, Dinah (2004), 'Strong, sexy women save the day, get their man', *USA Today*, 26 October, p. D4.

Entwistle, Alice (2003), 'At home everywhere and nowhere: Denise Levertov's "domestic" muse', in Jane Dowson (ed.), *Women's Writing 1945–60: After the Deluge*, London: Palgrave, pp. 98–114.

Evans, Sally (2004), *Bewick Walks to Scotland*, Darlington: Arrowhead.

Ewing, Winnie (1999), Inaugural speech to the Scottish Parliament, www.scottish.parliament. uk/business/officialReports/meetingsParliament/or-99/or010104.htm#Col1.

Fabiani, Linda (2004), Section F: motions and amendments, in *Scottish Parliament Business Bulletin*, 70, 27 April, www.scottish.parliament.uk/business/businessBulletin/bb-04/bb-04-27f.htm.

Fanon, Frantz [1952] (1986), *Black Skin, White Masks*, trans. Charles Lam Markmann, London: MacGibbon and Kee.

Farquharson, Kenny (1993), 'Through the eye of a needle', *Scotland on Sunday*, 8 August, p. 55.

Fazzini, Marco (1996), 'Edwin Morgan: two interviews', *Studies in Scottish Literature*, 29, pp. 45–57.

Ferguson, Brian (2002), '"Obscene" book ads removed from shops', *Edinburgh Evening News*, 31 August, p. 5.

Ferguson, Frances (2004), *Pornography, the Theory: What Utilitarianism Did to Action*, Chicago: University of Chicago Press.

Findlay, Bill (ed.) (2004), *Frae Ither Tongues: Essays on Modern Translations into Scots*, Clevedon: Multilingual Matters.

Findlay, Bill and Martin Bowman (trans.) (2000a), *A Solemn Mass for a Full Moon in Summer (by Michel Tremblay)*, London: Nick Hern.

Findlay, Bill and Martin Bowman (trans.) (2000b), '*The Reel of the Hanged Man* by Jeanne Mance-Delisle', *Edinburgh Review*, 105, pp. 99–143.

Fitt, Matthew (2003), *Kate o Shanter's Tale*, Edinburgh: Luath.

Fleming, Maurice (1976), 'The Stewarts of Blair', *Tocher*, 21, pp. 165–88.

Flesch, Juliet (1996), 'A labour of love? Compiling a bibliography of twentieth-century Australian romance novels', *APLIS (Australasian Public Libraries and Information Services)*, 9, 3/4, pp. 170–8.

Flesch, Juliet (2004), *From Australia with Love: A History of Modern Australian Popular Romance Novels*, Fremantle: Curtin University.

Fletcher, Donna (2002), *Isle of Lies*, New York: Jove.

Foreign and Commonwealth Office (2005), *Second Periodical Report from the United Kingdom on the European Charter for Regional or Minority Languages*, www.fco.gov.uk/Files/kfile/UK2ndReportECRML2005pdf.

Forsyth, Bill (dir.) (1983), *Local Hero*, Goldcrest Films.

Fowler, Alastair (2004), 'Eco-friendly [review of Christopher Whyte's *Modern Scottish Poetry*]', *Times Literary Supplement*, 20 August, pp. 4–5.

Fraser, Lilias (2000), Interview with Don Paterson, *Verse*, 20, 2/3, pp. 95–105.

Fraser, Lilias (2001), 'Kathleen Jamie interviewed by Lilias Fraser', *Scottish Studies Review*, 2, 1, pp. 15–23.

Fraser, Lindsay (2002), *An Interview with J. K. Rowling*, London: Egmont.

Frater, Anne (2001), 'Mì Chinnt/Uncertainty', in Moira Burgess and Janet Paisley (eds), *New Writing Scotland 18*, Glasgow: ASLS, p. 49.

Freeman, Fred (2003), *Hamish Henderson Tribute Album – A' the Bairns o Adam*, Cockenzie: Greentrax.

Friedman, Susan Stanford (1998), *Mappings: Feminism and the Cultural Geographies of Encounter*, Princeton, NJ: Princeton University Press.

Friel, Raymond (1994), 'Women beware gravity', in Raymond Friel and Richard Price (eds), *Southfields: Criticism and Celebration*, London: Southfields, pp. 29–47.

Friel, Raymond (1995), 'Don Paterson interviewed', in Robert Crawford, Henry Hart, David Kinloch and Richard Price (eds), *Talking Verse*, St Andrews and Williamsburg: Verse, pp. 192–8.

Fukuyama, Francis (1989), 'The end of history?', *National Interest*, 16, pp. 3–19.

Gabaldon, Diana (1991), *Outlander*, New York: Dell.

Galbraith, Douglas (2000), *The Rising Sun*, London: Picador.

Galbraith, John K. (1963), *The Affluent Society*, Harmondsworth: Penguin.

Gallivan, Joseph (2002), 'Welsh takes return train with "Porno"', *Portland Tribune*, 8 October, www.portlandtribune.com/features/story.php?story_id=14162.

Galloway, Janice (2002), *Clara*, London: Cape.

Galloway, Janice (1989), *The Trick is to Keep Breathing*, London: Minerva.

Galloway, Janice (1991), *Blood*, London: Minerva.

Galloway, Janice (1994), *Foreign Parts*, London: Vintage.

Galloway, Janice (1995), 'Different oracles: me and Alasdair Gray', *Review of Contemporary Fiction*, 15, 2, pp. 193–6.

Galloway, Janice (1999), 'Reconstructions: new writing for the New Parliament', *Edinburgh Review*, 100, p. 72.

Gardiner, Michael (1996), 'Democracy and Scottish postcoloniality', *Scotlands*, 3, 2, pp. 24–41.

Gardiner, Michael (2003a), 'Writing the Scottish Parliament', *Edinburgh Review*, 112, pp. 3–12.

Gardiner, Michael (2003b), 'British territory: Irvine Welsh in English and Japanese', *Textual Practice*, 17, 1, pp. 101–17.

Gardiner, Michael (2004a), *The Cultural Roots of British Devolution*, Edinburgh: Edinburgh University Press.

Gardiner, Michael (2004b), '"A light to the world": British devolution and colonial vision', *Interventions*, 6, 2, pp. 264–81.

Gardiner, Michael (2004c), An interview with James Kelman, *Scottish Studies Review*, 5, 1, pp. 101–15.

Gardiner, Michael (2005), *Modern Scottish Culture*, Edinburgh: Edinburgh University Press.

Gardiner, Michael (2006), *From Trocchi to Trainspotting: Scottish Critical Theory Since 1960*, Edinburgh: Edinburgh University Press.

Germaná, Monica (2003), '*Une petite mort*: death, love and liminality in the fiction of Ali Smith', *Ecloga*, 3, www.strath.ac.uk/ecloga/editorial3.html.

Gibson, Ben (2002), '*Laissez faire* eats the soul', *Journal of Popular British Cinema*, 5, pp. 21–30.

Gibson, Mel (dir.) (1995), *Braveheart*, Paramount.

Giddens, Anthony (1998), *The Third Way: The Renewal of Social Democracy*, Cambridge: Polity.

Gifford, Douglas (forthcoming), ' "Nathaniel Gow's Toddy": the supernatural in Lowland Scottish literature from Burns and Scott to the present day', in Lizanne Henderson (ed.), *Fantastical Imaginations: The Supernatural in Scottish Culture*, East Linton: Tuckwell.

Gifford, Douglas and Dorothy McMillan (eds) (1997), *A History of Scottish Women's Writing*, Edinburgh: Edinburgh University Press.

Gifford, Douglas and Alan Riach (eds) (2004), *Scotlands: Poets and the Nation*, Manchester and Edinburgh: Carcanet/Scottish Poetry Library.

Gifford, Douglas, Sarah Dunnigan and Allan MacGillivray (eds) (2002), *Scottish Literature*, Edinburgh: Edinburgh University Press.

Gillies, Valerie (2002), *The Lightning Tree*, Edinburgh: Polygon.

Gilroy, Paul [1987] (1992), *There Ain't No Black in the Union Jack: The Cultural Politics of Race and Nation*, London: Routledge.

Gilroy, Paul (2000), *Between Camps: Race, Identity and Nationalism at the End of the Colour Line*, London: Allen Lane.

Gilroy, Paul (2004), *After Empire: Melancholia and Convivial Culture*, Abingdon: Routledge.

Gish, Nancy (2001), 'Adoption, identity, and voice: Jackie Kay's inventions of self', in Marianne Novy (ed.), *Imagining Adoption: Essays on Literature and Culture*, Ann Arbor: University of Michigan Press, pp. 171–91.

Givens, Kathleen (1999), *Kilgannon*, New York: Dell.

Glasgow City Council (2005), 'Regeneration – into the new millennium', www.glasgow. gov.uk/en/AboutGlasgow/History/Regeneration.htm.

Glendinning, Miles (ed.) (1997), *Rebuilding Scotland: The Postwar Vision, 1945–1975*, East Linton: Tuckwell.

Glendinning, Miles and Stefan Muthesius (1994), *Tower Block: Modern Public Housing in England, Scotland, Wales and Northern Ireland*, New Haven, CT: Yale University Press.

Goldstein, Kenneth (1971), 'On the application of the concepts of active and inactive traditions to the study of repertory', *Journal of American Folklore*, 84, pp. 62–7.

Gonda, Caroline (1995), 'An Other country? Mapping Scottish/Lesbian/Writing', in Christopher Whyte (ed.), *Gendering the Nation: Studies in Modern Scottish Literature*, Edinburgh: Edinburgh University Press, pp. 1–24.

Goodwin, Karin and Melanie Legg (2005), 'Book makes top 10 list with no sales', *Sunday Times*, 30 January, p. 8.

Gorman, Rody (1996), *Fax and Other Poems*, Edinburgh: Polygon.

Gorman, Rody (1999), *Cùis-Ghaoil*, Callander: Diehard.

Gorman, Rody (2000), *Air a' Charbad fo Thalamh/On the Underground*, Edinburgh: Polygon.

Gorman, Rody (2003), *Toithín ag Tlaithínteacht*, Belfast: Lapwing.

Graddol, David (2006), *English Next: Why Global English May Mean the End of 'English as a Foreign Language'*, London: British Council. www.britishcouncil.org/learning-research-englishnext.htm.

Graham, Colin (2001), *Deconstructing Ireland: Identity, Theory, Culture*, Edinburgh: Edinburgh University Press.

Gramsci, Antonio (1971), *Selections from the Prison Notebooks*, trans. Quintin Hoare and Geoffrey Nowell-Smith, London: Lawrence and Wishart.

Gray, Alasdair (1981), *Lanark*, Edinburgh: Canongate.

Gray, Alasdair (1983), *Unlikely Stories, Mostly*, Harmondsworth: Penguin.

Gray, Alasdair (1984), *1982 Janine*, New York: Viking Press.

Gray, Alasdair (1992a), *Poor Things*, New York: Harcourt Brace Jovanovich.

Gray, Alasdair (1992b), *Why Scots Should Rule Scotland*, Edinburgh: Canongate.

Gray, Alasdair (1994), *A History Maker*, San Diego: Harcourt Brace.

Gray, Alasdair (1997), *Why Scots Should Rule Scotland 1997*, Edinburgh: Canongate.

Gray, Alasdair (2000a), *The Book of Prefaces*, London: Bloomsbury.

Gray, Alasdair (2000b), *Sixteen Occasional Poems, 1990–2000*, Glasgow: McAlpine.

Gray, Alasdair and Adam Tomkins (2005), *How We Should Rule Ourselves*, Edinburgh: Canongate.

Greig, Andrew (1977), *Men on Ice*, Edinburgh: Canongate.

Greig, Andrew (1990), *The order of the Day*, Newcastle: Bloodaxe.

Greig, Andrew (1992), *Electric Brae*, Edinburgh: Canongate.

Greig, Andrew (1994), *Western Swing: Adventures with the Heretical Buddha*, Newcastle: Bloodaxe.

Greig, Andrew (1996), *The Return of John Macnab*, London: Headline.

Greig, Andrew (1999), *When They Lay Bare*, London: Faber.

Greig, Andrew (2001), *Into You*, Tarset: Bloodaxe.

Greig, Andrew (2004), *In Another Light*, London: Weidenfeld and Nicolson.

Greig, David (1999), *The Speculator* [and Lluisa Cunille, *The Meeting*], London: Methuen.

Greig, David (2000), *That Summer*, London: Faber.

Greig, David (2003), *San Diego*, London: Faber.

Greig, David (2004), 'Our new National Theatre: like an elephant let loose upon the machair', *Sunday Herald*, 'Seven Days' section, 14 March, pp. 1–2.

Greig, David (2005), *Pyrenees*, London: Faber.

Greiman, Lois (2001), *The MacGowan Betrothal: Highland Rogues*, New York: Avon.

Grosz, Elizabeth (2001), *Architecture from the Outside: Essays on Virtual and Lived Space*, Cambridge, MA: MIT Press.

Guha, Ranajit (ed.) (1982), *Subaltern Studies: Writings on South Asian History and Society*, Delhi: Oxford University Press.

Gupta, Suman (2003), *Re-Reading Harry Potter*, Basingstoke: Palgrave.

Hagemann, Susanne (1997), 'Women and nation', in Douglas Gifford and Dorothy McMillan (eds), *A History of Scottish Women's Writing*, Edinburgh: Edinburgh University Press, pp. 316–28.

Hague, Euan (2001), 'Haggis and heritage – representing Scotland in the United States', in John Horne (ed.), *Culture, Consumption and Commodification*, Eastbourne: Leisure Studies Association, pp. 107–30.

Hague, Euan (2002a), 'The Scottish diaspora: Tartan Day and the appropriation of Scottish identities in the United States', in David Harvey, Rhys Jones, Neil McInroy and Christine Milligan (eds), *Celtic Geographies: Old Culture, New Times*, London and New York: Routledge, pp. 139–56.

Hague, Euan (2002b), 'National Tartan Day: rewriting history in the United States', *Scottish Affairs*, 38, pp. 94–124.

Hall, Catherine (1996), 'Histories, empires and the post-colonial moment', in Iain Chambers and Lidia Curti (eds), *The Post-Colonial Question: Common Skies, Divided Horizons*, London: Routledge, pp. 65–77.

Hall, Peter (1988), *Cities of Tomorrow: An Intellectual History of Urban Planning and Design in the Twentieth Century*, Oxford: Blackwell.

Hallward, Peter (2006), 'Staging equality: on Rancière's theatrocracy', *New Left Review*, 37, pp. 109–29.

Haraway, Donna [1985] (2001), 'A manifesto for cyborgs: science, technology and social-ist feminism in the 1980s', in Vincent Leitch (ed.), *Norton Anthology of Theory and Criticism*, London: Norton, pp. 2269–99.

Harman, Claire (2005), *Robert Louis Stevenson: A Biography*, London: HarperCollins.

Harpham, Geoffrey (1999), *Shadows of Ethics: Criticism and the Just Society*, London and Durham, NC: Duke University Press.

Harrington, Kathleen (1999), *The MacLean Groom*, New York: Avon.

Harris, Anita (2004), *Future Girl: Young Women in the Twenty-First Century*, New York and London: Routledge.

Harrower, David and David Greig (1997), 'Why a new Scotland must have a properly-funded theatre', *Scotsman*, 25 November, p. 15.

Hart, Francis (1971), 'Scott and the novel in Scotland', in Alan Bell (ed.), *Scott Bicentenary Essays*, Edinburgh: Scottish Academic Press, pp. 61–79.

Hart, Francis (1978), *The Scottish Novel: From Smollett to Spark*, Cambridge, MA: Harvard University Press.

Harvey, David (1990), *The Condition of Postmodernity: An Enquiry into the Origins of Cultural Change*, Oxford: Blackwell.

Harvie, Christopher (1977), *Scotland and Nationalism*, London: Allan and Unwin.

Hassan, Gerry and Chris Warhurst (eds) (2002), *Tomorrow's Scotland*, London: Lawrence and Wishart.

Heaney, Seamus (1969), 'Delirium of the brave', *Listener*, 27 November, p. 757.

Heaney, Seamus (1998), *Opened Ground: Poems, 1966–1996*, London: Faber.

Hearn, Jonathan (2000), *Claiming Scotland: National Identity and Liberal Culture*, Edinburgh: Polygon.

Henderson, Hamish (1992), *Alias MacAlias: Writings on Song, Folk and Literature*, Edinburgh: Polygon.

Hendry, Joy (1983), 'Editorial', *Chapman*, 35/6.

Herbert, W. N. (2002), *The Big Bumper Book of Troy*, Tarset: Bloodaxe.

Herbert, W. N. and Matthew Hollis (eds) (2000), *Strong Words: Modern Poets on Modern Poetry*, Tarset: Bloodaxe.

Herd, Tracey (2001), *Dead Redhead*, Tarset: Bloodaxe.

Hey, Valerie (1997), *The Company She Keeps: An Ethnography of Girls' Friendship*, Buckingham and Philadelphia: Open University Press.

Hill, John and Kevin Rockett (eds) (2004), *National Cinema and Beyond: Studies in Irish Film*, Dublin: Four Courts.

Hill, John and Kevin Rockett (eds) (2005), *Film History and National Cinema: Studies in Irish Film*, Dublin: Four Courts.

Hird, Laura (1999), *Born Free*, Canongate: Edinburgh.

Holdsworth, Nadine (2003), 'Travelling across borders: re-imagining the nation and nationalism in contemporary Scottish theatre', *Contemporary Theatre Review*, 13, 2, pp. 25–39.

Hollinger, David (1995), *Postethnic America: Beyond Multiculturalism*, New York: Basic Books.

Hubbard, Tom and R. D. S. Jack (eds) (2006), *Scotland in Europe*, Amsterdam: Rodopi.

Hutcheon, Linda (1988), *A Poetics of Postmodernism: History, Theory, Fiction*, London: Routledge.

Jameson, Fredric (1988), 'Cognitive mapping', in Cary Nelson and Lawrence Grossberg (eds), *Marxism and the Interpretation of Culture*, Chicago: University of Illinois Press, pp. 347–60.

Jameson, Frederic (1991), *Postmodernism, or, The Cultural Logic of Late Capitalism*, London: Verso.

Jameson, Fredric (1994), *The Seeds of Time*, New York: Columbia University Press.

Jamie, Kathleen (1994a), 'Kathleen Jamie writes', *Poetry Review*, 84, 1, p. 13.

Jamie, Kathleen (1994b), *The Queen of Sheba*, London: Bloodaxe.

Jamie, Kathleen (1997), 'Dream state', *Poetry Review*, 94, 4, pp. 35–7.

Jamie, Kathleen (1999), *Jizzen*, London: Picador.

Jamie, Kathleen (2002a), *Among Muslims: Meetings at the Frontiers of Pakistan*, London: Sort of Books.

Jamie, Kathleen (2002b), 'Diary', *London Review of Books*, 24, 11, p. 39.

Jamie, Kathleen (2002c), *Mr and Mrs Scotland Are Dead: Poems 1980–1994*, Tarset: Bloodaxe.

Jamie, Kathleen (2004a), *The Tree House*, London: Picador.

Jamie, Kathleen (2004b), [Comments on] *The Tree House*, www.st-andrews.ac.uk/academic/english/jamie/treehouse.html.

Jamie, Kathleen (2005a), *Findings*, London: Sort of Books.

Jamie, Kathleen (2005b), 'Primal seam', *Scotsman*, 30 July, http://Living.scotsman.com/books.cfm?ca=1702392005.

Jarvie, Gordon (ed.) [1992] (1997), *Scottish Folk and Fairy Tales*, London: Penguin.

Jenkins, Simon (1994), 'An expletive of a winner', *The Times*, 15 October, p. 20.

Johnson, Dorothy (2000), 'Sink drama [review of Laura Hird's *Born Free*]', *Spike Magazine*, www.spikemagazine.com/1201laurahird.php.

Johnston, Paul (1997), *Body Politic*, London: Hodder and Stoughton.

Johnston, Paul (2002), *A Deeper Shade of Blue*, London: Hodder and Stoughton.

Jones, Carole (2004a), '"An imaginary black family": jazz, diaspora and the construction of Scottish blackness in Jackie Kay's *Trumpet*', *Symbiosis*, 8, 2, pp. 191–202.

Jones, Carole (2004b), 'The "becoming woman": femininity and the rave generation in Alan Warner's *Morvern Callar*', *Scottish Studies Review*, 5, 2, pp. 56–68.

Kane, Rosie (2005), 'Just another day at the office,' *Guardian*, 11 July, p. 12.

Kauffman, Donna (1999), *The Legend MacKinnon*, New York: Bantam.

Kay, Jackie (1991), *The Adoption Papers*, Newcastle: Bloodaxe.

Kay, Jackie (1998), *Trumpet*, New York: Pantheon Books.

Kay, Jackie (2002a), *Strawgirl*, London: Macmillan.

Kay, Jackie (2002b), *Why Don't You Stop Talking*, London: Picador.

Kay, Jackie (2005), *Life Masks*, Newcastle: Bloodaxe.

Kearney, Richard (1997), *Postnationalist Ireland: Politics, Literature, Philosophy*, New York: Routledge.

Keating, Michael (1996), *Nations Against the State: The New Politics of Nationalism in Quebec, Catalonia and Scotland*, Basingstoke: Macmillan.

Kellaway, Kate (1994), 'Prizing treasure maps', *Observer*, 20 March, p. 21.

Kelly, Aaron (2003–4), 'Farewell to the single-end? Alasdair Gray, Scotland and post-modernism', *Études Écossaises*, 9, pp. 431–46.

Kelly, Aaron (2004), Irvine Welsh in conversation with Aaron Kelly, *Edinburgh Review*, 113, pp. 7–17.

Kelly, Aaron (2005a), *Irvine Welsh*, Manchester: Manchester University Press.

Kelly, Aaron (2005b), 'Geopolitical eclipse: culture and the peace process in Northern Ireland', *Third Text*, 19, 5, pp. 545–53.

Kelly, Stuart (2005), 'Canons to the left of him, canons to the right of him: Kenneth White and the constructions of Scottish literary history', in Gavin Bowd, Charles Forsdick and Norman Bissell (eds), *Grounding a World: Essays on the Work of Kenneth White*, Glasgow: Alba, pp. 186–96.

Kelman, James (1994), *How Late It Was, How Late*, London: Secker and Warburg.

Kelman, James (2001), *Translated Accounts*, London: Secker and Warburg.

Kelman, James (2002), *And the Judges Said: Essays*, London: Vintage.

Kelman, James (2004), *You Have to Be Careful in the Land of the Free*, London: Hamish Hamilton.

Kemp Smith, Martin (1941), *Philosophy of David Hulme*, London: Macmillan.

Kennedy, A. L. (1990), *Night Geometry and the Garscadden Trains*, London: Phoenix.

Kennedy, A. L. (1993), *Looking for the Possible Dance*, London: Vintage.

Kennedy, A. L. (1995a), *So I Am Glad*, London: Cape.

Kennedy, A. L. (1995b), *Now That You're Back*, London: Vintage.

Kennedy, A. L. (1997a), *Original Bliss*, London: Cape.

Kennedy, A. L. (1997b), *The Life and Death of Colonel Blimp*, London: BFI.

Kennedy, A. L. (1999a), *Everything You Need*, London: Cape.

Kennedy, A. L. (1999b), *On Bullfighting*, London: Yellow Jersey.

Kennedy, A. L. (2000), 'Introduction' to Jean Rhys, *Good Morning, Midnight*, London: Penguin, pp. v–xii.

Kennedy, A. L. (2002), *Indelible Acts*, London: Cape.

Kennedy, A. L. (2004), *Paradise*, London: Cape.

Kennedy-Andrews, Elmer (2003), *Fiction and the Northern Ireland Troubles Since 1969: (De-)Constructing the North*, Dublin: Four Courts.

Kernan, Aoife (2003), Interview with Janice Galloway, *Trinity News* (Dublin), 16 February, www.galloway.1to1.org/Trinity.html.

Kerrigan, Catherine (ed.) (1991), *An Anthology of Scottish Women Poets*, Edinburgh: Edinburgh University Press.

Kidd, Helen (1997), 'Writing near the fault line: Scottish women poets and the topography of tongues', in Vicki Bertram (ed.), *Kicking Daffodils: Twentieth Century Women Poets*, Edinburgh: Edinburgh University Press, pp. 95–110.

King, Jeannette (2001), '"A woman's a man, for a' that": Jackie Kay's *Trumpet*', *Scottish Studies Review*, 2, 1, pp. 101–8.

King, John (2002), 'The boys are back in town', *New Statesman*, 2 September, pp. 36–7.

Kinloch, David (2002), *Un Tour d'Écosse*, Manchester: Carcanet.

Kinloch, David (2005), *In My Father's House*, Manchester: Carcanet.

Kirkpatrick, Kathryn (ed.) (2000), *Border Crossings: Irish Women Writers and National Identities*, Dublin: Wolfhound.

Kirkwood, Colin (2005), 'The persons-in-relation perspective: sources and synthesis', in Jill Scharff and David Scharff (eds), *The Legacy of Fairbairn and Sutherland: Psychotherapeutic Applications*, Hove: Brunner Routledge, pp. 19–38.

Knight, Stephen (1980), *Form and Ideology in Crime Fiction*, Basingstoke: Macmillan.

Kobialka, Michael (ed.) (1999), *Of Borders and Thresholds: Theatre History, Practice and Theory*, Minneapolis: University of Minnesota Press.

Koren-Deutsch, Ilona (1992), 'Feminist nationalism in Scotland: *Mary Queen of Scots Got Her Head Chopped Off'*, *Modern Drama*, 35, pp. 424–32.

Kravitz, Peter (ed.) (1997), *The Picador Book of Contemporary Scottish Fiction*, London: Picador.

Kravitz, Peter (2001), 'As it never was', *Variant*, 2, 13, pp. 22–7.

Kuppner, Frank (2004), *A God's Breakfast*, Manchester: Carcanet.

Laing, R. D. (1961), *The Divided Self*, Harmondsworth: Penguin.

Lamont, Claire (1991), '*Waverley* and the Battle of Culloden', in Angus Easson (ed.), *History and the Novel*, Cambridge: Brewer, pp. 14–26.

Lane, Richard, Rod Mengham and Philip Tew (eds) (2003), *Contemporary British Fiction*, Cambridge: Polity.

Lappin, Tom (2002), 'Brain rotting', *Scotsman*, 24 August, p. 6.

Larkin, Philip (2003), *Collected Poems*, London: Faber.

Law, Chris (1992), 'Urban tourism and its contribution to economic regeneration', *Urban Studies*, 29, pp. 599–618.

Lea, Daniel and Berthold Schoene (eds) (2003), *Posting the Male: Masculinities in Post-War and Contemporary British Literature*, Amsterdam and New York: Rodopi.

LeBlanc, John (2000), 'Return of the goddess: contemporary music and Celtic mythology in Alan Warner's *Morvern Callar*', *Revista Canaria de Estudios Ingleses*, 41, pp. 145–54.

Lee, Rebecca Hagan (2000), *A Hint of Heather*, New York: Jove.

Lehner, Stefanie (2005), 'Reassessing postcolonial criticism for (Northern) Ireland and Scotland: rewriting national paradigms', in Shane Alcobia-Murphy, Johanna Archbold, John Gibney and Carole Jones (eds), *Beyond the Anchoring Grounds: More Cross-Currents in Irish and Scottish Studies*, Belfast: Cló Ollscoil na Banríona, pp. 154–62.

Lennon, John (1970), 'Working class hero', *John Lennon/Plastic Ono Band*, London: Apple/EMI.

Leonard, Tom (1984), *Intimate Voices, 1965–1983*, London: Vintage.

Leonard, Tom (1990), *Radical Renfrew: Poetry from the French Revolution to the First World War by Poets Born, or Sometime Resident in, the County of Renfrewshire*, Edinburgh: Polygon.

Linklater, Alexander (2001), ' "I am still a petulant brat showing off" ', *Evening Standard*, 24 April, p. 29.

Lobban, Mairearad (ed.) (2003), *Lachann Dubh A' Chrogain/Lachlann Livingstone and his Grandson*, Strathpeffer: New Iona Press.

Lochhead, Liz (1984), *Dreaming Frankenstein and Collected Poems*, Edinburgh: Polygon.

Lochhead, Liz (1991), *Bagpipe Muzak*, Harmondsworth: Penguin.

Lochhead, Liz (2000), *Medea*, London: Nick Hern.

Lochhead, Liz (2002), *Miseryguts & Tartuffe*, London: Nick Hern.

Lochhead, Liz (2003a), *The Colour of Black and White*, Edinburgh: Polygon.

Lochhead, Liz (2003b), *Thebans*, London: Nick Hern.

Lockerbie, Catherine (1993), 'Pure dead demotic', *Scotsman*, 14 August, p. 13.

Lockerbie, Catherine (1994), 'We're the cultural equivalent of the casuals', *Scotsman*, 26 February, p. 13.

Lockerbie, Ian (1990), 'Pictures in a small country: the Scottish Film Production Fund', in Eddie Dick (ed.), *From Limelight to Satellite: A Scottish Film Book*, London: BFI, pp. 171–84.

Longley, Edna (1985), 'Poetry and politics in Northern Ireland', *Crane Bag*, 9, 1, pp. 26–40.

Longley, Edna and Declan Kiberd (2001), *Multiculturalism: The View from Two Irelands*, Cork: Cork University Press.

Lucas, Ian (1994), *Impertinent Decorum: Gay Theatrical Manoeuvres*, London: Cassell.

Lyotard, Jean-François [1979] (1984), *The Postmodern Condition: A Report on Knowledge*, trans. Geoff Bennington and Brian Massumi, Manchester: Manchester University Press.

Lyotard, Jean-François [1988] (1991), *The Inhuman: Reflections on Time*, trans. Geoff Bennington and Rachel Bowlby, Cambridge: Polity.

Lyotard, Jean-François [1974] (1993), *Libidinal Economy*, trans. Iain Hamilton Grant, London: Athlone.

Mac a'Ghobhainn, Iain (1968), *An Dubh is an Gorm*, Glasgow: Clò Chaillean. [*See also* Smith, Iain Crichton]

Mac a' Ghobhainn, Iain (2006), *Am Miseanaraidh*, Edinburgh: Birlinn. [*See also* Smith, Iain Crichton]

MacAmhlaigh, Dòmhnall (ed.) (1976), *Nua-Bhàrdachd Ghàidhlig/Modern Gaelic Poetry*, Edinburgh: Southside.

Mac an t-Saoir, Màrtainn (2003), *Ath-Aithne*, Edinburgh: Birlinn.

Mac an t-Saoir, Màrtainn (2005), *Gymnippers Diciadain*, Edinburgh: Birlinn.

MacAskill, Kenny (2004), *Building a Nation: Post-Devolution Nationalism in Scotland*, Edinburgh: Luath.

MacCabe, Colin (1999), *The Eloquence of the Vulgar: Language, Cinema and the Politics of Culture*, London: BFI.

MacDonald, Gus (1990), 'Fiction friction', in Eddie Dick (ed.), *From Limelight to Satellite: A Scottish Film Book*, London: BFI, pp. 193–206.

MacDonald, Norman Malcolm (1983), *Calum Tod*, Edinburgh: Canongate. [*see also* Dòmhnallach, Tormod Calum]

MacDonald, Norman Malcolm (2000), *Portrona*, Edinburgh: Birlinn. [*see also* Dòmhnallach, Tormod Calum]

MacFhionnlaigh, Fearghas (1997), *Bogha-Frois san Oidhche/Rainbow in the Night*, Carberry: Handsel.

MacGill-Eain, Somhairle/Sorley MacLean (1989), *O Choille gu Bearradh/From Wood to Ridge: Collected Poems in Gaelic and English*, Manchester: Carcanet.

MacGill-Eain, Tormod (2005), *Dacha Mo Ghaoil*, Edinburgh: Birlinn.

MacGillIosa, Donnchadh (2005), *Tocasaid 'Ain Tuirc*, Edinburgh: Birlinn.

Mack, Douglas (2006), *Scottish Fiction and the British Empire*, Edinburgh: Edinburgh University Press.

Mackenzie, David (dir.) (2002), *The Last Great Wilderness*, Glasgow: Sigma.

MacLeod, Anne (1999), *Just the Caravaggio*, Salzburg: Poetry Salzburg.

Macleod, Donald John (1976), 'Gaelic prose', *Transactions of the Gaelic Society of Inverness*, 49, pp. 198–230.

MacLeòid, Coinneach (1998), *Orain Red*, Stornoway: Acair.

MacLeòid, Iain F. (2005), *Na Klondykers*, Edinburgh: Birlinn.

MacLochlainn, Antain (trans.) (2006), *Malairt Scéil*, Dublin: Cois Life.

MacMahon, Deirdre (2004), 'Scotland at the Smithsonian: beyond the cultural cringe?', *Scottish Affairs*, 47, 4, www.scottishaffairs.org/onlinepub/sa/macmahon_sa47_spr04.html.

Macmurray, John [1954] (1969a), *The Self as Agent*, London: Faber.

Macmurray, John [1954] (1969b), *Persons in Relation*, London: Faber.

MacNeacail, Aonghas (1996), *Oideachadh Ceart agus Dàin Eile/A Proper Schooling and Other Poems*, Edinburgh: Polygon.

MacNeice, Louis [1938] (1968), *Modern Poetry: A Personal Essay*, Oxford: Clarendon Press.

MacNeil, Kevin (1998), *Love and Zen in the Outer Hebrides*, Edinburgh: Canongate.

MacNeil, Kevin (2005), *The Stornoway Way*, London: Hamish Hamilton.

Maguire, Tom (1995), 'When the cutting edge cuts both ways: contemporary Scottish drama', *Modern Drama*, 38, 1, pp. 87–96.

Mahkota, Tina (1998), 'Dealing with "Scottishness" in translating Janice Galloway's *The Trick is to Keep Breathing*', paper presented at the conference 'British Cultural Studies: Cross-Cultural Challenges', Zagreb, http://galloway.1to1.org/Mahkota.html.

Mahon, Alyce (2005), *Surrealism and the Politics of Eros 1938–1968*, London: Thames and Hudson.

Mahmutćehajić, Rusmir (2003), *Sarajevo Essays: Politics, Ideology and Tradition*, Albany, NY: SUNY Press.

Maley, John (2002), *Delilah's: Stories from the Closet till Closing Time*, Glasgow: 11–9.

Maley, Willy (2000), 'Subversion and squirrility in Irvine Welsh's shorter fiction', in Dermot Cavanagh and Tim Kirk (eds), *Subversion and Scurrility: Popular Discourse in Europe from 1500 to the Present*, Aldershot: Ashgate, pp. 190–204.

Maley, Willy (ed.) (2005), *100 Best Scottish Books of All Time*, Edinburgh: List.

Malzahn, Manfred (1988), 'The industrial novel', in Cairns Craig (ed.), *The History of Scottish Literature. Volume 4: The Twentieth Century*, Aberdeen University Press, pp. 229–42.

Manlove, Colin (1994), *Scottish Fantasy Literature: A Critical Survey*, Edinburgh: Canongate.

Manlove, Colin (ed.) (1996), *An Anthology of Scottish Fantasy Literature*, Edinburgh: Polygon.

March, Cristie (1999), 'Exchanges [interview with Janice Galloway]', *Edinburgh Review*, 101, pp. 85–98, www.galloway.1to1.org/Leighmarch.html.

March, Cristie (2002), *Rewriting Scotland: Welsh, McLean, Warner, Banks, Galloway and Kennedy*, Manchester: Manchester University Press.

Martin, Lorna (2005), 'We Scots are still recovering from our industrial tsunami [interview with Stuart Cosgrove]', *Observer*, 13 February, http://observer.guardian.co.uk/uk_news/story/0,6903,1411963,00.html.

Martin, Michael (2002), 'When pornography sneezes, pop culture catches gold [interview with Irvine Welsh]', www.nerve.com/screeningroom/books/interview_irvinewelsh.

Martin-Jones, David (2005), '*Orphans*: a work of minor cinema from post-devolutionary Scotland', *Journal of British Cinema and Television*, 1, 2, pp. 226–41.

Maslin, Janet (2004a), 'A sleuth's taste for harsh back talk and soothing spirits', *New York Times*, 9 February, http://query.nytimes.com/gst/fullpage.html?res=9E01E2DC163 AF93AA35751COA9629C8B63.

Maslin, Janet (2004b), 'In Edinburgh, a (No. 2) lady detective philosopher', *New York Times*, 27 September, www.nytimes.com/2004/09/27/books/27masl.html?ex= 1154836800&en=dd067d002608177f&ei=5070.

Massie, Alan (2002), 'Sir Walter's Scoterati', *Scotland on Sunday*, 16 June, pp. 1–2.

McAllester Jones, Mary (1991), *Gaston Bachelard, Subversive Humanist: Texts and Readings*, Madison: University of Wisconsin Press.

McArthur, Colin (ed.) (1982), *Scotch Reels: Scotland in Cinema and Television*, London: BFI.

McArthur, Colin (1994), 'The cultural necessity of a poor Celtic cinema,' in John Hill, Martin McLoone and Paul Hainsworth (eds), *Border Crossing: Film in Ireland, Britain and Europe*, Belfast: Institute of Irish Studies/BFI, pp. 112–25.

McArthur, Colin (2003), *Brigadoon, Braveheart and the Scots: Distortions of Scotland in Hollywood Cinema*, London and New York: I. B. Tauris.

McCall Smith, Alexander (1998), *The No. 1 Ladies' Detective Agency*, Edinburgh: Polygon.

McCall Smith, Alexander (2002), *The Kalahari Typing School for Men*, Edinburgh: Polygon.

McCall Smith, Alexander (2003), *The Full Cupboard of Life*, London: Abacus.

McCall Smith, Alexander (2004a), *The Sunday Philosophy Club*, London: Abacus.

McCall Smith, Alexander (2004b), *In the Company of Cheerful Ladies*, London: Abacus.

McClintock, Anne (1992), 'The angel of progress: pitfalls of the term "post-colonialism"', *Social Text*, 31/2, pp. 84–98.

McCrone, David (1992), *Understanding Scotland: The Sociology of a Stateless Nation*, London: Routledge.

McCrone, David (2001), 'Neo-nationalism in stateless nations', in John MacInnes and David McCrone (eds), 'Stateless nations in the twenty-first century: Scotland, Catalonia and Quebec', special issue of *Scottish Affairs*, pp. 3–13.

McCulloch, Fiona (2004), *The Fictional Role of Childhood in Victorian and Early Twentieth-Century Children's Literature*, Lewiston, NY, and Ceredigion: Edwin Mellen Press.

McDermitt, Barbara and Alan Bruford (1980), 'Duncan Williamson', *Tocher*, 33, pp. 141–87.

McDonald, Jan (1997), 'Scottish women dramatists since 1945', in Douglas Gifford and Dorothy McMillan (eds), *A History of Scottish Women's Writing*, Edinburgh: Edinburgh University Press, pp. 494–513.

McGavin, Patrick Z. (1996), '"Trainspotting" author "stumbled into writing"', *Chicago Tribune*, 30 July, p. 52.

McGonigal, James (2004), *Passage/An Pasáiste*, Glasgow: Mariscat.

McGonigal, James (no date), 'Interview 02: Jim McGonigal on *Passage/An Pasáiste*', Scottish Corpus document 612, www.scottishcorpus.ac.uk.

McGonigal, James, Donny O'Rourke and Hamish Whyte (eds) (2000), *Across the Water: Irishness in Scottish Writing*, Glendaruel: Argyll.

McIlvanney, Liam (2002), 'The politics of narrative in the post-war Scottish novel', in Zachary Leader (ed.), *On Modern British Fiction*, Oxford: Oxford University Press, pp. 181–201.

McIntyre, Steve (1994), 'Vanishing point: feature film production in a small country', in John Hill, Martin McLoone and Paul Hainsworth (eds), *Border Crossing: Film in Ireland, Britain and Europe*, Belfast: Institute of Irish Studies/BFI, pp. 88–111.

McLean, Duncan (1985), 'James Kelman interviewed', *Edinburgh Review*, 71, pp. 64–80.

McLean, Duncan (1999), 'Reconstructions: new writing for the New Parliament', *Edinburgh Review*, 100, p. 74.

McLeod, Wilson (ed.) (2006), *Revitalising Gaelic in Scotland: Policy, Planning and Public Discourse*, Edinburgh: Dunedin Academic.

McLiam Wilson, Robert (1996), *Eureka Street*, London: Secker and Warburg.

McLiam Wilson, Robert [1989] (1997), *Ripley Bogle*, London: Minerva.

McLoone, Martin (2001), 'Internal decolonisation? British cinema in the Celtic fringe', in Robert Murphy (ed.), *The British Cinema Book*, London: BFI, pp. 184–90.

McMillan, Dorothy and Michel Byrne (eds) (2003), *Modern Scottish Women Poets*, Edinburgh: Canongate.

McMillan, Neil (2003), 'Heroes and zeroes: monologism and masculinism in Scottish men's writing of the 1970s and beyond', in Daniel Lea and Berthold Schoene (eds), *Posting the Male: Masculinities in Post-War and Contemporary British Literature*, Amsterdam and New York: Rodopi, pp. 69–87.

McQuillan, Rebecca (2003), 'Welcome to monarch country', *Herald*, 5 September, p. 21.

McRobbie, Angela (1994), *Postmodernism and Popular Culture*, London and New York: Routledge.

McSeveney, Angela (2002), *Imprint*, Edinburgh: Edinburgh Review.

Mhàrtainn, Cairistìona (ed.) (2001), *Orain an Eilein: Gaelic Songs From Skye*, Breacais/ Skye: Taigh nan Teud.

Miller, Alison (2005), *Demo*, Harmondsworth: Penguin.

Miller, Gavin (2001), 'Literary narrative as soteriology in the work of Kurt Vonnegut and Alasdair Gray', *Journal of Narrative Theory*, 31, 3, pp. 299–323.

Miller, Gavin (2002), '"We are all murderers and prostitutes": R. D. Laing and the work of Alasdair Gray', *PsyArt*, www.clas.ufl.edu/ipsa/journal/2002/miller01.htm.

Miller, Gavin (2004), 'The cult of the White Goddess in Alasdair Gray's *Lanark*', *Studies in Scottish Literature*, 33–4, pp. 291–307.

Miller, Gavin (2005a), *Alasdair Gray: The Fiction of Communion*, Amsterdam and New York: Rodopi.

Miller, Gavin (2005b), 'National confessions: queer theory meets Scottish literature', *Scottish Studies Review*, 6, 2, pp. 60–71.

Miller, Gavin (2005c), 'How not to "question Scotland"', *Scottish Affairs*, 52, pp. 1–14.

Mills, Scott (2005), 'Guilty pleasures', *Independent*, 13 June.

Mina, Denise (1998), *Garnethill*, London: Bantam.

Mina, Denise (2000), *Exile*, London: Bantam.

Mina, Denise (2001), *Resolution*, London: Bantam.

Mina, Denise (2002), *Sanctum*, London: Bantam.

Minnelli, Vincente (dir.) (1954), *Brigadoon*, Metro-Goldwyn-Mayer.

Mitchell, Nicholas (2006), 'Interview with Suhayl Saadi', *Spike Magazine*, March/April, www.spikemagazine.com.

Moffett, Julie (1997), *The Thorn and the Thistle*, New York: Dorchester.

Moi, Toril (1999), *What Is a Woman? And Other Essays*, Oxford: Oxford University Press.

Moning, Karen Marie (2000), *The Highlander's Touch*, New York: Dell.

Moning, Karen Marie (2001), *Kiss of the Highlander*, New York: Dell.

Moning, Karen Marie (2005), *Spell of the Highlander*, New York: Delacourt.

Mooney, Gerry and Lynne Poole (2004), '"A land of milk and honey"? Social policy in Scotland after devolution", *Critical Social Policy*, 24, 4, pp. 458–83.

Moore, Clayton (2005), 'In the company of the cheerful author: an interview with Alexander McCall Smith', *Bookslut*, October, www.bookslut.com/features/ 2005_10_006827.php.

Moravec, Hans (1988), *Mind Children: The Future of Robot and Human Intelligence*, Cambridge, MA and London: Harvard University Press.

Morgan, Edwin (1974), *Essays*, Cheadle: Carcanet.

Morgan, Edwin (1990a), *Collected Poems*, Manchester: Carcanet.

Morgan, Edwin (1990b), *Nothing Not Giving Messages: Reflections on Life and Work*, Edinburgh: Polygon.

Morgan, Edwin (1994), 'Long live the queen', *Poetry Review*, 84, 1, pp. 16–17.

Morgan, Edwin (1996), *Cyrano de Bergerac*, Manchester: Carcanet.

Morgan, Edwin (1997), *Virtual and Other Realities*, Manchester: Carcanet.

Morgan, Edwin (2000a), 'Transgression in Glasgow: a poet coming to terms', in Richard Phillips, Diane Watt and David Shuttleton (eds), *De-Centring Sexualities: Politics and Representations Beyond the Metropolis*, London: Routledge, pp. 278–91.

Morgan, Edwin (2000b), *Phaedra*, Manchester: Carcanet.

Morgan, Edwin (2002), 'The demon', in *Cathures: New Poems, 1997–2001*, Manchester: Carcanet, pp. 91–115.

Morgan, Edwin (2004a), *Metrum de Praelio apud Bannockburn/The Battle of Bannockburn (by Robert Baston)*, Edinburgh: Mariscat and The Scottish Poetry Library.

Morgan, Edwin (2004b), 'Open the doors', www.scottish.parliament.uk/nmCentre/events/holyroodOpening/edwinMorgan.htm.

Morgan, Edwin (2005), 'Acknowledge the unacknowledged legislators', www.scottish-booktrust.com/cocoon/sbt/viewitem/article/417/1/146/365.

Morrison, Ewan (2005), *The Last Book You Read and Other Stories*, Edinburgh: Chroma.

Morton, Samantha (2004), 'Clara and more [interview with Janice Galloway]', www.galloway.1to1.org/incwriters.html.

Mugglestone, Lynda (1993), 'Lochhead's languages: styles, status, gender and identity', in Robert Crawford and Anne Varty (eds), *Liz Lochhead's Voices*, Edinburgh: Polygon, pp. 92–108.

Muir, Edwin (1935), *A Scottish Journey*, London: Heineman.

Muir, Edwin [1936] (1982), *Scott and Scotland: The Predicament of the Scottish Writer*, Edinburgh: Polygon.

Mulcahy, Russell (dir.) (1986), *Highlander*, Republic Pictures/Twentieth-Century Fox.

Mulholland, John (1995), 'Acid wit', *Guardian*, 30 March, p. T8.

Mulvey, Laura [1975] (1989), 'Visual pleasure and narrative cinema', in *Visual and Other Pleasures*, Basingstoke: Macmillan, pp. 14–26.

Murray, Jonathan (2001), 'Contemporary Scottish film', *Irish Review*, 28, pp. 75–88.

Murray, Jonathan (2004), 'Convents or cowboys? Millennial Scottish and Irish film industries and imaginaries in *The Magdalene Sisters*', in John Hill and Kevin Rockett (eds), *National Cinema and Beyond: Studies in Irish Film*, Dublin: Four Courts, pp. 149–60.

Murray, Jonathan (2005), 'Kids in America? Narratives of transatlantic influence in 1990s Scottish cinema', *Screen*, 46, 2, pp. 217–26.

Nairn, Tom [1977] (1981), *The Break-Up of Britain: Crisis and Neo-Nationalism*, London: Verso.

Nairn, Tom (2000), *After Britain*, London: Granta.

Nairn, Tom (2004a), '*Break-Up*: twenty-five years on', in Eleanor Bell and Gavin Miller (eds), *Scotland in Theory: Reflections on Culture and Literature*, Amsterdam: Rodopi, pp. 17–33.

Nairn, Tom (2004b), 'The world thing', *Scottish Left Review*, 23, www.scottishleftreview.org/php/public/pastissues.php?action=article&docid=188.

Neat, Timothy (1996), *The Summer Walkers*, Edinburgh: Canongate.

Neat, Timothy (1999), *Living Poets and Ancient Traditions in the Highlands and Islands of Scotland*, Edinburgh: Canongate.

Neely, Sarah (2004), 'Cultural ventriloquism: the voice-over in adaptations of contemporary Irish and Scottish literature', in John Hill and Kevin Rockett (eds), *National Cinema and Beyond: Studies in Irish Film*, Dublin: Four Courts, pp. 125–34.

Neely, Sarah (2005a), 'Scotland, heritage and devolving British cinema', *Screen*, 46, 2, pp. 241–5.

Neely, Sarah (2005b), 'British cinema studies and the "intimate epics" of the "national" past', in John Hill and Kevin Rockett (eds), *Film History and National Cinema: Studies in Irish Film*, Dublin: Four Courts, pp. 47–56.

Neilson, Anthony (1997), *The Censor*, London: Methuen.

Neilson, Anthony (2002), *Stitching*, London: Methuen.

Nelson, Robin (1997), *TV Drama in Transition: Forms, Values and Cultural Change*, Basingstoke: Macmillan.

Nesteruk, Peter (2000), 'Ritual, sacrifice and identity in recent political drama, with reference to the plays of David Greig', *Journal of Dramatic Theory and Criticism*, 15, 1, pp. 21–42.

Neubauer, Jürgen (1999), *Literature as Intervention: Struggles over Cultural Identity in Contemporary Scottish Fiction*, Marburg: Tectum.

Ní Annracháin, Máire (2001a), 'An creideamh eaglasta i nuafhilíocht Ghaeilge na hÉireann agus na hAlban', *An Aimsir Óg*, 2, pp. 104–17.

Ní Annracháin, Máire (2001b), 'Seanphort, gléas úr: athnuachan an traidisiúin mar shaintréith de chuid na nua-Aimsearthachta i litríocht Ghaeilge na hÉireann agus na hAlban', *Léachtaí Cholm Cille*, 31, pp. 110–27.

Ní Annracháin, Máire (2002), 'The force of tradition in the poetry of Aonghas MacNeacail', in Colm Ó Baoil and Nancy McGuire (eds), *Rannsachadh na Gàidhlig 2000*, Aberdeen: An Cló Gaidhealach, pp. 117–27.

Ní Annracháin, Máire (2003), 'An tírdhreach agus an teanga fhíortha i bhfilíocht iarchlasaiceach Ghaeilge na hÉireann agus na hAlban', in Máire Ní Annracháin and Wilson McLeod (eds), *Cruth na Tíre*, Dublin: Coiscéim, pp. 136–65.

Ní Annracháin, Máire and Wilson McLeod (eds) (2003), *Cruth na Tíre*, Dublin: Coiscéim.

Nicholson, Colin (1992), *Poem, Purpose and Place: Shaping Identity in Contemporary Scottish Verse*, Edinburgh: Polygon.

Nicholson, Colin (2002), *Edwin Morgan: Inventions of Modernity*, Manchester: Manchester University Press.

NicLeòid, Norma (2006), *Dìleas Donn*, Edinburgh: Birlinn.

Nicoll, Laurence (2000), '"This is not a nationalist position": James Kelman's existential voice', *Edinburgh Review*, 103, pp. 79–84.

Niven, Liz (1997), 'Extracted fae a drunk wumman sittin oan a thistle', in Kathleen Jamie and Donny O'Rourke (eds), *New Writing Scotland 15*, Glasgow: ASLS, pp. 116–20.

Niven, Liz (2002), *The Scots Language in Education in Scotland*, Ljouwert/Leeuwarden: Mercator-Education.

Norquay, Glenda (2000), 'Janice Galloway's novels: fraudulent mooching', in Aileen Christiansen and Alison Lumsden (eds), *Contemporary Scottish Women Writers*, Edinburgh: Edinburgh University Press, pp. 131–43.

Norquay, Glenda and Gerry Smyth (eds) (2002), *Across the Margins: Identity, Resistance and Minority Culture Throughout the British Archipelago*, Manchester: Manchester University Press.

O'Hagan, Andrew (1999), *Our Fathers*, New York: Harcourt.

O'Hagan, Sean (2005), ' "I'd rather look at the hills than get wasted" ', *Observer* (Review), 4 December, p. 3.

O'Regan, Tom (1996), *Australian National Cinema*, London: Routledge.

O'Rourke, Donny (2001), *On a Roll: A Jena Notebook*, Glasgow: Mariscat.

O'Rourke, Donny (ed.) [1994] (2002), *Dream State: The New Scottish Poets*, Edinburgh: Polygon.

O'Rourke, Donny (2005), *Aus dem Wartesaal der Poesie: Nürnberger Notizen/From Poetry's Waiting Room: Nürnberg Notebook*, Nürnberg: Spätlese.

Pacione, Michael (1995), *Glasgow: The Socio-Spatial Development of the City*, Chichester: John Wiley.

Parker, Alan (2002), *Building a Sustainable UK Film Industry*, London: Film Council.

Parker, Andrew, Mary Russo, Doris Sommer and Patricia Yaeger (eds) (1992), *Nationalisms and Sexualities*, London: Routledge.

Paterson, Don (1993), *Nil Nil*, London: Faber.

Paterson, Don (1996), 'The dilemma of the peot [sic]', in Tony Curtis (ed.), *How Poets Work*, Bridgend: Seren, pp. 155–66.

Paterson, Don (1997), *God's Gift to Women*, London: Faber.

Paterson, Don (ed.) (2001), *Robert Burns: Poems Selected by Don Paterson*, London: Faber.

Paterson, Don (2003), *Landing Light*, London: Faber.

Paterson, Don (2004a), *The Book of Shadows*, London: Picador.

Paterson, Don (2004b), 'The dark art of poetry [South Bank Centre T. S. Eliot Lecture, 30 October]', www.poetrylibrary.org.uk.

Paterson, Don and Charles Simic (eds) (2004), *New British Poetry*, Minneapolis: Graywolf Press.

Paterson, Lindsay (1994), *The Autonomy of Modern Scotland*, Edinburgh: Edinburgh University Press.

Patterson, Lindsay, Alice Brown and John Curtice (eds) (2001), *New Scotland, New Politics*, Edinburgh: Polygon.

Pelaschiar, Laura (2000), 'Transforming Belfast: the evolving role of the city in Northern Irish fiction', *Irish University Review*, 30, 1, pp. 117–31.

Petrie, Duncan (2000), *Screening Scotland*, London: BFI.

Petrie, Duncan (2004), *Contemporary Scottish Fictions: Film, Television and the Novel*, Edinburgh: Edinburgh University Press.

Phillips, Trevor (2000), Inaugural speech to the London Assembly, 12 May, www.london.gov.uk/view_press_release.jsp?releaseid=580.

Pittock, Murray (1991), *The Invention of Scotland: The Stuart Myth and the Scottish Identity, 1638 to the Present*, London: Routledge.

Pittock, Murray (1999), *Celtic Identity and the British Image*, Manchester: Manchester University Press.

Pittock, Murray (2001), *Scottish Nationality*, Basingstoke: Palgrave.

Plain, Gill (2002), *Ian Rankin's Black and Blue: A Reader's Guide*, London: Continuum.

Plain, Gill (2003), 'Hard nuts to crack: devolving masculinities in contemporary Scottish fiction', in Daniel Lea and Besthold Schoene (eds), *Posting the Male: Masculinities in Post-War and Contemporary British Literature*, Amsterdam and New York: Rodopi, pp. 55–68.

Plato (1935), *Republic*, trans. Paul Shorey, *Loeb Classical Library*, London: Heinemann.

Plato (1942), *Laws*, trans. R. G. Bury, *Loeb Classical Library*, London: Heinemann.

Poe, Edgar Allan [1846] (1984), 'The literati of New York City', in *Essays and Reviews*, ed. Gary Thompson, New York: Library of America, pp. 1118–22.

Poster, Mark (ed.) (1988), *Jean Baudrillard: Selected Writings*, Cambridge: Polity.

Potter, Russell (1993), 'Interview with Chuck D', www.ric.edu/rpotter/chuck.html.

Potter, Russell (1995), *Spectacular Vernaculars: Hip-Hop and the Politics of Postmodernism*, Albany, NY: SUNY Press.

Pow, Tom (2004), *Landscapes and Legacies*, Aberdour: Lynx.

Powell, Enoch (1968), 'Rivers of blood', http://theoccidentalquarterly.com/vol1no1/ep-rivers.html.

Press, Joy (2002), 'Unthanksgiving: *Lanark* by Alasdair Gray', *Village Voice*, November 27–December 3, www.villagevoice.com/books/0248,press,40123,10.html.

Price, Richard (2005), *Lucky Day*, Manchester: Carcanet.

Rancière, Jacques (2003), 'The thinking of dissensus: politics and aesthetics', paper presented at the conference 'Fidelity to the Disagreement: Jacques Rancière and the Political', Goldsmith College, London, 16–17 September.

Rankin, Ian (1997), *Black and Blue*, London: Orion.

Rankin, Ian (2000), *Set in Darkness*, London: Orion.

Rankin, Ian (2002), *Resurrection Men*, London: Orion.

Rankin, Ian (2004), *Fleshmarket Close*, London: Orion.

Ranney, Karen (2002), *The Irresistible MacRae*, New York: Avon.

Ransford, Tessa (2002), *Noteworthy Poems*, Kirkcaldy: Akros.

Ransford, Tessa (ed. and trans.) (2004), *The Nightingale Question: 5 Poets from Saxony*, Exeter: Shearsman.

Raymond, Marcel [1933] (1970), *From Baudelaire to Surrealism*, London: Methuen.

Redhead, Steve (2000), *Repetitive Beat Generation*, Edinburgh: Rebel.

Reinelt, Janelle (2001), 'Performing Europe: identity formation for a "new" Europe', *Theatre Journal*, 53, 3, pp. 365–87.

Reizbaum, Marilyn (1992), 'Canonical double cross: Scottish and Irish women's writing', in Karen Lawrence (ed.), *Decolonizing Tradition: New Views of Twentieth-Century 'British' Literary Canons*, Urbana: University of Illinois Press, pp. 165–90.

Relph, Simon, Janice Headland and Anita Overland (2002), *The Relph Report: A Study for the Film Council Examining the Costs of Lower-Budget UK Films and Their Value in the World Market*, London: Film Council.

Research Institute of Irish and Scottish Studies (RIISS), University of Aberdeen, www.abdn.ac.uk/riiss.

Reynolds, Matthew (2004), 'So much more handsome [review of Don Paterson's *Landing Light*]', *London Review of Books*, 4 March, pp. 25–7.

Reynolds, Nigel (1998), 'Jailed terror suspect on Whitbread Book shortlist', *Daily Telegraph*, 7 November, www.telegraph.co.uk/htmlContent.jhtml?html=/archive/1998/11/07/nbook07.html.

Riach, Alan (2004), 'Drumelzier', *Quadrant*, 405, 4, pp. 68–9.

Rice, Alan (2004), '"Heroes across the sea": black and white British fascination with African Americans in the contemporary Black British fiction by Caryl Phillips and Jackie Kay', in Heike Raphael-Hernandez (ed.), *Blackening Europe: The African American Presence*, London: Routledge, pp. 217–34.

Rich, Frank (2001), 'Naked capitalists', *New York Times Magazine*, 20 May, pp. 50–6, 80, 82, 92.

Ritchie, Gayle (2005), ‘*Magoons*’ creator condemns Channel 4 as “anti-Scottish”’, *Sunday Times*, 20 November, p. 13.

Roberts, Diane (1999), ‘Your clan or ours?’, *Oxford American*, 29, pp. 24–30.

Roberts, Michael (1936), *Faber Book of Modern Verse*, London: Faber.

Roberts, Nora (1998), *The MacGregor Grooms*, New York: Silhouette.

Robertson, Angus (1913), *An t-Ogha Mòr*, Glasgow: Mac Labhruinn.

Robertson, Charles (1997), ‘“A great ship in full sail”: Basil Spence and Hutchesontown “C”’, in Miles Glendinning (ed.), *Rebuilding Scotland: The Postwar Vision, 1945–1975*, East Linton: Tuckwell, pp. 92–102.

Robertson, David (2002), ‘Clara’s theme’, in *Scotsman*, 22 June, http://news.scotsman.com/archive.

Robertson, James (2001a), *Fae the Flowers o Evil: Baudelaire in Scots*, Kingskettle: Kettillonia.

Robertson, James (2001b), *Stirling Sonnets*, Kingskettle: Kettillonia.

Robertson, James (2003), *Joseph Knight*, London: Fourth Estate.

Robertson, James (2005), *Voyage of Intent: Sonnets and Essays from the Scottish Parliament*, Edinburgh: Scottish Book Trust/Luath Press.

Robertson, Stanley (1988), *Exodus to Alford*, Nairn: Balnain.

Robertson, Stanley (1989), *Nyakim’s Windows*, Nairn: Balnain.

Robertson, Stanley (1990), *Fish-Hooses: Tales from an Aberdeen Filleter*, Nairn: Balnain.

Robinson, Mairi (ed.) (1999), *Concise Scots Dictionary*, Edinburgh: Polygon.

Roddick, Nick (1998), ‘Show me the culture’, *Sight and Sound*, December, pp. 22–6.

Rodgers, Everett (1995), *Diffusion of Innovation*, New York: Free Press.

Rose, Dilys (1989), *Our Lady of the Pickpockets*, London: Minerva.

Rose, Dilys (1993), *Red Tides*, London: Minerva.

Rose, Dilys (1999), *Pest Maiden*, London: Review.

Rose, Dilys (2000), ‘Out of touch: an extract from a work in progress’, in *The Canongate Prize for New Writing: Scotland into the New Era*, Edinburgh: Canongate, pp. 187–97.

Ross, Andrew (1995), ‘Out of kilter’, *Artforum International*, 34, p. 114.

Rowling, J. K. (1997), *Harry Potter and the Philosopher’s Stone*, London: Bloomsbury.

Rowling, J. K. (1998), *Harry Potter and the Chamber of Secrets*, London: Bloomsbury.

Rowling, J. K. (1999), *Harry Potter and the Prisoner of Azkaban*, London: Bloomsbury.

Rowling, J. K. (2000), *Harry Potter and the Goblet of Fire*, London: Bloomsbury.

Rowling, J. K. (2003), *Harry Potter and the Order of the Phoenix*, London: Bloomsbury.

Rowling, J. K. (2005), *Harry Potter and the Half-Blood Prince*, London: Bloomsbury.

Rudberg, Eva (2002), ‘Utopia of the everyday: Swedish and un-Swedish in the architecture of functionalism’, in Cecilia Widenheim (ed.), *Utopia and Reality: Modernity in Sweden, 1900–1960*, trans. Henning Koch, Sylvester Mazzarella and David McDuff, New Haven, CT: Yale University Press, pp. 150–73.

RWA (Romance Writers of America) (2004a), ‘2004 romance-fiction sales statistics, reader demographics and book buying habits’, www.rawnational.org/pdfs/StatisticsBrochure2004.pdf.

RWA (Romance Writers of America) (2004b), ‘Reader statistics’, www.rwanational.org/statistics/reader_stats.htm.

RWA (Romance Writers of America) (2005), ‘RWA – what is it?’, www.rwanational.org/about_rwa/about.htm.

Ryan, Ray (2002), *Ireland and Scotland: Literature and Culture, State and Nation, 1966–2000*, Oxford: Oxford University Press.

Saadi, Suhayl (1997), *The Snake*, New York: Creation.

Saadi, Suhayl (2001), *The Burning Mirror*, Edinburgh: Polygon.

Saadi, Suhayl (2004), *Psychoraag*, Edinburgh: Black and White.

Saadi, Suhayl (2005), 'Storm in the valley of death', *Independent*, 9 September, http://enjoyment.independent.co.uk/books/reviews/article311385.ece.

Saadi, Suhayl (2006), 'The gods of the door: literary censorship in the UK', *Spike Magazine*, February, www.spikemagazine.com.

Saadi, Suhayl and Catherine McInerney (eds) (2005), *Freedom Spring: Ten Years On*, Glasgow: Waverley.

Saadi, Suhayl and Christopher Whyte (trans.) (2003), *M/other Tongues: Poems by Adel Karasholi and Dragica Rajcic*, Glasgow and Edinburgh: Goethe-Institut and Scottish Poetry Library.

Salmond, Alex (1996), Keynote address, Annual Conference of the SNP, 27 September, 'Poems, Prayers and Profits', www.highlanderweb.co.uk/snp/alex4.htm.

Salmond, Alex (1997), 'Irish show Scots road to success', *Irish Times*, 1 May, p. 14.

Sassi, Carla (2005), *Why Scottish Literature Matters*, Edinburgh: Saltire Society.

Schoene, Berthold (1995), 'A passage to Scotland: Scottish literature and the British post-colonial condition', *Scotlands*, 2, 1, pp. 107–22.

Schoene, Berthold (1998), 'Emerging as the others of our selves: Scottish multiculturalism and the challenge of the body in postcolonial representation', *Scottish Literary Journal*, 25, 1, pp. 54–72.

Schoene, Berthold (1999), 'Dams burst: devolving gender in Iain Banks's *The Wasp Factory*', *Ariel*, 30, 1, pp. 131–48.

Schoene, Berthold (2000), *Writing Men: Literary Masculinities from Frankenstein to the New Man*, Edinburgh: Edinburgh University Press.

Schoene, Berthold (2002), 'The union and Jack: British masculinities, pomophobia, and the post-nation', in Glenda Norquay and Gerry Smyth (eds), *Across the Margins: Identity, Resistance and Minority Culture Throughout the British Archipelago*, Manchester: Manchester University Press, pp. 83–98.

Schoene, Berthold (2004), 'Nervous men, mobile nation: masculinity and psychopathology in Irvine Welsh's *Filth* and *Glue*', in Eleanor Bell and Gavin Miller (eds), *Scotland in Theory: Reflections on Culture and Literature*, Amsterdam: Rodopi, pp. 121–45.

Schoene, Berthold (2006a), 'The walking cure: *Heimat*, masculinity and mobile narration in Alan Warner's *The Man Who Walks*', *Scottish Studies Review*, 7, 11, pp. 95–109.

Schoene, Berthold (2006b), 'The wounded woman and the parrot: post-feminist girlhood in Alan Warner's *The Sopranos* and Bella Bathurst's *Special*', *Journal of Gender Studies*, 15, 2, pp. 133–44.

Scott, Amanda (2000), *Border Fire*, New York: Zebra.

Scott, Joan (1986), 'Gender: a useful category of historical analysis', *American Historical Review*, 91, 5, pp. 1053–75.

Scott, Kirsty (2004), 'Publishers cash in as Scottish writers drop the doom and gloom', *Guardian*, 10 January, http://books.guardian.co.uk/news/articles/o,,1119949,00.html.

Scott, Kirsty (2005), 'In the nature of things', *Guardian*, 18 June, http://books.guardian.co.uk/poety/features/o,,1508838,00.html.

Scott, Paul (2000), 'The Scottish Parliament and Scottish culture: the opportunity of the new era', in Alex Wright (ed.), *Scotland: The Challenge of Devolution*, Aldershot: Ashgate, pp. 204–13.

Scottish Arts Council (2001), *Scottish National Theatre: Report of the Independent Working Group*, Edinburgh: Scottish Arts Council, p. 5.

Scottish Arts Council (2002), 'Literature, Nation: Literature Strategy, 2002–2007', www.scottisharts.org.uk/1/information/publications/1000307.aspx.

Scottish Arts Council (2003), 'International Interest in Scottish Translations', 28 March, www.scottisharts.org.uk/1/latestnews/1000724.aspx.

Scottish Arts Council (2004), 'Review of Scottish Publishing in the Twenty-First Century', www.scottisharts.org.uk/1/information/publications/1000311.aspx.

Scottish Executive (2000), 'Creating Our Future, Minding Our Past: Scotland's National Cultural Strategy', www.scotland.gov.uk/nationalculturalstrategy/docs/cult-00.asp.

Scottish Executive (2005), 'Our Next Major Enterprise: Final Report of the Cultural Commission', www.scotland.gov.uk/Publications/2005/09/0191729/17302.

Scottish Executive (2006), 'Scotland's Culture', www.scotlandsculture.org.

Scullion, Adrienne (1995), 'Feminine pleasures and masculine indignities: gender and community in Scottish drama', in Christopher Whyte (ed.), *Gendering the Nation: Studies in Modern Scotish Literature*, Edinburgh: Edinburgh University Press, pp. 169–204.

Scullion, Adrienne (2000a), 'Contemporary Scottish women playwrights', in Janelle Reinelt and Elaine Aston (eds), *The Cambridge Companion to Modern British Women Playwrights*, Cambridge: Cambridge University Press, pp. 94–118.

Scullion, Adrienne (2000b), '[David] Harrower et le theatre écossais contemporain', *Alternatives Theatrales*, 65–6, pp. 111–15.

Scullion, Adrienne (2001), 'Self and nation: issues of identity in modern Scottish drama by women', *New Theatre Quarterly*, 68, pp. 373–90.

Scullion, Adrienne (2002), 'Contemporary Scottish drama', in Douglas Gifford Sarah Dunnigan and Allan MacGillivray (eds), *Scottish Literature*, Edinburgh: Edinburgh University Press, pp. 794–833.

Scullion, Adrienne (2003a), ' "But why? But why? But why?" Storytelling and performance in new drama for children', in Kimberley Reynolds (ed.), *Children's Literature and Childhood in Performance*, Lichfield: Pied Piper, pp. 113–29.

Scullion, Adrienne (2003b), 'Changing expectations: Holyrood, television and Scottish identity', in Michael Scriven and Emily Roberts (eds), *Group Identities on French and British Television*, Oxford and New York: Berghahn, pp. 41–58.

Scullion, Adrienne (2004a), 'Byrne and the Bogie Man: experiencing American popular culture in Scotland', *Atlantic Studies*, 1, 2, pp. 210–27.

Scullion, Adrienne (2004b), 'Theatre in Scotland in the 1990s and beyond', in Baz Kershaw (ed.), *The Cambridge History of British Theatre*. Volume 3: *Since 1895*, Cambridge: Cambridge University Press, pp. 470–84.

Scullion, Adrienne (2005a), 'Le théâtre et l'art dramatique dans l'enseignement primaire en Écosse: le défi du programme de la Citoyenneté', *Repères*, 32, pp. 73–92.

Scullion, Adrienne (2005b), ' "And so this is what happened": war stories in new drama for children', *New Theatre Quarterly*, 84, pp. 317–30.

Scullion, Adrienne and Christine Hamilton (2003), 'Flagship or flagging? The post-devolution role of Scotland's "national" companies', *Scottish Affairs*, 42, pp. 98–114.

Scullion, Adrienne and Christine Hamilton (2005), ' "Picture it if yous will": theatre and theatregoing in rural Scotland', *New Theatre Quarterly*, 81, pp. 61–76.

Searle, John (1992), *The Rediscovery of Mind*, Cambridge, MA and London: MIT Press.

Sedgwick, Eve Kosofsky (1991), *Epistemology of the Closet*, London: Harvester Wheatsheaf.

Seeger, Pete (1956), *Where Have All the Flowers Gone*, Colorado Springs: Fall River Music.

Shone, Tom (1994), Review of Janice Galloway's *Foreign Parts*, *Sunday Times*, 24 April, p. 7.

Sinclair, Lise (2005), 'Literature across frontiers: poetry translation on the border of dialect', *New Shetlander*, 233, pp. 25–8.

Slater, Don (2000), 'Looking backwards', in Martin Lee (ed.), *The Consumer Society Reader*, Oxford: Blackwell, pp. 177–85.

Smith, Ali (2001a), *Hotel World*, London: Penguin.

Smith, Ali (2001b), 'Gothic', in Alan Bissett (ed.), *Damage Land: New Scottish Gothic Fiction*, Edinburgh: Polygon, pp. 48–55.

Smith, Ali (2004), 'Life beyond the M25', *Guardian*, 18 December, http://books.guardian.co.uk/departments/generalficlion/story/o,,1376171,00.html.

Smith, Anthony (2001), *Nationalism: Theory, Ideology, History*, Cambridge: Polity.

Smith, Donald (2001), *Storytelling Scotland: A Nation in Narrative*, Edinburgh: Polygon.

Smith, Donald (2003), 'Time for literature? Scottish literature after the first Scottish Parliament', *Chapman*, 102–3, pp. 5–8.

Smith, George Gregory (1919), *Scottish Literature: Character and Influence*, London: Macmillan.

Smith, Iain Crichton (1977), *The Hermit and Other Stories*, London: Gollancz. [*See also* Mac a'Ghobhainn, Iain]

Smith, Iain Crichton (1986), *Towards the Human*, Edinburgh: MacDonald. [*see also* Mac a'Ghobhainn, Iain]

Smith, Jules (2005) 'Critical perspective on Kathleen Jamie', British Council Contemporary Writers, www.contemporarywriters.com/authors/%20%2509?p=auth02C5P102112626707.

Solnit, Rebecca (2001), *Wanderlust: A History of Walking*, London and New York: Verso.

Somerville-Arjat, Gillean and Rebecca Wilson (eds) (1990), *Sleeping With Monsters: Conversations with Scottish and Irish Women Poets*, Edinburgh: Polygon.

Sontag, Susan [1964] (1967), 'Notes on "camp"', in *Against Interpretation*, London: Eyre and Spottiswoode, pp. 275–92.

Sontag, Susan (1969), *Styles of Radical Will*, New York: Farrar, Straus and Giroux.

Spark, Muriel (1958), *Robinson*, London: Macmillan.

Spark, Muriel (1961), *The Prime of Miss Jean Brodie*, Harmondsworth: Penguin.

Spivak, Gayatri Chakravorty (1995), 'Supplementing Marxism', in Bernd Magnus and Stephen Cullenberg (eds), *Whither Marxism? Global Crisis in International Perspective*, London: Routledge, pp. 109–19.

Stallybrass, Peter and Allon White (1986), *The Politics and Poetics of Transgression*, London: Methuen.

Stasio, Marilyn (2004), 'Essay: death takes a holiday', *New York Times*, 29 August, http://query.nytimes.com/gst/fullpage.html?sec=travel&res=9800E608/E3FF93AA1575BC.

Stenhouse, David (2005a), 'America is turned on by kilt ripping yarns', *Sunday Times*, 27 March.

Stenhouse, David (dir.) (2005b), *The Tartan Spangled Banner* [BBC Radio Scotland/WBUR Boston radio documentary], January.

Stephen, Jaci (2005), 'The Welsh are scotched again', *Mail on Sunday*, 16 January.

Stevenson, Deborah (2003), *Cities and Urban Culture*, Buckingham: Open University Press.

Stevenson, Randall (1993), 'Re-enter Houghmagandie: language as performance in Liz Lochhead's *Tartuffe*', in Robert Crawford and Anne Varty (eds), *Liz Lochhead's Voices*, Edinburgh: Polygon, pp. 109–23.

Stevenson, Randall and Gavin Wallace (eds) (1993), *The Scottish Novel Since the Seventies: New Visions, Old Dreams*, Edinburgh: Edinburgh University Press.

Stewart, Helen (2002), 'Television: a remote possibility', *Scotland on Sunday*, 29 December, http://scotlandonsunday.scotsman.com/spectrum.cfm?id=1431262002.

Stewart, Karen (2001), 'George, Lynne, page 3 and an old beat-up car [review of Alan Bissett's *Boyracers*]', *Sun*, 21 September.

Stirling, Kirsten (2001), 'The shape of things to come: writing the map of Scotland', in Catherine Di Domenico, Alex Law, Jonathan Skinner and Mick Smith (eds), *Boundaries and Identities: Nation, Politics and Culture in Scotland*, Dundee: University of Abertay Press, pp. 137–43.

Stoneman, Rod (2005), 'The sins of Commission II', *Screen*, 46, 2, pp. 247–64.

Strachan, Zoë (1999), 'Queerspotting: homosexuality in contemporary Scottish fiction', www.spikemagazine.com/0599queerspotting.php.

Strachan, Zoë (2002), *Negative Space*, London: Picador.

Strachan, Zoë (2004), *Spin Cycle*, London: Picador.

Sturm, Brian (2000), 'The storylistening trance experience', *Journal of American Folklore*, 113, pp. 287–304.

STV (Scottish Television) (2003–4), Review 03, Preview 04, www.scottishtv.co.uk/content/mediaassets/pdf/STV_Annual%20Review%20Preview%200304.pdf, pp. 1–24.

STV (Scottish Television) (2004–5), Programme Review, www.scottishtv.co.uk/content/mediaassets/pdf/SCOTTISH%20TV%20Report%2004.05.pdf, pp. 1–32.

Sumari, Anni (ed.) (2005), *How to Address the Fog: XXV Finnish Poems 1978–2002*, Manchester: Carcanet and the Scottish Poetry Library.

Sutcliffe, Thomas (2003), 'Last night's television: fagged-out clichés in need of a break', *Independent*, 17 September.

Sutherland, Luke (1998), *Jelly Roll*, London: Anchor.

Sutherland, Luke (2004), *Venus as a Boy*, London: Bloomsbury.

Tait, Theo (2006), 'Just a big silver light [review of Alan Warner's *The Worms Can Carry Me to Heaven*]', *London Review of Books*, 28, 10, p. 33.

Taylor, Alan (1995–6), 'Showcase: Scottish efflorescence', *New Yorker*, December/January, p. 97.

Taylor, Charles (2004), 'Paint it noir', *New York Times*, 22 February, http://query.nytimes.com//gst/fullpage.html?res=9F01E0DD103AF931A15751C0A9629C8B63.

Tew, Philip (2003), 'The fiction of A. L. Kennedy: the baffled, the void and the (in)visible', in Richard Lane, Rod Mengham and Philip Tew (eds), *Contemporary British Fiction*, Cambridge: Polity, pp. 120–41.

Thomas, Gerald (1983), *Les Deux Traditions*, Montréal: Editions Bellarmin.

Thomson, A. J. P. (1999), 'What time is Scotland? Scottish writing and the politics of the nation', *Edinburgh Review*, 100, pp. 146–53.

Thomson, Derick (1994), *Companion to Gaelic Scotland*, Glasgow: Gairm.

Tipler, Frank J. (1996), *The Physics of Immortality: Modern Cosmology, God and the Resurrection of the Dead*, London: Macmillan.

Todd, Richard (1996), *Consuming Fictions: The Booker Prize and Fiction in Britain Today*, London: Bloomsbury.

Torrington, Jeff (1992), *Swing Hammer Swing*, London: Minerva.

Trocchi, Alexander (1968), *The Sigma Portfolio*, privately printed and distributed.

Turczi, István (ed.) (2005), *At the End of the Broken Bridge: XXV Hungarian Poems 1978–2002*, Manchester: Carcanet and the Scottish Poetry Library.

Turner, Victor (1969), *The Ritual Process: Structure and Anti-Structure*, London: Routledge and Kegan Paul.

United States Congress (2005), 'Expressing the sense of the House of Representatives that a day should be established as "National Tartan Day"', *House Resolution 41 EH*, 9 March.

United States Senate (1997), 'A resolution designating April 6 of each year as "National Tartan Day"', *Senate Resolution 155 IS*, 10 November.

Varney, Laura (2005), 'Anger at "parading queers" jibe in row over gay marriage', *Edinburgh Evening News*, 5 October, http://edinburghnews.scotsman.com/index.cfm?id=2044002005.

Varty, Anne (1997), 'The mirror and the vamp: Liz Lochhead', in Donglas Gifford and Dorothy McMillan (eds), *A History of Scottish Women's Writing*, Edinburgh: Edinburgh University Press, pp. 641–58.

Venuti, Lawrence (1995), *The Translator's Invisibility: A History of Translation*, London: Routledge.

Venuti, Lawrence (1998), *The Scandals of Translation: Towards an Ethics of Difference*, London: Routledge.

Vidler, Anthony (1992), *The Architectural Uncanny: Essays in the Modern Unhomely*, Cambridge, MA: MIT Press.

Virilio, Paul (2000), *Art and Fear*, trans. Julie Rose, London: Continuum.

Wallace, Gavin (1993), 'Voices in empty houses: the novel of damaged identity', in Randall Stevenson and Gavin Wallace (eds), *The Scottish Novel Since the Seventies: New Visions, Old Dreams*, Edinburgh: Edinburgh University Press, pp. 217–31.

Warner, Alan (1995), *Morvern Callar*, London: Cape.

Warner, Alan (1997), *These Demented Lands*, London: Cape.

Warner, Alan (1998), *The Sopranos*, London: Cape.

Warner, Alan (2002), *The Man Who Walks*, London: Cape.

Warner, Alan (2006), *The Worms Can Carry Me to Heaven*, London: Cape.

Watson, Roderick (1995), *The Poetry of Scotland*, Edinburgh: Edinburgh University Press.

Watson, Roderick (2006), 'Living with the double tongue: modern poetry in Scots', in I an Brown, Thomas Owen Clancy, Susan Manning and Murray Pittock (eds), *The Edinburgh History of Scottish Literature*, Edinburgh: Edinburgh University Press, pp. 163–75.

Watson, W. J. (ed.) (1918), *Bàrdachd Gàidhlig/Gaelic Poetry, 1550–1900*, Inverness: An Comunn Gaedhealach.

Weber, Samuel (1996), 'Displacing the body: the question of digital democracy', www.hydra.umn.edu/weber/displace.html.

Weight, Richard (2002), *Patriots: National Identity in Britain, 1940–2000*, London: Macmillan.

Welfonder, Sue-Ellen (2001), *Devil in a Kilt*, New York: Warner.

Welsh, Irvine (1993), *Trainspotting*, London: Cape.

Welsh, Irvine (1995), *Marabou Stork Nightmares*, London: Vintage.

Welsh, Irvine (2001), 'Contamination: a novella in regress', in Alex Garland (ed.), *The Weekenders: Travels in the Heart of Africa*, London: Ebury, pp. 125–268.

Welsh, Irvine (2002), *Porno*, London: Cape.

Welsh, Irvine (2003), 'Absinthe makes sense of a crazy world', *Daily Telegraph*, 14 April, www.telegraph.co.uk/opinion/main.jhtml?xml=/opinion/2003/04/14/do1403.xml.

Welsh, Irvine (2004), 'Reality principle,' in Andrew O'Hagan (ed.), *The Weekenders: Adventures in Calcutta*, London: Ebury, pp. 155–225.

Welsh, Irvine (2005), 'Scotland's murderous heart', *Guardian*, 20 October, pp. 8–11, www.caledonia.org.uk/papers/Scotland's_Murderous_Heart.doc.

Welsh, Irvine (2006), *The Bedroom Secrets of the Master Chefs*, London: Cape.

Welsh, Louise (2002), *The Cutting Room*, Edinburgh: Canongate.

Wheatcroft, Geoffrey (2004), 'The tragedy of Tony Blair', *Atlantic*, www.theatlantic.com/doc/200406/wheatcroft/1.

White, Allon (1993), *Carnival, Hysteria and Writing: Collected Essays and Autobiography*, Oxford: Clarendon.

White, Kenneth (1964), 'Jargon Paper #1', privately printed and distributed.

Whyte, Christopher (1989), 'Translation as poetic paradise,' *Lines Review*, 108, pp. 21–7.

Whyte, Christopher (1991), *An Aghaidh na Sìorraidheachd: Ochdnar Bhàrd Gàidhlig/In the Face of Eternity: Eight Gaelic Poets*, Edinburgh: Polygon.

Whyte, Christopher (1995a), *Euphemia MacFarrigle and the Laughing Virgin*, London: Gollancz.

Whyte, Christopher (ed.) (1995b), *Gendering the Nation: Studies in Modern Scottish Literature*, Edinburgh: Edinburgh University Press.

Whyte, Christopher (1997), *The Warlock of Strathearn*, London: Gollancz.

Whyte, Christopher (1998a), 'Masculinities in contemporary Scottish fiction', *Forum for Modern Language Studies*, 34, 2, pp. 274–85.

Whyte, Christopher (1998b), *The Gay Decameron*, London: Gollancz.

Whyte, Christopher (2000), *The Cloud Machinery*, London: Gollancz.

Whyte, Christopher (2002), *An Tràth Duilich: An Darna Chruinneachadh de Dhàintean*, Callander: Diehard

Whyte, Christopher (2004a), *Modern Scottish Poetry*, Edinburgh: Edinburgh University Press.

Whyte, Christopher (2004b), 'Queer readings, gay texts: from *Redgauntlet* to *The Prime of Miss Jean Brodie*', in Eleanor Bell and Gavin Miller (eds), *Scotland in Theory: Reflections on Culture and Literature*, Amsterdam: Rodopi, pp. 147–65.

Widdowson, Peter (1999), *Literature*, London: Routledge.

Williams, Raymond (1961), *The Long Revolution*, Harmondsworth: Penguin.

Williamson, Duncan and Linda Williamson (1983), *Fireside Tales of the Traveller Children*, Edinburgh: Canongate.

Williamson, Duncan and Linda Williamson (1985), *The Broonie, Silkies and Fairies: Traveller's Tales*, Edinburgh: Canongate.

Williamson, Duncan and Linda Williamson (1991), *The Genie and the Fisherman, and Other Tales from the Travelling People*, Cambridge: Cambridge University Press.

Williamson, Kevin (2002a), 'Under the influence', in Phil Moores (ed.), *Alasdair Gray: Critical Appreciations and a Bibliography*, London: British Library, p. 183.

Williamson, Kevin (2002b), 'Welcome home', *Sunday Times*, 18 August, p. 1.

Wilson, Michael (2006), *Storytelling and Theatre*, Basingstoke: Palgrave.

Winning, Joanne (ed.) (1992), *The Crazy Jig*, Edinburgh: Polygon.

Winning, Joanne (2000), 'Curious rarities? The work of Kathleen Jamie and Jackie Kay', in Alison Mark and Deryn Rees-Jones (eds), *Contemporary Women's Poetry: Reading/Writing/Practice*, Basingstoke: Palgrave, pp. 226–46.

Wittig, Kurt (1958), *The Scottish Tradition in Literature*, Edinburgh and London: Oliver and Boyd.

Zipes, Jack (2002), *Sticks and Stones: The Troublesome Success of Children's Literature from Slovenly Peter to Harry Potter*, London and New York: Routledge.

Žižek, Slavoj (1989), *The Sublime Object of Ideology*, London: Verso.

Žižek, Slavoj (1992), *Looking Awry: An Introduction to Jacques Lacan Through Popular Culture*, London: MIT Press.

Žižek, Slavoj (1997), 'Multiculturalism, or, the cultural logic of multinational capitalism', *New Left Review*, 225, pp. 28–51.

Index